Islam, Communities and the Nation

MUSLIM IDENTITIES IN SOUTH ASIA AND BEYOND

Edited by

MUSHIRUL HASAN

Fellow, Wissenschaftskolleg, Berlin

MANOHAR
1998

First published 1998

© Mushirul Hasan, 1998

ISBN 81-7304-070-2

Published by
Ajay Kumar Jain for
Manohar Publishers & Distributors
2/6 Ansari Road, Daryaganj
New Delhi 110002

Lasertypeset by
A J Software Publishing Co. Pvt. Ltd.
305 Durga Chambers
1333 D B Gupta Road
Karol Bagh, New Delhi 110005

Printed at
Rajkamal Electric Press
B 35/9 G T Karnal Road Indl Area
Delhi 110033

CONTENTS

Introduction

MUSHIRUL HASAN

When, as is currently the case (national, social, occupational, ethnic or religious) identity is invoked and extolled on all fronts, this proves that it is in doubt, that it is no longer self-evident, that it is already lost.

André Gorz[1]

In his contribution to this collection, Aziz Al-Azmeh argues that the use of 'identity' as an analytical category is beset by a number of problems, not the least of which is the disappearance of the distinction between the self-identification of social, political and ideological actors to whom identities are ascribed or who claim them, with historical and social reality. This distinction, according to him, is all the more essential as identity is, above all a performative and practical category rather than an analytical one, and this renders it amenable above all else to ideological analysis.

During the past decade or so, however, the concept of identity and its ramifications has attracted world-wide scholarly interest.[2] The constant refrain in scholarly and popular writings is how ethnic and national identities operate in the lives of individuals by connecting them with some people, and dividing them from others. Such identities, often heightened by the perception of a 'threat' from a group external to it, are often deeply integral to a person's sense of self, defining an 'I' by placing it against a background of 'we'.[3] The Partition of India in August 1947,[4] the Yugoslav catastrophe and the

[1] Quoted in Ronald Inden, 'Transcending Identities in the Modern World', in Kathryn Dean (ed.), *Politics and the End of Identity* (London, 1997), p. 1.

[2] Ibid., p. 1.

[3] Kwame Anthony and Henry Louis Gates, Jr (eds.), *Identities* (Chicago, 1995), p. 3.

[4] Mushirul Hasan, *Legacy of a Divided Nation: India's Muslims Since Independence* (London, 1997); Sugata Bose and Ayesha Jalal (eds.), *Nationalism, Democracy and Development* (Delhi, 1997). See also, Paul Brass, *Language, Religion and Politics in North India* (Cambridge, 1974), and his *Ethnicity and Nationalism: Theory and Comparison* (Delhi, 1991).

continuing Sinhalese-Tamil strife in Sri Lanka illustrate this process.[5]

Why is the theme of identity, which lies at the heart of the current debate in cultural studies and social theory, so compelling and yet so problematic? Part of the explanation lies in the diversity of issues and the multiplicity of approaches and interpretations. Notice how a recent book, based on anthropological case studies, examines the intersection of cultural landscapes with political boundaries and the ways in which state power informs cultural identity.[6] A chapter in yet another volume, also recently published, suggests how national boundaries persist robustly within Europe and are likely to neutralize all attempts to construct a European identity above them, one inevitably lacking the affective bonds of myth and memory that alone cement a strong sensed of collective belonging.[7] Some other writers detail the multiple intersections of race, class and gender in feminist studies, and shed light on the interrelations of postcolonialism, nationalism, and ethnicity in ethnic and area studies. These intersections provide a site for the articulation and discussion of new theories and discourses on identity.[8]

Although historians, anthropologists and sociologist often cover common ground, some of their analytical categories and explanations, especially when somewhat insensitively applied to differentiated and diverse communities and nations, fail to uncover the complexity of social realities. This is not surprising: identities in South Asian history and politics have seldom been unified; in modern times they are increasingly fragmented and fractured, they are never singular but always multiple, and thus difficult to capture on a single axis. Constructed across different, intersecting and antagonistic sites, discourses, and practices, they are subject to a radical historicization, and are constantly in the process of making and unmaking. This is clearly demonstrated by Nathalie Clayer and Alexandre Popovic in their study of the Muslims of Bosnia-Herzegovina. These Muslims, who were Yugoslavs just the other day, are now seen simply as

---

[5] For Sri Lanka, see the collection of essays in H.L. Senevirante (ed.), *Identity, Consciousness and the Past: Forging of Caste and Community in India and Sri Lanka* (Delhi, 1997).

[6] Thomas M. Wilson and Hastings Donnan (eds.), *Border Identities: Nation and State in International Frontiers* (Cambridge, 1998).

[7] Anthony D. Smith, 'National Identity and European Unity', in Peter Gowan and Perry Anderson (eds.), *The Question of Europe* (London, 1997).

[8] Anthony and Gates (eds.), op. cit., p. 1.

Muslims.[9] This often imparts a misleading ideological fixity to what is always a much more fluid and open-ended process of identity formation.

In general, the debates about identity need to be situated within all those historically specific economic and political developments which have altered the relatively 'settled' character of many populations and cultures. Consider another example of the contingent and transactional nature of cultures and identities. The debate over legislative reform of personal laws in the early 1950s made accommodations to recognize Indians, notably minorities, as members of religious communities. This was considered necessary in the aftermath of Partition, when the Indian state endeavoured to gain the trust of the Muslims who had opted to stay on in their country of birth. But given the changeable nature of cultures, Jawaharlal Nehru, the architect of this policy, expected that these provisions would themselves be subject to change. He hoped that the Muslim communities would, in the fullness of time, respond to the winds of change. Meanwhile, he insisted that they should have the right to decide when.

Many of the identity debates seem to invoke an origin in an historical past to which they continue to correspond; 'actually identities are about questions of using the resources of history, language and culture in the process of becoming rather than being; not "who we are" or "where we come from", so much as what we might become, how we have been represented and how that bears on how we might represent ourselves'. Identities are therefore constituted quintessentially within, not outside, representation. And precisely because identities are constructed within, not outside, discourse, 'we need to understand them as produced in specific historical and institutional sites within specific discursive formations and practices, by specific enunciative strategies'.[10]

Some of these issues bear considerable relevance to contemporary South Asia, especially in countries like India, Pakistan and Sri Lanka where identity politics has gained so much salience in recent decades. The resurgence of Hindu nationalism culminating in the

---

[9] 'Muslim Identity in the Balkans in the Post-Ottoman Period', *Islam, Communities and the Nation*, pp. 405-24 of this volume.

[10] Stuart Hall, 'Introduction', in Stuart Hall and Paul Du Gay (eds.), *Questions of Cultural Identity* (London, 1997), p. 4.

destruction of the Babri masjid on 6 December 1992,[11] ethnic strife in Pakistan, including widespread Shia-Sunni violence, and the conflict between the Sinhalese and Tamil identities of Sri Lanka are some significant expressions of the complex processes that unfold themselves in several different ways. There are, in addition, a number of disparate but aggrieved groups in these countries who are not so strident at present but whose sense of identity—of being different and therefore privileged to seek concessions or guarantees from the nation-state—is periodically heightened by numerous grievances, especially their limited access to power, authority and material resources. These are precisely the elements who invoke the themes of group identity into their activities or who blend religious fervour with identity.

The Shah Bano affair, which became a cause celebre in India during 1986, is a case in point. The issue at stake was the preservation of Muslim identity, symbolized by Islamic religious law, which, many Muslims fervently believed, was under attack by secularizing forces.[12] Similarly, the Hindutva forces around the same time used the Babri masjid controversy to orchestrate a pan-Hindu identity so as to create more exclusivist ideas of India and purge the nationalist imagination of its tolerant and pluralist moorings. Both were political performances timed to gain either political concessions or electoral success. Sometimes, the insecurities of minorities are played on: Muslims in Uttar Pradesh, the Hindu minority in Kashmir, the Sikhs in Punjab and the *muhajirs* in Sind. By using the themes and idioms of dissatisfaction and dispossession, they have been mobilized to muster support for a singular identity.[13] This is invariably done in

[11] Vasudha Dalmia and H. Von Stietencorn (eds.), *Representing Hinduism: The Construction of Religious Traditions and National Identity* (Delhi, 1995).

[12] There is considerable literature on the subject. See, for example, Zoya Hasan, *Forging Identities: Gender, Communities and the State in India* (Delhi, 1994), and her 'Gender Politics, Legal Reform, and the Muslim Community in India', in Patricia Jeffery and Amrita Basu (eds.), *Appropriating Gender: Women's Activism and Politicized Religion in South Asia* (New York, 1998); 'Indian Islam: The Shah Bano affair', in John Stratton Hawley (ed.), *Fundamentalism and Gender* (Oxford, 1994); Deniz Kandiyoti, 'Women, Islam, and the State: A Comparative Approach', in Juan R.I. Kole (ed.), *Comparing Muslim Societies: Knowledge and the State in a World Civilization* (Michigan, Ann Arbor, 1992); Ritu Menon and Kamla Bhasin, *Borders & Boundaries: Women in India's Partition* (Delhi, 1998).

[13] For a near historical background into a variety of ethinic conflicts, see Dietrich Reetz, 'In Search of the Collective Self: How Ethnic Group Concepts were Cast through Conflict in Colonial India', *Modern Asian Studies*, 31, 2, 1997, pp. 285-315.

South Asia, a region marked by economic disparities and social diversities, to capture power or demand more active redistribution. In such situations, economic and power interests of the dominant strata of the group get camouflaged, submerged in, or blended with the passions of identity of particular communities or castes.[14] This trend, though intertwined with and inextricably woven into a complex tissue of history, fact and fiction, saw its apogee during the prolonged and protracted movements for a separate state in Punjab and in Kashmir.[15] The turn of events in both regions are a witness to the tragedy of misjudging the possibilities of a state being created on the basis of fragmentary identities.

This volume is principally concerned with the history and contemporary experiences of the Muslim communities in India, Bangladesh, Nepal, the erstwhile state of Yugoslavia, and the Arab world.[16] Although the bulk of this collection covers India, a country inhabited by 120 million Muslims, all the contributions reflect on the notion, definition and development of identity politics. Essays on the former state of Yugoslavia have been written by scholars who had bitter encounters with ethnic cleansing. Radha Kumar spent a couple of years in Sarajevo and her essay should prove useful to those embarking on cross-cultural research projects. Aziz Al-Azmeh describes the Ottoman Empire and its successor states in a specific respect: that of the processes by which colonial relations were confronted. These entailed, according to him, the recasting of the state and its functions, particularly its legal, cultural and social functions, along lines broadly positivistic and in line with modernist developments elsewhere in the world, including Europe. In this process, Azmeh argues, religion played a decidedly peripheral role.

This volume has been in the making for the last three years. It is intended to bring together scholars from different countries, from

[14] For Sri Lanka, see Seneviratne (ed.), op. cit., p. 5.

[15] For Punjab, see Harjot Oberoi, *The Construction of Religious Boundaries: Culture, Identity and Diversity in South Asia in the Sikh Tradition* (Delhi, 1993); Dipankar Gupta, *The Context of Ethnicity: Sikh Identity in a Comparative Perspective* (Delhi, 1997). See, also Nonica Datta, *Negotiating Identities: The Jats in Colonial Punjab* (Delhi, 1998, forthcoming).

[16] Some of the essays in this volume were initially guest-edited by me in *Comparative Studies of South Asia, Africa and the Middle East*. The first installment of papers appeared in Vol. XVI, No. 2, and the final installment in Vol. XVII, No. 2. I am extremely grateful to Vasant Kaiwar and Sucheta Mazumdar, editors of the journal, for their cooperation and editorial support.

widely different political standpoints and disciplines, which include history, political science and sociology, to provide an overview and assessments of developments within a revitalized field of study. The contributions therefore vary in structure and content, from ones that are interpretative to those that concentrate on offering an overview of major strands, patterns and processes. Each essay, however, suggests some effective ways of dealing with these processes, given the current state of our knowledge. Taken together, they exemplify some of the key features of recent scholarship on how individuals and groups negotiate the complex world of identities.

The main thrust of the book is historical in one sense, though not all the contributors are historians by discipline. The temporal perspective differs in scope in some cases, but several authors cover considerable portions of the twentieth century and some try to embrace even longer periods. The result is discussion of a broader range of subjects than standard treatments allow. Obviously, this still leaves significant gaps. Among others, there are no Pakistani or Sri Lankan voices. But this volume is still a wider constellation than has been customary for some time.

Finally, in selecting the topics and authors, a conscious effort was made to cover different regions of India and to uncover, so to speak, the regional and local dimensions of identity politics. Thus Joya Chatterji, Papiya Ghosh, Taj al-Hashmi, Mohammad Ishaq Khan, Shail Mayaram and Dietrich Reetz tackle key questions in their respective regions and localities and provide, with the aid of much source materials, a fitting starting point for an academic dialogue on the wider theme of this collection. In the context of Bengali Muslim identity, Joya Chatterji insists that scholars of Bengali Muslim history should give up their idealist and essentialist assumptions, the most tenacious of which is the idea of a 'true' and fundamentally knowable Islam. Pointing out that 'true Islam' has always been a matter of dispute, whose outcome (always temporary) has been bound up with power, she concludes that 'there is no "authentic" soul or spirit of Islam, or indeed of the Muslim community'. From her standpoint, 'authenticity can only be a fundamentalist claim that seeks to standardize, essentialize and sentimentalize a past which has been characterized by plurality, multivocality and bitter conflict'.[17]

---

[17] See, also, Asim Roy. *Islam in South Asia: A Regional Perspective* (Delhi, 1996), especially Chapter 5.

My own survey traces the roots of Shia-Sunni conflict in Lucknow and questions conventional wisdom on the homogeneity of the Muslim 'community' in India and its so-called shared experiences in a colonial context.[18] My overall concern is to identify the local factors that led to the breakdown of Shia-Sunni relations in a local context, and to relate them with the countrywide movements of religio-revivalism.

Hamza Alavi reveals the premises on which the Khilafat movement was founded and the paradoxes and contradictions behind the rhetoric of its ideologues. This is followed by an analysis of the role of Mohamed Ali, a key figure in the pan-Islamic upsurge in north India in the early 1920s, and his engagement with the construction of an Indian Muslim identity. Ian Copland discusses the literary paradigms in the historical construction of the Indian Muslim identity by focusing on Mohammad Ali Jinnah, the founder of Pakistan, and Nawab Hamidullah Khan, the ruler of Bhopal State in central India, now the capital of Madhya Pradesh.

The historian Gail Minault and the political scientist Niraja Gopal Jayal address questions about gender in another sphere of identity, religion. Mohammad Talib turns to the Tablighi Jamaat for their own self-understanding of the world around them. His sociological reflections reveal how the Tablighi identity is limited by the active presence of identity constructs upheld by other traditions in Islam. He underlines the need to portray the polyphony of ideological voices and the contested character of the social and cultural space where Tablighi identity is formed.

II

The expression Muslim identity has been widely in vogue in the Indian subcontinent for well over a century. It was used by Syed Ahmad Khan, the founder of the Muslim University at Aligarh, to lend weight to his educational and reformist mission. Muslim organizations like the All-India Muslim League (founded in December 1906) which represented just a handful of government servants and landlords in its early years, invoked the 'separate' and 'distinct' identity of their co-religionists to stake their claim in the imperial

---

[18] This is a revised and enlarged version of my paper published in Violette Graff (ed.), *Lucknow: Memories of a City* (Delhi, 1996), pp. 114-35.

system. Several reformers, publicists, writers and poets harped on the same theme to devise communitarian strategies, advance religious rights and political representation, and nurture the vision of a unified, pan-Indian Muslim community. Thus the poet Mohammad Iqbal argued that Hindus and Muslims were in fact aiming at different, and more often than not, conflicting concepts of the future. 'Muslim demand for the creation of a Muslim India within India, was therefore justified'. Iqbal further added 'I would like to see the Punjab, North Western Frontier, Sind and Baluchistan amalgamated into a single state.' This, he said, appeared to be the ultimate destiny of the Muslims. In March 1940, Mohammad Ali Jinnah, the 'Ambasssador of Hindu-Muslim unity', changed course to emphasize the separate and distinct civilizational identity of the Muslims. This was the cornerstone of his 'two-nation' theory and the central plank of the Muslim League's demand for a Muslim nation.

What is clearly discernible in the writings and pronouncements of these individuals and groups is their self-image of being part of a community themselves—a monolithic *umma*—that remained, or was normatively expected to remain, the same across divisions in space and time. This theme was often powerfully expressed across a number of elite scholastic factions, especially of Sunni Islam, for whom Sufi and Shia beliefs in general, were just so many deviations from the norm. Time and again the theme of eternal and unmitigated Hindu-Muslim hostility was echoed. So also the view that 'internal' differences among groups of Hindus and/or Muslims were secondary and irrelevant to the more fundamental religious cleavage.

Such views conformed to the colonial perception of Indian Islam and its followers. For most British travellers, missionaries, administrators and ethnographers, Islam was part of the 'Great Tradition'—codified, rigid, unchanging and closed to external influences. They cast its followers, whether converted or not, in a specifically Muslim/Islamic mould, and defined their identity, regardless of economic status, caste, language or region, in strictly doctrinaire terms. In the constitutional plans, which broadly reflected the colonial assumptions about Indian society, the British government showed no sensitivity to the wide-ranging differences that separated the followers of Islam from one another. Though the representatives of the Raj were familiar with and recorded the strength of strong intercommunity networks and syncretic practices in most parts of the country, their knowledge and understanding was not reflected in concrete political decisions or translated into constitutional decrees.

In the context, the Act of 1909 was a calculated master-stroke. Separate electorates, along with reservation and weightages, gave birth to a sense of Muslims being a religio-political entity in the colonial image—of being unified, cohesive and segregated from the Hindus. They were homogenized like 'castes' and tribes' and suitably accommodated within political schemes and bureaucratic designs. In consequence, self-styled leaders, mostly drawn from *Ashraf* (honourable) families and without any tangible links with the Muslim masses or *Ajlaf* (ignoble) were emboldened to represent an 'objectively'-defined community and contend with others for patronage, employment and political assignments. In this way, separate electorates created space for reinforcing religious identities, a process which was, both in conception and articulation, profoundly divisive. In effect, the Act of 1909 (Morley-Minto Reforms) ingeniously challenged those assumptions which guided many nationalists to cultivate a pan-Indian identity, and undermined, through a judicious mixture of concessions and guarantees, the broadly secular underpinnings of Indian nationalism. The ideological contours of the future Pakistan were thus delineated by British opinion and policy-makers long before Jinnah burst upon the political scene with his insistence on a Muslim nation.

III

In an important study published in 1989, Farzana Shaikh underlined 'the profound sense of the distinctiveness of being Muslim'. There was, according to her findings, 'an unmistakable awareness of the ideal of Muslim brotherhood, a belief in the superiority of Muslim culture and a recognition of the belief that Muslims ought to live under Muslim governments'.[19] Elements that sustained the politics of Muslim representation were also grounded deep in a tradition the sources of which were believed to lie in divine revelation. 'It is this tradition', she concludes, 'that imparted to Muslims in India the body of assumptions concerning the pivotal role of the religious com-

---

[19] Farzana Shaikh, *Community and Consensus in Islam: Muslim Representation in Colonial India, 1860-1947* (Cambridge, 1989), p. 230.

munity, its exclusive claim to individual allegiance, the nature of political consensus and the organisation of power in society.'[20]

Ayesha Jalal, on the other hand, points out that a decidedly elitist discourse should not be seen as reflective of Indian Muslims or their so-called communal consciousness. Nor can the politics of Muslim identity in the subcontinent be reduced to a mere rationalization of normative Islamic discourse. There is, according to her, 'much variation even within this elitist discourse, not all of which focused on the knotty issue of electoral representation, and still greater evidence of Muslim willingness to differ from rather than defer to the consensus of the community, however construed, in the rough and tumble of practical politics'.[21] Indeed, 'the problem of identity in South Asia has been more complex and nuanced than permitted by the protagonists of the "two-nation" theory of the practitioners of a historiography based on a binary opposition between secular nationalism and religious nationalism'.[22]

Notwithstanding the proliferation of scholarly literature on the Muslim communities in South Asia, there is still much resistance to the fact that Islam in India, past and present, unfolds a bewildering diversity of Muslim communities and that there is much variety in their social habits, cultural traits and occupational patterns. Given the fact that 'communal' solidarities are being forged at different levels of society for self-defence or self-assertion, much of the discussion in the subcontinent tends to centre around imaginary and invented notions of Muslim cultural homogeneity and continuity.

A simple fact that eludes the grasp of scholars and generalists alike is that Islam came to the subcontinent not in a single time span, but in succession divided unevenly in different periods; consequently, its diffusion took place in a variety of forms from class to class and from one area to another. The difference in the phases in which people 'experienced' Islam brought with it variations in the nature of challenges facing its followers in different regions. In its local and regional specificity, therefore, the 'essential' core of Islam, so to speak, was not immune to changes by historical influences. Ordinary Muslims were not, as one is often led to believe, members of a monolithic community sitting sullenly apart, but were active participants

---

[20] Ibid., p. 233.
[21] Bose and Jalal, *Nationalism*, op. cit., p. 80.
[22] Ibid., p. 103.

in regional cultures whose perspective they shared.[23] They took their commitment to Islam not only as one among other values, but also as something which was itself differentiated internally into a number of detailed commitments.[24]

In the terms of a typical Orientalist cliché, 'Islam' is still seen not just as a religion but a total way of life. It provides, as such, a complete identity, explanation and moral code for Muslims' actions. The mere fact of people being Muslim in some general sense is conflated with that of their adherence to beliefs and policies that are described as 'Islamist' or 'fundamentalist'. What these approaches share is the analytic primacy of culture and ideology and the privileged place assigned to Islam. It is thus commonly assumed, both in India and elsewhere, that Islamic religion are essentially distinctive and thus inherently incompatible with Western ideals of democracy and secularism.[25] Islam as a religion is considered to be essentially different from all the others in that the concepts of belief and political rule are fused through the unity of *din wa dawla*, the Prophet having both revealed a religion and founded a state. Predicated on this statement is an assumed resistance to secularism.[26]

In reality, the commitment of some Muslim groups to specifically Islamic ideas and symbols does not indicate a unified structure of consciousness or a community acting in unison. What should not be assumed is a monolithic conception of Islamic ideology and practice or a teleology dictating the actions of the Muslims or a general acquiescence in the actions of few. Instead of considering

[23] Peter B. Mayer, 'Tombs and Dark Houses: Ideology, Intellectuals, and Proletarians in the Study of Contemporary Indian Islam', *Journal of Asian Studies,* 25, 3, May 1981: Susan Bayly, 'Islam in Southern India: "Purist" or "Syncretic"', in C.A. Bayly and D.H.A. Kolff (eds.), *Two Colonial Empires* (Dordrecht, 1986); and Asim Roy, *Islam in South Asia,* pp. 45-78, for an incisive conceptual and historical revaluation of Islamisation in Bengal.

[24] Akeel Bilgrami, 'What is a Muslim? Fundamental Commitment and Cultural Identity', *Economic and Political Weekly,* 16-23 May 1992.

[25] See, for example, the entry on 'Islam' by Charles F. Gallagher, in *International Encyclopaedia of the Social Sciences,* Vol. 7 (New York, 1972, rpt.), especially, pp. 215-16.

[26] For a refutation of this argument in the context of Turkey, see Nilufer Gole, 'Authoritarian Secularism and Islamist Politics: The Case of Turkey', in Augustus Richard Norton (ed.), *Civil Society in the Middle East* (Leiden, 1996); and Jacques Waardenburg, 'Muslim Enlightenment and Revitalization: Movements of Modernization and Reform in Tsarist Russia (ca. 1850-1917) and the Dutch East Indies (ca. 1900-1942)', *Die Welt des Islams,* 28, 1988.

what political ideas and particular group of Muslims hold, and the relations between these and their social conditions and practice, the reification of Islam in the realm of political ideas leads to essentially circular suggestions that both practice and ideas conform with the 'Quranic Political Culture'.[27] Aziz Al-Azmeh has rightly pointed out:

The very premises of Islamic studies are radically and thoroughly unsound; their very foundation, the identification and the construal of relevant facts, is based upon a political and cultural imagination. . . . Any proper writing of Islamic history has to rest on the dissolution of Islam as an orientalist category. . . . It has to liberate itself from Islam, and scrutinise Islamic histories, societies, economies, temporalities, cultures and sciences with the aid of history, of economics, of sociology, critical theory and anthropology. Only then will Islam be disassociated, and reconstituted as historical categories amenable to historical study.[28]

If you are still not convinced, turn to scores of local and regional studies which reveal how large segments of the Indian population have been integrated with other communities, how their views and responses are more diverse and complex than the statements found within the corpus of received opinion on the subject. They illustrate, moreover, the disjunction between the formal ideology of Islam as constituted by certain political groups and the actual day-to-day beliefs and practices of Muslims,[29] and point to those regional and local traditions and cultural features of Indian Islam that were components of, and contributions to, what the liberal and secular nationalities meant by the concept of a composite culture.

Yet the debates on such themes are also exclusively based on writers and publicists who are known to stress the elements of discord and separation, while explanations boldly constructed around secular and pluralist conceptions and counterpoised to the essentialist view of Indian Islam remain neglected in the discourse. For a balanced, objective and rounded view, it is necessary to explore the terrian of those scholars, artists and creative writers who contested the definition of Muslim identity in purely religious terms and refuted the popular belief that Islamic values and symbols

---

[27] Mayer, op. cit., p. 496.

[28] Aziz Al-Azmeh, *Islams and Modernities* (London, 1996, 2nd edn.), pp. 181-2.

[29] Succession is the principal areas in Muslim social life where *Sharia* requirements have often been ignored. For details, see Peter Hardy, in *The Encyclopedia of Religion*, Vol. 7 (New York, 1987), p. 402.

provide a key to understanding the 'Muslim world-view'.[30] We may well discover that they, more than anybody else, discovered elements of unity, cohesion and integration in India's past, sensed the bitter consequences of political identity being built on religious ties, and questioned the conviction (or myth) in certain Muslim circles that the future of Islam was endangered by Hindu nationalism. Their notable contribution in providing historical legitimacy to multi-culturalism and religious plurality should not go unnoticed. And their sane and sober voices should not be stifled by the weight of Muslim orthodoxy, Hindu revivalism and the Orientalist discourse.

Who, then, is a Muslim? What, if any, specific identity is associated with the Muslims generally and with India's Muslims in particular? Is it divinely-ordained or related to features that have always been characteristic of Islamic governments and societies? How important is the Muslim self-image? Is it the outcome of colonial images and 'nationalist' constructions, of treating Muslims as an undifferentiated religious category? To what extent has the post-colonial state also viewed Muslims as an undifferentiated religious entity, who are also presumed to represent a separate political entity?

When the first all-India census was tabulated and analysed in 1881, the enumerators found that Muslims numbered only 19.7 per cent of the population. They uncovered a geographically dispersed aggregate of Muslims forming neither a collectivity nor a distinct society for any purpose, political, economic and social. Out of a total population of about 50 million, the Muslims in Bengal spoke Bengali and those in Punjab used largely Punjabi as their language.[31] Those living in Tamil Nadu spoke Tamil; those settled on the Malabar coast, mostly Mapillas, spoke Malayalam. They found Muslims whose religious rituals had a very strong tinge of Hinduism and who retained caste and observed Hindu festivals and ceremonies. In

[30] This aspect is merely hinted at by some Indian and Western writers. For example, Mohammad Mujeeb, *Indian Muslims* (London, 1967); Asim Roy, *Islam in South Asia*, op. cit. See my *A Nationalist Conscience: M.A. Ansari, the Congress and the Raj* (Delhi, 1989), and *Nationalism and Communal Politics in India, 1885-1930* (Delhi, 1991); V.N. Datta and B.E. Cleghorn (eds.), *A Nationalist Muslim and Indian Politics* (Delhi, 1974); and W. Montgomery Watt, *Islamic Fundamentalism and Modernity* (London, 1988), pp. 62-5. Some insights are also available in Marshall G.S. Hodgson, *The Venture of Islam: The Gunpowder Empires and Modern Times* (Chicago, 1974).

[31] On Punjabi Muslims, see J.M. Wikeley, *Punjabi Musalmans* (Delhi, 1991 rpt, 1st published in 1915). This was written as a handbook for the instruction of 'young officers' on 'the history, customs, etc., of men with whom they are serving'.

Bengal, where developed the second largest total (after Indonesia) of rural Muslims in the Islamic world, between the fifteenth and eighteenth centuries, many Muslim cultural mediators, writing in Bengali, expressed Islam in the local cultural medium, an idiom greatly enriched in the same period by translations of the great Hindu epics, the *Ramayana* and the *Mahabharata*, into Bengali, and the expression of Nath and Vaishnava teachings. In fact, the entry of Muslims in South Asia through so many and such separate doorways, their spread over the subcontinent by so many different routes, and the diffusion of Islam in different forms from one area to the other, ensured that this religion would present itself in those different forms. Neither to its own adherents nor to non-Muslims did Islam seem monochromatic, monolithic or indeed mono-anything.[32]

This is borne out by a report compiled by Justice Mohammad Munir in 1953, following the anti-Ahmadiya (Qadiani) riots in Pakistan. The committee he headed asked the *ulama* to define a Muslim. No two learned divines agreed. The committee's own dilemma was summed up succinctly: 'If we attempt our own definition as each learned divine has done and that definition differs from that given by all others, we unanimously go out of the fold of Islam. And if we adopt the definition given by any one of the *ulama*, we remain Muslims according to the view of that *alim* but *kafirs* according to the definition of everyone else'. In fact the enquiry was 'anything but satisfactory'. The report concluded on a wary note: 'If considerable opinion exists in the minds of our *ulama* on such a simple matter, one can easily imagine what the difference on more complicated matters will be'.[33]

The variety of meanings and perceptions in defining a Muslim are also revealed by an *alim* of Lucknow's Nadwat al-ulama, by an erudite liberal scholar who guided the affairs of the Jamia Millia Islamia for decades, and by a socialist writer, journalist and filmmaker.[34]

A distinguishing feature of the entire Muslim community, including Indian Muslims, is that the fundamental basis of their existence as a religious community (*millat*) is a well-defined, distinct and immutable faith and a divinely ordained canon (*Shariat*). [Syed Abul Hasan Ali Nadwi (1974)]

[32] Peter Hardy, 'Islam and Muslims in Asia', in Raphael Israeli (ed.), *The Crescent in the East: Islam in Asia Minor* (London, 1988), pp. 39-40.
[33] Quoted in my *Legacy of a Divided Nation*, p. 12.
[34] Ibid., pp. 12-13.

If we have to define the Indian Muslims, we can only say that they are Indians who call themselves Muslims, who believe in the unity and fraternity of the Muslims as a religious and social community, and are capable of showing in practice that they act in accordance with this belief, however they might differ in doctrine and observances. [Mohammad Mujeeb (1967)]

Maula Bakhsh, a peasant, lives in Tamil Nadu and speaks Tamil. In Andhra Pradesh he speaks Telegu. In Bengal his language is Bengali. Do we think of such a Muslim for whom I have invented the name Maula Bakhsh? . . . Jinnah, Khaliquzzaman, Maulana Azad, the Aga Khan, M.C. Chagla and the Raja of Mahmudabad . . . were Muslims. So was Hakku, the elderly grandmother of our locality. She was a weaver. She prayed five times a day. She was so deeply moved by one of Gandhi's speeches that she would repeat his name after Allah and his Prophet. At the age of seventy, she stitched her own *khadi* coffin, because she did not want her body to be wrapped and then buried in a foreign cloth. So when people discuss India's Muslims, I wonder who are they talking about. Maula Bakhsh? Jinnah and Co.? Or Hakku? [Khwaja Ahmad Abbas (1975)]

Such political and literary descriptions make it clear that boundaries are multiple, and that at no time is one boundary the sole definer of an identity. Yet at different times and for different reasons there is a 'relevant boundary' that gains prominence and defines the us/them divide. It tends to reject the 'other' and frequently reinforces itself by defining the 'us', not by its members specific positive attributes but by the elements in opposition to the 'other'. This mode stresses the negative, expands elements of separation, and sometimes makes it harder to identify the broader groupings that always exist, albeit in weaker form.[35]

IV

The us/them divide, created by the institutional and bureaucratic structures introduced by the colonial government towards the end of the nineteenth century, eventually led to the Partition of India along religious lines. The following decade was a period of trial and soul-searching for the Muslim communities, especially those who had hitched their fortune to the Muslim League bandwagon but stayed put in their country of birth. How did such people respond to their situation after Partition?

[35] Ismail Serageldin, 'Mirage and Windows: Redefining the Boundaries of the Mind', *The American Journal of Islamic Social Sciences*, 2, 1, 1994.

The first point that needs to be underlined is that the political and intellectual currents reflected the mixed and diverse aspirations of the highly segmented and stratified Muslim communities. Second, Islamic issues were not the sole concern of educated Muslims; in fact, many were inspired by and wedded to a broadly secularized view of politics and society. The religious and-political leadership, too, was concerned to come to terms with the socio-economic con- sequences of partition, assess the losses and gains, and work out arrangements, much in the nature of a social contract, with other social and political entities. The secular and democratic regime rather than the Islamic dimension provided the overarching framework to forge new alliances and electoral coalitions. In effect, those holding the reins of leadership had to locate problems and find answers to contemporary dilemmas within the democratic and secular paradigms and seek adjustments not as Muslims per se but as members of a larger Indian fraternity. They had to accept state laws enacted by parliament and not insist on the 'application' of the Islamic law, except in the case of marriage, divorce and inheritance. After the departure of their British benefactors, who had created their separate political identity and patronized them to counter nationalist forces, the remnants of an highly dispirited Muslim leadership had to tread warily in a world that was fashioned differently.

The Muslim divines themselves, many of whom had stoutly resisted the movement for a Muslim homeland, realized that Islam was a living and vital religion, appealing to the hearts, minds and conscience of millions, setting them a standard by which to live honest, sober and God-fearing lives.[36] Although they nursed many grievances, they did not find much evidence of an organized or concerted attempt to undermine their interests as a 'community'. If anything, Jawaharlal Nehru tried his best, despite stiff resistance from the Hindu right in the Congress Party, to draw Muslims into the political and economic structures.

Undoubtedly, the choices and casts within the emerging national theatre were manifold. Muslims could draw on their Indian Islamic inheritance and the secular legacy of the nationalist movement or combine elements from a variety of cultural and political entitle- ments. In other words, if they were to move forward in their quest

---

[36] For an elaboration of this argument, see my *Legacy of a Divided Nation*, Chapter 6, and Christian W. Troll, 'Sharing Islamically in the Pluralistic Nation-State of India: The Views of Some Contemporary Indian Muslim Leaders and Thinkers', in Y.Y. Haddad (ed.), *Christian-Muslim Encounters* (Florida, 1995), pp. 245-62.

for a better life, their representative organizations had to be guided by fresh responses to the challenges facing the nation and not just the community. They had to come to terms with an untested and unexplored social and political reality, for which they were accountable to the nation at large, a point emphasized by Maulana Abul Kalam Azad and the leading alim. Husain Ahmad Madani, of the seminary at Deoband's Dar al ulum. They had to demonstrate a new political imagination for rewriting their agenda within the ground rules being laid out on the Indian turf. Indeed, the critical issue before them was to strengthen, for their own survival and progress, the existing cross-community networks and to discover new meanings to their existence not in isolation from, but through close interaction with, other social and economic entities. They had to find new forms of expression within a secularized idiom and explore fresh avenues to articulate their aspirations, anxieties and misgivings.

What does one make of 'Muslim Identity', an expression widely in vogue but without any clear intellectual underpinnings? It is doubtless true that economic discontent, coupled with escalating violence, lend weight to notions of identity and act as a catalyst to community-based strategies. Yet Muslim scholars and activists, both before and after Independence, have taken recourse to a definition that has rested uneasily on the Islamic concept of a unified *millat* (community). Such a definition will always be problematic. So too its projection in the political arena, more so after fifty years of Independence when the political landscape has changed drastically and new social groups have come to the fore with higher levels of consciousness and greater stakes in the power structures. Community-based politics, which is so often backed and sustained by political parties for electoral reasons, may yield short-term gains, but in the long run is not likely to produce any tangible benefits to the majority of poor, backward and impoverished Muslims.[37] Hence

[37] This is especially true of the recent demand for Muslim reservations in the civil service and education. I agree with Theodore P. Wright, Jr, that it would be more fruitful for the Muslim leadership to 'forego the hopeless and politically counterproductive campaign for quotas in the civil service and to concentrate on literacy, technical education, and, if need be, FEPC (New York State Fair Employment Practices Commission in the 1950s) to open up the private sector to Muslim employment'. 'A New Demand for Muslim Reservations in India', *Asian Survey*, 37, 9 September 1997, p. 858. See also D.L. Sheth, 'Muslim Reservations: No Provision for Communal Quotas', *Times of India*, 20 September 1997.

the importance of drawing a sharp distinction between political polemics and the actual realities on the ground.

For the Muslim communities, in particular, it is important to reiterate secular positions, oppose the mixing of religion with politics, revive internal discussions on reforms and innovation, and ignore the rhetoric behind the pronouncements on 'Muslim identity'. Surely the nature and outcome of a meaningful dialogue along these lines will determine the direction of change and progress amongst them in the next millennium. A creative process of reform, initiated by Syed Ahmad Khan and some of his illustrious colleagues exactly a century ago in the small town of Aligarh, can no longer be postponed. For the contempoary Muslim leaders, many of whom are burdened by the past and preoccupied with inconsequential issues, the challenge is not to create 'communal' solidarities but to equip their constituency to compete in the wider world and fashion their lives in the 'Indian environment' as co-citizens in a society where most people conform to democratic and secular values. The turf is sticky but also negotiable.

Ironies of History: Contradictions of the Khilafat Movement

HAMZA ALAVI

The 'Khilafat' movement of 1919-24 is probably unique inasmuch as it has been glorified with one voice by Islamic ideologists, Indian nationalists and Communists together with Western scholars. An anti-colonial movement of Muslims of India, it was set in motion by the hostility of the British to the Sultan of Turkey, the venerated Khalifa.[1] Little attempt has been made to examine the premises on which the movement was founded, the rhetoric of its leaders being taken at face value. On closer examination we find extraordinary paradoxes and contradictions behind that rhetoric.

As for the 'achievements' of that movement, its lasting legacy is the legitimized place that it gave the Muslim clergy at the centre of the modern political arena. Armed with a political organization in the form of the Jamiyat al-ulama-i Hind (and its successors after the Partition), it has enabled the clergy to intervene actively in both the political as well as the ideological spheres. Never before in Indian history had the Muslim clergy ever enjoyed such a place in political life.

The Khilafat movement also introduced the religious idiom in the politics of Indian Muslims. Contrary to some misconceptions (and misrepresentations) it was not the Muslim League, the bearer of Muslim nationalism in India, that introduced religious ideology in the politics of Indian Muslims. Muslim nationalism was a movement of the Muslims and not a movement of Islam. It was an ethnic movement of disaffected Muslim professionals and the government-job-seeking educated Indian Muslim middle class, mainly those of Uttar Pradesh, Bihar and urban Punjab. Their objectives were modest, for they demanded little more than fair quotas in jobs for Muslims and certain safeguards for their interests. Muslim nationalism in India

---

[1] Gail Minault's study of the Khilafat movement is perhaps the best available, but she too subscribes broadly to the general consensus which the present study questions.

was a secular rather than a religious movement. Nor was it, in its origins, a Hindu-hating movement as is sometimes made out. On the contrary, by virtue of the Lucknow Pact of 1916 it had already moved decisively towards a common platform with the broader Indian national movement and unity with the Congress Party. The Khilafat movement intervened in that context in a way that decisively killed the politics of the Lucknow Pact. Its intervention has had considerable retrogressive ideological influence in the modern Indian Muslim mind that still reverberates in Muslim thinking and politics in India and Pakistan. For that alone, it deserves to be reviewed and re-evaluated.

THE KHILAFATIST CLAIMS

The arguments of the Indian Khilafatists were based on the claims that

(1) the Ottoman Khalifa was the 'Universal Khalifa' to whom all Muslims, everywhere in the world, owed allegiance;

(2) there was an ongoing war between the world of Christianity and the World of Islam, which, *inter alia*, caused loss of territories of the Ottoman Empire in Europe, a loss that Indian Muslims felt obliged to mourn;

(3) Britain in particular was an enemy of the Ottoman Khalifa; that after World War I Britain held the Khalifa captive in Istanbul. They demanded that the person and the office of the Khalifa be protected and preserved, and his sovereignty, including that over Ottoman Arab colonies and the Muslim Holy Places, be respected and preserved.

A dispassionate examination of the relevant facts shows that these claims were dubious.

ORIGINS OF THE OTTOMAN KHILAFAT

The acquisition of the status of Khalifa by the Ottoman Sultans is a disputed matter. When, in the modern era, they decided to describe themselves as *Khulafa*, they claimed that the Khilafat had been transferred three and a half centuries earlier to the Ottoman Selim I by al-Mutawakkil, a descendant of the Abbasids of Baghdad, who was living in exile in Egypt as a pensioner of the Mamluk ruler

Baybars, and who was defeated in 1517 by Selim. Baybars, the most distinguished of the Mamluk rulers, was originally a Turkoman slave. He had picked up al-Mutawakkil's father, an uncle of the last Abbasid Khalifa, and installed him in Cairo with great pomp as a 'pseudo-Khalifa',[2] who carried the name but none of the authority of the office. Baybars' object in installing him in Cairo was to confer honour and legitimacy on his crown and give his court an air of primacy in Muslim eyes.[3] Al-Mutawakkil succeeded his father in that role. He claimed to be the legitimate bearer of the (late) Abbasid Khilafat, although he was a man without a country and without authority. He had, at best, only a symbolic value for Baybars', in view of his connections with the Abbasid Dynasty. On his return to Istanbul Selim carried the hapless al-Mutawakkil with him, to deny a potential future Mamluk any shred of legitimacy.

The claim that the Khilafat was transferred by al-Mutawakkil to Selim is considered by historians to be dubious.[4] It has been argued that al-Mutawakkil was in no position to pass on the Khilafat to anyone, for he did not have it himself. What appears to the present writer to be a more telling argument against the veracity of that story is that for nearly three and a half centuries neither Selim nor any of his descendants called themselves *Khulafa*! There was no Ottoman Khilafat for all those centuries. The title the Ottoman Sultans took pride in using was that of *Ghazi*.

It had, however, become a common practice among medieval Muslim rulers to be addressed as Khalifa, but only informally so, along with other honorific titles, on ceremonial occasions. In Turkey such a practice also grew, imperceptibly and gradually. The title of Khalifa came to be added to the many honorific titles attached to the Ottoman Sultan. Yet the title of Khalifa was not officially used by the Ottomans until 1774, two hundred and fifty years after Selim's famous victory over the Mamluks. And this came about purely by coincidence. During negotiations with the victorious Russians of the Treaty of Kucuk Kaynarca, the Russian negotiators described their Empress, Catherine the Great, as 'the Head of the entire Christian Orthodox Church', thus laying a theoretical claim to the loyalties of Christian subjects of the Ottomans. Not to be outdone, a quick-witted

[2] For example, Arnold, 1924, p. 94.
[3] Hitti, 1960, p. 676.
[4] Ibid., pp. 676-7.

negotiator of the Sultan named his master the Khalifa of all Muslims. There was no more to it than that.

Despite the informal use of the title of Khalifa, the Ottomans did not yet claim that they were legitimate *Khulafa* and *religious* heads of all Muslims until much later. That was encouraged not least by the British who were staunch allies and patrons of the Ottomans, with an eye on the Muslims of India whom they hoped to influence through the Khalifa. Bernard Lewis writes: 'Under Abdul Aziz (1861-76) the doctrine was advanced for the first time that the Ottoman Sultan was not only the head of the Ottoman Empire but also the Khalifa of all Muslims and the heir, in a sense not previously accepted, of the *Khulafa* of early times.'[5]

LEGITIMACY OF OTTOMAN 'KHULAFA'

It was only in the late-nineteenth century that the Ottoman Sultans decided to lay claim to the Universal Khilafat. For that to be credible, they needed to establish an acceptable source of legitimacy in the eyes of the world. Turkish propaganda (which was greatly to influence Urdu journalism and Indian Muslim thought) dredged up the story of the transfer of the Khilafat to Selim by al-Mutawakkil in 1517. If the Ottomans could show that the Khilafat had been formally transferred to them by a member of the House of Abbas (who was supposed to be the custodian-in-exile of the Abbasid Khilafat and held that legacy until he could transfer it to a ruler who possessed secular powers that could do justice to that awesome office) their claim, they hoped, would thereby be unchangeable. The Ottomans resurrected al-Mutawakkil from the grave to prove their Khilafat credentials.

Indian Muslims were divided into at least two groups on the issue of recognition of the legitimacy of the Ottoman Khilafat, though it is remarkable that neither side questioned the veracity of the story that it had been passed on to Selim by al-Mutawakkil. Those who subscribed to the Barelvi tradition refused to accept the legitimacy of the Ottoman claim on an issue of principle. Barelvis did not disbelieve the story of al-Mutawakkil itself. Given years of Turkish propaganda about it in the Urdu press, they took it for granted, like other Indian Muslims. Their objection was that the Khilafat could be

[5] Lewis, 1961, p. 121.

held only by someone descended from the Quraysh clan, and the Ottomans were not of Quraysh descent. In taking that view they were in accord with an authoritative and established tradition in classical Islam. Eminent scholars such as Imam al-Ghazali and al-Mawardi had expressed the view that only a descendant of the Quraysh could be Khalifa.[6] In the light of the Barelvi rejection, and in order to rally Indian Muslims behind the Ottoman Khalifa, Maulana Abdul Bari of Firangi Mahal issued a *fatwa* in February 1919 laying down *inter alia* that Quraysh descent was not a necessary condition for Khilafat. Lined up against Bari were such major figures in Islamic learning as Imam al-Ghazali and al-Mawardi. His *ex cathedra* judgement was rejected not only by the Barelvis but also by influential groups of 'Deobandi' *ulama*. Gail Minault records the fact that several senior *ulama* refused to sign the *fatwa*. Amongst those who signed, the *ulama* of Deoband, Punjab and Bengal were conspicuous by their absence.[7]

The principled Barelvi position on this issue has been totally ignored by scholars although, arguably, they are the majority of Indian Muslims. Barelvis had a following not only in towns but also, and especially, amongst the vast majority of the rural population. A key difference between Barelvi beliefs and those of the so-called 'Deobandi Tradition' (the 'tradition' itself is much older than the eponymous Dar al-ulum at Deoband) is that Barelvis believe in intercession between ordinary humans and Divine Grace by an ascending, linked and unbroken chain of holy personages, *pirs,* reaching out ultimately to Prophet Mohammad.[8] It is a more superstitious but also a more tolerant tradition of Indian Islam. The views of the Barelvi tradition of South Asian Islam are, by and large, ignored by scholars. Usha Sanyal's pioneering study is an exceptional and excellent new beginning.[9]

[6] Ghazali, 1964, p. iv; al-Mawardi, 1960, Chapter I, section 1.

[7] List of those who signed it, and senior *ulama* who did not, can be found in Minault, 1982, p. 80.

[8] For comments see Alavi, 1988, pp. 84ff.

[9] *Devotional Islam and Politics in British India: Ahmad Riza Khan Barelwi and his Movement, 1870-1920* (Delhi, 1996). The Barelvi tradition is itself an old and time-honoured one. It was not created by Ahmad Reza Khan, who was its most able and articulate guide at the turn of the century.

THE UNEXAMINED CONCEPT OF 'KHALIFA'

Abul Kalam Azad, the principal theoretician of the 'Indian Khilafat Movement' summed up the fundamental ideological point of departure of the movement, quite succinctly, in the following statement:

It is an Islamic *Shar'i* law that in every age Muslims must have one [*ek*] khalifa and Imam.[10] By *Khalifa* we mean such an independent Muslim king or ruler of government and country who possesses full powers to protect Muslims and the territory that they inhabit[11] and to promulgate and enforce *Shar'i* laws and is powerful enough to confront the enemies of Islam.[12]

The Sultan of Turkey, it was held by the Indian Khilafatists, was such a Muslim ruler and Khalifa, and it was to him that Muslims of India should pay allegiance.

It is quite extraordinary that this 'basic religious premise' of the movement, as stated by Azad and others, is taken for granted and has not been subjected to critical examination. No adequate evaluation of it is possible without an analysis of its initial premises.

To begin with, there is a basic contradiction between the Ottoman claim that the Khilafat was transferred to them by al-Mutawakkil, which the Indian Khilafatists took as the Ottoman's charter, and the conditions for a legitimate Khilafat outlined by Azad. Those conditions render the Ottoman claim to Khilafat flawed from the start. By virtue of the conditions set out by Azad, al-Mutawakkil was not a legitimate custodian of the Khilafat. He was neither a Muslim king or ruler of any country nor was he independent, being a pensioner of Baybars, the Mamluk ruler. In the circumstances the question of his possessing the power to enforce *Shariat* laws obviously does

---

[10] Quoted by Abbasi (1986, p. 15) from Azad's Presidential Address before the Bengal Provincial Khilafat Conference on 28 Feb. 1920, taken presumably from the records of the *Zamindar*, a campaigning paper behind the Khilafat movement, of which Abbasi was the Deputy Editor. He was an important figure in the movement and, as such, a close colleague and friend of Azad. This passage cannot be found in the version of that Address in *Khutbaat-i-Azad* (Azad, 1944). Abbasi is the more reliable source and would have the full text of the speech in his files. This important address is, rather oddly, omitted in its entirety from *Khutbaat-i-Azad* as edited by Malik Ram (Azad, 1974).

[11] In conflating the titles of *Khalifa* (Khalifah) and *Imam*, Azad follows a discredited ideological position that dates back to the late Abbasid period when attributes of *Imam* were ascribed to *Khulafa*, imputing to them a religious role.

[12] This condition was not satisfied in the case of India where the Ottoman Sultan did not rule.

not arise. Al-Mutawakkil was in no position to transfer the Khilafat to the Ottomans. He had nothing to give. This objection to the validity of the Ottoman Khilafat is distinct from that put forward by the Barelvis. Azad's rhetoric, typically for him, is bound up in contradictions.

THE MEANING OF 'KHALIFA'

It is important to be clear at the outset about the meaning of the word *Khalifa* and the way in which that word was later transformed linguistically by the Umayyad *Khulafa* to legitimize a position that had been seized by military force. The word is derived from the Arabic root *khalafa* which means 'to follow' or 'to come after'. It means as 'successor' in the sequential sense, not in the sense of inheritance of properties or qualities. When Prophet Mohammad died, Abu Bakr was elected to succeed him. He was consequently called *Khalifat al-Rasool Allah* or the 'Successor of the Messenger of Allah'. In its true meaning, thus, the word *Khalifa* does not indicate rulership or a particular status, the sense in which it came to be used later. *Khalifa* meaning 'successor' could be used meaningfully only with reference to a specified 'predecessor'. Abu Bakr was *Khalifa* only with reference to his predecessor, *al-Rasool Allah*.

The head of the Muslim *umma*, Umar, who succeeded Abu Bakr, could have been called *Khalifat al-Khalif al-Rasool Allah*, or the 'Successor to the Successor to the Messenger of Allah'. With every succession thereafter one more '*Khalifat al . . .*' would have had to be prefixed to such a title of the previous one. That would have been quite absurd. The question of using the word *Khalifa* for those who came after Abu Bakr simply did not arise. Instead, Abu Bakr's successors, Umar, Uthman and Ali, the three successive elected heads of the *umma*, were each designated *Amir al-Mu'minin* or 'Commander of the Faithful'.

When the Umayyad dynasty was set up in Damascus, its legitimacy was contested. Unlike the elected headship of the *umma*, here was a seizure of power by military force. For that reason Maulana Abul Ala Maududi (1903-79) has called the rise of the Umayyad dynasty a 'counter-revolution against Islam' (*Inqilab-i-ma'koos*) and a reversion to *Jahiliya* or the age of ignorance that is said to have preceded the advent of Islam.[13] The Umayyad rulers

[13] Maududi, 1961, p. 38.

having become monarchs through military force, looked for a legitimating symbol to sanctify their regime. For that they chose the word *Khalifa*. They hoped thereby to attach to themselves the legitimacy that was associated with the title of Mohammad's successor, Abu Bakr. In so doing they changed the meaning of the word. It was no longer to mean 'successor' to a specified predecessor, but 'monarch' or 'ruler'.

A new word had been invented. It was a neologism, unconnected etymologically or semantically, with the original word meaning 'successor'. The new word was to mean 'monarch' or 'ruler'. Syed Ahmad Khan commented on that, saying:

The term *Khalifa* was abandoned by Hazrat Umar when he was elected to succeed Hazrat Abu Bakr. Instead of that he adopted the title of Amir al-Mu'minin [Commander of the Faithful]. . . . That title was used until the time of Hazrat Ali and for a time even after him. . . . After that and after the time of *Imam* Husain, the people who had taken over power [viz., the Umayyads] abrogated to themselves the title of *Khalifa*[14] because they thought that the title of *Khalifa* was more exalted (*muqaddas*) than that of Commander of the Faithful.[15]

The word *Khalifa*, having been misused by the Umayyad monarchs as their title, would have lost its force had it not been applied also to the four successors of Prophet Mohammad. But there was a general recognition of the obvious fact that the Umayyads were not in the same class as the latter. Therefore Abu Bakr and his three successors were redesignated *Khulafa-i-Rashidun*,[16] or 'The Rightly Guided *Khulafa*'. If any religious significance was attached to the first four, it was made clear that it did not apply to the later *Khulafa*, starting with the Umayyads.

Under the Umayyads the word *Khalifa* was not yet impregnated with any religious connotation. For them the word was to be only a symbol of legitimacy of their rule—a variant of the 'divine right of kings' as propounded in medieval Europe. It was only in later centuries that claims about the *religious* significance of the title were made. That was during the period of decay and decline of the late Abbasid Khilafat, when the Khalifa was reduced to a mere puppet

---

[14] Sir Syed Ahmad Khan writes, '*apné taeen Khalifa Ké lafz se apné app ko ta'bir kiya*'.

[15] Syed Ahmad Khan, 1962b, pp. 165-6.

[16] *Khulafa* is plural of *Khalifa*.

in the hands of military commanders or regional princes. These true holders of power needed to generate an ideology that would remove the Khalifa from the centre of secular state power, as the ruler, and relegate him to the sidelines as a nominal head of the state whose essential functions were supposed to lie in the religious sphere— where in practice, he had nothing of any significance to do.

GOD'S KHALIFA

In the Sunni tradition the religious domain is the domain of the *Imam*. But unlike the Pope, the *Imam* does not have religious *authority*. Islam, as is often said, does not recognize any priesthood: it is a religion of the individual conscience. *Imams* are therefore essentially guides, persons who by virtue of personal and religious perfection and excellence in scholarship come to be recognized as such. No one appoints them. In contradiction to that earlier usage, in the decadence of the late Abbasid period, a (nominal) religious significance began to be attached to the Khalifa. Increasing the practice grew of conflating the concepts of *Khalifa* and *Imam*. It is this later corrupted tradition that Azad follows in his words quoted earlier.

There was also an escalation in religious attributes attached to the Khalifa. The Khalifa was even called *Khalifat-Allah*, or 'Gods Khalifa' or 'successor'. Azad in fact takes the phrase *Khalifat-Allah* as his point of departure when expounding the meaning of the word *Khalifa*. The concept of *Khalifat-Allah* (God's Khalifa), which Azad uses freely when expounding the concept of the Khilafat was strongly denounced by classical Islamic scholars in works of which Azad could hardly have been ignorant. Al-Mawardi wrote in his classic, *Al-Ahkam as-Sultaniya*:

We disagree that he can also be called *Khalifat Allah*. . . . The consensus of the *Ulama* has prohibited this and condemned anyone who says it as a *fajir* (i.e., a sinner or liar) because there can be a *Khalifa* (successor) only of such a person who has disappeared or who has died. Allah can neither disappear nor can he die.[17]

Goldziher writes:

When the Umayyads used this pretentious title (*Khalifat-Allah*) it was merely

---

[17] Al-Mawardi, 1960, pp. 69-70.

intended to convey the unlimited power of the ruler. Under the later Abbasids the title was filled with theocratic content. . . . The Ottoman Sultans were . . . thought to have special claim for adopting these titles of the old *Khulafa* just as the name *Khalifat-Allah* was transferred to them.[18]

When Azad, in the corrupted late Abbasid tradition, begins his exposition of the concept of *Khalifa* with the discredited notion of *Khalifat-Allah*,[19] he follows the most backward and reactionary traditions in Islam.

Syed Ahmad Khan's position on this issue is emphatically the opposite. He distinguishes between *Khilafat*, the secular domain, and *Imamat*, the religious domain. 'After the death of the Prophet of Islam, Hazrat Abu Bakr was appointed. . . . Khalifat al-Rasool *Allah* . . . . (But) he had no religious authority (*dini ikhtiarat*). He repeatedly emphasized that the Khalifa was not like a Roman Catholic Pope. Hazrat Abu Bakr, he pointed out, was simply the administrative head of the community of Muslims.'[20] Shaban, a contemporary scholar, says exactly the same thing. He wrote: 'Mohammad could have no true successor, since no other man could ever have the same divine sanction. . . . Therefore Abu Bakr had no religious authority. . . . He was in no sense a grand combination of Pope and the Holy Roman Emperor.'[21]

Under the late Abbasids when 'the Khalifa had little left except the capital and even there his authority was shadowy',[22] there was an escalation in his religious attributes. The Khalifa being divorced from effective control over state power was presented to the people as a religious rather than a secular figure. The *Khulafa* were increasingly referred to as *Imams*. Goldziher notes that:

Under the later Abbasids the title with theocratic content. . . . (They, the *Khulafa*) claimed to be Representatives of God's rule on earth and even as 'God's shadow on earth'. The Ottoman Sultans, as the protagonists of Islam, were thought to have a special claim for adopting these titles of the old *Khulafa*, just as the name of *Khalifat-Allah,* or God's Khalifa, was transferred to them.[23]

[18] Goldziher, 1971, pp. 67-8.
[19] Azad, *Khutabat-i-Azad* (Lahore, 1944), p. 192.
[20] Syed Ahmad Khan, 1962, p. 165.
[21] Shaban, 1980, p. 19.
[22] Hitti, 1960, p. 465. See also Arnold, 1924, p. 57.
[23] Goldziher, 1971, pp. 67-8. The notion of *Khalifat-Allah* (God's Khalifa) is discussed later.

The Ottoman propaganda machine played a large part in spreading the notion of the Khalifa's supposed religious role, which by implication provided a basis for his claim to the loyalty of Muslims everywhere, including India. The Indian clergy in particular welcomed this, because it enhanced their place in Indian society and Indian Muslim politics as mediators between the Khalifa and 'his people'.

It was not long before 'Muslim' intellectuals and scholars came forward with 'authoritative' texts, inventing, emphasizing and exaggerating the supposed 'religious' role of the Khalifa as *Imam*. Gone was the notion of an elected secular head of state as it was under the *Khulafa-i-Rashidun*, the first four 'Rightly Guided *Khulafa'*. The notions about the supposed religious role of the Khalifa were in contradiction to the distinction made in original Islam between the secular head of state (an office that remained secular even when it was redesignated *Khalifa* by Umayyad rulers) and that of *Imam*, a religious guide who dwelt in the domain of faith. In the decadence of later days, the two concepts were often collapsed one into the other so that the words Khalifa and *Imam* were uttered in the same breath as if there was no distinction between the two.

THE UNIVERSAL KHILAFAT

Azad's speeches suggest that there could be only *one* Khalifa in every age. One would have to close one's eyes to much of Muslim history to accept this arbitrary condition at face value. The fact is that over many centuries there has been a plurality of rival *Khulafa* in the Muslim world. Several Khilafats have co-existed: contemporary with the Abbasids in Baghdad were the Umayyads in Spain and the Fatimids in Egypt. Besides these, there were numerous independent Muslim kingdoms whose heads claimed the title of Khalifa. Bosworth's comprehensive survey offers an account of no less than eighty-two such Islamic 'Khilafats'![24] Yet, the Ottomans propagandized the notion of a single 'Universal Khalifa' for the whole Islamic world as a basic component of Islamic polities. That was the basis on which they laid claim to the loyalties of Indian Muslims. The idea is of course pure fiction. And yet that is the assumption on which the Khilafat movement was premised.

[24] Bosworth, 1967.

Azad claimed that it was an Islamic *Shariat* law that in every age Muslims must have 'one' (*ek*) *Khalifa* and *Imam*, the Universal Khalifa. He does not indicate the source of that *Shariat* law where such a principle is laid down, or the basis on which he makes such a statement, for he had none. It was enough that his half-educated and ill-informed audiences were captivated by the fluency of the rhetoric he laced with long 'quotations' in Arabic, which was virtually Azad's first language.[25] They had little time to reflect on the veracity of what Azad said and claimed. In any case the content of what he (and others) said mattered little for they had already made up their minds 'to be carried away'! Those who pontificated to them were, for them, mere cheer-leaders.

Syed Ahmad Khan argued emphatically against the notion of a Universal Khilafat. His view was that every Khilafat was confined to territories which were directly under the control of the claimant of that title. The Khilafatists dismissed his argument *ad hominum* by accusing him of being a servile subject of the British. It was unworthy of them to say so. It was Azad and not Syed Ahmad who, on that issue, was in tune with the pro-Ottoman British policy which strongly supported the notion of the Ottoman Sultan as the Universal Khalifa. Considering the charges of servility to the British, it is even more significant that on the issue of the Universal Khilafat Syed Ahmad held his ground as a matter of principle, although his views were diametrically opposed to those of the British. It was quite another matter that his political project for the future of Muslims in India, as he saw it in the mid-nineteenth century, left him open to the charge of being a British puppet. Pro-British he may have been at the time, a puppet he was not, as this example shows. Syed Ahmad's stance on the Universal Khilafat defied both British and Turkish-inspired propaganda.

BRITISH RELATIONS WITH THE OTTOMAN KHALIFA

The British, far from being enemies of the Ottomans, as the Khilafat movement propaganda suggested, had remained their steadfast allies over many centuries. The enduring alliance was prompted by a threat to British imperial interests that came from expansionist ambitions of Czarist Russia. The Ottomans were equally worried about the

---

[25] Azad's mother was an Arab from Mecca.

Russian threat, the more so with their increasing weakness. They needed a strong and dependable ally, which they found in Britain. The Ottoman decision to ally (but belatedly) with Germany during World War I was a temporary break to centuries old British-Ottoman alliance. Turkey's aberrant wartime alliance with Germany arose due to a peculiar combination of circumstances within Turkey itself and despite every effort made by the British to prevent if from joining the Central Powers. Turkey stumbled into the War, in opposition to her traditional ally, by an uncalculated accident.

For Britain the Ottoman Empire was a valuable bulwark in Russia's way, in the context of a new age that had been inaugurated by the great explosion of maritime trade and the correspondingly increased importance of naval power, from the sixteenth century onwards. Global strategic priorities were radically changed. Control of the high seas, and not of large land masses, was now to be the secret of Imperial power. Britain soon emerged as a major maritime power and extended its imperial might around the globe.

Czarist Russia was handicapped in this new game, its naval power constrained by geography. Its Baltic Fleet was vulnerable at the narrow straits that separated Sweden from Germany and Denmark. Its Black Sea fleet was even more vulnerable at the Bosphorus and Dardanelles. Its Eastern fleet at Vladivostock was far too distant to play an effective role in the game. If Russia was to become a major world power, it had to have free and open access to the oceans of the world. The option before it was to push south to conquer territory that would place it in a dominating position on the Persian Gulf and the Arabian Sea. And that would be a direct threat to British imperial interests.

The Ottoman Empire stood in Russia's way to the warm waters to the south. It would have to break Ottoman power to mount a successful southward move. Russian policy was therefore consistently hostile to the Ottomans. Given that equation, the Russian threat to move south was an immovable foundation on which an enduring alliance between the British and the Ottomans was built. It was to last for centuries. They fought wars together as allies, most famously in the long and wasteful Crimean War of 1854-6. That war ended, as the British desired, in a Treaty that banned passage through the Bosphorus and Dardanelles of all naval units, which for all practical purposes meant Russian naval units. That effectively bottled up the Russian Southern Fleet in the Black Sea.

OTTOMAN EXPANSIONISM AND DECLINE

The Ottomans reached the height of their power by the end of the seventeenth century when the Sultan's army besieged Vienna for the second time but once again failed to conquer it. From that moment began the steady decline of Turkish power in Europe. Turkey was soon to lose her colonial possessions beyond the Danube and Sava rivers through expensive wars with Russia and the Habsburg in the eighteenth century. But the final Ottoman decline was only partly the result of conflicts between Turkey and those two great powers. In the main the Turkish retreat was forced by nationalist struggles of the southern Slavs who were as hostile to the colonial power of the Habsburg Austro-Hungarian Empire as they were to the Ottomans. In their wars of national independence the southern Slavs fought against both those colonial empires, the Ottoman as well as the Habsburg. In India, in the Urdu press particularly, this was mis-represented as a war of Christianity against Islam. It was in fact a war of nationalism against colonialism.

These were struggles for territory and power. Religion did not come into it. 'Muslim' Ottomans did not hesitate to fight Arab people and subjugate them. They also led repeated, though unsuccessful, campaigns against the 'brother' Muslim Safavid rulers of Iran. Likewise, Muslim subjects of the Ottomans were no less keen to gain their freedom. Stojanovic writes: 'The weakening of the Central Power encouraged the already strong separatist tendencies of Provincial Pashas. The Porte (the Centre of the Ottoman Govern-ment) had to cope with a series of Moslem revolts—including that of Mohammad Ali of Egypt.'[26]

As for the charge that independence movements in the Balkans were 'Christian' movements against 'Islam', we can hardly forget that it was the assassination of the 'Christian' heir to the Habsburg throne, Archduke Francis Ferdinand, by a 'Christian' Serb nationalist at Sarajevo, that triggered off the First World War. It is patently simplistic and absurd to describe the nationalist struggles in the Balkans, as it was being done by Indian Muslim publicists and bigoted *mullahs*, as a war of Christianity against Islam. The nineteenth century was an age of nationalist ferment everywhere—as indeed in India. The Balkan nationalist movements were a part of that global phen-omenon.

[26] Stojanovic, 1939, p. 2.

GREEK INDEPENDENCE

The Indian Khilafatists have made much of the idea that the British were pro-Greek and anti-Turk. That charge can be made against Lloyd George who was temporarily the Prime Minister of Britain in the war-time coalition government—the man who dictated the humiliating Treaty of Sèvres, which even his Conservative cabinet colleagues such as Bonar Law did not like. That was one reason why the Treaty was never ratified and implemented. After the end of the coalition government when Lloyd George was thrown out and a Conservative government returned, Britain returned to her traditional pro-Turkish or, rather, pro-Ottoman policy (that distinction is not without significance).

As for the long-term strategy of the British in the eastern Mediterranean, the idea that British governments were pro-Greek is false. Here again the threat from Czarist Russia entered into British calculations. In the Greek struggle for independence from Turkish colonial rule, despite strong popular support in Britain for the Greeks, the British Government itself was not at all in favour of Greek independence. They feared that it would give Russia an ally and a foothold in the eastern Mediterranean. However, following an enormous upsurge of public opinion in Britain, after the death in 1826 of Lord Byron, who had fought and died for the Greeks at Missolonghi, a reluctant British Government was finally pushed to join the alliance that had been initiated by the Russians in support of the Greeks. The outcome of that war was the Treaty of Adrianople in 1829. But the British Government was quite as unhappy about that Treaty as were the Turks. As Gewehr notes:

Due to British fears of Russian preponderance in the Balkans, it was not until 1832 that the final agreement regarding the territorial extent and the form of government in Greece was made. The new born Greek state was restricted to an area . . . (which) excluded from its boundaries many important centres. . . . A numerical majority of the Greek race was actually left under Turkish sovereignty. . . . That is explained by the fear of the English Prime Minister, The Duke of Wellington, that Greece would become a satellite of Russia and hence it must be restricted to a small area.[27]

Britain's commitments to the Ottomans remained unshaken.

---

[27] Gewehr, 1967, p. 28.

OTTOMAN SERVICES TO THE
BRITISH IN INDIA

The acceptance by Muslims of India of the Turkish Sultan as the Universal Khalifa was a relatively recent development. For Mughal India, there was no question of submitting to the overlordship of the Turkish Sultan, whom they rivalled in power and wealth and the size of the territory over which they ruled. It was during the period of British colonial rule in India that, with full British encouragement and support, the idea of accepting the Turkish Sultan as the Universal Khalifa was propagated amongst Indian Muslims as their venerated Khalifa to whom they owed allegiance. Given their alliance with the Ottomans, the British realized the value of the idea that the religious authority of the Ottoman Khalifa over Muslims everywhere could be brought into play to control Indian Muslims. The British welcomed that and encouraged propaganda on behalf of the Khalifa. In return, the Khalifa served the British well.

The first major example of this was in 1789 when Tipu Sultan, in defiance of the Mughals, paid formal allegiance to the Ottoman Khalifa who, in return, sent Tipu a *sanad* (charter of office) and *khilat* (robes of investiture) as ruler of Mysore. Tipu is a legendary figure in Indian history as a fighter against expanding British colonial rule. In 1798, therefore, at British request, the Ottoman Khalifa sent a letter to Tipu, telling him that the British were his friends and asking him to refrain from hostile action against them. The letter was sent to Tipu not directly but through Lord Wellesley who was leading the British forces against Tipu. Tipu replied to the Khalifa, professing devotion but also telling him that the Khalifa was too far away to know the situation in India. He had the impertinence to invite the Khalifa to join hands with him to throw out the infidel. Another major occasion when the Ottoman Khalifa came out in support of the British at a very difficult moment was at the time of India's War of National Independence in 1857 (downgraded by historians as 'The Indian Mutiny'). True to form, the Ottoman Khalifa Abdul Majid condemned the 'mutineers' and called upon Indian Muslims to remain loyal to the British. The British, he said, were the 'Defenders of Islam'.

The idea that the Ottoman Khalifa would be of value in controlling Muslims of India was at the forefront of British calculations in their relationship with the Ottoman *Khulafa*. That is illustrated by the reception they gave to the tyrant Sultan Abdul Aziz when he visited

London in 1867. The British went overboard with lavish enter-
tainment of the Khalifa. Significantly though the huge expenses
incurred were charged by the British Government to Indian revenues
'on the ground that cordial relations with the Sultan contributed
towards the good government of India. . . . The Sultan as head of
the Muslim religion, would propitiate Indian Muslims.'[28]

SHAPING OF PRO-TURKISH ATTITUDES
OF INDIAN MUSLIMS

Until the beginning of the nineteenth century Indian Muslims were
largely indifferent to Turkey and the Ottoman Khalifa. Quite apart
from British interests, two factors of major social change combined
to create conditions for successfully propagating pro-Turkish
sympathies among them. These two changes had quite separate
origins. But they were sufficiently intertwined to constitute a single
phenomenon.

The first of these was the emergence of a new educated Indian
Muslim middle class. This class of Muslims were brought up not in
the traditional education provided by the *madaris* and the *ulama*.
They were products of the new Anglo-Vernacular system of
education that was instituted by the colonial government, following
Macaulay's Minute of February 1835. It was a system of education
that was designed to produce men who would staff the colonial state
apparatus—civil servants and scribes. They were needed in state
employment to mediate between the English-speaking sahibs and
the local population. Nehru called it an educational system designed
to produce a 'nation of clerks'. It was a new class, which I have elsewhere named the *salariat*.[29] The *salariat* was that section of the
middle class whose goal was state employment. They sought not
'education' but 'educational qualifications', i.e. degrees and diplomas,
that would serve as a passport for a government job. In colonized
societies with an agrarian production base, the *salariat* tends to
dominate urban society and is the most articulate class which tends
to pre-empt issues in political debate. The *salariat* therefore came
to be a class of enormous social and political significance. It also
became a newspaper reading class, when newspapers became
affordable.

[28] Shukla, 1973, p. 123.
[29] Alavi, 1988, pp. 68ff.

The Muslim *salariat*, especially in Uttar Pradesh, was a rather disgruntled class, for it had lost ground in state employment, especially in the more prestigious upper ranks of jobs in which it had been preponderant. Psychologically, this class needed avenues through which it could channel its discontent. News of Turkey's defeats in the Balkans, which was represented to them as war of Christianity against Islam, struck a chord in increasingly communalists minds. The 'fate of the Turks' seemed to mirror their own sense of decline. They responded with deep sympathy to the news of the 'Tragedy of the Turks' (*turkon ka almia*). A powerful sense of solidarity was created and, poor as they were, they collected funds for Turkish aid. The British, on their part, did all they could to encourage this. They were happy to see a growing bond between their protégé, the Ottoman Khalifa, and Indian Muslims.

This potential political base on which strong pro-Ottoman sympathies were generated was fostered effectively by a new development, the emergence of Urdu popular journalism.[30] The early newspapers had a minimal circulation, catering as they did to a handful of the wealthy and powerful who needed to keep in touch with affairs of the state and of the world of commerce. Many of these 'newspapers' were produced in manuscript form. Urdu printing was in vogue too, for *naskh* metallic type for Urdu had been available for some time. But *naskh* was not popular with general readers, and was also expensive. Calligraphic *nastaliq* writing was immensely more popular. As it turned out, the best method for printing *nastaliq* script, lithography, became widely available precisely at that critical time in the history of the Indian Muslim *salariat*. Litho printing was invented in 1796. Further development were needed before it could be used to print newspapers in large numbers and cheaply. By 1850 the first mechanized lithographic press became available. Later in the nineteenth century it became possible to build rotary presses by replacing stone with a zinc plate which could be curved. These inventions made large scale litho printing in *nastaliq* script both possible and cheap. Urdu newspapers could now be turned out in large numbers which 'everyone' could afford. For Urdu readers, the age of the mass media had arrived. But the papers needed issues that could be sensationalized, to build up their circulation. The drama

---

[30] Abdus Salaam Khurshid's slim volume (Khurshid, n.d.) is very informative about the history of Urdu journalism, more so than Sabri's massive three volumes (Sabri, 1953).

of the 'Turkish tragedy' was just what they needed. They played it for all they were worth.

Events of the First World War were a traumatic shock to Indian Muslims. They had grown up with the knowledge about friendship between Britain and the Ottomans, which was regularly reflected in news items in the Urdu press. The news of Turkey and Britain being on opposite sides in the War was therefore a blow. Nothing illustrates this with more poignancy than Maulana Mohamed Ali's long article entitled 'The Choice of the Turks' in his journal the *Comrade*. After listing Turkish grievances against Britain, he expressed a fervent hope that the Turks would remain neutral in spite of these slights. He ended with an assurance of Muslim loyalty to Britain.[31]

TURKEY AND WORLD WAR!

Turkey's decision to join Germany and the Central Powers was a complete surprise to everyone, including the Turks themselves. In 1908 a radical group called the 'Committee for Union and Progress' (the CUP), the so-called 'Young Turk', seized power in a coup, deposing the tyrannical Khalifa Abdul Hamid II. In his place the CUP installed his brother Mohammad Reshed as Khalifa. The Young Turk regime itself soon degenerated into a military oligarchy. Behind the scenes there was an ongoing triangular 'struggle for power with the Turkish state between the Khalifa supported by conservatives and reactionaries, the High Bureaucrats supported by liberals, and (on the third hand) the radical Unionists',[32] the Young Turks.

Despite differences within the Turkish ruling élite on internal questions, it was remarkable that they were all unanimously pro-British. That was the legacy of their shared experience of centuries of British support. As far as the Turkish élites were concerned, the British had been their most consistent and reliable friends. Despite factional squabbles, there was no faction which was not pro-British. Turkey's decision to ally with the Central Powers was therefore completely at odds with her long-standing friendship with Britain and France. This requires explanation.

[31] Quoted by Minault, 1982, p. 51.

[32] Feroz Ahmad, 1993, p. 35. Feroz Ahmad, the distinguished historian of modern Turkey, must not be confused with Feroz Ahmad, the Pakistani Marxist and Sindhi nationalist scholar.

[33] Ibid., p. 40.

Initially, Turkey itself offered to join Britain and the Allies.[33] But, despite Britain's consistent alliance with Turkey over many centuries and her commitment to preserve the safety and integrity of the Ottoman Empire in pursuit of her own imperialist interests against Czarist Russia, the Western powers turned down the offer.

There are some clues to this puzzle to be found in the auto-biography of the Aga Khan. Although the British had declined the Turkish offer to join them in the War, they were, nevertheless, most keen that it should stay neutral. The Aga Khan writes:

Lord Kitchener requested me to use all my influence with the Turks to persuade them not to join the Central Powers but to preserve their neutra-lity. . . . His opinion was shared and supported by the Secretary of State for India, by the Foreign Secretary Sir Edward Grey and by the Prime Minister Mr Asquith. Indeed even the King, when I had the honour of lunching with him, referred to it.[34]

So the Aga Khan got in touch with his 'old friend' Tawfiq Pasha, the Turkish Ambassador in London. They both agreed that Turkey should be kept out of the War. The Young Turks were invited to send a ministerial delegation to London to enter into direct negotiations with the British Government. The Aga Khan writes: 'Britain was prepared on her own behalf and on behalf of Russia and her other allies to give Turkey full guarantees and assurances for the future.'[35] He added that neutrality would give the Turks, after their recent losses, the time they needed to carry out their programme of social, economic and military reforms. That seemed to make sense.

Tawfiq Pasha, having meanwhile been briefed by his own government, told the Aga Khan that their negotiations would have a much better chance of success if the Allies were to ask the Turks to come and join them instead of staying neutral, as Britain had proposed 'for at the end of the conflict no one would thank her for staying neutral'. (But would neutrality not have been better than joining the losing side? And would neutrality have been disastrous if it was at the suggestion of the winning side?) Why did Britain decline one more ally? The underlying problem as so many times before, was Czarist Russia. Given Russia's anti-Turk attitude, there was a strong possibility that Britain, by taking Turkey as an ally, would have been left isolated to face the rising tide of German

[34] Aga Khan, 1954, p. 163.
[35] Ibid.

power, on her own. That was a risk that the British did not wish to take. Tawfiq Pasha 'was also convinced that Russia would never agree to Turkey joining the Allies, as such a step would put an end to all Russia's hopes of expansion at Turkey's expense, either in the North-East around Erzerum, or Southwards'.[36] The British had little choice but to decline Turkey's offer. Accepting Turks as allies would have antagonized the Russians. Russian neutrality would have left Britain at the mercy of the Germans. After repeated Ottoman requests to the British to let them join in the War had been politely turned down, the Turkish Government adopted a policy of 'wait and see', initially at least, rather than join Germany precipitately. But they also carefully avoided showing hostility to the Germans. They were keeping their options open. While they were still debating which side to align with, or stay neutral, in October 1914 the Turks, as Lewis puts it, 'stumbled into a major European War'.[37] The Aga Khan writes that:

By the close of 1914 the Central Powers were confident of quick victory on their own terms. . . . Tragically misled by all these signs and portents dangled before their eyes by the exultant Germans the Turkish Government took the irrevocable step of declaring war on Russia. This automatically involved the Ottoman Empire in war with Great Britain and France.[38] This was a disastrous move for which they have to pay a heavy price later.

THE KHALIFA AFTER WORLD WAR!

The 'Young Turk' (CUP) leaders, who had led Turkey into the disastrous War, fled into exile on board a German gunboat. In July 1918 the wartime Khalifa Mohammad Reshed, the nominee of the CUP leaders, was deposed and Mehmet Vahdettin (Mohammad Wahid-uddin), was installed in his place. Friends of Britain were in the driver's seat again. The government was reshuffled and an armistice was signed on 30 October. According to Aksin, 'in March 1919 Damad Ferid Pasha, the Grand Vizier, sent a message to the British to the effect that "their entire hope was in God and in England, that a certain amount of financial aid was a must and that they were prepared to arrest anyone the British wanted" '.[39]

[36] Aga Khan, 1954, p. 164.
[37] Lewis, 1961, p. 233.
[38] Aga Khan, op. cit., p. 165.
[39] Aksin, 1976, p. 229. I am indebted to Hakki Rizatepe for his generous help with the translation of Aksin's Turkish text.

During the War Britain had directed all its anti-Turk propaganda against the Young Turks but had spared the Khalifa himself because of the possibility of having to cooperate with him again after the War. The decision to spare the Khalifa was based on the recognition of three facts. First, he was merely a figurehead and it was the Young Turk leaders who were responsible for going to War. Secondly, and even more importantly, the British who were confident of victory, knew that the sympathies of the Khalifa and the old ruling class in Turkey were wholeheartedly with them and would continue to remain with them. Thirdly, Britain was still looking forward to the value of being able to exploit the Khalifa's claim to be the religious head of the entire 'Muslim World', as they had done successfully in the past. The Khalifa had been a valuable asset for the British in the past who, they thought, was worth preserving.

When, at the end of the War, the Young Turk leaders fled precipitately into exile, there was a power vacuum which was instantly filled by the old ruling class with the Khalifa as their head. This suited the British. Their protégé was in charge once again. Contrary to the Khilafatist's charges Britain was fully committed, after her victory, to preserve the Khilafat, protect the Khalifa, and insofar as it was possible, reinforce his authority in Turkey and abroad. In accusing Britain of being hostile to their venerated Khalifa, the Khilafatists were fighting an imaginary enemy. The real threat to the Khalifa came from the rise of the powerful Turkish republican nationalism with its secular and democratic aspirations. The Khilafatists proved to be quite incapable of perceiving the nature and significance of that historic conflict between the monarchical rule of the Khalifa and the democratic aspirations of the republican nationalists. Paradoxically, they glorified the arch-adversary of the Khilafat, Mustafa Kemal, whom they gave the title of *Ghazi*, while at the same time they also glorified their venerated Khalifa. They could not see that they were irreconcilable forces in Turkish society and politics. Their failure to comprehend this is quite incredible. When the denouement finally came about, with the victory of Turkish republican nationalism and the end of the Khilafat, the Khilafatists were left totally bewildered, unable to comprehend the news that came to them.

A new Turkish state was emerging in Anatolia, led by men who rejected outright the Treaty of Sèvres and the principles that underlay it. They condemned those Turks who had accepted it, as traitors.

The Indian Khilafatists shed endless tears over the injustices of the Treaty, but could not yet see that it was not their beloved Khalifa but the forces of the republican nationalist who successfully repudiated it. They were too preoccupied lamenting the 'fate of the Khalifa' to see the Turkish reality as it was actually unfolding before their eyes. The supine Khalifa had acquiesced in the iniquitous Treaty inspired by Lloyd George's prejudices. But, thanks to the power of the republican nationalists, it remained a dead letter until the victorious nationalists later renegotiated a fresh Treaty at the Peace Conference that opened at Lausanne on 20 November 1922. In the word of Lord Curzon (quoted by 'Maulana' Mohamed Ali) the Treaty of Sèvres was 'dictation of terms at the point of the Bayonet. . . . Only when the terms had been drawn up was the beaten enemy admitted, to be told his sentence. . . . Far otherwise was it at Lausanne. There the Turks sat at the table on a footing of equality with all the other powers.'[40]

BRITISH INTRIGUES WITH THE KHALIFA

On 9 November 1918, with the Khalifa and his coterie back in charge, Calthorpe, the newly appointed British High Commissioner in Istanbul, wrote to Foreign Secretary Lord Balfour: 'The Turkish Ministers will try to present themselves as genuine friends of the British and will try to win you over.'[41] He emphasized to his government that the Khalifa was important to the Muslim world as a whole, as in Turkey itself. The Khalifa, he wrote, was very eager that they, the British, 'should settle in Istanbul'.[42]

With the backing of the British, the Khalifa's government prepared to confront the remnants of the Young Turks and following that the emerging force of the republican nationalists. From now on 'one of the first tasks of the Turkish Sultan and his ministers was to crush the remnants of the Young Turks'.[43] The new republican nationalist movement, under the leadership of Mustafa Kemal, had to be suppressed, decisively. On their part, the nationalists were getting organized for action. By July 1919 Kemal convened a Congress of

[40] Mohamed Ali's Presidential speech at the Indian National Congress at Cocanada on 26 Dec. 1923 in: Mohamed Ali, 1944, p. 299.
[41] Aksin, 1976, p. 93.
[42] Ibid., p. 168.
[43] Lewis, 1961, p. 235.

Delegates from every district which laid the foundations of a popular Grand National Assembly which began to function from April 1920 to preside over the liberation of Turkey from dynastic rule. That caused alarm to the Allies as well as their protégé, the Khalifa. By August 1919 a declaration known as the *Milli Misak* or the 'National Pact' was issued. In September, at the Second Congress of the Republican National Assembly, Mustafa Kemal was elected Chairman. The nationalist struggle was well and truly launched.

To forestall a possible nationalist coup against their friend, the Khalifa (who had desperately been calling for their help), British forces entered the Turkish quarter of Istanbul on 16 March 1920 (eighteen months after the Khalifa had been back in business) and began to round up known nationalists. True to the time-honoured role of *mullahs* in such situations the Sheikh-al Islam, Durrezade Abdullah Effendi, issued a *fatwa* on the invitation of the Grand Vizier Damad Ferid Pasha, declaring that killing of nationalists was a religious duty of Muslims.[44] The target of that *fatwa* included Mustafa Kemal himself, against whom a sentence of death was already pronounced. The Indian Khilafatists who venerated the Khalifa and glorified Kemal Attatürk at the same time, appear to have received this news in uncomprehending silence. Given the prevalence of nationalist influences in the Turkish army, the Khalifa continued the disarming of Turkish force.[45] To forestall a popular revolt or a *coup d'etat*, the Khalifa, with British help, organized an independent special force known as *quwwa-indibatiya* ('force for discipline and control') to fight the nationalists. The nationalists, however, went from strength to strength.

KEMAL ON 'THE FRIENDS OF ENGLAND'

Confronted by republican nationalism, the Khalifa turned to the British for survival. Mustafa Kemal, in his remarkable retrospective 'six-day speech' of October 1927, spoke about a 'Society of the Friends of England' that was formed, as he put it, by some 'misguided' persons. He pointed out that: 'At the head of the Society were Vahdettin, who bore the title of Ottoman Sultan and Khalifa,

---

[44] Abbasi, 1986, p. 210; and Lewis, 1961, p. 246. Whether the Sheikh-ul-Islam's *fatwa* was in favour of the Khalifa or aginst him, depended on who was in power and wielded the stick.

[45] Lewis, 1961, p. 242.

Ferid Pasha (the Grand Vizier), Ali Kemal, Minister of the Interior. . . .' (Kemal named other leading figures of the *ancien regime*).
Kemal charged that the Society 'openly sought the protection of
England . . .', that 'it worked in secret', and that 'its real aim was to
incite the people to revolt by forming organizations in the Interior,
to paralyse the National Conscience and encourage foreign countries
to interfere'.[46] Kemal pointed out that: 'without knowing it, the nation
had no longer any one to lead it'.[47] He continued:

The Nation and the Army had no suspicion at all of the Padishah Khalifa's[48]
treachery. On the contrary, on account of religious and traditional ties
handed down for centuries, they remained loyal to the throne and its
occupant. . . . That the country could possibly be saved without a Khalifa
and without a Padishah was an idea too impossible for them to
comprehend.[49] . . . To labour for the maintenance of the Ottoman Dynasty
and its sovereign would have been to inflict the greatest harm, to the Turkish
nation. . . . We were compelled to rebel against the Ottoman Government,
against the Padishah, against the Khalifa of all Mohamedans, and we had
to bring to whole nation and the army into a state of rebellion.[50]

Kemal made it clear that he had made a decision to get rid of the
Khalifa from the very start of the republican revolution, although
prudence and tactical considerations dictated that the ground must
be prepared for it before the Khilafat was ended, step by step. That
was finally done in 1924. He said: 'From the first I anticipated this
historical progress. But I did not disclose all of my views, although
I have maintained them all of the time. . . . The only practical and
safe road to success lay in dealing with each problem at the right
time.'[51]

Kemal's statement made it clear that the Khalifa was in league with
the British and the European powers, who considered the Khalifa a
bulwark against the advancing forces of Turkish nationalism. This

---

[46] Attatürk, 1963, p. 5. This 740-page long speech was delivered over a period of
six days in Oct. 1927 before Deputies and representative of the Republican Party.
One must admire Kemal's stamina in delivering it and the audience's patience in sitting
through it.

[47] Ibid., p. 8. One can see Kemal's anger and contempt for the Khalifa in long
passages in the speech.

[48] The glossary that accompanies the publisheed text of the 'six day speech' defines
'Padishah' as 'The ruler or sovereign of the Ottomans, (the) Sultan'.

[49] Ibid., p. 7. Nor could the Indian Khilafatists comprehend that.

[50] Ibid., p. 10.

[51] Ibid., p. 11.

reality was only partly obscured by the extravagant and chauvinistic anti-Turk and pro-Greek rhetoric of Lloyd George and Asquith, who had headed the War-time coalition government in Britain. They were both soon to be ousted with the fall of their government and the formation of a Conservative government under Bonar Law, which reverted to Britain's old policy, except for new plans, made in league with the French, to carve up between themselves Turkish colonial possessions in Arabia.

ARABIA: A CHANGE IN BRITISH
GEO-POLITICAL PRIORITIES

The British were still interested in maintaining their friend, the Ottoman Khalifa, at the head of affairs in Turkey, if they could manage it. But the War had brought about a basic change in the historical reasons for British strategic support for the Ottomans. Britain's centuries old alliance with Turkey had been founded on British fear about the threat of a southward drive of Czarist Russia. Until the War, Ottoman Turkey was a bulwark against Russian southwards expansionism. The Communist Revolution of 1917 in Russia radically changed the strategic map. There was now an entirely new configuration of strategic calculations for the region. One of the first things that the Soviets did after winning power was to renounce all unequal treaties with neighbouring states that were a legacy from the Czarist days. They had no ambitions, nor indeed any capacity, for a drive to the south. Britain no longer needed a strong Ottoman state as a bulwark against a possible Russian threat, as it had needed hitherto. Its priorities changed.

The British and the French could now contemplate carving up the Arab colonies of the Ottomans between themselves. But Arab nationalist movements had already begun to make themselves felt, demanding their freedom from all colonial rule. However, sadly, the Turkish republican nationalists were no less committed to hold on to their Empire, in Arab lands, than the *Khulafa* before them. Indian Khilafatists slavishly followed Turkish slogans demanding preservation of Turkish colonial rule over the Arabs, rather than take a principled stand on the question of the right of the Arabs to national self-determination. The Arab territories were already under the *de facto* control of Britain and France. The Khilafatist slogans therefore demanded reimposition of Turkish colonial authority rather than

Arab freedom. They asked for restoration of Turkish colonialism under the guise of a demand that Muslim holy places should remain under Muslim rule. The Khilafat slogan was patently untrue. Given the claim of the Khilafatists to be Indian nationalists, their stand on Arab nationalism was quite shameful. But this was hardly surprising, coming from a movement that was dominated by the ignorant and bigoted Indian Muslim clergy and reactionary *ulama* such as Azad.

The Indian Khilafatists not only betrayed Arab nationalism, but their slogan for the authority of the Khalifa to be preserved was also reactionary. They were asking for the preservation of an outmoded monarchy in the face of a rising tide of republican democracy. Their campaign was misconceived, based on ignorance and prejudice and, founded on discredited interpretations of the supposed religious role of the Khalifa. Their perception of reality was twisted by narrow dogmatic and utterly reactionary ideology.

THE KHALIFA AS PRISONER OF THE BRITISH

The whole case of the Khilafatist campaign was based on the charge that after the War the British held the Khalifa 'captive', that they had undermined his authority and threatened his existence. The reality, as we know, was exactly the reverse. The real threat to the Khalifa came from republican nationalists. On the other hand, the British were the Khalifa's patrons and protectors—and they were as hostile to the nationalists as the Khalifa himself. How did the Khilafatists come to hold such a false nation of the Turkish reality?

Republican nationalism was a direct threat to the Khalifa, for its aims was to put an end to monarchic rule. The Khalifa had one weapon that he could deploy against the nationalists, Islamic ideology, of which he claimed to be the guardian. The Khalifa played the religious card for all its worth, and denounced the nationalists as atheists and enemies of Allah and his Khalifa. By that he hoped to alienate the mass of the Turkish people from the republican nationalist leadership.

Despite their rapidly growing strength, nationalists were as yet at an early stage of their great enterprise. Threatened by the Khalifa's campaign, they felt they could not ignore it. As Kemal's speeches show, they feared that Islamic ideology could still be a powerful factor among the Turkish people and that the Khalifa's propaganda might do their cause much harm. Feroz Ahmad, commenting on this, writes:

The nationalists took great pains to counter the *Khulafa*'s religious propaganda, for they understood the powerful influence of Islam in Turkish society. Their task became easier when Istanbul was occupied by Anglo-French forces. Now they could describe the Sultan-Khalifa as the captive of Christian powers, waiting to be liberated.[52]

These forces had entered Istanbul on 16 March 1920. Nationalist counter-propaganda on this score did not have much ground to stand on, but it was an ideological war. And any weapon that came to hand was welcome. British forces came into Istanbul only when the republican nationalists were gaining ground. It was feared, not without reason, that there might be republican coup against the Khalifa. If it had been the intention of the British to keep the Khalifa their 'captive' they would have moved in a year and a half earlier.

Whatever the Turkish people themselves may have made of the propaganda that the Khalifa was a prisoner of the British, the leaders of the Indian Khilafat movement seem to have swallowed it. The liberation of the Khalifa from the clutches of the British became their central slogan. Indeed that became the *raison d'être* of their campaign. These worldly wise leaders did not consider the possibility that the Khalifa could actually be a willing collaborator with the British, acting in collusion with the Western powers with whom he had common cause. Nor was this a matter that could not have been easily verified—it was important enough for them at least to have made an effort. All that they needed to do was to send a delegation to Istanbul, to see things for themselves. They had extensive personal contacts at all levels, amongst all groups, in Istanbul. They would have had no difficulty in getting to the bottom of things if they had wanted to do so. But they did not.

One might suspect that they did not really want to get to the bottom of it, for that would have punctured the balloon of their movement before it even got off the ground. The *maulanas* and *mullahs* behind the campaign needed the movement for its own sake. Whatever it may not have done for their revered Khalifa, it was certainly doing a lot for them. The campaign was elevating them to the forefront of Indian Muslim politics, for a while totally eclipsing

---

[52] Feroz Ahmad, 1993, p. 48.

the secular educated Muslim leadership. Because of the Khilafat movement the Muslim clergy was able to secure a legitimate place for itself in the political arena and masquerade as men with a nationalist conscience. In the process they also built up a political organization in the form of the Jamiyat al-ulama-i Hind.

INDIAN KHILAFATISTS AND TURKISH REALITY

The Indian Khilafatists could not comprehend the significance of the forces that were reshaping Turkey and the momentous changes that were in train. Abbasi, an Urdu journalist and a leading participant in the Khilafat movement, for example, explains Turkish politics of that period in terms of purely personal differences and intrigues.[53] He praises Mustafa Kemal as a great Ghazi, for victories against Greek, but also bemoans the fate of the Khalifa. Abbasi goes on to write that 'Mustafa Kemal challenged the *Khalifat-i-Muslémeen* and the Sultan found himself to be helpless. At last he complained to his Western Masters (*aqayane firang*). . . . But they were not prepared to take any decisive step against the Republican Movement.'[54] That statement by an important figure in the movement exemplifies their confusion and utter lack of comprehension of events in Turkey. It is to be deplored that a leading Indian Khilafatist, a champion of the cause of anti-colonialism, bemoaned the absence of British intervention against the Turkish nationalists. Abbasi's contradictory posture was by no means unique. It reflects the widely held attitudes of the Indian Khilafatist and their inability to understand the forces that were at work in Turkey and historic struggles that were reshaping it. At no point did they reflect on the significance of Turkish republican movement and ask themselves whether their own movement on behalf of the Khalifa had not been overtaken by events.

It is not surprising that the Government of India was not only tolerant but even supportive of the Khilafat movement. Until the launching of Gandhi's Civil Disobedience (quite a different kind of issue), the British responded to the Khilafat movement in quite good humour. It is not without significance that it was at the time when the latter had only just begun to gather steam that the colonial

[53] Abbasi, 1986, pp. 199ff.
[54] Ibid., p. 208.

government released from detention Mohamed Ali, Shaukat Ali, Abul Kalam Azad and Zafar Ali Khan, who were leading and effective figures of the movement. In the post-War situation their pro-Khalifa sympathies were no longer a threat to British interests, quite the contrary.

Nothing reveals the stand of the Government of India on the Khilafatists more clearly than its decision to finance a Khilafat delegation to Europe. In January 1920 a Khilafat delegation, led by M.A. Ansari, met the Viceroy, Lord Chelmsford, who promised them every assistance. A telling 'petty detail' arising out of it is that, following the meeting, Shaukat Ali wrote a letter on 20 January 1920 to an official, Maffey, requesting the Government of India to provide five first class return tickets for the Khilafat delegation which had gone to England to plead the Khilafat cause before the British public and parliament and the Peace Conference in Paris—a curious request from champions of a supposedly anti-colonial movement to their colonial masters! The Secretary to the Home Department of the Government of India immediately cabled the Government of Bombay asking them to arrange the passages accordingly, emphasizing its political importance.[55] This is a clear illustration of the fact that the Government of India did not see the Khilafat as a dangerous anticolonial movement, hostile to the Empire. British repression was let loose only later with the launching of the Congress Civil Disobedience movement, when appeals were made by some individuals to Muslims not to serve in the British army. That indeed was a threat to British imperial interests. But those appeals were born out of the Congress Civil Disobedience movement and were disowned by some Khilafat leaders.

The Khilafat movement has been idealized as an anti-colonial movement. But its main 'achievement' was the turning away of Indian Muslims from a secular understanding of politics, towards a religious and communalist one. It has left a legacy of political activism of the Muslim clergy that bedevils Indian and Pakistani politics to this day. One final irony of it is that the movement betrayed both Turkish and Arab nationalism. Unfortunately, Gandhi's leadership of the movement has led Indian nationalist scholars to acclaim uncritically the movement and Gandhi's role in it. On the other hand, M.A. Jinnah (who in the present writer's view has been accused, quite

---

[55] Home Poll. 588, 23 Jan. 1920, 2-14, National Archives of India (NAI).

unjustifiably of being a 'communal leader' rather than one with a secular outlook) was physically beaten by 'Maulana' Shaukat Ali for opposing that atavistic religious movement, which has had such a major negative impact on Indian (and Pakistani) Muslim political thought. Finally, the Khilafat movement laid the foundations of political leadership of the Muslim clergy, for which it was to be acclaimed by Islamic ideologists.

REFERENCES

Abbasi, Qazi Mohammad Adeel, *Tehrik-e-Khilafat* (Lahore, 1986).

Aga Khan, The, *The Memoirs of Aga Khan* (New York, 1954).

Ahmad, Aziz, *Studies in Islamic Culture in the Indian Environment* (Oxford, 1964).

——— *Islamic Modernism in India and Pakistan* (London, 1967).

Ahmad, Feroz, *The Young Turks: the Committee of Union and Progress in Turkish Politics 1908-1914* (Oxford, 1969).

——— 'The Late Ottoman Empire', in Marian Kent (ed.), *The Great Powers and the End of the Ottoman Empire* (London, 1984).

Alavi, Hamza, 'Pakistan and Islam: Ethnicity and Ideology' in Fred Halliday (ed.), *State and Ideology in the Middle East and Pakistan* (London and New York, 1988).

Aksin, Sina, *Istanbul Hukumetleri va Milli Mucadele* (Istanbul, 1976).

Arnold, T.W., *The Khilafat* (London, 1924).

Atatürk, Mustafa, Kemal, *A Speech Delivered by Mustafa Kemal Atatürk, 1927,* p. 744. Speech delivered before the Deputies of the 'Republican Party' from 15 to 20 Oct. 1927 (Istanbul, 1963).

Azad, Abul Kalam, *Khutbaat-i-Azad*, edited by Shorish Kashmiri (Lahore, 1944).

——— *Khutbaat-i-Azad*, edited by Malik Ram (Delhi, 1974).

——— *Tazkira*, edited by Malik Ram (Lahore, n.d.).

——— *Azad Ki Kahani Khud Azad ki Zabani*, edited by A.R. Malihabadi (Lahore, n.d.).

Bosworth, C.E., *The Islamic Dynasties* (Edinburgh, 1967).

Evangelos, K., *Greece and the Eastern Question* (n.d.).

Gewehr, W.M., *The Rise of Nationalism in the Balkans: 1800-1930* (1967).

Ghazali, Imam, *Counsel for Kings (Nasihat Al-Muluk)* with Introduction by F.R.C. Bagley (London, 1964).

Gibb, H.A.R., *Studies on the Civilisation of Islam* (London, 1962).

Goldziher, Ignaz, 'Umayyads and Abbasids' in *Muslim Studies,* vol. II (London, 1971).

Greenwall, H.J., *His Highness the Aga Khan* (London, 1952).

Hardy, Peter, *The Muslims of British India* (Cambridge, 1972).

Hasan, Mushirul (ed.), *Communal and Pan-Islamic Trends in Colonial India* (New Delhi, 1985). ·

—— *Islam and Indian Nationalism: Reflections on Abul Kalam Azad* (New Delhi, 1992).

Hitti, P.K., *History of the Arabs* (London, 1960).

Husain, Mahmud, *A History of the Freedom Movement* (Karachi, 1957a).

—— 'Tipu Sultan' in Mahmud Husain (ed.) (Karachi, 1957b).

Ikram, S.M. *Mauj-e-Kauthar* (Lahore, 1965 rpt.).

Inalcik, Halil, *The Ottoman Empire: The Clasical Age 1300-1600* (London, 1973).

Jackson, Stanley, *The Aga Khan* (London, 1952).

Khurshid, Abdus Salaam, *Sahafat: Pakistan va Hind Main* (in Urdu) (Lahore, n.d.).

Lewis, Bernard, *The Emergence of Modern Turkey* (London, 1961).

Margoliouth, D.S., 'The Sense of the Title Khalifah' in T.W. Arnold and R.A. Nicholson (eds.), *A Volume of Oriental Studies Presented to Edward G. Browne* (Cambridge, 1922).

Maududi, Abul Ala, *Tajdid va Ahyay-e-Din* (Lahore, 1961 rpt.).

—— *Khilafat va Mulukiyat* (Lahore, 1982 rpt.).

—— *Al-Ahkam as-Sultaniya* (Cairo, 1960).

Minault, Gail, 1982, *The Khilafat Movement: Religious Symbolism and Political Mobilisation in India* (Delhi, 1982).

—— 'The Elusive Maulana: Reflections on Writing Azad's Biography' in Hasan (ed.), (Delhi, 1992).

Mohamed Ali, *Speeches and Writings of Maulana Mohamed Ali* (Lahore, 1944).

Owen, S.J. (ed.), *Selection from Wellesley's Despatches* (Oxford, 1877).

Sabri, Imdad, *Tarikh-é-Sahafat-é-Urdu* (Delhi, 1953), 3 vols.

Sanyal Usha, *Devotional Politics in British India: Ahmad Riza Khan Barelwi and his Movement, 1870-1920* (New Delhi, 1955).

Shaban, M.A., *Islamic History*, vol. I (Cambridge, 1980 rpt.).

—— *Islamic History*, vol. II (Cambridge, 1980 rpt.).

Shukla, R.L. *Britain, India and the Turkish Empire, 1853-1882* (New Delhi, 1973).

Stojanovic, M.D., *The Great Powers and the Balkans: 1875-1878* (Cambridge, 1939).

Sunar, Ilkey, *State and Society in the Politics of Turkey's Development* (Ankara, 1974).

Syed Ahmad Khan, *Maqalat-i-Sir Syed*, vol. I (Lahore, 1962), articles on 'Khilafat', 'Khilafat aur *Khalifa*' and 'Imam aur Imamat'.

My Life: A Fragment
Mohamed Ali's Quest for Identity
in Colonial India

MUSHIRUL HASAN

Mohamed Ali was a controversial figure for his contemporaries and for posterity. Government officials associated him with the 'extreme faction of the Muslim community', the 'Advanced Party' and the 'hot headed Nationalist Party'.[1] He led a clique of noisy and aggressive Muslims of the 'young party', who made the raja's house (raja of Mahmudabad) their headquarters and lived and agitated at his expense.[2] He left trouble wherever he went, reported the viceroy. He persuaded some students at the Lahore Medical College to raise the tribes against the government in Afghanistan, and caused 'discontent' at Aligarh's M.A.O. College. That is why he and brother Shaukat Ali were prevented from entering Punjab and the United Provinces (UP).[3]

In recent years some historians have seen in Mohamed Ali a charmer and nothing more; a politician greedy for power, an irresponsible declaimer who drove himself and his followers from one disaster to another. He is charged with inspiring the 'young party' Muslims to manufacture issues and whip up agitations to keep their newspapers going, their organizations active and their coffers full.[4]

---

[1] Sydenham to Hardinge, 18 March 1913, Hardinge Papers, Cambridge University Library, Cambridge.

[2] Meston to Chelmsford, 20 Aug. 1917, File No. 136 (1), India Office Library and Records (IOLR), London.

[3] Quoted in Afzal Iqbal, *Life and Times of Mohamed Ali* (Delhi, 1978 rpt), p. 113. In May 1915, the Ali brothers were asked to remain in Mehrauli and abstain from political meetings. They were described by Richard Burn (writing for Meston) as 'disseminators of mischief and would-be-traitors', who 'have done any amount of evil at Aligarh. They have tried to stir up trouble in Lucknow and their message is mischievous wherever they go.' Home Poll. D, Proceedings, May 1915, 36, National Archives of India (NAI).

[4] Francis Robinson, *Separatism Among Indian Muslims: The Politics of the United Provinces' Muslims, 1860-1923* (Cambridge, 1974), pp. 178-9; and Judith M. Brown, *Gandhi's Rise to Power: Indian Politics 1915-1922* (Cambridge, 1971), pp. 139-40.

There are other images as well: the image of an energetic, talented
and charismatic figure devoted to Islamic resurgence world over.
Writers in India stress Mohamed Ali's commitment to Hindu-Muslim
unity, his adherence to the Congress movement, his passion for the
country's freedom.[5] Scholars in Pakistan, on the other hand, eulogize
him as one who contributed 'to the march of the Muslim nation on
the way to its final destination'.[6] They romanticize the story of his
life and extol his achievements, some real but mostly imaginary.
Schools, colleges and streets in Karachi and Lahore are named, as
in Delhi, Aligarh and Bombay, after him. Maulana Mohamed Ali
'Jauhar', the *Rais al-Ahrar* (Leader of the Free Peoples), is indeed
among the most popular and venerated figures in Pakistan.

What lends credence to such images is the tendency among
sections of the Muslim intelligentsia to construct their as well as their
community's identity around leaders who had the energy, drive and
the skills to articulate the Muslim/Islamic world-view from public
platforms.[7] Thus Mohamed Ali is commonly perceived to be more
sensitive than others to the predicaments of the Islamic world and
more stridently committed to its well-being.[8] He attracts greater notice
because he possessed to the full the resources of traditional oratory—

[5] Moin Shakir, *Khilafat to Partition* (Delhi, 1972), pp. 70, 74, 86; S.M. Hadi, *Ali Biradaran aur Unka Zamana* (Delhi, 1978); Shan Muhammad, *Freedom Movement in India—The Role of Ali Brothers* (Delhi, 1978); *Aaj Kal* (Delhi, 1978); *Jamia* (Delhi), 'Mohamed Ali Number', April 1979, Jan.-Feb. 1980.

[6] Moinul Haq (ed.), *Mohamed Ali: Life and Work* (Karachi, 1978), p. 41; *Nigar*, Nov.-Dec. 1976; *Maulana Mohamed Ali Jauhar Sadi Conference* (Karachi, 1978), and for the view that the 'two-nation theory' had been forecasted by Mohamed Ali, see Aziz Ahmad, *Islamic Modernism in India and Pakistan, 1857-1964* (London, 1967), p. 162.

[7] Thus an address presented to Mohamed Ali following his release from internment, stated: 'It would require a volume to enumerate in detail your services in regard to the M.A.O. College, the Muslim University, the galvanizing of the Muslim community through your brilliant newspapers, the *Comrade* and the *Hamdard* . . . the raising of funds for Muslim victims in the Balkan War, the organizing of a competent and well-equipped medical mission for the Turkish wounded. Your restoration to liberty is a mark of profound rejoicing to us. . . . Your presence in our midst will stimulate our community into the solidarity seriously imperilled during the last five years of agonizing ordeal.' *Leader* (Allahabad), 12 and 15 Jan. 1917.

[8] Mazharul Haq and M.A. Ansari to Hony. Secretary, All India Muslim League, 3 Sept. 1917; and Ansari to A.M. Khwaja, 3 Sept. 1917, in Mushirul Hasan (ed.), *Muslims and the Congress: Select Correspondence of Dr. M.A. Ansari, 1912-1935* (Delhi, 1979), pp. 9-10.

its repertoire of tricks. Few orators or political journalists had his combination of qualities: his range of articulate emotions, his capacity for analytical arguments, his pathos, fantasy and wit, and his power to marshall all these towards ends clearly discerned and passionately desired. He also had considerable poetic talent, which combined with his fervour and the desperate situation in which Turkey found herself after the War, to create in him a feeling of impending martyrdom.[9] 'Such sufferings and privations as ours,' he wrote, 'have only too often been the lot of mankind, in all ages and climes.'[10]

سکھایا تہا تمہیں نے قوم کو یہ شور و شر سارا ۱.
جو اس کی انتہا ہم ہیں تو اس کی ابتدا تم ہو

It is you (Syed Ahmad Khan) that had
taught the community its mischiefs;
If we are its culmination;
you are its commencement.

(Mohamed Ali, in 1923)

Mohamed Ali was born on 10 December 1878 in Rampur where his grandfather Sheikh Ali Baksh (1813-67) served as a petty official in the court of Nawab Mohammad Yusuf Khan. He aided the British in quelling the disturbances at Bareilly and Moradabad during the 1857 revolt, and received a *khilat* two years later and a *muafi* or a rent-free land with an annual income of 13,000 rupees. The family reaped the rewards of loyalty even after Ali Baksh's death in 1867. Abdul Ali (1848-80), his son, enjoyed the patronage of Rampur's nawab. But he died of cholera in 1880 leaving Abadi Bano Begum (1852-1924), then only 28 years of age, the responsibility of bringing up her five sons and a daughter. The begum's family, which was in direct succession to a number of nobles connected with the Mughals, had suffered during the 1857 upsurge. Her father changed his name and lived for several years as a refugee in the Rampur State territory. Much of the family's property, having been acquired through the

---

[9] Mohamed Ali, *Kalam-i-Jauhar* (Delhi, 1938); A. Rauf (ed.), *Mohamed Ali aur Unki Shairi* (Karachi, 1963); Nur-ur Rahman (ed.), *Divan-i-Jauhar* (Karachi, 1962).

[10] Mohamed Ali to James DuBoulay, 18 Feb. 1919, in Mushirul Hasan (ed.), *Mohamed Ali in Indian Politics* (Karachi, 1985), vol. 2, pp. 192-3.

generosity of the Mughal rulers, was confiscated by the British government.[11]

Abadi Bano was undeterred by the family's limited resources and the heavy debt incurred by a spend-thrift husband. When approached by Azimuddin Khan, general of Rampur forces, she agreed to send her eldest son to Bareilly.[12] Mohamed Ali recalled:

How she managed to bring up her six little children and how she, an uneducated *purdah* lady, as education is understood in these days, managed to educate us better than our educated and richer uncles educated their own children, is a remarkable story which it is not through egotism that I would like to relate. . . . This miracle was not accomplished without personal privations that would do credit to a hermit living in a cave. It is not, therefore, egotism that has suggested this tribute to a mother's memory, but the sense of a heavy debt that can never be paid off. . . .[13]

In the graph of Mohamed Ali's life, the steep arc of youth is missing; we see only the flattened curve of maturity. We see him studying a few Persian classics, reading the Koran in Arabic, and observing the religious rituals in a Sunni home. While in Aligarh (1890-8), he is found writing for the college magazine, sharing Shaukat Ali's love for 'the noble and manly game of cricket', and nursing the ambition of securing 'a nomination for the post of Subordinate Magistrate or Land Revenue Collector'.[14] The 'Big Brother' was impressed with his 'unexpected success' at the B.A. examinations and arranged for his education in England. In Mohamed Ali's own words, 'So before the proverbial nine days of wonder were over, I was on the high seas in the Indian Ocean in the teeth of a raging monsoon, bound for England. . . .'[15]

Within weeks of his arrival in September 1898, Mohamed Ali made his way into English middle class society with the help of the family of T.W. Arnold, who had taught philosophy at the Aligarh College,

[11] The best source for Mohamed Ali's life and career is his own 'autobiography' and his articles published in the *Comrade* on 21 and 28 Nov. 1924. Much additional information is available in the works of Afzal Iqbal, Rais Ahmad Jafri, Shan Muhammad and Abu Salman Shahjahanpuri. These are listed in my *Mohamed Ali: Ideology and Politics* (Delhi, 1981).

[12] 'People wondered why any mother should be so lacking in love for her children as to send them away from home while they are still so young.' *Comrade*, 5 Dec. 1924.

[13] Ibid., 21 Nov. 1924.

[14] *My Life*, p. 30.

[15] Ibid.

and its controversial Principal, Theodore Beck. Fazl-i-Husain, also in England, found him to be 'a jolly good fellow, very quick in making friends'. They spent 'exceedingly pleasant evenings' discussing literary, philosophical and political issues.[16]

Mohamed Ali reached Oxford on 11 October to study modern history at Lincoln College. He matriculated a year later and secured a second in 1902, missing a first in History by a narrow margin.[17] He impressed his tutors with his vigour, common sense and resourcefulness.[18] James Williams, his guru in Roman and English Law, noticed his 'great capacity for acquiring and remembering information'.[19] His paper on *Macbeth* was written by 'a man of ability, capable of thinking for himself'. Yet these skills did not equip him to qualify the civil service examination, 'thanks to an English spring, and a youngman's more or less foolish fancy'.[20] Success eluded him even after returning to India in 1902. Having failed to secure a teaching position at Aligarh owing to sordid manipulations, he opted for the Education Department in Rampur, a position for which his tutors in Oxford had found him suitable. But his brief and inglorious innings ended in November 1902, when he sought refuge in the princely State of Baroda.

Gaekwad Sayaji Rao (1875-1936), the ruler, regarded the new recruit as one on whose shoulders he could place the burden of administrative work, the man who got papers drawn up, orders sent out, correspondence carried on and records kept. But jealous and conservative officials in Baroda, as in Rampur, resented him for his initiative, drive and his proximity to the Gaekwad. Though Mohamed Ali kept himself in the public eye by writing and speaking at conferences, he was set to leave for Bhopal by the end of 1906.[21]

[16] Azim Husain, *Fazl-i-Husain: A Political Biography* (Bombay, 1936), p. 20; Iqbal, *Life and Times*, pp. 31-2.

[17] Mohamed Ali to Dewan Tek Chand, n.d., Mohamed Ali Papers (MAP), Jamia Millia Islamia, New Delhi.

[18] Testimonial of Rector, Lincoln College, 19 Oct. 1901, MAP.

[19] Testimonial of James Williams, 14 Oct. 1901, MAP.

[20] *My Life*, p. 32.

[21] This is revealed in his exchanges with Syed Mahfuz Ali. It is, however, clear that he took a keen interest in political developments. Although exaggerated claims are made about his influence on the Muslim League deliberations in Dec. 1906, he was regarded as a potentially bright recruit. In Feb. 1907, he lectured in Allahabad. A month later he prepared a text of the Muslim League proceedings which was published as 'Green Book No. 1'. This prompted an explanation from an official. 'I

Dunlop Smith, private secretary to the viceroy, urged him to stay: 'I quite understand that your surroundings are not always congenial, but after all whose are in every respect.'[22] Around this time Mohamed Ali printed the *Thoughts on the Present Discontent*, based on articles published in the *Times of India* and the *Indian Spectator*. He sent a copy to the viceroy, hoping that it 'would meet with the sympathy and encouragement which India has learnt to associate now with the name of Edward the Peace-Maker'. The viceroy endorsed its contents and wished the book the wide circulation it deserved.[23]

Mohamed Ali stayed in Baroda until 1910, although his heart was not at rest.[24] Activity and companionship were the drugs he craved for. The drab and routine work in the Opium Department offered no solace to his buoyant and exuberant spirit. He yearned for the *mehfils* where he could transmit the flame of his intellectual excitement to others. 'I am fed up with this state . . . (and) tired of this job', he told his Aligarh friend Syed Mahfuz Ali.[25] He was conceited about his Oxford degree and contemptuous of those who sported degrees from Indian universities. He submitted, as he did with monotonous regularity during his internment a few years later, long representations to his superiors commending his own abilities, demanding higher pay, and criticizing those placed above him. 'In spite of being an Indian and having received a very similar education to the rest of the Baroda officials,' he complained to the Gaekwad, 'I found that I differ from them in almost everything, and that it was difficult if not impossible for me to be received by them as one of their own number.'[26] Shaukat Ali, himself a civil servant in the Opium Department, felt that his younger brother had crossed the limits of discretion; he admonished him 'to curb yourself a little—you have to work with certain people and you cannot always have your way.

---

sent in a reply,' wrote Mohamed Ali, 'before the Council. In response, a general confidential circular was issued to government servants. They were told not to contribute articles which were likely to create communal animosity.' Mohamed Ali to Mahfuz Ali, 14 Jan. 1910, M. Sarwar (ed.), *Khutut-i-Mohamed Ali* (Delhi, 1940), pp. 252-4. For Mohamed Ali's speeches, see Home Poll. B, 149, 1913, NAI.

[22] Dunlop Smith to Mohamed Ali, 31 Jan. 1907, MAP.

[23] To Dunlop Smith, 5 Dec. 1907, MAP; and G.K. Gokhale, 8 Feb. 1908, Gokhale Papers (341), NAI.

[24] To Mahfuz Ali, 14 Jan. 1910, *Khutut*, pp. 252-4.

[25] Ibid.

[26] To the Gaekwad of Baroda, n.d., MAP.

If I was your boss, I would strongly object to your correspondence. It borders on insubordination.'[27]

For the time being the prospect of a government job was held out by Dunlop Smith and Harold A. Stuart, the Home Member. But hopes were soon turned into despair, when Mohamed Ali was told that 'the expenses of an Indian private secretary would (not) be justified at present', and that his lack of experience of detective work was a bar for a post in the Home Department.[28] Michael O'Dwyer, later Governor of Punjab, recommended him to the nawab of Jaora. But this small princely State could hardly assuage Mohamed Ali's thirst for participation in great events, even in a subordinate capacity.[29]

A career in journalism was the only option, the only avenue through which Mohamed Ali could prove to be of 'any appreciable use to it (Muslim community), while still earning a livelihood'.[30] His journalistic ventures, beginning with the *Comrade* on 14 January 1911, were successful. His own articles were laced with long and tedious quotations and tended to be verbose and repetitive. Yet he created for himself a broad-based readership because he wrote, just as he spoke, with passion and fervour. The *Comrade*, manned by some of his friends and protégés from Aligarh, grew in size; its circulation shot up to 8,500 copies. Its office in Kucha-i-Chelan in the old city became a political salon after the paper moved from Calcutta to Delhi, the new capital of British India. 'No paper has so much influence with the students as the *Comrade*, and no individual has the authority over them which is exercized by Mohamed Ali', reported the UP government in 1914.[31] When he wanted to stop publishing the *Hamdard* at the beginning of his internment, Wilayat Ali, the well-known columnist, begged him not to do so: 'I do not approve of your decision and I do not think many will. . . . You cannot imagine what the loss of *Hamdard* will mean to us—the Musalmans.'[32] Wilayat Ali recognized, as did others, that the *Comrade*

[27] Shaukat Ali to Mohamed Ali, 4 July 1909, MAP.

[28] G.S. Clark to Mohamed Ali, 2 Nov. 1909; Dunlop Smith to Mohamed Ali, 30 Oct. 1909; H.A. Stuart to Mohamed Ali, 10 Dec. 1909, MAP.

[29] *My Life*, pp. 33-4, and Mohamed Ali to the nawab of Jaora, 23 Nov. 1910, MAP.

[30] Ibid., p. 34.

[31] Home Poll. D., Dec. 1914, 31, NAI.

[32] To Mohamed Ali, 20 Aug. 1915, MAP. See, Abu Salman Shahjahanpuri, *Maulana Mohamed Ali Aur Unki Sahafat* [Maulana Mohamed Ali and his Journalism] (Karachi, 1983).

and *Hamdard* contributed to a general awakening of educated Muslims who read and financially supported these newspapers.[33]

The *Comrade*, more than the *Hamdard*, served to voice some of Mohamed Ali's main concerns; for example, the promotion of the Aligarh College, his Alma Mater. He wanted the college to serve as a common centre where Muslims from all over the world would congregate and energize a common Islamic consciousness to uphold Muslim interests in India and overseas.[34] Thus, his maiden speech in 1908 on the subject, modelled on the style of Edmund Burke and with quotations from Latin, Arabic, Persian, Urdu and English literature, proved to be the swan song of the first phase of the Muslim University movement.[35]

Mohamed Ali supported—some said fomented—a students' strike in 1907. His involvement in college affairs, a story detailed by David Lelyveld, Gail Minault and Francis Robinson, made him the *bete noire* of the board of trustees. The British staff complained to the English novelist E.M. Forster, then visiting India, that they were neither 'trusted to give the help they had hoped nor could they make some way with the students—not much, owing to the influence of the *Comrade*, a forward Islamic newspaper'. The Muslims 'had an air of desperation, which may be habitual, but was impressive'.[36] The college was transformed into a hot-bed of 'sedition'; officials wondered if anything could be done to prevent its students from 'being tampered with' by Mohamed Ali who, for all his professions of loyalty, was 'a dangerous malcontent', 'an element of strife'.[37]

[33] For the influence of *Comrade*, see K.M. Ashraf, 'Aligarh ki Siyasi Zindagi', in *Aligarh Magazine*, 1953-5, p. 164. 'Throughout the country, only one voice was heard by the people of the north and the south, the east and the west, by the educated and the illiterate, the *ulama* and the ignorant. . . .' Abdul Majid Daryabadi, *Maqalat-i Majid* (Bombay, n.d.), pp. 233-4.

[34] *Comrade*, 28 Jan. 1991.

[35] See Gail Minault and David Lelyveld, 'The Campaign for a Muslim University', *Modern Asian Studies*, vol. 8, 1974, p. 145; David Lelyveld, 'Three Aligarh Students: Aftab Ahmad Khan, Ziauddin Ahmad and Mohamed Ali', *Modern Asian Studies*, vol. 9, 1975, pp. 103-16, and his *Aligarh's First Generation: Muslim Solidarity in British India* (Princeton, N.J., 1978), pp. 330-6.

[36] Quoted in P.N. Furbank, *E.M. Forster: A Life: The Growth of the Novelist, 1879-1914* (London, 1978), p. 227.

[37] Hardinge to Meston, 14 Nov. 1912; Hardinge to Butler, 29 Oct. 1912; Butler to Hardinge, 3 Nov. 1912, Hardinge Papers. Malcolm Hailey, Chief Commissioner of Delhi, described Mohamed Ali as 'the centre and inspiration of the Pan-Islamic movement'. To H.H. Wheeler, 1 May 1915, Home Poll. D, May 1915, 36, NAI.

جو گمیں یاد رکھ، قیدِ قفس کا غم نہ کر! 2.
چمن کب اے بلبلِ ناداں تجھے گلشن میں تھا

Grieve not over imprisonment in the cage, but
    do not forget the actions of the plucker of the rose.
Oh foolish nightingale! When free in the garden,
    When did you ever find repose?
                (Mohamed Ali, translated by Gail Minault,
                    The Khilafat Movement, p. 160)

Historians have traced the breakup of the Anglo-Muslim *entente cordiale*, the growth of political radicalism among some Muslims, and their stridency in areas where colonial policies disturbed the *status quo* most. Some have examined how the anti-Muslim bias of UP's Lieutenant-Governor Anthony Macdonnell, the reunification of Bengal (1911), the rejection of the Muslim University scheme (1912), and the fracas over the Kanpur mosque (1913) convinced a number of educated Muslims that radical self-help was a better solution than mendicancy. Much secondary literature also delineates the role of the men of *Nai Raushni* and the representatives of 'new ideals' and 'new force', many of whom endorsed the Congress policies and programme. Mohamed Ali emerged as the rallying point for such 'younger men', for he himself held the opinion that the Congress, then dominated by the 'moderates', embodied the 'genuine and vigorous aspirations which move educated India for a well-organized and common national life'.[38] He emphasized, as did Maulana Abul Kalam Azad with greater rigour and consistency, the need for Hindu-Muslim amity and understanding. Without mutual cooperation Hindus and Muslims would 'not only fail but fail ignominiously'. He talked of a 'concordat like that of Canada' and '*a marriage de convenance* [*sic*], honourably contracted and honourably maintained'.[39] In another article—'The Communal Patriot'—he maintained that the two communities, despite their differences, should be mutually tolerant and respectful, and that eventually education and the 'levelling, liberalizing tendencies of the times'

[38] *Comrade*, 30 Dec. 1911.
[39] Ibid.

would create political individuality out of diverse creeds and races. He compared the Congress and the Muslim League to two trees growing on either side of a road:

Their trunks stood apart, but their roots were fixed in the same soil, drawing nourishment from the same source. The branches were bound to meet when the stems had reached full stature. . . . The soil was British, the nutriment was common patriotism, the trunks were the two political bodies, and the road was the highway of peaceful progress.[40]

Such views, which were beginning to be aired in many quarters, gained wide acceptance. Still, Mohamed Ali's fame spread far and wide only after he and Shaukat Ali were gaoled on 15 May 1915 for an article entitled 'The Choice of the Turks'.[41] On that day thousands congregated to offer their Friday prayers at Delhi's Juma Masjid and 'to bid adieu to the two patriots who had done all they could to promote their cause'.[42] They were first interned at Mehrauli, then transferred to Lansdowne and, finally, to Chhindwara where they arrived on 23 November 1915 wearing 'grey astrakhan cap with large Turkish half moons in the front, also Khuddam-i Kaba badges'. Located 'a considerable distance from their friends' and 'far removed from centres of Muhammadan feeling', Chhindwara was chosen because 'pan-Islamism is faintest' and 'the journey there from the United Provinces as regards visitors is exceedingly tedious'.[43]

The Ali brothers were well on their way towards martyrdom, with various organizations vying with each other to record their 'noble services rendered at the most psychological moment in the history of the community'. Their fame was kept fresh through many protest meetings, and also through the incident, covered by the historians

[40] Quoted in Gail Minault, *The Khilafat Movement: Religious Symbolism and Political Mobilization in India* (New York, 1982), p. 19.

[41] The article gave the government 'ample justification for suppressing such writings'. An official note stated on 6 Oct. 1914: 'I do not see how anyone can read the article except as a direct incitement to Turkey to go to war, and practically what it says is that if this does bring them up against Russia and France, they have no cause to love these Powers and it does not matter much. England is practically threatened if she does not evacuate Egypt, and Germany is extolled. If this is not attacking our allies and siding with our enemies it is difficult to know what it is?' Home Poll. A., Oct. 1913, pp. 142-9, NAI. The Ali brothers maintained that they were interned because they freely expressed their allegiance demanded by their Islamic faith. To Viceroy, 24 April 1919, MAP.

[42] *Leader*, 12 and 15 Jan. 1920.

[43] Home Poll. D, Proceedings, Oct. and Dec. 1915, NAI.

Gail Minault and B.R. Nanda, of the government's conditional offer of their release in 1917. They refused to sign the undertaking suggested by the government; instead they signed another, adding the qualification: 'Without prejudice to our allegiance to Islam'. Leading Congressmen, especially Gandhi, also courted them and pressed for their release. The Mahatma, having met the Ali brothers in Aligarh and Delhi in 1915 and early in 1916, assured Bi Amman— 'Mataji'—that he was 'leaving no stone unturned' to secure their immediate and honourable release.[44]

Having made Hindu-Muslim unity an essential part of his mission in India since his return from Africa in 1915, Gandhi assumed that Mohamed Ali was an ideal instrument in his hand for creating Hindu-Muslim alliance with the aim of obtaining Swaraj. He was valuable to Gandhi both as an issue on which to cement a communal concordat, and also because he considered him to be a splendid example of that mingling of Hindu and Muslim cultures which had taken place in the Indo-Gangetic belt.[45] His interest in Mohamed Ali's release was 'quite selfish':[46] 'We have a common goal, and I want to utilize your services to the uttermost in order to reach that goal. In the proper solution of the Mohammedan question lies the realization of Swaraj.'[47]

Gandhi's initiatives made him popular among north India's Muslims, many of whom participated in the *hartal* organized on 6 April 1919 against the Rowlatt Bills. M.A. Ansari extolled him as the 'intrepid leader of India . . . who has . . . endeared him as much to the Musalman as to the Hindu'. Mohamed Ali's younger colleagues, who regarded the Mahatma as a 'Tolstoy and Buddha combined', endorsed his non-violent programme. Satyagraha, according to Maulana Abdul Bari, the renowned *alim* of Lucknow's Firangi Mahal, was consistent with the Islamic principles.[48] In many parts of the country 'Gandhi', 'Khilafat', 'Swaraj', 'Mohamed Ali' were

---

[44] Mahadev Desai (ed.), *Day-to-Day with Gandhi* (Varanasi, 1968), vol. 1, pp. 93, 211.

[45] Brown, *Gandhi's Rise to Power*, p. 152.

[46] After arriving in India, Gandhi told a Khilafat meeting that he began to find out 'good Mohammedan leaders'. He was satisfied when he reached Delhi and met the Ali brothers. 'It was a question of love at first sight between us.' Speech at Bombay, 9 May 1919, *The Collected Works of Mahatma Gandhi* (*CWMG*), vol. 15, p. 295.

[47] Gandhi to Mohamed Ali, 18 Nov. 1918, ibid., p. 64.

[48] Hasan (ed.), *Muslims and the Congress*, Appendix 1; Abdur Rahman Siddiqi to Mohamed Ali, 24 March 1919, MAP; WRDCI, March 1919, Home Poll. B, April 1919,

words that conjured up in the minds of the people a picture of bringing about a better world under the direction of better leaders.

Around this time the portrayal of Mohamed Ali as a fiery and relentless anti-colonial crusader was based on the strength of his involvement in nationalist as well as pan-Islamic causes. This image is sustained in much secondary literature produced in India and Pakistan. In reality, however, Mohamed Ali's utterances on the Raj and his frequent references to the good that was to accrue from the 'beneficent contact' with Western culture and civilization explode the myth of his being consistently hostile to the colonial government.[49] Notice, for example, how he assured Meston, whose advice he followed in shifting the *Comrade* from Calcutta to Delhi, of his 'anxious desire' to cooperate with him and other well-wishers of his country and community,[50] and pleaded, on another occasion, for 'some pegs' on which to hang his moderate stance on the annulment of Bengal's partition. He insisted that 'well-merited concessions wisely made at a suitable moment' would curb an agitation far more effectively than the strenuous efforts of Muslim leaders.[51] He even suggested that the presence of the British monarch in India should be utilized to bind still more firmly the seventy million Muslims of India to the Empire.[52] No wonder, high-ranking British officers subscribed to the *Comrade* when it began publication in Calcutta. No wonder, the Viceroy Hardinge allowed Mohamed Ali to collect and advance a loan to Turkey, patronized the Delhi Crescent Society and supported Ansari's medical mission to Constantinople.[53]

Even when officials rebuffed Mohamed Ali in London during his stay from September to 1 December 1913, he declared his loyalty and appreciated the manifold blessings of British rule in India.[54] When the War with Germany broke out, he was on the side of the

---

pp. 148-52, NAI; also see, A.M. Daryabadi, *Mohamed Ali: Zaati Diary Ke Chand Auraq* (Hyderabad, 1943), p. 20.

[49] W.J. Watson, 'Mohamed Ali and the Khilafat Movement' (unpublished M.A. thesis, McGill University, 1955), p. 14.

[50] To Meston, 19 Feb. 1913, MAP.

[51] To James DuBoulay, 3 Jan. 1912, MAP.

[52] To F.H. Lucas, 3 Jan. 1912, MAP.

[53] For correspondence with the Viceroy on these issues, see Hardinge Papers (84); Iqbal, *Life and Times,* pp. 77-8.

[54] *Comrade,* 13 Sept. 1913; and Mohamed Ali to James Le Touche, 4 Nov. 1913, MAP.

British, urging India's Muslims to place their services at the disposal of the government. The article 'The Choice of the Turks' proclaimed the hope that the Khalifa would stay out of the war and save his Muslim countrymen from a conflict of loyalties. Talking to Abdul Majid, the C.I.D. officer, Mohamed Ali defined his position thus:

His quarrel (Abdul Majid recorded) was not at all with the British Government. He was certainly not so advanced as Messrs. Mazharul Haq, M.A. Jinnah and Lajpat Rai. He believed that is was necessary for Muhammedans that the British Government should and would remain in India much longer than the nationalists desired. . . . The Government did not know its real enemies. They will receive in audience Lajpat Rai and other nationalists, . . . but they would consider Mohamed Ali as their enemy.[55]

Mohamed Ali's antipathy towards Pax Brittanica may well have developed during his trip to Europe in 1913, though it was still not explicitly articulated. Meeting writers, journalists and civil servants enabled him to see Turkey from the outside, to observe the strife of the peninsula magnified into the terms of international politics, to watch and appraise the forces remoulding, sometimes deliberately, sometimes almost casually, the destiny of the Ottoman Empire. His exchanges convinced him, perhaps for the first time in his public career, that the British were insensitive to Muslim feelings over the Khilafat, and their ignorance of conditions back home was 'driving them fast to the brink of the precipice'. Hence his indignation at being denied access to senior officials of the Indian House. 'If we are unable to see even His Lordship,' Mohamed Ali told John Morley, 'what could we say to our people on our return except that because some local officials were desirous that we and our co-religionists and many others in our country should be misjudged by our superiors.'[56] Furious at the lack of sensitivity, he was drawn into a kind of *egoisme a deux* in defying their stuffiness. He commented that the government, having taken Muslim loyalty and support for granted, undermined the temporal power of Islam with scant regard for Muslim religious susceptibilities.[57]

Mohamed Ali's internment was the last proverbial straw; Ziauddin

[55] Quoted in B.R. Nanda, *Gandhi, Pan-Islamism, Imperialism and Nationalism* (Bombay, 1989), p. 138.
[56] To John Morley, 2 Nov. 1913, MAP.
[57] To Chelmsford, 24 April 1919, MAP.

Ahmad Barni (d. 1968), a Sub-editor of *Hamdard*, traced his mentor's anti-government stance to his confinement in Chhindwara.[58] From here, as also from Lansdowne and Betul, Mohamed Ali expounded on the government's repressive measures, targeting the Indian Civil Service in particular, 'a political party perpetually in office (with) the power to crush its political opponents with all the resources of the State'.[59] He told Delhi's Chief Commissioner, Malcolm Hailey, that he understood 'how hateful must be a man of my character to officials of a certain type'. He recognized the implications of the Defence of India Act, 'which makes even the Archangel Gabriel liable to internment by local governments on the secret testimony of Beelzebub'.[60] In June 1915, he announced that the law under which he was interned was 'tyrannous and unjust'.[61] No government was expected in the twentieth century to claim, even by implication, the right to force a man's conscience. He dwelt on 'the spirit of tyranny', the 'gag of prodigious proportions' prepared 'for silencing more than three hundred million of God's articulate creatures'. The Rowlatt Act 'has ended the reign of law, and substituted a reign of terror in its place'.[62] As a symbol of his protest, Mohamed Ali began to wear half-moons in his grey cap and Khuddam-i Kaaba badge, compared with his European style of dress in previous years.

The enforced leisure made Mohamed Ali more profoundly religious, enabling him to steep himself afresh in his Islamic heritage and to turn to the study of Islam—charting out an unfamiliar subject, getting at its rudiments, and exploring its nuances. In *My Life*, a document of deep religious feelings, he laments not having had access to the traditional Muslim learning. 'It is not without a feeling of deep shame that I have to confess, we boys and girls born and bred in Muslim households were taught far less of our religion than most English boys and girls of our age and position.' He bemoaned that Aligarh 'furnished' students with 'little equipment in the matter of knowledge of faith'. Though he attended Shibli's lectures and referred to the elation of sitting in the Principal's Hall attending his lectures with all the dignity of a quasi-'Undergrad', the Koran

[58] 'Maulana Mohamed Ali Jauhar', *Naqqush (Shakhsiat Number)*, Oct. 1956, p. 1161.

[59] To Chelmsford, 24 April 1919, MAP.

[60] To Malcolm Hailey, 24 May 1915, ibid.

[61] To Malcolm Hailey, 2 June 1915, ibid.

[62] To Chelmsford, op. cit.

practically remained a closed book, and the traditions of the Prophet was no more than a name. In the seclusion of his internment at Mehrauli, however, he studied Maulvi Nazir Ahmad's translation of the Koran and found 'the consolation and contentment that was denied to us outside its pages'.[63] He discovered, after years of ignorance of his Islamic heritage, that the Koran was a 'perennial of truth' and offered a 'complete scheme of life, a perfect code of conduct and a comprehensive social policy . . .'. Thus the main tenets of Islam, which were earlier 'little more than a bundle of doctrines and commandments', acquired 'a new coherence and, as it were, fell suddenly into place, creating an effect of units such as I had never realized before'. *Tauhid* grew upon him as a personal reality, man in the dignity of his 'service' as viceregent of God, and himself as part of this great strength. This was Mohamed Ali's 'unique discovery in that small volume revealed some thirteen centuries ago to an Arab of the desert whose name I bore'.[64]

Mohamed Ali read the *Sihah-i Sittah*, a compilation of the Prophet's Traditions (*Hadith*), the works of Imam Ghazali, T.W. Arnold, Shibli Nomani, the person who made the symbols of Islam a living reality for the Aligarh students, and the poems of Jalaluddin Rumi and Mohammad Iqbal. He experienced 'an exquisite thrill of delight' reading *Asrar-i-Khudi* (Secrets of Self), especially because its author Iqbal expressed 'the same basic truth of Islam, which I had in a blundering sort of way discovered for myself'.[65] Studying Islamic history enabled him to see its great men as figures to whom he could talk, and its crises as guides to action in current affairs.[66] Studying Islam was conventional enough for men like Syed Ahmad Khan, Shibli and Azad who did so with greater scholarship, but none with a greater personal need. Mohamed Ali recollected: 'Since I first commenced the study of the Koran I have read a fair amount about Islam from the point of view of Muslims and also of their critics; *but nothing that I have read has altered the significance of Islam for*

---

[63] *My Life*, p. 47; S. Abid Husain, *The Destiny of Indian Muslims* (New Delhi, 1965), pp. 24-5; S.M. Ikram, *Modern Muslim India and the Birth of Pakistan* (Lahore, 1970), pp. 42-3.

[64] *My Life*, p. 96; and Iqbal (ed.), *Selected Writings*, p. 170.

[65] Ibid., p. 127.

[66] A.M. Daryabadi, *Zaati Diary*, p. 14; To A.M. Daryabadi, 22 May and 25 July 1916, in Hasan (ed.), *Mohamed Ali in Indian Politics*, vol. 1, pp. 269-76.

me to which I had stumbled in the first few months of our internment eight years ago' (emphasis added).[67] To Gandhi, he wrote:

Whatever else my internment may or may not have done, it has I believe set the soul free, and that compensates me for so many items on the wrong side of the account. What I could dimly perceive before I now realize with distinctness, and it is this, that the whole aim and end of life is to serve God and obey His commandments. . . . I confess I had never before grasped this truth in all its fullness. . . . *Internment made us seek refuge in the Holy Koran, and for the first time, I have to confess it, I read it through and. with new eyes* (emphasis added).[68]

This experience was, in some ways, similar to that of Azad whose three-and-a-half year internment in Ranchi (Bihar) kindled his Islam into warmth and fervour. He began writing the *Tarjuman al-Koran* with his commentary on the opening *Surah Fatihah*, and its themes—Divine Providence, benevolence, justice, unity and guid-ance, *rabubiyah, rahma, adala, tauhid* and *hidaya*.

Both Azad and Mohamed Ali asserted the transcendental truth of Islam, 'a way of life, a moral code and social polity', a complete set of rules (*qanun-i-falah*), as Azad put it. Both believed in the rightness of the Islamic ideals—a complete way of life for an organized community living out Allah's plan under the kind of government which had prevailed in the days of the Prophet. Both held the Islamic principles to be compatible with reason or science. Mohamed Ali underlined this point in 'The Future of Islam', and Azad in the first three issues of *Al-Hilal*.

In Mohamed Ali's view there was just one world of Islam regardless of caste, class, linguistic and regional variations, one vast brotherhood stretching across the continents. This was summed up by the *Comrade* on 18 January 1916.

It is not only one God, one Prophet and one Kaaba that the Muslims of the world have in common, but in every degree of longitude and latitude they hold the same views of the relations of husband and wife, of parent and child, of master and slave and of neighbour and neighbour. . . . They follow among all races the same laws of marriage, divorce and succession. And they do this in the twentieth century of the Christian era exactly as they did in the sixth and hope to do so to the last syllable of recorded time. . . . There is still the one God to worship and the one Prophet to follow . . . , always

[67] Daryabadi, ibid., p. 14; Mohamed Ali to A.M. Daryabadi, 22 May, 25 July 1916 (Urdu), Daryabadi Papers, New Delhi.
[68] To Gandhi, 20 Feb. 1918, MAP.

one unaltered and unalterable Book to soothe and to stimulate, and the one Kaaba to act as the magnetic pole for all true believers from all points of the compass.

In this way Mohamed Ali underlined the primacy of religious loyalty, arguing that Muslims have had a pre-eminent sense of community in their *Weltanschauung*, and especially so in India, where their adherence to Islam made them unique and gave them their 'communal consciousness'. 'I have a culture, a polity, an outlook on life—a complete synthesis which is Islam', he stated in his magisterial style at the London Round Table Conference in 1930. 'Where God commands', he added, 'I am a Muslim first, a Muslim second, a Muslim last, and nothing but a Muslim. If you ask me to enter into your Empire or into your nation by leaving that synthesis, that polity, that culture, that ethics, I will not do it.'[69] He did not believe that by being a Muslim he was any less an Indian. His religious beliefs and nationality never appeared to him to be incompatible. He could—and must—be true to both Islam and India. He explained thus: 'Where India is concerned, where India's freedom is concerned, where the welfare of India is concerned, I am an Indian first, and Indian second, an Indian last, and nothing but an Indian.' On another occasion he spelt out his position in the following words:

I am a Muslim first and everything else afterwards. As a Muslim, I must be free and subject to no autocrat who demands from me obedience to his orders in defence of those of God. . . . Faith is my motive of conduct in every act . . . and my faith demands freedom. That Swaraj will give me, but it does not demand the subjugation of the Hindu or any one else differing from me in faith. . . . My own freedom and not the enslavement of any other is my creed.[70]

In sum, Mohamed Ali's earlier activities had been directed by 'communal loyalty', but his motivation after his religious experience was Islamic duty. This is not to suggest that he held his community in any lesser esteem or that its mundane welfare was less important to him. On the contrary, his awakening confirmed the rightness of what he had done in the past and made it necessary for him to intensify his endeavours along similar lines.[71]

---

[69] Afzal Iqbal, *Select Writings and Speeches of Maulana Mohamed Ali* (Lahore, 1944), p. 405.

[70] *Mussalman* (Calcutta), 13 May 1921.

[71] According to Watson, Mohamed Ali's loyalty to Islam was expressed in the days

مت سہل ہمیں جانو پھرتا ہے فلک برسوں ۰۳

تب خاک کے پردے سے انسان نکلتے ہیں

Don't think us cheap: the heavens revolve for years
To bring forth man out of the veil of dust.
(Mir Taqi Mir, translated by Ralph Russell and
Khurshidul Islam, in *Three Mughal Poets*, p. 184.)

Mohamed Ali's emotional disposition in religious matters had much to do with the nature and with the promptness of his response to events in Turkey. In this context his concerns cannot be doubted: the opinion that it was all feigned or that he was simply playing the pan-Islamic role cannot be defended. He passionately believed that the basis of Islamic sympathy was not a common domicile or common parentage but a shared outlook on life and culture, and that the Khilafat stood as 'the embodiment of that culture'. He endorsed Azad's description of a 'political centre' (*siyasi markaz*), and designated the Khalifa as the 'personal centre' of Islam and the *Jazirat al-Arab* as its 'local centre'. For these reasons Mohamed Ali warned the government that,

there should be no attempt to remove, whether directly or indirectly, from the independent, indivisible and inalienable sovereignty of the Khalifa, who is the recognized servant of the Holy Places and warden of the Holy Shrines, any portion of the territories in which such Holy Places and shrines are situated. . . . Nor should there be any such attempt to dismember and parcel out even among Muslim Governments, or in any other manner weaken the Khalifa's Empire with the object of weakening the temporal power of Islam, and thereby make it liable to suffer, without adequate power to prevent, the curtailment of its spiritual influence through the temporal power of other creeds.[72]

---

before the Turko-Italian War as loyalty to the Indian Muslim community rather than to an abstract way to Allah. His communal consciousness, as he said, was far more secular than religious: his decision to take to journalism was dictated by the 'secular affairs of my country' rather than by a 'religious call'. Then, in the seclusion of his internment, he read through the Koran. Islam possessed him and he discovered the dogmas and ethical codes of his religion. After this experience, argues Watson, his motivation was 'Islamic duty' rather than 'communal loyalty'.

[72] To Chelmsford, 24 April 1919; Hasan (ed.), *Mohamed Ali in Indian Politics*, vol. 2, p. 236 ; also, speech in London on 22 April 1920; Iqbal (ed.), *Selected Writings*, pp. 183-93.

Again, he stated in London:

Well, so long as there are your Bryces and your 'Big Sticks', we, too must have some sort of stick for the defence of our faith. . . . If you think you can please the Muslims of India by allowing the Turks to retain Constantinople in such a way that the Khalifa is worst than the Pope . . . for he would in fact be the prisoner of people of an alien race and faith, then, ladies and gentlemen, you know very little of Islam and the Muslims, or of India and the Indians. (*Cheers*) That affront shall never be tolerated, and if you think you can make out that all this 'agitation' is 'fictitious' and 'factitious', then you will be compelling the Indian Muslim soldiery to disprove this lie in a manner that will be far too unambiguous for your tastes or for ours. Beware, beware.[73]

Mohamed Ali envisioned a renascent Islamic world in which all Muslim peoples were united in a strong Islamic world—'the supernatural Sangathan of Muslims in Five Continents'—built around the Khalifa and supporting each other through that institution whenever Muslim security was threatened.[74] The new Khalifa, judged from his views at the Mecca Conference in 1928, was to be based on a democratic, elective rather than a dynastic institution like the *Khilafat-i Rashida*. And the person chosen would be virtuous and faithful to Islam. The Muslims of the world would direct the government and be responsible for its welfare, while his brethren in India—the largest single community—would lead the fight to emancipate Islam.[75]

Mohamed Ali infused vigour into the Central Khilafat Committee and its provincial and local units to realize the ideal of a renascent Islam. The *Hamdard* was started on 13 June 1913 to reach out to the Urdu readers. The Ali brothers travelled widely, delivered lectures, organized mass meetings and galvanized the *ulama* at the Dar al-ulum in Deoband, the Firangi Mahal and the Nadwat al-ulama in Lucknow.

The *ulama* decided to play to Mohamed Ali's tune. They were conscious that they must now be active in addressing themselves to the political, social and religious anxieties of fellow-Muslims, or else see true Islam as they understood it, and their own claims to guide

[73] Speech delivered in London on 23 March 1920, in *Selected Writings*, 2, pp. 20-1.

[74] 'Islam united Muslims by offering a set of common ideals and offered the only rational basis for unity and cooperation among its followers. The sympathies of a Muslim are co-extensive with his religion because they have been bred into him by the inspiring spirit of his creed.' *Comrade*, 12 April 1913.

[75] Watson, op. cit., p. 55.

them go by default. This led some amongst them 'to pocket their pride and in a way even accept the lead of men whom they had but a generation ago finally consigned to perdiction'. The orthodox and the anglicized 'were drawn together and as in a flash of lightning, saw that after all they were not so unlike each other as they had imagined'.[76] Once more, Mohamed Ali remarked:

Muslim society in India presented a level of uniformity and the bitterest opponents of a generation ago stood shoulder to shoulder. . . . If even a decade previously anyone had ventured to foretell such a result, he would have been laughed at for such a fantastic prophesy. . . .[77]

The annulment of Bengal's partition, the Turko-Italian War, the Kanpur mosque affair and the rejection of the Muslim University scheme added thrust to the converging courses in politics of the modern and the traditionally-educated. The 'temporal misfortunes' of Islam had such a profound impact that 'the wedge that Western education had seemed to insert between the ranks of the religious, and of the men of the "New Light" vanished as if by magic'. A general levelling took place 'without any dependence on the use of force or external authority'.[78]

Mohamed Ali played a pivotal role in strengthening these ties following his release on 28 December 1919. The 'disseminator(s) of mischief and would be traitors' reached Amritsar where, in keeping with the practice that had developed during the War years, the Congress and the Muslim League held simultaneous meetings. He had been imprisoned, Mohamed Ali told the Congress, for denouncing the injustices perpetrated on India and on Islam by the British, and now he must denounce them still, even if it meant returning to prison. At the Muslim League meeting, he expressed his readiness to sacrifice everything he had, including his life, for the sake of Allah and Islam. He made clear that Muslims were subjects of Allah and not of Great Britain. He echoed similar views in London as a member of the Khilafat delegation.

The delegation, having arrived in England at the end of February 1920 for six months, maintained an exhausting pace, spurred on by Mohamed Ali. He was the debonair gentleman, perfectly dressed, dispensing political wisdom, epigrams, jokes and anecdotes to representative audiences, impressing everyone except the British

[76] *My Life*, p. 46.
[77] Ibid., p. 47.
[78] Ibid., p. 46.

newspapers and Lloyd George—the man who mattered.[79] He lived well 'in a nice flat with heaps of good food, taxis to go about',[80] set up meetings with British leaders, spoke at length to various bodies and organized the publication of the *Moslem Outlook* in England and the *Echo de l'Islam* in Paris.

Mohamed Ali reached Bombay on 4 October 1920, nearly a month after the Calcutta Congress adopted the non-cooperation resolution. His advice was that Muslims must plunge into the campaign with their non-Muslim brethren to achieve the Khilafat aims. Words were soon translated into deeds. He redoubled his efforts, along with Gandhi, Azad and Ansari, to induce the trustees of the Aligarh College to give up the government grant-in-aid. When the demand was rejected, quite a few students set up a break-away national university. This is how the Jamia Millia Islamia was founded.

To begin with, Mohamed Ali devoted some time to giving the Jamia a solid Islamic footing. He revived Shibli's discourses on the Koran and ensured that 'our day began with a full hour devoted to the rapid exegesis of the Koran'. But he was a man on the move and his project in life extended far beyond the confines of a campus. Jamia was too small and too quiet a place for someone who was accustomed to the humdrum of national politics and who enjoyed being at the centre of every major event.[81] Predictably enough, he abandoned an institution he had himself founded, and headed for Nagpur to address the Congress, Muslim League and the Khilafat meetings.

Mohamed Ali was among the busiest men in India, speaking before crowds and local committees and galvanizing support for the non-cooperation programme. He travelled to eastern and western India from January to February 1921. His presence at the Erode session of the Majlis-ul-Ulama in March heightened the Khilafat euphoria, as did his presence in April at Madras where he attracted huge crowds of Hindus and Muslims. His fiery speech at Erode nearly

[79] Mohammad Mujeeb, *The Indian Muslims* (London, 1967), p. 537.

[80] Mohamed Ali to Shaukat Ali, 15 May 1920, MAP.

[81] Mushirul Hasan, *A Nationalist Conscience: M.A. Ansari, the Congress and the Raj* (Delhi, 1985), p. 104. Mohamed Ali is reported to have said in Sept. 1923: 'I never conceived of the Jamia's growth and permanence at all. The Jamia's existence today is rather like that of the refugees and the Prophet's helpers at Medina who were lying in wait for the conquest of Mecca. Our real objective is Aligarh which some day we shall conquer.' Quoted in A.G. Noorani, *President, Zakir Husain: A Quest for Excellence* (Bombay, 1967), p. 25. On this point, see Mujeeb, 'Oral History transcript' (407), p. 35, NMML.

got him into trouble again; an apology and an assurance that violence in every form would be eschewed led the government to withdraw the prosecution. From April to August, he spoke in Meerut (9 April), Bulandshahr (12 April), Lucknow (1 May and 7 August), Moradabad (26 July and 6 August), Pilibhit, Sitapur (7 August), and Allahabad (10 August). He was joined by his mother who threw off the veil, appeared before the public and began addressing vast audiences. Her journeys brought hundreds of thousands of rupees to the Khilafat fund. The whole of India was astir. A popular song of the era reflected the spirit:

> So spoke the mother of Mohamed Ali
> Give your life, my son, for the Khilafat.

During this tumultuous period, Mohamed Ali's relationship with Gandhi, with whom he had so little in common, was ambivalent. He was undoubtedly moved by the Mahatma's interest in his release and in the Khilafat cause, but he was uncomfortable with his world-view and could not grasp the significance of his political message. His own goals were limited to promoting pan-Islamism. As a result, it was not easy for him to make sense of the Mahatma's vision of a new social and moral order. Gandhi himself recognized that this was so. Yet he hoped that 'on seeing the success of my experiment in non-violence, (they) will come to realize its excellence and beauty later on'. In May 1920, he referred to a distinct understanding with the Ali brothers that violence would not be allowed to go on side-by-side with non-violence.[82] Mohamed Ali confirmed in December 1923 that he would not use force even if it was required for self-defence.[83]

Mohamed Ali did not press his own viewpoint because he needed Gandhi's support. In fact, he and other Khilafat leaders chose the path of non-violent non-cooperation to 'secure the interests of their country and their faith'. From Paris, he wrote: 'I only wish that I had a Musheer (adviser) here, and if possible Fazlul Haq, though of course the best man to have is Gandhiji himself.'[84] When he was accused of being a Gandhiphile, he replied: 'I cannot find in any community—Jewish, Christian or any other a man who has as noble

[82] Brown, *Gandhi's Rise to Power,* p. 331, fn. 2; *Day-to-Day,* vol. 2, p. 238.
[83] Brown, op. cit., pp. 330-1; Robinson, op. cit.
[84] To Shaukat Ali, 15 May 1920, MAP.

a character as Mahatma Gandhi. My *pir* and *murshid* is Abdul Bari whom I greatly respect. Yet I can say that I have not found anyone superior to Mahatma Gandhi.'[85] 'After the Prophet, on whom be peace,' he said, 'I consider it my duty to carry out the commands of Gandhiji.'[86]

While Mohamed Ali was reaffirming his loyalty to Gandhi, the Khilafat Conference at Karachi declared that serving in the army or police was *haram* for the Muslims. The expected happened. Mohamed Ali, the Chairman, was arrested two months later. On 26 October 1922 began the trial where he made the famous statement: 'The trial is not "Mohamed Ali and six others *versus* the Crown", but "God *versus* man". The case was therefore between God and man. The whole question was "Shall God dominate over man or shall man dominate over God?".' The jury listened to his rousing speech, but was not impressed. He and five other Muslim leaders were sentenced to two years' rigorous imprisonment on 1 November.

4.
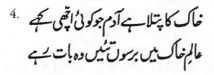

Man was first made of clay, and if the song you sing is good
This world of clay for years to come will listen to your voice.
(Mir Taqi Mir, translated by Ralph Russell and
Khurshidul Islam, *Three Mughal Poets*, p. 184)

Mohamed Ali was released on 29 August 1923, and in his first public address spoke of his gloom at finding on his shoulders the burden of freeing Islam and India. He said that he came out 'from a smaller prison to a large one', and that every executive member of the Congress must sign a pledge of readiness to sacrifice life itself for independence. Non-cooperation was still the main plank of his politics: 'If cooperation was "haram" according to the Islamic law two years ago, it cannot become "halal" today.'[86] He criticized the Swaraj Party and its leader, Motilal Nehru, for starting chamber practice in defiance of the Congress decision to boycott British law

[85] To Swami Shraddhanand, 26 March 1924, MAP.
[86] Quoted in Rajmohan Gandhi, *The Good Boatman: A Portrait of Gandhi* (Delhi, 1995), p. 104; and speech at Lahore, in *Bombay Chronicle*, 26 May 1924.

courts.[87] But three weeks later he himself proposed the compromise resolution at the Delhi Congress, permitting 'such Congressmen as have no religious or other conscientious objections against entering the legislatures . . . to stand as candidates', and calling for 'united endeavours to achieve Swaraj at the earliest moment'. He was concerned, as he wrote to Jawaharlal Nehru who was induced to accept against his will the Congress secretaryship in Mohamed Ali's year of presidentship,[88] to resolve the differences among Congressmen and to unite the factions. Appealing for unity, he stated:

Let the Provincial Congress [UP] assembly send for the sacred soil of Kashi itself the message of the greater and more solid *sangathan*, the *sangathan* of the National Congress. And let us go forth from this Conference truly *shuddh*, purged of all narrowness, bigotry and intolerance in order to free our country from the most cramping slavery—the slavery not only of the body but also of the soul. . . . If there is anything of the old world spirituality in Kashi, let us recommence the work of our great chief, Gandhiji, in the spirit of religious devotion and utter unworldliness.[89]

Whatever the reasons, Mohamed Ali's teaming up with the Swarajists enraged the *ulama*, whose *fatwa* against council entry was being repudiated by one of their own spokesman. The 'no-changers' too, accused their idol of having betrayed the Mahatma's heritage. The front-rank Communist leader, M.N. Roy, summed up his resentment:

Much was expected of Mohamed Ali. . . . The hope had been dashed to the ground. The idol showed its clay feet in such a hurry that the admirers were staggered. Mohamed Ali has failed to give the leadership which was expected of him. His pronouncements since he came out of jail are full of

[87] In September 1923 he complained that the Swarajists have 'completely gone back on the entire creed and policy of Gandhi'. 'I have been realizing every day that the leaders of the Swaraj Party want to throw Gandhism overboard without some of them having the courage to confess,' he wrote to his Khilafat comrade, Saifuddin Kitchlew. He wanted him to be a peacemaker between him and the 'Gujrati friends', although he advised 'caution and restraint'. Mohamed Ali to Kitchlew, 30 Sept. 1923, Hailey Papers, MSS. EUR. 220 (7-A), IOLR.

[88] Jawaharlal Nehru, *An Autobiography* (London, 1936), p. 99. 'I have just received your letter, and must "protest most indignantly" once more against your misplaced modesty. My dear Jawahar! it is just because some members of the Working Committee distrust and dislike your presence as Secretary that I like it.' Mohamed Ali to Nehru, 15 Jan. 1924, MAP.

[89] Mohamed Ali to Nehru, n.d., 1923, in *A Bunch of Old Letters* (Bombay, 1966 edn.), pp. 30-1.

mere platitudes and hopeless contradictions. No constructive programme, no positive suggestion as to the future of the movement is to be found in them. He authorises the removal of the ban on the councils, but holds up the edict of the ulemas [*sic*] on the question. He professes to be the standard-bearer of pure Gandhism, but sets his face positively against civil disobedience, without which the political programme of non-cooperation becomes meaningless. He indulges in fearful threats against the government, but finds the demand for the separation from the British empire 'childish and petulant'. He deplores the Hindu-Moslem feuds, but still insists on Khilafat propaganda, which contributed not a little to the success of the enemies of national freedom in creating communal dissensions. . . . In political questions, he has absolutely no programme to suggest. He harps on the threadbare 'constructive programme' which constructs naught but inaction. Such is the record with which Mohamed Ali goes to Kakinada to furnish the nationalist forces with a new direction.[90]

The main tenor of Mohamed Ali's address at Kakinada was that Hindu-Muslim unity was still necessary if Indians hoped to realize their aims. Similarly, non-cooperation was not outmoded even if one were to grant (only for the sake of argument) that it had failed. He also spoke of his long-standing dream of a 'Federation of Faiths', a 'United Faiths of India'. India's millions were so divided in communities and sects that providence had created for the country the mission to solve a unique problem and work out a new synthesis, which was nothing less than a 'Federation of Faiths'. The synthesis was to be of a federal type, for the lines of cleavage were too deep to allow for any other sort of union. He added:

For more than twenty years I have dreamed the dream of a federation, grander, nobler and infinitely more spiritual than the United States of America, and today when many a political Cassandra prophesies a return to the bad old days of Hindu-Muslim dissensions, I still dream of 'United Faiths of India'. It was in order to translate this dream into reality that I had launched my weekly newspaper, and had significantly called it the *Comrade*—'Comrade of all and partisan of none'.[91]

The motives for India's Muslim efforts towards achieving Swaraj were dual. They aimed at freeing India and freeing Islam. The relationship between Indians and the Turks was in the nature of a compact between countries who were oppressed by the same

[90] G. Adhikari (ed.), *Documents of the History of the Communist Party of India, 1923-1925* (Delhi, 1974), vol. 2, p. 181.

[91] Iqbal (ed.), *Selected Writings*, p. 256.

imperialism. Once India was free and her forces could not be driven to fight against the Turks, the two countries would be safe. Mohamed Ali's contention was that the Turks would have fought for the freedom of their co-religionists, including India's Muslims, and hence India, if they had not been so weakened. His lack of realism in assessing the Turkish aims did not stop here. He pictured them fighting for an ideal Khalifa, even though the Kemalist revolution was already on its way to achieving success. He believed that once the Turks were free from their 'distractions' they would revive the glories of Umayyad or Abbasid dynasties and the pristine purity of the *Khilafat-i Rashida*.

Mohamed Ali's elevation to the Congress presidentship legitimized his position in nationalist circles. But within months of his exhortations at Kakinada, he began drifting away from the Congress, or, perhaps, as he would have put it, the Congress drifted away from him. This had a great deal to do with worsening Hindu-Muslim relations and the feeling in some Muslim circles that the Congress was aiding the communal forces in order to establish 'Hindu Raj'. Mohamed Ali developed a point of view from which everything said or done by any Hindu was linked to the Hindu Mahasabha's influence. He saw 'the evil hand of the Hindu Mahasabha everywhere and its tainted mark on every forehead'. Indeed, his 'new mentality' recognized only two divisions in India, Hindu and Muslim, and not nationalist and reactionary or non-cooperating.[92] Commenting on Mohamed Ali's new stance, Nehru could not understand,

how a Hindu or a Moslem can have any political or economic rights as Hindu or Moslem. And I cannot conceive why Moslems or Sikhs or Hindus should lay stress on any such rights. No minority should be unjustly treated. But Maulana Mohamed Ali is well aware that minorities get on well enough as a rule. It is the great majority which requires protection. A handful of foreigners rule India and exploit her millions. A handful of India's rich men exploit her vast peasantry and her workers. It is this great majority of the exploited that demands justice and is likely to have it sooner than many people imagine. I wish Maulana Mohamed Ali would become a champion of this majority and demand political and economic rights for them. But this majority does not consist of Hindus only or Moslems only or Sikhs only. It consists of Hindus and Moslems and Sikhs and others. And if he works for this majority, I am sure he will come to the conclusion that he need attach

[92] Ansari to Mazharul Haq, 7 Sept. 1929; Hasan (ed.), *Muslims and the Congress*, pp. 86-7.

little importance to the imaginary rights of individuals or groups based on adherence to a religious creed.

Mohamed Ali's main grievance, however, was that Gandhi, whom he had only just described as 'the most Christ-like man of our times', gave a free hand to the 'Lala-Malaviya gang' to pursue the goal of a Hindu Rashtra. The Congress, according to him, was no longer a national party but a Hindu one, unprepared to condemn Hindu fanatics, and unprepared to work towards the creation of a secular society. Gandhi, with whom he worked for ten years through thick and thin, was keen to retain his popularity with the 'Hindus' and, for this reason, reluctant to resolve the Hindu-Muslim deadlock. Mohamed Ali's anxieties were heightened by the growing fissures in the Hindu-Muslim alliance in Bengal and Punjab and the rapid progress of the Arya Samaj, the Hindu Mahasabha, and the *shuddhi* and *sangathan* movements. Commenting on the Delhi riot of July 1924 specifically, and on the deteriorating communal situation generally, he wrote: 'And pray Mahatmaji forgive a pang of sorrow, the cry of a well-nigh broken heart, the credit of it all goes, in the first instance, to the misguided spirit of the *sangathan* movement, and the superfluous boastings of the *shuddhi* leaders. . . . I feel sick, positively sick of it all.'[93] At the same time, the 'pseudo-nationalists', he wrote in the *Comrade* on 17 July 1924,

talk and write as nationalists and run down communals; but only in the use of counters and catchwords of nationalism are they nationalists for their hearts are narrow and they can conceive of no future for India except it be one of Hindu dominance and the existence of the Musalmans as a minority living on the sufferance of the Hindu majority, forgetting that such ill-concealed dreams can have but one interpretation, the existence of the Hindu majority itself on the sufferance of the British masters of India. It is my sad conviction that not one of these pseudo-nationalists would have talked so glibly of nationalism, majority rule and mixed electorates, if his own community had not been in the safe position of an overwhelming majority. It is they who are real culprits as narrow communalists, but since the position of their community is safe enough they mouth all the fine phrases of nationalism and parade themselves as nationalists. The Cow question provides the best topic for the exposure of their pseudo-nationalism, for in the name of nationalism they make demands on their fellow-countrymen so absurd that none has ever heard of them in any other country or nation in the world, and it is time that their nationalism was fully exposed.

[93] Mohamed Ali to Gandhi, 21 July 1924, MAP.

The publication of the Nehru report in August 1928 set in motion the avalanche of Mohamed Ali's eloquence against Gandhi and the Congress. Soon after returning to India from Europe in October, he described the provision of dominion status in the Nehru report as being 'inconsistent with the independent spirit of Islam'. Its implication was that the creation was God's, the country was the viceroy's or of the parliament's and the rule was Hindu Mahasabha's.[94] 'Today', he said on 25 December 1928, 'Mahatma Gandhi and Sir Ali Imam would be sitting under our flag and over them would fly the flag of the Union Jack. The Nehru report in its preamble has admitted the bondage of servitude.'

He was equally outraged that Muslim representation in the central legislature was fixed at 25 and not 33 per cent, while separate electorates and weightages were done away with.[95] In his view, separate electorates guaranteed that a small minority was not swamped by an overwhelming majority, while weightages ensured that this majority would not establish 'a legalized tyranny of numbers'.[96]

Such views mostly mirrored the fears of government servants and landowners who, having gained political leverage through separate electorates and government nomination, faced the cheerless prospect of being eased out of legislative bodies. Equally, the proposal for adult suffrage was considered to be ominous. The enfranchisement of over fifteen million voters, mainly tenants, was certain to lead to the ouster of the landlords from the general constituencies as well. Not surprisingly, they resisted all forms of provincial advance if their interests were not safeguarded and insisted on having separate electorates, weightages, and 'effective' Muslim representation on autonomous institutions created by the legislatures.

Mohamed Ali was now identified with such elements and did his

---

[94] 'You make compromises in your constitution everyday with false doctrines, immoral conceptions and wrong ideas, but you make no compromise with our communalists—with separate electorates and reserve seats. Twenty-five per cent is our proportion of the population and yet you will not give us 33 per cent in the Assembly. You are a Jew, a Bania.' See Mushirul Hasan, *Nationalism and Communal Politics in India, 1916-1928* (Delhi, 1979), pp. 287-8.

[95] Ibid.

[96] In the very first issue of the *Comrade*, he had declared separate electorates to be necessary because of 'the distinct and well-defined Hindu and Muslim standpoints in regard to the common, immediate and everyday affairs of Indian life'. *Comrade*, 11 and 28 Jan. 1911, 29 March 1913, 19 Jan. and 6 Feb. 1925.

best to turn the tables against his detractors. The first opportunity arose on 21 December. The Ali brothers, in league with some others, disrupted a meeting which was tilted in favour of the Nehru report. When they employed similar tactics elsewhere, several delegates resigned and decided to boycott the forthcoming All India Khilafat Conference that was to be chaired by Mohamed Ali. A few days later Mohamed Ali tried his luck at the All-Parties Muslim Conference in Delhi. He did not need to stifle opposition, for this assembly of loyalists was already converted to the idea that the Nehru report jettisoned their interests.

Mohamed Ali's presence at the Delhi's conference was described as 'a tragedy of Indian public life'. *The Servants of India* commented: 'One's heart sinks at the thought that the Ali brothers should have been among the staunchest supporters of the conference.'[97] Ansari, once his comrade-in-arms, was anguished by his parleys with the 'Aga Khan and Co.'. He wrote:

Ever since the Lucknow Convention many of us have been making ceaseless efforts to come to an understanding with the Ali brothers and their friends. . . . They gradually but surely went on receding from us until at last they found themselves in the company of the Aga Khan and Sir Mohammad Shafi in January last. The willingness with which they associated themselves with people whose only distinction is that they have always been reactionary in regard both to Indian and Muslim affairs was surprising. . . . Indeed the differences that in their origin concerned a few provisions of the Nehru Report have now grown into a conflict of the very outlook. This to my mind explained why the Ali brothers are adopting an irreconcilable attitude although they know very well that they are thereby strengthening the government as well as the communalists, both Hindu and Muslim. . . .[98]

A striking feature of the All-Parties Muslim Conference was that Mohamed Ali sat beside Mohammad Shafi who he had so often derided as a government stooge, and that the Aga Khan was cheered by Azad Sobhani whose vitriolic speeches at Kanpur in 1913 had forced the Khoja leader to quit the Muslim League. Mohamed Ali actually seconded the resolution proposed by Shafi at the Delhi conference. Likewise, leaders like Jinnah, Mohammad Shafi and the Ali brothers, who had not shared a platform before, signed the 'Delhi

[97] *Servants of India*, 10 Jan. 1929.
[98] Ansari to Mazharul Haq, 7 Sept. 1929, Hasan (ed.), *Muslims and the Congress*, pp. 86-7.

Manifesto' on 9 March 1929 in order to persuade Muslims to stay away from Congress meetings and processions.

Nehru reacted angrily to Mohamed Ali's signing the 'Delhi Manifesto', declaring it a 'treason' against the Congress by one who had served as its president:

The ex-Presidents of the National Congress are certainly a mixed lot and not always amenable to discipline. Like the king they appear to be above the law. I had ventured to criticize a statement made by one of them forgetful of this truism in Indian politics because of my high regard for this gallant leader in the cause of Indian freedom. He has made history and, if he but will, can do so again. But just when India is stretching her limbs for another and a stiffer struggle, when drooping spirits are reviving, he cries 'halt' and calls back his regiments and battalions. And have not many of those with whom he consorts in this endeavour been the strongest bulwarks of British rule in India and the antagonists of those who strive for freedom?

In his sharp rebuttal on 13 March, Mohamed Ali condemned Congress leaders who defied the party's decisions on non-cooperation, non-violence, Hindu-Muslim unity and untouchability. As a price of his cooperation, Madan Mohan Malaviya, for example, 'wanted to place a revolver in the hands of every Hindu lady, no doubt as a token of non-violence, and of course all the Hindu-Muslim riots in which he has never said a word against Hindus are in full conformity with the Congress precepts of Hindu-Muslim unity'. He accused Motilal Nehru for 'killing non-cooperation just as he is killing the Congress today and merging it into the Hindu Mahasabha in spite of his well-known lack of Hindu orthodoxy',[99] and deplored Gandhi's endorsement of the Nehru report. Quoting from his writings of 1924 and 1925 to show that the Mahatma was converted to a different creed and striving for different goals, he pointed out:

Gandhi has defeated all Muslim attempts for a compromise. He is giving free rein to the communalism of the majority. The Nehru constitution is the legalized tyranny of numbers and is the way to rift and not peace. It recognizes the rank communalism of the majority as nationalism. The safeguards proposed to limit the high-handedness of the majority are branded as communal.[100]

Gandhi conceded that the Ali brothers 'had a fairly heavy list of

[99] *Nigarishat-i Mohamed Ali*, quoted in Abdul Hamid, *Muslim Separatism in India, 1858-1947* (Karachi, 1971 edn.), p. 201.

[100] *Times of India*, 5 March 1929.

complaints', and that he could not make an impression on them.[101] 'Whatever Maulana Mohamed Ali may think of me, I have nothing but kindly feelings about him. And I feel sure that time will remove misunderstandings. Having no feeling either against Islam or Mussalmans, I feel absolutely at ease', he wrote from the Yeravda Central Prison. He hoped in vain that 'if truth is in me, the brothers must capitulate'.[102] Some months earlier, Mohamed Ali had already leveled the baseless charge that Gandhi was 'fighting for the supremacy of Hinduism (and) the submergence of Muslims'. He refused to join 'Mr. Gandhi' not only because his civil disobedience movement was 'for making the seventy millions of Indian Muslims dependent on the Hindu Mahasabha',[103] but also doubted whether he would stick to his own programme:

Doubtless man who could suddenly call of the non-cooperation campaign at Bardoli in 1922 with the same astonishing about-face can inaugurate a civil disobedience movement in 1930. But what surety is there that he would not again order suspension, just as he did eight years ago, only a few days after serving an ultimatum to the Viceroy?[104]

Moreover, the country, according to Mohamed Ali, was not prepared for civil disobedience: it lacked unity, discipline and self-control. He warned Jawaharlal Nehru: 'Your present colleagues will desert you. They will leave you in the lurch in a crisis. Your own Congressman will send you to the gallows.'[105]

Mohamed Ali's appeal to Muslims to send delegations to London symbolized the collapse of the old alliance on which Gandhi had built the non-cooperation movement. He himself joined a delegation,

[101] Gandhi to Motilal Nehru, 12 Aug. 1929, Motilal Nehru Papers (G-1), NMML; see also Gandhi to Shaukat Ali, 17 April 1930, CWMG, vol. 43, p. 280.

[102] Gandhi to Horace G. Alexander, 23 Dec. 1930, CWMG, vol. 45, p. 26; Young India, 3 April 1930, CWMG, vol. 43, p. 126.

[103] Quoted in Reginald Coupland, The Constitutional Problem in India (Oxford, 1944), pt. 3, p. 111. The position of the 'Nationalist Muslims', on the other hand, was different. This was explained by Ansari to the raja of Mahmudabad: 'Whilst, on the one hand, we consider the policy and programme of the Congress entirely ill-conceived and detrimental to the larger interests of the country today, we do not consider the campaign of civil disobedience conceived in the spirit of antagonism to the Muslims'. To the raja of Mahmudabad, 11 May 1930, Hasan (ed.), Muslims and the Congress, p. 121.

[104] Jafri (ed.), Nigarishat-i-Mohamed Ali, pp. 237-72, quoted in Watson, op. cit., p. 92.

[105] Nehru, An Autobiography, p. 120.

led by the Aga Khan, with the firm conviction that critical collaboration with the British at the Round Table Conference would
bring greater political benefits than 'sedition' in Congress company.
But his departure was marked by gloom, for he knew that his mission
was condemned as traitorous by those people with whom he had
worked in the past. In fact, the Maulana felt in London that, 'his real
place was in the fight in India, not in the futile conference chamber
in London'.[106] In Oxford, his Alma Mater, he addressed the students
in their tail coats, talked cricket and made them laugh. But he 'made
little or no impression and quite failed to put across the case for the
Muslims to a youthful but intelligent audience who were to provide
a fair number of the nation's political leaders in later years'.[107]
His speech at the Round Table Conference, which turned out to be
his last sermon, appeared to be the raving of a man isolated,
inconsolably bereaved, dying. 'I want to go back to my country',
Mohamed Ali declared, 'with the substance of freedom in my hand.
Otherwise I will not go back to a slave country. I would even prefer
to die in a foreign country so long as it is a free country, and if you
do not give me freedom in India you will have to give me a grave
here.' In Mujeeb's view, Mohamed Ali's appeal to the British to give
India her freedom or else he would not return alive was no more
than a pathetic admission of his failure.[108]

Mohamed Ali, a chronic patient of diabetes, died in London on
3 January 1931 and was buried in Jerusalem. Gandhi, whom he
derided with such vehemence during the years 1928-30, had this to
say at his death:

In him I have lost one whom I rejoiced to call brother and friend and the
nation has lost a fearless patriot. We had differences of opinion between
us, but love that cannot stand the strain of differences is like 'a sounding
brass and thinking cymbal'.

Nehru was, likewise, equally charitable in his assessment.
Reflecting on his role in his *Autobiography*, he observed: 'It was a
misfortune for India that he (Mohamed Ali) left the country for
Europe in the summer of 1928. A great effort was then made to solve
the communal problem. If Mohamed Ali had been here then, it is

---

[106] Nehru, *An Autobiography*, p. 120.
[107] Benthall Papers (2), Centre for South Asian Studies, Cambridge.
[108] Mujeeb, *Indian Muslims*, p. 539.

just conceivable that matters would have shaped differently.' Nehru added:

For whatever the differences on the communal question might have been, there were very few differences on the political issue. He was devoted to the idea of Indian independence. And because of the common political outlook, it was always possible to come to some mutually satisfactory arrangement with him on the communal issue. There was nothing in common between him and the reactionaries who pose as the champions of communal interests.[109]

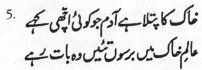

Man was first made of clay, and if the song you sing is good
This world of clay for years to come will listen to your voice.
(Mir Taqi Mir, translated by Ralph Russell and
Khurshidul Islam, *Three Mughal Poets*, p. 270).

Mohamed Ali had a supreme gift of expression, but he was not one to be identified with any great principle or order, or even a big idea. He relished the trappings of power, the drama of great debates, the high-sounding titles, his name echoing through history. He was too outspoken to be a good manager of people. He excelled at exposing the follies of others but had little to advocate himself; his own thinking was ruthless—he spared nothing and nobody. He had a nimble wit, but sometimes his devastating sarcasm hurt, and he lost many friends.[110] He and his brother Shaukat were 'splendid agitators and very little more'. 'They certainly are not the type of men in whom we would have much faith, were they placed to rule over us', commented Abbas Tyabji, one of Gandhi's lieutenants in Bombay.[111] Edwin Montagu, the Secretary of State who had not approved of

---

[109] *CWMG*, vol. 45, p. 203; Nehru, *An Autobiography*, p. 120.

[110] Nehru, *An Autobiography*, p. 117.

[111] Quoted in Brown, *Gandhi's Rise to Power*, p. 276. This opinion was shared by others. One of them wrote to Tej Bahadur Sapru: 'Frankly, I am not very much interested in the Ali brothers. I do not believe in them, and to the extent that they are doing right, it is because they are either attracted by Gandhi's glamour, or they feel that they can work more effectively under the kudos of his name'. S.L. Polak to Sapru, 8 July 1981, Sapru Papers, vol. 17, p. 241, National Library, Calcutta. Percival Spear, who met Mohamed Ali at Delhi's St. Stephen's College in 1924, wrote: 'He was

Mohamed Ali's internment, found him to be 'a quite typical specimen, full of incurable vanity'.[112]

Mohamed Ali was a passionate man, strong in his resentments as in his affections. He left a strong although not wholly pleasant impression on people who knew him, of a man devoted to his convictions. At the same time he was obstinate, impatient in temper, and choleric in disposition; quick to anger when honour or religion was touched; wild and untameable. He was the man for the people, impetuous, dashing, irrepressible, demanding sympathy by laying his heart open, crying and raising laughter, and believing in God and God's mercy with an intensity that made him at times completely irresponsible.[113] He advocated a strikingly wide range of ideas. Some grossly contradicted one another, some complemented one another, and some appear to have been floated simply to guage public reaction before being discarded. The Urdu scholar Maulvi Abdul Haq found Mohamed Ali lacking in 'balance and a sense of proportion'. He was no doubt a vocal champion of freedom, but was at the same time ruthless and dictatorial in his public and private conduct. He had an hysterical streak in his personality, lacked consideration for friends, and was, for these reasons, incapable of carrying through his numerous enterprises. Abdul Haq's final judgement was that Mohamed Ali, although a brilliant writer and orator, 'failed' to enhance his stature and reputation in public life.[114]

After all, Mohamed Ali wasted years of his life trying to make a hero out of the Turkish Sultan—as perverse a task as was ever attempted. In his enthusiastic, unrealistic moods, which were frequent enough, he regarded himself as a link not only between

---

a handsome bearded man with striking eyes and clothed in flowing robes. His speech was easy, his manner ingratiating, that of a willing sufferer for a noble cause. To me he seemed to be too suave to be sincere and too insincere to be noble. In fact I took an instant dislike to him.' Percival and Margaret Spear, *India Remembered* (Delhi, 1981), p. 15.

[112] To Chelmsford, 23 June 1920, File No. 6, Chelmsford Papers, IOLR. 'Why we should intern Mohamed Ali for pan-Mohammedanism', Montagu recorded in his diary on 11 Nov. 1917, 'when we encourage pan-Judaism, I cannot for the life of me understand.' S.D. Waley, *Edwin Montagu: A Memoir and an Account of his Visits to India* (Bombay, 1964), p. 141.

[113] Mujeeb, op. cit., p. 536.

[114] Abdul Haq, *Chand Humasr* (Karachi, 1952 edn.), p. 164. Muhammad Sadiq had described this sketch of Mohamed Ali as 'vitriolic'. *Twentieth Century Urdu Literature* (Karachi, 1983), p. 368.

Indian Muslims and the Turks, but also between the Turks and the rest of the world.[115] He was insensitive to the implications of the Turkish revolution, which was directed against the tyrannical rule of the Sultan as well as against Western imperialism. Similarly, he was unfamiliar with scholars like Ziya Gökalp, the intellectual leader of that period, who had dismissed the idea of uniting Muslim nations under one ruler as a messianic hope. That is why when Muslims elsewhere were establishing national states independent of external ties of domination, Mohamed Ali was striving to recreate the Khilafat of the classical theorists.

The invitation to the Amir of Afghanistan to liberate India from British imperialism was an act of indiscretion. On such matters Mohamed Ali seemed to be wanting to forget, as often as he could, the need to be tactful, in order that he might assert with ever greater vehemence the fact that he was a sincere believer in Islam.[116] The idea of Muslim migration (*hijrat*) to Afghanistan, which he endorsed, was both unrealistic and politically inexpedient. His credibility suffered, moreover, on account of the scandal over the 'misuse' of the Khilafat funds and his frequent outbursts that led to growing tensions between the Khilafatists and their Congress allies.[117] The *Comrade* was revived in November 1924, but ceased publication in

[115] Mujeeb, op. cit., p. 538.

[116] Azad stated that 'whatever Mohamed Ali said was quite compatible with the teaching of Islam'. Home Poll., 1921, 45, NAI. Later, of course, Mohamed Ali offered a clarification in order to remove the misunderstandings in many quarters. See his presidential address at the Allahabad District Conference in May 1921, Home Poll., 1921, 10, NAI.

[117] For example, the Urdu poet, Brij Narain 'Chakbast' stated that Mohamed Ali's speech at a Khilafat Conference in April 1921 had convinced him that the political turmoil in India was fomented to strengthen Islam and create conditions which would give Afghanistan the excuse to invade the country. He did not think that Muslims could be converted to Indian nationalism because of their extra-territorial loyalties. He was convinced that Mohamed Ali, a pan-Islamist, was not a friend of the Hindus. He argued that Muslim political movements revealed their lack of trust in the Hindus. Gandhi believed that the support of the Ali brothers would enable him to promote his objectives. But, in effect, the Ali brothers used him as their instrument. Chakbast to Sapru, 28 April 1921 (in Urdu), Sapru Papers. In an 'Open letter to the Maulana Sahebs', the editor of *Bharatwasi* took exception to the Khilafatists designating themselves as 'Khadim-i Kaaba' (Servants of Kaaba) and not as 'Khadim-i Hind' (Servants of India). He told the Ali brothers: 'For you swarajya for India is not the first duty. You build the whole edifice on religion, while we build the entire edifice on patriotic considerations.' P. Parasram to the Ali brothers, 8 July 1921, MAP.

January 1926. 'Poverty is pestering me', Mohamed wrote. He considered restarting the paper 'and see if I can wipe off the deficit due to those two journals [*Comrade* and *Hamdard*] or I shall retire from public life, and earn 50 rupees from tuitions'.[118] The Ali brothers, having spent more than their means, were in dire financial straits. Delhi's chief commissioner informed the viceroy that Mohamed Ali was 'thoroughly discredited and almost penniless'. He went cap in hand to his former associates and colleagues (the Karachi merchant Haji Abdullah Haroon had already donated 10,000 rupees to revive the *Comrade*), and having failed in almost all quarters he finally secured a grant of 6,000 rupees from the deposed maharaja of Nabha.[119] Some years later, the raja of Alwar bore his travel and treatment expenses in London. Even if these are not illustrations of Mohamed Ali's loss of credibility with his own community, they clearly reveal the gradual reversal of his fortunes.

The Congress politicians, including the 'Nationalist Muslims', gradually deserted Mohamed Ali;[120] yet he clung to the much-maligned Khilafat committees. His defence of Ibn Saud, who had demolished numerous sepulchers held sacred by Muslims, also alienated him from his spiritual mentor, Abdul Bari and other friends. But he was not impressed. Nor did he learn from his own experiences. During his visit to the Arab lands in June 1926 he discovered the squalor of Mecca and Medina, the barrenness of the surrounding land, the degeneracy of the social conditions, and the mismanagement of the *haj* traffic. Yet he continued to insist that the Khilafat committees were destined to bring about a truly Islamic rule in the Holy Land. He wanted India's Muslims to form a party around the nucleus of the Khilafat group, persuade other Islamic people to their way of thinking, and thus achieve a united Muslim voice. He wanted them to contribute money, time, technical assistance and moral support to the Hijaz, devote themselves wholeheartedly to the reformation of the Centre of Islam, and thus earn the good requital in both worlds. He was confident that it was possible to resist Ibn

---

[118] *Searchlight*, 17 April 1927.

[119] David Page, *Prelude to Partition: The Indian Muslims and the Imperial System of Control 1920-32* (Oxford, 1982), pp. 104-5.

[120] For example, one of his former colleagues, Arif Husain Hasvi, resigned from the *Hamdard* because of his communal posture. *Searchlight*, 14 May 1926. Page, op. cit., pp. 100-1.

Saud's arrogation of control of the Holy Land and help reestablish a genuine Islamic rule.[121]

Such romantic visions were nurtured by Mohamed Ali's inflated ego. That is why he paid scant regard to his own comrades who had followed his lead in the past but were no longer prepared to do so in the changed political scenario. His protégés in UP—Khaliquz-zaman and Shuaib Qureshi—opposed his plan of sending three deputations to the Middle East.[122] In neighbouring Delhi, Ansari resigned from the Khilafat committees in July 1926, stating that 'as an Indian owing allegiance first to the motherland' he had to sever his ties with communal and sectional organizations.[123] In Punjab, after their success in the 1924 elections, the Muslim Swarajists took less interest in the Khilafat committee; the main opposition to the Ali brothers came from the Khilafatists under the leadership of Saifuddin Kitchlew. One of Punjab's leading public figures, the poet Iqbal, believed that the Khilafat movement in its dying moments unfolded aspects in which 'no sincere Muslim could join for a single minute'. Turkey, he pointed out, was the first Muslim country to shake off the fetters of medieval mentality and found a way of life of her own.[124]

In sum, Mohamed Ali failed to recognize that 'Muslim identity' in a plural society had to be defined not in relation to his Islamic world but in response to the specific historical and contemporary experiences of the Muslim communities in the subcontinent. This fact had been underlined in Syed Ahmad Khan's rejection of pan-Islamism towards the end of the nineteenth century and was creatively expressed by Azad, Ajmal Khan and Ansari. But Mohamed Ali was swayed by his own religious/Islamic rhetoric. He could not reflect, as did Azad after 1922-3, on the wider implications of the Khilafat movement on inter-community relations. He even refused to accept that Muslims themselves had played the final part in destroying what he was almost single-handedly fighting to maintain. He continued charging at the windmill, hugging an illusion which

[121] Watson, op. cit., p. 87; Ahmad, *Islamic Modernism*, p. 139; Rais Ahmad Jafri, *Karawan-i Gumgushta* (Karachi, 1971), pp. 16-18.

[122] Page, op. cit., p. 502.

[123] Ansari to Shaukat Ali, 16 July 1926, Hasan (ed.), *Muslims and the Congress*, p. 19.

[124] Page, op. cit., pp. 503-4. For Iqbal, see Annemarie Schimmel, *Gabriel's Wings: A Study into the Religious Ideas of Sir Muhammad Iqbal* (Leiden, 1963), p. 47.

had become irrelevant to his own community.[125] As he once put it, he had 'an inherent and almost ineradicable tendency towards diffusion and a fatal attraction for tangents'.[126] He could not build the bridges for retreat, because he did not possess the skill to do so. Instead, he aimed 'to destroy all that did not conform to his ideal, even though he could not reconstruct what he had destroyed'.[127] Although he was popular with those who thought it a point of honour to wear Islam on their sleeves, he ultimately undermined his own position and damaged the very causes he aspired to serve.[128]

NOTE ON MOHAMED ALI'S
MY LIFE: A FRAGMENT

Since its publication in January 1942, Mohamed Ali's *My Life: A Fragment* has been widely read in academic circles in India and Pakistan. Afzal Iqbal, the Editor, secured the 'manuscript' from Mohamed Mujeeb, the Vice-Chancellor of Delhi's Jamia Millia Islamia, and published this 'autobiographical sketch'.

Mohamed Ali was a prolific writer; yet he did not consider writing a book until he was interned in 1923, following the famous Karachi trial. This is what he told Abdul Majid Daryabadi in 1916 while in Chhindwara, then a small town in the Central Provinces (now Madhya Pradesh):

You suggest to me that I should write some book during my enforced leisure, and that our people expect one from me. If that is so, I am afraid they don't know me. Firstly, I have not the patient perseverance nor the temper of the researcher. Secondly, my emotions are much too strong to permit what intellect I may possess to be exerted in the writing of a book. . . . No, my friend, my brain is far too busy (and so is my heart) to allow of any leisure for such 'pastimes' as authorship.[129]

He did, however, write a great deal more than many of his contemporaries. He contributed to his own newspapers, and wrote hundreds of routine letters as an editor. Besides writing *My Life*, he wrote poems to fill a not-so-slim volume, and miscellaneous

---

[125] Iqbal, *Life and Times*, p. 413.
[126] Quoted in Nanda, op. cit., p. 201.
[127] Choudhry Khaliquzzaman, *Pathway to Pakistan* (Lahore, 1961), p. 69.
[128] Mujeeb, op. cit., p. 538.
[129] 25 July 1916, Abdul Majid Daryabadi Papers, NMML.

historical, literary and political pieces to fill another.[130] During his internment and trips to Europe, he corresponded with his friends and family members.[131]

These letters constitute a major corpus of pan-Islamic literature in India. They uncover major themes that concerned his generation of educated Muslims who turned to him for political inspiration and leadership. The tone in his correspondence constantly varies from boredom and depression, on the one hand, to exhilaration and conviction on the other, now relaxed and desultory, now indulging in flights of fantasy or burlesque. A flair for the dramatic, coupled with a wry self-awareness, a temperament that allowed the fullest reins to intellectual enthusiasm while never really realizing personal ones. This complexity, not rare but fascinating in Mohamed Ali's case, is also noticeable in his speeches.

My Life is much more reflective and analytical than any of Mohamed Ali's other published writings. It is an important personal statement on how some educated Muslims lived through the turbulent decades of early twentieth century. It is an individual's intellectual and spiritual journey, his engagement with a society and polity that was undergoing rapid changes. 'Experts often write for experts,' commented Mohamed Ali, 'but I am, so to speak, "the man-in-the-street", and I write for "the man in the street". The individual experience which I relate will make this clear, and being typical of the history of so many Muslim lives of my generation, it will not, I trust, be altogether lacking in interest.'

At the same time, *My Life* reflects the collective experiences of large numbers of people who shared the author's commitment to and his passion for 'rejuvenating' the Muslim communities in the subcontinent. It is no doubt inadequate in many ways—verbose, incoherent, repetitive and full of digressions. Besides, as Afzal Iqbal pointed out, of the four parts Mohamed Ali planned to write, only the first is complete. The second part—included by Iqbal as an appendix—is incomplete. Yet, *My Life* is a document of considerable

---

[130] Rais Ahmed Jafri (ed.), *Selections from Mohamed Ali's Comrade* (Lahore, 1965), and his *Ifadat-i Mohamed Ali* (Hyderabad, n.d.); Mohammed Sarwar (ed.), *Mazameen-i Mohamed Ali* (Delhi, 1938), 2 vols.

[131] Mushirul Hasan (ed.), *Mohamed Ali in Indian Politics* (Delhi and Karachi), 3 vols.; Shan Muhammed (ed.), *Unpublished Letters of the Ali Brothers* (Delhi, 1979); Abu Salman Shahjahanpuri (ed.), *Siyasi Maktubat Rais al-Ahrar* (Karachi, 1978); Mohammad Sarwar, *Maulana Mohamed Ali ke Europe ka Safar* (Lahore, 1941).

significance for students of modern Islam in South Asia, its historical value enhanced by the absence of a similar text written by any of the leading Muslim actors of the period. Maulana Abul Kalam Azad, for one, did not write much besides his commentary on the Koran; he expressed himself instead in the literary form of his letters, published as *Ghubar-i Khatir*. In fact, Jawaharlal Nehru commented in his prison diary: 'Free thinker and magnificent writer as he is, he should have turned out a host of splendid books. Yet his record is a very limited one.'[132]

At a time when scholars are attempting to delineate the contours of 'Muslim identity' in South Asia, Mohamed Ali's *My Life* enables us to understand how some Muslims constructed their identity in 'British' India. For this reason this book invites comparison with other texts written around the same time in other countries by Muslim scholars and publicists. At a time when frequent scholarly engagements with 'communalism' and 'separatism' are taking place around the globe, *My Life* reveals, more than any other contemporary account, the anxieties and aspirations of several Muslim groups in a colonial society that was being gradually transformed as a result of far-reaching political, administrative and bureaucratic changes.

[132] Christmas Day—1942, S. Gopal (ed.), *Selected Works of Jawaharlal Nehru*, vol. 13, p. 39.

The Qaid-i Azam and the Nawab-Chancellor: Literary Paradigms in the Historical Construction of Indian Muslim Identity

IAN COPLAND

This is not, primarily, an essay about Mohammad Ali Jinnah; but I want to begin with him because his story is so well-known and because of his acknowledged importance in the political history of late colonial India. Jinnah is seen not just as a major contributor but, as his Pakistani honorific Qaid-i Azam suggests, the man who created a nation. As Leonard Mosley puts it: 'Pakistan was the one-man achievement of Mohammad Ali Jinnah.'[1] Here is one individual who, it would seem, changed the course of history.[2]

Why, when the Great Man Theory of history has long been displaced elsewhere by theories of economic causation, by structuralist-functionalist theories of party and state and by theories of nationalist consciousness, all of which focus on society rather than the individual, is the history of the Pakistan movement still overwhelmingly presented as one man's biography?[3] Certainly, Jinnah was a dominant player—perhaps the key player—in the negotiations which led up to Partition. Nevertheless, it strikes me that his celebrity status among historians of Pakistan has rather less to do with objective reality than with the dramatic appeal of his life. Generally speaking, people are more interested in other people than

[1] Leonard Mosley, *The Last Days of the British Raj* (London, 1961), p. 247.

[2] Interestingly, this view has been expressed most stridently by non-Pakistani scholars. See the paper presented by Sir Penderel Moon to the Qaid-i Azam Centenary Congress, Islamabad, 1976, quoted in R.J. Moore, 'Jinnah and the Pakistan Demand', *Modern Asian Studies*, 17, 4, 1983, p. 529; H.V. Hodson, *The Great Divide: Britain—India—Pakistan* (London, 1969), p. 30; Stanley Wolpert, *Jinnah of Pakistan* (New York, 1984), p. vii; and Sailesh Kumar Bandopadhyaya, *Quaid-i Azam Mohammad Ali Jinnah and the Creation of Pakistan* (New Delhi, 1991), p. 334.

[3] I am aware that some recent writings have taken a different point of departure: for instance, Imran Ali, *The Punjab Under Imperialism, 1885-1947* (Delhi, 1988); and David Gilmartin, *Empire and Islam: Punjab and the Making of Pakistan* (London, 1988).

they are in things or concepts (which is why biography consistently outsells 'straight' history in the popular market). Likewise, while historians may not consciously strive for an audience, at least in the commercial sense, they, too, feel the emotional pull of the great human comedy. However in writing 'biographically', historians are doing more than satisfying a psychological need to engage with flesh and blood. They are also seeking a way to make the past intelligible. Patchy and unbalanced though it may be, the surviving historical record is still overwhelmingly vast; it is also formless and chaotic. Faced with an immensity of random events, historians are forced to select, to discriminate between the essential and the irrelevant. Frequently this is done, at least on the surface, from a proclaimed ideological standpoint or with reference to some model or theory. Could it be, however, that our choices are not always conscious ones? Is it possible that they are influenced, in part, by habits formed long ago, by deep-set cultural suppositions? Some philosophers of history believe so. Following R.G. Collingwood, Northrop Frye and Levi-Strauss, Hayden White argues that historical writing is 'essentially a literary, that is to say, fiction-making operation',[4] a *poetic* act' 'prefigured' by distinct topological strategies.[5] All histories, White says, conform as regards their 'plots' to one or other of the archetypal modes of Western narrative discourse—Romance, Satire, Comedy or Tragedy.

To return to Jinnah, notice how similarly writers of different ideological hues construct their narratives of his political career. Almost all political biographies of the Qaid-i Azam characterize his career as a sort of ideological journey.[6] They might disagree about why he moved; but all agree that he ended in a very different political milieu to that in which he began. Moreover, virtually all hinge upon the same two or three turning points, namely 1920, when Jinnah became estranged from the Congress as a result of the Non-Cooperation movement, 1929, when, dismayed by the cavalier rejection of his 'Fourteen Points' by the Calcutta All-Parties Convention, he went into retirement and exile in Britain, and 1937,

[4] Hayden White, *Tropics of Discourse: Essays in Cultural Criticism* (Baltimore, 1978), p. 85.

[5] Hayden White, *Metahistory: The Historical Imagination in Nineteenth Century Europe* (Baltimore, 1973), pp. x-xi.

[6] For instance Saad R. Khairi, *Jinnah Reinterpreted: the Journey from Indian Nationalism to Muslim Statehood* (Karachi, 1995).

when at the Lucknow session of the Muslim League he launched that hitherto moribund organization on a collision-course with the Congress.[7] I suggest that the tripartite narrative structure is so common-place because it lends a dramatic symmetry to the Jinnah/Muslim League/Pakistan story, a symmetry Wolpert makes explicit when he writes:

[The speech of 28 December 1928 to the All-Parties Convention] . . . marked a point of departure in Jinnah's life, an even sharper veering off from the road of Congress and all it represented than [the] Nagpur [session] had been eight years earlier. He had delivered his swan-song to Indian national-ism. . . . Born thespian that he was, Jinnah spoke his lines to a packed, if not always friendly, house before each curtain fell on a major act of his political life. Nagpur had ended Act one, Calcutta finished Act two. This time there would be a longer intermission.[8]

Jinnah, one presumes, did not construct his life around significant turning points. How could he, when in many cases (for example, the 1937 Lucknow speech) their significance only became apparent in retrospect? Wolpert is here doing what all writers of stories do: ordering life to make art.

Many may still feel that these literary aspects constitute only the icing on the cake; that they are mere packaging devices. Rather than argue the point with respect to Jinnah—which would involve going over a lot of well-trodden ground—I want to throw some new light on a much less well-known Muslim life, that of Nawab Hamidullah Khan, ruler of Bhopal State and twice Chancellor of the Chamber of Princes. As it happens, Jinnah and Bhopal were quite closely connected; and later in the paper I shall say something about the influence each had on the other. But in the first instance I want to focus more specifically on Hamidullah's own political evolution. As we shall see later, it appears to closely mirror Jinnah's. Does this show that history is replete with coincidences? Or that our narratives of the past are as much literary artifacts as records of what actually happened?

II

As far as I know Nawab Hamidullah Khan of Bhopal never turned to one of his aides and said, 'this is the parting of the ways'; yet he too started out as a Congress nationalist and ended his days as a

---

[7] This reading is suggested by, amongst others, Wolpert, op. cit.
[8] Wolpert, op. cit., pp. 101-2.

disillusioned Leaguer. Born in September 1894, Hamidullah Khan's outlook on the world was shaped by four intersecting influences. The first was his mother, the then ruler of Bhopal Sultana Jahan Begum. Hamidullah's daughter, Princess Abida, remembers that her grandmother 'had a horror of soft living and didn't want us to turn out like the spoilt darlings of other Princely families'.[9] Hamidullah, too, was brought up according to this philosophy and from an early age was made to 'learn the ropes'.[10] Hence, by the time he succeeded to the *musnad* in 1926, he was already an experienced administrator—one, moreover, with a zest for getting things done.[11]

The second, which overlapped with the first, was the Bhopali tradition of pan-Islam. Bhopal rulers had always been staunch defenders of their faith; and in the nineteenth century Bhopal became known as a sanctuary and centre of patronage for Muslim scholars and activists. Jamaluddin Afghani, for example, spent some time there.[12] During Jahan Begum's reign, however, these Islamic connections became more overtly political as a result of Turkey's entry into the War on the side of the Central Powers and Muslim concerns about the impact on the Khilafat, and on the Islamic holy places, of Allied peace-plans. The strongest links were with Aligarh. As the Political Agent noted acidly: 'the control [of affairs in Bhopal] lies wholly in the hands of one party, the young Muhammadan party, which hail mainly from Aligarh'.[13] But the steady stream of Muslim 'mischief-makers' also included some notables from Delhi, including M.A. Ansari, co-founder with Hakim Ajmal Khan of the Khilafat movement, who doubled as the family doctor, and Maulana Mohamed Ali, who served for a time as Hamidullah's private tutor.[14] As early as 1916, Jahan Begum revealed incipient nationalist leanings

[9] Mani Mohsin, 'A Princess Remembers', in *The Friday Times* (Karachi), 13 May 1993, p. 24.

[10] *The Evening News*, 21 March 1931, Bhopal Record Office, Bhopal, Chamber Section, File No. 22, C-4/9.

[11] Hamidullah served successively as President of the Bhopal City Municipal Board (1915-16), Chief Secretary (1916-22) and Law and Finance Member (1922-6).

[12] An asociation which cost the ruler of the time, Nawab Siddiq Hasan Khan, dearly: he was deposed by the British for fostering sedition. Francis Robinson, *Separatism among Indian Muslims: the Politics of the United Provinces' Muslims, 1860-1923* (Cambridge, 1974), p. 126n.

[13] Note by Political Agent Bhopal, dated 11 June 1922, India Office Records (IOR), British Library, R/2/418/2.

[14] P.A. Bhopal to A.G.G. Central India, 20 Dec. 1916, IOR R/2/418/2.

when she declined to endorse Allied War aims.[15] By 1919 she had become openly critical of British repression, particularly as practised by the Punjab martial law regime of General Reginald Dyer and Michael O'Dwyer, telling the Political Agent that she thought Dyer and O'Dwyer should both be stripped of their pensions.[16] By 1922 she was actively lobbying for a general amnesty and for a round table conference of Indian leaders, suggestions which the Political Agent equated with 'a general surrender to the terms of the non-cooperation party as a whole'.[17]

The third influence on Hamidullah was Aligarh itself, or rather the Muslim University there. After taking a B.A. at Allahabad, he went on to study law at Aligarh for two years. He did not complete the degree, but five years of university education made him easily the best-educated prince of his day. More importantly, his contacts with classmates at Aligarh gave him a direct entrée into the 'Young Party' These links were further cemented when Hamidullah, on his return, persuaded his mother to give several of them jobs in the Bhopal public service.[18]

The fourth and final factor that shaped Hamidullah's outlook was his relationship with the British. Partly on legalistic grounds, partly because they had him tabbed as an extremist, the imperial government in Delhi put every obstacle that it could in the way of Hamidullah succeeding, even though it was his mother's wish that he should do so. At length, and at great personal cost to herself, Jahan Begum managed to persuade the secretary of state to reverse Delhi's ruling;[19] nevertheless Hamidullah ascended the throne under

---

[15] P.A. Bhopal to A.G.G. Central India, 1 July, 12 July and 16 July 1916, IOR R/2/418/2.

[16] A.G.G. Central India, 1 July, 12 July and 16 July 1916, IOR R/2/418/2.

[17] Officer on Special Duty to G.O.I., 8 Feb. 1922, IOR R/2/418/2.

[18] Salamuddin of Meerut was appointed State Advocate in 1917 and was later elevated to the bench. In 1921 his brother-in-law, Khwaja Mohammad Akram was appointed Inspector-General of Police, and another relative, Fazl Azeem, to a tehsildarship. Hakim Syed Rafiq Hasan, 'The Cry of the Oppressed', A[ll] I[ndia] S[tates'] C[onference] P[eoples'] File Nos. I, 18, pt. II.

[19] The Political Department based its objection on the fact that succession in Bhopal had always followed the principle of primogeniture, this assumption turned out, after lengthy enquiries, to be false. But it took a special trip to England by the elderly begum, and a discreet word from the king, to get the matter resolved. Even then, Political Secretary Sir John Thompson remained unhappy, describing the decision as a 'triumph of evil'. Lord Stamfordham to the Marquess of Reading, 8 Oct. 1925, Reading Coll., British Library, 1; Reading to Birkenhead, 30 March 1926, Reading (Private) Coll.,

a cloud, and matters were not improved when his request, in the interests of comfort and informality, to be allowed to remain seated while the *kharita* of recognition was read out, was pre-emptorily refused.[20] Then, a couple of years into his reign he tried to get the Government of India to modify its practice of selling liquor on mainline railway stations (which ran counter to Bhopal's policy of prohibition). This appeal too was denied. Last but not least, in 1930, shortly before he was scheduled to leave for London to attend the first Round Table Conference, Hamidullah was accused by the Agent-to-the-Governor-General in Central India, Colonel Heale, of a breach of protocol in assuming to 'receive' a representative of the King-Emperor in shirt sleeves on a tennis court. Heale's successor K.S. Fitze noted, of these contretemps, 'the Nawab is a difficult character'.[21] But Linlithgow was later to wish that Hamidullah had 'been more suitably handled in the past'.[22]

Radicalized by these influences, Hamidullah gravitated naturally into the Muslim wing of the broad nationalist camp—the so-called 'Young Party'. In 1918 he lent his name to the appeal of Ansari and Ajmal Khan for funds for a new theological college in Delhi.[23] In 1923 he became a partner with Ansari and Ajmal in a trading company. Elected, shortly after his accession, to the Standing Committee of the Chamber of Princes, he encouraged the Chamber to enter into constructive dialogue with British Indian politicians and openly supported the nationalists' demand for dominion status. In the late-1920s, he took on as his private secretary Mohamed Ali's son-in-law Shuaib Qureshi, a former Editor of *New Era* and *Young India*, Khilafatist emissary to Gandhi, and member of the All-Parties Convention of 1928 who had twice gone to jail for his nationalist beliefs. When in 1930 Gandhi inaugurated civil disobedience, he urged the imperial authorities to show restraint and is alleged to have reprimanded Lady Willingdon to her face at a viceregal luncheon for making disparaging remarks about the Mahatma.[24]

British Library, 100; Thompson diary [coded] entry, dated 12 Jan. 1926, Thompson Coll., British Library, 20.

[20] A.G.G. Central India to G.O.I, 30 June 1926, IOR R/1/1/1503 (2)

[21] Ibid.

[22] Linlithgow to Zetland, 24 July 1936, Zetland Coll., British Library, 13.

[23] Gail Minault, *The Khilafat Movement: Religious Symbolism and Political Mobilization in India* (Delhi, 1982), p. 30.

[24] Sharif al-Mujahid, *Quaid-i-Azam Jinnah: Studies in Interpretation* (Karachi,

What is more, Hamidullah echoed the Congress stance on communalism. Like Jinnah, he strove to be an ambassador of unity. Speaking at a public function in Bhopal in September 1930, he declared:

We cannot aspire to achieve anything great until we learn to rise above petty jealousies and blind fanaticism which, under the cloak of religion, have become a curse to our motherland. . . . Mussalmans, who have lost touch with our traditions, may . . . find it difficult fully to imbibe the spirit which has all along kept the two communities together in Bhopal. . . . [But] it is their duty, as it should be of every Mussalman, to be extra-magnanimous, large-hearted, tolerant, and sympathetic towards . . . the other communities. . . . I need hardly reiterate that it shall be my duty and the duty of my Government to do our utmost to cherish and maintain that goodwill between the Hindus and Mussalmans which have been the proudest heritage of the people of Bhopal.[25]

This rhetoric was backed up, domestically, with a repeal of the law which had made apostasy from Islam in Bhopal a criminal offence, and, in the wider political arena, with a 1931 initiative aimed at resolving the separate electorates/joint electorates impasse. Unlike Jinnah's initiative of 1916, this attempt to reconcile the two sides failed; but that did not stop Muslim hard-liners from excoriating Hamidullah 'for endangering the future of the community'.[26]

It is true, as his critics never tired of pointing out, that Hamidullah's political liberalism did not extend to giving his own people a significant say in the way the State was run. Similarly, while Bhopal may have been largely free from communal violence, and while all communities seem to have enjoyed relative freedom of worship, the numerically dominant Bhopali Hindus did suffer considerable discrimination as regards education and job opportunities. For example, as late as 1931 they comprised just 3 per cent of the public service and were virtually underrepresented in the army.[27] However

1981), 713; and memo by Kanji Dwarkadas, dated 28 Jan. 1945, encl. in U.S. Consul-Gen., Bombay to Secy. State, Washington, 10 April 1947, U.S. State Dept. decimal File No. 845.00/4-1047.

[25] *The Times* (London), 18 Sept. 1930; and the *Indian Annual Register*, 1930, II, p. 472.

[26] *The Times*, 18 May 1931.

[27] Memo by All India Hindu Hitaishi Mandal to Viceroy, April 1932, IOR R/1/1/2234. Presidential address by Thakur Rai Singh to second session Bhopal Hindu Conf., 27 May 1938, AISPC, I, 18, pt. II, *The Tribune* (Lahore), 11 Dec. 1931.

these domestic contradictions—if such they were—do not seem to have had any significant impact upon Bhopal's attitude to the larger issue of Indian self-rule. All the evidence suggests that, until the early 1930s at least, he remained a sincere patriot[28]—one, moreover, whose political loyalties lay with the Congress rather than the Muslim League.

III

To repeat, there does not seem to have been, in Hamidullah's case, any defining moment that we could call a 'parting of the ways'. Nevertheless, like Jinnah, Bhopal underwent a political transformation. By slow degrees the liberal Congressite of the 1920s became conservative and communal. What caused this about-face?

As regards Hamidullah's estrangement from the Congress, one factor was the changing character of that organization. Several of the established Congress leaders with whom Hamidullah had built up a rapport died during the early 1930s: Motilal Nehru in 1931, Mohamed Ali in 1931, Syed Ali Imam in 1932, Ansari in 1936. What is more the men who replaced them—Jawaharlal Nehru, Subhas Bose, Rajendra Prasad, Vallabhbhai Patel—though roughly Bhopal's contemporaries in age—spoke with different voices. Nehru and Bose preached a levelling socialism, Prasad and Patel talked politics in a language steeped in Hindu metaphors. All favoured *purna* Swaraj, which meant severing India's constitutional links with the British Empire. For an aristocratic Muslim ruler whose family owed much to the patronage of the Crown, this was disconcerting. Hamidullah found it hard to move with the times. Until the end of his reign he remained thoroughly sceptical of democracy, equating it with 'chaos, corruption and suffering'. 'I feel that for a period the Ruler should have power to guide, criticize and if necessary to control those who have still far to go', he wrote to B.N. Rau in 1948.[29] While others trimmed their sails to changing circumstances, Hamidullah, like Jinnah, held fast to values and attitudes formed early in life, and in the process, became more and more isolated.

---

[28] The *Riyasat* of Delhi, a constant critic of the *darbar*, maintained that Hamidullah's support for the national cause was solely designed to keep the Congress off his back. It did indeed have that effect, but there is no reason to conclude that it was a masquerade. *Riyasat*, 2 March 1936, quoted in IOR R/1/1/2870.

[29] Bhopal to B.N. Rau, 28 Feb. 1948, IOR R/3/1/143.

Again, Hamidullah found himself increasingly at odds with the Congress over its policy towards the Muslims. Like Jinnah, he was offended by its refusal, at the Calcutta Convention of 1928, to concede the Muslim claim to one-third of the seats in the central legislature, a claim which seemed to him eminently fair and moderate. (Significantly, his stance on this issue began to harden after the arrival in Bhopal of Shuaib Qureshi, who had been the only Muslim on the All-Parties Convention drafting committee and the only member to file a dissenting report.) Later, after 1937, he took issue with some of the policies of the Congress provincial ministries, which struck him as discriminatory and harmful to the welfare of the Muslim masses. 'Many of us feel that it [the Muslim position in India] is steadily deteriorating', he told the viceroy.[30]

Third, Bhopal, like other princes, was badly shaken by Congress decision in 1938 to rescind its long-standing policy of non-intervention in the states and lend moral and material support to local campaigns for responsible government. Although the ensuing Satyagraha in Bhopal was fitful and easily contained, it marked the end of the state's political innocence; moreover, it put Nawab Hamidullah and the Congress High Command, for the first time, on opposite sides of the political fence.

Finally, such ties as still remained were snapped by the outbreak of War in 1939. From the outset Hamidullah supported the Allied cause vigorously and without reserve—not simply because he believed in it, and because his fealty to the Crown left him little discretion in the matter, but because War called to him, awakened primaeval urges, appealed to his self-image as the member of a martial race. If younger (he turned 50 in 1944) he would have sought leave to enlist; as it was, he pledged the support of his state 'in the name of Islam',[31] made several morale-building tours of the Middle-Eastern battlefields, donated his entire holdings of U.S. securities, valued at ten lakhs, to the British government for the purchase of American fighter planes, and spent another two crores of state revenues on war-related projects. Congress, meanwhile, having resigned from office over Linlithgow's declaration of War, steadfastly refused to support the Allied struggle so long as the conduct of War-policy remained in British hands—a course that culminated in the

[30] Bhopal to Linlithgow, 18 June 1941, IOR R/1/1/3751.
[31] Quddus Qureshi, member, WC, Bhopal SPC, n.d., AISPC, I, File No. 18, pt. I of 1938-42.

'Quit India' ultimatum of 1942. Hamidullah not only disapproved of this stance, he openly condemned it as 'tantamount . . . to collaborating with the enemy'.[32] He in turn was pilloried, along with the other princes, as an arch-collaborator and traitor to the national cause—a charge that wounded, but helped convince the nawab that the Congress he had known and admired no longer existed.

Of itself, this divorce from Congress did not turn Hamidullah into a communalist, certainly not into a Leaguer. During the 1930s, he and Jinnah met occasionally in Delhi, but they remained only casual acquaintances, as they had been since the first Round Table Conference. Indeed, Bhopal's closest links on the Muslim side of politics during this period were probably with the Punjab Unionist Party by virtue of his working-association with the Chamber of Princes Secretary Mir Maqbool Mahmud, who was a son-in-law of Sikander Hyat Khan and uncle of Unionist minister Shaukat Hayat.[33] Nevertheless, from the 1930s on, his outlook became more and more that of a committed Muslim.

One reason for this, perhaps, was Bhopal's propaganda-visit to Cairo and Palestine in May 1941 which greatly increased his familiarity with the wider 'Muslim World'.[34] Another was the 'Hyderabad factor'. Around 1930, Hamidullah's search for developmental capital as part of his scheme for 'the inauguration of an industrial era [in Bhopal], through the formal initiation of important schemes of industrial development',[35] drew him into the financial orbit of Nizam Osman Ali at a time when the Hyderabad ruler was flirting with the Muslim League. Although the full parameters of their relationship remain unclear, we know that Osman Ali prevailed on Hamidullah to go in to bat for him with the Government of India;[36] more than likely, the Nizam's hand also lay behind the initial private visit that Jinnah paid to Bhopal in 1938—a visit that laid the foundations of an enduring personal friendship between the two Muslim leaders.

[32] Bhopal to Linlithgow, 18 June 1941, IOR R/1/1/3751.
[33] During 1940-1 Maqbool put Sikander in touch with B. Shiva Rao, Sir Tej Bahadur Sapru and several dissident Congressmen in a bid to solve the wartime political deadlock. He shared Sikander's hope that this informal network might 'widen out into a Centre Party'. Shiva Rao to Sapru, 16 July 1941, B. Shiva Rao Papers, NMML.
[34] Bhopal to Linlithgow, 18 June 1941, IOR R/1/1/3751.
[35] Bhopal Govt. Publicity Office, 'Bhopal in 1936-7', *Asiatic Review*, XXXV, 1930 pp. 787-8.
[36] Bhopal to Lord Willingdon, 14 Aug. 1931, IOR R/1/1/2161.

However, probably the major factor behind Hamidullah's reorientation was the gradual breakdown of the class solidarity of the princely order as the tenure of the British Raj drew towards a close. While the princes had always been a jealous bunch, in the face of challenges from outside they had usually stuck together. In the 1940s this sensible policy was increasingly abandoned as the rulers jockeyed to win the support of the politicians who would inherit British paramountcy. Some tried to build bridges with Congress, but still more, in particular the Rajput and Maratha rulers of Rajputana and central India, worried by their exposure to the rising tide of religious conflict, took out insurance by giving money to the Hindu Mahasabha,[37] which, under V.D. Savarkar's presidency, had emerged as a champion of the Indian (that is to say, Hindu) system of monarchy.[38] As Maqbool observed during the lead up to the 1944 Chamber elections, 'our opponents . . . are moving under the inspiration of the Hindu Sabha'.[39] This defection was doubly anathema to Hamidullah, first, because it weakened the collective bargaining power of the princely body, and second because the Mahasabha had long been a patron of the (overwhelmingly Hindu) anti-*darbari* movement inside Bhopal.[40]

[37] For details of donations by Hindu rulers to the Hindu Mahasabha see, e.g. note by Bikaner, dated 7 Nov. 1931, Rajasthan State Archives, Bikaner, P.Ms. Office, A 984-7 of 1931; and correspondence from Bikaner and others in the B.S. Moonje Papers, NMML. When, during the 1944 chancellorial election campaign, Yadavindra Singh urged Indore not to vote for Bhopal on the grounds that would be a vote for an outside political party—the League—Indore retorted that the precedent had already been established since he, Baroda and Gwalior already supported the Mahasabha! Memo. by Kanji Dwarkadas, 28 Jan. 1945, encl. in Consul-Gen. Bombay to Secy. State Washington, 10 April 1947, U.S. State Dept. decimal File No. 845.00/4-1047.

[38] For Savarkar's pro-monarchical views, see his *Hindu Rashtra Darshan*, quoted in Bipan Chandra, *Communalism in Modern India* (New Delhi, 1984), p. 95; and his letter to the maharaja of Jaipur, 19 July 1944, Akhil Bharat Mahasabha Papers, NMML, C-39.

[39] Maqbool Mahmud to Liaquat Hyat Khan, 26 June 1943, BRO, Pol. Dept., Chamber Section, 94, 10/1.

[40] The Bhopal States Peoples' Conference formed in 1939 had a sprinkling of Muslims in its leadership. But its membership and orientation reflected its origins as an offshoot of the Bhopal Hindu Sabha movement which, in 1931, persuaded the Mahasabha's Bhai Parmanand to conduct a covert inquiry into the grievances of the Hindu majority ('the Bhopal Government', ran the report, 'leaves behind the Aurangzebian Government in tyrannising over the Hindus') and later established a local branch of the Rashtriya Swayam Sevak Sangh. For details see Tehri Singh Vidyarthi to L. Kushal Chand Kursand, Editor of *Milap*, 24 Dec. 1931, IOR R/1/1/2234;

At any rate, by the early-1940s there were unmistakable signs that Hamidullah had crossed over into the hard-line Muslim camp. As we have seen, the nawab had never been shy about stacking his public service with Muslims from north India. During the late 1930s, outside recruitment was stepped up, bringing to over 600 the total number of Punjabis in Bhopal service. Prominent amongst them was Punjab MLC Hisamuddin Khan, who was recruited in 1940 as Mir Bakhshi or Chief of Staff. According to Olaf Caroe, Hisamuddin was under the impression that he had been hired, not so much for his military expertise, but to provide a conduit into 'the inner councils of the Muslim League'.[41] This bold policy of 'Muslimization' or 'Punjab-ization', as it was variously described by Hindu and *mulki* critics, culminated in 1947 when about one lakh Muslim refugees from north and central India were railed into Bhopal and given liberal resettlement allowances, apparently with the object of increasing the Muslim share of the population and entrenching Muslim domination 'of Bhopal's economic, agricultural, industrial, commercial and political life'.[42] Meanwhile, the *darbar* cracked down heavily against dissent under the plea of war security. The houses of members of the Bhopal State Peoples' Conference were searched, public gatherings curtailed, and the use of posters and loudspeakers banned. When, eventually, municipal elections were held they were fixed. In April 1946 'hooligans', thought to be Khaksars affiliated to the Muslim National Guard, attacked Hindu shops while police looked the other way.[43] Benefiting from this repression but also from covert *darbari* patronage, the hitherto miniscule state branch of the Muslim League grew strongly, its ranks further swelled after 1946 by the influx of refugees.

However the most dramatic manifestation of Nawab Hamidullah's new communal consciousness was his decision in 1944 to contest the chancellorship of the Chamber of Princes for a second time. Like

---

Offg. Supt. Police, Delhi to Asst. Director, Intelligence Bureau, GOI, 21/22 March 1932, IOR R/1/1/2234; and Inspector-General of Police, Bhopal, to Private Secy, nawab of Bhopal, 10 Feb. 1948, Bhopal, Pol. Dept. A, 126, 2/21.

[41] Sir Olaf Caroe to Sir Bertrand Glancy, 4 April 1940, IOR R/1/1/3533.

[42] Presdt., Sehore Prajamandal to States Minister [1 Nov. 1947], AISPC, I, 19, pt. I; and Rajendra Verma, *The Freedom Struggle in Bhopal State (A Gambit in the Transfer of Power)* (New Delhi, 1984), p. 99.

[43] Verma, op. cit., pp. 74-5; Report to Gen. Secy., AISPC by Gen. Secy. Bhopal SPC, 15 Dec. 1947, AISPC, I, 19, pt. I.

Jinnah's in 1929, Bhopal's parting of the ways was accompanied by a withdrawal from political life. His term as chancellor in the early 1930s had been a distressful experience, marred by a deep and savage rift within the princely order over the pros and cons of all-India federation. Frustrated and disgusted by the growing factionalism of the princely body, in 1933 he walked out of the Chamber altogether, not to return until 1940. Indeed, by 1942 he was privately questioning whether the organization had a future at all.[44]

On further reflection, however, Hamidullah came around to the view that the Chamber was too firmly entrenched, too much part of princely tradition, to be casually swept aside. Besides, he was sick of semi-retirement. He itched to again exercise his considerable talents on the all-India stage, to realize the great destiny which he believed had been carved out for him. And the passage of time had eliminated almost all of his potential rivals. The two princely giants of the inter-War years, Bhupinder Singh of Patiala and Ganga Singh of Bikaner, were both dead, which left only one prince of real stature in the field, the incumbent Chancellor, Digvijaysinhji of Nawanagar. The latter, however, was no certainty to run (he later withdrew his nomination). This left only the likeable but lightweight Udaibhan Singh of Dholpur. As Hamidullah's campaign manager, Maqbool Mahmud, pointed out, this was a contest he could hardly fail to win.

However Hamidullah's decision to run was not simply rooted in ambition; there was also a sectarian agenda. During 1943, Chamber Secretary Maqbool spent many hours in close conclave with his father-in-law, Sikander Hyat Khan, and Sikander's brother, the Patiala Foreign Minister Liaquat Hyat Khan. In the course of these discussions the three men came to the conclusion that Bhopal's leadership of the princely order was 'vital to the [Muslim] cause' in the current climate of 'crisis' precipitated by the imminent end of the War and the prospect of far-reaching post-War reforms. When this proposition was put to him, Hamidullah responded, as they knew he would, enthusiastically: 'he would be prepared to take over the Chancellorship if it helped the Moslem cause'.[45] The very next day

---

[44] Draft memo. by Sir Joseph Bhore, Constitutional Adviser, Bhopal, dated [?] Jan. 1942, as amended by Hamidullah in his own hand, BRO, Bhopal, Pol. Dept., Chamber Section, 55, 4/44 of 1941.

[45] Maqbool to Liaquat, 26 June 1943, BRO, Bhopal, Pol. Dept., Chamber Section, 94, 10/1. The fact that Maqbool and Liaquat had in the past both worked for non-Muslim rulers (Jhalawar and Patiala respectively) suggests that something quite fundamental was happening to the once proudly ecclectic *darbari* polity.

he formally announced his candidacy. Prudently (for he needed the votes of some of the Hindu princes to get elected) Hamidullah played down the communal angle during the campaign but could not fool his opponents. Gwalior's Kailash Haksar circulated a memorandum 'in which he endeavoured to convey the impression that His Highness was [an] out and out . . . Pakistani, and that if he were elected . . . the Chamber would be turned into a Pakistan stronghold',[46] while Yadavindra Singh of Patiala urged the maharaja of Indore not to vote for Bhopal for that would be tantamount to a vote for the League.[47] Nor, once the election was concluded, did Hamidullah take long to make good his pledge to Maqbool. As part of a general overhaul of the Chamber (of which more later), Bhopal jockeyed the nawab of Chattari into the chairmanship of the strategic Committee of Ministers, and selected Sultan Ahmad (over excellent candidates in V.T. Krishamachari and C.P. Ramaswamy Aiyer) for the new post of constitutional adviser to the secretariat. For three years the Chamber of Princes would operate to all intents and purposes as a sleeping partner of the Muslim League.

However, the alliance with the League was never simply an end in itself. Even as a committed Muslim, Bhopal remained every inch a monarchist, and he saw his primary task as chancellor to prepare the states for the external challenge that was sure to come with the transfer of power. Hitching the states to the rising star of the League (to create a blocking anti-Congress majority in the federal legislature) was one means to this end. Other elements in this 'rearguard' strategy included the further rebuilding of the Chamber; accelerated internal reforms, to cement the bond between ruler and subject; the maintenance of some elements of the imperial connection; and, though this was never high on the agenda, a bilateral settlement with the Congress. Moreover, since the princes regarded their own salvation as of prime importance, they generally supported Bhopal's strategy, despite their misgivings about his orientation towards the League. In 1945 Bhopal obtained the Chamber's permission to upgrade its secretariat. A new post of personal advisor to the

[46] Liaquat to Palanpur, 20 Jan. 1944, BRO, Bhopal, Pol. Dept., Chamber Section, 94, 10/1, 1943. K.M. Panikkar saw him as 'a Muslim partisan and enemy of the Hindus'. *An Autobiography* (Madras, 1977), p. 138. For an insight into why, none the less, Hamidullah prevailed in the polls (by a big majority), see Palanpur to Bhopal, 13 Jan. 1944, BRO, Bhopal, Pol. Dept., Chamber Section, 94, 10/1.

[47] Memo. by Kanji Dwarkadas, dated 28 Jan. 1945, encl. in Consul-Gen., Bombay to Secy. State Washington, 10 April 1947, U.S. State Dept. decimal File No. 845.00/4-1047.

chancellor, carrying a salary of Rs. 4000 a month, was created for Maqbool, five new assistant-secretaryship were added to the senior establishment, a public relations bureau was set up, and the general office staff was expanded. The costs were heavy, about six-and-a-half lakhs, which translated into an additional contribution from member-states of between Rs. 5000 and Rs. 25,000 a year. However, despite some initial grumbling, most rulers paid up. Even more remarkably, Hamidullah in May 1945 managed to persuade a general meeting of rulers at Bombay's Taj Mahal Hotel to agree to recast their administrations 'along democratic lines in preparation for the part which the Indian States expect to play in the event of a national government in India'.[48] The following June, the Standing Committee of the Chamber, at Bhopal's request, fixed a twelve month time-limit for the commencement of this process.[49] At the same the chancellor achieved considerable success in repairing relations with the Political Department, now under the control of the monarchophile Conrad Corfield. Impressed by Hamidullah's arguments about the residual treaty rights of the states, Corfield used his position to wind down paramountcy ahead of the British departure to improve their chances of staying out of the clutches of the Congress-led Interim Government which took office in 1946, and his influence with Viceroy Wavell to push the princes' case for independence in London. Thanks in part to these representations, the Cabinet Mission which reported in the spring of 1946 opted for a position on paramountcy which, if ambiguous, indicated that all the rights ceded by the princes to the Crown would return to them upon the British departure. This left the door open for the states to go it alone, outside the Indian dominion. By any reasonable measure this was a pretty remarkable—one might almost say triumphal—record.

Again, comparison with the career of Jinnah are suggestive. Jinnah emerged from a period of political seclusion to take supreme charge of the Muslim League. As president, he forced through badly needed structural reforms which made the organization more flexible and

[48] Panikkar, *Autobiography*, pp. 142-6; Consul-Gen. Bombay to Secy. State Washington 12 May 1945, U.S. State Dept. decimal File 845.00/5-1245; and circular from Chancellor dated 18 July 1945, BRO, Bhopal, Pol. Dept., Chamber Section, 54, 4/24.

[49] Press-statement by Standing Committee, 11 June 1946, encl. in Bhopal to Wavell, 19 June 1946, quoted in Nicholas Mansergh *et al.* (eds.), *Constitutional Relations between Britain and India: the Transfer Of Power, 1942-7 (TOP)*, (London, 1970-83), VII, pp. 980-1. *Bombay Chronicle*, 11 June 1946, headed its coverage of the Standing Committee meeting: 'INDIAN PRINCES PLUMP FOR DEMOCRACY'.

responsive. He built bridges with the government, winning strategically important promises from Linlithgow and Stafford Cripps. He developed a plan for Muslim salvation in the post-colonial era. However, there are differences. Jinnah's triumphs occupied an extended period, from the mid-1930s until his death in 1948. Hamidullah's period of glory lasted just three years, from 1944 until 1946. The Qaid-i Azam's career had its apotheosis in the creation of Pakistan; the Nawab-Chancellor's dream of a princely Pakistan remained unfulfilled.

IV

Bhopal's strategy for preserving the integrity of the princely states after the transfer of power hinged, in the last resort, on two things: persuading the League to abandon its scheme of Pakistan in favour of the federal constitutional scheme mapped out by the Cabinet Mission; and persuading the princely order to present a united front in negotiations with the successor government in New Delhi. He failed miserably on both counts.

Turning the League away from Partition was always going to be a difficult task; and it was made considerably harder by Prime Minister-elect Jawaharlal Nehru's off-handed rejection of a key aspect of the Cabinet Mission Plan—the compulsory grouping of the provinces into 'sections', which caused the League, on 29 July 1946, to withdraw its initial acceptance of the Plan. But Hamidullah did not give up. He pestered Jinnah to reverse his decision, and in the autumn hosted talks at Bhopal and at his residence in Delhi in an effort to bring the parties together. What is more, this quixotic venture almost succeeded. Early in October, after many hours of face-to-face discussion, Hamidullah and Gandhi reached agreement on a formula for the selection of Muslim members of the Interim Government. Overnight Bhopal had this typed up. And the following morning, against the objections of his secretary Pyarelal, Gandhi signed it, saying that 'he was sure he could safely place himself in the Nawab's hands'. However when, later that day, the Bhopal draft was published, Gandhi claimed that it did not 'explicitly' match his recollections—and repudiated it.[50] Whether Hamidullah tried to 'pull

---

[50] D.G. Tendulkar, *Mahatma: Life of Mohandas Karamchand Gandhi* (rev. edn., Delhi, 1961-3), pp. 230-1.

a fast one' or the Mahatma simply changed his mind, we will never know. What we do know is that the incident killed the talks. On 31 January 1947 the Muslim League reaffirmed, this time in words of absolute finality, its decision to boycott the Indian Constituent Assembly.[51]

By 1947, then, it was clear that the states could not expect much from the Muslim League beyond moral support.[52] However Hamidullah still had the British card to play. The prospects were still good, he believed, if the princes could but 'hold together'.[53] In a bid to rally the troops, Bhopal summoned a general meeting of princes and ministers at Delhi and put to them a bold, if utopian, scheme for a confederation of states to be called 'Rajasthan'. But the idea did not find favour. On the opening day of the conference (28 January), Bikaner's K.M. Panikkar accused Hamidullah of proposing a 'vivisection of Hindu power', and on the second day Ramaswamy Aiyer effectively torpedoed further discussion by announcing that even if such a grouping were to be formed, Travancore would not agree to be part of it.[54] Angry and disillusioned, Hamidullah began to talk openly of abdicating and devoting the rest of his life to helping his co-religionists. 'I am unhappy', he confided to Corfield,

about everything in this country. The British seem to have abdicated power and what is worse they have handed it over . . . to the enemies of all their friends. . . . I look upon it as one of the greatest, if not the greatest, tragedies that has ever befallen mankind, and I find it difficult to overcome the shock.

[51] On Bhopal as 'honest broker', see Sir Sultan Ahmad's interview with the *Daily Telegraph*, 21 Sept. 1946; and Sir J. Colville (acting Viceroy) to Lord Pethick-Lawrence, 18 Dec. 1946, *TOP*, IX, pp. 380-1.

[52] Jinnah and Liaquat Ali Khan did stand by the states during this period, affirming, inside and out of the Interim Government, that the states had an absolute right to determine their own constitutional futures. How much this was due, however, to a sense of loyalty to Bhopal and Hyderabad and how much to a desire to spite the Congress, it is hard to say. For the League's policy on paramountcy and the states in the post-War period see Ian Copland, 'The Princely States, the Muslim League and the Partition of India In 1947', in *The International History Review*, XIII, i, Feb. 1991, pp. 38-69.

[53] Circular from Chancellor, 31 Dec. 1946, BRO, Bhopal, Pol. Dept., Special Branch, 78, 30/SB/46.

[54] Panikkar, *Autobiography*, pp. 149-50. Afterwards, Panikkar opined to Mountbatten's aide Alan Campbell-Johnson that the chancellor seemed to be 'trying to enunciate a new doctrine of paramountcy—namely that no action should be taken by States individually, but only in concert, with approval of the Chamber of Princes'. Campbell-Johnson, *Mission with Mountbatten* (London, 1951), p. 38.

The States, the Moslems, and the entire mass of people who relied on British justice, and their sense of fairplay, suddenly find themselves totally helpless, unorganized and unsupported. . . . What should a Prince, who has some life, honour and ambition left in him, do in such circumstances? . . . I am tired of leading a team who have neither the will nor the desire to survive. I am tired of intrigue, calumny and communal feelings of the worst type. I want to resign the Chancellorship . . . I want to die in the cause of the Moslems of the world. . . . The Princes betrayed by the British are already a lost cause and I feel I am wasting my energies . . . in trying to protect their case. I am a Moslem in a crowd of Hindu Princes, who suspect me all round, who are blind to their own interests and who are at the moment only guided by one desire, namely . . . to kill, destroy . . . and wipe off the Moslems from the face of the earth. I am a complete misfit in this crowd and I am sure my place lies somewhere else.[55]

Somewhat against his better judgement, Hamidullah was persuaded by Corfield to stay on; but relations between the chancellor and his Standing Committee continued to cool to the point where the Committee felt obliged to complain about his behaviour. This, in turn, prompted Bhopal to raise—unsuccessfully—with Corfield the question of keeping official correspondence between himself and the viceroy 'secret' from his colleagues on the plea that most of them had 'now definitely . . . gone over to the Congress side'.[56]

Nevertheless, for a time the Chamber of Princes managed to maintain a facade of public unity, while their crumbling solidarity was bolstered temporarily by Prime Minister Clement Attlee's announcement of 20 February, which reaffirmed London's commitment to the Cabinet Mission line on paramountcy, and Nehru's speech in April to the Gwalior session of the All-India States Peoples' Conference, which threatened the princes with extinction if they did not join the Indian union.[57] Sensing an opportunity to make up lost ground, Hamidullah called the Chamber's Constitutional Advisory Committee together and in the face of vehement objections from Maharaja Sadul Singh of Bikaner got its permission to draft a motion,

[55] Bhopal to Corfield, 23 Nov. 1946, TOP, IX, pp. 156-7.

[56] Corfield to Abell, 10 Feb. 1947, IOR R/3/1/112; and note by Wavell on interview with Bhopal, dated 3 March 1947, TOP, IX, p. 834.

[57] For the text of the Nehru speech see IAR, 1947, I, pp. 214-16. For reaction see Ambassador New Delhi to Secy. State Washington, 24 April 1947, U.S. State Dept. decimal File No. 845.00/4-2447; Note of interview between Nehru and Mountbatten, 22 April 1947, TOP, X, p. 361; and minutes of Viceroy's 19th Staff Meeting, 21 April 1947, TOP, X, p. 352.

to be put to a general conference of princes at Bombay, authorizing him as chairman of the States Negotiating Committee to suspend discussion with the Constituent Assembly until such time as the latter agreed to the Chamber's long list of conditions for participation.

More than ever convinced of the justice of his cause, and as always supremely confident of his power to sway a crowd, it never for a moment occurred to Bhopal that this motion might not get up. Yet, no sooner had the Bombay meeting opened than the first signs of rebellion appeared. At a preliminary Standing Committee meeting on 1 April, Bikaner sat patiently but silently as a string of rulers—Dungapur, Dholpur, Alwar and Nawanagar—indicated their support for the chancellor's motion; then, after about fifteen minutes, he rose and 'went quietly out of the room' and back to his suite where he penned two notes: one, very short, to Bhopal asking to be excused from further meetings of the Standing Committee; the other, much longer, to the assembled delegates imploring them to 'act in the larger interests of India' and warning them of the dire consequences that could follow from an impetuous decision to hold aloof from the Assembly.[58] Many were impressed by its arguments. Thus, by the time the conference proper commenced next morning, Sadul Singh's group had already gained a number of new adherents. Yet even then Bhopal might have prevailed had he restricted himself to moving the Standing Committee's motion about *sine qua non*. He did not. Determined to make Bikaner pay for his trouble-making, he proposed a second, linked resolution to the effect that no state should enter the Assembly until it had finished its initial work of drafting constitutions for the sections and the provinces—work which was expected to consume at least a further six months. As soon as this clearly mischievous motion was read out there was an uproar: and when it had subsided Bikaner announced, to a chorus of resounding cheers, that if the resolution was passed his state would ignore it and enter anyway. This gave the maharaja of Gwalior, a Bikaner symphathizer but also a firm believer in the virtue of princely unity, an opportunity to move an amendment to the motion, which was carried, that the question of entry to the Constituent

---

[58] Consul-Gen. Bombay to Secy. State Washington, 7 April 1947, U.S. State Dept. decimal File No. 845.00/4-747; Bikaner to Mountbatten, 3 April 1947, *TOP*, X, p. 107; and minutes of Standing Committee meeting, 1 April 1947, BRO, Bhopal, Pol. Dept., Special Branch, 106, 61/SB/47. For the full text of Bikaner's note see the *Free Press Journal*, 3 April 1947.

Assembly should be a matter for the discretion of individual states.

Afterwards Bhopal assured the press that the conference had 'ended happily' and that there was 'no rift',[59] but the truth of the situation became plain a few weeks later when, on 28 April, delegates from Cochin, Patiala, Baroda, Jaipur, Rewa, Jodhpur and Bikaner took their seats in the Assembly. There may not have been a formal 'split', but with the public defection of these seven important states the princely order ceased to be, in any meaningful sense, united. As that veteran of so many princely quarrels, Udaibhan Singh of Dholpur sadly remarked to the viceroy, no 'two different views conspicuously mark the division of thought and action of the Order'.[60] What is more, its leadership had been fatally compromised. While the Congress' K.M. Munshi might have had an axe to grind, his observation that the conference 'marked an end to the domination of the Nawab of Bhopal'[61] was a shrewd and, with hindsight, accurate one. Although Hamidullah tried valiantly to pretend that he was still in charge, his policy statements now rang hollow. At length, persuaded by Corfield that his duty henceforward lay in looking after the vital interests of his own state,[62] he resigned the chancellorship on 3 June.

The rest of the Bhopal story can be quickly told. On 5 June Hamidullah informed the viceroy that, in the light of the 3 June Plan for devolution, Bhopal intended to boycott the Constituent Assembly and to work towards the establishment of diplomatic relations jointly with India and Pakistan. But the independence option, while it seems to have enjoyed considerable popular support within Bhopal,[63] was

[59] Consul-Gen. Bombay to Secy. State Washington, 7 April 1947, U.S. State Dept. decimal File No. 845.00/4-747.

[60] Dholpur to Mountbatten, 20 July 1947, IOR R/3/1/138.

[61] Consul-Gen. Bombay to Secy. State Washington, 14 April 1947, reporting conversation with Munshi on 12 April, U.S. State Dept. decimal File No. 845.00/4-1447. On 9 June the Deccan states announced that they had chosen former M.L.A. M.S. Aney to represent them in the Assembly; on 24 June Mysore sent delegates. By the end of July all but a handful of states, of which Bhopal and Hyderabad were the most notable, had joined.

[62] Note by Corfield, dated [?] March 1968, Corfield Coll., BL, 4.

[63] About this time a rumour got about in Bhopal, probably started by the *darbar*, that the Nawab intended to abdicate. When he returned in July 1947 from Delhi, fifty thousand people met his plane at the airport, and refused to let him leave until he had made a speech, pledging to stay on. The three 'popular' ministers in the Bhopal government all backed the independence bid, as did the Muslim League and—paradoxically—the Hindu Sabha.

never a realistic one. Surrounded by hostile territory, the state was too weak to survive unaided, and the promised assistance from Pakistan, not surprisingly, failed to materialize.[64] Hamidullah pleaded and procrastinated, but on 14 August bowed to the inevitable and acceded to the Union for foreign affairs, defence and communications. Two years later the Bhopal state was merged with Madhya Pradesh.

Now out of a job (for the merger effectively extinguished what was left of the monarchy's power) Hamidullah looked to restart his political career in Pakistan; his friendship with Jinnah, he thought, ought to be worth at least a provincial governorship. (Indeed, his long-term ambition was to succeed to the governor-generalship of Pakistan after Jinnah's death.) However these plans foundered on the rock-like opposition of Liaquat Ali Khan (which Hamidullah attributed to the prime minister's fear that he might 'outdo him in popularity'), and he eventually had to settle for a modest and secluded retirement in the Middle East, where he died in 1960.[65] Thirty years later his grandson, Shaharyar Khan, became Pakistan's Foreign Secretary, a role that in other circumstances Hamidullah himself might have filled with distinction.

V

Two lives. One well-known, the other relatively obscure. Yet seemingly much alike. Both Jinnah and Hamidullah were (in their separate spheres) important Muslim leaders; both were trained in the law; both started out as Congress liberals and ended up as Muslim chauvinists; both suffered mid-career setbacks, only to make spectacular comebacks; both believed in evolution rather than revolution.

But were Jinnah and Hamidullah aware of these parallels? Did each have a sense of the other as a sort of *alter ego*? Would Bhopal have relished the suggestion that he was basically just a pale

---

[64] The only real help—some 50 lakhs worth—came from another would-be rebel state, Travancore. See *Malayala Manorama*, 10 March, 23 Nov. and 28 Dec. 1949. I am indebted to Professor Robin Jeffrey for this reference.

[65] For a while the Government of India refused to let Hamidullah go abroad. In the end they agreed on condition that he used his good offices to help bring about a settlement with the Nizam. Before leaving Bhopal Hamidullah abdicated in favour of his eldest daughter, princess Abida. Abida herself later moved to Pakistan.

reflection of another man? I think not. The two men were in fact not particularly close. True, they met frequently, interacted politically, and for a while shared a joint anti-Congress platform, but the acquaintance did not extend to important rites of passage. Although he sent his condolences, Hamidullah could not find time in September 1948 to attend Jinnah's funeral in Karachi. And there is nothing in the Jinnah papers or in the Bhopal archives to indicate that the two were regular correspondents, as one would expect friends to be. Thus, while the juxtaposition of the careers of Jinnah and Hamidullah Khan makes logical sense, has a pleasing *dramatic symmetry*, it does not reflect, necessarily, how the two men envisaged the world they inhabited. My guess is that the notion of a pairing would have struck both of them as somewhat bizarre.

The point can be strengthened by noting some significant contrasts. Hamidullah was born to power; Jinnah had to make his own way in the world. Hamidullah's personal life was benign and fruitful; Jinnah's steeped in disappointment. Jinnah was a consistent opponent of British imperialism in India; whereas Hamidullah, whilst often critical of British intolerance of dissent and impatient with their fussy overlordship, never wavered in his loyalty to the Crown or in his attachment to the imperial connection. (Which is why, like many other princes, he felt betrayed and humiliated by Britain's decision, in 1946, to sever its treaties with the states.) Jinnah's public career was capped by a lasting achievement, namely the creation of Pakistan; Hamidullah's ended in failure. The Qaid-i Azam died famous, revered by millions; the Nawab-Chancellor died in forlorn obscurity. Applying Hayden White's taxonomy, one might say that Jinnah's life invites a romantic treatment, Hamidullah's a prefiguring in the mode of tragedy.[66]

Laying stress on the commonalties between Jinnah and Bhopal may be a literary device; yet the approach is not without intellectual benefit, for it puts the political careers of the two men in a different light, and raises interesting questions about the interaction between

---

[66] Hayden White: 'The Romance is fundamentally a drama of self-identification symbolized by the hero's transcendence of the world of experience, his victory over it. . . . It is a drama of the triumph of good over evil, . . . of light over darkness.' Tragedy moves 'inexorably towards a fall'; but the hero acquires nobility in resisting his fate; and at the end there is a certain reconciliation as the characters in the drama become resigned 'to the conditions under which they must labour in the world'. *Metahistory*, pp. 8-9. The points of convergence here are fairly obvious.

princely and provincial politics, an interaction which has so far
eluded the hindsight of most historians. Certainly, what we peddle
in the name of history has far more to do with art than with science.
Certainly it does not constitute a 'truthful' record of the past in a literal
sense. Yet, paradoxically, the history we write is replete with
meaning. Studded with insights, deductions and second-guesses—
'truths' if you like—our historical narratives illuminate a past that lay
hidden from contemporaries. As the Darley character in Lawrence
Durrell's *Alexandria Quartet* laments:

I wonder why only now I have been told all this? My friends must have
known all along. Yet nobody breathed a word. But of course the truth is
that nobody ever does breathe a word, nobody interferes, nobody whispers
while the acrobat is on the tightrope; they just sit and watch the spectacle,
waiting only to be wise after the event.[67]

---

[67] Lawrence Durrell, *The Alexandria Quartet* (London, 1962), p. 297.

Muslim Identity: Self-Image and Political Aspirations

A.G. NOORANI

A minority's sense of identity is shaped by its understanding of its own history. Its self-image is influenced, no less, by the image the majority groups have of the minority—an image shaped, in turn, by their understanding of history. Not infrequently, historical perceptions clash. History does not address itself in the same language to different peoples.

This paper is concerned primarily with the Indian Muslim identity and self-image as shaped by events. It is but a beginning towards a fuller study, and is made in the belief that such an exercise will be of academic interest and practical value. For, a minority's participation in national life and its expectations, and the demands of the state are governed by that one inarticulate major premise which dominates its thinking—its sense of identity. The perceptions of others will be mentioned only in the context of some important events.

A community that considered itself to be a distinct nation by itself, rather than a part of a nation, demanded the Partition of the country for the establishment, ironically, of another majoritarian state. The United Nations secretary-general submitted to the sub-commission on the Prevention of Discrimination and Protection of Minorities a memorandum on 'Definition and Classification of Minorities' on 27 December 1949. It noted that

some minorities feel that they form a real nation, different from the nation of the predominant group and different from that of other minorities which may exist within the state. Other minorities consider themselves to be only regional groups having particular distinguishing characteristics. Some minorities wish to obtain autonomy, while others only wish to keep alive the particular characteristics (language, culture, etc.) which distinguish them from the dominant group. The sense of solidarity of some minorities with their co-nationals is intensified when they are placed under another state's jurisdiction, and they are willing to accept the authority of the new state only on condition that they are permitted to retain their particular distinguishing characteristics and to carry on their own collective life by means of an autonomous regime.

The alternative to Partition for long seemed to be protection, constitutionally and in some cases (as in the case of the 'minority clauses' of the post-World War I Treaties), internationally. As British rule was consolidated all over the country and the first stirrings of political life were felt, Indian Muslims sought precisely that in the decades preceding Partition. They were a part of the nation but needed constitutional protection. Experience has demonstrated that constitutional protection without political participation provides no satisfaction or security to either group.

It is not possible to understand the political mind of Indian Muslims today nor their politics except against the historical background. The same holds good for the approach which political parties have adopted towards them. To anticipate, both have tended to be protectionist; participation has been largely formal; empowerment remains a distant goal. This is the result to no small extent of the course which Muslims and political parties adopted in the early years of Independence and to which most Muslims continue to cling. The roots of such politics lie in a self-image which is unreal and warped.

When the debate began a century ago, two rival viewpoints were put before Muslims. Syed Ahmad Khan said at the Lucknow session of the Muhammadan Educational Conference on 28 December 1887,

they want to copy the British House of Lords and the House of Commons. Now let us imagine the Viceroy's Council made in this manner. And let us suppose that all the Muslim electors vote for a Muslim member and now count how many votes the Muslim members will have and how many the Hindu. It is certain that the Hindu members will have four times as many because their population is four times as numerous.

He denied that India constituted a nation at all.

The president of the Congress was Badruddin Tyabji who wrote to Syed Ahmad and other Muslim leaders on 13 January 1888, in an effort to allay their misgivings,

It does seem to me to be a great pity that on matters affecting all India as a whole, any section of the Mussalman community should keep aloof from the Hindus and thus retard the national progress of India as a whole. I understand your objection to be that the Hindus being more advanced than ourselves would profit more by any concessions made by Government to educated Natives but surely it is our duty, if possible, to raise ourselves in the scale of progress, other than to prevent other people from enjoying the rights for which they are qualified. If any proposal is made which would subject the Mussalmans to the Hindus or would vest the executive power in Hindus to the detriment of the Mussalmans, I should oppose it with all my strength, but the Congress proposes to do no such thing.

Tyabji urged Muslims to participate in national politics on the Congress platform on the understanding that they would have a *decisive* say on matters affecting their rights. He did not ask for any separate representation. That was done nearly two decades later when a deputation of some Muslim leaders led by the Aga Khan called on the viceroy, in 1906.[1]

Two pronouncements, each by a Muslim political figure of the highest eminence (but with wholly different backgrounds), reflect remarkable self-assurance and identification with Indian nationalism. They bear quotation *in extenso*:

It is said that we are going on at a tremendous speed, that we are in a minority and the government of this country might afterwards become a Hindu Government. I want to give an answer to this. I particularly wish to address my Mahomedan friends on this point. Do you think, in the first instance, as to whether it is possible that the government of this country could become a Hindu Government? Do you think that government could be conducted by ballot boxes? Do you think that because the Hindus are in the majority, therefore they could carry on a measure, in the Legislative Assembly, and there is an end of it? If seventy millions of Mussalman do not approve of a measure, which is carried by a ballot box, do you think that it could be enforced and administered in this country? (Cries of "No, No"). Do you think that the Hindu statesmen, with their intellect, with their past history, would ever think of when they get self-government enforcing a measure by ballot box? (cries of "No, No"). Then what is there to fear? (cries of "Nothing"). Therefore, I say to my Moslem friends not to fear. This is a bogey, which is put before you by your enemies (cries of "Hear", "Hear") to frighten you, to scare you away from the cooperation with the Hindus which is essential for the establishment of self-government.[2]

The other read thus:

Politically speaking, the word minority does not mean just a group that i

---

[1] A.G. Noorani, *Badruddin Tyabji* (New Delhi, 1969), pp. 81, 167, 173.
[2] R.K. Prabhu (ed.), *An Anthology of Modern Indian Eloquence* (Prombarj, 196
p. 132.

124   ISLAM, COMMUNITIES AND THE NATION

numerically smaller and therefore entitled to special protection. It means a group that is so small in number and so lacking in other qualities that give strength that it has no confidence in its own capacity to protect itself from the much larger group that surrounds it. It is not enough that the group should be relatively the smaller, but that it should be absolutely so small as to be incapable of protecting its interests. . . . If this is the right test, let us apply it to the position of the Muslims in India. You will see at a glance a vast concourse, spreading out all over the country; they stand erect, and to imagine that they exist helplessly as a "minority" is to delude oneself. The Muslims in India number between eighty and ninety millions. . . . Can such a vast mass of humanity have any legitimate reason for apprehension that in a free and democratic India, it might be unable to protect its rights and interests. These numbers are not confined to any particular area but spread out unevenly over different parts of the country. In four provinces out of eleven in India there is a Muslim majority, the other religious groups being minorities. If British Baluchistan is added, there are five provinces with Muslim majorities. Even if we are compelled at present to consider this question on a basis of the religious groupings, the position of the Muslims is not that of a minority only. If they are in a minority in seven provinces, they are in a majority in five. This being so, there is absolutely no reason why they should be oppressed by the feeling of being a minority.[3]

The first was Jinnah's speech to the Muslim League session at Calcutta in December 1917. The second was Azad's presidential address to the Ramgarh session of the Indian National Congress on 2 March 1940. The logic and language are alike.

In his initial expositions Jinnah's two-nation theory did not imply Partition at all but sharing of power in a united India. His famous article to *Time and Tide* (London) published on 19 January 1940— only two months before the Lahore Resolution of 23 March 1940 demanding a separate state—combined two nations in a united India: 'a Constitution must be evolved that recognizes that there are in India two nations who both must share the governance of their common motherland . . . so that India may take its place amongst the great nations of the world'.[4] Hence his plea against enforcing Western democracy without qualification and his rejection of a Constituent

[3] P.N. Chopra (ed.), *Maulana Azad: Selected Speeches and Statements 1940-1947* (New Delhi, 1990), pp. 16-17; Syeda Saiyidain Hameed (ed.), *India's Maulana* (New Delhi, 1990), vol. II, pp. 158-9.
[4] Jamiluddin Ahmad (ed.), *Speeches and Writings of Mr. Jinnah* (Lahore, 1960), vol. I, p. 124.

Assembly unless it was based on a pact with the Muslims.[5] On 28 September 1939, he said: 'Within the honest meaning of the term, I still remain a nationalist. I have always believed in a Hindu-Muslim pact.'

Jinnah was groping for an arrangement which would avoid 'brute majority rule' in a pluralist society in united India. But instead of evolving a formula on this basis, he demanded Partition expecting the Congress to come forth with a formula to preserve India's unity. The theory broached by him in his address to Pakistan's Constituent Assembly on 11 August 1947 was shot down.[6] He then spoke of a nation of 400 million souls in subjection and used those oft-quoted words: 'Hindus would cease to be Hindus and Muslims would cease to be Muslims in the political sense as citizens of the State.'

By then, to be sure, the theory had spread far and wide in the minds of millions, as damage far more grave than the Partition of India. 'The pact' was central to the League's strategy and made sense in its historical context and within the framework of a united India. Such pacts lie at the core of Arend Lijphart's 'Consociational Democracy'. As he explains: 'In a consociational democracy, the centrifugal tendencies inherent in a plural society are counteracted by the cooperative attitudes and behaviour of the leaders of the different segments of the population. Elite cooperation is the primary distinguishing feature of consociational democracy.'[7]

The pacts and understandings on minority demands continue to linger in India even after Partition in a context that has changed radically. Evidently, no one had given the slightest thought to the role Indian Muslims should play after the Partition, least of all Jinnah. Since he was the unquestioned leader, his neglect had a devastating effect on Muslim morale, all the more so because of the expectation he had so irresponsibly and recklessly built up.

The Lahore Resolution envisaged 'adequate, effective and mandatory safeguards' for the minorities in the constitutions of both countries. The Partition plan of 3 June 1947 did not contain a word about minorities in either countries. Only one person was concerned.

---

[5] Jamaluddin Ahmad (ed.), Speeches and Writings of Mr. Jinnah (Lahore, 1960), vol. I, p. 110.

[6] Ahmad, *Speeches and Writings*, vol. II, p. 403.

[7] Arend Lijphart, *Democracy in Plural Societies* (Bombay, 1989), p. 1.

The Viceroy, Mountbatten, envisaged a 'Charter of Liberty' for the minorities.

Jinnah's speech to the League's Council on 9 June urging support for the plan was no more encouraging. It was a question of the minorities to take up in their Constituent Assembly, he said.[8] Questioned by representatives from UP, Bengal and Bombay, Jinnah said that he could disclose nothing beyond his personal opinion that the safeguarding of the rights of Muslim minorities would depend upon the future relations between Hindustan and Pakistan.[9]

This remark was made in the presence of the future leaders of Indian Muslims who he was soon to designate. As Governor-General designate of Pakistan, Jinnah told a press conference in New Delhi on 14 July about the dangers of a disloyal minority, intolerable to any state. 'I advise Hindus and Muslims and every citizen to be loyal to his state.'[10]

Choudhry Khaliquzzaman, asked by Jinnah to assume leadership of the Indian Muslims after he had left for Pakistan and was elected leader of the League Party in the Constituent Assembly (also the Provisional Parliament) on 11 June, offered support to Jawaharlal Nehru's motion on the national flag and implicitly pledged loyalty to the new state.[11] The only League leader who began articulating a strategy in the new situation was H.S. Suhrawardy, former Premier of Bengal. His letter to Khaliquzzaman of 10 September 1947 listed the options. He raised an important question which is relevant still:

What I fear is, will they have respect for you if you have not strength, that is to say if you give up your particular group solidarity? At the same time, any attempt to acquire solidarity and strength will raise suspicion in their minds as regards bona fides. Here the question, what should be our attitude towards the Hindus is very important. Shall we treat with them as League treating the Congress or shall we create a political party of Hindus and Muslims? They may refuse to accept you as the League treating with the Congress and in a system of joint electorate will support the breed known as the Natonalist Muslims.

---

[8] S.S. Pirzada (ed.), *Foundations of Pakistan* (Karachi, 1970), vol. II, p. 567.

[9] Z.H. Zaidi (ed.), *Jinnah Papers*, first series, vol. II, National Archives of Pakistan, p. 840.

[10] M. Rafique Afzal (ed.), *Speeches and Satements of the Quaid-i Azam: Mohamed Ali Jinnah* (Lahore, 1973), p. 421.

[11] C. Khaliquzzaman, *Pathway to Pakistan* (Lahore, 1961), pp. 397-9.

Several other options were mentioned, only to be dismissed. But Suhrawardy was categorical on one point: the Muslims of the minority provinces must chalk out their own plan. He suggested a convention of Muslim legislators, but Khaliquzzaman was not interested and settled in Pakistan in October 1947.

There next occurred an event of seminal importance for the future of Indian Muslims. Jinnah had repeatedly counselled them to organize themselves and professed that they should chalk out their own future. This, however, is precisely what he prevented them from doing, with consequences that are still with us. The Muslim League Council met in Karachi on 14-15 December 1947 and decided that 'there shall be separate Muslim League organizations for Pakistan and the Indian Union'. The assets and liabilities were to be 'equitably divided' between the two. The significance of this resolution lay in the nomination of Mohammed Ismail as convenor of the Indian Union Muslim League, and of Madras as the venue for the Council meeting. Two of the most powerful units, of UP and Bombay, were by-passed. The newspapers of the following day (*Statesman, Times of India* and the *Daily Gazette* of Karachi) yielded few secrets. That was left to the Communist Party's *People's Age* of 11 January 1948, on which Sharifuddin Pirzada's volumes draw.

The proceedings quoted *in extenso* from Pirzada's volumes reveal the *damnose hereditas* which Jinnah imposed on Indian Muslims over the opposition of some of their leaders:

The Qaid-i Azam recalled the charges that were being levelled against Pakistan and its leaders about the betrayal of the Muslim masses in the Indian Union. He said, he was full of feelings for the Muslim masses in the Indian Union who were, unfortunately, facing bad days. He advised the Indian Muslims to organize themselves so as to become powerful enough to safeguard their political rights. A well-organized minority should be powerful enough to protect its own rights—political, cultural, economic and social. On his part, he assured them of his full realization that the achievement of Pakistan was the outcome of the labour and toil of the Muslims in India as well as of those who were now enjoying its fruits. Pakistan would help them in every possible way.

A member interrupted and asked the Qaid-i Azam if he would once again, be prepared to take over the leadership of the Muslims of India in the present hour of trial. The Qaid-i Azam replied that he was quite willing to do so if the Council gave its verdict in favour of such a proposal. He recalled his statement at the time of the achievement of Pakistan that his job had been done, and with the achievement of Pakistan, the cherished goal of the

Muslim nation, he wanted to lead a retired life. But if called upon, he was quite ready to leave Pakistan and share the difficulties of the Muslims in the Indian Union and to lead them.

Jinnah said: "There must be a Muslim League in Hindustan. If you are thinking of anything else, you are finished. If you want to wind up the League you can do so; but I think it would be a great mistake. I know there is an attempt.

"Maulana Abul Kalam Azad and others are tying to break the identity of Muslims in India. Do not allow it. Do not do it. I again appeal that those who have moved their amendments will not press for them."

At this stage, Maulana Jamal Mian of Mahal withdrew his amendment. M. Husain Imam then moved his amendment: "In the resolution, '. . . in place of the All-India Muslim League, there shall be separate League organizations for Pakistan and the Indian Union', the word 'shall' should be replaced by 'may'." Mr. Imam said, "People here do not know the difficulties the Muslims are facing in India. They should be left free to decide their future according to the circumstances." No one supported Mr Husain Imam's amendment.

Mr Jinnah said, "I sympathize with Mr Husain Imam. He has not read the resolution properly. You should constitute the Muslim League in India. If you do not, you would go back to 1906. You are 40 millions; you can have a leader—if not one, then two or more. We cannot give directives to you. When you are strong and Pakistan is developed, the settlement will come."

Speaking next, Mr Suhrawardy first made a reference to the fact that those who like him were opposing the resolution were men who had refused or given up Ministries. He added: "I oppose this resolution. I am amongst those who had proposed some time ago that the League should be split. So, some might be surprised at my opposition. But before we split, my concern is to do something practical about the protection of minorities. I say when our objective is achieved, then why should we not organize ourselves in such a manner that the minorities are given the opportunity, on a national basis, to join us in the same organization? If you do that in Pakistan, it would help us in the Indian Union. If you form a national body here it would strengthen the hands of Nehru and Gandhi. The AICC passed a very good resolution we should have also passed a similar resolution."

Sardar Abdur Rab Nishtar made an appeal to the members and said, "Our two friends want to finish the League. I say if the League exists, Islam exists, Musalmans exist. We shall never allow the League to be wound up. The protection of minorities in India depends on the strength of Pakistan. we shall do all to protect them."

Mr Liaquat Ali Khan supported Sardar Abdur Rab Nishtar. The resolution was passed with an overwhelming majority. Some 10 members, including Mr Suhrawardy and Mian Iftikharuddin, voted against it.

This belied Jinnah's claim on 19 December that Indian Muslims were entitled, and by implication allowed, 'to form their own independent policy'. The course which the League subsequently adopted is ably traced in a neglected work which contains excellent material. Mohamed Raza Khan was a member of the League Council since 1943, of the IUML till 1963, and of the Madras Legislature from 1946 to 1962. His memoirs describe the Muslim mood at Partition, the short-sighted policies which the IUML pursued, and his own disillusionment.[12]

Having worked for the creation of Pakistan, they found themselves left without an organization and leadership, with nobody to guide them, Mr Jinnah left for Karachi to lead the new State. Most of the top leaders, who were on the League Working Committee and prominent Leaguers in different States, either left for Karachi to build up their own careers, as they felt they had no political future in India, or went into complete retirement. A fear complex had overtaken the Muslim community throughout the country. They could not think in terms of their political rights or their material welfare. All that they wanted was that there should be no communal trouble in their areas. They practically lost all interest in politics and wanted that they should be left to themselves. This mood of withdrawal lingers till today.

The Leaguers need not have worried about Azad providing the leadership. His address on 23 October 1947 to the Delhi Muslims assembled at the Juma Masjid has been much lauded for its oratorical qualities. He was full of reproach that his advice had not been heeded. A heavy dose of nostalgia was administered in order to instill courage.

Another exercise in providing leadership was his speech at the Indian Union Muslim Conference at Lucknow on 27 December 1947. (Strangely this finds no place in any of the compilations of his speeches.) The audience numbered more than 60,000 Muslims, including some Leaguers. The Maulana was heard in silence. Muslim leadership was his for the asking. 'All communal organizations must be liquidated. Even the Jamiyat al-ulama.' Its main task had been to guide the Muslims in the cultural and religious spheres, but it entered the political field in the cause of Indian nationalism. It, 'will have to cease its political activities, stated Azad, now that India had achieved liberation'.

Azad declared that any political organization of the Muslims—and

---

[12] Mohamed Raza Khan, *What Price Freedom?* (Madras, 1969).

for that matter of any other community—however nationalist and progressive it may be, would be harmful to the interests of the Muslims and the country as a whole, and could not be tolerated in the changed circumstances.

Azad did not explicitly advise Muslims to join the Congress; that was left to the Chairman of the Reception Committee, Hafiz Mohammad Ibrahim. On 28 December the Conference passed a resolution moved by the Vice-president of the Jamiyat al-ulama, Maulana Ahmad Saeed, declaring that 'Muslims of all shades of political opinion must take a united decision and abjure communal politics'. Another resolution moved by S.A. Brelvi, Editor of the *Bombay Chronicle*, advised them to join the Congress.

There were few takers for the Lucknow recipe. This was the last time Maulana Azad ventured to provide leadership. Suhrawardy, still in India, issued a statement in Calcutta asking Muslims to await Gandhi's signal before joining the Congress. 'Shall we be welcomed wholeheartedly and sincerely, shall we be trusted?' (*Times of India*, 27 December 1947), he asked.

He was taking his cue from Gandhi's following remarks at his prayer meeting on 22 December:

In my opinion, while they should hold themselves in readiness to join the Congress, they should refrain from applying for admission. Until they are welcomed with open arms and on terms of absolute equality. . . . Because the Congress has not always been able to live up to its professions, it has appeared to many Muslims as a predominantly caste Hindu organization. Anyway, the Muslims should have dignified aloofness, so long as the tension lasts. They would be in the Congress, when their services are wanted by it. In the meantime, they should be of the Congress, even as I am. . . . Today, every Muslim is assumed to be a Leaguer and, therefore, to be an enemy of the Congress. Such, unfortunately has been the teaching of the Muslim League. There is now not the slightest cause for enmity. Four months is too short a period, to be free from the communal poison.

Gandhi was emphatic, however, that the aspirations of communal bodies 'could only be satisfied by the Congress'.

The Lucknow Conference evoked a strange response from Vallabhbhai Patel. Addressing a huge public meeting in the same city on 6 January 1948, he angrily asked: 'To Indian Muslims I have only one question. Why did you not open your mouths on the Kashmir issue? Why did you not condemn the action of Pakistan?' It was a clear reference to Azad's Conference held only a fortnight earlier.

Patel was, obviously, prescribing a loyalty test to Muslims—support to the Government of India's stand on the Kashmir dispute with Pakistan.

On 14 August 1951, fourteen distinguished Muslims led by Zakir Husain, Vice-Chancellor of the Aligarh Muslim University, presented a memorandum to the U.N. mediator on Kashmir.[13]

Organizations of Muslims and even meetings of Muslims were a taboo then. But a Convention of Muslim legislators held in Lucknow on 19-20 March 1958 drew praise for its support to the Indian cause.[14] Muslims of riot-torn Sambalpur met, in 1964, not to demand greater protection, but to send cables to the president and members of the UN Security Council stating that 'Kashmir's accession to India is irrevocable'.[15]

Dissent was confined to those who supported Jayaprakash Narayan's viewpoint. Very few Muslims joined him. The Jamaat-i Islami's stand on Kashmir was in keeping with its bigoted outlook: one result of the acceptance of this test on a contentious issue has been to create an emotional barrier between Indian Muslims in the country at large and those in Kashmir. This did not deter Sheikh Abdullah from exploiting the former for his political ends, yet it did render interaction difficult.

Patel did not stop at prescribing the loyalty test. In the same speech he said: 'Select one horse. Those who want to go to Pakistan can go there and live in peace', and 'I appeal to the Hindu Mahasabha to join the Congress' (Bombay Chronicle, 7 January 1948). Azad relapsed into silence. The reality of a Congress so divided and the atmosphere in the country after Gandhi's assassination had little effect on the League's strategy. On 3 April 1948 the Constituent Assembly passed a resolution advocating 'all steps' to prevent any communal body from participation in 'any activities other than those essential for the bona fide religious cultural, social and educational needs of the community'. The Muslim League members of the Assembly met under the presidentship of Nawab Ismail Khan and decided to dissolve the party. In Bombay the League became a fourth party, and one of its prominent members, A.K. Hafizka, joined the Congress.[16]

[13] B.L. Sharma, The Kashmir Story (Bombay, 1967), pp. 258-64.
[14] Sisir Gupta, Kashmir (Bombay, 1966), p. 450.
[15] Noorani, India's Constitution and Politics (Bombay, 1970), p. 362.
[16] Mohamed Raza Khan, op. cit., pp. 366, 367.

Pursuant to the Karachi Resolution, the League's Council met at Madras in March 1948. Barely thirty members turned up. There were no representatives from Bengal, Orissa, Bihar or Delhi. UP had a sole representative in Maulana Hasrat Mohani. 'It was decided to continue the League with emphasis on non-political activities.' Mohammad Ismail was elected President and was authorized to establish branches in the states. The League, however, continues, albeit as a regional body with a strong base in only Tamil Nadu and Kerala.

In the Constituent Assembly the League members' approach was reactionary. As late as 25 May 1949, two of its members moved amendments to ensure that separate electorates for Muslims should be retained, drawing a sharp response from Patel. Mohammad Ismail supported the amendments. Z.H. Lari opposed both reservations and separate electorates: 'I am no longer satisfied with sending some Muslim advocates of certain causes. It is my ambition that my representative, be he a Muslim or a Hindu, *shall have an effective voice in the governance of the country*.'[17] Not long thereafter, Lari joined the League leaders who went over to Pakistan, not to forget others like the poet Josh Malihabadi. This exodus only added to the demoralization. No Muslim leader cared to develop the Lari line— how to proceed beyond protection to participation.

Two lines of approach emerged—one was to join or support the Congress, the other was to buttress the League. They were not mutually exclusive, for in time the League became a staunch supporter of the Congress. But it speaks a lot for the impress of the Karachi Resolution on some Muslim minds that under Ismail's leadership the League in Madras began by according 'full and complete support to the Congress' but sought thereafter 'some sort of private understanding between the Congress and the League'. In all this it received encouragement from the Congress leaders, particularly Kamaraj Nadar who sought the League's support, albeit on his terms. But Ismail, as *Qaid-i Millat,* was the poor man's Qaid-i Azam. When his emissaries reported back to him, 'he rejected Kamaraj's offer offhand and insisted that the Congress should recognize the League as the sole representative organization of Muslims'.

In 1961 Raza Khan broke ranks. In a speech on 19 August, he deplored that instead of working amongst the Muslim masses to raise

---

[17] C.A.D., vol. 8, p. 283 and pp. 269-355 for the debate.

their social, educational and economic levels, 'we bother ourselves only with elections in Madras and Kerala, and that too without any corresponding benefit'.

As a minority spread throughout the country, the Muslims could not afford to antagonize the majority community or the major parties. But by then the League had gained respectability as a valued ally of the Congress in its campaign to oust the first Communist government in Kerala, in 1959. Even if a ministerial berth proved difficult, the League bagged the speakership. Political marriage had been arranged which has served both parties eminently to this day. That it has ill-served the Muslims is beyond question. Not one tangible gain accrued to the community; no grievance was redressed; no reform carried out. The insecurities yet remain. Muslims continue to perceive their identity to be under threat. The principal gainer was, of course, the League leadership.

While it would be unfair to lay all the blame at the door of the party, it would be unwise not to notice the near total failure of intellectual creativity in the community. Saif F.B. Tyabji was a popular Bombay attorney deeply committed to the cause of Muslim education and to the success of the Anjuman-i Islam. In September-October 1955, he wrote eight articles in the Urdu daily *Inqilab* which were translated into English and circulated widely in mimeo form. His earnestness is not in question. But he was utterly unrealistic in prescribing the recipe. He was opposed to communal parties. He was equally zealous of preserving the Muslim identity. What, then, should be the aim of the Muslims? He wrote:

This has happened before. In 1856 the last Emperor of Delhi was deposed and his sons were shot. The wells of Delhi and Lucknow were heaped with the bodies of the flower [sic] of the Muslim aristocracy, and there was no water to drink, because there was only blood. The rule of the British had finally arrived. But our forefathers did not see the writing on the wall. They did not realize that a new world had dawned, and this new world would require a new way to live in. Decades passed without this being realized, and it was only many years later that farsighted thinkers such as the founders of Aligarh University in the UP and of the Anjuman-i Islam in Bombay, made efforts in new directions, often against the strong and persistent opposition of the conservatives, and ultimately, many years later, these efforts began to bear small and stunted fruit. We must not make this mistake again. We must realize what has happened in this country. We must ascertain the facts and act as they require.

Muslims had two objectives—economic and political. Tyabji analysed the letter and spirit of the Constitution of India and the Congress programme. Both provided a shortcut to the attainment of those objectives. Muslims

must be numbered amongst the poorest sections of the population Fortunately for the Muslims all the important political parties of India are now finally and irrevocably attached to socialism. By the now famous Avadi resolution, the Congress has set before itself the aim of creating a Socialist State in India. The Socialist Party by its very name stands for socialism. And the Communist Party differs from the others only as regards the means and the timing of the steps that must be taken and adopted for introducing socialism.

He maintained that Muslims must play an active role in shaping India's composite culture: 'I would like that a three-quarter part of the inspiration for the new culture of India should be in the Hindu culture and a one-quarter part in the Muslim culture.'

Tyabji emphasized that for the economic regeneration of Muslims the first step was their political awakening. Muslims must become active in politics and, above all, join and become influential in the ruling Congress. Only those influential in the Congress decided candidature for important posts, such as the chairmanship of banks and the major state-owned institutions and factories, 'and it is in these institutions and factories that commercial and industrial employment will be available to Muslims'.

The flaws are obvious. To speak of the evolution of a new culture, based on Hindu and Muslim cultures in crude proportions merely because the country became free from foreign rule, is to play into the hands of those who wish to evolve such a culture; notably, the Rashtriya Swayam Sewak Sangh (RSS). It would be more pertinent to speak of the development of India's composite culture. Politically, it is significant that a secular-minded person of that time could think of nothing better than Muslims joining a political party *en bloc*. We have come to realize that it is wrong to lay stress on political participation alone, and that too from the standpoint of Muslims. The best course for the Muslims is to participate in the entire spectrum of activities that constitute national life—the trade union movement, cooperative movement, women's and students bodies, etc.

There is a yet more important duty for us to perform: the political platform for expression on *national* issues from a *national* perspective. Not a single Muslim leader has emerged as an expert on economics, defence, foreign policy, and other matters of national concern. Were such a leader of proven identification to voice the grievances of the Muslims, the impact of his pleas would be much stronger. Both the nation and the community would be the richer for his contribution. What inhibits Muslim politicians and Muslim organizations is a *misconceived* notion of Muslim identity within the nation as a whole. The grievances are genuine; the politics of grievance redressal is wrong.

In 1961 Jabalpur was hit by riots, the worst since Partition. The veteran Congressman Syed Mahmud convened a convention in New Delhi in June 1961. One of its moving spirits was Maulana Hifzur Rehman. The most vital issue before the convention was to secure a 'due share' for Muslims in government services and in other walks of life, such as trade and industry. Due recognition of Urdu was another, as also the withdrawal of offensive textbooks. Among the participants were Brij Mohan Toofan, President Delhi Pradesh Congress Committee, Subhadra Joshi, Member of Parliament, Father J.S. Williams, a Bombay Bishop, G.M. Sadiq, the leader from Kashmir, Z.A. Ahmed of the Communist Party of India, and Mohammad Mujeeb, Vice-Chancellor of Delhi's Jamia Millia Islamia. About 600 delegates participated.[18]

There was no follow-up to the 1961 convention. No organization was established which would be open to all groups, to fight wrongs against a particular group. Muslim grievances were genuine, even if their validity had been long denied.[19]

These grievances cover a whole range of matters—employment in the public and private sectors, representation in the legislature and government, educational opportunities, glaring communal bias in textbooks, *wakf* properties, police partiality, and the State's utter and persistent failure to protect Muslim lives and properties.

Syed Mahmud abandoned his own effort of 1961. The Muslim Leaders' Convention he convened at the Nadwat al-ulama, Lucknow in August 1964 set up a united front of Muslim organizations—the All India Muslim Majlis-i Mushawarat comprising the League, the Jamaat-i Islami, the Progressive Muslim League, the Anjuman-i Tamir-i Millat, the Ittehadul Muslimeen of Hyderabad, and prominent leaders including A.J. Faridi. The very first paragraph on the

[18] *Times of India*, 11-12 June 1961.
[19] Noorani, 'The Grievances of Indian Muslims drawn up for the Union Home Ministry', reprinted in *Opinion*, 8 and 15 July 1969; also Noorani, pp. 366-407.

objectives of the Mushawarat required it 'to bring about better under-standing and promote unity amongst the various communities. . . . ' Another mandated it 'to enlist the support of the members of all communities for the full implementation of the Constitution of India . . . '. That remained only on paper.

On 3 June 1968 the Uttar Pradesh unit decided to form a new political party, the Muslim Majlis, led by Faridi. On 13 October 1968 the All-India Federation of Muslims and Scheduled Caste and Backward Classes was formed under the auspices of the Majlis. It comprised also representatives of the Republican Party, Sikhs and Christians. Faridi's contempt for Congress Muslims was unconcealed.

Faridi died an untimely death, but the strategy he had in mind is not to be dismissed out of hand. The state of Uttar Pradesh's politics is a cruel reminder that it can have *some* value in the short run and yet wreak havoc eventually. Any success in exploiting differences among political parties to extract concessions for Muslims will lead to a Hindu backlash and a consolidation even more hostile to Muslims.

Muslims do have a problem. Alas, they do not perceive its dimensions. Any charter of grievances is regarded by others rather like Jinnah's fourteen points and a 'harbinger' of Partition. The solution lies not in denying the reality of the grievances, but in devising a form and context of agitation which simultaneously draws Muslims into the political mainstream and enlists the support of non-Muslims as well. This has never been tried.

The Mushawarat never concerned itself with any but Muslim questions. It provided a platform for Sheikh Abdullah in 1971. When alienated from Indira Gandhi, he exploited it to push through a resolution markedly soft on Pakistan on the crisis in Bangladesh. He later led a deputation of Muslims to Mrs Gandhi to plead for redressal of specific Muslim grievances. One of them concerned Aligarh's Muslim character; another the new Criminal Procedure Code which sought to confer on divorced wives the right to maintenance till re-marriage and did not exclude Muslims from its ambit. Indira Gandhi had no hesitation at all in conceding their point. The provision was amended. Thus were sown the seeds of the Shah Bano question.

Two points Indira Gandhi made are noteworthy. She complained that 'the Muslim community had sought the support of the opposition parties' and she objected to their leaders adopting 'an agitational approach' (mimeographed minutes). Her counsel to Gen. Shah

Nawaz Khan was the same. She warned that 'confrontation and the spreading of an atmosphere of desperation is likely to be more damaging to the minorities themselves by arousing reaction in other community'.[20]

Such fears of Hindu reaction did not prevent the then Prime Minister from writing to the so-called Shahi Imam of Juma Masjid, Delhi, Syed Abdullah Bukhari on 20 November 1979 pledging redressal of Muslim grievances, listed in detail in her letter, while soliciting his support in the elections. It was preceded by a meeting between the two on 17 September 1979 at his residence, at which Sanjay Gandhi was present.[21]

Indira Gandhi was not interested in drawing Muslims into the mainstream of national politics. Her attitude was strictly protectionist and largely cynical.[22]

Nor was Rajiv Gandhi more principled. The Muslim Women's (Protection of Rights on Divorce) Act, 1986, gave the Muslims a bad name, but it followed and did not precede the unlocking of the gates of the Babri Masjid.[23]

When the Babri Masjid question erupted in 1986, leaders of Muslim organizations made little effort to enlist the support of non-Muslims in order to make it an issue of the rule of law. They treated it as a Muslim issue so as to neglect even the elementary duty of collecting documents and historical materials in order to arouse enlightened public opinion. The best studies emerged from the labours of non-Muslim scholars like Sushil Srivastava, Romila Thapar, S. Gopal and Neeladri Bhattacharya.

The demolition of the Masjid on 6 December 1992 did not induce any rethinking in Muslim political circles. The All-India Muslim Personal Law Board became even more active than before. It was set up at a convention in Bombay on 27 December 1972. It is highly significant that *uniquely* among the Muslim bodies, it was this one body which the Bohra chief patronized and used for his own ends. There is no danger of a uniform civil code being enacted. There is,

[20] *Mulk-o-Millat Bachao Tehrik*, Correspondence of the Amir with Prime Minister Indira Gandhi, p. 14.

[21] 'A Call of 150 Million Muslims to UN . . .', 1 March 1983, published by Bukhari, op. cit., pp. 10-11.

[22] Noorani, 'Indira Gandhi and Indian Muslims', *Economic and Political Weekly*, 3 Nov. 1990.

[23] Neerja Choudhary's disclosures in *Statesman*, 20 April 1986.

however, little prospect of this Board consenting to the reform of Muslim personal law either, not even in order to make it in accord with the *Shariat*.

The current drive is for reservation of seats in public services and educational institutions. It is only fair to mention that many a non-Muslim politician has endorsed the demand; not a few with tongue firmly in cheek. (Farzand Ahmed and Javed M. Ansari, *India Today*, 30 November 1994 and *Nation and the World* Issues of 1994; and Masood Ali Khan's article 'Reservation for Muslims', *Mainstream*, 20 May 1995).

None of this should blind us to the fact that the communal atmosphere has deteriorated to an alarming degree. But there is a fundamental flaw in the fight against communalism as Professor K.N. Panikkar pointed out in the Fourth V.P. Chintan Memorial Lectures in 1990.

The anti-communal struggle is a negative struggle. It is a struggle which tries to evolve ways and means to oppose communal propaganda. The agenda is set by them and the secular forces are made to respond to it. At every stage the secular forces are either trying to counter, say, a Mahant Avaidyanath or an Advani. They are ahead of us. It is necessary to reverse this order. If so, we have to transform our struggle against communalism to a struggle for secularism. Such a struggle can be meaningful only if it is a part of a struggle for a humane society—a society in which human beings are recognized and respected as human beings and not as "Hindu", "Muslim" or any other religious denomination. Such a struggle is possible only if we integrate the struggle for secularism with the larger struggle for a just society.

That is a distant political goal. But the first step towards it will have been taken if Muslims do not let mistaken notions of identity hinder their participation in the struggle for a just society and the leaders of secular political parties assist them in participation by responding to the genuine needs of Muslims, while enlisting them in the common struggle.

Women, Legal Reform and Muslim Identity

GAIL MINAULT

In Urdu writings of the late nineteenth century, Muslim reformers as diverse as Syed Ahmad Khan of Aligarh (1817-98), Maulana Ashraf Ali Thanavi of Deoband (1864-1943), and Syed Mumtaz Ali of Lahore (1860-1935) evolved a critique of contemporary Muslim life and culture in response to the pressures of colonial rule. The themes of this critique were threefold. First was the consciousness of the decline brought about by the loss of political power to foreign rule. Second was the analysis of the causes of that decline that included the squandering of power and resources by the military and landed élites, and the loss of religious and cultural vitality. Third was the evolution of a programme of reform that would remedy that decline. Foremost in this programme of reform was the need for improved education. Whether that education was a Western curriculum that included an Islamic element for the male leaders of the community (Sir Syed), or a reformed Islamic curriculum for the religious guides of the community (Deoband), or else a literary and practical education for both men and women (Mumtaz Ali), was a matter of considerable controversy.

There was nevertheless one point upon which all reformers could agree: the status of Muslim women required amelioration. In this, their discourse resembled that of Hindu social reformers of the time. Both Hindu and Muslim social reformers saw the roots of decline in a subsoil of rituals and customs that they regarded as unnecessary accretions, corruptions of a pure standard embodied in a reinterpreted past. For both Hindu and Muslim reformers, the solution to their current decline included the purification and rectification of religious life, and to that end, the reform of the role of women who were viewed—paradoxically—as both the chief perpetrators of wasteful and invidious customs and as the chief victims of such customs. For the reformers, therefore, women needed to be rescued from ignorance and superstition and also from abuse. Social reform, as articulated in the late nineteenth century, was thus the responsibility of men. Women were to be the beneficiaries of the actions of men, not actors on their own behalf. Women became symbolic, not only of all that was wrong with cultural and religious life, but also all that was worth preserving.

If their discourse was similar, however, Hindus and Muslims looked to different textual sources for their inspiration. For Hindus, the golden age was variously Shastric or Vedic, but certainly pre-Muslim. For Muslims it was scriptural, prophetic and non-Indic. As their discourses concerning the reform of women's intellectual and religious lives evolved, Hindus and Muslims either revived or created certain norms and boundaries for their communities. Reformers thus helped to articulate separate identities, to define what it meant to be either a Hindu or a Muslim, for both men and women.[1]

DISCOURSES OF MUSLIM REFORM:
CUSTOM VS. *SHARIAT*

Syed Ahmad Khan, regarded as the father of Indo-Muslim reform, was a champion of Western education for Muslim men. He regarded such education for women as premature, but was in favour of home education for Muslim women and, to his further credit, felt that the custom of purdah, as practised in India, had been carried to extremes. Such isolation, he argued, was the cause of women's ignorance. They were credulous and clung stubbornly to outmoded customs; they made men's lives difficult. In the great days of early Islam, he claimed, women had been educated. They could inherit property and had to be able to manage it. Hence, they needed to know not only how to read the scriptures, but also how to write and calculate. Islamic civilization had fallen on evil days and thus the status and rights of women had been abridged. This was not true

[1]Other discussions of community and boundary definition include Roasalind O'Hanlon, 'Historical approaches to Communalism: Perspectives from Western India', in Peter Robb (ed.), *Society and Ideology: Essays in South Asian History* (Delhi, 1993), pp. 247-66; and Sudhir Chandra, *The Oppressive Present: Literature and Social Consciousness in Colonial India* (Delhi, 1992).

[2]Syed Ahmad Khan, 'Hindustan ke Auraton ki Halat,' and 'Auraton ke Huquq', in M. Ismail Panipati (ed.), *Maqalat-i-Sir Syed*, vol. 5 (Lahore, 1962), pp. 188-99; on Sir Syed's educational reforms, see David Lelyveld, *Aligarh's First Generation* (Princeton, N.J., 1978).

Islam, but the result of adherence to bad custom.[2]

Sir Syed's argument found echoes among other reformers, younger men who were even more outspoken about the potential benefits of education for women. Education would break down women's isolation, and combat superstition and bad custom. This was a line of reasoning heard again and again in Muslim reformist discourse. Muslims thus seemed to accept the British cultural critique that Indian weakness was a result of moral as well as political collapse.[3] But such an argument had been present in Muslim discourse well before the British displaced Mughal power. Shah Waliullah in the eighteenth century, and before him, Shaikh Ahmad Sirhindi in the seventeenth, had lamented the loss of religious compass in the Muslim élite and linked it to the loss of political power.[4] Re-establishing the authority of God's law (Shariat) as opposed to spurious custom in Muslim lives was thus a prelude to regaining political and cultural ascendancy. By the late nineteenth century, women were viewed as an essential part of this process.

For Muslims in favour of change, challenges—whether external or internal—had to be met by arguing for a return to a pristine Islam, as variously interpreted. For Muslim reformers as for Hindu, social and religious change did not mean aping the West, but rather arguing for a revitalization of tradition. The *ulama* were very much a part of this effort. Indian *ulama* in the late nineteenth century, in the absence of a Muslim state, resorted to two main strategies to perpetrate Islamic learning. The first was to institutionalize founding a number of *madarsas* that were not only repositories of the Islamic curriculum, but that incorporated ideas derived from Western institutions such as academic departments, examinations and the offering of degrees. The second was to emphasize individual piety and dedication to the faith, based not on custom but on personal knowledge of the scriptures and the laws. That, of course, involved literacy. The *ulama* were heavily involved in publication: popular guides to religious practice, polemical pamphlets, scholarly

[3] Good summaries of this critique appear in Francis Hutchins, *The Illusion of Permanence* (Princeton, N.J., 1967), pp. 3-19; and Gauri Viswanathan, *Masks of Conquest* (New York, 1989), pp. 118-41.

[4] Waliullah and his line are the subject of a voluminous literature. One useful summary is Barbara Metcalf, *Islamic Revival in British India* (Princeton, N.J., 1982), pp. 16-63; see also Aziz Ahmad, 'The Political and Religious Ideas of Shah Waliullah of Delhi', *Muslim World*, 52, 1962, pp. 22-30.

quarterlies and less scholarly monthlies. A number of *madarsas* had their own lithographic presses that contributed to the expansion of Urdu as a medium of public discourse.[5]

The Deoband *madarsa* was one of the major manifestations of these trends. Deobandis sought to purify personal religious observance and to spread the knowledge of the *Shariat* more widely among Muslims in India. To advance this project, some *ulama* also championed women's education. To purify household rituals, to increase knowledge and observance of scriptural religion as opposed to folk customs, and to improve individual piety in the Muslim community, it was important for women to be educated in their religion.[6]

Maulana Ashraf Ali Thanavi of Deoband accordingly decided to write a compendium of useful knowledge for women, a guide not only to learning, but to the pious life.[7] He began by citing a tradition of the Prophet Mohammad: 'It is a duty incumbent on every Muslim man and every Muslim women to acquire knowledge.'[8] This *Hadith* was frequently cited by Muslim educational reformers as evidence that the Prophet himself favoured education for women. Maulana Thanavi then went on to explain the rationale for this book, *Bihishti Zevar* (The Ornaments of Paradise):

For many years, I watched the ruination of the religion of the women of Hindustan and was heartsick because of it. I struggled to find a cure, worried because that ruin was not limited to religion but had spread to everyday matters as well. It went beyond the women to their children and in many respects even had its effects on their husbands. To judge from the speed with which it progressed, it seemed that if reform did not come soon, the disease would be nearly incurable. . . . [T]he cause of this ruination is nothing other than woman's ignorance of the religious sciences. This lack [sic] corrupts their beliefs, their deeds, their dealing with other people, their character, and the whole manner of their social life. . . . I have for some time, therefore, realized that in order to manage women, it is absolutely

---

[5] Metcalf, *Islamic Revival*, pp. 87-137, 198-234; Francis Robinson, 'Technology and Religious Change: Islam and the Impact of Print', *Modern Asian Studies* (*MAS*), 27, 1, 1993, pp. 229-51.

[6] Metcalf, *Islamic Revival*, pp. 146-52; idem., 'The Madrasa at Deoband: A Model for Religious Education in Muslim India', *MAS*, 12, 1978, pp. 111-34.

[7] Ashraf Ali Thanavi, *Bihishti Zevar* (Lahore, n.d.). I am greatly indebted to Barbara Metcalf's partial translation of this work, entitled: *Perfecting Women* (PW) (Berkeley, 1990).

[8] *PW*, p. 47.

necessary to teach them the science of religion—even if it must be through the medium of Urdu.[9]

Maulana Thanavi here echoes a number of themes articulated by other reformers. Women's ignorance of religion is a problem for the society as a whole, for they infect their children and husbands with a contagion of indiscipline, ignorance and decline. Women are singled out as the carriers of that illness, an imagery suggesting the need to treat not just symptoms, but the root causes of the contagion. In evidence here is a second idea: that what happens in the home is of importance to the society at large, and that through social relations, women's influence extends well beyond the home. There is also the idea of control. Women need to be 'managed' via proper instruction in Islam. According to this reasoning, women are deficient, but this deficiency can be remedied by discipline and instruction. Women are, therefore, potentially equal to men in their capacity for understanding, and hence their reform and 'management' is central to the religious reform of all Muslims.

Given Maulana Thanavi's egalitarian assumption, which derives from the preaching of Islam, if women have inferior status, it is not due to their inherent inferiority—for their souls are the equal of men's—but because of degenerate custom, falsely identified as religion. *Bihishti Zevar* devotes a lot of space to attacking and rooting out false custom, as did other reformers. Thanavi's concerns are religious, although one also hears echoes of economic concerns about excessive expense and ostentation. The material and spiritual consequences of useless custom are closely allied for both middle class reformers and reformist *'ulama'*. Maulana Thanavi describes marriage customs:

[T]he women of the family gather and confine the girl in a corner. . . . Etiquette calls for the girl to be seated on a low platform, for ointment to be placed on her right hand, and for her lap to be filled with rice and sweets. Rice and sweets are also distributed among those present. From that day on, the women continually rub the girl with ointments. This custom involves much foolishness. The first objection is to the requirement of seating the girl alone. Whether it is hot, whether it is stuffy, whether all the doctors and physicians in the world say she will get sick . . . this obligation must not be missed. This entails the evil of strict adherence to set customs. . . . [P]lacing

---

[9] *PW*, pp. 47-9; Metcalf calls attention to Thanavi's implication that using Urdu is second best (to learning about religion in Arabic), but necessary in order to reach a popular audience.

the ointment on her right hand and filling her lap with puffed rice and sweetmeats seem to be some kind of omens or superstitious acts. If this is so, it is polytheism. What Muslim does not know that that is opposed to the *Shariat*?[10]

The rich composite of Hindu and Muslim observances that evolved over the centuries in the *zenana* in connection with marriage and childbirth is here attacked as both wasteful and un-Islamic.

Maulana Thanavi goes on to object to ostentatious charity and to the use of silver implements and silken garments also as wasteful and irreligious, particularly the latter. The mark of a pious Muslim is his or her devotion to God's will, not these vestiges of the nawabi lifestyle which, in his view, convey false status.[11] Thanavi's insistence on the egalitarian message of Islam has striking implications for the Islamic society as a whole, implications that the Maulana—even with his theme of women's need to become more like men in matters of self control and religious observance—does not fully explore. His emphasis on individual piety meets the needs of a time when an aristocratic culture based on birth was gradually being displaced by a middle-class culture based on individual achievement. This ethic of individual achievement for both men and women was rendered more possible by the culture of print, which made easier the dissemination of works such as *Bihishti Zevar*. But the equal status of all believers when face-to-face with God was, in practice, superseded by the hierarchical relationships of the society. Members of the middle-class service élite, generally speaking, remained preoccupied with status, both among social groups and within families.[12]

One reformer whose views on women's status were egalitarian in practice as well as in theory was Sayyid Mumtaz Ali of Lahore, founder in 1898 of one of the first Urdu journals for women, the weekly newspaper *Tahzib un-Niswan*. It was edited by his wife, Muhammadi Begum. Mumtaz Ali was also the author of *Huquq un-Niswan* (Women's Rights), a treatise in defence of women's rights

[10] *PW*, p. 116.

[11] Ibid., p. 107.

[12] Ibid., pp. 21, 79-83; a congruent case in the European reformation is discussed by Natalie Zemon Davis, 'City Women and Religious Change', in her *Society and Culture in Early Modern France* (Stanford, 1975), pp. 65-95. As she shows, it was one thing for women to be learned in the scriptures; it was quite another for them to challenge the male hierarchy in the society and the church.

in Islamic law, inspired by both his early Deobandi education and his experience of debating with Christian missionaries in Lahore. The missionaries criticized Islam, as well as other Indian religions, for the low status accorded to women and blamed these religions for the lack of education among Indian women. Mumtaz Ali knew that the position of women in Islamic law was theoretically higher than their actual current status. The cause of this discrepancy he felt, was adherence to false customs—in this, as we have seen he was not alone. Answering missionaries with theoretical arguments, however, was not enough. Changing Muslim practice had to be the highest priority. Women's adherence to false custom had to be combatted, but so too did the views of men, who felt that keeping women in ignorance and isolation was part of their religion. To attain these aims, he wrote *Huquq un-Niswan*.[13]

Mumtaz Ali denied all English influence upon his writing, arguing that anyone who knew the *Shariat* and who followed the example of the Prophet and his family must be prepared to reject ignorant customs. He thus placed himself firmly within the framework of Deobandi reform, seeking to revalidate Islamic law and prophetic example in Muslim daily life, and to eradicate superstitious customary accretions. The first section of *Huquq un-Niswan* addressed all the various reasons why men are considered superior to women. He showed that the distinctions made between men and women that are justified on religious grounds are, in fact, the products of social custom. If these distinctions were subjected to the scrutiny of reason, well bolstered by a knowledge of the religious sciences, the fallacy and injustice of male supremacy would become clear.[14]

Mumtaz Ali points out that even though men and women have different physiques and fulfil different biological functions, both are human and hence equal in God's sight. Mumtaz Ali's arguments, however, go beyond the equality of souls found in Ashraf Ali Thanavi's *Bihishti Zevar* and encompass greater egalitarianism in gender relations as well. While admitting that men have greater physical strength than women, he states that this does not automatically give men the right to rule over women. A donkey can carry more on its back than a man, but does that mean that donkeys

[13] Abu Athar Hafiz Jalandhari, 'Maulvi Syed Mumtaz Ali', *Tahzib un-Niswan*, 38, 6 July 1935, pp. 607-17; *Huquq un-Niswan (HN)* (Lahore, 1898).
[14] *HN*, pp. 3-42.

are superior to men? Perhaps in the dark ages, 'might made right', but with the advance of civilization, rulers needed to have more understanding and compassion. Thus the right to rule should belong not to the strong, but to the wise. As for men's supposed greater intellectual capacity, he notes that men and women are of the same species. Any differentiation between the brain powers of the two genders must be something that the society has attributed to them, not that God has created. Indeed, if the intelligence of women were less than that of men, the human race would rapidly become stupid, for intelligence would be transmitted in lesser degree to each succeeding generation.

Mumtaz Ali argues for a broad, humanistic education for women, not a narrow, household-centred one. Based on the assumption that men and women have equal rational and moral faculties, the education of women needs to be as complete as that of men, with some additional emphasis on household skills.[15] He also discusses purdah in Islamic law, maintaining that purdah as practised by Indian Muslims goes far beyond anything that the *Shariat* intended. Such customs have debilitating social results, but, he admits, they are very difficult to dislodge. Arguing from verses in the Koran that refer to the need for modest behaviour, and from *Hadith* in which the Prophet ruled on various aspects of social interaction, Mumtaz Ali draws a clear distinction between what is customary—and thus subject to change—and what is normative or desirable according to the *Shariat*. He does not argue for the abolition of purdah, but rather for a pattern of *Shariat*-inspired modest behaviour on the part of both men and women and for allowing women greater freedom of movement and social discourse, as befits their status as responsible human beings.[16]

Mumtaz Ali then discusses marriage, and here too his emphasis is egalitarian.[17] He notes that the Prophet decreed that a marriage contracted without the consent of the partners is unlawful, but that this consent is usually simply assumed. The boy is cajoled by his parents; the girl is supposed to sit passively during the ceremony, mutely accepting her fate. These customs go completely against the *Shariat*. He also discusses certain reforms in the payment of dower

[15] *HN*, pp. 42-60.
[16] Ibid., pp. 60-102.
[17] Ibid., pp. 102-42.

(*mahr*) and in the granting of divorce (*talaq*). In Islamic law, the wife has a right to the payment of *mahr* by the husband, part of which is given upon marriage and part of which can be deferred. Parents often demand a huge dower at the outset, in the hope that this will discourage divorce, but this only embitters family relationships. More beneficial in terms of protecting the wife's interests is the placing of stipulations in the marriage contract (*nikahnama*). For example, the husband might agree to pay a higher amount only in the event of a divorce or a second marriage, and the wife would agree not to demand payment except under such circumstances. In this way, there would be mutual understanding, and both partners would benefit. The wife would have security without demanding ruinous *mahr*, and the husband would know that he would not be liable to a high payment except under certain specific conditions.[18] Other stipulations in the marriage contract could limit polygamy and give the wife more control over her fate, i.e. the husband could agree to give his wife the right to divorce if he took a second wife. She would thus retain her right to *mahr*, but also the right to initiate divorce under certain conditions.[19] These suggested reforms are fully in line with the *Shariat*. Some benefit the wife, some the husband, but all emphasize the need for mutual agreement and equality in contractual dealings, which are absolutely necessary to ensure equitable and happy marriage based on the free choice of the partners.

Mumtaz Ali's approach to marriage emphasizes close adherence to Islamic law, and human relations based on mutual respect between men and women and understanding between the families concerned. Such considerations carry over into his discussion of relations between spouses. When men recognize that women's rights in Islamic law are equal to their own, and grant them an education commensurate with their abilities, then it will not be necessary to consider the problem of marital relations, he maintains—rather too optimistically—since he feels that the problem will disappear of itself.

[18] The Hanafi school of Muslim law divides the *mahr* into prompt and deferred payments, the latter due upon termination of the marriage. Mumtaz Ali's recommendation differs only slightly from standard Hanafi prescription. Cf. John L. Esposito, *Women in Muslim Family Law* (Syracuse, NY, 1982), pp. 24-6.

[19] Cf. Lucy Carroll, '*Talaq-i-Tafwid* and stipulations in a Muslim Marriage Contract: Important Means of Protecting the Position of the South Asian Muslim Wife', *MAS*, 16, 2, 1982, pp. 277-309.

He admits, however, that this is not currently the case. The cure for injustice is for men to become more enlightened and to realize that their wives are human, he argues. Until women are treated like human beings, it is no use blaming them for not living up to their potential. Mumtaz Ali, who heretofore had emphasized mutual responsibility for improving marital relationships, here places greater responsibility upon men for bringing about social change.

He also emphasizes that simply talking about the need for change in public is not enough; men must begin by setting an example in their private lives. Educated men, government servants, professionals, and the like who talk about the need for self-government in India should realize the connection: if they are unwilling to grant greater education and rights to their women, how can they, in all serious-ness, demand greater self-determination for themselves? The edu-cated sections of the community must lead the way in recognizing the rights given to women in the *Shariat*, which have been forgotten. One of the legal reforms that Mumtaz Ali advocates in *Huquq un-Niswan* is the passage of a divorce law that would recognize a Muslim woman's right to initiate divorce (*khula*). This right is present in the *Shariat*, provided the woman gives up her right to the payment of *mahr*, but it is not in force in India. He thus anticipates by some forty years the Dissolution of Muslim Marriage Act of 1939.[20]

LEGAL REFORM AND MUSLIM POLITICAL IDENTITY

The discourses of Muslim reformers deprecated useless custom, particularly as observed by women, and placed heavy emphasis on the need to observe the *Shariat* in everyday life. The recom-mendations of these reformers involved changing personal habits and eliminating household rituals. In some cases, however, reformers advocated legislative enactments in order to bring Muslim personal law closer to the spirit of the scriptures, as well as to improve women's rights in the context of family relations. Mumtaz Ali's thoughts on the need for a reformed divorce law was one such instance. Other reformers were concerned about British legal actions invalidating certain types of *waqf* (pious endowments) that had been used in the past to support the donor's surviving family members—

---

[20] *HN*, pp. 142-88.

frequently women. Thus, the revalidation of such *auqaf* would benefit indigent Muslim women.

Another matter that concerned reformers was succession to property. Under the *Shariat* a daughter is entitled to inherit a share of her father's property—half that of a son, to be sure—but nevertheless her right to property is specified in the Koran and *Hadith*. In many places in British India, however, 'customary law' was enforced, custom that favoured sons to the exclusion of daughters. This was to the benefit of rural landed magnates, cultivated as political allies by the British, in the interests of keeping landholdings intact. The nature of rural landholdings varied greatly from place to place, but in general, the issue of *Shariat versus* custom among Muslims pitted rural landholders against urban reformers and some *ulama*.

In the early part of the twentieth century, therefore, an unlikely coalition of *ulama*, Muslim middle-class reformers, and Westernized politicians with nationalist leanings came together—for very diverse reasons—to enact a series of legal reforms. The Waqf Validating Act of 1913, the Muslim Personal Law (*Shariat*) Application Act of 1937, and the Muslim Dissolution of Marriage Act of 1939 were laws that specifically applied to Muslims. In this period also the Sarda, or Child Marriage Restraint Act of 1929, was enacted that applied to all religious communities. The latter was heartily endorsed by the All-India Women's Conference (AIWC), founded in 1927, representative of the growing voice of Indian women in the social and educational reform arena.[21]

In addition, a growing body of opinion among Muslim women, whether writing in Urdu magazines or speaking from the platforms of women's associations, objected to polygamy and unilateral divorce, and supported greater property rights for women and the right of a women to initiate divorce when her marriage was cruel or insupportable. Muslim women's resistance to legal inequities included a resolution against polygamy passed by the All-India Muslim Ladies' Conference (Anjuman-i Khavatin-i Islam) at its annual meeting in Lahore in 1918 that caused considerable outrage in the

---

[21] Amrita Basu and Bharati Ray, *Women's Struggle: A History of the All-India Women's Conference, 1927-1990* (New Delhi, 1990); Janaki Nair, *Women and Law in Colonial India* (New Delhi, 1996), pp. 79-84.

Muslim press.[22] In addition, a movement in favour of 'delegated divorce' (*talaq-i tafwid*) was spearheaded by Mrs Sharifa Hamid Ali, who served as President of the AIWC in the late 1930s. Mrs Hamid Ali, the wife of a Muslim member of the Indian Civil Service who was a member of the distinguished Tyabji family of Bombay, had a draft prepared of a Muslim marriage contract containing stipulations allowing the woman to divorce under certain conditions. She urged educated Muslim women to see that such stipulations were incorporated into all marriage contracts.[23] Such delegated divorce was permitted under Hanafi law, the school of Muslim law most prevalent among Indian Muslims, and the least latitudinarian in matters of divorce for women. Under *talaq-i tafwid*, for example, the contract could specify that if a man married a second wife, the first could seek a divorce without forfeiting her *mahr*. This was significant, for if a woman initiated divorce (*khula*), she would lose her right to *mahr*, often her only means of support after divorce. This was a major disincentive to women seeking divorce, even in dire circumstances; whereas delegated divorce gave women a way out of marriage that preserved her right to some support.[24]

Such evidence of women's resistance to legal inequities caused some consternation among men and added to pressures in favour of reform. Mumtaz Ali had anticipated a number of these laws, but it is unlikely that these would have been passed if reformers like him had been their only advocates. Without the evolution of opinion that produced the coalition of men who favoured legal reforms, the chances of an improvement in Muslim women's rights would have been slim. A brief examination of the debates among men that led to the passage of the *waqf*, *Shariat* and divorce legislation is necessary in order to ascertain the impact of those laws both on women's rights and on the emergence of Muslim political identity.

The Waqf Validating Act of 1913, proposed by Mohammad Ali Jinnah, sought to reinstate endowments that benefited the donors'

---

[22] For a detailed examination of this resolution and the response to it, see Gail Minault, 'Sisterhood or Separatism? The All-India Muslim Ladies' Conference and the Nationalist Movement', in Gail Minault (ed.), *The Extended Family: Women's Political Participation in India and Pakistan* (Delhi, 1981), pp. 83-108.

[23] Basu and Ray, *Women's Struggle*, p. 188.

[24] Lucy Carroll, '*Talaq-i-Tafwid* . . .', *MAS*, 16, 2, 1982, pp. 277-309; Azim Beg Chughtai, *Tafwiz* (Karachi, 1957, 1st pub. 1932).

families. This type of *waqf*, as opposed to endowments for public religious and charitable purposes, had been voided by a Privy Council judgment. Jinnah's bill sought to undo what the Privy Council had wrought. In this effort, Jinnah secured the support of a number of leading *ulama* and Muslim politicians, including representatives of the *madarsas* of Deoband, Firangi Mahal, and Nadwat al-ulama (achieving agreement among such diverse *ulama* was no small feat in itself), plus Mian Mohammad Shafi of Punjab (a Muslim Leaguer), Hasan Imam of Bihar (Muslim League and later Congress), and Aftab Ahmad Khan of Aligarh (generally, loyal to the British). Others, however, felt that Jinnah was simply using the issue to further his political career by establishing himself as a spokesman for Indian Muslim opinion, a collectivity that he and other Muslim leaders of the day sought to bring into being.[25]

In a discussion of the passage of the *waqf* legislation, Kozlowski points out that Jinnah, like the British jurists whose ruling he sought to undo, emphasized the ancient and unchanging nature of Muslim religious law. As this line of reasoning confirmed British suppositions, it was effective. Muslim politicians thus participated in the tendency, prevalent under British rule, to codify—and hence to rigidify—what was understood as Islamic law.[26] In the process of negotiating with colonial authorities, Muslim political leaders represented both Islamic law and their own community as more unified than they actually were, or had ever been. But, Kozlowski wryly notes: 'Muslim leaders could not be blamed for choosing the line of argument most likely to obtain their goal.' He further argues that:

Jinnah and the others might have chosen another away of presenting their case, one which did not depend on so abstract a reading of Islam or the people who professed it. Sir Syed, for example, tried to place the institution [of *waqf*] in the context of changing economic conditions in the Muslim world and India in particular. Sir Syed readily admitted that the use of endowments as family settlements suited the conditions created by British rule.[27]

---

[25] For a full discussion of the passage of this legislation, see Gregory Kozlowski, *Muslim Endowments in British India* (Cambridge, 1985), pp. 177-91.

[26] This tendency is analysed in Michael Anderson, 'Islamic Law and the Colonial Encounter in British India', in Chibli Mallat and Jane Connors (eds.), *Islamic Family Law* (Boston, 1990), pp. 205-23.

[27] Kozlowski, *Muslim Endowments*, p. 186.

Jinnah, as a British-trained lawyer, had a considerably more abstract understanding of Islamic law than did Sir Syed.

The Shariat Application Act of 1937 also addressed economic conditions created by British rule, particularly in the Punjab. In that important agrarian province, British authority rested firmly upon the recognition and codification of 'tribal' custom, wherein women were deprived of rights to inherit immovable property. As pointed out earlier, customary law tended to keep landholdings intact, or at least more intact than if daughters could inherit land along with sons. The recognition of custom, by tying the interests of landholders to that of the British administration, was a cornerstone of British policy in the Punjab, but it contravened the *Shariat*, which gave a daughter a share of her father's property, albeit half that inherited by a son. For Muslim women, therefore, support for the *Shariat* had definite, if limited, advantages.[28]

In such a situation, support for the *Shariat* not only denoted ties to the Islamic moral order, but also implied support for nationalist aspirations. In the 1930s in the Punjab, support for customary law was found in the Unionist Party, composed of large rural landholders of various religious communities, who generally spoke in favour of the British connection. Support for the *Shariat* emerged among the Muslim League, which was urban and (relatively speaking) more nationalistic. The Jamiyat al-ulama, the political party representing many Indian *ulama,* supported legislation to validate the *Shariat* for both religious and nationalistic reasons. A Bill to apply the *Shariat* in the Punjab, which specifically sought to improve women's rights to land inheritance, was blocked by the Unionists in the provincial Legislative Council in the mid-1930s, but the issue persisted, and in 1937, Muslim League members introduced a similar measure in the Central Legislative Assembly, which ultimately passed.

During the legislative debates, the point was repeatedly stressed that this Bill, representing a consensus of Muslims throughout India to have their personal lives guided by the *Shariat*, would grant women greater rights. Speakers as diverse as Sir Mohammad Yaqub

---

[28] David Gilmartin, 'Customary Law and Shari'at in British Punjab', in Katherine Ewing (ed.), *Shari'at and Ambiguity in South Asian Islam* (Berkeley, 1988), pp. 43-62; idem., 'Kinship, Women and Politics in Twentieth-Century Punjab', in Minault (ed.), *The Extended Family*, pp. 151-73.

from Moradabad,[29] Dr Ziauddin Ahmad from Aligarh,[30] the poet and journalist Zafar Ali Khan from Lahore, the former Khilafat leader Maulana Shaukat Ali,[31] the urbane Congress lawyer Asaf Ali from Delhi, the even more urbane M.A. Jinnah from Bombay, and regional leaders such as Maulvi Syed Murtaza of Madras, Maulvi Mohammad Abdul Ghani from East Bengal and Abdul Qayyum from the North-West Frontier Province all voiced their sympathy for downtrodden Muslim women and their desire to see their lot bettered. Jinnah was able to secure passage of the Bill, however, only after a number of major compromises left adoptions, wills, and legacies entirely up to individual Muslims. On the inheritance of agricultural land, furthermore, the Bill was silent, for under the Government of India Act of 1935, this was a subject reserved for the provinces and outside the scope of central legislation. The Shariat Application Act of 1937, for all the sympathetic rhetoric of the debate, had an extremely limited effect on Muslim women's rights. It did, however, express a consciousness of Muslim identity in the legal structure of the state and further enhanced Jinnah's claims to speak for that collectivity.[32]

The debate on the Sarda, or Child Marriage Restraint Act of 1929 showed a similar concern to apply the *Shariat* as a generalized scriptural prescription and to represent Muslims as an undifferentiated community. A number of Muslims, including Jinnah, at first opposed the application of the Sarda Act to Muslims, on the grounds that it was irrelevant, as child marriage had no sanction in Islam. T.A.K. Sherwani argued that if Muslims in India did practice child marriage, it was because they were following a Hindu custom—a familiar reformist argument, though not always stated so blatantly. Ultimately, Jinnah and other Muslim representatives were convinced by the select committee's report that child marriages were also

[29] He was not, incidentally, the son-in-law of Mumtaz Ali. His late wife, Wahida Begum Yaqub, was Mumtaz Ali's daughter by his first marriage and a former editor of the Urdu newspaper for women, *Tahzib un-Niswan* of Lahore, managed by her father.

[30] On his career, see David Lelyveld, 'Three Aligarh Students: Aftab Ahmad Khan, Ziauddin Ahmad and Mohamed Ali', *MAS*, vol. 9, 1975, pp. 103-16.

[31] For these two, see Gail Minault, *The Khilafat Movement* (New York and Delhi, 1982).

[32] Gilmartin, 'Kinship, Women, and Politics', pp. 166-9; Archana Parashar, *Women and Family Law Reform in India* (New Delhi, 1992), pp. 146-50; Govt. of India, *Legislative Assembly Debates*, 1937, vol. 3, pp. 2528-44; 1937, vol. 5, pp. 1426-48, 1819-65.

common among Muslims, to vote in favour of the Act. Muslim women members of the AIWC also strongly supported the Act, which outlawed marriages under the age of fourteen in all communities.[33]

The legal reform that had the most significant impact on Muslim women' rights was the Muslim Dissolution of Marriage Act of 1939. Major credit for its passage must go to Maulana Ashraf Ali Thanavi whose writings were an enabling factor in assembling the coalition that backed the legislation. As a background, in 1913, Maulana Thanavi had issued a *fatwa* in a case involving a Muslim husband who had applied to a British court in India for restitution of conjugal rights. The wife's family refused, on the grounds that she had renounced Islam and her marriage was no longer valid. The judge asked the claimant to secure a *fatwa* clarifying this point in Islamic law, and Maulana Thanavi ruled that the marriage was indeed annulled as a result of the wife's apostasy.[34]

As previously noted, the Hanafi school of Islamic jurisprudence, followed by a majority of Muslims in the subcontinent, is strictest in matters of divorce and gives a wife almost no grounds for initiating the dissolution of her marriage. In the early twentieth century, the number of Muslim women who resorted to the device of renouncing Islam in order to secure judicial divorces increased alarmingly. This was partly a result of missionary activity, but partly because many Muslim women found no other way out of cruel and abusive marriages. The press took notice of this phenomenon and the influential voice of the poet Iqbal urged Muslim scholars to reform Hanafi law, in order to find a solution within Islam for this problem, so that Muslim women would not have to adopt this desperate tactic.[35]

Ashraf Ali Thanavi, therefore, returned to the subject of his 1913 *fatwa* and consulted with a number of other *ulama*, including Mufti Kifayatullah of Delhi, Husain Ahmad Madani of Deoband, and

---

[33] Geraldine Forbes, 'Women an Modernity: The Issue of Child Marriage in India', *Women's Studies International Quarterly* (1979), pp. 407-19.

[34] M. Khalid Masud, Brinkely Messick and David S. Powers (eds.), *Islamic Legal Interpretation: Muftis and their Fatwas* (Cambridge MA, 1996), pp. 193-203; Ashraf Ali Thanavi, *Imdad ul-Fatawa, Ma'ruf be Fatawa-i-Ashrafiya* (Deoband, n.d.), vol. 2, pp. 55-77.

[35] Khalid Masud, 'Apostasy and Judicial Separation'; idem., *Iqbal's Reconstruction of Ijtihad* (Lahore, 1995), pp. 155-78; cf. Furqan Ahmad, 'Contribution of Maulana Ashraf Ali Thanavi to the Protection and Development of Islamic Law in the Indian Subcontinent', *Islamic and Comparative Law Quarterly*, 6, 1, March 1986, pp. 71-9.

various Maliki *ulama* in Arabia. In 1931, he issued a lengthy revision of his earlier *fatwa*: *Al-Hilat un-Najiza li'l-Halitat al-'Ajiza* ('A Successful Legal Device for the Helpless Wife').[36] He ruled that apostasy did not annul a Muslim marriage, but that a wife might obtain a judicial divorce based on grounds permitted by the Maliki school of Muslim jurisprudence. This device of jurisprudential electicism (*takhayyur*), recognized by some legal scholars and commentators, opened the way to a reform of Muslim divorce law. The Jamiyat al-ulama seconded Maulana Thanavi's view, after which Qazi Mohammad Ahmad Kazmi, a lawyer from Meerut and a Jamiyat al-ulama member of the Central Legislative Assembly, in 1936 introduced the Bill that became the Muslim Dissolution of Marriage Act. The Bill was first referred to a Select Committee composed of a majority of Muslims, then debated thoroughly in the assembly and finally passed in 1939.[37] The Act provided that apostasy of the wife did not annul a Muslim marriage, a point greeted with some relief by Asaf Ali who was married to a Hindu and was shocked to hear that a marriage between a Muslim and a non-Muslim might be considered invalid *ab initio*.[38]

The Act permitted the wife to seek a judicial divorce on grounds permitted by the Malikis, including the husband's cruelty, insanity, impotence, disappearance, or imprisonment and his failure to perform his marital obligations or to provide maintenance—for specified periods of time ranging from two to seven years. The Act also provided for divorce based on the 'option of puberty', that is: if a woman had been married off by her elders before puberty, and the marriage had not been consummated, she could ask for its dissolution.[39] It is worth remarking that the legislative debate and the law as enacted were concerned with the suffering of Muslim women that resulted from the inability of men to fulfil their marital duties, or from custom that permitted her to be married off without a choice. This vision of women as victims is familiar, and in this context, very

---

[36] A new edition of this treatise, ed. by Taqi Usmani, is: Ashraf Ali Thanavi, *Hilat-i-Najiza, ya'ni: Auraton ka Haqq-i-Tansikh-i-Nikah* (Karachi, 1987).

[37] Debate on the Bill is contained in Govt. of India, *Legislative Assembly Debates*, 1938, vol. 1, pp. 318-23, 509-13; 1938, vol. 5, pp. 1090-1124, 1951-88; 1938, vol. 6, pp. 2831-43; 1939, vol. 1, pp. 615-54, 863-95.

[38] Ibid., 1938, vol. 5, p. 1113.

[39] Masud, 'Apostasy', Parashar, *Women and Family Law Reform* (Delhi, 1992), pp. 151-8.

useful politically. Begum Hamid Ali, on the other hand, in her campaign in favour of stipulations in marriage contracts was working to empower women, as well as their relations, in marital negotiations.

The Act differed in several respects from the recommendations of the *ulama*, most notably in not reserving jurisdiction in cases of Muslim divorce to Muslim judges. It was also made to apply to all Muslims, not only Sunnis, but Shias as well. Consequently, Maulana Thanavi and the other divines who had originally urged reform of the divorce law were displeased with the Act in its final form and condemned the Muslim Dissolution of Marriage Act as un-Islamic.[40] More secular parliamentarians, however, including Abdul Qayyum of the North-West Frontier and Asaf Ali from Delhi, were loath to risk governmental defeat of the Act by amending it to reserve jurisdiction to Muslim judges and they accepted its application to Shias as well in the interest of maintaining their claim to represent the interests of Muslims as a whole.[41] Once again, compromises in the legislature made for a law that was passable, if not strictly *shari'i*. For all its strange bedfellows, this episode showed that reformers, politicians and *ulama* could work together to bring about the reform of Muslim personal law in a parliamentary context, even where Muslims were in a minority. The evidence of Muslim women's discontent and their resistance to the existing state of affairs, whether within élite organizations such as the AIWC or via apostasy, had acted as a catalyst. Maulana Thanavi's careful scholarship, broad consultation and invocation of the principle of jurisprudential eclecticism had made consideration of divorce reform possible.

The *waqf, Shariat* and divorce laws had several results that were cumulative: (1) They recognized that women had certain rights in Islamic law. (One should be careful, however, not to regard these laws as a victory for individual rights, but rather as a recognition of rights that were women's by virtue of their being members of families as well as Muslims.) (2) They created a distinct body of law, within the context of the state, with which both Muslim men and women could identify. (3) They created a fragile political coalition in support of issues that were clearly labelled Islamic. These laws, with their concern for women in the family, with demarcating boundaries

---

[40] Masud, 'Apostasy'; the text of the law is contained in B.R. Verma, *Muslim Marriage and Dissolution* (Allahabad, 1971), pp. 251-97.

[41] Govt. of India, *Legislative Assembly Debates*, 1939, vol. 1, pp. 621-2.

around the Muslim community and defining its legal system in religious terms, and with bringing together Muslims of different ideological persuasions on the basis of their Islamic identity, fitted well into the structure of the British colonial state that allowed considerable latitude for organization around 'private' matters such as religion. It also appealed to the coalition-building skills of the man who shepherded the first two bills through the central legislature, Mohammad Ali Jinnah.[42]

This is not to suggest that Jinnah's political career was mainly associated with the movement for Muslim women's reform, nor still less with the movement for scriptural reform. He was, however, able to articulate issues raised by those interlocking movements within a political and legislative context. It is significant that his most successful efforts at coalition-building among Muslims prior to the Pakistan resolution of 1940 were those focused on legal issues that linked women and family life to Islamic legal identity, and that further linked the concerns of urban and small-town professionals and *ulama* at the expense of rural landed interests. The defence of the Muslim family and the definition of the Muslim community in India as a legal entity were issues at stake in the enactment of these laws. They were also issues that had linked these two important groups of educated Muslims since the late nineteenth century, groups whose support was essential to Jinnah and the Muslim League's claim to be the political representatives of all Indian Muslims. This linkage among concerns for women's status within the family, Muslim personal law and Muslims' sense of distinctive identity persists into the present.

CONCLUSION

The writings of Muslim social reformers in the late nineteenth century portrayed women as embodying all that was wrong with their culture as well as all that which was worth preserving. Most of what was wrong could be summed up by the phrase 'useless custom' (*fazul rasum*). Women were its practitioners as well as its victims. The solution to the ambivalence of the reformist message was provided by a return to a purified practice of the faith which, in turn, would

---

[42] Jinnah took no part in the debate over the Muslim Dissolution of Marriage Act.

improve and preserve the family life that reformers both valued and found deficient. Part of that return to the faith involved a reassertion of scriptural religion over household ritual, another involved the revived observance of the *Shariat* in matters such as the inheritance of property (including charitable endowments), marriage and divorce.

All of the legal reforms that were enacted in the early part of the twentieth century are extensions of this ideology of reform. Scriptural authority, as reinterpreted in the colonial context—increasingly restricted to certain specific texts and clearly defined readings of them—was asserted over customary practice. Since reformers viewed the female and the indigenous as the bases of such customary practice, their educational, social and later legal reforms increasingly asserted male control and values over women's lives. On the other hand, women were central to the family, and their dignity and honoured roles essential both to the preservation of family life and to its improvement. Legal reforms were thus a logical extension of men's concerns to improve women's status and their adherence to the faith of Islam. Women were the symbols of what men wanted their community to be. Women, when consulted, were expected to agree. Concern for Muslim women's rights, as individuals, was another matter. From a feminist perspective one may fault the reformers for doing little to improve Muslim women's rights,[43] but that was not their main concern. Their concern was with establishing norms for community behaviour, and in the process, establishing an irreducible Muslim identity within the political process.

[43] As do, for example, Janaki Nair and Archana Parashar in their insightful works cited earlier.

Secularism, Identities and
Representative Democracy

NIRAJA GOPAL JAYAL

This paper argues that the question of identity poses two kinds of difficulties for the project on secularism, and seeks to locate both these in the context of institutions of representative democracy. The first of these difficulties is the familiar one of determining the adequacy of democratic institutions for the expression and recognition of claims of particularistic identity within the context of a secular state. The second is a more unusual difficulty that attends societies in which the claims of community identity sometimes conflict with claims to other kinds of identity (e.g. gender), raising important questions about the adequacy of representative institutions—as a guarantee of both procedural and substantive democracy—as well as about the state's avowed commitment to secular political practice and discourses. Both these issues are illuminated by an examination of an episode in the recent political history of India, viz., the controversy around the Supreme Court judgement in the Shah Bano case in 1985, and the subsequent enactment of the Muslim Women (Protection of Rights on Divorce) Act, 1986.[1] This episode, apart from its yet unresolved legacy in terms

---

[1]The case of *Shah Bano* vs. *Mohammed Ahmed Khan* (Criminal Appeal No. 103 of 1981) was decided by the Supreme Court in a landmark judgement delivered in April 1985. The case pertained to the claim for maintenance of a seventy-three-year-old divorcee, Shah Bano. Her husband, Ahmed Khan had moved the Supreme Court in appeal against a High Court judgement making the payment of a small maintenance allowance incumbent upon him. Ahmed Khan argued that since he had fulfilled his obligations under Muslim Personal Law by paying her an allowance for the three months of the *iddat* period, and paid her *mahr* as well, he was not bound to do more. The Supreme Court was thus implicitly asked to pronounce on the relationship between the personal law and some provisions of the Criminal Procedure Code of 1973 which relate to destitution and vagrancy, and were being regularly invoked for maintenance petitions by abandoned wives. The Court upheld the High Court judgement, ruling that the criminal law of the country overrides all personal laws and is uniformly applicable to all, including Muslim women. This judgement sparked off

of the problems of both secularism and gender justice, also explicates the dimension of representative democracy in a way that possibly no other comparable event does.

Majoritarian democracy, almost everywhere, has shown itself to be less than capable of handling the problems of multicultural heterogeneous societies. Institutions of representative democracy, arguably designed for more or less homogeneous societies, have therefore been modified to allow for special provisions (of a protective nature) for minorities, as well as efforts to rule out what Dworkin has called 'double counting'.[2] In practice, however, these institutions remain open to the charge that they function in ways that give majorities greater purchase in the polity and also undermine the constitutional guarantees of equal citizenship enjoyed by individuals belonging to minority social groups, however defined. In India, the state's policy response to the competing claims of identity, historically and most influentially articulated on the basis of religion, was the strategy of state secularism, a strategy that cohered with the adopted ideology of liberal neutrality, as this principle was extended to cover the relationship of the state with a culturally plural society. This extension was altogether too neat to be effective, for it rested upon a mistaken equivalence between interest and pressure groups, on the one hand, and cultural and religious communities, on the other, and nonchalantly offered an identical liberal pluralist solution for both. Consequently, the charge of majoritarianism as an institutional bias is manifestly not mitigated by the state's formal adoption of secularism as a goal, especially as this does not translate into a sufficiently widespread consensus on secularism as a valuable social and political objective, much less into

---

a political storm in which guarantees were demanded for safeguarding personal law, grounded in the claim of rights to cultural community. In deference to the opinion of the politically influential community leadership, the Rajiv Gandhi government hastily drafted a legislation which explicitly excluded Muslim women from the purview of the criminal law, to which all citizens otherwise have recourse.

[2]The idea of double counting is, in Dworkin, premised upon the distinction between personal preferences (for one's own enjoyment of some goods and opportunities) and external preferences (for the assignment of goods and opportunities to others). Given that external preferences, political or moral, are generally not independent of personal preferences, but grafted on to the personal preferences they reinforce, counting them as if they were independent has grave consequences for equality, e.g. racism. Cf. Dworkin, 1977, pp. 235-6.

a consensus on the substance and content of a secular doctrine. This paper argues that such a consensus presupposes and is premised upon a prior consensus on procedures by which to establish the value and determine the content of secularism in Indian society, and that such procedures are conspicuous by their absence.

At least one available philosophical defence of secularism implicitly seeks to underpin a project of state proselytization of toleration in society. It is also, in a not dishonourable sense, a majority-oriented conception, to the extent that it seeks to provide members of the majority community with good reasons why secularism is a worthwhile value (Bhargava, 1994). While both these are important and positive tasks for a philosophy of secularism, equally deserving of concern is the problem of finding ways in which minority communities can be persuaded that the institutions and practices of the majority and of the state are not weighted against them. Only the provision of effective safeguards for minority rights— which are institutionalized enough for it to be difficult, if not impossible, to subvert them—can give minorities greater purchase in the polity. While these safeguards must be such that non-secular majorities cannot tamper with them, they should also, at the same time, disallow the possibility of being monopolized by the most conservative elements within the minority.

The controversy around the Supreme Court judgement in the Shah Bano case, and the public as well as parliamentary debate on the Muslim Women (Protection of Rights on Divorce) Bill, tended to be focused around the conflict between, on the one hand, the right of a religious minority to a separate civil code as an important legal guarantee of its identity and, on the other, the claims of the state, legitimized through representative institutions, to define, articulate and realize the 'common good'. The criticism that the debate altogether ignored the important question of women's rights remained confined to feminists and a few progressives. Politically, this criticism was appropriated only, and rather incongruously, by parties of the right, clearly for the wrong reasons. The political centre stage was thus decisively occupied by two dominant strands of argument, advancing respectively the claims of minority rights ('communal' to its critics) and of majoritarian democracy ('secular' by self-proclamation). Thus, claims to minority rights came to be identified with 'communalism', while 'secularism' came to be defined in terms of majoritarian democracy. Such equivalence seemed to suggest a certain incompatibility between the claims of minority rights and majoritarian democracy, now posited as irreversibly opposed, in much the same way as secularism and communalism are.

This debate explicates an important theoretical paradox in liberal political theory, viz., the conflict between liberal-individualist and communitarian claims to political voice, but it also impels us to reconsider the institutional conditions for secularism, by problematizing the notion of representation, and calling into question the adequacy of institutions of representative democracy in evolving even a minimal consensus on institutional secularism, let alone securing a more substantive normative endorsement for it.

The idea of representation draws our attention to a major problem inherent in making democracy receptive to the claims of communities, rather than confining it to the customary claims to representation on the basis of individual rights. The lack of institutional mechanisms for determining the authentic community voice is, in the present case, complicated by the further difficulty of discovering the authentic voice of the Muslim woman citizen, and of determining whether this voice, when it speaks as one with the community voice (but apparently at the expense of the material interests of Muslim women) should be privileged over the latter. This generates an additional problem for democracy, viz., the question of democratic citizenship in situations in which it is possible to construct more than one identity on behalf of the same 'community'. In our case, the religious and gender identities of the Muslim woman citizen were counterposed to each other. However the choice of which identity should be politically privileged as the critical criterion of collective self-definition is not an easy one. The search for a substantive conception of democracy must necessarily therefore encompass a search for ways of rendering compatible conflicting identities, without the effacement of either.

II

Going beyond the minority rights *versus* majoritarian democracy formulation, we may recast the controversy around the judgement in terms of the tension between the claim of rights for cultural communities *versus* the claim of women's rights of equal citizenship, underpinned by essentially liberal-individualist assumptions. Viewing this as an issue of community claims can yield both a conservative and non-conservative argument. The conservative position was argued by the religious leadership of the Muslim community at the time of the formulation of the Bill. The non-conservative position that may follow from the assertion of community has been spelt out in some recent writings on secularism which, it is held, mandates the giving of 'participatory negotiating voice to the different communal interests' in the creation of a consensus on this value (Bilgrami, 1994: 1755). On such a view, the Rajiv Gandhi government's consultation of the *ulama* in the formulation of the Bill would be at best inadequate and at worst objectionable precisely because the *ulama* are assumed not to be authentic representatives of the Muslim community. On this account, then, heeding the un-representative voice of the community leadership cannot advance the secular ideal, while hearing community voices not only does so, it also provides the foundations of genuine or 'substantive' secularism.

The view of secularism as being properly rooted in an adequate recognition of community voices may be seen to be, for all its eclectic attractiveness, problematical on three counts:

- the institutional problem of representation: how do we discover the authentic voice of a community? If, in the case at hand the *ulama* are no acceptable representatives of Muslims where is this voice to be found? Are there institutional mechanisms to discover it, and, if not, is it possible to devise such institutions?
- the problem of the hegemony of a community leadership, and the possibility of such leadership not allowing for internal dissent or questioning of community norms; as also the possibility of oppressive and, in this case, patriarchal, social practices internal to the community.
- the problem of women's rights: suppose, even hypothetically, that an authentic community voice was hostile to or dis-approved of gender equality, and indeed believed it to be violative of the norms of the community. Would the state be obliged to heed it? Would the average citizen be obliged to hedge her/his belief in gender equality accordingly?

On the other hand, viewing the Shah Bano issue as one of gender justice implies approaching it from an essentially liberal-individualist perspective. The consequences of this view—asserting claims expressed in terms of women's rights—for secularism are that religious affiliation and minority status are deemed irrelevant to certain fundamental rights, in this case, the claims of gender justice and the equal rights of citizenship. While this second perspective is self-evidently and emphatically a rights-based one, even the first view (secularism based on an adequate recognition of community voices) does not altogether eschew rights-claims. Indeed, it may be seen to be arguing for a recognition of communities, rather than individuals, as agents or bearers of rights. That this category of rights-claims may be detrimental to or diminishing of certain categories of individual rights is an unavoidable consequence of this position. Where the rights of minorities as cultural communities are to be weighed in the balance against the rights of women belonging to that minority, the problem is rendered more complex. There are difficulties in upholding the right of a community to practise certain rituals or forms of worship which impinge on the rights of others, or are seriously repugnant or offensive to them. But the difficulties are manifestly greater in situations where the conflict remains internal to the community, insofar as the community leadership's claim to certain cultural rights may adversely affect, rather than advance, the interests of some of its own members.

This perspective also entails some contradictions. First there is the institutional problem of representation: how may we discover what Muslim women really want? Can we assume that all Muslim women are united in their opinion? Is there any way of knowing how many Muslim women actually endorsed the judgement or the Bill? Is it desirable that Muslim women should themselves decide whether their minority identity should be privileged or their position as women, whether they would rather have a separate personal law and no maintenance allowance, or maintenance and no separate civil code? Is it possible or desirable to allow the female voice of the community to speak independently of—even if to the same effect as—the community voice? For instance suppose many Muslim women believed—in line with Shah Bano's own recantation—that the protection of minority identity was more important than maintenance, could advocates of women's rights legitimately force them to accept maintenance and give up on minority identity? There is also the problem of how to accommodate the minority status of women and assimilate it to their position as women.

The deep contradiction between these two positions is resolved if and only if we can unambiguously claim that the genuine community voice is supportive of women's rights and that this voice is discoverable by some known or devisable procedure. If these two distinct, but linked, claims cannot be asserted, sustained or proved, we are left with our original paradox. Thus, those who advance the thesis of cultural communities as self-determining and self-authenticating sources of rights-claims have to insure every vulnerable—in this case, female—member of the community against the possible effects of patriarchal hegemony. The burden of proving the authenticity of the community voice also rests upon them. On the other hand, advocates of women's rights need to be sensitized to the claims of cultural identity. The tension between these two positions clearly encompasses one critical area common to both, viz., the problem of adequate and authentic representation. The next section of this paper briefly discusses varying usages of the concept of representation, before proceeding to examine the deployment of this concept in the debate on the Muslim Women (Protection of Rights on Divorce) Bill.

III

'The benefits of the representative system,' said James Mill, 'are lost in all cases in which the interests of the choosing body are not the same with those of the community.' Did the political contention around the Muslim Womens' Bill express a situation of this nature? The textbook account of representation suggests at least three senses in which the concept may be, and has been, used. Following Birch, we may identify these three 'logically distinct' usages as:

(a) *Delegated representation*, which denotes an agent or spokesman who acts on behalf of his principal, e.g. a sales representative or an ambassador.

(b) *Microcosmic representation*, in which a person shares some of the characteristics of a class of persons, e.g. a representative sample, which suggests that the main characteristics of a population are mirrored in the sample; or an assembly, which reflects the social composition of a nation.

(c) *Symbolic representation*, in which a person symbolizes the identity or qualities of a class of a persons, e.g. Adam as the symbolic representative of all mankind (Birch, 1971, p. 39).

Historically, in the liberal tradition, the role of the elected political representative has been conceptualized in two ways: first, in accordance with the Whig theory of representation, the idea of the elected representative as an independent maker of national policies, obliged to consult only his own judgement and not, on every issue, the wishes of his constituents. This position has been most famously defended in Edmund Burke's Address to the Electors of Bristol in 1774. The second conception, expressed in the ideas of the Levellers, is underpinned by a radical notion of popular sovereignty, and sees the political representative as an agent sent to Parliament by his electors to give or withhold *their* consent to measures of taxation and legislation proposed by the executive.

It has often been argued that the adoption, by independent India, of Western liberal representative institutions, though based upon the assumption of the rational self-interested citizen, actually created spaces, within these derivative political forms, for the furtherance of interests based on traditional social divisions, such as caste and religion (Rudolph and Rudolph, 1967; and, more recently, Khilnani, 1993). What these arguments ignore is the fact that these supposedly new political forms had already been in existence for some considerable time, and in a form adapted to the colonial perception of Indian social reality, as well as colonial categories of its representation, viz., the division of the Indian electorate (itself a limited category) on the basis of religion through the institution of separate or communal electorates. These electorates could be seen to be appealing to the microcosmic idea of representation, though this in no way commits us to the assumption that separate electorates are the only or even the best way of achieving microcosmic representation. After independence, however, elected delegated representation became the dominant mode, with a few notable exceptions such as the two reserved seats for Anglo-Indians in the Lok Sabha, which could be interpreted as forms of symbolic representation. The shift from microcosmic to delegated representation, in turn, became possible precisely because the creation of Pakistan was perceived to be the fulfilment of the microcosmic ideal.

The Islamic critique of principles of liberal representation, based on majority rule and shifting political loyalties, has been persuasively documented by Farzana Shaikh in her study of Muslim politics in colonial India, and the construction of a case for Pakistan on the ideological divide between Muslims and non-Muslims. This critique, which provided the rationale for the claim to separate electorates towards the end of the nineteenth century, is explained by reference to the alienness of the Western liberal notion of individual political autonomy to the normative framework of Islam (Shaikh, 1991). Indeed, the main elements of this critique may be seen implicitly to continue to furnish the chief challenge of heterogeneous societies to liberal democratic institutions, though these manifestly do not form a part of even Muslim members' opinions in the parliamentary debate on the Muslim Womens' Bill in 1986. It is possible to identify, in this debate, five strands of argument about representative majoritarian democracy, the first two of which pertain exclusively to majoritarianism as a procedural principle.

(i) The first strand fuels the argument of parliamentary competence to legislate to counter the effect of the court's judgement. It seeks to privilege the legislature over the judiciary by pointing out that while judges are merely nominated/appointed, members of parliament are elected and therefore better placed to express the will of the people they represent. A sort of *carte blanche* mandate is here implied and asserted, with the theory of democratic representation serving to legitimate parliamentary action. There is also an implicit claim, by the government, of the power to enact law and make public policy, while the judiciary should remain confined to the tasks of enforcement. Underlying this claim, of course, is the idea of the state as the embodiment of the common interest. Regardless of the substance of the legislation, or of the extent to which it upolds the principles of rights or equality or justice, on this interpretation of democracy, it is the representativeness of the legislature that is the sole determinant of the legitimacy of its actions.

Thus Syed Shahabuddin of the Janata Party argued that the court's judgement had triggered off a hostile reaction because it contained unworthy remarks against Islam; made a gratuitous observation about the desirability of a common civil code; interpreted the relationship between Sections 125 and 127 (3) (b) of the Criminal Procedure Code in a manner that contradicted the intent of Parliament as expressed in 1973; and took it upon itself to interpret holy scriptures. He supported the Bill, he said, because 'the Bill places beyond challenge the legitimacy, the legal supremacy, the constitutional supremacy of Parliament of India to legislate on matters of concern to the Muslim community as a religious community beyond all doubt (*Lok Sabha Debates*, 5.5.1986, p. 503).

(ii) The argument of parliamentary sovereignty was reinforced by the assertion of a second (and vulgar) type of majoritarian argument, invoking the notion of majority as a procedural rule for decision-making within the legislature. This most common—though usually unstated—usage of the majority principle is evident in the following statement by the Lok Sabha Speaker: '. . . this is a democracy. It is a question of whose will prevail [sic] and the will of the majority will prevail, and the will of those who get the backing will prevail' (ibid., p. 308).

(iii) The third type of majoritarian argument draws upon the identification between the state and the majority community, and prescribes legislative restraint in the matter of the personal law of minorities. The sanctity of Muslim personal law is established by reference to historical precedent—viz., the debate in the Constituent Assembly and the promises made by the Congress Party under Indira and Rajiv Gandhi—as well as by reference to the insecurity and alienation of the minority community, and its perception of threat to its religious and cultural identity. The government, in projecting itself as the protector of Muslim minority rights, implicitly identified itself with the majority community. There is a strong underlying strain of argument in the 'us' and 'them' mode, 'they' being seen as in need of protection, guarantees and safeguards provided by 'us'. This identification is embarrassingly sharp in the speech of minister K.C. Pant:

Gandhiji, Panditji and all the others, have repeatedly emphasized that every minority has a guarantee that it could conduct its own affairs; it could have its own way of life; preserve its own cultural identity, have full freedom to practice its religions and so on. We are familiar with this and have taught tolerance to the majority. After all, the majority has a certain duty in this matter. The majority if it is not sensitive to the needs of the minority can steamroller sometimes the view of the minority. . . .

. . . I think we have to be sensitive to the fact that since they are in minority we have all to be very careful that this House does not steam-roller. . . . (ibid., pp. 389-90)

The sudden switch from the majority identified as an impersonal 'it', in the first paragraph, to the more personal 'we' in the second, is notable, as is the corresponding shift in the description of the minority from the neutral 'it' to 'they'. The legislation was thus defended on the grounds that 'they' felt threatened by the Supreme Court judgement, which they feared imperilled their basic right to profess and practice religion. The conception of secularism implied in this debate is clearly one that presupposes that the majority is doing the legislating, while the minority is in a position of being legislated for, or even possibly against.

(iv) The fourth argument, apparently considered most persuasive by the advocates of the Bill, centered around the wishes of Muslims. It is perhaps ironical that various Congress speakers, including several ministers, repeatedly sought to establish the legitimacy of the Bill by citing the percentage of Muslims who, in their estimation, supported it. This majority was held up as the acid test of the Bill's acceptability. A derivative argument was that the so-called progressive and liberal members of the Muslim intelligentsia who had petitioned the prime minister against the Bill, were a mere minority in the Muslim community, the exception rather than the rule. Thus when members of the opposition asked the government whether it had consulted all Muslims, the government spokesmen clung to the prime minister's statement that 90 per cent of the Muslims were supporting the Bill. Some Congressmen even upped this figure to 99 per cent leading the Opposition benches to demand a referendum of Muslim women on this issue (Saifuddin Chowdhary, *Lok Sabha Debates*, 5.5.86, p. 363). Members tried to establish support for the Bill numerically, by resorting to a variety of indicators: Tariq Anwar said that had the Bill been supported by only 10 per cent of Muslims this Bill would not have been brought forth, and the fact that it had showed that 90 per cent Muslims were in favour of it (ibid., p. 467); Santosh Mohan Deb, who had recently won the election in Silchar, Assam claimed that as 80 per cent of the Muslim voters in his constituency voted for him and the Congress in an election where the Bill was an issue, they clearly supported it (ibid., p. 483). Meanwhile Indrajit Gupta asked the government if it had corresponding figures for Muslim sentiments on the Babri Masjid, and if 99 per cent of them were exercised about that issue, why the government had not acted on it (ibid., p. 605).

In the Rajya Sabha, P.V. Narasimha Rao, Minister of Home Affairs, put the government's case as baldly and preposterously as possible:

We happen to be in charge of the Government. We happen to be the body which has to make an assessment of the situation. We have made it. You have every right to differ. You may say 90 per cent of the Muslims don't want this Bill, but only 5 per cent want it. Whether it is 95 per cent or 5 per cent it is up to you.

. . . We stick to our assessments. There is no question of your arithmetic changing ours. Only time will show. Maybe a time will come when it will be possible for us to verify in a more verifiable manner what the Muslim opinion in this country thinks about this Bill, but at the moment, we are convinced, this party is convinced, this Government is convinced that an overwhelming [sic] Muslims are for this Bill. (*Lok Sabha Debates*, 8.5.86, pp. 420-1)

(v) The opinion of those who would be directly affected by the legislation is barely mentioned, except by the Opposition. Clearly, if the government was at all seized of the question of minority rights it was concerned exclusively to protect male minority rights. Muslim women—divorced or otherwise—are clearly a minority within a minority, and as such too miniscule to be entitled to a solicitation of its opinion by the government. One sympathizer of the Bill expressed this starkly in the Rajya Sabha, when he said that the press and public figures had become so 'obsessed' with this issue.

that one would think that India's population consists mainly of Muslim women...that too divorced women and that India had no greater problem to solve than this. Sir, as a matter of fact, the Muslim population is 12 per cent. Of them children and adolescents form 6 per cent. Then males are 3 per cent and females another 3 per cent. Among them married women will be 1 per cent and the divorced will be .001 per cent, a miniscule minority within the minority . . . there are far more serious problems involving millions of Indian women, both Muslim as well as non-Muslim. (*Rajya Sabha Debates*, 8.5.86, p. 329)

While the opposition asked why the government chose to disregard the views of 'those educated Muslim women who demonstrated in the streets of various capitals' (P. Upendra, ibid., p. 379), the government remained firm in its resolve, with C.K. Jaffer Sharief exhorting his fellow-members to not look merely to the Muslim women, but to the Muslim minority as a whole 'which needs your moral support today' (*Lok Sabha Debates*, 5.5.86, pp. 373-4).

These five versions of the majoritarian principle serve to under-write its validity both as a procedural rule for decision-making and as a normative principle, at times justifying the overriding of minorities if they are numerically insignificant or powerless, and at other times justifying their 'protection'. At the same time, many of the statements in the debate contain a tacit admission of the idea that if the satisfaction of minority opinion can be useful in securing ballot paper endorsements, then it is perfectly legitimate to do so.

Thus, even though it is the promise of the legislation, situated in a certain political rhetoric, that is used to garner votes, success in elections is taken to signify its popularity and wide acceptability.

The minoritarian argument is much less layered and complex. The first strand in this is the familiar one which sees minority identity as endangered. Not surprisingly, this argument was also enthusiastically advanced by Hindu Congressmen, who emphasized the need to provide 'protection' for minority identity defined in religious or cultural terms. The government saw its role as one of providing conditions for the safeguarding of culture, religion and tradition, asserting that the impetus for change, if any, must come from within the Muslim community and be initiated by it.

The second important strand in the minoritarian discourse was the idea, frequently expressed, of the authenticity of the representative voice. Several Muslim members argued that *Shariat* law is sacred, and not everyone is competent to speak, much less to legislate, on it, thus implying some rejection of the principles of representative democracy. The government also on occasion adopted this discourse, as when the Law Minister A.K. Sen, introducing the Bill, said, 'When we hear all the representatives of the Muslim community on the floor of the House' (*Lok Sabha Debates*, 5.5.86, p. 318), and was swiftly countered by Saifuddin Chowdhary: 'How can he say this? Nobody is a Hindu representative or a Muslim representative in this House. . . . He is communalizing the whole country' (ibid.).

It is not a little ironical that those who expressed minoritarian views of this nature were also expressly supporting the Bill, even as its chief initiators and defenders in the Congress Party used a complex majoritarian discourse to ensure its passage. Thus, the theory of representative democracy provides: (a) the grounds from which the legislative competence of parliament and its priority over judicial interpretation are established; (b) the grounds on which the procedural correctness of the legislation—as supported by a majority of members of both chambers, as well as by an alleged majority of Muslims outside—is established; and (c) the ground from which questions are raised about the authenticity of representatives, and of who is entitled to speak on the issue. At one level, all these arguments belong with the Ayes on the Bill. But, at another level, they signify a deep contradiction within the ranks of the Ayes: between the Congress politicians who would endorse (a) and (b), but much less (c); and conservative Muslim leaders who would support (c) remain ambivalent on (b) and reject (a). Thus the same theory of representative democracy ordains and justifies and enactment of the Muslim Womens' Bill from a majoritarian perspective, and subverts the notion of undifferentiated representation from a minoritarian perspective.

The minoritarian argument in the public (as distinct from parliamentary) debate on the Bill also addresses itself to the vexed question of representation. We find here a much greater acceptance of the principle of liberal representation among Muslim leaders than Shaikh's account of colonial India suggests. The writings of Syed Shahabuddin, Member of Parliament and Editor of the monthly magazine *Muslim India*, provide an influential though perhaps not strictly representative, view of this kind. In 1985-6, Shahabudin made extensive editorial comment on the judgement and the Bill, arguing that the Supreme Court had transgressed permissible limits and interfered with Muslim personal law. In doing so, it had set itself up as a 'super legislature, or a third chamber of the legislature' (*Muslim India*, May 1985). Its constitutional mandate, however, was to interpret the Constitution and not the Holy Koran. It was for the Muslim community to reform itself on the question of maintenance and such reform is consonant with religious texts. In this task, Muslim Indians needed leadership, distinct from the national leadership, which they could trust.

Addressing himself to the Burkean question of whom the Muslim legislator represents—the people of his constituency, the people of his religious community, or the nation as a whole—Shahabuddin argues

a Muslim legislator also represents the Muslim community. He acts as a channel of communication between the community and the system. . . . When he promises to carry the legitimate and felt grievances to the powers-that-be, he builds up the confidence that justice will be done. The Muslim Legislator is thus both an advocate of the community and a pillar of the system. With his presence in the corridors of power, he is the agent of History for bridging the psychological gap that still exists between the community and the administration. (*Muslim India*, July 1985)

On the eve of a national convention of Muslim legislators, he suggested ways of institutionalizing these ideas:

Time has come to institutionalize such democratic processes in order to discover what a social group wants, to moderate its demands, to balance its perceptions, to determine what is feasible and then to engage the system to implement what is feasible. It would be a glorious day if in every legislature, by convention, if not by regulation, the Muslim legislators—cutting across party lines—would meet in order to render advice on a matter of interest or on a problem the community faces. (ibid.)

These arguments have two significant implications: first that the question of representing community interest cannot be left to the undifferentiated representative institutions of democracy, viz., political parties and legislatures; and, second, that the community is defined as an internally coherent monolith, presumed to be devoid of differences of opinion, much less differences of interest such as those generated by gender inequalities.

While Muslim leadership in India has shown itself to be flexible on some matters, it has been much less inclined to review the women's question. Thus, while the theological validity of the oral triple *talaq* had remained a contentious issue, 55 leading theologians of different schools collectively decided in 1992 that the grave damage caused by communal riots warranted a reinterpretation and modification of the *Shariat*, such that Muslims could be permitted to insure their persons and property. Four years earlier, the process of *ijtehad* (interpretation of the *Sharia*) was revived on the grounds that *Shariat* law lacked the dynamism essential for any jurisprudence. The recognition of the importance of modern science and the consequent legalizing of organ transplants as well as the recognition of earnings in the form of *pagri* followed.

The opponents of the Bill use the theory of representation differently. They point to the unrepresentativeness of government opinion arguing that it is undemocratic insofar as it disregards the wishes of most of many or some of the Muslims who disapprove of the Bill, and takes into account only the approval of the conservative or affluent and male sections of Muslim society. They also suggest a referendum of those affected, again implying that electoral procedures of representation are insufficient and unreliable guarantors of democracy. They point to the forthcoming elections in Kerala, West Bengal and Jammu and Kashmir—all with sizeable Muslim populations—as keys to understanding the haste with which this legislation was passed. The by-elections in Bihar, Assam and elsewhere had already established the electoral efficacy of the Bill in no uncertain terms.

IV

The preceding pages have argued that the problem of representation, both as discourse and practice, is a critical though long neglected area in the debate on secularism. Though two categories of questions about representation have been identified, viz., representation of community voices and representation of affected interests, in this case women, only the first category of questions has been dealt with so far. To return briefly to the argument in the first section of the paper, the assertion of community rights refutes the liberal conception of individual citizens as the sole legitimate subject of rights, and advances instead the claim that collective entities such as culturally homogeneous communities are entitled to rights, too. It is a well-worn dilemma of communitarian arguments that romanticizing the community can undermine the sovereignty of its individual constituents as self-defining and self-determining subjects, possessing consciousness and agency, resurrecting in its place the autonomy of collective entities based on common descent or other cultural attributes of an heritable nature.

In the present case, as the Muslim woman's community identity is privileged over her identity as a citizen, there is a filter of community control through which alone she has access to the state, and that access is further restricted by the state's self-limiting assumption of the role of a mere arbiter in determining who shall be responsible, and in what measure, for the care of a divorced Muslim woman. In the absence of a reformed divorce law, women are unequal *vis-a-vis* men and vulnerable to unilateral divorce; they are also now rendered unequal *vis-a-vis* other women who have recourse to the law in respect of maintenance. Through this legislation, the primacy of cultural/community rights over political/citizenship rights is endorsed and the state willingly circumscribes its own domain by editing even its criminal legislation so as to exclude some citizens from rights uniformly available to others. It withdraws its telluric laws to make way for those of ecclesiastical origins, in a gesture that is portentous, a dangerous precedent.

This debate about the rival identities of gender and religion also challenges standard ways of thinking about democracy and citizenship. Multiple identities are, as caricatured in Benjamin Barber's 'portrait in pieces', of the man whose 'life is splintered into quarters and fifths' (1984, p. 208) a fact of modern societies, and political sociology draws professional sustenance from exploring the relationships between such identities, in particular those of class, sex and race. What is notable, however, is that these are frequently overlapping, rather than conflicting, identities. Thus, the oppression of a female black worker in an advanced capitalist society stems from different, but mutually reinforcing social structures of patriarchy, race and class. Here, on the other hand, we have a case where identities which, not altogether but in certain critical respects, conflict with each other. The Muslim female citizen is disadvantaged both as a member of a minority religion and as a woman. The source of her oppression—material as well as ideological—may also on occasion be mutually reinforcing, as when the state and patriarchy act *in tandem*. But there is a third dimension yet to her oppression. Her membership of a religious minority renders her simultaneously vulnerable as a Muslim (in a predominantly Hindu society and in relation to the state) and as a woman (*vis-a-vis* the state and Muslim men). Ironically, it is the realization of the community's project of obtaining recognition for its cultural rights and the securing of legal safeguards for these, that compounds her vulnerability. But must her emancipation as a woman be necessarily contingent upon her disengagement from her religious community affiliations? What implications does this have for the theory of democratic citizenship?

The secular project cannot merely be a negative project of state abstinence, or even simply a positive project of proselytizing toleration in society. It must also necessarily be a project of democratic citizenship, to achieve which may involve transcending the existing framework of representative institutions and abandoning the search within these for a space for secular practices in both state and society. There is a need for a procedural consensus by which to establish the value of secularism as a social and political goal for every citizen, and by which to determine an acceptable content for it. Minorities, being disadvantaged, have a greater stake in a secular framework, and therefore need to have a greater say in mandating both the value and the content of this goal.

A secular society may be difficult to achieve unless it is under-written and accompanied by two requirements of democratic citizenship:

- the requirement of uniform conditions of citizenship, i.e the necessity of generating a procedural consensus, including a consensus on principles of representation.

- the requirement of the equal rights of citizenship, which requires that community voices be rendered receptive to the goal of gender equality (and any other kind of equality necessary for the equal rights of citizenship to be effectuated) or else that gender questions be removed from all community agendas.

Securing the uniform conditions of citizenship and guaranteeing equal rights of citizenship could arguably limit and circumscribe the potential of non-secular agenda, and possibly even serve to delegitimise it. In the Western context, feminists have influentially advanced the claim that the liberal theory of citizenship is flawed, being premised upon the liberal separation between the public and the private realm. Men and women, it is argued, are incorporated into citizenship on a differential basis, and 'membership of the political community is itself profoundly gendered' (Phillips, 1993, p. 108). Hence the suggestion for finding mechanisms for giving voice to women through policies akin to affirmative action, even if for a transitional period, until the conditions of full and equal citizenship are achievable (Young, 1993).

In the Indian case, any proposal for representative mechanisms which recognize gender differences and seek to redress gender inequalities, is bound to come into conflict with the rival claims of cultural community. A political sensibility which is willing to endorse the claims to rights of such communities has to prepare itself to meet the challenge of gender injustice and inequality, especially if the latter is interpreted as a core component of the community's way of defining itself, or the symbolic objective of its search for protection.

A Rawlsian solution, such as an overlapping consensus, may be able to suggest ways in which people subscribing to different religious and philosophical doctrines can coexist in a plural polity (Rawls, 1993). But it has little to offer when relations of domination and power between men and women of the same religion are justified by invoking cultural community norms, and seeking political recognition for the inequalities so engendered. The problem is how to arrive at a conception of democratic citizenship that (a) provides sufficient space for the articulation of both (and more) kinds of identities without securing one at the expense of the other, and/or (b) ensures that the expression and recognition of neither identity is subversive of the principles of equality and justice. Such an emphasis on the equal rights of citizenship should eventually mandate the removal of gender questions from all community agendas.

It has been argued that whenever communities have asserted collective cultural rights, these have been backed by popular consent through democratic processes (Chatterjee, 1994). It is, however perfectly possible that on questions like gender, patriarchal practices might be endorsed even with 'democratic' consent. The experience of women in the erstwhile socialist societies has established quite clearly the fact that even within an egalitarian ideological framework, gender inequalities tend to persist. That being so, how can religious communities—generally known to be conservative with respect to the position of women—be reasonably expected to allow the women's question and family law to be taken off their agenda, more so if these are perceived to be inextricably linked with the markers of their cultural identity?

Presently, the privileging of community identity over gender identity and its protection in law fails to secure for Muslim women their constitutionally guaranteed equal rights of citizenship. These rights have, with disconcerting ease, been formally abridged, and call for restoration. If it is recognized that the articulation of diverse identities can contribute to the expansion of democracy, but can also be detrimental to it, it is not undemocratic to speak of a polity or society where space for plurality is created and guaranteed while at the same time defining, delimiting and reserving a core democratic space which is non-negotiable. Such a core would necessarily have to be insulated from rights-claims, whether or not these are identity-based, or at least be indifferent to them. But it would have to provide justifiable criteria against which such claims could be tested. Thus, for instance, new claims to rights would be admitted if found to be consistent with the democratic core, but rejected if incompatible with it. Likewise, diverse identities would be not merely tolerated, but encouraged, respected and recognized if they passed the same test. While different societies would need to specify the democratic core differently, in the Indian context, gender justice would clearly have to form a part of such a non-negotiable core, and the claims of religious identity would be expected to respect the democratic project. An institutional framework for secularism might then be in place, possibly rendering easier the task of arriving at a societal consensus on its value as a social and political objective.

REFERENCES

Barber, Benjamin, *Strong Democracy* (Berkeley, 1984).

Bhargava, Rajeev, 'Giving Secularism Its Due', in *Economic and Political Weekly*, vol. XXIX, no. 28. 9 July 1994.

Bilgrami, Akeel, 'Two Concepts of Secularism: Reason, Modernity and the Archimedean Ideal', in *Economic and Political Weekly*, vol. XXIX, no. 28, 9 July 1994.

Birch, A.H., *Representation* (London, 1971).

Chatterjee, Partha, 'Secularism and Toleration', in *Economic and Political Weekly*, vol. XXIX, no. 28, 9 July 1994.

Dworkin, Ronald, *Taking Rights Seriously* (London, 1977).

Khilnani, Sunil, 'India's Democratic Career', in John Dunn (ed.), *Democracy: The Unfinished Journey* (New Delhi, 1993).

————— *Muslim India* (New Delhi, 1985-6).

Phillips, Anne, *Democracy and Difference* (Oxford, 1993).

Rawls, John, *Political Liberalism* (New York, 1993).

Rudolph, L.I. and S.H. Rudolph, *The Modernity of Tradition* (Chicago, 1967).

Shaikh, Farzana, *Community and Consensus in Islam: Muslim Representation in Colonial India 1860-1947* (New Delhi, 1991).

Young, Iris Marion, *Justice and the Politics of Difference* (Princeton, N.J., 1990).

Parliamentary Debates: Lok Sabha and Rajya Sabha (1985-6).

All India Reporter of the Supreme Court of India (1985).

On the Nature of Muslim Political Responses: Islamic Militancy in the North-West Frontier Province

DIETRICH REETZ

When talking about Islamic militancy on the north-west frontier,[1] the objective is to understand the conceptual framework by which movements coming under this description were driven. Muslim militancy in the frontier can provide clues to understanding the mechanism of the fusion of politics and religion within Islam, or, more specific, within South Asian Islam. This paper is an attempt to look closer at the pretension of Islamic movements of harbouring a radically and fundamentally different world-view, to see how their Islamic ideals fared when confronted with Western political concepts and with local power considerations. Since the problem is relevant even today, it may provide some insights into how Islamic religious injunctions are reconciled with the need to adapt to Western political concepts. The latter prevailed at the time in India through colonial domination and continue to dominate the political discourse in Islamic countries today.

There has been no extensive research on the specific political views and concepts of regional Islamic movements. The north-west frontier region comprised the North-West Frontier Province belonging to British India, carved out of the Punjab in 1900, and the independent tribal territories ruled directly through the chief commissioner of the Frontier Province on behalf of the Government of India. Frontier politics in the north-west have so far mainly been described within the framework of the Pathan movement under Abdul Ghaffar Khan (1890-1988), the so-called Red Shirt movement which started out as the Khudai Khidmatgaran, or Servants of God, doing social service in the countryside. Other researches are focused on frontier politics as part of the Pakistan movement. Thus, frontier politics have been mainly treated in the perspective of the two

---

[1] An earlier version of the paper was contributed to the 14th European Conference on Modern South Asian Studies at Copenhagen on 21-4 Aug. 1996.

dominating discourses of (1) the nationalist Congress movement, with which the Red Shirts were aligned,[2] and (2) the Pakistan movement, led by the Muslim League.[3] While there has been research on local Islamic traditions of the frontier, the political implications of local Islam have rarely been discussed. It is assumed that mainstream politics on the north-west frontier of the 1930s and 1940s, which have been widely covered by researchers, originated from that kind of local political mobilization, an important part of which was the Islamic discourse.

Most of the case studies conducted provide little more than an assemblage of random facts on the movements covered by this paper. They often lack in clarity and concept as far as political consequences or historical meanings are concerned. Attempts are also made to appropriate these movements exclusively either for doctrinal Islamic traditions or for a separate Muslim liberation movement, leading up to the creation of Pakistan. This is typical of the studies on the *mujahidin* where another drawback is also that, except the article by Lal Baha, they do not shed light on the twentieth century.[4] On the 1920 *hijrat*, an unpublished dissertation written at Peshawar University, Pakistan, treats the subject strictly within the parameters of an Islamic ideology framework.[5] The same is true of a number of articles on the *hijrat* that cover only selected aspects of the phenomenon.[6] A recent monograph by this author limits itself to one British file from the India Office Library, though within a more

[2] Stephen Rittenberg, *Ethnicity, Nationalism, and the Pakhtuns: The Independence Movement in India's North-West Frontier Province* (Durham, N.C., 1988); E. Jansson, *India, Pakistan or Pakhtunistan? The Nationalist Movements in the North-West-Frontier Province, 1937-47* (Acta Universitatis Upsaliensis Studia Histokrica Upsalilensia, 119) (Uppsala, 1981).

[3] Ian Talbot, *Provincial Politics and the Pakistan Movement* (Karachi, 1990).

[4] On the *mujahidin* movement, see Qeyamuddin Ahmad, *The Wahhabi Movement in India* (Calcutta, 1966); Lal Baha, 'The Activities of the *Mujahidin* 1900-1936', in *Islamic Studies*, 18 (1979), pp. 97-168; Maulana Ghulam Rasul Mehr, *Jama'at-i-mujahidin* (Lahore, 1955); N.D. Ahmad, 'Mujahidin-Triumph of the British diplomacy', in *Journal of the Research Society of Pakistan*, 12, iii (1975), pp. 33-45.

[5] Noshad Khan, *The Khilafatists 'Hijrat to Afghanistan* (unpublished Ph.D. thesis, University of Peshawar, 1995), p. 282.

[6] F.S. Briggs, 'The Indian Hijrat of 1920', in *Moslem World,* 20 (Princeton, N.J., 1930), pp. 164-8; Lal Baha, 'The Hijrat movement and the North-West Frontier Province', in *Islamic Studies* 18 (Islamabad, 1979), pp. 231-42; M. Naeem Qureshi, 'The Ulema of British India and the Hijrat of 1920', in *Modern Asian Studies,* 13 (1979), pp. 41-59.

comprehensive regional framework.[7] Little is available on the 'provisional government' at present. It is usually mentioned in passing.[8] Activities of militant *mullahs* on the frontier have not been politically conceptualized so far. They have either been mentioned in reports and writings on tribal uprisings,[9] or in anthropological studies of Muslim customs in the frontier region.

I

Conceptually, the question arises if Indian Muslims had a political concept of their own sufficiently different from mainstream nationalism to merit a special distinction. It would be illuminating to understand to the extent to which they produced indigenous concepts of political power, authority and society and how these were linked to classical political concepts of the time. Islamic movements were trying to position themselves within a triangular reference scheme of (1) the Islamic doctrine, (2) the Western constitutional reforms project pursued by colonial British Government in India, and (3) the nationalist movement led by Gandhi and Jawaharlal Nehru from the Indian National Congress, with the latter through Gandhi substantially drawing on Hindu ethics and

[7] D. Reetz, *Hijrat—The Flight of the Faithful: A British File on the Exodus of Muslim Peasants from North India to Afghanistan in 1920*. (Förderungsgesellschaft Wiss. Neuvorhaben mbH, FSP Moderner Orient, Arbeitshfte, 5) (Berlin, 1995), p. 140. It is being revised and extended for re-edition at present.

[8] See note by the Criminal Investigation Department, later published in book form by the author of the note: P.C. Bamford, *Histories of the Non-cooperation and Khilafat Movements* (Delhi, 1925). Cf. also Sir Cecil Kaye, *Communism in India: With Unpublished Documents From National Archives of India (1919-1924)*, compiled and edited by Sobodh Roy (Calcutta, 1971), p. 384, although this note discusses M.N. Roy mainly as founder of the Communist Party of India. Recent historical studies add more details: from a leftist, Marxist perspective, see Ashok Kumar Patnaik, *The Soviets and the Indian Revolutionary Movement, 1917-1929* (Delhi, 1992), p. 345; and Shashi Bairathi, *Communism and Nationalism in India* (Delhi, 1987), p. 248.

[9] A typical example is by Akbar S. Ahmed, *Religion and Politics in Muslim Society* (Cambridge, 1983) on the controversial *mullah* in Wana, Waziristan, which mentions historical antecedents only briefly and concentrates on the post-Independence history of the area. For Ahmed, history and conflict of this kind in the tribal belt, in keeping with his anthropological training, is mainly *agnatic rivalry* which has to be sorted out in order to be solved. See also his 1978 dissertation published as *Pakhtun Economy and Society: Traditional Structure and Economic Development in a Tribal Society* (London, 1980).

Unitarian religious beliefs. The British-sponsored political projects aimed at the slow but gradual and steady process of introducing parliamentarian constitutional reforms increasing a certain measure of self-rule and popularly elected local government. The reality of the Indian constitutional reforms in terms of limitations and conditions imposed upon India fell considerably short of the radical demands of Indian nationalists who wanted a fully responsible government elected by a parliament based on adult franchise. The Acts of 1919 and 1935 nevertheless broadened and strengthened Western political institutions and structures. Indian Muslims constituted the largest religious minority in India, comprising 21 per cent of the population. Their impact on political life and on society increased further by way of clustered settlement in certain areas where they constituted the majority, i.e. Punjab, the North-West Frontier Province and Bengal in British-India and Kashmir and Hyderabad among the larger principalities. However, centres of Islamic learning and culture were located in UP, the largest and most populous province until today, where Muslims made up a minority of 15 per cent.[10] Based on the comprehensive interpretation of Islam as *deen*, i.e. way of life, instead of the narrow approach as *mazhab* or religion, politics were supposed to form part of Islamic doctrine by implication. But it was not formulated as a concept on its own, as yet.

This changed with the concept of Muslim nationalism which assumed that all Muslims belonged to one separate nation, as did Bengalis or Indians in general. This concept presumed that the Muslim community in India would seek self-determination for very much the same reasons as the all-India nationalist movement fought for independence. The Muslims were seeking constitutional safe-guards against alleged domination by a non-Muslim statutory majority in elected bodies. Otherwise, goals and methods of policy-making were hardly different from secular nationalist movements. To demand a separate territory for this imagined Muslim nation was supposed to be the aim of the Pakistan movement when it demanded a homeland for Indian Muslims. It was led by the Muslim League founded in 1906 which had come to be a synonym for Muslim politics in pre-Independence India. The Pakistan movement was no doubt the major political movement of Indian Muslims both in terms

[10] Peter Hardy, *The Muslims of British India* (Cambridge, 1972).

of scope and resulting success and it has also been covered extensively by researchers.[11] However, from the point of view of Islamic doctrine, the Pakistan movement could only partially and in a very limited way be called an Islamic movement. It was conducted by the Muslim League, a political party which—beyond its Muslim subject members and its Muslim majority area concept—followed rather orthodox bourgeois political ends, that is power and control of legislatures and over the allocation of resources, for which it also employed fairly established political means. The Muslim League was a mainstream party which more or less strictly followed the example of the British parliamentarian system, complete with office-bearers and conventions, programmes and all the trimmings of Westminster-style democracy. In this respect it can hardly be considered representative of a particularly Islamic way of politics. In terms of size and influence before 1935 it also remained a small, so-called leader party, representing a certain élite. It broadened its support only after the rather disastrous outcome of the 1937 provincial elections in which it could not prove its claim to be a major spokesman of Indian Muslims.

To study specific Islamic responses, one may have to consider other parties and movements in order to discern a specific Islamic response to Western political categories. For purposes of this study, a movement or party will be considered to be Islamic which primarily was not founded to participate in a parliamentary system, whose aims were directly related to Islamic doctrine or the furtherance of Islamic belief.

Colonial India sported a great variety of Islamic parties and movements. As related to political identity, one could broadly distinguish four major groups:

(i) *Islamic mass activism* where a large number of Muslims showed more or less spontaneous responses to political challenges, like demonstrations, unrest, riots and where these responses were legitimized with reference to a threat to Islam. If organization proceeded these outbreaks it played the role of a trigger and was mostly eclipsed by the magnitude of the spontaneous mass response

---

[11] Ayesha Jalal, *The Sole Spokesman: Jinnah, the Muslim League and the Demand for Pakistan* (Cambridge, 1984); Mushirul Hasan, *Legacy of a Divided Nation: India's Muslims Since Independence* (London, 1997).

which often moved away from the original intention of the organizers. This category would perhaps include movements like the Indian Wahhabis or *mujahidin*, the Moplah rebellion of Muslim peasants on the west Indian Malabar coast in 1921, the Khilafat movement in the 1920s in support of the continued authority of the Turkish Khalifa, despite Turkey's defeat at the side of Germany in the First World War by Britain, the Frontier *hijrat*, being an exodus of Muslim peasants from the north-west frontier in 1920. Presumably, communal riots would also qualify for inclusion in this category.

(ii) *Institutional Islamic activism* centered around Islamic institutions of learning such as the Dar al-ulum, the religious seminary, in Deoband, of the Barelwi and of the Nadwa in Lucknow. They represented different doctrinal approaches when responding to political issues with reference to Islam. Their political influence and also their interest in politics, was often substantial. Building up a large cross-regional following, they wielded significant social and cultural influence with political implications. The Muslim University in Aligarh would qualify for inclusion in this category insofar as it also represented a distinct school of doctrinal thought which stood for a reconciliation of Islam with modern Western influences. Though being a university and not a seminary, teaching Islamic subjects was an important part of Aligarh's brief.

(iii) *Islamic sectarian and revival movements* usually wanted to restore some of the original meaning of the Koran and the *Hadis* within the Islamic practice. In a way, they were reform movements representing sort of purification drives inspired by Shah Waliullah and emphasized by the Deobandi school. Their political impact was mainly felt by implication, usually emphasizing one or the other element of the Islamic discourse which was then seized upon by more established political forces. For the purpose of self-definition and self-projection, they gave prominence to certain Islamic injunctions or institutions and their re-interpretation. These movements included the Ahl-i Hadith, the Ahrar, the Ahmadiyya, the Khaksar, and also the *Tabligh* and the *Tanzim* movements.

(iv) *Established Muslim political parties and mainstream movements* would then form a separate group characterized by their intention to participate in the elective institutions and processes for which they were often—but not always—founded. They mainly operated within the parameters of Muslim nationalism and its regional variations. These parties comprised the Muslim League, the Unionist Party in Punjab, the Red Shirts from the Frontier Province, the Bengal Peasants Party, Krishak Praja, and the Jammu & Kashmir Muslim Conference under Sheikh Abdullah.

The aforementioned definition of an authentic Islamic response to political challenges would imply that it was group (i) to (iii) from which such a response could be expected. While Muslim nationalists wanted to participate in the game but wanted to change the rules of the game in their favour, the first three groups were not constituted for this purpose. Yet, although they had not intended to play by the rules of the British game, they were forced to respond because the gradual introduction of popularly elected representation created a set of pressures which threatened to undermine the place of the Islamic and all traditional, non-political religious and cultural élites in society. Although their control over society had eroded, elected representation was going to put the seal on their demise. In order to retain their mostly local place of influence and importance they had to adapt to the new system. The purpose of the larger project is to show how they adapted to these circumstances and what responses they developed.

The movements which will be briefly discussed here in relation to the North-West Frontier Province belong to the first group, Islamic mass activism. The period covered is the 1920s, when these movements were at the height of their activities, leaving aside earlier peaks in the nineteenth century.

II

The twentieth century *mujahidin* in the Frontier area had taken their name, meaning holy warriors, from the Koran. They had survived from a nineteenth-century movement which contemporaries called the Indian Wahhabis. Yet, their link with Arabian Wahhabism was remote. The eighteenth-century Islamic scholar Shah Waliullah had been inspired by Wahhabi ideas to cleanse Islam and to free it from later accretions, to restore the central place of the Koran and the *Hadis* in the teachings and practice of Islam, although Indian Sunni Muslims and their reformers mostly continued to follow the Hanafi *fiqh* and not the Wahhabi rite. In this sense, the term Indian Wahhabis was a misnomer. But their idea of the purification of Islam proved a powerful influence, also with Sayyid Ahmad Shahid of Rai Bareilly who founded the *Mujahidin* movement. Their *jihad* activities started from 1826. Being also called the *Tariqa Mohammadiyya*, they wanted to follow the way of life of Mohammad the Prophet. They engaged first the Sikhs and later the British in military encounters, their form of *jihad*, by which they hoped to liberate their homeland from alien forces, though their strongholds were limited to relatively small areas in Punjab, on the north-western frontier and in Bengal. They were militarily defeated and many of their members were tried in the sequence 'Wahhabi trials' in the 1870s. Groups of activists withdrew into the Black Mountains in Mansehra subdivision, where they founded colonies in Smasta and later near Chamarkand in Bajaur. Since 1915 they were ruled by Amir Nimatullah of Smasta. In 1915 and 1916 they participated in local attacks on British positions. By the end of 1916 the Government of India decided to get tough on the *mujahidin*, keeping in mind the ongoing war with Germany and Turkey both of which exploited the special relationship they supposedly had with Indian Muslims. The Government instituted a blockade of *mujahidin* settlements and intercepted messengers and money. The Amir then started secret negotiations with the Government, claiming his *mujahidin* were sandwiched between the fighting Mohmands and the British troops. Against opposition from its governor on the Frontier, who felt that the defeat of the *mujahidin* was close at hand, the British-Indian administration made a deal with the Amir, signed in December 1917, in exchange for a grant of some land. The deal was to remain secret for most of the time but during the 1920s the influence of the *mujahidin* steadily declined.[12] A few were tried in 1921-2. The colonies of *Hindustani Fanatics* were declared unlawful associations.[13] The Chamarkand colony acted more independently after 1923. They provided shelter to various political activists and

[12] Files from the India Office Library give more details about the *mujahidin*. For example: British Library India Office Collection (BL IOC) File No. 4261/16 'Hindustani fanatics, NW Frontier: relations of the Soviet Legation in Kabul with the Chamarkand colony; GOI recommended no action, 29-7-12–18-6-26'.

[13] The Peshawar Frontier Archives keep multi-volume files on the *mujahidin* as File Nos. 9/12/7, vols. I-VI and 9/12/9, vols. I-VII, with single items also included in other files.

participated in tribal risings of the Mohmands in 1933 and 1935.[14]

The British also labelled the *mujahidin* as *Hindustani Fanatics* under which name they gained prominence in the intelligence reports from the frontier province.[15] They show how their movements were followed in detail and their activities in terms of contacts and travels covered a large area of the province as well as the so-called independent territories. Political responses were visible in two ways. One was the emphasis on a code of conduct or guidelines for their camps at Charmakand and Smasta which were supposed to bring life in conformity with Islamic tenets.[16] This implied contrasting and critiquing the social and political ills of life which had come to dominate the Frontier areas, loosely called the commercialization of society and the oppressive rule of the British. Another political response was their thorough opposition to British rule over the frontier province. They would seek to support tribal forces who rose against the British. This often took the form of local encounters or skirmishes for which the *mujahidin* provided weapons, collecting money, sometimes calling the tribes into action when a local dispute arose, and sometimes participating themselves. Their political response was mostly violent and unrelenting, hardly to be called withdrawal protest. Yet, they withdrew into mountainous areas which were difficult to access, in order to protect themselves from the British. At the same time, their solitary settlements also betrayed elements of cultural isolation. Their violent protest culture could only function through withdrawal into seclusion. Another prominent feature of their protest is the linkage they provided between different strands of anti-British activities. Acting in a strategically important region, they had links with Afghanistan, the Russian Bolsheviks, Turkey, Germany and the Indian nationalist. At one time or the other, they played host to activists belonging to these affiliations.

The *Hijrat* movement was a mass movement of excited Muslims from the frontier province and the Punjab, mainly peasants or landless agricultural workers from rural areas, who wanted to leave India in 1920 in the wake of calls and rumours that Islam was in

[14] Lal Baha, 'The Activities of the Mujahidin 1900-1936', op. cit., pp. 113-14.

[15] BL IOC File No. 1229/19, 'Provincial and Intelligence Bureau Diaries 9-7-21'.

[16] Cf. Lal Baha, 'The Activities of the *Mujahidin*', op. cit., passim; Ghulam Muhammed Jaffar, 'Agreement between the British Government of India and the Amir of Mujahidin, Mawlawi Ni'inat Allah', in *Journal of the Pakistan Historical Society*, 41 (Islamabad, 1993), pp. 53-62.

danger.[17] India was considered to be no longer *dar al-Islam*, but became *dar al-harb*, which meant there were major obstacles to practice Islam. This was partly inspired by the Khilafat movement. Since Britain was a party to the negotiations that resulted in the dissolution of the Ottoman Empire and the reduction of Turkish sovereignty to its Anatolian heartland, it was accused of willfully undermining the authority of the Turkish Khalifah, the spiritual head of all Muslims. The cause of the Khilafat was made popular in India by radical Muslim nationalists like Mohamed Ali who agreed with Gandhi that strong emotional impulses were required to start a nationwide protest campaign against British rule in India. They calculated that India's Muslim minority should be made a prime target for mobilization as it had been sitting on the sidelines so far. They considered not without reason, as was to be found later, that success for the Indian nationalist movement without Muslim participation was not impossible but would be difficult. Muslim participation would make the nationalist movement almost irresistible.

The logic of Muslim activists was that when Britain had become an enemy of Islam by its deeds against the Khalifa, Muslims were obliged by their religious duty to migrate, possibly to Afghanistan, where the young Amir was striking a strong Islamic posture for his own ends. What was thought of as a kind of publicity stunt, no more than designed to increase pressure on the British, turned into a grim reality. The call for migration or *hijrat* was taken up in 1920 by local politicians and the Islamic clergy on the frontier and met with an overwhelming response. At the height of the campaign in August 1920, almost 40,000 people had migrated to Afghanistan. They had done so under the most difficult personal conditions, selling all their belongings, going practically bankrupt, banking on the good promises of the Afghan Amir. The Afghans, however, were overwhelmed by the magnitude of the response and feared a catastrophic drain on their own meagre resources. When the migration was halted by them in August 1920, the *muhajirin* party which was stopped at the frontier could not believe it, but being turned back they did not meet with the same fate of their fellow pilgrims who had made it to the other side but were often plundered by marauding tribes. Several hundred *muhajirin* died on way.

---

[17] For a more detailed exposition of the *Hijrat* movement, see D. Reetz, *Hijrat— The Flight of the Faithful*, op. cit.

Compared to the *mujahidin*, the *muhajirin's* political response was, likewise, directed against British rule, particularly against its un-Islamic character. The debate about the inception of the 1920 *hijrat* was derived from the question whether or not India under the British, and particularly owing to the war with Ottoman Turkey, was inimical to Islam, that is *dar al-harb*.

There was no unanimity on this issue among the *ulama*. The influential but pragmatic Abdul Bari from Firangi Mahal in Lucknow wanted to keep his option open. He refused to outrightly declare India *dar al-harb*, probably because he feared the repercussions of a mass exodus of Indian Muslims which would have been its logical consequence. Bari carefully argued:

In my opinion migration is neither obligatory nor is it meant for one's own advantage or good. It is only to attain the object of protecting Islam and hence no one has a right to stop those who want to migrate and in the same way no one has a right to compel those who do not want to go.[18]

By contrast, Maulana Abul Kalam Azad in his *fatwa* was satisfied 'that from the viewpoint of the *Shariat*, the Muslims of India have no choice but to migrate from India. . . . Migration from India before World War I was desirable, now it is mandatory' in order to restore the Khilafat.[19]

Yet, the local mullahs and the organizers of the *hijrat* campaign in the frontier and Punjab remained somewhat aloof from this theological dispute. In order to compel people to join the movement they made strong references to the spiritual advantages of going on *hijrat*. From their arguments, as well as from activities related to the establishment and regulation of the *muhajirin* colonies in Afghanistan, it appears that the whole affair had infused its followers with strong millenarian hopes of deliverance from earthly dilemmas. They sought to establish a counter-model of an Islamic society of brotherhood and common good. This was evident from the spirit of some of their *karawaan* journeys, their *qafilas*, by which they travelled to Afghanistan, which were conducted in an exulted and celebratory, almost festive mood.[20] Also the way by which they

---

[18] Letter from Maulana Abdul Bari, *Al Bureed* (Kanpur), 4 June 1920.

[19] Hafeez Malik, *Moslem Nationalism in India and Pakistan* (Washington, 1962), Appendix B.

[20] F.S. Briggs, a contemporary, thus described the arrival of one of the *qafilas* at the Indian-Afghan border in an article 'The Indian Hijrat of 1920', in *Moslem World*, 20 (Princeton, N.J., 1930), p. 166.

intended to manage the affairs of the settlers' colonies in Afghanistan, through committees with common guidelines, strangely reminiscent of the Communist collective communes, pointed to the ideal of an Islamic community.[21] However, in contrast with the *mujahidin*, the *hijrat* was not primarily thought of as an offensive measure against the British. If force or pressure were applied, it was done so indirectly and by implication. Pressure was mounted on the British through resignations by government, police and army officers in the course of the concurrent civil disobedience movement. Those officers resigned in order to go on *hijrat* which made the *hijrat* also appear to be part of the non-cooperation campaign. Pressure was also exerted on the Muslim masses in the frontier region by the local mullah who threatened the unwilling in case of failure to join the *hijrat* with dire consequences like foregoing their marital rights in case of 'un-Islamic' behaviour. The convergence of the *hijrat* and the civil disobedience movement that Gandhi had launched at the time along with the Khilafat movement, was significant. The withdrawal of the intending *muhajirin* from public life in India, and from India as such, was in a way civil disobedience carried to the extreme where you not only give up cooperation with colonial power but also leave its territorial domain. This form of response is sometimes called 'avoidance protest' and as a form of archaic social protest it is found in other cultures and countries as well.[22]

Another form of local unrest proceeded in the name of the Provisional Government of India. It had been set up by Mahendra Pratap (b. 1886), a *taluqdar* or landowner from Awadh, in 1915. As he remembered in his autobiography, it was 1 December, his birthday, when a few friends had come together to start this undertaking. He had graduated from the M.A.O. College in Aligarh, the first and only one of its kind, later the first Muslim University of India. Under the strong influence of Islamic values and Persian

[21] For various copies and versions of the rules regulating the settlement of the *muhajirin* in Afghanistan, see the India Offce dossier on the movement, BL IOC L/P&J/6/1701, File No. 5703/1920, 'Hijrat in N.W.F. Province etc.', File pp. 26-7; and Confidential Political Diaries and Special Branch Record, B. No. 30, File No. 475, which also includes a version of the *Nizam-e-Muhajirin* in Dari, quoted in Noshad Khan, *The Khilafatists's Hijrat*, op. cit., pp. 96-8, 197-211.

[22] Michael Addas, 'From Footdragging to Flight: The Evasive History of Peasant Avoidance Protest in South and South-East Asia', in *The Journal of Peasant Studies*, 13, 2, January 1986, pp. 64-86.

education imbibed in Aligarh, yet setting his eyes on a rather romantic militant nationalism, he travelled from Afghanistan around the world to make friends with other governments and courts willing to assist militant Indian nationalists against the British. This desire made strange bedfellows, first with the German and Turkish courts, and later with the Bolsheviks and the Third International. Strangely enough, this small group of activists always sounded strong tones of pan-Islamism which at the time was regarded by a certain faction of Islamic activists as somewhat akin to Communism in its desire to have a world and a society of the equal. Maulana Ubaidullah Sindhi (1872-1944) and Maulvi Barkatullah (1870-1928) were the better-known of the Islamic activists. Sindhi functioned as the 'Administrative and Foreign Minister' of the Provisional Government. Ahmad Aziz called his views a kind of 'Pseudo-Waliullahi Communism'.[23] Barkatullah was the 'Prime Minister'. In March 1919, he went to Soviet Russia as the Afghan representative to negotiate the establishment of diplomatic relations. When Pratap came to Moscow in May 1919, he joined his party and participated in an interview with Lenin. He stayed on in Soviet Russia for several months, closely involved in Pratap's activities to popularize Marxism and Socialism among Muslims in Central Asia. For this purpose he had written a number of articles and pamphlets, the better known among which was on 'Bolshevism and Islam' explaining Marxist Socialism as a return to the concept of the *Bayt-al Mal,* the common treasury for the community. From a pan-Islamic perspective, he shared with the Bolsheviks the abolition of private property which he believed to be the 'cause of all evil on earth',[24] and a rejection of Western parliamentary democracy which he called 'a children's toy made to dupe the people'.[25]

Like in the two preceding cases, the support base was located in the North-West Frontier Province from where the 'Provisional Government' helped train militants and sent out propaganda literature, weapons and explosive. Through Sindhi and Barkatullah the 'Provisional Government' remained in close contact with the Pathan tribal areas and the Frontier Province of British India, particularly with the bases of the *mujahidin* in the Black Mountains.

---

[23] Moin Shakir, *Khilafat to Partition 1919-1947* (Delhi, 1983, 2nd edn.), pp. 41-6.
[24] Quoted in Patnaik, *The Soviets and the Indian Revolutionary Movement,* op. cit., p. 62.
[25] Ibid., p. 63.

Local skirmishes occurred in Mansehra subdivision of the Frontier Province in 1920 when the British raided the positions of their supporters. Maulvi Muhammad Ishaq and Maulvi Muhammad Irfan had been successful in organizing a series of mass meetings in Hazara district in 1920, coinciding with the *hijrat* movement and culminating in the declaration of a 'provisional government' of 'self-rule' in some localities. About 30 thousand people participated in their meeting at Khaki village on 22 August 1920. After their arrest, this movement petered out.[26] On this occasion, the British-Indian government noted with imperial arrogance and ferocity that 'the efforts of fanatical agitators in the Mansehra subdivision resulted in the working up of wild excitement which culminated in the repudiation of the British administration and the erection in many places of a 'Provisional Government'. This movement collapsed with the arrest of the ringleaders; but the neighbouring Black Mountain tribes, having been persuaded that they were invulnerable to rifle fire, 'burnt and sacked some of our posts until they were brought to their senses by a severe repulse followed by aerial operations'.[27]

Prior to these events, the activists of the 'Provisional Government' gained prominence in the 'Silk Letter Conspiracy' in 1916 when a messenger was caught carrying a letter written on yellow silk, addressed by Sindhi to his teacher, the *Shaikh al-Hind,* Mahmud Hasan of Deoband, in which he gave detailed instructions how Indian Muslims should be mobilized against the British. However, none of the major activists caught at the time, except that Mahmud Hasan was externed to Malta.[28]

Politically, the 'Provisional Government' sought to address alienation from British rule. Coming from a radical nationalist background, their primary concern was not the un-Islamic character of British rule, but through the participation of Muslim leaders in their activities, their goals became fused with Islamic injunctions on the basis of the liberative potential of Islam and its potential inspiration for a quasi-Communist utopian society. Initially, Pratap himself believed in the potential of true religion for the liberation of India.

---

[26] BL IOC File No. P/CONF/59, protocol no. 306, Nov. 1920.

[27] L.F. Rushbrook Williams (ed.), *India in 1920* (Delhi, 1985 rpt.), p. 13.

[28] For further details on the 'Silk Letter Conspiracy' and Obaidullah Sindhi, see BL IOC File No. 4260/16, 'Afghanistan: the Silk Letter case 1916-1918'. For books, partly based on these files, see Maulana Muhammed Mian, *Tehrik-e-reshmi rumal,* 1971; Muhammad Hajjan Shaikh, *Maulana Ubid Allah Sindh: A Revolutionary Scholar* (Islamabad, 1986).

Lenin, when confronted with his book *Religion of Love*, called his views 'Tolstoyan' which supposedly had already failed Russia.[29] Though their group did support acts of violence against the British, this was rather sporadic. They did not form the kind of closed community as the *mujahidin* did. They were rather a network of radical and militant activists, moving as individuals and linking up with local activities.

A fourth kind of Islamist political activity highly typical of the frontier region was the militant *mullah*, or preacher. This was local Islamic mass activism inasmuch as the *mullahs* aroused one or the other tribe into action against the British on various occasions. Mostly, these were tribal insurrections.[30] The *mullahs* sometimes were people of spell-binding influence. A high profile during the 1920s and 1930s was retained by the Haji of Turangzai,[31] the Babra Mullah,[32] the Fakir of Alingar,[33] the Mullah of Chaknawar,[34] who at

[29] Patnaik, *The Soviets and the Indian Revolutionary Movement*, op. cit., p. 39.

[30] For accounts of the role of religious figures in the tribal wars on the North-West Frontier, see Arthur Swinson, *North-West Frontier* (New York, 1967); Akbar S. Ahmed, *Millenium and Charisma among Pathans* (London, 1976); Olaf Caroe, *The Pathans* (London, 1964).

[31] His real name was Fazal-i-Wahid (1885-1937). He was named after a place where he was given some land: in the Maira near Turangzai, not far from Charsadda, in Peshawar district, which he used to build a large mosque and a hostel for his Sheikhs and disciples. He was mostly active among the Mohamands of Peshawar district, especially since 1914 and during the Third British-Afghan War of 1919-20. In 1915 he fled to the tribal belt of the independent territories which were losely controlled by the British through a political agent but where tribal law reigned supreme. He played a significant role in the Mohmand uprisings of 1915 and 1927 and acted as an intermediary in the relations of the Afghans with the Mohmands. Two of his sons also achieved prominence: Fazl-i-Akbar, known as Badshah Gul I, was the eldest son and succeeded his father in his spiritual duties and political callings. However, while his father was regarded as a *faqir* or saint, he was not. Collected tribute from the Safis whose *de facto* ruler he was. Lived in Lakarai, in Safi country. He was the leader of the Mohmands in the operations of 1933 and 1935. Was assisted by his two brothers Badshah Gul II and III (Fazl-i-Malbud and Fazl Shah). See Government of India, *Who's Who in the Peshawar District. Corrected up to 1 January 1931* (Peshawar, 1931), p. 33. Confidential. BL IOC L/P&S/20B.296/10.

[32] He was one of the leaders of the Mohmand tribal uprisings in 1915 and 1927. See BL IOC L/PS/12/3125 Coll. 23/4, *'North-West Frontier. Tribal disturbances 1930-31. Peshwar and District Situation, 7-5-30–14-12-32'*.

[33] Active during the 1927 Mohmand uprising and more influential then the Haji of Turangzai at the time. See also BL IOC L/PS/12/3125 Coll. 23/4.

[34] See BL IOC L/PS/12/3125 Coll. 23/4. Led a force of Afghans into Mohmand territory in the 1915 trouble.

one stage or the other were all involved in the Mohmand disturbances of 1915-17, 1927 and 1937-8. What the Haji of Turangzai
was for the Mohmands, Haji Abdul Razzaq was for the Wazirs. In a
duly signed and sealed letter to the British Agent he claimed in 1920
that he had set up an independent government for the political
agency of Waziristan. He believed that he had the support of a
Bolshevik minister, that Afghanistan was 'compelled' to assist him,
and that Indians 'approved' of his actions.[35] The Sandaki Baba was
active in Upper Swat in the Malakand Agency in the 1920s.[36] Some
notoriety was achieved by the so-called *Shami Pir* in 1938. Coming
from Syria, as the honorary appellation '*Shami*', his name was Syed
Muhammad Sadi, nephew of Suriya, the former Queen of
Afghanistan and wife of the deposed Afghan King Amanullah. He
belonged to the Qadiri order for which he allegedly came to collect
tribute from certain tribes. But his real intention was to overthrow
the Afghan King Zahir Shah in order to avenge the downfall of
Amanullah. The *Shami Pir* succeeded in mobilizing a sub-section
of the Waziris but were however stopped by the British.

The usual pattern of action was that a *lashkar* or group of
volunteer fighters was raised from among the tribals. The latter were
either lured by the promise of loot or attracted by oratory of the
mullahs. The *mullahs* were not averse to using crafty imagery to
impress the tribals. The *Shami Pir* was believed to be capable of
rendering the weapons of the adversary ineffective. For a sum of
£ 25,000 he was finally bought off by the British and externed from
South Waziristan.[37]

The *mullahs* largely shared the political response to British rule
with the first two groups discussed here. They were enraged by its
un-Islamic character but they were also very much concerned with
securing a place for themselves in the local power equation which
was disturbed by British rule in general, and, more specifically,
through the impending introduction of elected institutions. Generally,
they were associated with one, or sometimes two particular tribes,
or sub-tribes, for some time. Beyond recruiting followers from these
tribes for certain campaigns, they did not head any particular party
or movement.

[35] Para 398 of the Frontier Intelligence Diary (FID) No. 15, 8 April 1920, in BL IOC
L/P&S/10/813, *Provincial and Intelligence Bureau Diaries 1919-20*.
[36] FID No. 8, 21 February 1920, in L/P&S/10/813, op. cit.
[37] BL IOC L/P&S/12/3255-9, *Shami Pir*. adherents, movement, identity, arrest.

III

The political responses of these four groups, being remarkably similar in many ways despite the very pronounced differences in terms of their inception, activity and response, suggest a number of common compulsions underlying their reactions. By way of conclusion the following points are suggested for deliberation:

First, there was a close interaction between local, national, i.e. Indian, and international factors.

Muslim unrest on the frontier, and elsewhere in India, in the 1920s took its root from a number of earlier political campaigns in which Muslim political opinion was polarized. One such root cause was the wars led by Turkey or affecting it, like the Turko-Italian war and the Balkan wars, and more significantly, the beginning of the World War I in 1914. Attacks on Turkey were taken close to heart by Indian Muslims. Solidarity movements were started by those who later played a prominent role in other forms of protest like Mohamed and Shaukat Ali.[38] Germany raised hopes of becoming a potential ally to defeat British rule over India. Another root cause inspiring Muslim political mobilization was, no doubt, the strengthening of the Indian nationalist movement which concluded and, albeit short-lived, strategic pact between Hindu and Muslim forces at a conference in Lucknow in 1916.

Afghanistan played a central role in these affairs. Its struggle for greater independence from the British became another Muslim cause on the frontier.

The fundamental changes in Bolshevik Russia also captured the imagination of Islamic activists, particularly between 1917 and 1923, when pan-Islamic schemes for a while banked on support from Russia against the British, and more so after the Bolshevik success against the allied armies in the civil war, in which Britain also played a role. It was typical that Maulana Mohammad Irfan at a meeting for

---

[38] Cf. their efforts for medical relief to Turkey through a Red Crescent missions during the Turko-Italian and the Balkan wars, and more prominently the foundation of the *Anjuman-i-Khuddam-i-Kaaba* in 1913, the 'Servants of Ka'aba Society', where they were joined by Maulana Abdul Bari (1879-1926) from the Nadwa in Lucknow who later played a key role during the Khilafat and the *hijrat* campaigns. Afzal Iqbal, *The Life and Times of Mohamed Ali: An Analysis of the Hopes, Fears and Aspirations of Muslim India from 1778 to 1931* (Lahore, 1974); Mushirul Hasan, *A Nationalist Conscience, M.A. Ansari, the Congress and the Raj* (Delhi, 1985).

the *muhajirin* in Abbottabad declared:

A strong flood would shortly set in from Baku which would sweep away everything from its path. He praised the Amir of Afghanistan who had drawn the sword in defence of Islam and would not sheathe it until he had accomplished something. The non-existence of the Khilafat was the death-blow of Islam.[39]

Pan-Islamic causes, such as the support for the Ottoman Empire or for Afghanistan, were a strong motivating force, but they almost always underwent significant mutations to the extent that they became unrecognizable or inconsistent with the original source of inspiration. The compulsions for Indians to defend the Khilafat were unacceptable for Islamic militants from Arabia who wanted to break free from the Ottoman Empire. Likewise, the classical *hijrat*, undertaken by Mohammad, the Prophet, was generally a topic of consent in the *umma*, the Muslim world community. When this pan-Islamic issue of undertaking *hijrat* was appropriated by the Indian frontier Muslims who went to Afghanistan, their motives became somewhat divorced from the *hijrat* of the Prophet, as they were driven by dissatisfaction with the Indian political situation, pursuing the campaign to an extent which took Afghanistan by surprise. The Khilafat and the *hijrat* campaigns showed that Indian Muslim leaders, both local and national, selected pan-Islamic courses rather at random to illustrate or support their political intentions.

Second, all the four forms of local political mobilization were closely interrelated. Activists frequently passed from one stream of action on to another. The *mujahidin* colonies played host to almost all of them at one time or the other. In the localities, a number of people who would be known to be active and interested in politics would take up one or the other causes as it came along. Organizing committees for the Khilafat movement and the *hijrat* campaign was identical or overlapped in many cases. The mullah would wait for a new tribal conflict to consolidate his influence to embarrass the authorities. In a way, local activists would make up an informal Islamic network which could be called into action whenever the need or the desire arose.

Third, these were emotional and spontaneous responses on the mass level, invoking strong images of Islam in danger—except in the case of the 'Provisional Government', where Islam was held out

<hr>

[39] BL IOC P/CONF/59, op. cit., p. 22.

rather as a romantic promise. At the same time, at least on the part of some of the organizers of these campaigns, these were intentional responses which were used to demonstrate to the British how easy it was to mobilize a large following for 'the right cause'. They knew very well that the British were extremely uneasy with religious fervour, which was irrational to them and difficult to deal with. Causes could rarely be explained to the superiors in a manner that they could be removed or dealt with administratively, forecasts were difficult to make about the duration and outcome of such action. It was very clearly a potential for blackmailing the British administration into caution and compromise. This, for instance, is supported by the decisions of the British to deal leniently with the *hijrat* agitation where wide rehabilitation measures were taken on after the return of many *muhajirin*, and also in the case of the *Shami Pir*, who was bought off rather than arrested. Fear of the outcome of such religious campaigns prompted compromise rather than confrontation.

In the fourth place, morality was important to the campaigns as a means of making the Muslims seem superior to their British detractors. People were offered an utopian vision of a different life which would not be as competitive, cheap or materialistic as under the British. The *mujahidin* tried to establish model communities in Smasta and Chamarkand with a clear code of conduct. The 'Provisional Government' offered a utopian vision of a better life on Communist lines, merged with Islamic ideals. The *muhajirin* colonies in Afghanistan in 1920 were also to follow strong moral and religious guidelines. The mullahs invoked moral injunctions branding the infidels and the irreligious ways of the British, where state schools and a state administration supposedly undermined the traditional religiosity of the people. The topic of moral improvements was later picked up by others like the Red Shirt movement. But it was equally shared by non-Muslim movements like the Sikhs and the Tamils in the 1920s and 1930s.[40] Gandhi had appropriated the subject for the Congress all along.

Fifth, the movements seemed surprisingly oblivious to traditional measures of political success or failure. They were often blessed with little success by Western political standards. Yet this did not in any

[40] Cf. D. Reetz, 'Religion and group-identity: Comparing three regional movements in Colonial India', in Annemarie Hafner (ed.), *Essays on South Asian Society, Culture and Politics* (Förderungsgesellschaft Wiss. Neuv. mbH, FSP Moderner Orient, Arbeitshefte, 8) (Berlin, 1995), pp. 73-89.

conceivable measure discourage their followers, or reduce the stature of the organizers or of Islam as a motivating force. Though there was sometimes a short-lived rage against the mad *mullah* who had misled them, people rather quickly settled back to their daily routine. The long-term effect was surprisingly positive. Political awareness and the readiness to engage themselves in protest against British rule or in defence of Islam increased. These campaigns also served as training grounds for a new generation of politicians who later entered mainstream local or national politics like Abdul Ghaffar Khan, the so-called Frontier Gandhi. In 1914-15 he considered himself a disciple of the Haji of Turangzai, particularly in the latter's educational enterprises. He had started a chain of Islamic schools which were meant to serve as an alternative to the state schools and were also used to increase public awareness about resistance against Britain. Ghaffar Khan later founded the Red Shirt movement which after the introduction of elected provincial representation under the Government of India Act of 1935 came to form the Government of the Frontier Province.

Next, against the background of developments in India, these movements sought to anticipate, forestall or rival the imminent introduction of elective representation. Although representative and elective provincial autonomy was introduced in India by the 1919 Constitutional Reforms Act, it was done so in the frontier province only in 1932. But the *mullahs* and tribal elders could clearly see the importance of the principle of public representation. Traditional political authority which was mostly inherited—also the position of the mullah was practically very often hereditary—would then be challenged by people who were voted into office. This is borne out by evidence to various inquiry commissions by the British Government in preparation for the constitutional and administrative reforms like the Public Service Commission in 1913[41] and by the 1922

[41] United Kingdom, Parliamentary Papers, *Royal Commission on the Public Services in India: Appendix Vol. X, Minutes of evidence relating to the Indian and Provincial Civil Services taken at Lahore from the 9th to the 15th April 1913, with appendices* (London, 1914), Cd. 7582, passim. The fear of the impending changes was, for instance, reflected in the evidence by Khan Bahadur Khan Abdul Ghaffar Khan, Khan of Zaida, who demanded special consideration for the traditional tribal chiefs and Khans, as the aristocracy is 'a very large and important class, and their history, traditions and ideals are based on loyalty to the Crown and support of the British rule' (p. 301). He saw no further need to broaden recruitment.

North-West Frontier Enquiry Committee led by the Foreign Secretary of the Government of India, Dennis Bray, which set out to take evidence whether or not the frontier province, created in 1900, should be re-amalgamated with the Punjab province, an issue which was raised by Hindu politicians from the frontier and at the centre, ostensibly to extend the 1919 reforms to the frontier districts. Witnesses like the Pathan members of the Civil Service, Abdul Qaiyyum Khan and Khan Bahadur Khan, repeatedly demanded limitations on the elective principle, reservation for special interests and classes like the Khans.[42]

Seventh, the campaign contributed to an Islamic discourse on the political scene at the time of nationalist mobilization. The Islamic campaigns during the First World War and immediately afterwards contributed—for better or worse—to linking politics with Islam and Islam with politics. Islamic activists succeeded in preserving and adapting their traditional system of influence to elective represent-ation and future independence. This was helped by the general trend in Indian politics during the anti-colonial movement not to separate politics and religion but to join them to reinforce their impact on British rule. Events in India and Pakistan since Inde-pendence have shown that religious institutions, not of the Islamic denomination only, have survived the arrival of Independence and elective democracy remarkably well. Politics in India and Pakistan are still largely, though not exclusively, governed by similar assumptions on a close and inherent nexus of religion and politics as in the 1920s and 1930s. To argue that this has only been to the detriment of politics will fall short of the complexity of the issues involved. The example of the Islamic militant campaigns on the frontier in the 1920s shows that it may, instead, be necessary to understand the rational of these movements better and evaluate the motives and perspectives of participants within the framework of these movements. Only then a clearer picture of their place in national politics would emerge. The militant Islamic discourse, just as any other religious discourse, should be seen as a means to negotiate a place in society for the local cultural norms, and for the local political and religious establishment.

Last, the tendency to separate people on the basis of religion

---

[42] Govt. of India, *North-West Frontier Enquiry (Bray) Committee 1922. Proceedings Vols I-III: Evidence and Appendices.* BL IOC V/26/247/2-4, vol. 1, 4, p. 190.

should be contrasted with the syncretism of religious movements and practices throughout South Asia. Time and again, religiosity *per se* and the wider issues of morality and spirituality have helped to foster a certain degree of understanding between the adherents of different religions. Also, the peculiar meaning the concept of secularism had acquired in South Asia has contributed to religious traditions and institutions. In Europe the term secularism and secularized society has rather come to mean a society which moves or has moved way from religion where people have stopped following religious practices, whereas in South Asia it amounts to the coexistence of different religions where religion is protected from the state and one faith from the other. This has meant that religiosity and religious institutions have continued to remain highly visible and influential under Indian secularism.

In a nutshell, concepts of Islamic militancy in South Asia owe their specific character as much to Islam as to local traditions and cultures and to South Asian religiosity in general. They are less rooted in the abstract categories of Islam than in the need and motivations of local leaders and their followers to survive and assert a place of their own in the existing structures of power and influence in society.

Kashmiri Muslims:
Social and Identity Consciousness

MOHAMMAD ISHAQ KHAN

In Kashmir lives one of the oldest Muslim communities in the Indian subcontinent. Being homogeneous in respect of history, religion and culture, the community has, by and large, shared a distinct identity. Having experienced the trauma of negative changes, particularly since the sale of Kashmir by the British to Gulab Singh, the Dogra Raja of Jammu, in 1846,[1] Kashmiri Muslims have faced the dilemma of simultaneously discrediting and inheriting the imperialist legacy. While their valiant political struggle against the oligarchy of the princely state forms an important watershed in the history of the liberation struggle against British imperialism in South Asia, the role of their leaders in the post-1947 period to preserve the 'Muslim character' of the state of Jammu & Kashmir presents a paradox.[2] It is beyond the scope of this paper to go into the details of the impact of the amalgamation of Jammu, Ladakh and the Kashmir Valley into one entity, but not difficult to delineate certain inherent tensions underlying the crucial question of Kashmiri identity. The clue to the understanding of the Kashmir problem comes not so much from the year 1947, as 1846.

Long before the establishment of the Muslim Sultanate in 1320 Kashmir was known to Islam through traders, travellers, scholars, artists and adventurers. When Sufi missionaries began to arrive from

[1] For a rebuttal of the argument that Kashmir was not sold to Gulab Singh, see Mohammad Ishaq Khan, 'Was Kashmir Sold to Gulab Singh?', in *The Kashmir Times*, 17 April 1988.

[2] The avowed struggle for independence in contemporary Kashmir is, among several other factors, also the outcome of a fear-psychosis which has threatened Kashmiri Muslims since 1953. Whether in power or out of power, Shaikh Mohammad Abdullah seldom failed to emphasize the need for preserving the 'Muslim character' of Jammu & Kashmir, particularly in speeches at the *dargah* of Hazratbal. Having been an eye-witness to many political developments in Kashmir since 1953, I have made use of my personal diaries dating back to 1964 without referring to them in the notes in the concluding part of the article.

Central Asia and Persia from the fourteenth century onwards, Kashmiri society began to experience several changes of far-reaching importance. While the immigrant Sufis endeavoured to bring about Iranian and Central Asian orientations to Kashmiri culture, their egalitarianism and philanthropy reshaped and reoriented the indigenous mystic traditions in the emergence of the Rishi order in the Valley. Under the inspiring leadership of Shaikh Nuruddin Rishi (1379-1442) and a host of his disciples dispersed in every nook and corner of the Valley, Kashmiri folk—agriculturalists, artisans and boatmen—gradually assimilated Islam through a process of acculturation during the fifteenth to eighteenth centuries. Two significant developments were integrally bound up with such a historical process: first, the orderly evolution of Kashmiri Muslim society, and second, the indomitable urge of Kashmiri Brahmins, better known as Pandits, to preserve the distinct and somewhat ethnocentric character of their community. That they succeeded, at least, in keeping alive their convictions about superior birth and social position, and contempt for manual labour even as the socially-oppressed sections of Kashmiri society searched for a just social order.[3]

The Kashmiri Pandits were a tiny but not insginificant minority. Their numerical insignificance was overshadowed by their preponderance in the administration of the state under the Mughals (1586-1757), Afghans (1757-1819), and Sikhs (1819-46). They were so well entrenched that the Dogra rulers found it impossible to displace them. Thus when Maharaja Pratap Singh (1885-1925) began to shower favours on Punjabis, the Pandits raised the issue of *mulki* and non-*mulki*. Their agitation resulted in the appointment of the State Subjects Definition Committee soon after the accession of Maharaja Hari Singh in 1925. The definition arrived at by the Committee was accepted by the new Maharaja in 1927. It was by forcing the government to define a genuine state subject that the Pandits succeeded in driving Punjabis away from state service and thereby continued their monopoly of the services.[4] In more than one important sense, then, the initial credit for preserving the distinct identities of J & K may be given to Pandits.

[3] See my *Kashmir's Transition to Islam: The Role of Muslim Rishis* (Delhi, 1994); and *Perspectives on Kashmir: Historical Dimensions* (Srinagar, 1983).

[4] Ishaq Khan, *Histoy of Srinagar, 1846-1947: A Study in Socio-Cultural Change* (Srinagar, 1978).

Of the several identities existing in J & K, Kashmiri Muslim, Kashmiri Pandit, Dogra and Ladakhi are most important. Kashmiri Muslims are overwhelmingly concentrated in the Valley, comprising 97 per cent of its total population. In district Doda, comprising Poonch, Rajouri and Doda, although Muslims form 65 per cent of the population, only those living in Badarwah and Kistawar have linguistic and some cultural affinity with their brethren in the Valley.[5] In striking contrast to Kashmiri Muslims long settled in 'Azad Kashmir' and Pakistan, Kashmiri-speaking Muslims of the Doda district have enriched Kashmiri literature in several forms. While Kashmiris long settled on the other side of the border are proud of their cultural identity, their children can neither speak nor understand the language of their motherland (*Mouj Kashmir*). That Kashmiri Muslims inhabiting 'Azad Kashmir' and Pakistan have been assimilated in the mainstream of Punjabi culture is reflected in their style of living and speech.[6]

Significantly, Kashmiri Pandit families settled in the plains of India have an acute sense of identity. This is reflected not merely in their occasional displays of taste for salted tea, *nadru, kawah* and so on, but more importantly, in keeping alive the concept of their ancient cultural and modern political identity at the all-India level. Various nuances of the Pandit identity crisis in the context of the development of Kashmiri Muslim society have been studied elsewhere;[7] suffice to say here that our understanding of this enables us to examine the crucial question of Muslim identity during Dogra rule as an integral part of a historical process, rather than a conflict between Hinduism and Islam.

[5] Pampori, *Kashmir in Chains, 1819-1992* (Srinagar, 1992), p. 450.

[6] Based on the impressions of my visit to Pakistan in connection with an international symposium organized by 'Pak-German Research Project on Karrakorum' in Islamabad (28 Sept.-2 Oct. 1995). Although at the invitation of our hosts, I reached Islamabad in the company of four Indian scholars on 17 September for participating in an excursion to Gilgit, Baltistan and other parts of 'Northern Pakistan', we were not granted permission to visit the areas of my own state. Sardar Abdul Qaiyyum Khan, Prime Minister of 'Azad Kashmir' who invited us over a cup of tea at his Kashmir House in Islamabad, expressed his helplessness in arranging a visa for us. However, until about 150 foreign scholars returned to Islamabad from their 'exciting' trip to parts of the Jammu & Kashmir, several Kashmiris settled in Pakistan, through the display of traditional Kashmiri hospitality, afforded me an opportunity to share my awkward predicament with them. Among several others must be specially mentioned the veteran journalist Mir Abdul Aziz, Khwaja Abdus Samad Wani and Sayyid Javed.

[7] See Ishaq Khan, *Kashmir's Transition to Islam*, op. cit.

The deep-seated changes that Muslim society of the Valley underwent after the sale of Kashmir to Maharaja Gulab Singh in 1846 has yet to receive the attention it deserves. The contours of change, however, are clear: a pattern of new economic relations emerged when the new rulers declared themselves absolute owners or lords of the soil. The new rulers often invoked the Treaty of Amritsar to establish their legitimacy and to perpetuate the notion of their superior ownership of land. The treaty was also invoked to thwart British machinations for establishing a Residency in the state.[8] It is no wonder that Maharaja Pratap Singh drew on it in moments of despair to legitimate and consolidate his authority. His letter to the chief minister is worth quoting here:

As you are already aware the proprietary rights in all the lands of Kashmir belong to the ruling Chief exclusively, for the simple reason that the territories of Kashmir were purchased by my late lamented grandfather, Maharaja Gulab Singhji, and hence any sale of such land by anyone else is illegal.[9]

It is hard to deny that the Treaty of Amritsar conferred both *de jure* and *de facto* rights on the Dogra maharajas to regard Kashmir as their personal property.[10] In fact, it was understood to imply that Gulab Singh had purchased against cash payment all lands, rivers, forests, mines, natural products,[11] and indeed even the skill of weavers of shawls. The Kashmiri Muslim response was first reflected in both Kashmiri and Urdu literature produced during Dogra rule. The philosopher poet Mohammad Iqbal remarked:

O breeze, if you happen to go Geneva way,
Carry a word from me to the Nations of the whole world.
A land and people, its streams and forests all were sold.
In fact the whole nation was sold and fancy at how
    cheap a price.

Although the recognition of the Dogra ruler's prior ownership of land formed the basis of government policy, throughout the period from

[8] JKA (Jammu & Kashmir Archives), File No. 191/H-75, Bloc C of 1906.

[9] For British policy towards Kashmir, see D.K. Ghosh, *Kashmir in Transition* (Calcutta, 1974).

[10] Walter Lawrence describes Kashmir of the 1880s as an 'absolute monarchy'. *The Valley of Kashmir* (Srinagar, 1967), p. 2.

[11] Mirza Muhammad Afzal Beg, *On the Way to Golden Harvests: Agricultural Reforms in Kashmir* (Jammu, 1951), pp. 22-3.

1846 to 1931, the Dogra administration worked directly to create a landed aristocracy comprising mainly Kashmiri Pandits and Dogra Rajputs.[12] In the process, land grants, *jagirs*[13] and *chaks*[14] were institutionalized. The use of these assignments was a major device for ruling-class support. What the founding of Dogra rule brought about was the creation of a new system of agrarian exploitation, on which a parasitical urban growth was based. The new polity combined political authority with economic power more fully than did the previous regime.

Demographically the Pandits by 1891 formed less than 7 per cent of the population of Kashmir,[15] but they were a highly urbanized group, located in large numbers in Srinagar.[16] The Pandits developed a class consciousness much earlier than the rest of the population. Though few in numbers they were interrelated, and functioned in part through their direct relationship to institutions which expressed or symbolized society as whole.

In fact this part of the society had no particular economic function other than parasitic consumption. The founder of modern education in Kashmir, while writing about the two hundred and fifty boys who first sought admission in the Mission School of Srinagar, says:

They are the sons and grandsons of those officials who had bullied and squeezed the Mohammedan peasants for years past, and their large houses in the city with all their wealth were a standing witness to their looting powers, for the salary they received from the State was quite insignificant.[17]

Corruption was rife in the ranks of the revenue staff manned by the Pandits, who made common cause with the revenue officials,

[12] The Dogra Rajputs who were given land grants in Kashmir were (kinsmen) of the Dogra rulers.

[13] The *jagirs* of the Dogra period should not be confused with the Mughal *jagirs*. While the Doga *jagirdar* enjoyed unlimited powers and considered himself to be the virtual owner of the landed estate, the Mughal *jagirdar* was a mere functionary of the government.

[14] *Chaks* were the landed estates mainly under the possession of the Pandit officials of the Dogra government.

[15] *Census of India* (J & K), 1891.

[16] 'The Hindus who preponderate in the urban population and comprise well known literate castes like Kashmiri Pandits and the urban Brahman population of cities and towns claim 70 literates out of every 1,000.' Ibid. (Part 1, 1921), p. 111. In Srinagar, the Pandits formed nearly 20 per cent of the population of the city in 1868, see Lawrence, *The Valley of Kashmir*, p. 225.

[17] Tyndale Biscos, *Kashmir in Sunlight and Shade* (London, 1922), p. 268.

tampered with deeds and contracts so as to serve the latter's interests, and made their own fortunes out of such corruption. It is, therefore, in the context of these emerging agrarian relations that the opposition of the Pandit officials[18] to Sir Walter Lawrence's reforms needs to be studied.

Closely connected with the creation of the landed aristocracy is the system of forced labour (*begar*) which remained until the beginning of this century the most prominent feature of the Kashmir administration. After 1846 the magnitude of forced labour grew not only owing to the military expeditions to Gilgit and the adjoining border areas of Kashmir, but also to the emergence of an organized landed aristocracy and an underdeveloped exchange economy, especially in the agrarian sector which was characterized by localism. By accentuating localism the official class made the intensity and the scope of subjection and dependence of the peasants in Kashmir no less than the servitude of the peasantry in Western feudalism, which overburdened the peasant with service on the lord's farm and payment of various dues and rendered them dependent on the lord as well as the land.[19]

The destruction of the Kashmiri peasants' proprietary rights and the reduction of peasants to virtual 'serfdom' are thus two marked features of agrarian economy in the beginning of Dogra rule in Kashmir. In spite of restrictions on the movement of peasants imposed by the feudal government, the peasants started fleeing to the Punjab as coolies. A good number of artisans also emigrated to the Punjab owing to feudal exactions.[20] Other factors such as recurrent famines, cholera, epidemics, floods and scarcity of grains, added to the pressure to migrate.[21]

It is this background against which we shall study phases in the growth of social consciousness among the Muslims of Kashmir between 1846 and 1947.

When Kashmir came under Dogra rule, Muslims formed more than 93 per cent of the population of the Valley. The cultivation of land was their principal source of livelihood, although a fair

[18] Lawrence, op. cit, p. 6.

[19] For details, see Ishaq Khan, 'Some Aspects of Corvee in Kashmir', in *Research Biannual*, vol. 1, no. II, Directorate of Research, Srinagar, 1976, pp. 58-71.

[20] The system, under which no person could leave the Valley without permission, was known as *Rahdari*.

[21] For details, see my *History of Srinagar*, op. cit.

population was engaged in small scale business, shopkeeping and trade in towns like Baramulla, Sopore, Anantnag and Srinagar. An overwhelming majority of the Muslim peasants were illiterate and unskilled. In Srinagar, Muslims were 80 per cent of the population.[22] Of these the artisans in the shawl industry alone formed 30 per cent.[23] The shawl trade, the mainstay of Srinagar's economy, had flourished during Afghan and Sikh rule, but it began to show signs of decline after 1846.[24] Educationally, Muslims were backward; as late as 1921, 978 Muslims out of 1000 were unable to read or write. As against this, the Pandits claimed 70 literates out of every 1000.[25]

It is no wonder, therefore, that Muslims of Kashmir remained politically inactive until the 1920s, in contrast to their co-religionists in India. Their political inertia may also be attributed to the ban on the formation of societies and even the publication of newspapers in the Valley. As late as 1921 the Dogra government hesitatingly permitted the formation of an association whose object was the teaching of the Koran, but ordered the police to ensure that the Anjuman did not take part in political matters.[26]

However, it should not be supposed that there was total absence of social consciousness among the Muslims of Kashmir. If, on the one hand, they had developed a fatalistic outlook owing to oppression, exploitation and misery, on the other, they had developed a spirit of revolt against intolerable conditions. Earlier in 1847, the shawl weavers, comprising the bulk of the Muslim population in Srinagar, resorted to a strike[27] and demanded the reduction of various kinds of taxes.[28] They also demanded that wages be fixed[29] and urged the government to establish the rule of law in

[22] See Lawrence, op. cit., p. 25.

[23] Foreign Dept., March 1883, no. 86, National Archives of India; also Census 1921, vol. 1, p. 181.

[24] *History of Srinagar,* p. 62.

[25] Census, 1921, vol. 1, p. iii; see also *The Civil and Military Gazette* (Lahore), 1 Nov. 1923, p. 13; Kashmir Government Records (General), File No. 204/9-C (1920).

[26] Kashmir Government Records (General), File No. 66/102/C of 1921. The government also accorded permission to Sanatan Dharam Sabha to open its branch in Srinagar in 1923 on the distinct understanding that the Sabha will take no part in politics. The Sabha was a purely religious institution, ibid., File No. 46/G-39 of 1923.

[27] *Lahore Political Diaries,* 1847-9, vol. VI, p. 48.

[28] K.M. Panikkar, *The Founding of the Kashmir State* (London, 1930), p. 139.

[29] Again in 1853, the workers of shawl industry expressed their resentment against the *Karkhanadars* over wages. There broke out some riots in the city. See Mirza Saif-ud-Din, *Akhbarat-i-Darbar-i-Maharaja Gulab Singh,* MSS, 1853, vol. VI, ff. 9a, 10b.

respect of the shawl industry.[30] Though the agitation died down owing to the intervention of Maharaja Gulab Singh, there remained an undercurrent of hostility among the weavers against feudal exactions. In 1855 the workers of the shawl industry staged a demonstration in Srinagar against extreme forms of exploitation.[31] Lacking organization, effective leadership and ideology, the shawl weavers' uprising was essentially pre-political and was ruthlessly suppressed. Nevertheless, the outcome of their uprising and their ceaseless agitation over the scarcity of gains did provide an impulse to other Muslim sections to fight for their rights. In 1877, for example, the first signs of agrarian discontent became manifest when the peasants appealed to Maharaja Ranbir Singh during his sojourn at Achabal in Kashmir against official high-handedness and corruption. The intensity of the peasant's discontent is reflected in the manner in which revenue officials were forced to return the bribes they had taken from the peasants. But Wazir Punnoo was able to dissuade the Maharaja from taking stern action against corrupt officials. This was not all. Wazir Punnoo had officials search the houses of the peasants and seize their meagre rations.[32]

These developments did, however, make the Muslims of Kashmir introspective. In 1886 some seventeen or eighteen Muslims who had landed interests sent two signed petitions to the viceroy and the British resident in Srinagar, requesting a compassionate, just and courteous Englishman as settlement officer there. The petitioners hoped that they would be able to explain to him 'their circumstances without fear'.[33] As a result Wingate was appointed the Settlement Commissioner in 1887. He was succeeded by Lawrence in 1889.

From 1890 onwards Muslim consciousness was heightened by several factors. Although the opening of the Jhelum Valley road in 1890 brought advantages to Kashmir, it caused economic dislocation to many Muslim trading families as a large influx of Punjabis moved

---

[30] Panikkar, op. cit., p. 139.

[31] *Cashmere Misgovernment* (typed copy in the J & K Archives, pp. 18-19). Mir Saifullah, *Tarikh-nama Kashmir* (Ibn Mahjoor's collection), pp. 100-1; Khalil Mir-Janpuri, *Tarikh-i Kashmir,* vol. II, MS no. 800, Research Library Srinagar, p. 910; Pir Hasan, *Tarik-i Hasan* (Ibrahim's Ur. tr.), III, p. 577.

[32] Pir Hasan, op. cit. (Persian text), vol. II, pp. 860-1. See also Pandit Hargopal Khasta, *Guldasta-i Kashmir* (Lahore, 1983), pp. 222-4.

[33] NAI/Foreign, S.E., Oct. 1886, nos. 235-300, p. 20; J. C. Bose, *Cashmere and its Prince* (Caluctta, 1889), p. 3.

into Kashmir in search of business or employment. New markets like the Maharaja Bazar and Maharaj Gunj, meant entirely for enterprising Punjabi traders, sprang up. The old trading community of Kashmir, mainly situated in the Juma Masjid area and Nowhatta in the city, could not compete with the Punjabis owing to lack of enterprise and capital. The result was that the export trade passed entirely into the hands of Punjabis who established a trading monopoly. Little wonder that there were few indigenous traders left in Srinagar at the close of the nineteenth century.[34]

It is well to remember that the Muslims of Srinagar had a strong link to commerce, but this was overshadowed by their unfortunate political circumstances.[35] That the development of trade was greatly hampered by the system under which the state itself monopolized all trade, can hardly be denied.[36] For example, the rice trade was practically in the hands of the Dogra government.[37] Silk, saffron, violets, various kinds of forest products, hemp, tobacco, waternuts and paper were at different times monopolized by the state which also enjoyed a monopoly of the shawl industry.[38] Apart from this, the government subjected various other trades to impositions.[39] It was the policy of Gulab Singh and his successors to make every product of the Valley a state monopoly.[40] Even prostitutes were taxed[41] and, in the words of Lawrence, everything save air and water was under taxation.[42] Thus the Dogra rulers killed initiative and the enterprise

[34] *History of Srinagar*, pp. 39-49, 77-80.

[35] Bates, *Gazetter of Kashmir* (Calcutta, 1973), p. 71; Arthur Brinckman, *Wrongs of Kashmir* (London, 1868), typed copy in the J & K Archives, Chapter II, p. 12. See also Henvy's note on famine. NAI/Foreign Sec. E, March 1883, nos. 83-5.

[36] Lawrence, op. cit., pp. 387-90.

[37] Ibid. Papers relating to Kashmir (London, 1890), p. 52. See also Khan Bahadur Gulam Ahmad Khan, 'Note on High Prices of Shali' (State Archives, Jammu, 1903), p. 4.

[38] Lawrence, op. cit., p. 417.

[39] The right to legalize marriage was farmed out and the office of grave digger was also taxed. Lawrence, op. cit., p. 417; Prinsep, *Imperial India* (London, 1879), p. 214; Richard Temple, *Journals kept in Hyderabad, Kashmir, Sikkim and Nepal*, vol. I (London, 1887), p. 302; Henry Torrens, *Travels in Ladakh Tartary and Kashmir* (London, 1863), p. 301. For greater details, see *History of Srinagar*, p. 79 and n.

[40] Lawrence, op. cit., p. 17.

[41] Younghusband, *Kashmir* (Edinburgh, 1909), p. 161; Bates, op. cit., p. 101; NAI Foreign, Pol. Sec. E., March 1883, no. 86.

[42] Lawrence, op. cit., p. 417; *The India We Served* (London, 1928), p. 134; Arthur Brinckman, op. cit., p. 13; Bates, op. cit., p. 101.

of many trading families. And this explains why, after the abolition of many vexatious taxes on the trade in 1885 and a marked improvement in the means of communication and transport, the Punjabi traders succeeded in weakening the financial predominance of the old Muslim trading classes of Kashmir.

However, one important consequence of the opening of the Jhelum-Valley road[43] was that the Muslims of Kashmir were no longer isolated from their brethren in the rest of the country. As a result of their contact with the outside world, the Muslim education movement was started in the 1890s by Mir Waiz Maulvi Ghulam Rasool Shah to safeguard against Muslims being driven towards Christianity. He believed that education on Western lines, supported by Koranic teachings, would produce young Muslims of capacity and character. In order to mobilize public opinion in his favour the Maulvi founded an Anjuman-i Nusrat-ul Islam which was devoted to religious and educational subjects of the Msulims. The climax of his efforts was the creation of a primary school in which religious instruction was imparted. With this initial purpose, the school slowly developed into a High School and began to follow the pattern of the Christian missionary schools in Srinagar. Interestingly enough, the local Muslims under the leadership of fanatic *mullahs* raised a violent agitation and attempts were made on the life of the Maulvi.[44]

The advent of modern education had a mixed effect. Kashmiri Muslims, in spite of the best efforts of Maulvi Rasool Shah, could not keep pace with educational developments. The Pandits, the first to take to modern education, were better equipped to adapt themselves to changing circumstances and could capture both low as well as high government posts.[45] It is, therefore, not surprising that concessions and privileges in education and appointment to government jobs in were the subject of petitions of 1907 and 1909. In the 1907 petition, Muslim petitioners implored the Government of India to take effective measures for the propagation of education

---

[43] See *History of Srinagar*, p. 80.

[44] Muhammad Din Fouq, *Mashahir-i-Kashmir* (Lahore, 1930), p. 123.

[45] In Oct. 1931 Maharaja Hari Singh expressed these words to a deputation of the Kashmiri Pandits: 'I am certain you will be the first to recognize that with the steady growth of education in other communities the position of advantage which your community enjoyed in the past in regard to the State service cannot continue.' *The Tribune*, 27 Oct. 1931.

among Kashmiri Muslims.[46] In 1909, thirty self-claimed represent-atives of the Muslims expressed the hope that the British would relieve the Muslims of Kashmir of the tyranny of their rulers.[47] The growing Muslim public opinion was also expressed through the press outside the state. As the press was practically non-existent in Kashmir, the Muslims utilized the Punjabi press to give vent to their feelings.[48]

The introspection of the Muslims is not only explicit in their petitions and letters addressed to the viceroys, Residents and the Maharaja, but also in the desire to keep pace with changing social conditions. In 1904, Muhammad-din Fouq, a prominent Kashmiri, moved by the ignorance, superstition and poverty of his brethren, requested the Maharaja to grant him permission to start a social magazine in Srinagar. But he was refused permission.[49] The noted writer did not, however, budge from the path he had chosen. In 1906, he started the *Kashmir Magazine* in Lahore which, no doubt, was influential both among the Muslims of India and Muslims of Kashmiri origin who had long settled in Punjab. The interest shown by the All-India Muhammadan Educational Conference in the welfare of Muslims of Kashmir in the 1920s was evidently the culmination of a process started by Fouq.[50]

Between 1900 and 1930, Muslim consciousness was further heightened by the propaganda carried in newspapers in Punjab that constantly reminded their readers of the inadequate enrolment of Muslim students in government schools in Kashmir, owing to the failure to employ adequate numbers of Muslim teachers.[51]

Although the Muslims of Kashmir were not affluent, a small core of wealthy merchants had emerged during the period when Kashmiri shawls were in demand in foreign countries. Among these were trading families like Shawls,[52] Ashais, Jehaz and Bachh. In spite of the decline of the shawl industry, the Shawls, for instance, made

---

[46] NAI/Foreign Intl., Feb. 1907, nos. 163-4.

[47] Ibid., Genl. B., Jan. 1909, nos. 15-16.

[48] See *The Observer*, Lahore, 16 Sept. 1911; also Report on Native Newspapers (Punjab, 1911), p. 975.

[49] Kashmir Government Records, General, 117, p. 51 of 1904.

[50] See Sir Henry Sharp's Report on Education in Kashmir (Calcutta, 1916), p. 40.

[51] See *History of Srinagar*, pp. 154, 186-7; also Abdus Salam Khurshid, *Suhafat Pakistan Wa Hind Maen* (Lahore, 1963), p. 450; *The Amrit Bazar Patrika*, 15 Aug. 1931; Prem Nath Bazaz, *Inside Kashmir* (Srinagar, 1941), pp. 116-17.

[52] Shawl is also a family name among Kashmiri Muslims.

handsome profits. This is shown not only by big business houses in the Punjab, Calcutta and Bombay, but also by their display of wealth during the great famine of 1877-9 when they rendered relief to thousands of famine-stricken people.[53] With developed communications after 1890, the commercial contact of some merchant families with northern India improved further, and drew some prominent Muslims into the mainstream of modern social and cultural activity in northern India. The Urdu-speaking Muslims of Kashmir were courted by north Indian Muslim organizations, such as the All-India Muhammdan Educational Conference, the Majlis-i Ahrar[54] and the Anjuman-i Himayat-i Islam, which attempted to weld Indian Muslims together to respond to the increasing social and political activity among non-Muslims and growing Muslim self-consciousness. In September 1913, a deputation of the All-India Muhammadan Educational Conference approached Maharaja Pratap Singh. Among the remedies suggested for the removal of Muslim backwardness was religious education; assistance to raise the schools run by Anjuman-i Nusrat-ul Islam to collegiate grade; special stipends and scholarships for Muslims; the appointment of Muslim professors, teachers and inspectors; and the appointment of a special inspector for Muslim education.[55]

The Muslims of Kashmir responded readily to the stimulus of some north Indian Muslim religious movements. The establishment of the Anjuman-i Ahl-i Hadith in Srinagar in the 1920s marked a further step in the growth of Muslim consciousness. Rich merchants like Haji Muhammad Shahdad and Ahmad Ullah Shahdad were among the founders of the Anjuman. The Anjuman achieved prominence under

---

[53] Mohammad Din Fouq, *Tarikh-i-Aqwam-i-Kashmir*, p. 336.

[54] The Ahrar movement began with the establishment of the All-India Majlis-i-Ahrar-i-Islam at Amritsar in 1931 with Habib-ur-Rehman as its President and Daud Ghaznavi and Mazhar Ali as its Secretaries. It aimed at working for the economic, educational and social uplift of Muslims. Besides, its object was to awaken political consciousness and to infuse the spirit of Islam among Muslims and also to work for the freedom of the country by peaceful methods (a note on Muslim political organizations, NAI/Home Pol., File No. 150 of 1934, p. 27).

Though the movement was started by pro-Congress Muslims with the main purpose of maintaining the position of the Muslims in the Congress itself and to secure seats in the working committee, the Ahrars did not stick to any consistent policy. See J.B. Mathur, *Muslims and Changing India* (Delhi, 1972), pp. 102-10.

[55] *Sharp's Report*, pp. 40-1; see also Kashmir Government Records (O.E.R.), File No. 217, 1913, p. 96.

the inspiring leadership of Maulvi Ghulam Nabi Mubaraki who was in close contact with the Ahl-i Hadith leaders of Punjab.[56]

A careful reading of *The Muslim*,[57] the official organ of the Anjuman-i Ahl-i Hadith, reveals that the aim of the north Indian inspired organization was to purge contemporary Islam of excessive rituals and practices, such as the extravagant funeral ceremonies. Yet the leaders of the Anjuman often held the custodians of the shrines responsible for much of the ills of Muslim society.[58] The hypocricy, greed and degeneration of the *mullahs* is shown by their misuse of holy shrines for the organized exploitation of the masses. Instead of exercising a moral influence on the people, the *mullahs* had contributed a great deal to superstition, ignorance and poverty of their credulous believers. Interesting to note is the fact that *noufal* processions in Srinagar were often organized by the *mullahs* at the command of the Dogra rulers.[59]

The leaders of the Anjuman were thus justified in describing the condition of the Kashmiri Muslims as worse than that of political slaves.[60] True, the influence of the Anjuman was limited to a few families in Kashmir; yet by attacking the social evils, which like a cancer were eating into the vitals of Muslims society, the Anjuman did fill an important gap by providing intellectual leadership.

The 1920s was a formative decade in the awakening of Kashmiri social consciousness. The All-India Muslim Kashmiri Conference, started in the Punjab by Kashmiri Muslim settlers, had done a great deal for the Muslims of Kashmir. In 1920 a deputation sought an interview with the Maharaja regarding the inaction of his government in implementing Sir Henry Sharp's recommendations for the improvement of education among Muslims, but the interview was refused.[61]

This rebuff made it impossible for the Muslims of Kashmir to keep

---

[56] Based on the present writer's interview with late Maulvi Ghulam Nabi Mubaraki.

[57] Maulvi Mubaraki was kind enough to donate some rare issues of *The Muslim* to my personal library.

[58] *The Muslim*, 2 Oct. 1941; 2 March 1942; Safar, 1360; The Hijri, Moharram, 1360 H.

[59] *Akhbarat*, 1852, vols. Vff. 37 ab, 63, vol. VIII, 1855, ff. 129 ab. Ghulam Nabi Shah Khanyari, *Wajeez-ut-Tawarikh* (MS), CCAS. f. 69b. For more details on *noufal*, see *History of Srinagar*, p. 106.

[60] *The Muslim*, Safar, 1360 H.

[61] Kashmir Government Records, File No. 2/Misc. 14, 1920.

silent and they showed their resentment against the government in various forms. The first signs of unrest appeared in Srinagar, the political, intellectual and commercial capital. Situated in the centre of the Valley and commanding trade routes to Central Asia and Punjab, the city contained the wealthiest and most articulate section of Muslims, the Naqshbandis, the Shawls and the Shahdads. While the Naqshbandis had large landed estates in the Valley and had also been the leading merchants, the Shawls and the Shahdads had a monopoly of the carpet and shawl trade in Kashmir. Srinagar also provided religious leadership to the entire Valley. In fact, before 1931 the Muslims of Kashmir were completely under the spell of the two religious heads of Srinagar, the Mir Waiz of Juma Masjid and the Mir Waiz of Shah Hamdan Mosque, the two quite often at loggerheads. The religious, merchant and landed élite were the first to articulate the grievances and aspirations of the Muslim middle class. Thus, when Viceroy Reading visited Srinagar in 1924,[62] some of the prominent members of the Muslim community (including Khwaja Saad-ud-Din Shawl, Khwaja Nur Shah Naqshbandi, Khwaja Hasan Shah Naqshbandi Jagirdar, Mir Waiz Kashmir Maulvi Ahmed Ullah of Juma Mosque, Khwaja Maqbool Pandit, Khwaja Sayyid Hasan Shah Jalali) submitted a memorandum to him. They not only demanded a larger representation of Muslims in government services and an improvement in the condition of Muslim education in the state, but also the grant of proprietary rights in land to the peasants, and abolition of the hated corvées. This shows that middle class leaders wanted to utilize the support of the masses for the further-ance of their demands.

As stated earlier, the 1920s mark an important stage in the growth of public opinion in Kashmir. At this stage in the awakening of social consciousness all classes of the Muslim population in Kashmir were seething with discontent. The shawl trade which had been subjected to rigorous impositions had declined.[63] This had caused unemployment among the weavers.[64] Even though the carpet

---

[62] *The Ranbir*, 23 Aug. 1927; *The Pioneer*, 4 Sept. 1931; *Inside Kashmir*, p. 84; *Daur i-Jadeed*, 8 July 1955.

[63] NAI/Foreign Sec. E., March 1883, no. 86, p. 15; see also Diwan Kishan Lal's report, Foreign Sec., 31 March 1846, nos. 66-70 (MS); ibid., Foreign Pol., July 1863, nos. 73-5.

[64] Duing the reigns of Maharaja Gulab Singh and Ranbir Singh there were 30,000 to 40,000 shawl weavers in Srinagar alone (NAI/Foreign Sec. E., March 1883, no. 86).

industry had absorbed some shawl weavers,[65] there were many who were wandering in search of employment. Equally deplorable was the condition of the *papier maché* artists, most of whom were thrown out of work on account of the non-availability of raw material. As a result of the recession caused by World War I, many artisans were unemployed and most of them are said to have sold their ordinary clothes so as to provide themselves with food.[66] Workers in the silk factory of Srinagar, who were demanding reasonable wages and medical facilities, were equally distressed and frustrated. In 1924, the workers in the state-owned silk factory went on strike.[67] It did not last long. None the less, it signaled a new development, the emergence of the working class.

It should be borne in mind that the rich merchant of Srinagar, Khwaja Saad-ud-Din Shawl, had not only played a leading role in submitting the memorandum to the Viceroy in 1924, but was also involved in the silk factory riots. This explains why he was banished from the state. But so great was the pressure of public opinion that the new Maharaja, Hari Singh, was obliged to lift the ban in 1927. On his return home, Sadd-ud-Din Shawl was given a hero's welcome. However, the government in its vendetta against the emerging leaders deprived them of their landed property. Two religious heads were warned, and some official privileges which they had been hitherto enjoying were withdrawn.[68]

It was in the late 1920s that the merchant leadership was reinforced by the emergence of some young Muslim men, fresh from universities like Aligarh, where they had come in contact with Muslim leaders and propagators of pan-Islamism. In April 1930 the Reading Room[69] was inaugurated in Srinagar and under its auspices several

---

Census of India (J & K) 1891 records that there were 5148 shawl weavers. The level to which shawl trade of Srinagar had declined may be judged from the fact that only 148 persons were found working at it when an industrial enumeration was held in 1921. See *Census* 1911, vol. 1, p. 232.

[65] *The Valley of Kashmir*, p. 375; Marion Doughty, *A Foot Through the Kashmir Valley* (London, 1901), p. 158. See also *Imperial Gazetteer*, p. 120.

[66] Kashmir Government Records, General, File No. 278, p. 16, 1915. For the decline of *papier maché* craft, see *East and West*, XV, July-Dec. 1916, p. 661.

[67] NAI/Foreign Pol. File No. 19(2) of 1924, nos. 1-4. See also *The Ranbir*, 2 Sept. 1934; *Amrit Bazar Patrika*, 25 Aug. 1931.

[68] Rashid Taasir, *Tahreek-i-Huriyyat-i-Kashmir*, vol. I (Srinagar, 1968), p. 72. See also *The Ranbir*, 23 Aug. 1927.

[69] *Inside Kashmir*, pp. 97-8.

meetings were held. Azad Subhani of Calcutta's Juma Mosque was in Srinagar on the eve of the formation of the Reading Room Party. He held secret meetings with the religious heads of Srinagar urging them to support the young men.[70] Thus the members of the Reading Room Party were definitely drawn into the maelstrom of the politics of the Muslims of undivided India. This is also supported by the activities of the leaders of the All-India Kashmir Committee in Punjab and the Majlis-i Ahrar-i Islam Hind.[71]

From 1930 to 1932 when Kashmir witnessed the persecution and repression of Muslim agitators, politics remained under the direction and virtual control of the Punjabi Muslims. The Ahrars launched a people's movement in Kashmir and carried on intense propaganda in the form of a press campaign, meetings, processions of Kashmiri labourers, and the celebration of Kashmir day, against the state.[72] In June 1931, the Ahmadiyas in their bid to gain a firm foothold in Kashmir sent Syed Wali Shah Zain-ul-Abidin and Chaudhari Bashir Ahmad to Srinagar to guide them.[73] Even Shaikh Muhammad Abdullah, the emerging champion of Muslim sentiment and a very active member of the Reading Room Party, did not lose sight of the contribution of the 'Muslims of Punjab and Hind' and the Muslim Press to the ferment of the early thirties when he presided over the first session of the Jammu and Kashmir Muslim Conference in October 1932. In his presidential address the Shaikh thanked them for all that they had done for Kashmiri Muslims.[74]

Yet, the ideology of some Muslim leaders of the Punjab did not fit into the social milieu of Kashmir. Their constant harping on the

---

[70] *Tahreek-i-Huriyyat-i-Kashmir*, vol. I, p. 77.

[71] The Kashmir Committee was formed after the meeting of some well-known Muslims like Mian Afzal Husain, Zulfiqar Khan, Maulana Abul Kalam Azad, Dr. M.A. Ansari, Maulana Shaukat Ali, Dr. S.M. Iqbal, the Nawab of Dacca, Shaikh Sadiq Husain Ansari, Saifuddin Kitchlew and the Nawab of Kanchore in Simla on 24 July 1931. Mirza Mian Bashiruddin Mehmud Ahmad, Khalifa of the Quadain Party, was made its President. Though initially started with the object of rendering financial assistance to Kashmir leaders for organizing the movement against the maharaja, the Kashmir Committee openly supported the Muslim movement by sending *jathas* to Kashmir in 1931. Ibid., pp. 141-2; also *Inside Kashmir*, p. 142.

[72] NAI/Home Poll. File No. 150 of 1934; see also *Civil and Military Gazette*, 4 Feb. 1932.

[73] *Tahreek-i-Huriyyat-i-Kashmir*, vol. 1, p. 95.

[74] Proceedings of the Jammu and Kashmir Muslim Conference, 1932.

'Hindu Raj' of Kashmir did rouse the Muslim sentiments.[75] But soon the Kashmiri leaders' sense of history convinced them of the hollowness of the idea of a religious conflict against the Dogras. This also explains why, from the very start of the foundation of the Muslim Conference in 1932, its aims and objects remained secular in principle.[76]

It is necessary to examine here why after 1932 or so the Muslim leaders of Kashmir did not allow their minds to be influenced by the Muslim politics of Punjab. In the first place, the association of Kashmir leaders with the All-India Kashmir Committee which had some Ahmadiyas as its members, generated doubts among their co-religionists regarding their religious beliefs. Mir Waiz Muhammad Yusuf Shah made much of the Shaikh's association with the Ahmadiyas. His diatribes against the Shaikh[77] were, however, understandable. In fact, the Shaikh's growing popularity[78] marked the gradual eclipse of the influence of the religious leadership among the people. But so vehement was the propaganda carried on against what they called the Shaikh's 'unholy alliance' with the Ahmadiyas, that the Kashmir leader had to write to Allama Anwar Shah (Shaikh-ul-Hadith) in 1932 affirming his faith in the finality of Prophethood (*khatam-i-nabuuwat*).[79]

---

[75] The observations of Maulana Abdus Salam Hamdani on the eve of the celebration of 'Kashmir Day' in Amritsar on 14 Aug. 1931 are worth quoting here: '. . . the Muslim subjects of Kashmir were greatly oppressed. There was nothing communal in this agitation and it was a pity that some people were trying to give a communal colour', *The Tribune*, 8 Aug. 1931.

[76] See, for example, *Inside Kashmir*, p. 187.

[77] On 30 January 1933, Mir Waiz Mohammad Yusuf Shah in a sermon at Khanqah-i-Naqshbandia alleged that the Shaikh was paving the way for spread of Ahmadiya movement in Kashmir.

[78] That the Mir Waiz felt the growing popularity of Abdullah as a challenge to his leadership is clearly noted in a letter dated 31 Oct. 1933 addressed by a Qadiani, Mirza Bashir Mehmud Ahmad to the people of Kashmir. Cited in *Tahreek-i-Huriyyat-i-Kashmir*, vol. 1, pp. 270-4.

[79] A copy of this letter is with Abdul Rehman Kundoo of Gojwara in Srinagar. One should not however, lose sight of the fact that Abdullah received firm-support from the Ahmadiyas. That Abdullah was closely associated with the Ahmadiyas is evident from a reference by the British Resident in his report of 30 Oct. 1931 in which he referred to the arrest of S.M. Abdullah 'Qadiani'. NAI, File No. 35, Foreign and Pol. Report on Kashmir for the period ending 31 Oct. 1931. But it sould not be supposed that the Kashmir leader had turned an Ahmadi, for 'the record of a conference of the All Jammu and Kashmir Muslim Conference held at Sialkot on 10 February 1940 shows

The pressure of Hindu public opinion in Kashmir also helped to loosen the grip of the Muslim leaders of Punjab on Kashmir politics. Understandably, the Kashmiri Pandits were initially reluctant to join the Muslim leaders against the Dogra government. But soon some prominent leaders among them realized the futility of their opposition. Thus the formation of a party on the lines of the All-India National Congress 'having a common flag, common slogans, common programme and a common goal' was advocated time and again in certain sections of the 'Hindus Press'[80]. Last but not least, the gradual association of the Muslim leadership of Kashmir with Gandhi and Nehru also began to influence the course of Muslim politics in the Valley. In November 1934, Abdullah while on a visit to various parts of India came into contact with Nehru and other nationalist leaders. Addressing a press conference in Lahore, the Kashmir leader accused the Muslim leaders of Punjab of interference in Kashmiri affairs and also inciting communal tensions in Kashmir. Abdullah also expressed his desire to lay the foundation of an organization that would support the programme of the Indian National Congress.[81]

Abdullah's address at the press conference caused much reaction in Punjab. The nationalists applauded him, but the Hindu and Muslim communalists launched a virulent attack on him. While the Punjabi Muslims carried on vehement propaganda against Abdullah, the Punjabi Hindus described his statement as mere 'eyewash'. The Kashmir leader, however, proved true to his convictions. Soon after his return from Lahore, he began to mobilize public opinion in favour of a united party of Hindus and Muslims of Kashmir. It was not an easy task to prepare the ground for the foundation of a nationalist party, considering that a sizeable number of Muslim leaders (particularly Chaudhari Ghulam Abbas) wanted to retain the Muslim character of the Muslim Conference. However, it was Shaikh Abdullah's convictions that ultimately triumphed. He succeeded in winning over to his side even a diehard like Chaudhari Ghulam Abbas of Jammu. It was Chaudhari Abbas who, in a presidential

---

that Abdullah staunchly denied being an Ahmadi!' Spencer Lavan, *The Ahmadiyah Movement: A History & Perspective* (Delhi, 1974), p. 159.

[80] *Kashmir Times*, 7 Aug. 1937, also 3 April 1937; *Hamdard*, 19 March 1938; *Inside Kashmir*, p. 365.

[81] *Tahreek-i-Huriyyat-i-Kashmir*, vol. 1, pp. 327-8.

address at the annual session of the Muslim Conference in October 1935, made a fervent appeal to the non-Muslims of the state to join Muslims in their struggle against the maharaja for 'social justice'. In May 1937, in his address at the annual session of the Muslim Conference at Poonch, Abdullah reiterated his party's stand for protecting the rights of the minorities and even pointed out that the Muslim Conference had gone a step further in this direction than the Indian National Congress.[82]

It was under these circumstances that the All Jammu and Kashmir National Conference took place in 1939. The conversion of the Muslim Conference into the National Conference was an event of far-reaching importance in Kashmir's modern history. The change, besides giving a fresh impetus to the movement against the maharaja, gave a definite political unity and political identity to Kashmiris. The reason why the All-India Muslim League could not make much headway in Kashmir was the opposition of the National Conference which had no faith in the ideology of the League. The National Conference articulated the need for political and economic programmes, strengthened by a strong regional identification and leadership which for all practical purposes wished the group to continue as a functional part of Kashmir society. Furthermore, the orientation of the National Conference was purely Kashmiri; its outlook was not based on the lack of social integration with non-Muslims, but on close cooperation with them. It reflected a broader trend in Kashmiri society like the Kashmiri writers of the 1930s and 1940s who were both self-conscious and socially conscious in their endeavour to preserve what was of abiding value in their own culture and to assimilate from the outside what was vital for the building of a new society.

Ghulam Ahmed Mahjoor, among others, was the most potent force who popularized the concept of 'Kashmiri nation' in his patriotic songs. To him, religious humanism was one of the chief character-istics of Kashmiri nationalism: 'Hindus will keep the helm and Muslims play the oars; Let us together row ashore the boat of the country.' Small wonder, therefore, one of Mahjoor's patriotic poems was adopted as the anthem (*Qaumi Tarana*) of the National Conference.

---

[82] Ibid.

Significantly, the emerging nationalism of the Muslims of Kashmir was not centred on the symbols of Islam or past Muslim supremacy. The leaders of the Indian National Congress were, therefore, drawn to Kashmir. A certain distinctiveness about the cultural foundations of the politics of the Muslims of Kashmir was particularly recognized by a keen observer and statesman like Pandit Nehru. Personally, Nehru was not only fond of Kashmir but profoundly proud of his familial ties with the picturesque Valley. He often talked about the distinctive character of Kashmir and its people. Not only did Nehru regard Kashmir as 'a definite historical cultural and linguistic unit', but he even described it as 'as rich and lovely county to live in'. While 'India', according to Nehru, could not compare with China in craftsmanship, in Kashmir, he felt, 'there was something which could equal China'. He was full of praise for the Kashmiris' skill in handicrafts and their prominent role in many walks of life in 'India'. He was proud of the fact that Kashmiri Pandits were 'recognized in India as Kashmiris'. But he was sorry to note that many of the 'Muslim Kashmiris' were 'not known as Kashmiris'.

One might be tempted to say that Nehru touched the right chord by popularizing the concept of Kashmiri identity or *Kashmiriyat* to counter the influence of the two-nation theory on Kashmiri Muslims. But, then, he also struck the right balance by discovering the roots of the dilemma of Kashmiri identity. He was conscious of the sad reality that 'impelled by a desire for self-protection' the Kashmiri Pandits had organized themselves as a 'communal group' after the rise of the 'popular mass movement' in 1939. He therefore warned his 'own people' not to 'fall into the trap which minorities so easily fall' and urged them to join the National Conference which under Shaikh Abdullah's leadership had steered the mass movement 'out of the narrow waters of communalism into the broad sea of nationalism'.[83]

That Nehru was determined to give a subtle direction to Kashmiri nationalism is further illustrated by his assiduous interest in the affairs of the National Conference and constant association with Shaikh Abdullah. Since both Nehru and Abdullah were men of lofty vision, the latter found in Nehru an ardent champion of Kashmiri nationalism.[84]

[83] Ibid.
[84] See my letter in *The Times of India*, Sept. 1981.

Given the nature of the Kashmiri Muslim struggle for political recognition during the Dogra rule, the possibility of J & K acceding to either India or Pakistan on the eve of Partition inevitably carried serious implications. The possibility of either was bleak, not only due to the distinctive character of Kashmiri Muslim nationalism, but also owing to the Maharaja's desire to preserve the unique character of his state with a large Muslim population.[85] However, the riots of the Muslim 'rebels' in Poonch and the consequent infiltration of Pathan tribesmen from the North-West Frontier to assist Muslims against the Dogra army proved to be a turning-point in sealing the fate of J & K as an independent state. Fearing the forcible annexation of the state to Pakistan, the Maharaja fled to Delhi. Under these rather exceptional circumstances,[86] he appealed to the Indian Government for help and offered to accede to the Indian Union. Delhi was, however, cautious in its response, for two basic reasons: first, J & K was a Muslim majority area and, second, the mass participation of Muslims in the struggle against the Maharaja had convinced Indian statesmen of the cultural and regional roots of their nationalism. Thus Delhi did not risk the possibility of annexing J & K on the principle of complete integration. This explains the somewhat hesitant acceptance of the offer of accession and the stipulation that the accession would be ratified ultimately by popular consultation. However, the Indian forces that landed in Kashmir were able to drive the Pathans out of the Valley, though the ceasefire called by the United Nations divided the area into two administered territories, 'Azad Kashmir' and Indian-administered Kashmir. On 5 March 1948, the Maharaja conceded full governmental powers to the National Conference. Shaikh Abdullah became the Prime Minister and the Constituent Assembly of Indian-administered Kashmir, elected in October 1951, ratified the accession, while ratifying the autonomy of the state. The accession of the state was given legal and constitutional validity by the incorporation of Article 370 in the Indian Constitution which defined its special relationship with India.

It would appear that the Kashmiri Muslim leadership set at naught the most widely-accepted view that Islam and nationalism are opposed to each other and worked out a harmonious relationship

[85] Shaikh Mohammed Abdullah, *Astish-i-Chinar* (Srinagar, 1986), p. 397.
[86] See Alstair Lamb, *Kashmir: A Disputed Legacy, 1846-1991* (London, 1991), pp. 148-56.

between the two. Kashmiri Muslims, under the leadership of Shaikh Abdullah, generated both a positive conception of what they wanted and the political means to attaining it, attested to by their mass participation in the elections to the State Assembly and the Indian Parliament in the aftermath of the Indira Gandhi-Abdullah accord of 1975. Significantly, even after the accord, Kashmiri Muslims remained deeply concerned to preserve Article 370. Even those who vehemently opposed the accord felt constrained to participate in the elections in the face of perceived threats to the cultural and religious identity of Kashmiri Muslims from Hindu communalist forces out-side the Valley which launched a campaign for the*abrogation of Article 370. The Jamaat-i Islami's participation in the elections in the wake of the accord, for instance, was apparently prompted by a resolve not only to liberate the state form the 'Indian yoke' but also by the contradictory aim of capturing political power to enforce the *Shari'a* from above. Paradoxically, the Jamaat's earlier attempt to fulfil such an objective, even though partial and superficial, had come to naught in 1971.

The Jamaat-i Islami's failure to overthrow the government resulted in a strange admixture of Islam and politics in the life of a certain section of Kashmiri Muslim youth. The Jamiyat-i Tulaba, led by Shaikh Tajamul Islam[87] and by Dr Mohammad Ayub Thakur,[88] attempted to organize an international conference of Muslim youth in Srinagar as a response to Hindu communal endeavour to undermine Kashmiri Muslim identity. Having been denied permission to hold the conference at the last moment, the Jamiyat-i Tulaba raised the slogan of 'Brahmin imperialism'. After going underground, the youth leaders succeeded in enlisting support in Pakistan and Saudi

---

[87] I chanced to exchange ideas with Shaikh Tajmul Islam for nearly half an hour during my visit to Islamabad. While he was driving me to Rawalpindi after offering me a lift to the Faisal Mosque, I was wondering, with my eyes open in his air-conditioned imported car, whether the adherents of 'Islamic ideology' would ever be able to deal with the Kashmir problem in a deeper historical perspective. For challenging views on 'Islamic ideology', see Ishaq Khan, *Experiencing Islam* (Delhi, 1997).

[88] During my fellowship period (Feb.-Sept. 1992) at Oxford, Dr Ayub Thakur played host to me on several occasions. In spite of our different perceptions and perspectives on the Kashmir problem, both of us would frequently burst into tears while listening to a patriotic Kashmiri-cum-Urdu poem sung by Hemal:

Karyo manz jigars jaai chhamna maai mashae ne, meray watan, meray watan.

Arabia where they gradually evolved the strategy of indoctrinating Kashmiri youth with the spirit of *jihad*.

However, it must be pointed out that more than any other religious or political group, the National Conference played a crucial role in perpetuating a fear psychosis about Delhi's policies. Its determination to exercise effective control over the famous shrines and mosques of the Valley, through its subsidiary wing, the Auqaf, was intrinsically aimed at buttressing the ideology of Muslim *Kashmiriyat*.[89] Even after assuming the reins of government, Shaikh Abdullah continued to make the shrine of Hazratbal subservient to the need for preserving the bruised identity of his people. He roused anti-Indian sentiment at Hazratbal by his diatribes against Hindu communalist forces. The controversy over the Resettlement Bill gave a semblance of respectability to Shaikh Abdullah as a champion of Kashmiri Muslim sentiment.[90]

The tables, however, were turned on the National Conference soon after the so-called Rajiv-Farooq accord, denounced as a total sell-out. Under the influence of his personal understanding with Rajiv Gandhi, Farooq Abdullah began to equate *Kashmiriyat* with regionalism and fundamentalism. What, in fact, hurt the susceptibilities of Kashmiri Muslims was the attack made on the concept of their historic identity from the pulpit of the *dargah* of Hazratbal by the once flamboyant champion of 'your country, my country! It is Kashmir, it is Kashmir'.[91]

Consequently, the concern for preserving the Muslim character of the state reached a crescendo in the unification of various religious and political groups as the Muslim United Front. In the changed political scenario in the Valley, the sole aim of the enthusiastic adherents of Kashmiri Muslim identity was to ensure the defeat of the National Conference at the next elections. However, the slogan-

---

I wish I could carve out a place for you (Kashmir) in my lacerated heart
(Alas!) there is no room in it except the deep sense of longing for (you), my country, my country.

[89] See Ishaq Khan, 'The Importance of the dargah of Hazratbal in the Socio-Religious and Political life of Kashmiri Muslims', in C.W. Troll (ed.), *Muslim Shrines in India* (Delhi, 1989).

[90] For an analysis of the controversy over the Bill, see Lamb, op. cit., p. 320.

[91] In the early 1970s, Farooq Abdullah roused the sentiments of Kashmiri youth by raising the slogan of '*choun desh meuon desh, Koshur Desh, Koshur Desh*' by leading several processions in Srinagar.

mongering of the MUF afforded an opportunity to the National Conference leadership to project the suppressed concern for Kashmiri Muslim identity as 'fundamentalism'. The Centre thus had no qualms about giving free licence to the National Conference to rig the elections. The victory of the National Conference, however, proved to be a nightmare in that it served to confirm the widespread, though orchestrated, belief of Kashmiri Muslims about the insidious designs of the 'Brahmin imperialism' against them.

Seen in a deeper historical perspective, however, the problem of Kashmir Muslims is in essence the legacy of both British imperialism and the post-1947 developments resulting in the division of J & K and the expulsion of Shaikh Abdullah from the prime ministership in 1953. What is more, Nehru's idealism and stand as the champion of the right of self-determination for the people of J & K, even in the aftermath of Shaikh Abdullah's removal, further complicated the problem by internationalizing it.[92] Pakistan's 'petty quibbles' over 'Nehru's suggestion for a new plebiscite administrator'[93] kept the problem alive instead of solving it. Little wonder, then, that after the foundation of the All Jammu and Kashmir Plebiscite Front in 1955, Kashmiri Muslims found themselves interlocked between an urge to free the Valley from India's control and a subtle strategy of arrogating to themselves the leadership of the Buddhists and Hindus of the Ladakh and Jammu regions. Thus, with the passage of time the variegated complexities of the Kashmir problem were compounded by the complex role of Muslim leadership in the post-1953 period.

[92] Nehru wrote to Bakshi Ghulam Mohammad: 'Obviously I cannot ignore the wishes of the people of Kashmir. If our efforts thus far have been, as it now appears, in vain and the only result that we can expect is some sort of tragedy, even so we have to behave decently and honourably, adhering to what we have stood for.' Cited in S. Gopal, *Jawaharlal Nehru: A Biography* (Delhi, 1975), vol. 2, pp. 181-2. Realizing the implication of Nehru's sentiments, the then Prime Minister of Jammu & Kashmir threatened to resign. But Nehru seems to have been prepared to lose Kashmir in a plebiscite rather than hold it against the widespread resentment among Kashmiri Muslims over Abdullah's arrest. Thus he advised Bakshi: 'We have to consider the various forces at work and—try to fashion our policy so as to get the best advantages out of it—we have to think to the future . . . (and) choose a path which not only promises the greatest advantages but is dignified and in keeping with our general policy.' Ibid.

[93] See Gowher Rizvi, 'India, Pakistan, and the Kashmir Problem, 1947-1972', in *Perspectives on Kashmir: The Roots of Conflict in South Asia* (Boulder & Co., 1992), pp. 58-9.

Ironically, later in the mid-1970s, no less a person than the founder of the Plebiscite Front himself described the twenty-year-old movement for the right of self-determination of Kashmiris as *awara gardi* (a movement that had lost its way).

The contradictory character of the politics of Kashmiri Muslims, therefore, consists, on the one hand, in their historic role in discrediting the imperial designs behind the foundation of J & K as contradictory on the one hand and in inheriting the colonial legacy by assuming the leadership of Hindus and Buddhists of Jammu and Ladakh regions on the other.

In the 1930s, the Kashmiri Muslim struggle was directed against the sale of the Valley to the Dogra chief of Jammu. The culmination of such a struggle was the Quit Kashmir movement launched by the National Conference in 1946 against the Dogra occupation of the Valley. Perhaps the Kashmir problem would not have assumed complicated and perilous proportions had the Kashmiri leadership been content with liberating the Valley from the chains of the Dogras. Such a freedom movement would have led to the separation of the Valley from Jammu and Ladakh. However, the most complex feature of the freedom struggle, though the most significant in historical terms, was that it was fundamentally aimed at overthrowing the imperial yoke. The struggle for freedom was not merely suffused with the Kashmiri ethos but had widespread ramifications for the politics of the subcontinent. The unfolding of this process was visible in the gradual submergence of the Kashmir movement in secular ideologies of nationalism, socialism and democracy. Such a development was bound to be in conflict with the ideologies of Hindu communalism and Muslim separatism. Little wonder that the Muslim Conference, though rejuvenated by Chaudhri Ghulam Abbas of Jammu,[94] was overshadowed by the National Conference under the leadership of Shaikh Abdullah. While the Muslim Conference sought the integration of J & K with Pakistan, the National Conference advocated the right of the oppressed and enslaved Kashmiris to be the architects of their own future destiny on the firm ground of the 'New Kashmir' Manifesto. The mass popularity of Abdullah therefore lay in his identification with the problems of the region rather than that of a particular religious group.

[94] For his autobiography and political role, see Chaudhri Ghulam Abbas, *Kashmakash* (reprint Pakistan, n.d.).

Yet post-Partition developments leading first to the Islamization and subsequently Indianization and internationalization of the Kashmir problem obstructed a lasting solution. And, indeed, it was the Indianization aspect that assumed prominence over others. In the first instance, the presence of Indian troops in J & K was overloaded with moral connotations of international dimensions. Not only did Shaikh Abdullah always try to justify their presence as 'saviours' in terms of the historical experience of Kashmiri subjugation to Mughal, Afghan and Dogra rule, but the presence of Indian forces was also deemed necessary in order to enable India to play its role as the international guarantor of the right of self-determination for the people of J & K. However, extraneous circumstances like Shaikh Abdullah's hobnobbing with the US, the agitation launched by the Hindus of the Jammu region against Shaikh Abdullah's government and the machinations of Kashmiri Pandits in the corridors of power in Delhi in the wake of the introduction of radical land reforms—all combined to knock the bottom out of the 'Naya Kashmir' of Shaikh Abdullah's dreams. Consequently, Kashmiri Muslim nationalism, based intrinsically on a secular foundation, was bound to reorient or redefine itself in the fear psychosis of being swamped by Hindu nationalism. Shaikh Abdullah's expulsion as the Prime Minister of J & K in 1953 and his subsequent imprisonment for fourteen years did not mean a change of government but a subversion of the ideology of secular nationalism fostered by the Congress and the socialist leadership in the pre-1947 period.[95] The tragedy of Kashmiri Muslims thus lies not only in Shaikh Abdullah's failure in securing a respectable position for them in the comity of nations but also in his acquiescence and then defiance of the Indian presence in J & K. What is more, his uncompromising and somewhat ambiguous position in retaining the colonial legacy threw a wet blanket over Kashmiri Muslim nationalism. What has seldom been emphasized in the extant literature is the Kashmir Assembly's decision to ratify the accession to the Indian Union without taking

---

[95] See, for example, ibid., p. 254. Ever since the deposition of Shaikh Abdullah on 9 Aug. 1963, there was hardly a home in the Valley which did not tune into 'Azad Kashmir' and Pakistan radio. It may sound strange that before the 1953 episode Shaikh Abdullah's governement had put a ban on listening to Radio Pakistan and 'Azad Kashmir'. The present author constantly listened to 'Azad Kashmir' Radio particularly from the mid-fifties to the emergence of Bangladesh. Its favourite theme was the liberation of Kashmir by means of *jihad*.

into confidence the people living in 'Azad Kashmir', notwithstanding the reservation of seats for the representatives of 'Azad Kashmir' and also that of the latter. Shaikh Abdullah did realize the implications of the unconstitutional and unilateral manner in which his Assembly had proceeded. Therefore, after 9 August 1953, for nearly a quarter of the century when Kashmiri Muslims remained cut off from the Indian national mainstream, their undisputed leader did not mince words about challenging the accession issue in numerous and fiery speeches to mammoth public gatherings that he delivered following his release in 1958 and 1964.

The emergence of Bangladesh, however, brought about a great change in Shaikh Abdullah's outlook. If on the one hand, the changed circumstances in subcontinental politics convinced him of Pakistan's inability to play the desired role of championing the fragile cause of Kashmiri Muslims on the international forums, on the other, Bangladesh's separation from Pakistan on the basis of cultural democracy revitalized his faith in *Kashmiriyat*. Abdullah, though deeply conscious of the failure of his life-long mission in wooing his Pandit compatriots, not to mention the Hindus and Buddhists of Jammu and Ladakh, and even a considerable number of Muslim Punjabis and Gujjars, was at long last compelled to accept the *de facto* division of J & K into 'Azad Kashmir' and Indian-administered Kashmir. Against the historic background of his valiant struggle for vindicating his stand on the sale of Kashmir, the policy of assimilating the Dogra and Ladakhi identities into *Kashmiriyat* in one form or the other was an embarrassing blunder. Worse, the abysmal *faux pas* of Delhi in perpetuating the false interpretation of *Kashmiriyat* as a basis for ensuring Kashmiri Muslims integration with the Indian Union led to a blurring of perspectives and a clouding of judgment on the centuries-old identity crisis of an ethnic nationality with a distinct Central Asian and Persian ethos. For this reason alone, the pendulum has swung back to the side of those who wish to use the Valley's shrines as means of preserving the 'Muslim character' of the colonial inheritance.

The story of Kashmiri Muslims is a conundrum not only for the experts, but paradoxically even for Kashmiri Muslims themselves. Their story has been a long one, with many vicissitudes. Neither India nor Pakistan have garnered much glory in their policy of maintaining the balance of terror at the cost of suffering of the teeming millions of poverty-stricken inhabitants. The point is that this story is not over, particularly as the psychological genocide with which Kashmiri Muslims have felt threatened since 1953, has now, unfortunately, a reality in the over-reaction of state power to the challenges of militancy. And what has turned the second great tragedy in the subcontinent after Partition into a comedy of contemporary politics is the ingenuity of Delhi and Islamabad in allowing the centuries-old Kashmiri urge for preserving a cultural and religious identity to flounder in a whirlwind of political romances inspired paradoxically by battered ideologies like Indian secularism and Muslim separatism.

Partition's Biharis

PAPIYA GHOSH

This paper will focus on the bonds of region and *biradari* that pushed through the homogenizing political trajectories of the 1940s and explain some of the complexities within the Bihari Muslim community in the Partition diaspora, as well as in contemporary Bihar.[1] But first a preliminary mapping of the community.

Bihar did not form a single political entity in the medieval period. Within the broad regions, north and south of the Ganges, the frontiers of the local chiefs shifted constantly. It was during the first half of the fourteenth century that the political boundaries of Bihar underwent several changes. The first was the merging of Tirhut and Bihar, i.e. south Bihar. The other was that Bihar was constituted as a province, though its boundaries were not quite the same as those of the subsequent Mughal *suba* of Bihar.[2]

It appears that factors other than political power explain the spread of Islam in Bihar from around the twelfth century. Thus although the area north of the Ganges came under Turkish rule later than the south, today 8/9 of the most populous Muslim districts lie north of the Ganga.[3] Here, as elsewhere, Muslims comprised local converts largely from the Hindu artisan caste and foreign immigrants.[4]

[1] Mushirul Hasan, 'Muslim Intellectuals, Institutions and the Post-Colonial Predicament', *Economic and Political Weekly*, vol. xxx, no. 47, 25 Nov. 1995, p. 2997, and his *Legacy of a Divided Nation: India's Muslims since Independence* (Delhi, 1997).

[2] Qeyamuddin Ahmad, 'Aspects of Historical Geography of Medieval Bihar', *The Indian Historical Review*, vol. 5, nos. 1-2, July 1978—Jan. 1979, pp. 119-20, 122-3 and 125-6. For details of the Mughal *suba* of Bihar see pp. 130-2; and Irfan Habib, *The Atlas of the Mughal Empire* (Delhi, 1982), pp. 44-2 and sheets 10 A and 10 B.

[3] George Koovackal and Paul Jackson, 'The spread of Islam' in Paul Jackson (ed.), *The Muslims of India: Beliefs and Practices* (Bangalore, 1988), p. 119.

[4] Fritz Lehman, 'The Sufi Khanaqahs in Modern Bihar' in Yohanan Friedman (ed.), *Islam in Asia* (Jerusalem, 1984), vol. 1, p. 227. For the conversion of Rajputs in Saran and Shahabad and the Babhans and Kayasthas in north-west Gaya see L.S.S. O'Malley, revd. by A.P. Middleton, *Bihar and Orissa District Gazetteers: Saran* (Patna, 1930), p. 43; Francis Buchanan, *An Account of the District of Shahabad in 1812-13* (New Delhi, 1982), p. 179; P.C. Roy Chaudhury, *Bihar District Gazetteers: Gaya* (Patna, 1957), p. 129.

Of the twenty-six Sufis of the Shattari order known to have worked in north Bihar, nine belonged to the period 1412-1588.[5] The oldest and the most widely dispersed Sufi orders in Bihar, the Suhrawardy and the Chishti, were later eclipsed by an offshoot of the former, the Firdausia, under Sharfuddin Yahya Maneri.[6]

Linguistically, the Bihari Muslims were far from homogeneous. Awadhi was spoken as far east as Muzaffarpur district and south of the Ganges, as far east as Gaya. In Champaran district the Awadhi spoken by the better-off Muslims was called Shekhai or Musalmani. On the other hand the Awadhi spoken by the low-caste Muslims was called Julaha Boli, but was different from the Maithili Julaha Boli of Darbhanga district. The version of Maithili spoken by the Muslims of eastern Purnea was locally known as Gaonwari.[7] It has been argued that Bihari Urdu, unlike the Urdu evolved in Delhi and UP, was overwhelmingly plain and simple and influenced by Magahi and Bhojpuri,[8] with scores of authors and writers being based in villages and qasbahs.[9]

Even today, most Bihari Muslims speak Magahi, Maithili and Bhojpuri rather than Urdu.[10] However, a higher percentage of Urdu speakers were recorded in the 1961 census. This was because until then the potential population of Urdu speakers had not been fully mobilized to identify with Urdu.[11] The fact that the Hindi-Urdu controversy in pre-1947 Bihar was 'somewhat less intense' than in UP is attributed to 'Muslim and Urdu culture' being more deeply

[5] Lehman, op. cit., p. 230. For a list of major khanqahs, see p. 232. Also Syed Hasan Askari, 'Aspects of Society and Religion' in S.H. Askari and Q. Ahmad (eds.), The Comprehensive History of Bihar (Patna, 1987), vol. 2, pt. ii.

[6] S.H. Askari, Islam and Muslims in Medieval Bihar (Patna, 1992), pp. 228 and 297.

[7] See G.A. Grierson (ed.), Linguistic Survey of India (Calcutta, 1903), vol. v, pt. ii, pp. 118-19 and (Calcutta, 1904), vol. vi, pp. 14, 86 and 118.

[8] K.A. Azij, 'Persian and Urdu Literature' in Kali Kinkar Datta (ed.), The Comprehensive History of Bihar (Patna, 1976), vol. 3, pt. ii, p. 490. See p. 488 for the characteristics of Bihari Urdu.

[9] Ibid., p. 487. Page 490 lists the villages and qasbahs. Surendra Gopal, Patna in the 19th Century (A Socio-Cultural Profile) (Calcutta, 1980), p. 70, mentions the famous Urdu poet Shaad Azimabadi writing poetry in Bhojpuri and in Magahi as well.

[10] Paul R. Brass, Language, Religion and Politics in North India (Cambridge, 1974), p. 106.

[11] Paul R. Brass, ibid., pp. 196-7.

entrenched in UP and the Muslim League being stronger there than in Bihar.[12]

According to the 1931 census, Hindus comprised 83 per cent of the population and Muslims 10.1 per cent. Most Muslims lived in the north, totalling 40.5 per cent in Purnea; 16.5 in Champaran, 11.2 in Bhagalpur, and 10 in Patna, Gaya, Hazaribagh and the Santhal Parganas.[13] The Julahas (who called themselves Momins after the turn of the century) were the only *biradari* for which statistics were tabulated in the census: they fell just short of 25 per cent of the Muslim population. They were also the only *biradari* for which statistics of literacy were collected. They ranked midway between the Kurmis and Goalas, but Julaha women were more literate than those of any of the other intermediate Hindu castes.[14]

The Bihari Muslims were a slightly smaller minority than their UP counterparts, much less urbanized and hence less organized.[15] But like the UP Muslims they had a distinct lead over other communities, both in literacy and in Western education.[16] And like the UP Muslims they held a commanding position in government service.[17] According to a July 1928 tabulation, the percentage of Bihari Hindus and Bihari Muslims in the Indian Civil Service was 2.7 and 0.9, in the Provincial Civil Service, Executive Branch 24.2 and 20.0, in the Subordinate Civil Service, Executive Branch 28.9 and 8.9, in the Indian Police Service 4.8 per cent and 6.4 per cent, in the Provincial Police Service 39.2 and 17.8, and in the Provincial Civil Service, Judicial Branch 35.0 and 21.2.[18]

With regard to occupations too, the situation in Bihar approximated to that of UP. The percentage of Muslims in the category of farm servants and field labourers (8.04) was below their proportion in the population. However their representation among ordinary

---

[12] Paul R. Brass, ibid., p. 212.

[13] Vinita Damodaran, *Broken Promises: Popular Protest, Indian Nationalism and the Congress Party in Bihar, 1935-1946* (Delhi, 1992), p. 338, fn. 136.

[14] W.G. Lacey, *Some Aspects of the Census Operations of 1931 in Bihar and Orissa* (Patna, 1933), pp. 78 and 104.

[15] Janet Mary Rizvi, 'Muslim Politics and Government Policy: Studies in the Development of Muslim Organization and its Social Background in North India and Bengal, 1885-1917' (unpublished Ph.D. thesis, Cambridge, 1969), pp. 80 and 82.

[16] Ibid., pp. 46-7.

[17] Ibid., p. 82.

[18] *Bihar and Orissa Legislative Council Debates* (Patna, 1930), pp. 18-20.

cultivators (9.30 per cent) approximated to the proportion. The percentage of Muslims living on income from rent of agricultural land (12.72) was above their proportion in the population. In 1871, Muslims comprised 12.42 per cent of the population in Patna district but held 41.8 per cent of the land. In Gaya they comprised 11.33 per cent of the population but held 43.4 per cent of the land. In Munger the corresponding figures were 10.1 and 30.28 per cents.[19]

Up until the interventions of reformist orthodoxy and political communalism in the late nineteenth and twentieth centuries, regional rather than religious categories predominated among Muslims.[20] Briefly, South Asian Muslims are regarded to have acquired a sense of political community from the late nineteenth century.[21] Subsequently what became of the bonds of region via the intersectedness of the agendas of different strands of composite nationalism, the Pakistan movement and Hindu Rashtra, is well worth considering though not entirely within the scope of this paper.[22]

I would like to argue that the denominational nation-makings of the 1940s not only deeply metamorphosed the ethnoscape of subcontinental migrancy[23] but were crucial to the spawning of multiple identities such as 'aqliat suba (minority province) Muslims', 'Bihari refugees' (of 1946), 'Biharis', 'Bangladeshi/Pakistani Biharis', 'Stranded Pakistanis' and 'Bihari Muslims' (as post-1971 'infiltrators' in India). This was also the decade when the Muslim League was opposed by the Momin Conference to replace the 'Islam in Danger' agenda with one aimed at correcting the un-Islamic *razil-sharif* (labouring and well-born) divide: a strand of politics that is now

---

[19] Rizvi, op. cit., pp. 48, 50-1 and 54.

[20] Peter Robb, 'The Impact of British Rule on Religious Community: Reflections on the Trial of Maulvi Ahmadullah of Patna in 1865', in Peter Robb (ed.), *Society and Ideology: Essays in South Asian History presented to Prof. K.A. Ballhatchet* (Delhi, 1993), p. 146.

[21] Ibid., Peter Robb, 'Texts, Communities and the History of Change in Modern South Asia', p. 20.

[22] See my f.c. 'Community and Nation: Bihar in the 1940s'.

[23] L.S.S. O'Malley, *Census of India, 1911: Bengal, Bihar and Orissa and Sikkim* (Calcutta, 1913), vol. v, pt. ii, pp. 180-1, mentions that the bulk of the labourers from Bihar and Orissa and UP, in Dhaka (35,000), Mymensingh (75,000) and Faridpur (12,000) were Hindus (Kurmis, Kahars, Nonias, Kandus, Mallahs and sweepers). 'The number of Muslims coming for employment [as coachmen, cart-drivers and railway servants] being very small.'

centre-stage in post-Mandal Bihar, but in a different context.[24] All this is to be situated between the early twentieth century movement for the separation of Bihar from Bengal which was led by *both* the Bihari Hindu and Muslim professionals and landlords,[25] and the post-1947 phase of provincial boundary disputes during which the demarcations of the Mughal *suba* of Bihar were invoked by the Biharis to resist Chotanagpur being given away to Bengal.[26]

As early as 1940 and the Muslim League's Lahore session, it was amply evident that the *aqliat suba* Muslims were going to be excluded from the Pakistan that was to come.[27] Thus, though the constitution sub-committee considered creating 'independent homelands already having Muslim Majority' [*sic*] in the *aqliat* provinces of UP, Bihar and Madras, or alternately, 'arranging some migratory zones to which Musalmans may migrate and thus form a majority in due course of time', the idea was given up as impractical and unworkable because of the low percentage of Muslims involved.[28]

The partitioning of the Bihari Muslim community and its refugee lives started in the aftermath of the 1946 riot in October-November, in which 30-50,000 Muslims were killed. By December, 60,000 of them had moved to camps in the Muslim League-ruled Bengal. The same month the exodus of refugees from Bihar split between Bengal

[24] See my 'Community questions and Bihar Politics 1917-23', *The Indian Historical Review*, vols. xvi, nos. 1-2, July 1989-January 1990; 'The Virile and The Chaste in Community and Nation Making: Bihar 1920s to 1940s', *Social Scientist*, 22, 1-2, Jan.–Feb. 1994.

[25] See Vijay Chandra Prasad Chaudhury, *The Creation of Modern Bihar* (Patna, 1964), pp. 97-9, 172, 175, 196-7, 199.

[26] Sachchidananda Sinha, Member Constituent Assembly, *A Memorandum to be presented to President, Constituent Assembly, by the representatives of Bihar in the Constituent Assembly as a rejoinder to the note submitted by the representatives of West Bengal in the Constituent Assembly, on the question of the Amalgamation of certain parts of the districts of Bihar with West Bengal* (Patna, 1948), pp. 9, 11-12; *Bengal Bihar Boundary Issue: Speech delivered by Shri Krishna Sinha, Chief Minister, Bihar, in the Bihar Legislative Assembly on 15th May 1953* (Patna, 1953), p. 13.

[27] Contrary to the argument in Anita Inder Singh, *The Origins of the Partition of India 1936-1947* (Delhi, 1987), p. 56, that the League had concentrated on Pakistan without letting the Muslims in the minority province know what their position would be in it.

[28] Ikram Ali Mailk, compiled, *Muslim League Session 1940 and the Lahore Resolution (Documents)* (Islamabad, 1990), pp. 381-9.

and Sind.[29] H.S. Suhrawardy hotly denied the Bihar Congress premier's charge that the Muslim League's propaganda was responsible for the exodus to Bengal.[30] Meanwhile in Sind, though there was some opposition from the 'middle class, educated' Sindhi Hindus to the rehabilitation of 'Bihari Muslims . . . preaching for revenge' in 'a purely Hindu locality',[31] the Sindhi government was keen that Biharis 'be encouraged to leave Bihar and settle in Sind'. However, the preference was for 'cultivator and who can plough' rather than the 'mostly middle-class' emigrants 'pouring into' Sind.[32] Closer to Partition the Sind League Council recommended more facilities for Bihari refugees.[33] Again, in July 1947, the president and general secretary of the Sind Provincial Muslim League issued a statement 'reflecting the consciousness of deep sympathy of Sind Musalmans for the Biharis' and summing up its enlistment of 'influential people and zamindars and firms' and of the government in the 'worthy cause' of the rehabilitation of Biharis.[34] A month later, however, the general secretary expressed horror at the rush of immigrants, 'even from Muslim majority areas', and categorically stated that only Muslims from Hindu majority areas were welcome

[29] Papiya Ghosh, 'The 1946 Riot and the Exodus of Bihari Muslims to Dhaka', in Sharifuddin Ahmed (ed.), *Dhaka: Past Present Future* (Dhaka, 1991), pp. 282-3.

[30] Z.H. Zaidi (ed.) *Quaid-i Azam Mohammad Ali Jinnah Papers: Prelude to Pakistan, 20 February-2 June 1947* [hereafter *Jinnah Papers*] (Islamabad, 1993), first series, vol. i, pt. i, p. 95.

[31] Ibid., vol. ii, pp. 313-14.

[32] Ibid., vol. i, pt. i, pp. 353-4, Yusuf A. Haroon to Jinnah, Karachi, 22 March 1947: 'If you see Mr Yunus or the Bihar leaders personally, you may kindly impress on them the necessity of Muslims coming to settle in this part of the country.' The Sind Government's communique, 'Bihar Immigrants To Be Settled In A Colony': 'We declare that the government of Sind has got full sympathy with the Bihar immigrants and is ready to help with all possible facilities. We warn the Bihar Muslims not to get misled by the Press. Our Government is very anxious for urgent relief of the oppressed Bihari immigrant and is preparing a plan for settling Bihar immigrants in a colony near Karachi commercial city.' About getting 'misled' the reference was to a controversy about when 60,000 acres of land, earmarked for cultivation by the Biharis would get water from the Lower Sind barrage, i.e. in 1948/9 or 1952. See *Karachi Pictorial Guide* (Karachi, 1983), for the Bihar Colony and Sher Shah Colony.

[33] *Morning News*, 28 Feb. 1947, 24 June 1947, mentions Jinnah approving of a sum of rupees 42,000 being used as railway fares for Bihari refugees.

[34] *Jinnah Papers*, vol. ii, pp. 557-8, 'Press Statement by Yusuf A. Haroon and Agha Ghulam Nabi Pathan, president and general secretary, Sind Provincial Muslim League', Karachi, 27 July 1947.

even while indicating pointedly that Sind had 'room for Muslim labourers and cultivators'.[35]

Shortly after the 1946 riot, the partition of Bihar preoccupied the Bihar Provincial Muslim League (BPML). In a foreword to a pamphlet entitled *Divide Bihar*, which was issued by the Muslim Students' Federation to coincide with the second session of the 'Division of Bihar Conference' held at Gaya in April 1947, Jafar Imam, the BPML President, made a case for it in categorical terms.

The Musalmans living in Pakistan zones will soon have their own independent sovereign state. . . . But what will happen to the five million Muslims of Bihar, who form a minority of 13 per cent and are surrounded by a hostile majority all over the Province?. . . . After full consideration, we have come to believe now that our salvation lies only in establishing an independent homeland for us *in some part of the Province of Bihar* where we may be able to concentrate our entire population.[36] (emphasis added)

As a run up to this conference, meetings were held in Bhagalpur, Bakhtiarpur, Siwan, Jehanabad and 'other important places' to select delegates and popularize the move. The BPML general secretary stated that as both the government and the masses of Bihar had been involved in the massacre of the Muslims in 1946, it was imperative that the Bihari Muslims had a homeland of their own to develop themselves 'socially, politically and economically'.[37]

[35] *Morning News*, 12 Aug. 1947: 'They (the immigrants) seem to think that Pakistan is confined only to the city of Karachi, where every one of such immigrants wants to have a house, free plot of land, government job or facilities for business.' See 19 Sept. 1947 and *Star of India*, 21 Jan. 1948, for the Sind premier's concern at the influx of refugees.

[36] Pyarelal, *Mahatma Gandhi: The Last Phase* (Ahmedabad, 1956), vol. i, pp. 681-2. 'The contention that since the Muslim population is scattered in Bihar and nowhere forms a majority they cannot have a homeland is absurd. Rights belong to human beings and not to lands or areas. Five million Muslims of Bihar . . . want to live their own lives free from the fear of domination and annihilation by others. . . . The districts demanded as a homeland for the Muslims of Bihar form a contiguous area and may form some sort of union with Chotanagpur and Santhal Parganas and make a strong independent sovereign state.' Regarding the last bit, also see L/P&J/5/182, Fortnightly Report [FR] May (1)/1947.

[37] *Morning News*, 18 April 1947. See 23 April 1947 for M.A. Warsi's (General Secretary, Division of Bihar Conference) statement that if any province was to be divided at all, it must be Bihar, for the case of Bihar Muslims was 'the strongest'. Thus if the Hindu majority of Bengal consisting of 46 per cent of the total population felt weak against Muslims, who were about 54 per cent, how could the unprotected Muslims of Bihar who were only 13 per cent of the population face a fully armed aggressive majority?

The resolutions passed at Gaya on 19 April went like this. The province of Bihar 'hastily carved' out from Bengal in 1912 was not only 'heterogeneous' but also 'artificial' (therefore its support for an autonomous Jharkhand). And since 'the caste Hindu-dominated Congress Ministry' had failed to protect the life, honour and property and religion of the Muslim minority and had not conceded their 'just and simple demand' for the consolidation of Muslims in selected pockets, Bihar should be forthwith partitioned 'into Hindu and non-Hindu autonomous provinces'. The conference decided on a provisional thirteen-member Committee of Action of the Division of Bihar Conference. In a follow-up meeting in Patna on 11 May, it was decided that a deputation was to wait upon Jinnah to impress upon him 'the imperative necessity of carving out 1/6th area in Bihar for the formation of a national homeland for the 50 lacs of helpless, unprotected and oppressed Muslims of the province'.[38]

The homeland envisaged by the *Divide Bihar* pamphlet included the entire district of Purnea, south Bhagalpur, south Munger, the entire district of Patna, the subdivisions of Jehanabad and Nawadah and some parts of the Sadr subdivision of Gaya district. The logic behind this detailing was that the population of Purnea district was already predominantly Muslim and the districts of south Bihar had been 'the seat of Muslim culture and therefore must be given to the Muslim'.[39]

It appears that Jinnah did not respond to the Gaya proposal. Instead, he made a case in May 1947 for amalgamating those areas of the Purnea district which were contiguous to Eastern Bengal (and had a Muslim majority) with Eastern Bengal, in the event of the partition of Bengal, in the same way as the Muslim-majority areas of Assam were being allowed to amalgamate with Eastern Bengal.[40]

See 30 April 1940 for Latifur Rahman's (member, All-India Muslim League Working Committee, from Gaya) statement that this was the 'only solution' for the Bihari Muslim, for the Congress Ministry had completely failed to protect the Muslims. The partition of Bihar demand therefore had the 'full and universal support of the entire Muslim population of the province'. In fact separate homelands were to be allowed not only to Muslims but to the tribals and scheduled castes as well.

[38] *Jinnah Papers*, vol. i, pt. i, pp. 801-3 for copies of the Division of Bihar Conference held at Gaya on 19 April 1947 and at Patna on 11 May 1947, and Mahboob Ahmad Warsi to Jinnah, 19 May 1947.

[39] Pyarelal, op. cit.

[40] *Jinnah Papers*, vol. i, pt. i, pp. 780 and 846 for Note by Jinnah on the revised draft proposal, New Delhi, 17 May 1947; and Jinnah to Eric Mieville (for the Viceroy), 22 May 1947.

Later that month a BPML conference at Kishanganj in Purnea district and attended by 15,000, including a large number of volunteers from Punjab and Bengal, passed resolutions on the inclusion of Purnea, north Bhagalpur and northern Munger and Santhal Parganas in Bengal.[41]

Meanwhile, the secretary of the Purnea district Muslim League made a case for the twenty *thanas* of eastern Purnea which had a 53 per cent Muslim population, being made a part of Eastern Bengal.[42] Subsequently the Kishanganj subdivisional Muslim League decided on presenting a separate memorandum to the Boundary Commission for the inclusion of Kishanganj, Araria, Amaur, Baisi and Barsoe in Eastern Pakistan because of their 'great racial, cultural and linguistic unity with Bengal'.[43] In late July, a meeting in Kishanganj resolved that the Boundary Commission be moved to include the whole of Kishanganj subdivision, Kadwa, Araria, Azamnagar, Karandighi, Amour, Baisi, Barsoi and Sikti *thanas* of Purnea into East Pakistan, as Muslims comprised 'seventy per cent' of the population and had linguistic and cultural affinities with Bengal, whose integral part in any case they were till the separation of Bihar from Bengal (in 1912).[44]

A telling shift had therefore been made, from seeking a homeland in Bihar for Bihari Muslims, to a homeland in Eastern Bengal for the Purnea Muslims because of their bonds with Bengal. Thus the Statistical Bureau of the BPML worked on maps, tables and pamphlets to claim that the north-east of Purnea be joined to Eastern Pakistan.[45] Likewise, some prominent leaders of the BPML, including Jafar Imam and Husain Imam, wanted the incorporation of fifteen out of twenty-nine Purnea *thanas* which had a Muslim population totalling 59 per cent, within Eastern Pakistan. The argument was that this area was linguistically, topographically, economically and historically part of Bengal. Thus 'on the principal of the community of race, language and culture' the people were 'Bengalis pure and simple'. Moreover, Eastern Pakistan would be more viable with the incorporation of eastern Purnea, which produced surplus foodgrains and jute. In their appeal to the viceroy and to Cyril Radcliffe,

[41.] L/P&J/5/182, FR May (2)/1947.
[42] *Morning News,* 4 May 1947.
[43] Ibid., 15 July 1947.
[44] *Star of India*, 28 July 1947.
[45] *Morning News*, 20 June 1947.

chairman of the Boundary Commission, however, the bottom line was that what was involved was the 'political emancipation and freedom of lakhs of Muslim of Bihar who had recently been subjected to terrible rioting'. Therefore, *'the ten lakh Muslim of Purnea'* were not to be denied their emancipation.[46]

On the other hand, the secretary of the Santhal Parganas Boundary Committee sent a memorandum to the Boundary Commission on behalf of the Muslims of Rajmahal, Barharwa, Hiranpur, Pakur and Maheshpur *thanas*, in support of their inclusion in Eastern Pakistan. The grounds were that Muslims comprised 60 per cent of the population of these areas and their language and culture was common to that of Eastern Pakistan.[47]

The president of the Bihar Refugees Union, Asansol, together with the Calcutta and Kidderpore Muslim Leagues, wrote to Jinnah in May 1947 that the Muslims of West Bengal and the Bihar refugees settled in Burdwan and Midnapur districts strongly felt that 'the idea of sacrificing West Bengal' would be 'most unjust to the refugees of Bihar who sacrificed one lakh Muslims to secure a free Homeland in Bengal'.[48] Jinnah was therefore persuaded 'never' to agree to give up Calcutta or West Bengal, and more obliquely to 'do something to organize and win over the tribals of Assam, West and North Bengal and Chotanagpur and the depressed classes of Bengal and Assam'.[49] Four days later, Raghib Ahsan of the Calcutta district Muslim League recommended to Jinnah that Chotanagpur and the Santhal Parganas and Assam be given the option to join either Pakistan or Hindustan.[50]

Although the 1946 Bihar refugees expected the East Pakistan

---

[46] *Morning News*, 29 July 1947; and *Star of India*, 26 July 1947.

[47] Ibid., 19 July 1947.

[48] *Jinnah Papers*, vol. i, pt. i, p. 950. 'The Muslims of Bihar fought and died in thouands for Pakistan with the hope that they will get refuge in Bengal and an asylum in Calcutta. Actualy no less than three lakh Bihar Muslims got refuge in West Bengal and in Greater Calcutta. Now what will be the fate of the homeless victims of the fight for Pakistan? Where will they go now? Will they be forced to *shuddhi*, serfdom and slavery? Where is the living space for more population in the most thickly populated East Bengal where the density of population is more than 1000 persons per square mile and which is deficit in foodgrain and has no industry at all?'

[49] Ibid., pp. 950-1.

[50] Ibid., vol. ii, pp. 52-3, Raghib Ahsan, Calcutta District Muslim League to Jinnah, Delhi, 4 June 1947 and Suggestion Re. India Plan, Right of Option For the Excluded Areas of Assam and Santhal Parganas and Chotanagpur. Ahsan was also a signatory of the letter mentioned in fn. 48.

government to settle them there,[51] its premier, Nazimuddin, clearly awaited a Muslim League decision to be taken about their fate.[52] Meanwhile, even in late-1947, there was a growing feeling that the Pakistan Government was 'averse to their miserable plight' and that 'the blood of the Bihari martyrs' which 'served as the foundation stone of Pakistan' had been callously forgotten.[53]

The Biharis who made it to East Pakistan had to cope with *dalals* (middlemen)[54] for their housing and with Bengali provincialism in their workplaces.[55] This was serious enough for Jinnah to underline that Pakistanis were basically Muslims, and that if they wanted to build up a nation they should give up provincialism.[56]

By all accounts, after 1946, 1971 was the next watershed for the Biharis in East Pakistan. Stigmatized as collaborators of the Pakistan Government, only 118,866 out of 534,792 Biharis were granted repatriation by the Pakistan Government.[57] The Stranded Pakistanis' General Repatriation Committee, formed in 1977, deploys the language of 'refugees' with the UN and of 'Muslim refugees' with the Islamic heads of states. But with Pakistan, it is a reinvocation of the two-nation theory, to reinscribe an evasive nationhood. The 1980s retrospective of the Partition emerging from the Bangladesh camp-sites idealizes the Bihari homeland and squarely blames the Muslim League's Pakistan logic that dislodged them twice over, in 1947 and in 1971.[58]

[51] For example, *Morning News*, 28 July 1947.

[52] Ibid., 25 Aug. 1947, statement asking Biharis not to move to Jessore from Murshidabad till a decision was taken about them.

[53] Ibid., 17 Oct. 1947, letter to the editor, Nurul Ainan, Asansol Camp, '. . . to our utter disappointment we find ourselves totally forsaken and coldly neglected'.

[54] Ibid., 1 Oct. 1947, letter to the editor, 'A Bihar Refugee', Dhaka.

[55] Ibid., 6 Sept. 1947, letter to the editor, 'Non-Bengalee Muslim', Chittagong, that the railway staff were being 'victimized by Muslim Bengalis in general' and that the Muslim League should intervene on their behalf; 9 Sept. 1947, editorial: 'Muslims not Bengalee'; 23 Sept. 1947, letter to the editor, from Abdur Rafay Desnavi (Desna is a village in Patna district), Chittagong, about his disillusionment with the slogan of Bengal for Bengalis and their being treated as 'blood-sucker', 'exploiters and aliens and treated as foreigners and despised'. Also that many of them were considering returning to India.

[56] Ibid., 2 March 1948, in a Dhaka speech.

[57] David Ennals, 'The Biharis in 1981', in Ben Whitaker et al., *The Biharis in Bangladesh* (London, 1982), p. 30; *The Muslim Refugee*, Feb.-March 1992, p. 10.

[58] Papiya Ghosh, 'Reinvoking the Pakistan of the 1940s: Bihar's Stranded Pakistanis', *Studies in Humanities and Social Sciences*, ii, 1995, p. 134.

That both the Stranded Pakistanis General Repatriation Com-mittee[59] and the Muhajir Qaumi Movement[60] have agreed not to insist on the repatriation of the 'Stranded Pakistani' to Pakistan's Sind province is in itself indicative of an acknowledgement of how deeply the two-nation theory had metamorphosed following the Bihari Roko (Stop the Biharis) movement. The repatriation of Biharis from Bangladesh to Pakistan has been resisted by the Jeay Sind Students' Federation, the Jeay Sind Tehrik, the Jeay Sind Mahaaz and the Jeay Sind Taraqi Pasand Party.[61] Benazir Bhutto had at one point of time threatened that Sind would cut adrift from Pakistan if the Biharis were settled there.[62] In fact, she pointedly refers to them as 'Bangladeshi Biharis'.[63]

Since the early 1970s, the Bihari Muslim diaspora in the UK and USA intervened to salvage the Biharis from their existence in the Bangladesh camps, initially through voluntary organizations, then through the Asian Committee of the British Refugee Council and the Makka-based Rabita al Alam al Islam.[64] In February 1972 Ghulam Sarvar, the Editor of *Sangam,* floated the Bihari Bachao (Save the Biharis) Committee, which urged the Indian Government to allow the uprooted Biharis to return to Bihar.[65] While some of them did, others made their ex-homeland a temporary base, *en route* to Pakistan, via Nepal, Sri Lanka, Burma and Thailand.[66] This provoked a huge debate in parliament and inaugurated the tracking of the 'Bihari Muslim influx' from Bangladesh.[67]

---

[59] *The News*, 23 Aug. 1991, Nasim Khan, chief patron, Stranded Pakistanis General Repatriation Committee.

[60] *Muslim India*, no. 67, July 1988, p. 331.

[61] See, for example, *Dawn*, 1 and 22 Dec. 1983; *Star*, 22 Dec. 1983; and *Frontier Post*, 17 Aug. 1991, 21, 24 and 25 Sept. 1992.

[62] 'Reinvoking the Pakistan of the 1940s', p. 134.

[63] *The Herald*, Jan. 1990, p. 51.

[64] 'Reinvoking the Pakistan of the 1940s', p. 138. Also see Forum columns of *The Muslim*, 23, 25 and 31 May 1983 for representative *muhajir* letters in support of the repatriation of Biharis to Pakistan from Bangladesh. *Daily Jang* (London), letter to the editor, Israrul Haque, 27 Feb. 1994, about the sacrifices of Biharis for the creation of Pakistan is just another example of the centrality of this self-image among the Biharis.

[65] Ali Ashraf, *The Muslim Elite* (Delhi, 1982), pp. 50-1 and 115-16.

[66] Interviews in Kishanganj, Purnea, Ghazipur, Tarapur, Manianda, Munger and Gaya in Jan. 1995 and in Ramzanpur, Asthawan, Desna and Nagarnausa in Feb. 1996.

[67] See, for example, *Lok Sabha Debates, 1972*, vol. 13, nos. 21-30, 11, 13, 19 and 20 April 1972.

Simultaneously with the Bihar Muslim League's rallying the Biharis round the Pakistani homeland and later and unsuccessfully, of a Bihari homeland within it, the Abdul Qaiyum Ansari-led Momin Conference situated its political intervention in the *razil-sharif* differentiation within the putative community, to contest the Muslim League's *sharif*-solespeak.[68] The Momins, who numbered 20 lakhs in the mid-1940s,[69] comprised more than 20 per cent of the Bihari Muslim population.[70] (See Tables 1 to 4 on the *biradaris* in Bihar.)

The Julahas who were of weaver descent were regarded as among the lowest of the Muslim *biradaris* and in many areas forced labour was taken from them freely. The *zamindars* of Gaya and Shahabad, for example, employed them as customary porters. An illegal tax— *kathiari*—was exacted on their handloom by *zamindars*, as also a royalty on the net monthly profit of each loom, called *masarfa*. In many areas *zamindars* claimed an illegal house tax known as *ghar dwari*.[71] The stories and proverbs at the expense of Julahas that circulated both in Urdu and colloquial dialects, were common to UP, Bengal and Bihar,[72] and were perceived as yet another confirmation of their oppression by *sharif* Muslims.

From the late nineteenth century, many north Indian Julahas shed their preconversion Hindu prefix and rejected the name Julaha altogether. This was in favour of 'Momin', meaning 'the faithful', or 'Ansari', after the name of their Arab ancestor who used to weave, or 'Momin Ansar' or 'Sheikh Momin'. The term 'Momin' was probably in use even before the nineteenth century, at least in Purnea district. However, the trend became more noticeable in the 1911 census returns. The change was made both to gain an equal standing with the upper classes and to establish a 'purer Islamic status'.[73]

---

[68] Papiya Ghosh, 'Contesting the Sharif: The Momin Conference—Muslim League Interface In Bihar, 1938-1947', seminar on 'Caste and Class in India', Joshi-Adhikari Institute of Social Studies, New Delhi, 4 April 1929 (unpublished). The Momin Conference split in 1938.

[69] Political Department, Special Section, 1 (4)/1945, A.Q. Ansari, President, Bihar Provincial Jamiyat al-Momineen to Deputy Secretary to Govt. of Bihar, n.d.

[70] Paul Brass, op. cit., p. 245.

[71] Hasan Nishat Ansari, 'Socio-Economic Status and Condition of the Momins Under British Rule', *Journal of the Bihar Research Society,* lxvii-lxviii, Jan.- Dec. 1981-2, pp. 496-502.

[72] Ibid, p. 497; H. Risley, *The People of India,* edited by W. Crooke (Delhi, 1969 rpt., first published, 1915), pp. 136-7.

[73] Gyanendra Pandey, *The Construction of Communalism in Colonial North India* (Delhi, 1990), pp. 88-9. Contrary to his observation on p. 89, however, the term 'Julaha'

Although the Julahas were the most largely represented *biradari* in the 1891 census, their number was believed to have formerly been much larger than that returned that year, i.e. before the introduction of English cotton fabrics.[74] The 1906 district gazetteer of Gaya recorded that if Julahas had depended on the produce of their looms they would have long since disappeared. Many had shifted to agriculture and labour of various kinds. Every year large numbers of them, from Gaya and Munger in particular, sought work in the jute mills on the Hoogly or as menials in Calcutta.[75] It was the performance of menial and other work for the upper castes and landowners that has been identified as perhaps the most important indicator of the community's *razil* status. Equally indicative was the proportion of women in the community who went out to work. In 1911, while there were 8 female workers to every 100 male workers among the Bhumihars, 29 among Syeds, 30 among Pathans, 52 among the Kurmis, and 54 among the Ahirs and Koeris, the figures were as high as 69 and 71 among the Julahas and Dusadhs, and 61 and 71 among the Dhuniyas (cotton carders) and Kunjras (vegetable growers and sellers), respectively. On the basis of this calculation, then, the Julahas ranked with some of the lowest of the Hindu castes.[76] Upper class Muslims as well as theologians and scholars were known to insist on a separate system of education for themselves and the *razil* masses.[77] This came to be resented as the Momin movement expanded. Among the *razil biradaris* in 1931, the Julaha men ranked midway between the Kurmis and Goalas in Bihar's literacy statistics, but among its women literacy was more prevalent than in any of the 'intermediate castes'.[78]

The son of a contractor, Abdul Qaiyum Ansari, belonged to a family which had moved in the late nineteenth century from

---

is still used among the *ashraf* Muslims; Hasan Nishat Ansari, 'Origin and Appellation of the Momins', *Journal of the Bihar Research Society*, lvii, i-iv, Jan.-Dec. 1971.

[74] *Census of India, 1891* (Calcutta, 1893), vol. iii, p. 270.

[75] Ibid., *1921* (Patna, 1923), vol. vii, pt. i, p. 111; Amiya Kumar Bagchi, 'Deindustrialisation in Gangetic Bihar, 1809-1902', in Barun De (ed.), *Essays in Honour of Prof. S.C. Sarkar* (New Delhi, 1976), p. 516; Pandey, op. cit., pp. 77-85; Ansari, 'Socio-Economic Status', p. 581.

[76] Pandey, op. cit., p. 85.

[77] Ansari, 'Socio-Economic Status', pp. 492-3.

[78] W.G. Lacey, *Some Aspects of the Census Operations of 1931 in Bihar and Orissa* (Patna, 1933), p. 78.

Ghazipur in UP to Dehri-on-Sone in Shahabad district. His political career, like that of Latifur Rahan (who led the Momin Conference affiliated to the Muslim League), began during the Khilafat and non-cooperation movements. He was secretary of the Shahabad District Congress Committee between 1930 and 1931.[79] Two years later in a two-part article, 'Quo Vadis Muslims?,[80] Ansari criticized the 'Muslim leadership' in Bihar for concentrating on the 'protection of the much coveted 'Muslim rights', while remaining 'visionless and totally blind to the needs and interests of the distressed (in the) community'. As though a few more jobs, for which Muslims could not qualify in open competition, would bring 'the promised millennium' to the community. According to Ansari, the leadership having ignored the lot of the Muslim masses, needed to be changed.[81]

When the Muslim League passed its Lahore Resolution, a Bihar Provincial Momin Conference meeting declared that the 'entire community' intended opposing the Partition 'tooth and nail'.[82] Since the Momins 'formed a single race and unity' they would not tolerate the attempt to destroy their identity and integrity. It was pointed out that Partition would vitally affect the Momins which comprised the majority in the Muslim population of the proposed 'Hindu state'. Moreover, since the Muslim League did not represent the Momins it did not have the right to decide their fate.[83] As elsewhere, it was pointed out that, even in the Muslim majority provinces, Momins and other working class Muslims were regarded and treated as *razil*. There was therefore no logic in supporting Pakistan.[84]

The Momin Conference maintained that the slogan of 'Islam in Danger' was merely a ploy to distract the Momins from organizing themselves. Momins were therefore alerted to the parenting act[85] of the 'capitalist and power-hunting' Muslim League.[86] Every 'true' Momin was to see to it that the un-Islamic Muslim League ceased to

[79] S.P. Sen (ed.), *Dictionary of National Biography* (Calcutta, 1972), vol. i, p. 64.

[80] *Indian Nation*, 28 Dec. 1934 and 3 Jan. 1935.

[81] Ibid.

[82] *Searchlight*, 23 April 1940.

[83] Ibid., and 9 May 1940.

[84] Ibid., 23 April 1940.

[85] Ibid., 12 Oct. 1938 (Ranchi); 18 Dec. 1938 (Arrah) and 22 Dec. 1938 (Chatra).

[86] Ibid., 2 March 1940, Ansari at the Muzaffarpur District Momin Conference.

exist.[87] What seemed to elude the Muslim League was that the idea of Pakistan would be seen as a 'defeat for Islam'.[88] Islam being a proselytizing religion, its followers were enjoined to propagate their faith. But Pakistan would end all such activities as the 'Hindu states' would not permit propagation within their territories. The *hijrat* implied by the scheme would mean that Muslims would have to leave behind their holy places and graves in the hands of the *kuffar* (plural of *kafir*). A resolution was therefore moved to oppose the Lahore Resolution on the ground that it would turn a major part of India into a *Kafiristan*.[89]

Ansari described the Pakistan scheme as contrary to 'true' Islam. The Muslim League's argument of cultural binationality did not take into account patterns of cross-community coexistence. After all, he asked, what did the Indian Muslim have in common with the Muslims of Arabia and Turkey? The Muslims of Bengal had more in common with the Hindus of their region than with their co-religionists in the NWFP.[90] As Asim Bihari of the Bihar Momin Conference put it, Momins had no religious, linguistic or cultural fears. Wherever they lived was their Pakistan.[91] At the All India Momin Youth Conference at Patna, A.A. Muhammad Noor described the Pakistan scheme as 'unIslamic . . . and absolutely impracticable'. It was absurd to work for a divided India, he said, since the communities inhabiting the country led an 'intermingled' existence.[92]

Ansari explained that Pakistan would not protect Muslims in the minority provinces as they would remain in the 'hand of the majority community', with the crucial difference of not having any control over the administration. This would endanger the Muslim culture and language, about whose protection the Muslim League had been crying itself hoarse.[93] There was a point of view in the Momin Conference that the Muslim Leaguers were leaving the Momins in the lurch to find security for six crore Muslims in Pakistan. But till the Muslim Leaguers themselves showed a readiness to leave behind

[87] *Searchlight.*, 22 June 1940, Ansari at the Shahabad District Momin Conference.
[88] Ibid., 23 April 1940, Ansari's presidential address at the the first session of the Bihar Provincial Momin Conference.
[89] Ibid.
[90] Ibid., (Patna); 9 May 1940 (Begusarai); 29 Dec. 1940 (Dhaka).
[91] Ibid., 23 April 1940.
[92] Ibid.
[93] Ibid.

their property and migrate to Pakistan,[94] the Momin Conference would view the Pakistan scheme as merely a move to overawe the Congress and the Hindus.[95]

In November 1939, Ansari sent telegrams to Gandhi and Rajendra Prasad that the four-and-a-half crore strong Momin community did not accept the League as its representative and wanted separate representation in all matters.[96] Their differences were constantly underlined in the Momin Conference meetings.[97] On 27 and 29 December 1939, A.A. Muhammad Noor, MLC from Bihar, moved a resolution that the future constitution of the country should only be framed by a constituent assembly based on adult franchise with separate electorates for the Momins.[98] The demand was made on the ground that the electoral roll prepared on the basis of the existing franchise rested on property, tax-paying and educational qualifications and protected the interests of the *sharif* Muslims represented by the Muslim League. Thus the existing system worked against the principle of democracy by 'turning the minority among the Muslims into (the) majority'.[99]

The Muslim League's claim to be speaking for Indian Muslims was contested by the Momin Conference from now on. Ansari's argument was that the League did not represent the eight crore 'working class' Muslims; it represented just the upper class and 'capitalist' Muslims.[100] The Conference therefore decided to launch a vigorous campaign against the League's unIslamic attitude towards the Momins.[101] Ansari found it surprising that the League which claimed to be an Islamic body would have taken such an 'unmanly' and unIslamic stance

[94] *Searchlight*. As it turned out, most of them including Latifur Rahman did not leave India in 1947.

[95] Ibid., 1 Dec. 1940.

[96] Ibid., 3 Nov. 1939.

[97] For example, CID SB 71/1942, Conf. Dhanbad, 18 March 1942; Momin meetings in Katras and Conf. Dhanbad, 26 March 1942; Momin meetings addressed in the coalfields by Asim Bihari, General Secretary, All India Momin Conference.

[98] Hasan Nishat Ansari, 'Momins, Cripps Mission and Aftermath', *Journal of the Bihar Research Society*, lxiii-lxiv, 1977-8, pp. 689-90.

[99] Hasan Nishat Ansari, *The Momin-Congress Relation: A Socio-Historical Analysis* (Patna, 1989), p. 16.

[100] *Searchlight*, 15 Oct. 1940; the 22 June 1940 issue mentions a resolution of the Shahabad Momin Conference against the anti-Momin policy of *Ittehad, Asre Jadid* and *Star of India* and called upon the Momin community to 'effectively and totally' boycott those newspapers.

[101] Ibid., 22 June 1940.

against it.[102] In late 1940 he offered to respond to Jinnah's call to muster under the League's banner along with four-and-a-half crore Momins, provided his Six Points (see later) were conceded.[103]

The description of the Muslim League as a party of 'nawabs, capitalists and *zamindars*' prefaced the conclusion in Momin Conference meetings that it was imperative for the Momins to have an organization of their own.[104] More so because neither the Jamiyat al-ulama-i Hind nor the Congress shared its concerns.[105] It was emphasized that despite the Muslim League propaganda and the attempt of the upper class Muslims at weaning away the Momins, their movement had come to stay.[106] The Momin Conference pointedly summed up the outcome of a 'centuries long' oppression of the Momin *biradari*.[107] Its agenda, therefore, envisaged a correction of the un-Islamic *razil-sharif* divide.[108]

Narrations of the oppression of the *razil* by the *sharif* Muslims were common. Maulvi Hafiz Din Muhammad, *rais* of Chainpatia and President of the Champaran district Jamiyat al-Momineen, detailed the 'un-Islamic' oppression of the Muslims who were 'described as inferior'.[109] A.A. Noor catalogued the treatment meted out to Momins by upper class Muslims.[110] Hafiz Manzoor Hussain quoted several instances of the exploitation of Momins at the hands of Muslim *zamindars*.[111]

At the first Bihar Provincial Momin Conference Noor pointed out that ironically, while high class Muslims had in the past demanded a royal commission to enquire into their oppression by the Hindus, they seemed completely unmindful of the atrocities they had been perpetuating on the Momins. He revealed that several reports had been pouring in on the 'cruel' behaviour of Muslim *zamindars* towards the Momins, especially in Gaya, Latifur Rahman's home district. At Tappa Deoraj in Bettiah the graveyards of Momins were desecrated and 'everything' was done to wound their feelings. Noor

[102] *Searchlight.*, 22 June 1940.
[103] Ibid., 1 Dec. 1940, Ansari at a meeting in Ramdachapra, Shahabad.
[104] Ibid., 23 April 1940.
[105] Ibid.
[106] Ibid., 29 Dec. 1940, Ansari at Dhaka is an example.
[107] Ibid., 22 June 1940, Hafiz Manzoor Husain at the Shahabad Conference.
[108] Ibid., 10 Feb. 1940, A.A. Noor at the Gaya Momin Conference.
[109] Ibid., 7 March 1940.
[110] Ibid., 9 May 1940.

therefore moved a resolution to form an enquiry committee to go into the 'volumes' of grievances that the Momin Conference had received about the Muslim *zamindars*.[112]

This committee was set up under the chairmanship of Dr Aminuddin Ahmad of Biharsharif and asked to submit a report within three months.[113] A month later, Ahmad made a statement about some Momins of Deawan (a village in Hilsa, Patna district) being framed in a false case, because they had refused to give up the Momin Conference at the behest of the local Muslim League president. Ahmad observed that it looked like the 'legendary animosity of Bani Umayya (Umayyad) and Bani Abbasya (Abbasid) of Islamic history' would be replayed in India. His forecast was that the 'trial of strength' would end in the political retirement of the Muslim League and its withdrawal to the homeland it had mapped out in 1940.[114]

Condemnation of the *sharif* viewpoint of the League remained a major electoral thrust of the Momin Conference in 1946. Thus a leaflet of the Momin Students' Federation in Dehri-on-Sone (Ansari's hometown) deployed a narration of the situation in Latifur Rahman's *zamindari* in Nagmatia in Gaya to embarrass the Momin supporters and candidates of the League. It carried a mention of Rahman insisting on forced labour from his *biradari* and extorting fowl from his tenants and neglecting the fate of the Momins during the yarn famine.[115] A pamphlet in support of Ramzan Ali, a Momin Conference candidate, '*Zila Palamau Ke Momin Biradari Se Appeal*', circulated that the Momin panchayats had decided against voting for the League which was being openly funded by Bhaiya Saheb whose *zamindari* covered much of the district.[116] The Palamau Momin Conference campaign was directed against the vagueness of the Pakistan scheme and the abolition of the *zamindari* system.[117] '*Momin Conference Zindabad*', an election pamphlet doing the rounds of Manbhum and

[112] *Searchlight*, 24 April 1940.

[113] Ibid., 23 April 1940. I have not come across the report.

[114] Ibid., 1 June 1940.

[115] Political Department, Special Section (hereafter PS) 644/1945, leaflet of the Momin Students' Federation, Dehri; also see Appointment Department, Election Branch, 1E/BLA/11/1946; Report of the Returning Officer, South Santhal Parganas, Muhammadan Rural Constituency, 23 March 1946.

[116] Appointment Department, Election Branch, 1E/BLA/11/1946.

[117] Ibid., Conf. R.H. Prasad, Returning Officer, Palamau Muhammadan Rural Constituency to the Election Officer, Daltonganj, 17 March 1946.

the Jharia coalfields, summed up that it was the 'five crore' 'Momin nation' that the League wanted to obliterate. Predominantly an organization of nawabs and khan bahadurs, the League had only 'a look of contempt' for them. The Momins had 'an immense numerical superiority' which was not to be wasted, or else their fate would be sealed forever. In any case, the Prophet had always instructed them to 'first' see to their own community.[118]

In the mid-1930s Abdul Qaiyum Ansari had disapproved of the Bihari Muslim leadership concentrating solely on representation of Muslims in the legislature and services, but the Momin Conference led by him ended with a similar agenda. Perhaps, that flowed from a reciprocal contestation of the League's main focus. Ansari therefore repeated that the Momins wanted nothing less than a 'proper and legitimate' share and representation in the services and legislature.[119] His *Nukate Momineen* (Six Points) were as follows: At least one minister of the central and the provincial governments was to be Momin. Half the seats allotted to Muslims in the federal and provincial legislatures were to be reserved for the Momin *biradari*, and seats in local self government bodies and government and semi-government services in proportion to their population in the areas concerned. Also, special government facilities were demanded for the technical education of Momin boys and girls and state protection and aid for the handloom industry. These demands were compiled in *A Statement Regarding the Aims and Objects, Policy and Programme of the All India Momin Conference* and submitted to Cripps on 8 December 1939.[120]

Central to the Momin Conference efforts at enumerating the *biradari* as a prelude to a definitive political intervention was the contestation of the League on the question of the 1941 census entries.[121] The League opposed the entry of individuals under caste and sub-caste heads.[122] The Bihar Provincial Muslim League therefore

[118] Ibid., Patna City subdivisional officer's report on general elections, 21 March 1946.

[119] *Searchlight*, 23 May 1940.

[120] Ibid., 16 May 1939 and 10 Feb. 1940; PS 644/1945; Ansari, 'Momins, Cripps Mission and Aftermath', p. 687.

[121] H.N. Mitra (ed.), *Indian Annual Register, 1942* (New Delhi, 1990), pp. 329-30 for the All India Momin Conference Working Committee Resolutions, 6 April 1942.

[122] *Searchlight*, 11 Dec. 1940, letter to the editor from Syed Badruddin Ahmed, General Secretary, Bihar Provincial Muslim League.

directed Muslims to enrol themselves as Muslims, their language as Urdu and their religion as Islam.[123] The Momin Conference interpreted this as an obvious attempt to reduce the number of Momins in the colonial records.[124] According to Ansari the move was directed at depriving the Momins of their 'rights' because the Momins, who formed the largest single group among Muslims, had demanded them on the basis of their population.[125] It was conveyed to the League that the Momins would only consider joining it if their 'rights on the basis of their population' were assured.[126] The Momin Conference therefore called upon all members to be enumerated as Momins, and not Muslims, in the forthcoming census.[127]

An important dimension of the interrogation of the *sharif* politics of the Muslim League by the Momin Conference was its attempt to forge a transformative *razil* collective. Its verdict about the homogenizing politics of the League was that it was 'impossible' to coalesce all Muslims on a common platform given the divergence between the 'rich and poor'.[128] The very fact that labouring Muslim communities *other* than the Momins had organized themselves was, according to the Momin Conference, a confirmation of the 'selfishness' of the League leadership.[129]

The Momin Conference had two considerations in rallying the other 'backward' *biradaris*. First, numbering eight out of nine crore Indian Muslims as they did, they could together 'overthrow' the 'capitalist' Muslim League leadership and 'put India on the road to freedom'.[130] In any case, the Momins and the *peshawar* (occupational) Muslims 'never had any confidence in the Muslim League', which had neglected them completely.[131] The Momin Conference therefore aimed at the 'amelioration' not just of the Momins but of

---

[123] *Star of India*, 27 Jan. 1941.

[124] *Searchlight*, 24 April 1940.

[125] Ibid., 1 Dec. 1940, Ansari at the Ramdachapra Momin Conference; and 19 Dec. 1940, Letter to the Editor from the Secretary, Hazaribagh Jamiyat al-Momineen.

[126] Ibid., 23 April 1940.

[127] Ibid., 22 June 1940; 1 and 29 Dec. 1940. Zahiruddin, President, All India Momin Conference, advised that all those who described themselves as Ansars, Ansaris, Safed-bufs and Nur-bufs, Momins or Julahas were to return themselves as one community, i.e. Momins.

[128] Ibid., 28 March 1940.

[129] Ibid., 15 Oct. 1940.

[130] Ibid., 23 April 1940.

[131] Ibid., 15 Nov. 1940.

the Rayeen (vegetable sellers and growers), Mansoor (cotton carders), Idrisi (tailors) and the Quraish (butcher) com-munities.[132] According to Ansari's computation this would mean the uplift of not only 45 million Momins but of 35 million other backward Muslims as well.[133] Second, the Jamiyat al-Momineen aimed at achieving for the Muslim depressed classes at least some of the 'privileged treatment, recognition and tangible amenities' that had been given to the scheduled castes among Hindus.[134] Around this time several 'backward' Muslim associations had sent in a number of appeals to the Congress seeking 'protection' from the hostility of upper class Muslims.[135]

While the apex body of the Anjuman Rayeen-i-Hind was set up in April 1915 by the Rayeens of Punjab, in Bihar the Rayeen Conference was established only on 2 October in 1938, under the presidentship of Dr Abdus Shakoor of Biharsharif.[136] However, his directive to the Rayeens in 1946 to stand 'solidly behind the Muslim League',[137] conceals contrary political perceptions within the *biradari*. Thus in 1939 an outraged letter to the editor indicated that the League's criticism of the recruitment of backward Muslims by the Congress ministry would make Rayeens keep their political options open.[138] Similarly, speaking at the Rayeen Conference at Arrah in 1940, Zainuddin, a pleader from Samastipur, indicated that if their 'rights' were not recognized they would arrive at them with the 'combined forces of the 'so-called inferiors' and even explore seeking the protection of the Congress 'as the Momins had done'. As things stood, he said, the 'so-called' *sharif* Muslims looked down upon them and treated them worse than untouchables. But considering that their numerical strength stood next only to that of the Momins, i.e. at two and a half crores, their rights as Muslims had to be recognized and their position brought on par with the *sharif* Muslims.[139]

[132] *Searchlight*, 26 May 1939.

[133] Ibid., 10 Feb. 1940, at the Gaya Momin Conference.

[134] Ibid., 30 Dec. 1939.

[135] Ibid., 16 Feb. 1939, Binodanand Jha in reply to M. Yunus.

[136] Written communication from Zafar Ahmad, Bihar Jamiyatur Rayeen, Patna, 25 Feb. 1992.

[137] *Dawn*, 2 March 1946. This contrasts with the Jamiatur Rayeen communication of 25 February 1992, that the Rayeens in Bihar were 'not enthusiastically disposed' towards what was 'an elitist (Pakistan) movement'.

[138] *Searchlight*, 11 June 1939. A. Samad, 'Rayeen (Kunjra)'.

[139] Ibid., 9 Jan. 1940.

The Bihar Provincial Jamiyat al-Mansoor appears to have been functioning from at least the late 1930s.[140] On the eve of the 1946 election it appointed a committee 'to decide the election issue and direct the [voting of] Mansoors ascertaining the views of the leading political parties'.[141] It appears that ultimately a sub-committee of the Bihar Jamiyat decided to vote for the Momin Conference.[142] Much later in the year, the working committee of the Hazaribagh District Jamiyat al-Mansoor passed resolutions against the Muslim League Parliamentary Board, because it had not 'provided' any seat to the Mansoor *biradari* in the provincial legislatures, though it had to other backward Muslims such as Momins and Rayeens.[143]

The self-image of the Momins that grew out of the politics of the 1930s and the 1940s reflected their agenda for breaking with their *razil* experience. Thus a Momin Conference election pamphlet in 1945 recalled that when Ansari had contested the Muslim League candidate in the 1938 Patna by-election, S.M. Ismail of the Muslim League expressed his unconcealed horror at a 'Julaha trying to get elected from the city of nawabs'.[144] Not surprisingly, a resolution passed by the first session of the Bihar Provincial Momin Conference suggested that the Bihar Text Book Committee should reject textbooks containing offensive references to Momins and other backward Muslims.[145] The Momin Conference projected itself as an organization that had redeemed the *biradari* from the backwaters and made it conscious of 'its power without clashing with either the Hindus or the British'. The League had been able to dupe the other Muslim organizations, but not the Momin Conference.[146] The Momins were no political greenhorns after all, and had learnt how to cope with their exploiters.[147]

On the eve of the 1946 election when Rajendra Prasad worried

---

[140] *Searchlight*, 13 Feb. 1940.

[141] V. Chaudhury (ed.), *Rajendra Prasad Correspondence and Select Documents* (heareafter *RPCSD*) (New Delhi, 1986), vol. vi, pp. 62-3.

[142] Appointment Department, Election Branch, 1E/BLA/11/1946, April 1946, No. 87, 'Important Decision of the Sub-Committee and Leaders of Provincial Jamiyat al-Mansoor of Bihar'.

[143] *Searchlight*, 14 Dec. 1946.

[144] PS 644/1945, 'Brethren in Islam Beware: Momin Ansars Be Watchful!'.

[145] *Searchlight*, 24 April 1940.

[146] Ibid., 23 April 1940.

[147] Ibid., Asim Bihari at Patna and 15 Dec. 1940, Hafiz Manzoor Hussain at Nasriganj.

over the fate of the forty Muslim seats of the provincial legislature, he noted that of the Congress Muslims, the Muslim Independent Party and the Jamiyat al-ulama-i Hind and the Momins, 'the only active body' was the Momin Conference.[148] Ultimately the Jamiyat contested nine, the Congress ten and the Momin Conference twenty seats.[149] The Muslim League swept thirty-four, the Jamiyat got none, the Congress one and the Momin Conference five.[150] The League candidates were defeated by the Momin Conference by margins of between 254 to 1095 votes.[151] Subsequently, on Patel's intervention and 'as special case', Ansari was included as a cabinet rank minister (Public Works Department and Cottage Industries), without having to sign the Congress pledge.[152]

The A.Q. Ansari-led Momin Conference had understood the potential of deploying the colonial census returns to correct the inequitous *razil-sharif* divide.[153] In ranging itself against the homogenizing politics of the League, the Momin Conference demonstrated that the community was not perceived as a monolith by its adherents.[154] What was invoked was not the ideal of Medinite fraternization of the *biradaris* (subscribed to by Latifur Rahman of the Muslim League), but the enumeratedness of the *aksariyat* within the *aqliat* to reclaim the rights trampled upon and 'usurped' by the *sharif* Muslims in the League.[155] The Rayeen and Mansoor *biradaris* that the Momin Conference sought to rally round itself, explored similar exercises themselves. In addition to their separate organizations, there was a Peshawar Muslims Federation, with which Ansari had links.[156] In the early post-independence period, he

[148] *RPCSD*, vol. vi, pp. 46-7, from railway train, 7 Nov. 1945, and Patna, 12 Nov. 1945, to Vallabhbhai Patel.

[149] Ibid., pp. 96-7, Patna, 8 March 1946, to Vallabhbhai Patel.

[150] *Return Showing Results of the Elections of the Central Legislative Assembly and the Provincial Legislatures in 1945-46* (New Delhi, 1948).

[151] Ibid.

[152] Khurshid Anwar Arfi (General Secretary, All India Momin Conference), 'The Momin Movement', *The Hindustan Times*, 7 July 1988.

[153] *Searchlight*, 23 April 1940, at the Bihar Provincial Momin Conference in Patna, Abdul Jalil observed that it was after their enfranchisement by the 1935 Act that the Momins had mustered the strength to consolidate themselves.

[154] See Mushirul Hasan, 'Muslim Intellectuals and the Post-Colonial Predicament', p. 2997.

[155] See my forthcoming, 'Community and Nation: Bihar in the 1940s'.

[156] PS 1 (47)/ 1945, A.Q. Ansari to deputy secretary, Political Department, Patna, 11 April 1945. Ansari sought permission for the publication of 'Payam-e-Momin' to

established a short-lived federated organization of the backward Muslims, called the Bihar State Backward Muslim Federation.[157]

Following Partition, the Bihar Muslim League leadership that stayed on, was invited to join the Congress. There were two shifts in the Bihari community that stayed. The large proportion of Muslims in north Bihar meant more political leverage than for Muslim in south Bihar, who though only 7 per cent of the total had till then dominated education, the services and professions The other was at the level of the leadership structure within which the consolidation of the Momins has been attributed to the advancement of the backward *biradaris*.[158]

Blair points out that the backward classes movement had been active in Bihar since the 1940s, but it was only in the late 1970s during the chief ministership of the Janata leader Karpoori Thakur that 'Backward Raj' was inaugurated,[159] and the number of Most Backward Class (MBC) Muslim communities rose form 6/7 in 1955 to 14/20 in 1978. By 1992, only 4/9 Muslim *biradaris* remained in the Other Backward Class (OBC) category (see Table 5). Even as Blair notes that a part of the Muslim community has been included in all the listings of the backward classes, he proceeds to exclude Muslims from the analysis.[160] That Muslims are 'generally' thought of in Bihar 'simply as Muslims' rather than as belonging to caste groups within their religion and that the entire community is thought of as either 'backward or not backward'. Also, that it is 'relatively easy' to keep track of Muslims as a single group in the analysis without having to 'add portions of them to the Forward and Backward groups'. Though the history of the Backward Classes annexure is a 'tangled one',[161] it is important to map the mobilizations of the Muslim *biradaris* for social justice.

---

represent the views of both the Momin Conference and the Peshawar (Functional) Muslims' Federation. I have not come across any details about the latter.

[157] Brass, op. cit., p. 247.

[158] Ashraf, op. cit., p. 44.

[159] Harry W. Blair, 'Rising Kulaks and Backward Classes in Bihar: Social Change in the Late 1970s', *Economic and Political Weekly*, 12 Jan. 1980, p. 72.

[160] Ibid., p. 65.

[161] Ibid., p. 64; Annexure 1 listed the Most/Extreme Backward Classes and Annexure 2 the Other Backward Classes. Also see Papiya Ghosh, 'Enumerating for Social Justice: Religious Minorities and the Indian Constitution' in Ajit Bhattacharjea (ed.), *Social Justice and the Indian Constitution* (Shimla, 1997).

A.Q. Ansari was one of the 11 members of the 1955 Kalelkar Backward Classes Commission and the President of the All India Backward Muslim Federation for 1952.[162] The working committee of the All India Momin Conference, held in Patna on 18 June 1966, had appealed to the government to draw up a comprehensive scheme towards bringing the backward Muslims on par with other citizens, for the backwardness of a sizeable population, it pointed out, did not conform with the 'prestige' of the country.[163]

When the Bihar State Momin Conference negotiated for the Momins to be moved from the Other Backward Class (Annexure 2) to the Most Backward Class (Annexure 1) category, the argument was not merely one of backwardness but the claim that they comprised more than half the entire Muslim population not only in Bihar but in India. The Momin Conference also emphasized the point that Momins had been 'traditional nationalists', 'pillars of strength to secularism and democracy and the unity and integrity of the country'.[164] The demand was accepted in 1984.[165]

A similar move by the Bihar Jamiyatur Rayeen[166] to move from Annexure 2 to 1 has been more uphill. Comprising 26 per cent of the Bihari Muslim population, 'just two less than the Momins', the Jamiyatur Rayeen attributes its Annexure immobility to discrimination by the Congress on account of its association with the opposition.[167] In support, the following sequence is elaborated by the organization. On 13 September 1977 the Janata government decided that the facility of freeships in educational and technical institutions, available to communities classified in Annexure 1, would be extended to all Muslim Other Backward Classes. While this was withdrawn in the case of the Muslim *biradaris* when the Congress returned to office

[162] Ashraf, op. cit., pp. 108-9; *GOI Report of the Backward Classes Commission, 1980*, part i, vol. ii, appendix i, p. 67.

[163] Ansari, *The Momin-Congress Relations*, p. 28.

[164] Ibid., p. 51.

[165] Ibid., pp. 51-2; see Govt. of Bihar, Dept. of Personnel and Administrative Reform Resolution no. 11/S, 1-105/84, 14 Nov. 1984 for the enlistment. The resolution justifies the change in the light of having received 'several' representations to that effect.

[166] Significantly the Rayeens as also the Mansoors had not been keen during the 1940s to be part of a collective 'together with the Idrisis and Quraishes' that the Momin Conference had tried to float.

[167] Interview with Zafar Ahmad, Secretary, Bihar Jamiyatur Rayeen (BJR), 29 December 1993, Patna. The reference is to Ghulam Sarvar being active in the J.P. Narayan movement.

in 1980, the Momins not only continued to avail of it but were in fact moved to Annexure 2.[168] When the Chief Minister Laloo Yadav did not keep to his 1991 assurance of conceding the demand, the Jamiyatur Rayeen organized a massive rally in Patna on 28 December 1993. (see Appendix 1). The memorandum submitted to Yadav mentioned that the Rayeens had much expectations from the chief minister, whose political arrival was itself a manifestation of the constitutional provision for social justice.[169]

The Kulahia Vikas Sangathan's enumeration mobilization came in the wake of the September 1993 announcement regarding the implementation of the Mandal Commission Report and its decision to revise the Backward Classes lists. The *biradari* totalling '11,17,949' and living in '653 villages' according to a survey that it conducted in September 1993, lives in Purnea, Araria and Katihar and claims to have its 'own culture, civilization and language'. To establish their backwardness its memorandum to the government mentions that only 0.5 per cent of them are in government service and that thousands work as agricultural labourers or as labourers in Delhi, Punjab and UP. The clincher is the point that forty-five years after Independence they remain extremely backward, they who as a majority had voted against Pakistan.[170]

On the other hand, in 1994, the Mehtars, Lalbegis and Halalkhors who are entered as MBC agitated to be shifted to the Scheduled Caste list.[171] There are also differences of opinion about categorizing the entire or part of the Muslim community as backward. When the Karpoori Thakur government was working out its reservation formula, Ghulam Sarvar, a Rayeen, and till recently the Bihar Assembly Speaker, is reported to have categorically opposed the declaration of all Muslims as backward.[172] More recently, however, the Janata Dal has demanded that the entire Muslim community be declared backward.[173] Even so in December 1993 the Bihar Pradesh

[168] BJR representation, Feb. 1991.

[169] For yet another postive assurance from Yadav, see *Aaj*, 29 Dec. 1993.

[170] Press statement of the Kulahia Development Organization addressed to *Jansatta* to coincide with a day long fast by 300 Kulahia students in Patna on 29 Dec. 1993. I am grateful to Surendra Kishore for a copy.

[171] *Hindustan Times*, 12 Jan. 1994.

[172] Interview with U.N. Sinha, Chairman, Creamy Layer Committee, 25 Jan. 1994, Patna.

[173] *Telegraph*, 15 Aug. 1993. The stand is shared by Jabir Hussain, Chairman, Bihar State Minorities Commission: telephone conversation on 29 Jan. 1994, Patna.

Janata Dal Momin Conference demanded the inclusion of Momins in the list of Scheduled Castes and Tribes.[174]

The deployment of the bonds of region and *biradari* in the context of the pre- and post-Partition politics point to their having been crucial rallying points for the interrogation of the Islamicate identity referred to at the outset. Initially, this was occasioned by the contingencies of coping with the homelessness (in the case of *aqliat* Biharis, in particular after the dimensions of the 1946 riot) and the homogenization implied in the *sharif*-led Pakistan movement. Subsequently, Bihar's *muhajirs* are still bitterly coming to terms with having been 'sacrificed' for the 'creation and preservation' of the denominational homeland, both in 1946 and 1971. This has evoked both a nostalgia about the 'rich' province of Bihar that they were unyoked from by the Muslim League's agenda and a downfocusing of their Bihari past, to invisiblize their *gairmulki* (alien)-ness in ethnicized Pakistan. On the other hand, as is evident from the more recent mobilizations by the backward Muslims for social justice, their having contested Partition politics continues to be an important reference point.

[174] *Hindustan Times*, 13 Dec. 1993.

TABLE 1: DISTRICT-WISE PERCENTAGE DISTRIBUTION OF
MUSLIM *BIRADARIS* IN BIHAR, 1870s

Saiyid:	Patna 5.0; Saran 1.5; Gaya 4.5; Shahabad: 1.2; Hazaribagh 0.2; Lohardaga 1.8; Bhagalpur 0.8; Tirhut 1.4; Champaran 1.0; Munger 3.0; Purnea 1.1.
Shaikh:	Patna 21.2; Saran 17.8; Gaya 17.0; Shahabad 9.9; Hazaribagh 2.3; Lohardaga 7.2; Bhagalpur 24.9; Santhal Parganas 4.6; Tirhut 29.2; Champaran 21.1; Munger 21.6; Purnea 54.1.
Mughal:	Patna 0.1; Saran 0.2; Gaya 0.4; Shahabad 0.3; Tirhut 1.9; Champaran 0.1; Munger 0.3.
Pathan:	Patna 3.3; Saran 4.7; Gaya 8.4; Shahabad 5.7; Hazaribagh 4.3; Lohardaga 7.6; Bhagalpur 2.9; Santhal Parganas 0.6; Tirhut 3.2; Champaran 3.7; Munger 3.4; Purnea 0.8.
Julaha:	Gaya 0.1; Hzaribagh 52.7; Lohardaga 44.0; Bhagalpur 11.0; Santhal Parganas 0.9.
Kalal:	Hazaribagh 4.6; Lohardaga 0.5.
Kunjra:	Hazaribagh 1.1; Lohardaga 0.3.
Dhuniya:	Saran 0.1; Bhagalpur 0.1; Tirhut 0.1; Champaran 0.3; Munger 0.4.

SOURCE: W.W. Hunter, *A Statistical Account of Bengal [1877]* (Delhi, 1976), vols. xi-xvi.

TABLE 2A: MUSLIMS RETURNED BY TITLE, 1891

	Bihar			Chotanagpur		
	Total	Male	Female	Total	Male	Female
Provincial Total	2,208,363	1,071,734	1,36,629	209,835	106,553	103,282
Gasi	—	—	—	—	—	—
Khan	—	—	—	—	—	—
Mir	2,173	1,037	1,136	1	1	—
Mughal	7,152	3,334	3,818	764	395	369
Pathan	157,423	75,718	81,705	12,627	9,066	3,561
Sardar	—	—	—	219	111	108
Saiyid	92,302	45,026	47,276	6,380	3,198	3,182
Sheikh	194,876	945,383	1,001,993	184,727	93,719	91,008

SOURCE: C.J.O' Donnell, *Census of India, 1891* (Calcutta, 1893), vol. iii, p. 268

TABLE 2B: MUSLIMS RETURNED BY OCCUPATION, 1891

	Bihar			Chotanagpur		
	Total	Male	Female	Total	Male	Female
Provincial Total	1,155,325	550,484	604,841	43,715	21,004	22,711
Darzi	31,319	15,103	16,216	467	211	246
Dhopa	45,626	21,128	24,498	167	92	75
Dhuniya	187,479	86,929	95,550	334	166	168
Fakir	48,857	20,660	22,197	1,047	511	536
Hajjam	30,739	14,470	16,269	229	84	145
Julaha	572,596	272,416	300,180	34,510	16,529	17,981
Kalu	4,851	2,362	2,489	49	18	31
Kangar	—	—	—	—	—	—
Kunjra	126,006	59,702	66,297	693	327	366
Laheri	10,786	5,232	554	162	75	87

SOURCE: C.J.O'Donnell, *Census of India, 1891* (Calcutta, 1893), vol. iii, p. 268.

TABLE 3: *BIRADARIS*: A DIVISIONAL BREAKDOWN, 1911

Biradari	Division	Male	Female
Darzi	Patna	4,909	5,189
	Tirhut	10,199	11,477
	Bhagalpur	1,083	1,060
	Chotanagpur	1,476	1,694
Dhuniya	Patna	8,145	10,142
	Tirhut	60,490	70,068
	Bhagalpur	25,276	26,828
	Chotanagpur	627	609
Julaha	Patna	71,746	91,482
	Tirhut	148,011	173,575
	Bhagalpur	79,404	81,684
	Chotanagpur	89,376	90,082
Kasai	Patna	2661	3000
	Tirhut	2889	2990
	Bhagalpur	368	370
	Chotanagpur	929	979
Kunjra	Patna	8958	10,128
	Tirhut	41,359	45,061
	Bhagalpur	37,544	42,556
	Chotanagpur	1,325	1,679
Mughal	Patna	509	539
	Tirhur	671	784
	Bhagalpur	439	470
	Chotanagpur	332	274
Pathan	Patna	26,317	30,925
	Tirhut	28,716	32,166
	Bhagalpur	16,631	16,167
	Chotanagpur	12,631	11,805
Saiyid	Patna	15,092	16,125
	Tirhut	10,092	10,858
	Bhagalpur	10,429	10,927
	Chotanagpur	3,602	3,222
Shaikh	Patna	59,899	66,964
	Tirhut	194,491	223,206
	Bhagalpur	505,968	500,284
	Chotanagpur	46,813	40,715

SOURCE: L.S.S. O'Malley, *Census of India, 1911* (Calcutta, 1913), vol. v, pt. iii, pp. 125-7.

TABLE 4: OCCUPPATIONAL BREAKDOWN OF *BIRADARIS*

DHUNIYA		
Actual workers	M	55,946
	F	34,036
Income from rent of land	M	212
	F	259
Cultivators of all kinds	M	24,744
	F	9,254
Field labourers	M	18,886
	F	9,254
Commissioned/Gazetted officers	M	—
	F	—
JULAHA		
Actual workers	M	228,877
	F	165,842
Income from rent of land	M	1,595
	F	1,068
Cultivators of all kinds	M	116,589
	F	71,704
Field labourers	M	32,427
	F	48,735
Gazetted officers	M	11
	F	—
Lawyers, doctors, teachers	M	394
	F	25
KUNJRA		
Actual workers	M	52,525
	F	37,113
Income from rent of land	M	57
	F	22
Cultivators of all kinds	M	28,187
	F	6,829
Field labourers	M	10,501
	F	5,640
Commissioned/Gazetted officers	M	3
	F	—
PATHAN		
Actual workers	M	48,530
	F	15,476
Income from rent of land	M	1,284
	F	751

TABLE 4 (Cont.)

Cultivators of all kinds	M	23,985
	F	5,171
Field labourers	M	5,057
	F	3,329
Commissioned/Gazetted officers	M	86
	F	—
Lawyers, teachers, doctors	M	553
	F	22

SAIYID		
Actual workers	M	21,547
	F	6,541
Income from rent of land	M	3,257
	F	1,710
Field labourers	M	1,155
	F	536
Commissioned/Gazetted officers	M	82
	F	—
Lawyers, etc	M	1,176
	F	50

SOURCE L.S.S. O'Malley, *Census of India, 1911* (Calcutta, 1913), vol. v, pt. iii, pp. 239, 241, 244 and 247.

TABLE 5: ANNEXURES OF BIHARI MUSLIM OTHER BACKWARD AND
MOST BACKWARD CLASSES 1951-93*

Names	1951	1955	1976	1978	1980	1992	1993
Bhat			O&M	O&M	O	M	O
Bhathiara	M	M	O&M	O&M	O	M	O
Chik	M	O	O&M	O&M	O	M	O
Churihar	O	M	O	O	O		O
Dafalange					O		
Dafale	M	M	O&M	O&M	O	M	O
Dhobi	M	O	O&M	O&M		M	O
Dhunia	M	M	O&M	O&M	O	M	O
Faqir					O		
Gadihar					O		
Hima, Karanjia, Qassar					O		
Ibrahimi		O					
Idrisi	O	O	O	O	O	O	
Kassab	M	O	O&M	O&M	O	M	O
Mehtar, Lalbegi, Halalkhor, Bhangi	M	M	O&M	O&M	O	M	O
Madari	M		O&M	O&M	O	M	O
Miriasin	M	M	O&M	O&M	O	M	O
Mirshikar	O	O	O&M	O&M	O	M	O
Momin	O	O	O	O	O	M	O
Mukero	O				O	O	O
Nalband	O		O	O	O		O
Nat	M	M	O&M	O&M	O	M	O
Pamaria	M	O	O&M	O&M	O	M	O
Rangrez	O	O	O	O	O	O	O
Rayeen	O	O	O	O	O	O	O
Sayee	O	O	O&M	O&M	O	M	O
Thakurai					O		

KEY: O: Other Backward Classes; M: Most Backward Classes.

NOTE: There was a common list in 1980 and 1993, i.e. there was no O and M classification in these years.

SOURCE: 1. 1951 and 1976: Mungeri Lal Commission Report, pp. 114-15 and 118-19,
respectively.
2. 1955: GOI Report of the Backward Classes Commission (1955), vol. ii,
pp. 16-23
3. 1978: Govt. of Bihar, Dept. of Personnel and Administrative Reforms:
Circulars, etc., up to 1988 (10 Nov. 1978), pp. 118-23.
4. 1980: GOI Report of the Backward Classes Commission (1980),
vol. vi, pp. 178-9.
5. 1992: Govt. of Bihar Gazette, 10 March 1992, pp. 9-12.
6. 1993: GOI, Extraordinary Gazette, 13 Sept. 1993, pp. 40-3.

28 दिसम्बर को राईन भाईयों का विराट प्रदर्शन

राईन भाईयों ।

जिन्दगी के समस्त क्षेत्रों में हमारी स्थिति दयनीय है । इस दयनीय हालत के लिए एक ओर जहाँ हम स्वयं जिम्मेदार हैं, वहीं दूसरी ओर यह भी एक निर्विवादित सत्य है कि स्वतंत्रता, के पूर्व और उसके बाद भी हमारी प्रजातांत्रिक सरकारों की ओर से लगातार हमारे सामूहिक वजूद की अपेक्षा होती रही है । हमारी अत्यन्त दयनीय स्थिति और पिछड़ापन के बावजूद न तो सरकारी स्तर पर हमें कभी कोई सुविधा मिली और न ही हमारी सामाजिक उत्थान के लिए हमारी किसी भी माँग की पूर्ति हुई । बिहार में मुसलमानों की कुल आबादी का 26% होने के बावजूद हमारी न कोई पहचान है और न ही कोई सामाजिक एवं राजनैतिक छाप !

यह समझने और समझाने के लिए कि हमें भी एक अभिभाणित नागरिक की तरह जीवन व्यतीत करने का हक है ।

28 दिसम्बर को बिहार विधान सभा के समक्ष विराट प्रदर्शन का कार्यक्रम है ।

- अपने आत्म सम्मान की रक्षा के लिए,
- अपनी पहचान बनाने के लिए,
- सामाजिक असमता और अन्याय के विरूद्ध अपनी कटिबद्धता को दुहराने के लिए,
- अपने अस्तित्व का एहसास दिलाने के लिए,
- मुख्यमंत्री को उनका वायदा याद दिलाने के लिए,

हजारों हजार की संख्या में पटना के गाँधी मैदान में **28 दिसम्बर 93'** को **11 बजे दिन** में जमा होकर अपनी एकता और जागरूकता का परिचय देते हुए इस ऐतिहासिक प्रदर्शन को सफल बनायें ।

बिहार जमिअतुराईन
गोलारोड बाकरगंज, पटना-4
दूरभाष-657791

मनव्यर प्रिंटिंग प्रेस, सब्जीबाग, पटना-४

The Bengali Muslim: A Contradiction in Terms? An Overview of the Debate on Bengali Muslim Identity

JOYA CHATTERJI

The Bengali Muslim has long been regarded as a living oxymoron, his Muslimness vitiated to the extent that he is a Bengali. The idea that outside the Middle East, Islam exists in contradistinction with a 'host' culture is widely accepted, and pervades much of the literature on Islam in South and South-East Asia. It is certainly not unique to the discussion of Islam in Bengal. But in the case of Bengal it is particularly powerful because it appears to have been vindicated by history. The formation of Bangladesh is widely interpreted as a re-assertion of a latent Bengali identity, hitherto suppressed by the triumphant pan-Islamism of the Muslim League political alliance.[1]

Bengali Muslim identity is thus commonly perceived as being riven by a fault line, with Bengaliness and Muslimness coexisting uneasily on the opposite sides of a deep and fundamental divide. Bengali Muslim culture is almost invariably written about in terms of a series of binary opposites which loosely correspond to the primary Muslim *versus* Bengali opposition: *ashraf* (Muslims of foreign ancestry) *versus atrap* (Muslims of regional origins); orthodox *versus* heterodox; *sharia* (Muslims who adhere to the *Shariat*) *versus basharia* (those who follow practices such as *pir* worship[2] which are not sanctioned by the *Shariat*); Urdu-speaking *versus* Bengali-speaking, élite *versus* popular, pan-Islamic *versus* regionalist, and so on. Moreover, it is readily assumed that each corresponding series of attributes—Muslimness, foreign antecedents, orthodoxy, *Shariat*-following, Urdu-speaking—are clustered together, so much so that

---

[1] See, for instance, Rafiuddin Ahmed, 'Contradictions in Bengali Islam: Problem of Change and Adjustment', in Katherine P. Ewing (ed.), *Shariat and Ambiguity in South Asian Islam* (Delhi, 1988), pp. 138-9.

[2] A *pir* is (literally) a mystic saint of a Sufi brotherhood. As we shall see later, this was not the only meaning of the word in Bengal.

their relationship with each other is deemed to be one of continuity, even interchangeability. In other words, if one were told that a certain group of people were of *atrap* (or local) origin, it would be considered safe to assume that they were also Bengali-speaking, *pir*-worshipping, heterodox in religious practice, and all in all more 'Bengali' than 'Muslim'.

Corresponding to this paradigm, the history of Bengali Muslims until 1947 has been understood as a history of 'Islamization': as the history of a process by which the first series of attributes (Muslimness, *ashrafism*, orthodoxy, *shariat*-following, Urdu-speaking) gradually replaces the second (Bengaliness, *pir* worship, heterodoxy, idolatry, Bengali-speaking). In other words, it is perceived as linear progress, albeit partial and halting, towards the Islamic ideal. Conversely, the history of East Pakistan between 1947 and 1970 is written as a history of a triumphant 'Bengaliness'[3].

This sort of narrative rests, in turn, on a particular understanding of 'Islam' as a pure, transcendent idea, the 'essentials' of which are indisputable. Traditionally, these 'essentials' are understood as being inscribed in certain core texts of Islam: whether the Koran, *sharia, Sunnat* or *Hadith*. Not only are they obvious and indisputable, their true meaning, for many scholars, is unproblematic. For one historian, 'the moral ideal established by the Koran is at once objectively knowable [and] universally applicable to all people and all times. . . .'[4] Even Cliford Geertz, more sceptical than most scholars of the value of treating Islam as a single unified religion, tends to slip back into the describing Islam as 'a universal, in theory standardised and essentially unchangeable system of ritual and belief'.[5] More recently,

[3] So, for instance, one scholar argues that immediately after Partition, *Bengali distinctiveness* was asserted within the Pakistani structure, that the struggle for language drew fresh attention to the *other* traditon (the first being Islam) both liberal and secular, the tradition of Bengali culture nurtured in the course of two thousand five hundred years. Ali Anwar, 'Muslim Mind and Society in Bangladesh: A Historical Retrospect' in Ashgar Ali Engineer (ed.), *Islam in South and South-East Asia* (Delhi, 1985). Also see Ahmed, 'Contradictions in Bengali Islam', pp. 138-9; Tazeen Murshid, *The Sacred and the Secular: Bengali Muslim Discourses 1871-1977* (Calcutta, 1995), p. 443; Harun-or-Rashid, *The Foreshadowing of Bangladesh: Bengal Muslim League and Muslim Politics, 1936-1947* (Dhaka, 1987), p. 346.

[4] Richard M. Eaton, 'The Political and Religious Authority of the Shrine of Baba Farid' in Barbara Daly Metcalf (ed.), *Moral Conduct and Authority: The Place of Adab in South Asian Islam* (Berkeley, 1984), p. 333. As we shall see later, Eaton has moved away from this position in his recent work.

[5] Clifford Geertz, *Islam Observed: Religious Development in Morocco and Indonesia* (New Haven and London, 1968), p. 14.

scholars have attempted to uncover in the diversity of Islamic practice certain 'core values' which reflect a universal Islamic code of conduct or *adab*.[6] In her introduction to a collection of essays devoted to defining and describing *adab*, Barbara Metcalf speaks of her 'wonder at having approached . . . the core of what has given the Islamic tradition its resilience throughout times and places of such increasing diversity. . . .'[7] She insists not only that there is one Islam ('the teachings of Islam are one')[8] but that 'there is a general *adab* shared widely in Muslim society'.[9] This general moral essence can be distilled, by careful scholarship, out of the medley of Islamic practice.

Following from this definition of Islam as having a pure, irreducible kernel, the process of conversion to Islam has often been explained with the analogy of implantation. It is frequently described as the process by which the pure seed of Islam was implanted in the 'soil' of the host society. Biological metaphors of insemination, implantation and germination[10] abound in scholarly writing on conversion to Islam. Inevitably, the role of the host society is seen as passive,[11] merely receiving the living seed which takes root, grows and struggles to survive. And where the cultural distance between the host society and western Asiatic cultures is great, the 'soil' is deemed to be too poor to sustain a healthy tree: the Islam that grows in such soil will inevitably be a poor, debased sort of faith. In medieval Bengal, a humid, tropical, riverine, frontier society on the farthest eastern reaches of Gangetic civilization, the product was 'inevitably' a grossly distorted, almost unrecognizable version of Islam.

Another popular variation on this theme is the idea of 'local accretions' which are believed to have obscured the pure Islamic core beneath. The metaphor of accretion or sedimentation of layers of local (cultural) matter is used to explain, for instance, the 'invisibility' of Islam in Bengal.[12] So, for instance, the story of the first British census officers who were surprised to find so many

---

[6] Metcalf (ed.), *Moral Conduct and Authority*.
[7] Barbara Daly Metcalf's 'Preface', ibid., p. viii.
[8] Ibid., 'Introduction', ibid., p. 9.
[9] Ibid., p. 4.
[10] See, for instance, Geertz, *Islam Observed*, p. 14.
[11] Ahmed, *The Bengali Muslims*, p. 8.
[12] Ahmed, 'Contradictions in Bengali Islam', p. 127.

Muslims in Bengal is retold to demonstrate the density of the local accretions that hid Bengali Islam from British view.

Yet for all this, the fact remains that it is this very 'stunted', 'unrecognizable' version of Islam which prevails amongst the second-largest Muslim society in the world. Bengali-speaking Muslims are second only to the Arab Muslims in number.[13] If their version of Islam is an exception to the rule, it is indeed a massive exception. As one scholar has remarked in a different context, rules which require such gigantic exceptions to sustain themselves can only have the most limited power to explain.[14]

This paradigm has limited the discussion of the history of Bengali Muslim society to a static and increasingly sterile reaffirmation of the 'basic contradictions' and 'inherent ambiguities' between true Islam and the Bengali reality. Moreover it has forced us for too long into the untenable position of regarding the Bengali Muslims as victims perpetually trapped in a dilemma of identity, forever torn between their (irreconcilable) Bengaliness and Muslimness. We cannot but help see this dilemma as being engendered by their own failure to grasp what we scholars comprehend so easily, i.e. the true meaning of Islam. From the traditional standpoint, the very density of 'local' Bengali culture makes it opaque: Bengalis cannot see through it into the heart of Islam. So it is their lot to be Muslims only in name, or else Bengalis only in name.

This is, of course, a position that none of the scholars involved in the discussion would explicitly take. There is a strong element of parody in my description of what is undoubtedly a very rich and informed body of scholarship. But the parody is deliberately intended to bring out what I would argue is the underlying rationale within which the subject has been defined. Rafiuddin Ahmed, in his enormously influential and learned study of the Bengali Muslims, actually insists that 'a Bengali identity was in no way inconsistent with their faith in Islam'.[15] Yet his avowal is unconvincing because Ahmed accepts the main features of the model I have set out above:

[13] Richard V. Weekes (ed.), *Muslim Peoples: A World Ethnographic Survey*, (Westport, 1984), p. 137.

[14] Rajnarayan Chandavarkar, *The Origins of Industrial Capitalism in India: Business Strategies and the Working Classes in Bombay, 1900-1940* (Cambridge, 1994), p. 1.

[15] Rafiuddin Ahmed, *The Bengal Muslims 1871-1906: A Quest for Identity* (Delhi, 1981), p. 113.

that there are certain 'basic tenets of faith' that characterize Islam,[16] that Bengali Muslims, for the most part, 'were semiliterate with a bare knowledge of the rudiments of Islam',[17] their faith was dominated by the 'un-Islamic' practices such as *pir* worship[18] and idolatry[19] and that, despite a century of reformist efforts, they are very little closer to seeing the light today.[20] Inevitably, for Ahmed, 'there was something curiously self-contradictory in the Muslim masses' quest for an Islamic identity.'[21] And Geertz, whose writings on Indonesia and Morocco have deeply influenced scholarship on Islam outside western Asia, goes even further to conclude that Muslims in these cultures are 'rather thoroughly mixed up'.[22]

Is this a tenable point of view? Can one be comfortable with a paradigm which regards the people who are its subjects as somehow unable to see the main point? If Geertz, Ahmed, Metcalf and a host of other scholars, writing from cultural positions no closer to the Arabia of the Prophet, can easily and unproblematically grasp the 'core' values and 'basic tenets' of Islam, why have the Bengali Muslims failed to do likewise? Surely no one would argue that as a race they lack the mental equipment. Nor would I suggest for a moment that any of the scholars cited here would take such a stance. Yet the way in which they have argued the issue leads us, albeit unwillingly, into this position. How are we to extricate ourselves from it?

This essay aims critically to examine the paradigm within which the discussion of Bengali Muslim identity has been circumscribed. It will suggest more fruitful ways of looking at the subject and point to recent research which is beginning to engage with these questions in a new and dynamic way. I should stress at the outset that this paper is not based on original historical research and makes no claims to specialist competence in this area. It is no more than an idiosyncratic overview of the literature by a reviewer whose entry into the subject has been by a circuitous route.

---

[16] Rafiuddin Ahmed, ibid., p. 57.
[17] Ibid., p. 29.
[18] Ibid., p. 60.
[19] Ibid., p. 186.
[20] Ibid., pp. 186-90.
[21] Ibid., p. 184.
[22] Geertz, *Islam Observed*, p. 18.

I

The first and most obvious problem with the traditional paradigm is its deployment of very idealistic notion of 'Islam'. In the framework outlined above, Islam appears an autonomous subject which acts on society. This is clearest in the discussion of conversion, where Islam appears as the living seed and society as the inert soil in which it grows. In other words, Islam is treated as a subject or agent and Bengali society as merely a passive predicate.[23]

This gives rise to a particular problem. If we think of Bengali society as a 'thing' that was acted upon by Islam, it encourages us to regard that society as a fixed entity with a given structure. This is to think in a way that deprives the Bengalis of agency and also to de-historicize Bengal, to reduce it to a context whose basic elements are unchanging. This has led to some extraordinarily careless history-writing from otherwise painstaking scholars. For instance, Rafiuddin Ahmed writes that 'Bengal, particularly the low-lying districts of eastern and southern Bengal where Islam found most of its adherents, *has been a peasant society for the whole of her recorded history*, agriculture . . . has [always] provided the foundations of the region's distinctive culture.'[24] The point about this is not so much that it is incorrect (as we shall see later, the areas where Islam has flourished in Bengal were brought under the plough much more recently), but that the author is so comfortable with this picture of an unchanging peasant society because the uncritical idealism of his paradigm predisposes him to think of society as an inert object.[25] If Bengal appears to have had no history, it is because history itself—in the sense of diachronicity and change—is not a dynamic variable in this model.

If we turn to the second part of this binary—i.e. Islam—the problem is slightly different. Problems arise from the tendency to

[23] The theoretical difficulties of this approach were pointed out a long time ago, though in a different context. See Marx's polemic against Hegel in his 'Critique of Hegel's Doctrine of the State' (1843), in Karl Marx, *Early Writings* (London, 1975).

[24] Ahmed, 'Conflict and Contractions in Bengali Islam', p. 115. Emphasis added.

[25] Similarly, he speculates that 'a plausible explanation for such a massive Muslim population . . . is the *possibility* of large-scale conversions of indigenous tribes who *probably* has never been fully Hinduized, either professing a localized form of Buddhism or adhering to the animistic rituals and beliefs of their ancestors', ibid., p. 119. Here again, we sense that it would make little difference to the author's argument if these assumptions actually turned out to be wrong.

think of Islam as a set of 'core values' with an unambiguous meaning. There are two ways in which this notion is problematic. It does not allow for the possibility that Islam's 'core values' might be historically constituted: in other words, that at different places and times in history and in response to different sorts of challenges, different constellations of ideas might have been represented as being the 'core values' of Islam. It does not grant that this terrain might in fact be a contested one, in which different and even contradictory readings of Islam compete for hegemony. And yet even a cursory reading (against the grain) of the history of Muslims in Bengal, suggests that it is possible to argue this case. So, for instance, one might argue that the early battles between the *ulama* and the Sufis were actually a debate about the 'true meaning' of Islam, with the *ulama* insisting that dualism, the transcendence of God and the *shariat* laws were the non-negotiable truth of Islam, while the Sufis argued for God's immanence and monism, asserted that the *shariat* was only a primer for the uninitiated and that there was a higher and final truth revealed only to those who pursued the mystic path. Similarly one could argue that the subsequent Tariqah and Fairazi campaigns against the 'corrupted' practices of both the *ulama* and the *pirs* were actually re-inventing the 'fundamental tenets' of Islam in ways that allowed for no intermediaries between man and God. Yet even the reformers themselves did not agree about the key texts (some argued that 'only' the Koran and *Sunnat* were the core texts of Islam, others insisted that the *Hadith* be included). The Wahabis did not accept any of the four established schools of Islamic jurisprudence, the Fairazis accepted the Hanafite school,[26] and so on. One might extend this further to argue that in the modern period, when communal friction with the 'Hindus' increasingly dominated religious discussion, non-Hindu practices (such as cow-slaughter, silence before mosques, iconoclasm) were elevated by some Muslims (such as Pir Abu Bakr) to the status of core values, while others argued that universal brotherhood, equality and tolerance were the 'true' meaning of Islam.[27]

This is not to suggest that this scheme or history is the 'correct' one. It is merely to argue that it is one among many readings opened

---

[26] Ahmed, *The Bengali Muslims*, pp. 58-60.
[27] Pradip Kumar Datta, 'Hindu Muslim Relations in Bengal in the 1920s' (Delhi University, Ph.D. Thesis, 1995), pp. 132, 134.

up once we give up our habit of regarding Islam's 'core values' as an unchanging, universal and standardized essence about which there can be (and has been) no dispute.

The second order of problems arises from thinking of Islam (and Islamic texts) as having an unambiguous, fixed meaning. It is a little surprising to have to raise this point, vis-a-vis a body of scholarships so deeply influenced by Geertz. After all it was Geertz who so eloquently argued for the impossibility of a correct or final interpretation of culture.[28] And yet even Geertz himself lapses from his own position when it comes to discussing what Islam is.[29]

The arguments against the possibility of establishing the 'true meaning' of any text are well-known in the social sciences and I will not go over this ground here. But it has important implications for any discussion about Bengali Muslim identity. If (as has generally been the case) the 'core texts' of Islam are credited with a fixed and unambiguous 'meaning', then 'true' conversion must be regarded as the process of correctly apprehending their message. Conversely, 'false' conversion is failing to comprehend the true meaning. When there is only one possible meaning, you either 'get it' or you don't. In this sense, it has been argued the 'Bengali masses' were not proper Muslims because they failed to understand the true meaning of Islam. This is explained partly as a failure of pedagogy (those who tried to 'teach' them—the rural priests—did not understand 'it' themselves[30]); and partly as a failure of translation (Bengali culture was so different, in essence, from Islam that all attempts at translation failed). But for whatever reason, goes the argument, the Bengali Muslims did not

---

[28] See, for instance, 'Thick Description: Towards an Interpretive Theory of Culture', in Clifford Geertz, *The Interpretation of Cultures* (no place mentioned, 1973).

[29] The isolation of the study of Islam from the main currents of the social sciences is remarkable. But as Edward Said has pointed out, this isolation has a long history. He argues that 'the history of Islamic Orientalism is relatively free of sceptical currents and almost entirely free from methodological self-questioning. Most student of Islam in the West have not doubted that despite the limitations of time and place, a genuinely objective knowledge of Islam . . . is achievable . . . I have been unable to find any contemporary example of the Islamic scholar for whom the enterprise [of 'knowing' Islam] was itself a source of doubt. . . . ' Edward W. Said, *Covering Islam: How the Media and the Experts Determine How We see the Rest of the World* (New York, 1981), pp. 128-9. Perhaps Geertz's lapse from his hermeneutic positon can be understood in the context of this tradition of scholarship.

[30] Ahmed, *The Bengal Muslims*, p. 29.

(and still do not) get 'it', while to us scholars 'it' is as obvious as 'it' is indisputable.

Now the problem with this is not only that this is an uncomfortable arguement to justify. It also lends weight to fundamentalism. If there is only one true meaning of Islam, then the fundamentalist reformers must be understood on their own terms as pedagogues who were trying to teach people this true meaning. We cannot help inferring that they were right. So, for instance, Rafiuddin Ahmed cannot help but reach the conclusion that the fundamentalists launched the process of true 'Islamization' in Bengal,[31] however much he might deplore fundamentalist politics.

If, on the other hand, we accept as valid the idea that 'meaning' is impossible to fix, the whole picture changes. Conversion then becomes an act whose agents are the converts themselves. They become, like Barthes' readers, creative agents who write the text anew with each reading.[32] From this standpoint, fundamentalism is not an effort to impart 'true meaning' but an effort to foreclose the possibility of reading itself by valorizing one reading above all others. Islamization can then be understood not as a process of gradual purification of belief, or as a movement in the direction of the truth that Islam actually is, but as a project of imposing on society one construct or reading of Islam as the correct one.

In other words, it opens up the whole field of discussion in a historical way. Or rather, it allows one to write history differently. When seen from the old standpoint of 'Islamization', Islam itself—eternal, essential and unique, standing outside time—was the subject of history, and history could be written in only one way, as 'an alternate in a continuity of decadence and health'.[33] In Bengal, this meant that history could only be a narrative of gradual (and still incomplete) recovery of an Islam rendered diseased by the hostile 'local culture' of Bengal.

But if we can accept that what is put forward as 'true Islam' is itself a social construct, we can then begin to think about when, how and why that construct was fashioned. We can begin to consider the

---

[31] He thus argues that the process of Islamization in Bengal began only in the nineteenth century with the rise of fundamentalist movements. Ahmed, 'Contradictions in Bengali Islam', p. 115.

[32] Roland Barthes, 'The Death of the Author' in his *Image Music Text* (London, 1977-90).

[33] Aziz al-Azmeh, *Islams and Modernities* (London and New York, 1993), p. 42.

processes by which it came to exercise hegemony, shutting out alternative readings. We could see these alternative readings not as 'accretions' or corruptions but as powerful and compelling creations with a rich history of their own. We can think about how particular readings of Islam came to be bound up, at different times, with power and privilege. We would have to seek the answers to these questions in Bengali society itself, in its history. We would have to think, in other words, about these issues in ways that break down the dichotomies between religion and society, 'Islam' and 'Bengal', 'Muslimness' and 'Bengaliness'.

II

Two recent books have made a breakthrough in this direction, Asim Roy's history of Islamic syncretism in Bengal,[34] and Richard Eaton's study of the rise of Islam in Bengal.[35] Both these books are histories of the origins and growth of Islamic society in Bengal. Essentially they cover the same period, the thirteenth to eighteenth centuries. Both books complement each other. Eaton's is the more ambitious, including in its ambit the consideration of socio-political, geo-graphical, technological as well as ideational changes which accom-panied the rise of Islam in Bengal. Roy's focus is more specifically on culture, on the emergence of a syncretistic Islamic tradition in Bengal. Neither extends further in time than the eighteenth century. Neither deals, therefore, either with the rise of fundamentalist movements in the nineteenth century or with the emergence of modern (twentieth-century) Muslim identity politics in Bengal. Yet both books, read together, throw new and (in my view) significant light on the whole question of Bengali Muslim identity.

Richard Eaton's books is the first work seriously to engage with the question of the exceptional expansion of Islam in Bengal. How did it come to pass that the people of a far-flung delta, never thoroughly subjugated by Delhi, embraced Islam in such large numbers, while those of the north-Indian heartland—more closely integrated into the political and cultural systems established by successive 'Muslim' monarchs—did not? This is a paradox that has

---

[34] Asim Roy, *The Islamic Syncretistic Tradition in Bengal* (New Delhi, 1983).
[35] Richard Eaton, *The Rise of Islam and the Bengal Frontier, 1204-1760* (Delhi, 1994).

long baffled observers. Eaton provides, at long last, some persuasive answers.

The great strength of Eaton's work is that it deploys the terms 'Islam' and 'Bengal' in a remarkably open-ended and dynamic way. In his analysis, neither are closed or discrete cultural systems: they are constantly in flux. For Eaton, deltaic Bengal was far from being *a peasant society for the whole of her recorded history,* with an ancient (primordial) culture founded in agriculture.[36] Instead he describes the Bengal delta as frontier zone in which different frontiers—each moving by its own dynamic gradually from west to east—overlapped. The first, and oldest, frontier defined the long-term eastward movement of Sankritic civilization. The second, agrarian, frontier divided settled agricultural zones from the uncultivated marshes and forests. The third was the political frontier, which defined the territories within which the Sultans and Mughal governors 'minted coins, garrisoned troops and collected revenue'. And the fourth was the porous Islamic frontier between Muslim and non-Muslim communities.[37] Eaton explains the growth of Islam in Bengal as the product of a complex interaction between each of these dynamic frontiers.

Eaton's argument is a complex and sophisticated one, and I will not attempt to summarize it here. Instead, I will draw upon it in parts to bring out themes which are significant to any discussion of modern Bengali identity.

Briefly and simply put, Eaton argues for two stages in the advance of the Islamic frontier in Bengal. The first began when Mohammed Bakhtiyar led his Turkish cavalry into Bengal in the beginning of the thirteenth century, ending with the consolidation of Mughal power over Bengal at the end of the sixteenth century. In this period, the Sultans of Delhi struggled to keep Bengal in their ken, but with very little success. In 1359, Firuz Shah Tughlaq's effort to establish his hold over Bengal failed disastrously, and after this Delhi left Bengal alone for two-and-a-half centuries. Successive ruling dynasties established their capitals in the older, more settled areas of western Bengal and governed them, always with one eye on the threat from Delhi. It was a period characterized by conflict, whether intense or simmering, between the rulers of Bengal and the court at Delhi.

[36] Ahmed, as cited earlier. 'Conflict and Contradictions in Bengali Islam', p. 115. Emphasis added.

[37] Eaton, *The Rise of Islam*, p. xxv.

In this first phase, Islam came to Bengal as a religion of the court capital and garrison towns where Turks, Arabs and Afghans settled. Most of the important Sufi brotherhoods grew up in the capital cities and for the most part shared ties of mutual patronage and dependency with the courts. Islam did not become a mass religion in this period. Nevertheless, some crucial themes of Bengali Islam were born in this period: the most significant being Ashrafism or the cult of 'foreign origins' that is still so much in evidence in modern Bengal.

Eaton's work suggests that as the Bengal Sultans struggled to break free of Delhi, they sought ways of articulating their political authority without reference to the Sultanate. One strategy was to claim a direct relationship with the 'centre' of Islam and with the Caliphate. In the titles they adopted, the coins they minted and the grand mosques they built, they used motifs that deliberately replicated Sassanian and Iranian traditions. This was a strategy that sought to bypass the authority of Delhi and to appeal over its head directly to the 'highest' authorities of Islam in Persia. They cultivated a version of Persio-Sassanian culture so as to distance themselves from their would be overlords at Delhi.[38] Gradually, as the threat from Delhi grew weaker and the need grow to coopt local 'Hindu' notables into their political system, local motifs were incorporated into the paraphernalia of power. It was this cultural complex that survived as ashrafism: in the valorization of Persian, the insistence on foreign origins, the habit of tracing lineage back to the Khalifat, in a version of pan-Islamism that ignored Delhi and looked only towards Mecca-sharif and the Khalipha.

Several points emerge from this that bear upon the question of modern Bengali Muslim identity. The first is that Ashrafism was a construct, born of the political history of medieval Bengal. Later attempts to impose *ashraf* culture as genuinely Islamic culture must be seen in this context. Ashrafism was in no sense congruent with what passes for 'Islamic orthodoxy': indeed the earliest (and some of the most popular) Sufi orders were partonized by *ashraf* kings, courtiers and soldiers. There is a real tendency in scholarly writing to mistake Ashrafization for Islamization.[39] Eaton's work cautions us against this error.

---

[38] Eaton, pp. 47-50.
[39] This perspective is particularly pervasive in all of Rafiuddin Ahmed's writings.

The second point is that ashrafism is as 'Bengali' as the more popular sorts of Islam that emerged at a later date. It was born in Bengal, in response to very local and particular political contingencies. Despite its deployment of 'foreign' pan-Islamic idioms, it was basically the ideology of a regional elite seeking to protect and legitimate its regional power against the centre. In its first incarnation, therefore, ashrafism was not fashioned in opposition to popular '*atrap*' Islam. There were in fact no *atrap* Muslims to speak of at the time when ashrafism was first elaborated. So the scholarly habit of posing *ashraf* and *atrap* as eternal opposites is ahistorical.

'*Atrap*' Islam, according to Eaton, is a recent development. He argues that mass conversion only began in the Mughal era, in the seventeenth and eighteenth centuries. Several things happened simultaneously, 'by momentous coincidence', to create the conditions for the rise of Islam in the delta. The first was the change in the course of the Ganga, so that its main channel now met the Padma. Its main discharge, which had hitherto flowed into the Bhagirathi-Hooghly river system in the west, now surged through the eastern land mass into the sea. This meant that for the first time, a channel of communication was opened up directly linking eastern Bengal with the Gangetic heartland. It also meant that as the active delta moved eastwards, it created new possibilities for intensive settled cultivation in the marshy and forested tracts of the east.

It so happened that these natural changes took place at about the same time that Akbar launched his campaign to integrate the entire delta into the Mughal revenue system. The spread of settled cultivation went hand in hand with the spread of Mughal authority, and according to Eaton, the via-media for both were pioneer-saints. These men (some, but by no means all, of whom claimed divine inspiration) organized the clearing of the forests and the sowing of the first rice crop. They did so with the backing of the Mughal state, which gave them titles to the land they cleared in expectation of enhancing its agricultural output and revenue collections. These pioneers were the first '*pirs*', who brought Islam to this frontier zone together with the axe and the plough. They were remembered by later generations of east Bengali Muslims as much for their power over nature as for their Islamic teaching. The shrines that were built in their memory, together with the rough mosques that they erected, were the social and cultural nuclei of new communities that grew up around them.

So Islam did not descend upon a ready-made ancient agrarian civilization (as Rafiuddin Ahmed contends). On the contrary, it advanced hand in hand with a new agricultural civilization. It developed in eastern Bengal as a vector not only of religious change, but of social and technological revolution. It was 'locally understood as a civilization-building ideology', a religion of the axe and the plough and was analogous with economic development and agricultural prosperity.[40] It is in this context that one must interpret the extraordinary popularity of Islam in rural Bengal, as also its depth and tenacity.

Most of the first Muslim 'converts' were tribal forest-dwellers only weakly influenced by Sanskritic civilization. They did not 'convert' from Hinduism to Islam: instead they incorporated 'Islamic' super-human agencies into dynamic local cosmologies. Eaton and Asim Roy both give us some fascinating insights into this process. Roy argues for an 'orthogenetic' model of interaction between the two cultures, with each acting as a stimulus in the generation of growth and change in the other.[41] Islamic belief in Bengal was born of the interaction between two vigorous systems, so that by now it is impossible to extricate the 'foreign' from the 'indigenous' elements in popular rituals and beliefs.

Eaton and Roy both stress the crucial importance of the *pir* cults in the creation of popular Islam. Both argue, however, that it is unhelpful to regard the *pir* tradition in the standard way as simply the veneration or worship of mystic guides and holy men, though some *pir* cults did begin in this way.[42] Many other founder-*pirs* were leaders of men canonized for the secular part they had played in the taming of the forest.[43] As Eaton argues, 'in such cases, the vocabulary of popular Sufism stabilised in popular memory those persons who had been instrumental in building new (agricultural) communities', persons who often had little acquaintance with the intricacies of Islamic mysticism.[44] In other cases, *pir* cults grew up around older (pre-Muslim) mythical figures attributed with special superhuman powers. Even inanimate objects, venerated for their particular powers over nature, over the forest, snakes, crocodiles,

[40] Eaton, *The Rise of Islam*, p. 308.
[41] Roy, *The Islamic Syncretist Tradition,* p. 250.
[42] Ibid., p. 208.
[43] Ibid.
[44] Eaton, p. 257.

tigers and diseases, were 'pirified.'[45] Eaton suggests that these forces were 'Islamized' as Islam itself came to represent the force of civilization (agrarianization) against the vagaries of nature.

If Eaton and Roy are correct, their works have important implications for the discussion of modern Muslim Bengali identity. They demonstrate, for one, that the growth of folk or popular Islam went hand in hand with the extension of Mughal authority in the southern and eastern deltaic tracts of Bengal. The Mughal state was a key player in the process by which forests were cleared, lands brought under the plough, little mosques and shrines constructed and peasant civilization built up in these areas. The early pioneers in these frontier regions were partronized by the Mughal court, receiving from it land titles, grants-in-aid and religious endowments. The revenue-paying Muslim peasant communities that emerged in these areas were thus substantially integrated into the centralized state structure. In this sense, these Muslim communities were far less parochial than their predecessors in Bengal, the '*ashraf*' Muslims of the towns. The latter might have had foreign ancestors and might have looked to Iran and Mecca for the symbols of their authority, but their political allegiances were the more strongly regional.

This picture shakes some of our deepest assumptions about the sources of the regional identity of Bengali Muslims. For too long, a continuity has been readily assumed between the adherents of folk Islam or the *atrap* Mussalmans, and a sense of regional 'Bengali' identity. The *atrap* Mussalmans had Bengali ethnic origins: they spoke 'Bengali' dialects and followed a heterodox local version of Islam, hence the argument that they must have had a strong sense of regional 'Bengali' identity (which was 'ready-made' for mobilization during the struggle for Bangladesh).[46] Conversely, it is assumed that because the *ashraf* Muslims had non-Bengali ancestors, spoke non-Bengali languages and followed (though this is debatable) a more orthodox sort of Islam, they must have had a more trans-regional, pan-Indian and pan-Islamic worldview (which was 'ready-made' for mobilization by the Muslim League). Yet the arguments outlined above turn these assumptions on their heads. If nothing else, they force us to question these assumptions and to think afresh about the processes (political as well as cultural) by which a regional 'Bangla' identity was constructed.

[45] Roy, *The Islamic Syncretist Tradition*, p. 208.
[46] See, for instance, Murshid, *The Sacred and the Secular*, pp. 440-4.

This work also throws new light on another hoary shibboleth in the discussion of Bengali Muslim identity: the 'class'-'community' paradox. Scholarly discussion of Muslim communalism in Bengal has almost invariably drawn attention to the ways in which 'agrarian' (class) issues were 'given a communal colouring' in twentieth-century Bengal. There has been a search for the 'culprits' responsible for this unfortunate twist, and the so-called *kath mullah*, the itinerant Muslim preacher, has been a handy peg on which to hang the blame.[47] Increasingly, there has been dissatisfaction with this paradigm, as more and more scholars ask why it is that class interests have lent themselves so easily to communalization.[48] If Eaton is right, then we have the beginnings of an answer. If Islam was a part of the very process by which agrarian civilization was born, if Islam was a vector of social and technological transformation, if it was indeed the 'world-building ideology' of a nascent agrarian civilization, we can see how the hard distinction between class and community ideologies might break down.

This is not to suggest that 'Islam' was the same thing for the peasant-pioneers of the eighteenth century as it was for the *jotedars* and *adhiars* of twentieth-century Bengal. What Islam signified for Bengali peasants must undoubtedly have been transformed and re-invented countless times even as agrarian society grew more complex and stratified with the onset of colonial rule and the elaboration of intricate tenurial hierarchies under the Permanent Settlement. But there are suggestions, for instance in the recent work of Pradip Datta, that in the twentieth century being a Muslim was imagined in ways that sought to tie Islam to notions of a peasant ethic. Datta describes the emergence of a genre of writing by rural Muslims that preached peasant 'improvement', in ways that combined practical advice on day-to-day agriculture with ethical ('Islamic') exhortations. Their message was that the path to collective ('Muslim') betterment lay in pursuing individual economic advancement and piety. In these texts, Muslim peasants were given

---

[47] Taj ul-Islam Hashmi, for instance, writes that 'as agents of orthodoxy and Islamic revivalism, the *pirs* and other categories of *ulama* aroused religious solidarity and fanaticism among a large section of the peasantry. . . .' Taj ul-Islam Hashmi, *Pakistan as a Peasant Utopia, the Communalisation of Class Politics in Bengal, 1920-1947* (Boulder, San Francisco and Oxford, 1992), p. 103. Also see Suranjan Das, *Communal Riots in Bengal, 1905-1947* (Delhi, 1991), pp. 2, 211.

[48] Datta, 'Hindu Muslim Relations', p. 78.

practical advice, for instance, on how to form cooperative banks and credit societies in order to pursue more capital-intensive 'improvements' in their agricultural practice.[49] They were also warned— always with reference to appropriate parables from the life of the Prophet—against the dangers of extravagance and improvidence.[50] We can see how, in their emphasis on agricultural pedagogy, they might have resonated powerfully with older, perhaps still familiar images and messages of Islam.

Datta points out that the discourse of improvement was not intentionally communal, although it did cast the Hindu moneylender in the role of enemy, setting him up as a corrupt figure of temptation who lured hard-working Muslim peasants into the trap of debt.[51] But in the hands of a powerful thinker and organiser such as Abu Bakr (who, interestingly enough, called himself a *Sharia-pir*) improvement could be reworked so as to make it, without too much difficulty, available for absorption into a more deliberately communal agenda.[52] Here then, was yet another version of 'true Islam', which raised cow-slaughter, iconoclasm and silence before mosques[53] to the status of 'core values' for an idealized Muslim peasant community.

Where does all of this leave the question of Bengali Muslim identity? We can see that very little might remain of the familiar 'crisis of identity' paradigm if scholars of Bengali Muslim history were to give up their idealist and essentialist assumptions, the most tenacious of which is the idea of a 'true' and fundamentally knowable Islam. If this lynchpin is removed, the entire structure built around the idea of oppositional essences of Bengali Islam—Muslimness *versus* Bengaliness, *ashraf versus atrap*, elite *versus* popular, *sharia versus basharia*—collapses. All of these become porous concepts which have overlapped with each other at different times and in a variety of ways. So in the early twentieth century, Pir Abu Bakr could describe himself as a *Sharia pir*, straddling 'orthodoxy' and 'heterodoxy' by means of a new rendition of Islam. Similarly, as we have seen Ahsrafism could and did overlap with Bengali regionalism and

---

[49] Datta, op. cit., p. 99
[50] Ibid., pp. 87-90.
[51] Ibid., p. 95.
[52] Ibid., pp. 120ff.
[53] Ibid., p. 132, 134.

with *basharia* practices. It is clearly time to dispense with a model that insists on presenting Bengali Islam itself as a paradox. In its stead, we need to fashion a new historiography which takes very little for granted and subjects even the most cherished notions to sceptical scrutiny and doubt.

The recent breakthrough that scholars have made in this direction may not be only of academic or historiographical interest. It might also have implications for our understanding of contemporary political questions. If, as I have tried to show, 'true Islam' has always been a matter of dispute, whose outcome (always temporary) has been bound up with power, it follows that there is no 'authentic' soul or spirit of Islam, or indeed of the Muslim community. From this standpoint, 'authenticity' can only be a fundamentalist claim that seeks to standardize, essentialize and sentimentalize a past which has been characterized by plurality, multivocality and bitter conflict.

Rethinking Meo Identity: Cultural Faultline, Syncretism, Hybridity or Liminality?

SHAIL MAYARAM

This paper on questions of Muslim identity is based on the research carried out over the last decade on the Muslim community of Meos.[1] For over a millennium a major concentration of the group has inhabited the region called Mewat. Beginning south-west of Delhi, the rural terrain inhabited by the Meo peasantry spreads over eastern Rajasthan and Haryana, with substantial clusters also in Uttar Pradesh, Madhya Pradesh and (after Independence particularly) Pakistan.

The problematic of identity discussed here relates not just to one obscure community but to several communities that fall between religious traditions. The Muslim Merat, Bhatti, Musalman and Kayamkhani Rajputs and Khanzadas of Rajasthan and the Malkana Rajputs of central India inhabit an interstitial space between Hinduism and Islam although the precise configuration of each displays substantial variations. The volumes of the Anthropological Survey of India's mammoth survey titled *People of India* suggest that approximately 15 per cent of Indian communities inhabit a terrain of intermediate identities.

I must emphasize how my work on the Meos radically altered my own expectations, indeed certainties, about ethnic boundaries. Elsewhere, I have suggested that the notion of 'fuzzy' thinking grounded in the multivalent logic of philosophical traditions, such as Taoism, Zen and Buddhism, provide an alternative to the bivalent, either/or logic of the Western philosophical tradition that has held sway from the Greeks to the logical positivists. Sudipta Kaviraj also uses the term 'fuzzy' but his usage suggests the absence of enumera-

[1] Some of the concerns draw upon an earlier paper titled, 'Rethinking Meo identity: cultural faultline, syncretism or liminality?' The theoretical framework is indebted to discussions with Daya Krishna and Ashis Nandy. I am grateful to Mukund Lath, Abdul and other Mirasis for help with the Mewati sources; and to the feedback from participants of the Seminar on Muslim Communities in western India, Centre for Social Sciences, Surat, 14-17 December 1995.

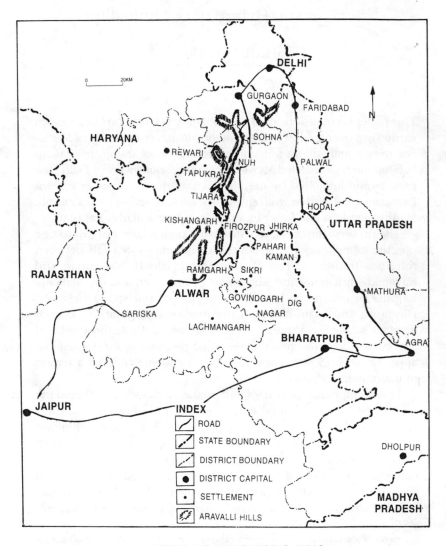

MEWAT AND SURROUNDING AREAS

tiveness grounded in census figures so that there would be a 'a relative lack of clarity of where one's community, or even one's region, ended and another began'. This is not a notion of fuzziness with respect to traditional identities *per se*, which in Kaviraj's conception are clear-cut in terms of their sense of belonging to a village, neighbourhood, caste or religious denomination (1992). In this essay fuzziness means a deliberate ambivalence, a preferred ambiguity regarding identity claims, and a resistance to denominational boundaries.

At some level I feel strongly the need to talk about the pedagogies of the academy that propel one to look for boundaries, difference, and identity so that the ground level situation is revealed as something of a shock. This essay, however, is particularly concerned with how the Hindu-Muslim relationship has been understood and represented. A dominant approach to Hindu-Muslim relations in politico-administrative and academic writings sees their two respective lifeworlds as bifurcated and separate. A contemporary Western political theorist has identified the future global faultline in terms of the conflict between the Western and Islamic civilizations— all preceding battles (including the World Wars) having been civil wars. In line with this, recent writings on Hindu-Muslim relations have identified a similar geological metaphor of 'the Muslim and non-Muslim lifeworlds' as 'distinct and even contradictory. . . . The cultural faultline can be accepted as a boundary not to be transgressed or tampered with.'

The faultline is theoretically symptomatic of division by dichotomy. The crisis, it is said, reveals the master cleavage, it exposes reality. The faultline then comprises the image of standard normality, whereas the world of the everyday, by definition, is reduced to the abnormal. Shashi Joshi and Bhagwan Josh read the terrain of interreligious, intersubjective existence in terms of overriding Hindu-Muslim conflict, polarity, and sustained animosity through the medieval and modern periods. Even if interethnic intersubjectivity exists, it is held that this apparent and illusory world will sooner or later give way to the absolute reality of faultlines. The authors' own investigation does not lead them to explore the sensibility of multiple lifeworlds. Instead, the lifeworld is predefined by the master cleavage. Further, they do not ask whether the world of 'crisis' is a normal world. And if it is the case that human effort is impelled towards its resolution, surely this suggests that it is the crisis which is abnormal. Enormous energies are therefore usually directed to its resolution, so that a return to the everyday becomes possible.

The insights of K.S. Singh's *People of India* surveyors are useful in this respect: they indicate how the quotidian practices of everyday living bring about a sharing between communities. Hence, also the relative harmony that prevails over a large part of the countryside and the impetus to return to normalcy quickly after every searing experience. Singh argues that the region itself constitutes a matrix. Communities look more at commonalities than at differences and easily establish rapport when they discover that they have 'traits' in common. Hence, the vast terrain of sharing between low castes and tribal peoples; between tribals and Hindus; Hindus and Sikhs; and particularly between Hindus and Muslims. A forthcoming volume of the Anthropological Survey of India series on cultural traits demonstrates that lower castes and tribes have more in common with Muslims than with upper caste Hindus.

A deeper problem concerns the very nature of thought and logic that tends to impute a bivalent logic. Rationality itself seeks order and strives towards classification and taxonomy. The processes of classification mean a sorting out of the conceptual or material world into either this or that. Identification is implicit in naming. For example, an object can be red or not red, action can be good or bad. Binarism is intrinsic to thought itself which proceeds by the logic of either/or and p or not p. The knowledge systems of the human sciences for long have been impelled along the directions of the biological sciences that have sought to classify life forms into genus and species. The latter tend to ignore the constant mutation of species and the production of intermediate lifeforms. The legal, political and social sciences are similarly grounded in classification. Kierkegaard comments that true eternity does not lie behind either/or but before it. What are our conceptual frameworks then, for understanding identities that defy classification, that transgress an either/or status?

Bhabha's notion of hybridity is one of the most recent concepts of cultural theory that express the intercultural encounter. It has dominated contemporary discussion of identity and politics. Although hybridity emphasizes transgression of religion and language and is juxtaposed to purity and exclusivity, it is restricted in time and space to the metropolitan First World characterized by diasporic mass migration, cross-cultural marriage and transnational identities. Hybridity suggests how two entities combine to produce a third. In Bhabha's usage it is associated with the post-coloniality and with globalization. Bhabha derives the term from Bakhtin's formulation but reinterprets it restricitvely to refer to cross-cultural kinship/marriage.

In effect, however, the hybrid constitutes as its other the pure. So if interracial marriages in the Western world are 'hybrid' their racial derivatives, by definition, are vested with forms of purity. This not only reproduces a racial understanding of the universe (in contrast to the multiraciality of the hybrid), but is also ahistorical as it ignores the constant intermixing, intermarriage, and migratory diasporas that have occurred across the centuries. But the problem with the hyphen is that difference is in relation to fixity. Bhabha writes, 'hybrid hyphenations emphasize incommensurable elements—the stubborn chunks as the basis of cultural identification'. Bakhtin's work is far more nuanced with respect to historicizing the hybrid than Bhabha's as he suggests how in interstitial periods such as the Carolingian Revival or between the Middle Ages and the Renaissance languages and genres become dialogized (1981).

K.S. Singh points out that there are few Indians who are not immigrants, and that every community recalls migration in its folklore and history. Bilingualism characterize 64.2 per cent of all communities in India. M.N. Srinivas writes with respect to his own context how it draws from both Tamil and Kannada cultures although he is a Kannadiga. He comments on the constant production of ethnic identities by mutation so that the Vokkaligas who as a category are demanding a greater share in political power, are different from the Vokkaligas for endogamous purpose or for social dining. The British, he points out, classified caste Hindus in opposition to animists whereas even Brahmanical groups are known to go to a witch doctor.

Bhabha's work certainly lends the trajectory of identity an inherent elasticity, suggesting the mixing and crossings of globalized cultures. For him the hybrid is the site of resolution of conflict. In fact, tensions are not always resolved and oppositions and tensions continue within. Jussawalla cites Aamir Hussein's comment that hybridity smacks far too much of the biological process of generating new species and of gene pools and argues that hybridity denies the simultaneous existence of local, older, or minority cultures.

Syncretism is the term most often used to describe the encounter between religions. Notwithstanding the considerable slippage between the terms, I find it necessary to distinguish between the hybrid and the syncretic. Both medieval historians and writers such as Rushdie have seen Mughal and post-Mughal culture as syncretic (not as hybrid) in terms of music, poetry, architecture, devotion and language. Syncretic, I have argued elsewhere, retains an ontology of poles, the dualism of the self and the other. It tends, moreover to signify the abnormality of the moment. As in the case of hybridity the dualism is transcended only on the margins by figures such as Rushdie's Saladin Chamcha who is a 'borderline' figure representing the migrant culture of the in between, a minority.

The analysis of the syncretic is invariably in terms of the building blocks of 'cultural traits'. The problem with this understanding is that it sees cultures, and particularly religions, in terms of essences. Further, the mixing tends to assume mechanistic proportions. Religious authority becomes a single voice rather than the competing bazaar of interpretations that it usually is. Religions become the legitimate great traditions while the margins are seen as inhabited by aberrant little traditions. The latter are rendered transient and anomalous and evoke the bizarre and the eccentric and hence, elicit surprise. The discussion tends to ignore the ways in which human agency seeks a multiplicity of meaning and anchorage in its quest to comprehend, understand and explain the cosmos and to negotiate an intersubjective existence. I have preferred the term liminality to suggest ways in which binary identities are contested. The liminal helps constitute a third space that does not presuppose binarism but seeks to transcend the binary mode of thought and understanding.

Despite the conceptual distinction one must also recognize that there is translatability between the hybrid, syncretic and liminal. Cultural syncretism is generally seen as enhanced by the diasporic experience. As a hybrid product of an Asian Indian-American marriage, I could empathize with the liminalism of Meo culture. For instance, I could wear Western clothes and speak 'American' when I was in the US. On the other hand, I could sit for hours at length with old Indian women and share their downgrading of Western culture where people had no time for the family. This was not the mere manifestation of a schizophrenic personality, but a sense of alternative and multiple selfhood in which authenticity is redefined, as Taylor puts it, in terms of biculturalism. With the Meos I noted a distinct ability to do similar switching. Among Hindu castes they can talk in terms of Puranic genealogies. They can also in the presence of theologians speak a more Arabic-Persian vocabulary that emphasizes, say, their affiliation to particular Muslim sects.

The liminal of religion relates to the hybridity of kinship in terms of analogous metaphors such as of the staircase connecting two floors, the bridge across two shores and the harbour that links land and ocean. Both critique the binarism of race—black and white— or of culture—self and other. If hybridity is read as heresy by fundamentalisms and in metropolitan contexts is desacralized by the author and the critic, liminality denotes a peculiar combination of reverence and irreverence to the gods. But if temporally hybridity relates the space 'beyond' to the present, what Bhabha calls 'revisionary time beyond', liminalism also relates to the preceding, the past future.

This paper methodologically stresses that we decenter our way of talking about identity so that we examine it as being constituted in process at multiple sites, rather than in terms of fixity and cultural traits. Identity has to be seen not in terms of essences and thingness but temporally as the site of tremendous upheaval. I have found it enormously useful to use as my point of departure narratives of the Meo oral tradition. These consist of multiple folk epics, legends, myths, folktales, an eclectic mix of genres that are variously authored and performed to different audiences across time and space. Both the texts and other Meo voices are a useful point of entry into thinking about the ways in which identities are constituted and contested. In his essay I draw up Meo poetic myths (*bat sahitya*, from the Rajasthani *vat*), folktales or *qissas*, women's songs or *git* and Meo authored histories or *tarikhs*.

It is particularly exciting to see what happens at what Lacan calls the cusp of language. Poetic folk literature has a tremendous vigor that expresses itself, among other ways, in the strength to desire. Music, as Kierkegaard puts it, is an even more perfect medium than language. Language involves reflection but the spoken word cannot express the mood which is too heavy for speech to carry. Music expresses a mood, a moment. It is the demonaic and has its absolute object in the erotic sensual genius. The combination of verse and music is devastating for popular consciousness. Poetry is also the domain of the chaotic. It is hardly surprising that the rhythms of the poetic are regarded as the other of philosophical order and of science epitomized by taxonomic regimes. No wonder Plato dispelled from his utopia what could potentially be the authors of disorder, the dissipators of harmony and classification, namely the poets!

Let me begin with poetic verse citing a passage of the *Meo Mahabharata* as a clue to the question of how mythic cosmologies get established:

Gandharan (Gandhari) tells Jarjot (Duryodhan), 'Son, make me an elephant of cowdung and mud.'

Jarjot makes the elephant in a single day. Gandharan offers water (*arak*) to the sun as it is setting.

Kaunta (Kunti) who is watching says to herself, 'men are fortunate, they can do as they will. Today I will tell my sons to make an elephant in one month.'

Kaunta approaches Arjan, her strongest son, who is tightening the *kamandi* bow that he has received from Indra. He says, 'O mother, why is there such sadness on your face.'

Kaunta tells him that her sister, Gandharan's sons, the Kairu, have made their mother an elephant from cowdung and mud so that she can make an offering of water to the Sun god. 'But if I tell you, it will take six months.'

Arjan responds, 'Is that all mother?' He promises to make her a real elephant while the Kairu have one of only cowdung and mud. Till then he vows that both water and grain will be *haram* (prohibited) for him. He picks up his bow and aiming the bow addresses Indra saying:

arak taind sandesva
meri mata kino kukh kahto
airavat kun bhej dai
nahin to tero ambar karun do tuk

The sacred offering of water is a message.
I am born of my mother's womb.
Either send an elephant
Else I will rent your sky in two.

Raja Indra sends the elephant. It comes and does *salam* to Arjan. He takes the elephant to his mother and tells her that 'while the cousins have been able to provide their mother only an elephant of cowdung and mud. Indra has sent an Airavat (elephant) for her.'

Kaunta joyfully says, 'Go son. You already ave the strength of one thousand elephants and now here is the strength of twenty more on my behalf. If you are ever in trouble remember this.'

It is significant to see how the Puranic tradition is colloquialized so that the elephant does *salam*. Both grain and water are *haram* for him (possibly an imagery derived from the Ramzan fasts), while he tries to get the special elephant he has promised his mother. His threats to Indra succeed in getting for her the Airawat, Indra's celestial elephant which is visually portrayed as having seven trunks. The elephant of cowdung and mud is pushed aside in favour of the divine one.

The oral text that most clearly addresses the question who are we for the Meos is the *Palon ki Bansabli*. It describes the Meo *pals* whose *bans* (*vamsh*) are traced to various Rajput clans: the Tonwar Rajputs of Delhi, Mathura's Jadus, Jaipur Kachhawahas and Ajmer's Chauhans. The thirteen Meo *pals* and the multiple *gots* are ideally exogamous and territorial units of Meo social structure. The *Bansabali* further links the villages and patrilineages of the *paliya* Meos with gods and heroes and thereby sacralizes political and social structure.

Both in the case of the *Pandun ka kara* and the *Bansabali* we notice how genealogy is a metaphor for thinking about the self in relation to time and space. Myth establishes the connection of blood and flesh with the gods. Spatialized, it relates the sacred terrain of Brajbhumi to the space of everyday living. Temporalized, it relates cosmologies to the here and now. As genealogy is the clue to caste the genealogical castes are central to social organization. As performers they help create the poetics and aesthetics of cultural identity.

Both the Meo folk epic and the genealogy are attributed individual authorship. But let me cite a passage from an oral text composed by a Meo in the early half of this century which hints at the character of intertextuality within the oral tradition and the larger sub-continental Puranic tradition:

gokul nagri bich hue krisna autari
jisne maro kafir kans nath basak ke dari
manthura mandal bich
gopika mohin sari
pundlot duhlot hai jabro chiraklot ko dall
daimrot nai nasal jadu ki pachun pal saball

In Gokul city
   the incarnate Krishna was born
Who killed the coward (kafir) Kansa
   and pierced the nose of Basak.
In the midst of the Mathura region
He enchanted the milkmaids.

Pundlot and Duhlot
    and the Chiraklot all,
Daimrot and Nai
    are the five powerful Jadu *pal.*

It is interesting to see how the Muslim classification of believer and non-believer (*kafir*) is applied to Krishna and Kansa. Basak refers to one of the divine serpents on whose hooded head the earth rests.

Meo clans are derived from the gods of the *Mahabharata* and the *Ramayana*. The Singhal and the Dhaingal Pals are called the Suryabansis:

raghubans main hue ram chandra autari
jane dhanus diyo ho tor sitaji jiski nari
jako lav kush lav kush huya sitaji mata pyari
donun kuchhvaha ki pal han tevi aganban nirban

In the Rama lineage was born
    the incarnate Ram Chandra.
Who broke the bow (and so)
    Sitaji was his woman.
To whom Lav and Kush were born
    Sitaji, their beloved mother.
Both are Kachhawaha *pals*
    and the third is the agan *bans* Nirban.

Although some scholars have tried to, one cannot understand the Mewati oral tradition with reference merely to the *rasa* theory even if the notion of *bhakti* as an additional *rasa* is particularly helpful). The crux is the relationship between the text and the context. Lest it be assumed that these are only traditional identities characteristic of pre-modern societies prior to modernity and streamlined religious ideologies, let me cite an episode of the epic that was told to me by a Deobandi Mewati *maulvi* in Delhi. This person is well equipped with knowledge of *gunah* and *shirk* and is also an activist who works with the Tablighi Jamaat. Trying to rectify my recorded version of the folkepic, he said my narrator had missed out the description of the *lakhamandar* episode in which Jarjot sets fire to the wax temple (palace in the *Mahabharata*). Bhim comes to see his mother when he learns that she is mourning their death. She is overjoyed that they are alive and no one is dead. She insists that all the rituals must be performed for the Brahmans who died in their place so that none suspects that the Pandun are still alive. She gives Bhim, who already had the strength of a hundred elephants, stated the *maulvi*, the strength of another ten. This later helped him to fight the Kichak of Bairath who had his eye on 'Daropada' (Draupadi). Cultural memory, thus, has a tenuousness and is a deep-seated part of the self that persists despite ideological overwriting.

Eaton comments on the absence of a zero-sum-game cosmology among Bengali Muslims. The arrival of the Muslim holy man in rural settings did not require a rejection of other cults dedicated to other gods and goddesses. Processes of inclusion and identification occur so that Islamic superhuman agencies are accepted alongside Bengali, primarily Hindu deities in popular cosmologies. He examines inscriptions and a range of Bengali literature including epics, romances and devotional poems to suggest the multiple names for god and the attempt to adapt the whole range of Perso-Islamic civilization to the Bengali cultural universe so that Fatima is *'jagat-janani'* or mother of the world and god is *Prabhu, Niranjan* and *Isvar*. The Meo oral tradition reveals a large number of names for god including *Kartar* (Creator), *Datar* (Giver), *Har* or *Hari, Sain,* and *Mata.* Simultaneously there are also Islamic referrents of divinity such as *Rab, Allah* and *Rasul.*

Rajasthan's religious traditions indicate that agricultural castes, of whatever religious denomination and tribal groups such as Bhils share Shaivite and Shakta traditions of worship. Shiva is popularly referred to as Mahadev and the *devis* or goddesses variously called Shitalamata (the deity against small pox), Chavanda, etc. Artisanal and specialist groups such as tailors, washermen, barbers, potters, genealogists, leather tanners, liquor brewers, cloth printers, and others consist of both Hindu and Muslim branches who share the same deities (Singh, 1895). Goga Pir and the Devi, for instance, are deities venerated by both Hindu and Muslim Rajputs just as *kuldevi's* or clan goddesses and *istadevs* are shared by family lineages across religious boundaries, Hindu, Muslim and Jain.

Meo Muslims worship Allah and also practice cults of animism and the worship of *pirs* and other deities. For the Meos the gods are not 'out there' but inhabit this world as well. Mahadev, in particular, is a benevolent god who along with his wife Gaura is constantly concerned about the welfare of the Meos even to the extent of supporting them against 'Hindu' castes. The gods are in the world and intervene not only to save the world but in their own everyday conflicts. In the *Qissa* of *Lal Mohammad* the hero falls in love with the *shehzadi* or princess Hira. Lal Mohammad becomes a *faqir* as he removes the clothing from his body and covers his body with ashes and prays to Krishna that he be united with his beloved. Eventually he gains Hira but, in a twist to the story, she kills him. Hira is now advised:

> *mahadev age kharo jako parbat main bas*
> *tera karaj pura hovenga tiriya parja yake panv*

> Mahadev who lives in the mountains
>   stands before you.
> Woman, fall at his feet
>   he will bring life to the dead.

Mahadev, however, refuses to help the *manas khani nar* or maneating woman. In *Ghurchari Mev Khan*, composed at the end of the nineteenth century, Meo bandits isolated by the state police pray to Mahadev. Gaura (Parvati), his wife, appeals to her husband to help their 'sons' who are in trouble. He intervenes and they are saved. I might mention that this cosmological imaginary is different from Islamic cosmology where the human and superhuman domains are more sharply demarcated.

Chandraval Gujari is about the passionate submission of Chandraval, body and soul, to the universal beloved, Krishna. Possibly this can be explained as deriving from a north Indian performative repertoire shared among both Hindu and Muslim bards. But how does one explain the retelling of popular Mulim folklore? It is apparent from the Lal Mohammad story that narratives that belong to the 'Muslim' genre of *qissa* and *dastan* undergo a peculiar transformation in their Mewati versions. The *dastan* was a genre of Urdu prose romance that drew upon Persian traditions and was particularly influential in the nineteenth century. The stories usually describe the adventurous journeys, battles and encounters of a hero in a monarchical context. *Shamsuddin Pathan* in its Mewati telling begins with an entreaty to the goddess of Dhaulagarh. She is offered meat and wine in return for the fulfilment of wishes:

> *daru bakro mas dun kardun toy madh chak matvali*
> *laj rakhle sabha main mata tu dhaulagarh vali*

> I offer you goat meat and wine
>   that will make you intoxicated.

Uphold my honour in the assembly
  mother-goddess of Dhaulagarh.

As benefactress in the story she enables Sulaiman's employment for two thousand rupees.

The self-other relationship is tossed around and reordered in poetic consciousness so that the other is part of the self. Further, the sacred-profane exist on a continuum making it possible to have fun at the expense of gods. In the Mewati version of a popular story called *Mahadav Gaura Ka Chal,* Siva tries to dupe Gaura by pretending to be a cobbler, but Gaura betters him in the guise of a Bhil woman. Siva is tempted by the Bhilni who agrees to stay with him only on condition that he shave his hair and beard. In the process the Jogi loses both woman and his identity. Shamefacedly he explains that he lost his hair while cooking!

In the Mewati *Mahabharata* Bhim is associated with much of the comic relief in the folkepic. He is depicted as a phenomenal consumer of food and his elephant drinks up a lake of water. Bhim encounters the demon's daughter, Rani Hadamba, on a swing in her garden. She calls out to Bhim to give her a push. When Bhim pushes her gently she mocks him that since he cannot push the swing he can hardly be expected to help his brothers. When she commands him to push the swing harder, Bhim gives her such a push that she and the tree roam the sky:

> *kaunta ka roi jodhiya tainai dar sun dal mein ger*
> *tol pai parungi bhinvra nay tu mero girto ambar jhel*

Kaunta's warrior son
  your push has made me fall.
I will fall on you, Bhim,
  unless you catch me as I fall from the sky.

When she comes down, wherever her urine falls, the ground turns salty. This is the peasant community's explanation of soil salinity, an outcome of Hadamba's fear.

If divinities are profaned, political structures are often mocked. The Rajput prince of Alwar, author of a Hindu Vaishnavization of state and society, was awarded the title of 'Bharat Dharma Prabhakar' by the Bharat Dharma Mahamandal. Sacrifice at the Shaivite centers of worship such as Bhartrihari was banned even as the prince was free to hunt all over. The attempted '*Ram Rajya*' became the target of many a Mewati poet.

Noor Mohammad often narrates a folk story as part of his performance, that allegorizes the Mughal empire. The central figure of this and a series of comic stories is Dada Haija. He belongs to Kol in Kishangarh tehsil (Alwar district) which is a village of fools. So goes this story:

The Muslims of Kol do not keep the *roza*. The Badshah wants to instruct them to keep the *roza* fast. He summons them and tells them that *roza* is to come during the month and they must keep it. The villagers return. The entire village gets ready and waits for the appointed day. They wait all day long. 'What is the matter *roza* has not arrived,' they say. By evening they say, 'Perhaps the king was lying, *roza* has not arrived.' Dada Haija tells them, 'the king will not lie. Go around and look in all four corners of the village. If it comes be sure not to let it go. The Badshah has told you, remember, we must keep the *roza*.'

In the evening a camel and a young boy arrive. The boys descend on the arriving party. The youth escapes but they catch the old camel saying, 'At last *roza* has come.' Another man says, 'the smaller one has escaped, but let us keep the bigger one for a month. After that we will take it to the king's court.'

For a whole month they give fodder and grain to the camel who becomes healthy. A month later they present him to the king's darbar. The king asks all his courtiers, 'Have you kept the *roza*.' 'Yes, the villagers of Kol respond. We've fattened him well. The smaller one escaped. We couldn't help it. But here is the big *roza*.'

The darbar bursts into laughter.

Meo performers have a repertoire of subversive stories. In this case 'keeping the *roza*' is identified with the religion of the Mughal rulers. In the presentation of the camel to the *darbar* by the so-called village of fools there is an iconoclasm of the subcontinental sovereignty claimed by the Mughals who are also seen as authorizing forms of religious practice. The act of storytelling, as Clayton puts it, becomes 'an oppositional technique because of its association with un-authorized forms of knowledge'. The Badshah's command becomes caricature. Folklore carnivalizes the power structure that is sub-verted in the exercise of laughter and religious structure is mocked in the pairing of the sacred and blasphemous. Aileen Kelly writes that 'it was through the muted laughter of the grotesque that Dostoevsky demonstrated the capacity of human beings to define them'. It is in this sense that symbolic capital is truly the inverse of political and economic capital. Elsewhere I have referred to Meo resistance to the Tablighi Jamaat with respect to their own social organization. '*Mev to mulla ki nay mane*' (the Meos do not follow religious leaders), Jahaz Khan of Alwar informed me when I asked him about the extent to which they were electorally amenable to religious influence.

Little wonder that nineteenth century ethnographers described the Meos as 'very lax Muhammadan, sharing in most of the rites and customs of their Hindu neighbours, especially such as are pleasant to observe; their principle of action seems to have been to *keep the feasts of both religions and the fasts of neither*'. With the Meos, however, identity is not only the *neti neti* of denial but an affirmation of both, of 'this and that'. Elsewhere I have cited the historian Ashraf's account of an incident when his father censured his mother's brother for his *gunah* (sin) in placing flowers before an image of Mahadev that stood in the field. The family belonged to the community of Malkana Rajputs. The uncle responded, 'How do you know about the state after death? Has anyone ever returned after he has died?' His father fell silent and his uncle added that since one does not know what will happen after death, it is better that both all the gods should be placated. He said in Brajbhasha, '*patu nain he dad na kaon kam ai ja*' (who knows what will work after death?). So follow both ways, this and that. At least one will succeed, being the logic.

Intermittently there were signs of change and it was reported in the last quarter of the nineteenth century that 'Recently religious teachers have become more numerous among them, and some Meos now keep the Ramzan fast, build village mosques, say their prayers, and their wives wear trousers instead of the Hindu petticoat,—all signs of a religious revival.' Simultaneously the work of the S.P.G. and Cambridge Mission was also in progress and in 1872 twenty-five Muslims were baptized including the Imam of the mosque. In the early 1920s Mewat became a battleground for Arya Samajists and Tablighi Jamaat activists.

It is often assumed that identities are subject to an automatic displacement following sustained religious resocialization. But does this progressive linear displacement tell the whole story? Let me cite a conversation with the most venerated religious leader of the Meos, Mufti Jamaluddin, who lives in Alwar, 'Bhupan (a major Meo Chaudhari) of Chandoli is a Singhal. He is from the Ram Lachman *pal*. The Jadu *vamsh* of five Meo *pals* are from Kishanji. We are Suryavamshis. All the Tomar Pals are Suryavamshi.' It is interesting to see how the Mufti's sense of identity is constituted by an intersection of collective mythic memory and religious belief. His lineage derives from the sun, for whose worship his ancestor, Arjun, fetched an elephant from Indra. The myth of lineage descent is not seen in contradiction to *tauhid* or the Islamic doctrine of the unity of godhead.

Muzaffar Alam (1996) comments on the attempt to understand medieval society in terms of exclusively either conflict or amity. Although there was Mughal and Rajput conflict in Awadh between the seventeenth and nineteenth centuries, the Nawabs also consolidated in a variety of ways their alliance with Rajput *zamindars*. In particular, he points out the role of the Qadiri Sufi Shah Abd-ur-Razzaq Bansawi in attempting to reduce conflicts between diverse communities. Although he was known to be an orthodox Sufi, in recognition of prevailing social realities he avidly watched the *bhakti-baz* performance at a marriage which depicted the life of Narsimha *Avatar* and Krishna although it violated the *sharia*. On one occasion he even fell into a trance during a Krishna *bhakti* dance-drama and helped *Bairagi* followers and other Muslims have a vision of the Lord and his *gopis* and subsequently one of Ram and Lakshman. He saw himself as a Sufi who could violate on occasions the *sharia*. Although he tried to integrate both orthodox and heterodox Sufism, the role of an *alim* was preceived differently and hence he kept Mulla Nizam-ud-Din away from such a performance.

The medieval world of Islam for the Meos was similarly complex. It comprised *pirs, murids, faqirs, shaikhs, khwajas, sayyids, sajjada nashins* and Sufi lineages such as the Qadiris and Chishtis. This was an extraordinarily heterogeneous universe incorporating a diversity of theology and practice. Different notions of piety were invoked by sectarian groups. There were confrontations between the respective supporters of Salar Masud on the one hand, and Madar Sahib and Khwaja Sahib, on the other. Whereas intoxication was held as aiding mystical experience by some, it was proscribed by others. Syed Rasul Shah of Alwar in the eighteenth century became Peshwa of a wandering sect whose members wore a handkerchief on the head, participated in rites that induced ecstatic *madhoshi*, and hence, were prohibited from sweeping at night. The *tariqa* was said to be unconcerned with material, worldly concerns of clothing or eating. Intoxication and sexual and other rites were practiced by several secret cults. Similarly, Fida Husain, a *faqir* who drank alcohol, refused to read the *namaz* and covered his body with ash. When confronted once by a *maulvi* sent by the famous Sufi Shaikh Abid ul Aziz, his magical powers overcome the other's opposition to the extent that the *maulvi* shaved off his own beard.

Since oral literatures are a performed art let us pause and think for a moment about the authors of Mewati texts and their audiences. As Bourdieu puts it the artistic work does not merely reflect the collective conscious of the group and it is important to look at the agent, the literary producer (1993). Kanvar Khan, a Mirasi, was the composer of the *Bansabali*. Sadulla and Nabi Khan are believed to have composed the *Pandun ka Kara* in the early eighteenth century. Choto Meo, a participant of the Meo revolt of 1932, wrote a narrative, *Dhamukar*, largely in response to growing representation of the Meos as an alien Muslim presence by the princely state and its erosion of local community autonomy by an assertion of juridico-territorial sovereignty. In the story of the *sajra* or (lineage trees) of the Meos are presented to the viceroy in defiance of the Alwar ruler's stigmatization of the Meos as Shudras. Meo *chaudharis* mobilize to 'prove' their Kshatriya status and to counter what they see as a prelude to displacement and deterritorialization. Genealogy plays a critical contestatory role in politics as it establishes counter-claims to both status and power.

I have frequently attended and recorded performances of Abdul, a 70-year-old Mirasi. Abdul learnt his craft from his *ustad*, Bhure Khan, of Roshiyaka village in Kaman tehsil of Bharatpur. Like other Mirasis Abdul's narration begins with the veneration of the *ustad* and the Lord (*Khuda*) who is *pak* (pure) and *subhan*. The *ustad* teaches knowledge and Allah shows the right way. To the Devi, however, is attributed all inspiration. She is seated in the midst of his *hriday* (a combination of *dil* or heart and *man* or the mind) and guides him in opening the 'box of knowledge'. The performer plays an important role in interpreting and colloquializing myths. Abdul explains to his audience the story of Krishna going to get the ball from the sea, and Basak Nag, the divine serpent, getting hold of him; so that Krishna can control him only by putting a loop through his nose.

It is interesting to note that it is not only the customary invocation of the teacher and the divine that is part of a larger Western tradition. In fact, the language, metaphors, and rhetorical devices of the Mewati poetic tradition are reminiscent of the form and content of a much longer tradition of Dingal *kavya*. Over a period of time the literary *apabhramsha* developed into Old Western Rajasthani or Maru

Bhasha. The Mewati oral tradition is a complex web of intertextuality. Hence, for instance, the reference to the *paras* stone whose touch was believed to turn iron into gold; to the *sagun shastra* or science of omens; the description of taking up a challenge in terms of eating the betel-leaf (*biro pan ka*). This explains also the striking resemblance between the Mewati *Darya Khan ki bat* and Kallol's *Dhola Maru ra duha*, a well-known narrative of the thirteenth-fourteenth century. The separation and reunion of Darya and Sasbadni following their marriage in childhood closely resembles the episodes and metaphors of *Dhola Maru*. As Marvani grows up she yearns for her husband and sends a series of messages. Likewise Sasbani sends the barber and the Mirasi to her husband.

Let me move now to another section of this essay on the strategies of representation of Urdu texts authored by regional writers, and how they imagine the group and the world. Although these texts are classified as *tarikhs* or histories and draw upon the Perso-Arabic traditions of history writing they maintain a cross genre character. Maulana Abdul Shakur's conception of *tarikh* weaves into it the poetic and the mythic. Both the *Ramayana* and the *Mahabharata* belong in his work to the category of history as the Meos trace their descent from the Suryavamshis and to the house of the Kairu and Pandu. It is possibly because of this entwining of myth and history that the historiographical status of these works becomes suspect. A Persian specialist once told me when we were working on manuscripts at the Arabic and Persian Research Institute of Tonk that he would not think of these works as 'reliable' histories. None the less, the texts are eloquent statements of identity.

Maulana Habibur Rahman Khan Mewati is the author of a text whose subtitle evokes the forgotten Sufi traditions of the Meos. A knowledgeable *maulvi* with a command over languages, he works at the library of Jamia Hamdard in Delhi. Although he has considerably internalized the Deobandi-Tablighi discourse of *shirk*, i.e. condemnation of forms of polytheistic practice, and is committed to *dawat* and *tarbiyat*, he acknowledges that it was really Sufi *tasawwuf* or the idea of giving oneself totally up to God that historically held sway over the area. Although there is considerable ambivalence when it comes to *tablighi* Islam, Habibur Rahman's narrative also simultaneously sees the Muslim invader-ruler as the other. In the face of a large number of historians who tend to gloss over the violence associated with Turko-Afghan rule in India, Habibur Rahman's description foregrounds the very troubled relation of the Mewatis (as they were called by Persian chroniclers) with the Muslim rulers of Delhi. The following are commemorated as episodes dishonouring the claims of the Mewatis: the killing undertaken by Sultans Nasiruddin Mahmud and Balban; Firoz Tughlaq's setting up of a *chavni* in Firozpur to improve the troubled situation in Mewat; the repeated attacks on Mewat in 1413 and 1447 by the Saiyads; Bahlol Lodi's victory over Ahmad Khan Mewati in 1458 and the taking of the seven parganas of Tijara. Babar's looting of Mewat is elaborated prior to the battle of Fatehpur Sikri, as also the eviction of people from their homes so that they would not be fully prepared to fight against him. Habibur Rahman remarks on Akbar's final defeat of Mewat that ends approximately three whole centuries of very distressed relations for the Mewatis with both the Turko-Afghan Sultanate and the Mughal rulers.

I am mystified when writers such as Joshi and Josh refer to a faultline between cultural enclosures that is revealed in 'crises'. Urdu histories by Mewati authors even as they derive from Islamic traditions with respect to the form and language of their texts, invariably highlight the tortuous history of the Mewatis with a series of central Muslim rulers. In fact the Meos seem to have had far better relations with the Jat kingdom of Bharatpur than with the Mughals and their Rajput allies. Some sections of the community participated in the Jat attacks on Mughal armies led by Suraj Mal and others in the seventeenth century. In the Jat uprising of 1669 Raja Ram Singh carried other castes such as the Meos, Minas and Gujars with him against the Mughals. Another section of Meos accompanied Raja Jawahir Singh on his famous pilgrimage to Pushkar in defiance of the Jaipur state and fought against the Rajputs. Suraj Mal is said to have addressed Ali Azam, the Chaudhari of Pahari in Bharatpur, as '*bhayya*', suggesting a fictive kinship that often charactered Meo-Jat relationships.[2]

The historiographical narrative of Hindu-Muslim relations that sees only the faultline of enmity, conflict and tension ignores how other emotions such as friendship and love also constitute the lifeworld. The representation of intercommunity relations almost seems to refuse to take cognizance of the everyday. But unless the historian takes heed of this, histories will be incomplete, if not distorted. Let

---

[2] *Ali azam chaudhari tu bara bara tumhara dil, bhayya kahke bolta yako suraj mal.* Interview, Ganga Singh Chaudhari, Bharatpur, April 1996.

me illustrate: If I were, at the turn of our century, to write a history of the Meos between 1890 and 1990 I would have as 'record' the Hindu-Muslim judicial dispute on the Lal Das property of Dhauli Dhup; the record of partition violence in which an initial Ahir-Meo hostility degenerated into an organized programme against the Meos; the contemporary conflict over the Karbala graveyard with the district administration. What record would there be of the quotidian, of the mundane and the uneventful? Would I know of the relationship of Sardara Gujar and the Meo Chaudhari Bhupan characterized as *dant kati roti?* And how would I get access to the traditional feud and rivalry of the Ahir and non Ahir castes that is evoked in the saying, '*thakar aur pahar ki thokar bhali*'. Indeed, one of the central features of contemporary Mewat politics is the Ahir-non Ahir divide.

To conclude, the emphasis on multiple subject positions in this essay is not to suggest a dissolution of collective identity but to see how identities are articulated, preserved and revised at multiple sites. Contemporary theorists have only recently begun to perceive the flux that characterizes identity. Rudolph suggests that identities follow undulating patterns, that differences can surface and become envigorated but can also lie fallow. This is in contrast to colonial knowledge projects that both dichotomized and froze Hindu-Muslim as a master cleavage. Stuart Hall perceptively remarks that identity is neither simple nor stable but 'a structure that is split; it always has ambivalence within it'. Further that it is more of a 'process of identification' than 'one thing, one moment' so that it is 'something that happens over time, . . . that is subject to the play of history and the play of difference'

Modern taxonomic systems create categorial identities. What implications does this have for knowledge? Clearly the crossings and the overlapping spaces are left out. Applied to the sphere of religion, identities are clearly demarcated. There is no acknowledgment of any intermediate reality in this dichotomous mode of thinking. One must none the less, create spaces in theory for the simultaneity of this *and* that.

The other problem has to do with our understanding of social process. If I am writing a history of rural India the question arises as to how the archive gets constituted. To do a village history one would go to police records, land disputes, and so on. But reading an FIR by itself suggests the marking of otherness. The self-other compartmentalization can be further collaborated by stereotypes available in the administrative record. But we know from our own lives that there is also present a different terrain of intercommunal, intersubjective existence. We know of how in everyday living people work out relationships, negotiate, compromise, collaborate, have friendships, share pain and suffering and moments of pleasure, participate in celebration and mourning. The problem for the historian is how to access this other archive, avail of this other record which is omnipresent in quotidian, routine living, but constantly submerged by the record of ethnic conflict and tension.

Meo identity exists at the interface between Hinduism and Islam. There is then a need to recover Bakhtin's usage of the dialogical that brings out the mixing of languages that takes place within a text and how it bears immense subversive possibilities of critiqing a monological language. Although there are multiple identifications for the self it is also the case that structures constrain, limit and also take away the human freedom to define one's identity. Selfhood is then also shaped by the ways in which others view us. Political and legal practice and religious regimes can play a major role in sharpening identities by promoting strategies of exclusivism or inclusivism.

Myth and memory, we have seen, pervade narration and along with language help comprise a complex web that is a community. This then is hardly a confused space. But is it the case, as has been claimed, that liminal identities are weak identities? They are certainly seen as troublesome and unmanageable. For this reason these identities are extremely vulnerable being viewed as transgressive of the mainstream and in defiance of merger and doctrine. They are perceived as a challenge to be shaped and tamed by the modernizing sectors of bureaucratic governance, transnational religious institutions and electoral politics. Needless to say, the latter are committed to classificatory procedures and the policing of boundaries.

Lest it be assumed that the foregoing is a critical statement on modernity, let me conclude with a footnote that underlines the democratic process as a counter process. The functioning of electoral politics suggests also the ways in which alliances across religious and caste divisions are formed and mobilized in larger networks such as political parties. Aggarwal emphasizes the Hindu-Muslim lines of division of Mewat politics in terms of the Meos vis-a-vis resettled Sikhs and the upwardly mobile Dalits. But I have seen Mewat politicians in recent years strategize a Brahmin, scheduled caste and Meo alliance to counter Ahir dominance of the Alwar parliamentary constituency.

REFERENCES

Aggarwal, Pratap, *Caste Religion and Power: An Indian Case Study* (New Delhi, 1991).

Alam, Muzaffar, 'Assimilation from a distance: Confrontation and Sufi accomodation in Awadh society', in *Tradition Dissent and Theology: Essays in Honour of Romila Thapar,* edited by R. Champalakshmi and S. Gopal (Delhi, 1996).

Ashraf, Kunwar Mohammad, 'K.M. Ashraf on himself', in *Kunwar Mohammed Ashraf: An Indian Scholar and Revolutionary 1903-1962,* edited by Horst Kruger (Delhi, 1969).

Bakhtin, Mikhail, *The Dialogic Imagination: Four Essays,* edited by M. Holquist and translated by Caryl Emerson and Michael Holquist (Austin, 1981).

Bhabha, Homi K., *The Location of Culture* (London, 1994).

Bourdieu, Pierre, *The Field of Cultural Production* (1993).

Clayton, Jay, 'The narrative turn in recent minority fiction', in *American Literary History* 2 (1990), 375-93.

Eaton, Richard, *The Rise of Islam and the Bengal Frontier, 1204-1760* (Delhi, 1994).

Habibur Rahman Khan Mewati, *Tazkirah Sufiane Mewat: Islami Hind ki tarikh ka bhula hua ek aham bab* (Gurgaon, 1979).

Hall, Stuart, 'Ethnicity: identity and difference', in *Radical America,* 23, 4 (1991), 9-20.

Huntington, Samuel. 'The clash of civilizations', in *Foreign Affairs* (Summer 1993), pp. 22-49.

Joshi, Shashi and Bhagwan Josh, *Struggle for Hegemony in India 1920-47,* vol. 3 (New Delhi, 1994).

Jussawalla, Feroza, '*Of The Satanic Verses*' mohajirs and migrants: Hybrid vs. syncretism and the Indigenous aesthetics of postcoliality', in *Third Text* 32 (Aug. 1995), 85-94.

Kaviraj, Sudipta, 'The imaginary institution of India', in *Subaltern Studies; Writings on South Asian History and Society,* vol. 7, edited by Partha Chatterjee and Gyanendra Pandey (Delhi, 1992), pp. 1-39.

Kelly, Aileen, 'Revealing Bakhtin', in *The New York Review* (24 Sept. 1992), 44-8.

Kierkegaard, Soren, *Either/Or,* vol 1, translated by David F. Swenson and Lillian M. Swenson (Oxford, 1944).

Mayaram, Shail, *Resisting Regimes: Myth, Memory and the Shaping of a Muslim Identity* (Delhi, 1997).

———, 'Recognizing whom?: Multiculturalism, Muslim minority identity and the Mers', in *Multiculturalism: India and Beyond,* UNDP Seminar volume, edited by Rajeev Bhargava, Amiya Bagchi and Sudarshan (Delhi, forthcoming).

————, Selection from the Mewati oral tradition, transcribed in Devnagari and Roman and translated into English, unpublished manuscript.

Nandy, Ashis, 'Coping with the politics of faiths and cultures: between secular state and ecumenical tradition in India', unpublished paper for Culture and Identity Project of International Centre for Ethnic Studies, Colombo. 1995.

Pritchett, Frances W., *Marvelous Encounters: Folk Romance in Urdu and Hindi* (Riverdale, 1985).

Punjab District Gazetteer vol. 4A, Gurgaon district, 1910 (Lahore, 1911).

Rudolph, Susanne Hoeber, 'Now you see them, now you don't: historicizing the sailence of religious identities', unpublished paper presented to panel on Modern Religion and the State, Conference on 'Religious Forces in the New World (Dis) Order', University of California, Santa Barbara, 23 Feb. 1995.

Singh, Munshi Hardyal, *Report Mardumashumari Raj Marwar* (Hindi), 3 vols. (Jodhpur, 1895).

————, *The Castes of Marwar*, translated into English and introduced by Komal Kothari (Jodhpur, 1990).

Singh, K.S. (ed.), *People of India: An Introduction*, vol. 1 (Calcutta, 1992).

Singh, Kesri, Translation of Dingal Poetry, Sahitya Akademi, forthcoming, typescript.

Srinivas, M.N., 'On the people of India project', in *People of India: An Introduction,* vol. 1, edited by K.S. Singh (Calcutta, 1992).

Taylor, Charles, *Sources of the Self* (Cambridge, MA, 1989).

Shakur, Abdul, *Tarikh Mev Chatri* (Urdu) (Nuh, Gurgaon:, 1974).

The *Tablighis* in the Making of Muslim Identity

MOHAMMAD TALIB

Muslim identity in India has been expressed in several modes, be it in scholarly works or in political articulations. This identity has invariably been a complex of social and cultural referents, its crisis a lament, and the strategies of its reproduction proof of allegiance to the community. However, the objects of reference, the target at which the lament of the community is directed and the site wherein the strategies of reproduction are deployed, have varied among Muslims from one perception to another.

CONTRASTING THE *TABLIGH* IDENTITY: A DETOUR

At the outset it may be useful to juxtapose identity construction amongst the *tablighis* (the central theme of the present paper) and that in the nine-point manifesto of the Majlis-i Mushawarat (the federation of various Muslim organizations) released in July 1966, to highlight the contrasting and contending principles of identity formation, articulation and dissemination among the followers.

The *tabligh* and *majlis* define themselves as *Khair-e Ummat*, as the 'noblest of all peoples who enjoin the good, forbid the evil and believe in Allah'. Both position themselves in the essentialized narrative of the phylogeny of Allah's revelation through the long succession of Allah's Prophets up to Prophet Mohammad and his biographical accounts and those of his companions. The identical self-definitions are grounded in a common concern for the malaise of the Muslim community. Both appropriate different segments of valorized meanings and their social and cultural forms, strategies of reproducing Muslim identity, and articulate different sites of operation.

Issued as a charter of demands, the nine-point manifesto of the Majlis (1966), outlined the broad motifs of Muslim identity in terms of its salience and crisis. It included the inadequate Muslim representation in the legislative assemblies and parliament, and state interference in Muslim Personal Law. Furthermore, the manifesto records that Urdu is being ignored in schools as a medium of instruction. Aligarh Muslim University is cited as another source of dismay. Muslims showing up poorly in jobs and business is attributed to inadequate financial and institutional support to establish industries. The manifesto thereby goes beyond representation of the grievances of Muslims, to threats to the survival of the community's inherited cultural goods. The angst of the manifesto describes the Muslims as those who bear the deaths and damages after recurring communal riots.

The manifesto constructs Muslim identity in terms of endangered yet chosen emblems such as Aligarh Muslim University, Urdu and Muslim Personal Law. Constituted as social and cultural simulacrum, this ensemble of objectified emblems denotes the Muslim community.

In the Mushawarat's strategy 'Islam in danger' was not merely a slogan but a symbolic axis which sought to galvanize 'unity among all sections of Muslims'. The lament of the identity crisis was directed at the state. But the strength to negotiate with the government drew its sap from the Muslim voters who were exhorted to elect candidates who subscribed to the manifesto.

Muslim identity was objectified and mobilized as moments in negotiation with state agencies, particularly as preparation for the elections. The objective was to secure 'my share of the pie' in this world from the state and its various offices.

Muslim identity, in the mode thus delineated, is a positive exteriorized ensemble in this world. It draws upon the emotive basis of faith (without involving faith and its overt manifestation in the course of action). It also connotes, though seldom explicitly, a projection of the source of predicament on to an external principle, be it the majority's prejudices or discriminatory practices of the law and policy enforcers. Here, the paradigm for understanding identity may be described in terms of resource mobilization. This construction of identity is but one manifestation of the differentiated terrain called Muslim identity, involving diversified resources of tradition-specific valorized meanings and their social and cultural forms.

Scholarly writings commenting upon this mode often tend to naturalize the concrete endowments of identity. In the same vein, the disaffection of a section of Muslims towards the dismemberment of the identity ensembles is generalized as the homogeneous response of all Muslims. Thus, discrimination against Urdu, interference in Muslim Personal Law, the affair of Babri Masjid demolition are expected to evoke a fairly uniform response from the Muslims. That such a view is far from reflecting the reality of Indian Muslims is what the present argument is about.

This paper represents the case of the *tablighis* in the making of Muslim identity. If the *tablighis* are called upon to comment on the discriminatory treatment meted out to the valorized social and cultural emblems of Muslim identity, they may, first of all, question the uncritical expectation of a typical Muslim response. They may reserve comment on the futility of suffering either dismay or outrage during moments of identity crisis. One may even hear from them that Urdu, Muslim Personal Law, Babri Masjid and other elements in the list are distractions from what the central concerns of 'true' Muslims should be.

PRELIMINARY ENCOUNTERS WITH THE *TABLIGHIS*

Four encounters with the *tablighis* in Delhi and Uttar Pradesh may perhaps be in order, as precursors to enquiry into the world of the *tablighis*:

1. Commenting on the Urdu being granted the status of a second official language in Uttar Pradesh during the chief ministership of Mulayam Singh Yadav in 1980s, a *tablighi*, Qamaruddin from the district Bijnor (western Uttar Pradesh) said it was unfortunate that the Muslims identify themselves with the status of Urdu in the government's statute book. The jubilation among Muslims was, in fact, a waste of precious emotions over a timely and finite matter. Our (Muslims') language is one that understands the divine commands (*Amr-i Ilahi*). Urdu and *Farsi* (Persian) where indifferent to Allah's commandments may even become the language of Satan.

2. Shakir Husain from Delhi recalled the arguments against joining the rally of protesting Muslims in 1986 over the Supreme Court's judgement in the Shah Bano case. He was of the view that the Muslim Personal Law was of little value in comparison with

personal conduct that follows the command of *Allah-Taala* and adopts Mohammad's way of life.

3. Responding to the Babri Masjid demolition, a *tablighi* from South Delhi, Karam Ilahi, opined, 'Let them take away the mosque but can anyone rob you of your *imaan* (faith) which makes you a *namazi* (regular performer of the prayers at the mosque)? What is awful is to have mosques without *namazis*. Our effort (of *tabligh*) is to build faith in the commands of Allah. Everything else shall follow.' Karam Ilahi recollected his experiences concerning retrieval of medieval mosque in R.K. Puram, New Delhi, which had fallen into disuse because of non-Muslim urban migrants squatting in its premises. He said,

the regular visits of the *jamaats* to the mosque over a span of few years helped in retrieving the place of worship. The regular *namazis* had a required magical spell over the illegal occupants of the mosque. When they (the families of the squatters) saw us in the serious business of relating to Allah, they left the mosque on their own. This involved no blood spilling or heart burn. Perhaps *hikmat* (prudence) imbued with *hukm-e Ilahi* (the command of God) is a more potent weapon than the politics of the unsheathed sword.

4. Contrary to the expected outrage towards Salman Rushdie's *Satanic Verses*, Anwar Ahmad from Moradabad district of Uttar Pradesh, a *tablighi* in the early fifties, was almost nonchalant. In a carefully worded response he said,

If someone insults the Prophet, then how should we behave with him? Should our behaviour follow the tradition of the Prophet or the tradition of his adversaries? We know for sure that our Prophet provides us with numerous instances where he dealt with personal insults and insinuations with forbearance and love. It is because he knew the Koranic distinction between the sick and its sickness. Love the sick and fight sickness is a Koranic instruction. The more sick a person, the more compassion should be shown towards him and even more intensive should be the measures of combat against sickness. So with Rushdie. In my judgement, Rushdie is sick. His sickness is that the biographical account of the Prophet Mohammad's character does not enchant him. As a matter of fact, his portrayal of him is obnoxious. In writing the book (*Satanic Verses*) Rushdie behaved like the *kafir* woman who hurled the visceral remains of the slaughtered animal upon the Prophet while he was offering *namaz*. The Prophet showed compassion towards the woman and won her on his side. Why didn't we do the same with Rushdie? And, if you say that Rushdie is a case beyond remedy, then what stops you from dealing with Rushdies of the world through the example of your own conduct which conforms to the ways of the Prophet?

The most apt rebuttal to the *Ahanat-i Rasool* (insult to the Prophet) is *Ishaat-i Rasool* (the propagation of the Prophet's ways). If I meet him (Rushdie) and if he has time to listen to me I will extend him a *dawat* (invitation). Of course, the key to the doors of the heart is in the hands of Allah.

The persons I have quoted above refused to accept what has been hitherto considered to be the typical Muslim valuation, one of strong affiliation to the ensemble of chosen objects of valorized meanings and the related concrete forms. The attitudes of a section of Muslims towards the plight of Urdu, Muslim Personal Law, and the recent additions in the list, Babri Masjid demolition and Rushdie's *Satanic Verses,* step out of the stereotypical Muslim response. This call for an indepth analysis of the alternative mode charted out by the *tablighi* movement. While accounting for its different response, the enquiry should disclose the instrumentalities and expressive forms mobilized to socialize the Muslims differently.

The purpose of our analysis is to see how meaning templates and strategies for creating their objective forms find expression in the specific *tablighi* context. In other words, the present enquiry focuses on how general principles and precepts of *tabligh* are explicated in particular encounters and experiences. The constitution of general meanings in particular settings involves a double task for a *tablighi*. On the one hand, a *tablighi* is expected to be aware of the corpus of this movement's discursive resources which are to be reproduced. On the other, a sensitivity is demanded towards the hitherto unknown concrete settings which the *tablighi* confronts but which are to be incorporated within the fold of general meanings. This involves a continuous interpretation whereby in concrete cases the explication and application of meanings is carried out simul-taneously. In brief, we explore the ideological grid of the cosmology or larger worldview of the *tablighis* that lends *meaning* (subjective disposition) and *attention* (objective engagement) to the everyday conduct of a *tablighi*. This, in turn, provides a medium wherein the believers define themselves and others while making and re-making the identity of the 'true' Muslim community.

EXPLORING THE *TABLIGHI* COSMOLOGY

Sociologists have scarcely ventured into an analysis of *tablighi* ideology. One probable reason seems to be that they have not been able to analyse, in a meaningful way, the claim of the believer to be in communication with Allah.[1] In making that claim, the believer commits himself to the belief that he can orient to and conform with the command of Allah. Subsequently, he can seek Allah's favour, approval and assent through participation in a prescribed complex of activities. As a matter of fact, in the relation between a *tablighi* and Allah, an alter and an ego are interlocked as in any social relationship in the secular world.

This paper pursues the proposition that the communion between the believer and Allah (Object of belief) is dyadic or relational.

The *tablighi* is inducted into the structured engagement in the *tabligh's* schedule through which he gets to know Allah, read his moods and manners and feels his presence as if before him. The call for *tabligh* may be described as an invitation to join the drill to practise believing in the omnipresence of Allah who also watches the believer all the time (*hazir-o nazir*). The claim further enjoins the believer to conform to Allah's commands in practice after which he can relate to Allah's being and apprehend His characteristics (*zat-o sifat*).

Ahmad Ali from Delhi describes how Allah sent help when his father was hospitalized and needed rare medicines for which he had no money. In the midst of utter desperation he turned to Allah as if to a friend for succour. He beseeched Allah through prayers. He told Allah that he could not take the burden any longer and that he was passing it on to Him. Ahmad Ali felt relaxed after taking Allah into confidence.

Prior to receiving help from Allah, Ahmad Ali chose not to speak to Allah about his particular problem, for in his judgement, He had turned indifferent to him. This did not mean ceasing to pray. He

---

[1] Bryan S. Turner, 'Allah and Man' in Bryan S. Turner, *Weber and Islam: A Critical Study* (London, 1974), pp. 39-55, offers an analysis to take the actor's claim to communication with the supernatural seriously. The sociological account of the actor's subjective world must incorporate the actor's description of his social environment. Taking the actor's definition of the situation as a critical step in the interpretation of action, a sociologist might want to ask how social actors interact with beings who are not physically present or who cannot exist. The analysis builds up to include God as a social actor, as a culturally postulated superhuman being.

maintained the minimum contact with Allah expected of him through the *farz namaz* (compulsory prayers). For Ahmad Ali, Allah is a friend who looks after him and has never let him down, except in the case of the tragic event which Allah did not explain. But faith tells Ahmad Ali that even tragic events have a rationale, which Allah alone knows. Obviously, He wouldn't go against us, if our routine conforms to His mandate. Ahmad Ali describes his experience of Allah as a co-presence in life which quite often fades out of mind but gets re-charged during the course of a *chilla*. He quotes from *Fazail-i Amal* to embellish his beliefs that his relationship with Allah is indeed very personal and intense.[2]

For the Tablighi jamaat, Muslim identity is grounded in the individual physical being of the believer—the site where faith is constituted.[3] In fact, the *jamaat* dissociates itself from those engagements which in the name of Islam seek their identity through enhancement of the objective endowments within the matrix of status and power in society. A *tablighi* finds little value in struggling to acquire state power even as an instrumentality to institute the will of Allah in this world.[4] To the query why Muslims are not conferred state power (by Allah), the response of Maulana Ilyas often quoted by *tablighi* respondents, was

when you (Muslims) are not able to defend and maintain Allah's commands in your own individual being and in your life (for which you are sovereign and face no barriers), then how could the task of governing the affairs of the world be entrusted to you? Allah's purpose to hand over the affairs of

[2] Shiekhul Hadis Hazrat Maulana Mohammad Zakariyyah, 'Fazail-i-Zikr' in the same author, *Fazail-i Amal* (New Delhi, n.d.), p. 4.

[3] Mohammad Nejatulla Siddiqui, *Tehrik-i-Islami Asre Hazir Main* (Delhi, 1995), p. 38, a well-known proponent of Jamaat-i Islami, does not name Tablighi jamaat but criticizes the ailing religiosity (read: *tablighi* faith) which gives a disproportionately high emphasis on individual's subjectivity (read: the valorized meanings) and lessens the importance of objective goals in reform and guidance of humanity. The ailing religiosity, Siddiqui submits, considers the fulfilment of the objective mission of the *Ummat* (Muslim community) as the by-product of the reform of the individual self.

[4] The principles of identity formation in the *tabligh* and the *Majlis* have drawn upon the conceptual distinctions proposed by Jean L. Cohen and Andrew Arato, *Civil Society and Political Theory* (Cambridge, MA, 1992), pp 492-563, between two competing paradigms in the field of social movements: resource-mobilization, and the identity oriented paradigm. The first entails conflict of interest, moblization for increased material benefits. The latter refers to the capacity of movements to develop and alter their own orientations.

the state to the community of the faithful is to implement in the world the will and commands of Allah. When you are not practising it within your limited prerogative, then with what hope could the guardianship of the world be delegated to you?[5]

Yet the *tablighis* have found themselves defending their position from the uncomfortable question posed by their critics. One such question that appears in a well-known essay by the *tablighi* scholar, Maulana Ehteshamul Hasan,[6] continues to be repeated by those outside the fold

How can the Muslims develop in the circumstances when they have neither a state of their own nor any power to rule, neither wealth nor a financial stature, no army and armament nor any influence, they lack even the physical stamina. . . .[7]

The crux of the *tablighi* response is that it does not matter if Muslims lack any of these means. It is always possible for them to practise in their daily life the commands of Allah. All solutions to the community's regeneration are premised on the acceptance of *tabligh*.

A *tablighi* does not recognize that certain circumstances are congenial and others inimical to the spread of Islam. The classical distinction between *dar al-Harb* and *dar al-Islam* is, for a *tablighi*, an empty distinction.

A *tablighi* faces the contrast between the way of life which relates to the world through the mediation of an internal communication with Allah and the other way of life which seeks things as a precondition to the relation with Allah. This leads us to a distinction between two different techniques for acting in the world to attain one's goal: (*a*) First acquire power, then prevail upon people (by dint of force) to live up to one's principles. (*b*) First strive among the people with heart and soul and then, upon receiving favours from Allah, employ these again in seeking more favours from Him.[8] The field of action for the first option is also described as the earth on which we live, and for the other, it is the faith constituted corporeal

[5] Maulana Mohammad Manzoor Naumani (ed.), *Malfuzat: Hazrat Maulana Mohammad Ilyas* (Luknow, 1988), p. 20.

[6] M. Ehteshmul Hasan, *Muslim Degeneration and its only Remedy* (New Delhi, 1981).

[7] Ibid., pp. 19-20.

[8] Maulana Mohammad Ilyas, *A Call to Muslims* (New Delhi, 1981), p. 12.

self. The first striving produces worldly goods, while the other effort allows one to reap dividends in the next world.

The two differing emphases on control over the self and control over sources of power evoke a common metaphor—the train—in the writings of Maulana Mohammad Ilyas and Maulana Abul Ala Maududi.

For Maulana Ilyas,

> . . . life is a moving train. The hours and minutes are its bogies and our engagements (the way we spend our time) are the travelling passengers. What has happened is that our worldly and materially based engagements have crowded the bogies of the train to such an extent that they do not allow the affable and other-wordly commitments to enter in. Our task is to lodge, with determination, the exalted schedule (which pleases Allah and ensures our security in the *akhirat*) on the seats and make the degenerate passengers move out.[9]

In the metaphor, the train of life moves within the boundary of the individual self of the *tablighi*. And the problem in life can be overcome through changing the orientation of the schedule of an individual.

Maulana Maududi uses the metaphor of the train to relate the state of human collectivity with the role of those who exercise control over the sources of power and direct the affairs of society. Thus goes the metaphor:

> a train will move in the direction the driver intends it to go. The passengers are in his hands. They will have to go in whatever direction the train goes. If they want to go in some other direction, they will have to change either the train or the driver. In the same way, human civilization travels in the direction determined by the people who control the centres of power.[10]

The *jamaat's* reason for existence, as described by Maulana Ilyas, is propagation of faith (*Ala Sabilid-Diayah*) and not politics (*Ala Sabilis-Siyasah*). One is admonished not to follow the latter option as Muslims, in the present state, are bereft of the requisite qualifications of character and conduct.[11] Perhaps it is the 'politics

[9] Maulana Muhammad Manzoor Naumani, op. cit., p. 38.

[10] Syed Abul Ala Maududi, *The Islamic Movement: Dynamics of Values, Power and Change*, edited by Khurram Murad (London, 1985), p. 77.

[11] Iftikhar Faridi, *Irshadat-o-Maktubat bani-e-Tabligh, Hazrat Maulana Shah Mohammad Ilyas Sahib* (New Delhi, 1980), p. 16.

of the Prophet'[12] which orients the axis of the heart towards Allah and builds up the required character to pursue *din*.

A *dai* (a *tablighi* would like to be called by this term) accomplishes a true self-image while engaging in the work of *dawat*, and becomes conscious of the tremendous reserves of resources at his command. This, according to a *tablighi*, is a source of real power. The point was explained by a respondent from Uttar Pradesh who invoked the story of a lion and a donkey who were brought up together without knowing who they were. One day, as they strayed to a nearby river, the lion sighted his image in the water. The moment he sensed that he was a lion, he pounced on the donkey to tear him into shreds. The *tablighi* evoked another story to extend the earlier metaphor to tell us what would happen to the world when the lion awoke to its true identity. All false ones would be driven into oblivion. The *tablighi* clarified that the false lion here refers to the donkey who wears the dead skin of a lion but considers itself a true lion. The reference here is to a tradition in politics which seeks to draw (false) strength by capturing state power or other institutions in society (the dry skin of a lion) as a precondition for reconstruction of the world. But without working hard for *din* (an internal strength), the *Ummat*, despite its growing numerical strength, will become like the foam of an ocean, lifeless in content. And if such a state would continue, then the *Ummat's* enemies would invite each other to devour them as though sitting near the dining spread.

TABLIGH RULES ABOUT RELATIONSHIP TO ALLAH

An attempt is made here to construct the paradigm which a *tablighi* invokes to explain his relationship to Allah and His Prophet. The aphorisms and maxims assembled for the construction are drawn from the *Irshadat-o-Maktubat* of Maulana Ilyas.[13] They have become household exressions among the common *tablighis* as well. This exposition employs the vocabulary of the *tablighis* so as to explain how the two modes of identity among Muslims are aligned and appropriated.

In constructing the discursive logic which regulates the *tablighis*

---

[12] Saeed Ahmed Khan, *Ek Qeemti Mashwarah: Tablighi Kaam Karne Walon Ke Liye Chand Rehnuma Usool* (Lahore, 1992), p. 24.

[13] Faridi, op. cit., pp. 106-7.

relation to Allah, we have only selected those articles of faith that are constantly invoked:

An individual relates to Allah in two modes: (i) as *makhlooq* (creature) and (ii) as *banda* (servant). An individual as *makhlooq* is unaware of his duties towards Allah. S/he nurtures *nafs* (lower self) and worldly desires, and constantly indulges in *rizq talabi* (hankering after material goods). *Rizq* is not just food and nourishment, but the aspirations . . . worldly wants. The individual as *banda* is aware of his duties towards Allah. S/he nurtures *din* (the ensemble of Allah's command) and constantly engages in *Khuda talabi* (seeking Allah). Nurturing of desires leads to *rizq* (material provisions) while nurturing of *din* draws you closer to the *razzaq* (Provident).

Tabligh is the practice of instilling in the heart of the believer that Allah is *hazir-o-nazir* (present everywhere and beholding you all the time). The believer's devotions for Allah is put to a constant test by pitching Allah's commands against those of the *nafs*. A *tablighi* consolidates *imaan* which is the state of mind where one's belief in Allah's sayings overshadows the sayings of everyone else in the world. To have *imaan* is to have before you (*pesh-i nazar*) the characteristics of Allah, the accounts of great deeds of Prophet and the *Sahabah*, the happenings in the grave and in the *hashr* (the day of judgment in the after life). A *tablighi* is expected to observe commands of Allah specific for different parts of the body. For instance, the *qalb* (heart) is to be awe-stricken and imbued with Allah's tremendousness. The tongue is to talk about Allah and engage itself in the *zikr* (rememberance) of Him. The eye is to look at things, to learn lessons and be forewarned. And for all this one wouldn't care for the loss of one's life or honour.[14]

THE FUNDAMENTALS OF *TABLIGH*

For *tablighis* there are six or seven fundamentals in life, which are internally related to each other. They can be contracted to form a brief synopsis or expanded to cover the entire syllabus of the relation of the believer with Allah. The *saat batein* are orally narrated during the *bayan* (presentation) in the mosque and constitute the norm on which daily life is modelled.

---

[14] Other relevant texts published by Idara Ishaat-e-Diniyat, New Delhi, are:
    (i) Shaikhul Hadees Hazrat Maulana Mohammad Zakariyyah, *Jamaat-e-Tabligh Par Aitrazat Ke Jawabat* (n.d.)
    (ii) Syed Abul Hasan Ali Nadvi, *Ek Ahm Dini Dawat* (1982).
    (iii) Syed Sulaiman Nadvi and Ali Nadvi, *Dawat-o-Tabligh Ka Ta'aruf* (n.d.).
    (iv) Ali Nadvi, *Makateeb: Hazrat Maulana Mohammad Ilyas* (1991).

The seven fundamentals are a living phenomenon to the extent that in each presentation of *saat batein* there is a speaker and a group of people listening with rapt attention. The listeners sit close to each other on the floor of the mosque. They usually keep their heads down, and punctuate the presentation with deep sighs and even kindling the emotions of the speaker. The allegories, meta-phors, stories from the tradition enjoy a permutation which is specific to the speaker. The more seasoned a *tablighi*, the more permissible are his strayings.

It is claimed that the *tablighi* programme outlined in *saat batein* has the blessings of Allah. The programme, said to replicate the ways and methods of Prophet Mohammad,[15] is expected to show to the volunteers the glimpses of life led by Prophets and the *Sahaba* and instil among them a deep communication with Allah. The seven principles, as broad recognitions, are both precepts and practices.

1. The first fundamental instils the significance of *Kalima* (profession of faith, *tauhid*—Allah as the only God and *risala*—Mohammad as the Prophet of Allah). Allah is the sole guardian and helper in distress and is *hazir-o-nazir*— present everywhere, seeing and hearing everything in the world.

During the programme of the *jamaat,* a volunteer engages in exercises to remember the words of *Kalima* with correct intonation, memorize its literal translation, understand its meaning and follow the practical implications of *Kalima* in terms of the expenditure of self and resources.

2. The second fundamental, *namaz*, is the first demand on the physical self of the believer as witness to the *Kalima*. Regular prayers, five times a day, is the first most exalted command of Allah. During the *namaz*, every part of the worshipper's body is supposed to be engaged in an exercise of obedience to His commands.

The call for *namaz* from the mosque was quite often compared by the *tablighis* to exercises in military camps, where soldiers are trained to learn how to perform their duties during the war. As a part of the exercise, a bugle is blown at unexpected hours of the day or night. The soldiers are commanded to assemble at a particular place and a drill is necessary to inculcate the habit of carrying out orders at whatever hour. This also serves the purpose of weeding

---

[15] Ilyas, op. cit., pp. 12-13.

out the lazy and lethargic. In the same way, the muezzin (the caller for the prayers) plays the bugle of *namaz* so that the soldiers of Allah assemble in the mosque, and affirm thereby their preparedness to obey Allah's commands under any circumstances. Those indifferent to the call are those who do not recognize the *farz* (duty) or too lethargic to comply, thereby unsuited to remain in the army of Allah.[16]

Who says 'Allah, Allah' but does not go beyond the movement of the tongue is no true *momin'*, is a clarification adduced to support the belief that *namaz* should be a full bodied engagement of the believer. The idea is raised to a high pitch through a story of a saint whose leg had to be surgically amputated. The saint requested that this be done while he was offering *namaz*. In the state of communion with Allah, his body was so benumbed that it experienced no pain.

3. The third fundamental emphasizes *ilm* (knowledge of Allah's commands) and *zikr* (remembering Allah and His Prophet). The emphasis on knowledge is laid to make one's faith in Allah pure and strong. Knowledge should equip the believer to observe Allah's commands in an informed way, to know about *namaz, roza* (fasting), *zakat, haj*, mutual deals and obligations to others. But, more importantly, one must acquire knowledge of those observances in life, ignorance about which may lead the believer to sin. Here, knowing means to recognize and belief in the ultimate reality of *din*.

Knowledge of Islam is a vast subject. But during the course of the *jamaat*, the themes that receive maximum attention refer to the functional knowledge about *namaz* its basic conditions, practical imperatives and memorization of what is recited during the *namaz*. Emphasis is also laid on explaining the gains of being a regular *namazi* and also the sufferings that follow for neglecting it. A *tablighi* learning session invokes Koranic verses and accounts of *Hadis* to interpret the *Kalima, zikr, saat batein,* etc. Special care is taken not to commit the mistake of incorrect pronunciation and intonation, particularly with the Arabic sounds.[17]

Zikr is a continuous remembrance of Allah so as to intensify one's devotion to Him. While no time slot is allotted to *zikr*, it is expected

---

[16] Author not specified, *Majmua Tablighi Tehreek ke Saat Number* (New Delhi, n.d.), p. 24.

[17] Maulana Mohammad Ashiq Elahi Bulandshahari, *Chhey Batein* (Delhi, 1983), p. 32.

that every second of spare time should be devoted to it. Allah is remembered through special Koranic verses for every detail of life. There are special verses for falling asleep and waking up, *Dua* at the end of meeting people, *Dua* before and after having the meals, for stepping in and out of one's house, *Dua* while setting out for a journey and then upon returning, *Dua* while boarding a vehicle or entering a new town.[18]

How important *zikr* is in the life of a *tablighi* can be inferred from an interesting interlocution between Allah and His angels.[19] As the favoured form in sophisticated communication among the *tablighis*, the interlocution presented in the following has the dramatic quality.

Prophet Mohammad is believed to have narrated a story of a group of angels who were given a special duty by Allah to perform a patrol of the entire earth, looking for those who are engaged in remembrance of Allah, chanting His name. When such assemblies are discovered, the angels are so amazed and pleased that they call more angels to join them and, placing their wings together in embrace, they make a column that reaches up into the Heavens.

When the assembly of *zikr* has ended, these angels return to Heaven, and Allah asks them where they have been. (Even though He is already aware of what has transpired, He is pleased to hear of it.)

The angels tell Him that they are returning from an assembly of persons engaged in remembrance of Him and that they were glorifying and praising

---

[18] The nature of authority in *ilm* and *zikr* vis-a-vis the *tablighi* needs to be distinguished. In *ilm* the authority is exteriorized while in *zikr* it is interiorized. The corpus of *ilm* requires an authority which helps the *tablighi* to appropriate knowledge from outside; the pedagogic authority is the senior *tablighi*. In *ilmi majlis* (study circle), wisdom is transmitted from outside to the learner. This relates to the tradition of the *madarsa* education. But in the case of *zikr,* realizations are drawn out from the inner layers of consciousness. Here, the inner resources of the mind are retrieved. The *tablighi* is a spiritual midwife to its own self. This relates to the Sufi tradition in self-realization. To be sure, in both *ilm* and *zikr,* the tradition of Islamic thought is the ultimate authority. For an insightful discussion of Islamic tradition and authority, see Mohammed Arkoun, 'Concept of Authority in Islamic thought' in Klaus Ferdinand and Mehdi Mozaffari (eds.), *Islam: State and Society* (London and New York, 1988). In discussing tradition as a source of authority, Arkoun takes into account not only the technical concept of Prophetic Tradition or *Sunnah* but all practical knowledge, beliefs, habits and values which assure the identity of a group or community. Scriptural traditions assuming valuable elements of local traditions, is the historical consciousness of the community. The process of this concentration of history in tradition and control of history by tradition is the focus of enquiry.

[19] *Majmua Tablighi Tehreek Ke Saat Number,* op. cit. pp. 53-5. This interlocution is also quoted in the Sufi exposition by Shaikh Hakim Abu Abdullah Ghulam Moinuddin, *The Book of Sufi Healing* (New York, 1985), pp. 142-3.

Him. Allah ask the angels, 'have they seen Me?' The angels reply, 'No, Lord, they have not.' Allah then asks the angels, 'What would those people think if they had seen Me?' The angels reply that in such a case, they would have been engaging themselves even more in His worship.

'What do they ask of Me?' Allah then asks. 'They long for your Paradise,' the angels respond. 'Have they seen my Paradise?' Allah asks. 'No, they have not seen it,' the angels respond. 'What would happen if they had seen it?' Allah inquires of the angels. 'They would long for it all the more,' is their reply.

Then Allah asks the angels, 'From what were the people seeking protection?' The angels inform Him that the people were seeking protection from hell. 'Have they seen my hell?' Allah inquires: 'No, Lord, they have not,' the angels reply, 'What if they had seen My hell?' Allah asks of the angels, who reply that the people would have even more sought refuge and protection from it.

Then Allah commands each of the angels present that He has forgiven all of those who were engaged in remembrance of Him. One angel says to Allah, 'But Lord, there was one among them who only accidentally sat down and did not belong there' (that is, he was insincere). Allah replies, 'Even that one have I forgiven, so exalted is the assembly that even one on the edge is not deprived of My reward.'

4. The fourth fundamental of *tabligh* is *Ikram-i Muslimeen* (respecting every Muslim). It is realized most visibly during the course of the *jamaat*, particularly by the senior *tablighis*. The head (*amir*) of the *jamaat* takes special care not to invoke the principle of seniority or merit in relation to novices in the *jamaat*. The *Amir* always takes the responsibility of *khidmat* (service through physical work), usually in the form of organizing the make-shift kitchen, arranging the provisions, cookings, and washing utensils. During the learning sessions, beginners are never made to feel ashamed of their errors. Those discussions are deliberately avoided which indulged in hair-splitting distinctions for their own sake and led to serious differences among people. Especially striking is the indifference of the senior *tablighi* to the background of the novice. 'How does it matter if he is a Shia, Communist, or Barelvi? It is enough that he is a Muslim who is eager to learn the commands of Allah and the ways of the Prophet,' said one *tablighi*. There is a constant forewarning that a *tablighi* should forever refrain from the allurements of invoking authority, seniority, racial superiority, economic status and nationality.

The following excerpts are invariably shared by *tablighis* in support of the fourth fundamental:

(a) 'Every Muslim must be considered as one's real brother and must always be given affection, sympathy and sincere attention at all times, particularly when he is in need. The fact that a person professes the faith of Islam automatically entitles him to brotherly respect and reverence from all Muslim who must at all times refrain from causing him any physical or mental harm.'[20]

(b) 'All fellow-workers and companions in this work must be given full respect, shown tolerance, be cared for and encouraged at all times by one another.'[21]

(c) 'No controversial matters or points of secondary importance be discussed at any time.'[22]

5. The fifth fundamental is pure intentions, sincerity and self-appraisal. It is invoked to forewarn a *tablighi* that the intention to relate to Allah is seldom monovalent. It can be tempered with wordly aspirations. A *tablighi* clarified, 'One may join the activities of *jamaat* for the purpose of learning the commands of Allah as well as for recreation, picnicking and shopping in the new places one visits. Here, the engagement of the person in the *jamaat* lacks in sincerity or purity of intention.'

The Prophet is believed to have said that another name for faith (*imaan*) is sincerity (*ikhlaas*). Not to have *ikhlaas* is like submitting to several considerations of which Allah is just one. This, in the words of the Prophet, is 'smaller polytheism'. It happens when one shows off one's prayer, fasting or charity, to please several authorities at the same time, one's *nafs*, the onlookers who matter and least of all Allah.

6. *Tafrigh-i waqt* (literally, to spare time) is the sixth fundamental. The believer is expected to spare as much time as possible for inviting others (and by implication oneself) to the commands of Allah and the ways of the Prophet. This may involve leaving home and family for a specified duration. One is constantly reminded by senior *tablighis* how the Prophet and his companions ate leaves or a single date and walked barefoot long distances. A *Hadis* is said to have declared: 'Anyone whose feet are covered with dust in the way of Allah, the fire of Hell will never touch them.' It is often clarified that sparing time for the work of *tabligh* does not mean giving up everything else in one's profession and employment. All what it

[20] M. Ehteshamul Hasan, op. cit., p. 30.

[21] Ibid., p. 34.

[22] Ibid., p. 35.

means is to spare time for the minimum schedule of *tabligh* in one's residential locality. This usually involves a weekly *gasht* (taking rounds) of the locality, around the mosque. The *tabligh* programme where one leaves one's home, requires spending once in a month full three days outside in a locality, a town or a village other than one's own. Once a year, a *tablighi* must spend forty days (*chilla*) in a distant area. Then, a *tablighi* is supposed to spend four months, once in a lifetime, in a given place or area.

Even a casual observer of *tablighi jamaat* would not fail to notice a group of ten or twelve people recognized by their beards and typical Muslim dress carrying their light beddings, travelling from one place to the other, inviting people to lead their life according to the six fundamentals of *tabligh*. When the group encounters opposition, threat or persecution, they have a theodicy to understand:

(a) 'Everyone is not lucky enough to be disgraced in the cause of Allah.'[23]
(b) '. . . (If our workers meet calamities in the path of Allah) they should tolerate them as a compensation for their sins, as a promotion of their ranks, and as a blessing of Allah.'[24]
(c) '. . . You should have an intention to please Allah only, and not your audience . . . (then) you will not get disappointed by the ill treatment of the person to whom you talk, nor will you be discouraged.'[25]
(d) 'What a foolish conception that if our audience does not follow our instructions, we take it to be our failure; whereas it is a failure of our listeners . . . (as) they have not honoured the teachings of their religion. . . . Our duty is to preach Islam in the most impressive manner. Even the Prophets were not held responsible if the audience did not follow them.'[26]

7. The seventh fundamental is *tark-i layani* (abdicating the pointless). This is to caution the believer that the six fundamentals in practice form a territory whose boundary is to be constantly defended. 'Pointless' is any thought or deed which takes the believer away from the commands of Allah. Maulana Ilyas instructs his followers:

Instead of wasting your time in telling lies, backbiting, picking up quarrels and other useless pursuits, utilize it in the study of books on religion and in

[23] Maulana Mohammad Ashiq Elahi Bulandshahari, op. cit., p. 46.
[24] Ibid.
[25] Ibid.
[26] Ibid.

profiting from the company of adherents to Islamic practices so that your knowledge about these may increase day to day. Be particularly cautious about saving yourself from useless and superfluous pursuits while you are out in the path of Allah. . . .[27]

DINING AND SLEEPING IN *TABLIGH* LIFE

The seven principles of *tabligh* in their implementation school the body of the believer to lodge Allah as a mediation in every activity (eating, drinking, sleeping, awaking, travelling, earning bread, etc.) The body is the province in the world wherein the nexus of valorized meanings and their concrete forms are instituted. We now describe the etiquette of dining meals and going to sleep[28] for the purpose of illustrating how *tablighis* overcome contested spaces in society by transferring valorized meanings and their concretizations primarily on to their bodies. These norms are important currencies of meaning that circulate within the *jamaat.*

1. Wash your hands before and after having the meals, as well as rinse your mouth.
2. Begin your meals by saying: '*Bismillah wa' ala Barkatillah.*'
3. While eating use your right hand.
4. Eat from the side of the plate that faces you, but if there is a variety of eatables in the plate then eat from whichever side pleases you.
5. Eat after laying out the food on a dining spread.
6. Do not take food from the middle of the plate, as it is the spot which receives Allah's blessings.
7. Once you are through, do not let remaining food stick to the plate as it will be devoured by the *satan.* When you do so, the utensils pray to Allah for your deliverance from Hell.
8. Lick the food off your fingers before washing your hand, for according to a *hadis,* 'You do not know which part of your hand is imbued with the blessing of Allah.'
9. Use three fingers of your right hand while eating.
10. If you drop a morsel, pick it up to eat, and don't leave it for the *satan.*

---

[27] Maulana Mohammad Ilyas, op. cit., p. 18.
[28] Maulana Mohammad Ashiq Elahi Bulandshahari, op. cit., pp. 38-41.

11. Do not recline on a pillow while taking your meals, for it smacks of arrogance.
12. Do not find fault with the food: take it or leave it as you please.
13. Eat together.
14. One *Sahaba* has reported, 'I saw the Holy Prophet taking His meals in a squatting posture.'
15. If others in the company are having sweetmeats or dates, do not take two pieces at a time, without seeking their nod.
16. If you forget to recite '*Bismillah*' at the time your meal begins, then say when you remember it: '*Bismillahi awwaluhu wa akirahu*', that is, with the name of Allah is the beginning and in the end of it.
17. Refrain from eating onions while in the mosque, and if you have had them outside, then enter the mosque after the smell has subsided.
18. When you have had your meals, say: '*Alhamdo lillahillazi at amana wasaqana wajalana minal Muslimin*. All praise be to Allah, who has nourished us, and has quenched our thirst, and has supported us to be Muslims.'
19. Fold up the dining spread before you get up from the meals.
20. Do not eat the steaming hot food.
21. If you have had your fill first, do not get up while others are still having theirs. Meanwhile nibble slowly so as to give company: and if you have to get up then say politely that you are already through, but others may take their time.
22. While drinking water, milk or some other drink, say '*Bismillah*' before and '*Alhamdo Lillah*' after taking it.
23. Do not gulp drinks down in one drought like a camel.
24. While drinking do not blow into the glass.
25. If a glass has a crack, do not drink from the broken side.
26. Rinse your mouth after taking milk, and say this prayer: '*Allahumma barik lana feehi wa zidna minho*'—'O Allah! let it be a blessing for us, and let it grow for us.'

FIELD NOTES

I now attempt to explore *tablighi* ideology and consciousness, both valorized meanings and their concretizations in terms of the entire repertoire of descriptions and evaluations. These are charted out in the range of metaphors, images, ideas and affectivities which a *tablighi* harbours and shares with other *tablighis*. Society is for a *tablighi*, both *meaning* (subjective disposition) and *attention* (objective engagement).[29] These resources also furnish material for a dual construction of identity: the identity of affirmation and the identity of negation. Identity referents as ensembles of chosen meanings and their objects are made and re-made. In situations where meanings and their concretizations are constantly threatened, *tablighis* invoke a comprehensive rationale to come to terms with them.

I conducted research as a participant-observer joining various activities of Urdu-speaking *tablighis*, randomly chosen at various places in Delhi and Uttar Pradesh. The study employed what has been termed a mundane phenomenological method of free attention. This requires that a researcher hold in abeyance any concern with formal tools of research and slip into the roles and situations as they unfold. The method facilitated access to the ethos and culture which the *tablighi* ideology develops in the lives of its members. The respondents interviewed are long-term *tablighis* whose exposure to the ideology is spread over a minimum duration of four *chillas*. They are also regular participants in the three-day *jamaat* organized every month in the mosques of their respective localities.

In the three case studies of *tablighis* which follow, the first respondent is a small landowning farmer, the second is peasant-carpenter, and the third a college teacher. The material is then interspersed with observations and explanations collected from the remaining thirty-two respondents.

Abdul Azeem

Abdul Azeem, aged 45 years, is a peasant owning approximately ten *bighas* of land and belongs to a town called Azampur in western Uttar Pradesh. His ancestors were share-croppers on the land owned by the local (absentee) *zamindars*. During his short life, Abdul Azeem claims to have witnessed several upheavals and catastrophes in the little world around him. This gave him sufficient evidence to

---

[29] This paper benefits immensely from the theoretical and methodological considerations of an insightful study by John R. Hall, *The Ways Out: Utopian Communal Groups in an Age of Babylon* (London, 1978), p. 247.

ground his faith in the omnipotence of Allah. He illustrated his argument by pointing out how the *zamindari* system produced landlords whose *havelis* wealth, servants and animals created an impression among people that their glory would never end.

Do you know what happened over a period of time? As the *zamindari* system was legally abolished, their splendour burst like a bubble. The wooden beams that supported the sprawling roofs were eaten by termites, the walls collapsed under the weight of time. The real inhabitants of these dilapidated mansions are skylarks and bats. Doesn't it provide the required jolt to wake up to recognize how the entire universe capitulates before Allah? We look for security in our land, material resources, family and business. But in the work of *dawat*, I have realized that my security lies in the deposits I make in the bank of Allah by working for *din* (through *gasht, chilla,* etc.). This bank balance will never perish.

Worldly resources that one possesses are either lost in the event of one's death, or due to extravagance or some misfortune. Every paisa that one spends in working for *dawat* would multiply a thousand-fold in the *akhirat*. But if one goes there with empty pockets, then one would really be in trouble, as there would not be any means to earn wealth. What one spends on Allah's will now are your true savings. Worldly resources (*maal*) never belong to anyone, they merely change hands. It is with me today, it will pass on to someone else tomorrow. It is never loyal to anyone. My real *maal* is that which I consume or spend for Allah. But my savings in worldly resources actually belong to its inheritors, usurpers or buyers. The interesting thing is that one laboriously accumulates wealth for those with whom one would not willingly share even a paisa. The irony is that one maintains an account of one's expenditure. But leaves it unaccounted for those who appropriate it after one's death. One saves due to a lurking fear that if one spends now one may need it against some greater exigency tomorrow. This fear is due to a disbelief in Allah, for one doesn't realize that he who offers you today will protect you tomorrow as well.

Abdul Azeem recalls the immediate precursor to his decision to go for a *chilla*. In those days he had lost a patch of land in a dispute over ownership with his brother. When he met the *Amir* of a visiting *jamaat*, he narrated to him how he was robbed of land through a legal procedure and that too by his brother. The *Amir* patiently listened and asked him how much land he expected to receive in the *akhirat*, the land which no one can steal.

Abdul Azeem quickly pursued the logic and discovered during the *chilla* a world he had not known so vividly,

Till then, I believed in Allah's Will but my practice never reflected it.

Moreover, in a short span of two years, after I began working for *dawat*, I could buy four more *bighas* of land. On the other hand, my brother suffered family losses. Was Allah not responsive enough? All that I can say is that he protects me from those who intend to harm me for no fault of mine.

I asked Abdul Azeem if by spending so liberally on Allah's Will, he would not deprive his children (three sons and three daughters) from their inheritance. What have you thought about your children's future?

Abdul Azeem remained unruffled but paused before answering the battery of questions:

I pray to Allah that they inherit from me what I lack so conspicuously. This is the wealth of character and morality which makes one distinguish between the legitimate (*halal*) and illegitimate (*haram*). I can leave behind *Qaroon's* treasure but without knowledge of the distinction, it can be squandered in barely a few days time. But mere knowledge of the distinction is not enough. Its practice with an alert mind is a difficult task. Earning one's wealth through *halal* ways doesn't automatically guarantee that one would not spend it on *haram* resources. A *halal* purpose, such as building a house, may become a point of deviation where the same house absorbs the owner in its cosmetics to such an extent that one's attention is deflected from thinking and working for Allah. Prayers demand a heart emptied of the anxiety for worldly affairs. Owning too much of worldly resources imply owning too many anxieties. . . . The time one ought to spare for one's *din* slips out of hand.

I am struggling hard that my children are familiarized with Allah's dictates and Prophet Mohammad's life and, if they practice it, they would lead their life without penury or dependence. I'll show you in my own village a number of people who were pauperized in no time, for they only inherited wealth, without *din*. Leaving behind a *dindar* (person possessing *din*) progeny is better than a *maldar* (wealthy) one.

If you own one mango grove now, you will feverishly strive to buy another tomorrow. If you had a mountain of gold today you would burn your blood to secure two in future. Is there an end to it? Yes, in death. It is the mud of one's grave which satisfies the limitless hunger for material wealth.

The real future lies not in the present world but in the *akhirat*— world whose life is perennial and where pleasures and fulfilments are real. The world and *akhirat* are each others counterpoints, like two co-wives, they compete for seeking common allegiance of their husband (believer). The believer usually finds himself in a quandary. If one is kept in good humour, the other is automatically displeased.

They are like the two pans of a balance. If one tilts downward, the other goes upward. It is the strength of one's *imano-yaqeen* which enables one to recognize that the pleasure of the world contains the pain of this world as well as the *akhirat*.

This interview, which took place in instalments, ended at a time when the last prayer of the day (*Isha*) was drawing near. Abdul Azeem instructed his sons to attend to his bullocks and buffalo. He also allotted them their duties in successive shifts at night to water the crops from the tube-well of the neighbouring landlord. The children were reluctant, but there was hardly any option, as the timing for the supply of electricity for agriculture was the timing of *tahajjud* (between *Isha* and *Fajr*). The children were cajoled and subtly coerced into accepting their duties. And at least for this little segment of reality, Abdul Azeem accepted the constraining reality of the world *in toto* and even prevailed upon his own children into accepting it.

Azam Ali

Azam Ali, aged 48, hails from Rajabpur, a small town in western Uttar Pradesh. He owns five *bighas* of land, which supports the family's need of vegetables, cereals and pulses. His carpenter's shop earns him money for clothing, house repairs, medicines, several exchanges and social reciprocities in the *biradari*[30] (clan).

When he decided to join a *jamaat* for one year, he closed his carpentry shop. It took him almost ten months to prepare himself before he could implement his decision. Surely, it was Allah alone, Azam Ali confessed, who enabled him to leave his home against several odds. His eldest son Rashid, 21-year-old, was a school dropout, and was generally irregular in earning for himself, even through unskilled work. It was only when local orchards owned by big landlords were ripe in their fruits, mango or guava, that Rashid could make a living for himself by selling fruits in the neighbouring market. Two other sons, adolescents, were studying in a *madarsa* about 5 km away. Ali lamented that his sons were not mature enough to shoulder family responsibilities.

---

[30] For an anthropological clarification of the term *biradari*, see the contributions of Hamza Alvi, Pnina Werbner and Aparna Rao in T.N. Madan (ed.), *Muslim Communities in South Asia: Culture, Society and Power* (Delhi, 1995).

What made Ali join the *jamaat* programmes as a regular participant? He found in them a reinforcement and an elaboration of his religious convictions. The *jamaat* people were exceptionally simple and sincere in their dealings. A year's absence from home was less a loss to his family, even when the children were still economically dependent on him, than a gain. Azam Ali explained that there was no other way of waking his sons to family responsibility, their own life and above all towards the *akhirat*. He recalls how the family members were stunned when he decided to invest one year to work for *dawat*. Ali read out a letter from his eldest son reporting that the family was doing well. His sons were growing vegetables and wheat on the agricultural land. Neighbours were especially considerate. Ali explained in low whispers how Allah is always responsive to believers who sacrificed for him. He added, 'if you walk towards Allah, He runs to receive you (to protect you). Isn't it astonishing that my sons matured in my absence and learnt to be more responsible towards the family and also Allah?' He added that working for the path of Allah is mandatory as we are all indebted to him for being blessed so lavishly in numerous ways. At this point, I asked if his material conditions was not a poor example of Allah's blessings. Ali was not impressed.

One needs to have an eye imbued with *din* to be able to discern thousands of blessings that shower over living beings all the time, but which generally go uncounted. Even the blessings of deep sleep, fresh water and uninterrupted breathing deserves gratitude. And these blessings are common to both the rich and the poor. On the last judgement day, one will be held accountable if the piece of bread which satisfied hunger, water that quenched thirst and the clothes one wore to protect the body were received without gratitude to Allah.

Ali surmised that the degenerate world around us makes us want goods and resources which add to our conceit and make us so haughty as to forget Allah. We are constantly made to feel poor amidst plenty.

Ali confided how the association with the work of *dawat* made him richer, as now he could cater to all his needs as well as wants. On the face of it, this pronouncement did not make much sense. When prodded, Ali remarked wittily, 'I attend to all my wants by requesting some to wait for another day'. He added, 'sometimes, I borrow from immediate needs to attend to a given urgency. I prefer this to borrowing from the *mahajan* (local moneylender)'. For nstance, on the wedding of his daughter, he extended simple nospitality to the *baraat*, contrary to the standard set by the *biradari* as well as other community elders. In the heat of disapproval, people did not even spare Ali's association with the work of *dawat*, stating that this had made him selfish and stingy. He could not convince others that he was answerable to Allah if he borrowed money from the *mahajan* to promote his pride. But Ali prayed to Allah beseeching him to change their hearts and asking forgiveness if he had erred.

Afaq Ahmed

Afaq Ahmed, aged 42 years, has two daughters and a son. A regular participant in the programme and activities of *tabligh* for the last ten years, he is a teacher in a college in Muradnagar, western Uttar Pradesh. At a small gathering of Afaq's neighbours and colleagues, incidentally Muslims but outsiders to the *tablighi* movement, Afaq was asked about the *tablighi* movement. Afaq Ahmad's responses recapitulate the predominant belief and practice of a serious participant of *tablighi jamaat* who confronts the world through the mediation of *tablighi* ideology.

Afaq was happy to be grilled by his friends, as he felt that the doors of *hidayat* may open any time for anyone and, who knows, a person in the gathering may receive it during the discussion. He was asked to explain why he spent substantial time and money on *tabligh* activities but did not send his daughters to a good school. It was remarked that the wife and children of a *tablighi* always suffer from the frequent absence of the head of the family.

Afaq explained that public schools help pupils to be inducted into the world at large and to be successful in every sphere of life. But have we ever thought about the content of this success? It consists of a persistent acquisition of status, power and wealth. But what would you do with it after you die? Whatever you accomplish in this world has to perish, but the life of *akhirat* never ends. The choice is open to a wise man to run after shadows or pursue real objects. This world is for me like a waiting room of a railway station. As soon as the train (here death) will arrive, I'll have to board it. It would be folly on my part to forget the incoming train and instead start decorating the waiting room. But where would the luggage be and how would he board the train without preparation? 'The train has to leave and my luggage is scattered. This is the plight of most of us when death knocks at our door. We are least prepared to receive it.'

Afaq said he was sending his daughters to learn the Koran, *namaz*, and other fundamentals of Islam. It is only when the basic foundation of *din* was prepared that his daughters would be sent to any school.

Afaq clarified that it was not true that he spent a lot of time organizing and attending *tablighi jamaat* activities, which made his family suffer. On the contrary, his wife shared his concern for building an atmosphere wherein it becomes easier to abide by the dictates of Allah.

Afaq was asked if he was not turning himself into a recluse, contemptuous of worldly success: he did not allow his daughters to attend birthday parties or college cultural programmes.

Afaq replied that most birthday parties provide a setting to display conceit and status as well as consumerism. Similarly, the cultural programme promote vulgarity and blind submission to degenerate culture. Above all, birthday parties as well as cultural programmes invariably clashed with *namaz* and recitation of Koran, he pointed out.

Worldly success and riches are like a venomous snake. If a person is skilled to handle it, he can extract its venom to convert it into medicine, which will cure ailing people. But if the snake is handled clumsily, the person will be instantly killed and perhaps anyone else within the range of the venomous bite. Worldly status and wealth are like lush vegetation, pleasant to the senses, only if lived according to the restraints prescribed by the *Shariat*. But if the world is acquired without heed to Allah's dictates, then such a person will resemble a glutton who fills his stomach without a slightest sense of fulfillment.

Afaq Ahmad took a little pause before extending the theme he had meticulously built:

One must bear in mind that worldly riches and status are not intrinsically evil. . . . But in so far as they carry a streak of venom, one finds that Koran and *Hadith* usually admonish the believer to keep away from excessive indulgence. As it is difficult to walk across water without wetting one's feet, similarly one cannot pursue worldly success and riches without contaminating oneself with the sins it breeds.

Another question hurled at Afaq was regarding his callous indifference to his father's ailing condition when during the same time, he left for Malaysia for a four-month *jamaat*. Furthermore, he spent ten thousand rupees on his travel expenses but hardly a paisa on his father's medical expenses. Afaq replied that his friends had only heard of his father's ailment but not of his immediate recovery, as soon as Afaq left for his *tablighi* tour. This recovery was so amazing and contrary to the doctor's expectations that Afaq considers it as a *ghaibi madad* (divine help). Afaq did not wish to make a public mention of ten thousand rupees, but surmised that such an amount was usually spent by even an ordinary teacher in decorating his toilet. With ten thousand rupees he was building a house in *akhirat*, a house whose spaciousness and comfort was unfathomable in this life.

What we build in this world, a house, bank account, status, name, etc., are ephemeral. They are like vigorous and shining flora that grow temporarily during the monsoon, and then . . . disintegrate, as particles scattered at the mercy of the wandering breeze. Only a person grounded in *iman-o-yaqeen* knows that worldly status and riches are but brief passing glories. What survives till *akhirat* is a person's virtuous deeds and they alone should provide foundation for one's hopes.

Afaq finally commented,

ten thousand rupees were also being used to build a sanatorium on the earth, a moral order whose climate would attract the battered and tattered people and also those who are suffering the wrath of God in the form of affluence, power, progress, communication, etc. In the sanatorium they would regain their lost spirits. This sanatorium is being built by thousands and millions of people, labouring day and night in the work of *dawat*. The people in the sanatoruim will look after each other. They'll work with pleasure, and sleep contented. If a person would have an opportunity to rest under its trees for just an hour, he would refuse to go back to the material world, which would look like a cobweb to be cleared.

DISCUSSION AND ANALYSIS

The three case studies invite us to understand how the *tablighi* codified cosmology mediates the individual's encounters with his micro world. It is at this level that the general principal come into contact with the organized social order and cultural setting, with a given constellation of objects of meaning and attention. The *tablighi* cosmology at this moment of appropriation mediates insofar as it offers general principles to describe and evaluate the existing conditions and possibilities of life.

In each of the cases the relationship of the *tablighis* with Allah provide a vantage point to critique the social setup. The vantage point also enables the *tablighi* to reorganize his life story so as to rethink relations and associations worthy of meaning and attention.

Abdul Azeem was traditionally a sharecropper and had learned to live under the supremacy of the local *zamindars*. For a share cropper to question the dominance of the *zamindari* system was hardly thinkable within the symbolic resources of the village. But Abdul Azeem was able to see through the splendour of the *zamindars* only on the basis of his affiliation to the *tabligh*. Abdul Azeem's initiation into the ideology of the *tabligh* was in fact a constant induction into the enduring symbols, moods and activities whose longevity and emotional reality was intensely lived as if it were the entire world in its own right. The valorized object for a small peasant in rural India continue to be patch of cultivable land. Much of the violence in the rural countryside emanates from land disputes. Abdul Azeem was able to detach himself from a possible land feud with his brother because Allah was on his side. When Abdul Azeem said that the inner accomplishments of *din* were far more valuable than material possessions, he was merely hinting at the transference of valorized objects in the world onto the physical self of the *tablighi* as subjects of his beliefs.

Azam Ali, the marginal peasant who inherited carpentry as his caste occupation, found himself in a changing village society. Perhaps more data are required to find out why his two sons could not follow the ancestral occupation. But Azam Ali claimed to have exercised control on his two sons and brought them back into becoming earning members of the family. This was possible only due to his engagement in the work of *tabligh* and his relation with Allah. Ali's interaction with Allah also gave him the moral strength not to bow down to customary demands of his caste network or *biradari* in maintaining standards of reciprocity and hospitality.

Afaq Ahmad's relation with Allah gave him that little space on the basis of which he could maintain a critical distance from the 'rule of fashion' or the 'model of life' in vogue. Association with the activities of *tabligh* provided him a cherished space into which he could escape temporarily. The three cases reveal rather vividly the underlying commonalities of principles and precepts around which the world is encountered and experienced by *tablighis*. Their ideology is an intervention, insofar as it offers an alternative blueprint for society through a radical remoulding of the individual and his/her identity. This is manifested in the common concern to forge the moral alternative at various levels of identity and practice. While drawing upon the above for analysis, we shall weave in related material and observations collected from interviews with thirty-two *tablighis* at the *markaz*, in the setting of the *jamaat*, in the mosque after the *bayan* or *taleem* following *Isha* prayers, and at their respective residences. Most of the respondents belong to Uttar Pradesh, the rest to Delhi (though their ancestral places are Bihar, Orissa, Assam, West Bengal, Kashmir, etc.).

For many of them, joining the work of *tabligh* involves in reality, a major shift away from existing compulsions and associations, rejections and modifications of various components of one's existing identity. There is somewhere in the mind of the believer, discursively expressed or silently lived, a long dialogue with his received identity which is now seeks to review and alter. The world outside the fold of the *din* is morally disdained. Its power and grandeur are grotesque and false, even if it presents itself to people as an object of ultimate concern. Abdul Azeem tells us how the absentee landlords turned pauper in no time, as also his brother, after winning land through litigation. Ali's absence from his home, despite his being the only breadwinner, was indeed a veritable gain to the family. The world's claims are unwarranted, its promises illusory. The security it posits in wealth, status and power seldom protect people from penury, dependence or death.

During the course of fieldwork, certain images of the world were collected. The respondents appropriated images from the standard texts of the *jamaat* entitled *Fazail-i Amal* and/or *Hayatus Sahabah* even if in the act of projection, these were not formal, cited quotations. The images provide the narrational and moral presentation of reality, out of which, in the subsequent derivation, the moral alternative is constructed. Here are some images striking for their salience and intensity of communication.

(*a*) The world is a house of dishonour where the destiny of a settlement is destruction, its inmates enter their graves alone, its solidarity suffers from dissensions, its spaciousness breeds poverty, its abundance survives on labour and its penury begets pleasure.

(*b*) The world deceives its lovers by decorating itself with a colourful costume. And like the bride on the first nuptial night, it casts its spell on the lover to captivate his soul in its clutches. But beware, this bride is a different one because it poisons its lovers in their trance. It kills them as it did a number of its lovers in the past.

(*c*) Prophet Muhammad once came across a heap of garbage where stray bones and human skulls were rotting amidst decaying waste and tattered pieces of worn out garments. He explained to his followers that the garbage heap was the world's ultimate destination. He elaborated that these skulls once nurtured a mind that aspired to conquer the world. The human excreta which now repel, were once colourful cuisines prepared with great pains and whose aroma evoked a craving in people. The tattered costumes were once worn by people to enhance their conceit. The bones are of the horses upon whom rode arrogant warriors. Surely, the world is not worthy of being held as a pinnacle of all concerns and desires.

(*d*) On the day of *qiyamat* an old hideous woman, condemned to hell, would be brought before people. Her eyes would carry a cruel tint and the crooked teeth would project out. People would be told that she was the personification of world.

(*e*) In a diagrammatic presentation of the plight of man in this world, Prophet Mohammad drew a square, which was divided by a vertical line in the middle. This line extended a little beyond the square. A number of small horizontal lines were shown emanating from the vertical walls of the square which ended halfway without touching the middle dividing line. The middle dividing line represents the man in the world, surrounded by the four lines of the square that are his death. The little protrusion at the top of the square are the tall hopes which attempt to outlive death. The incomplete horizontal lines are the trials and tribulations which constantly surround the individual without letting him escape. The *Ummat's* well-being, according to the Prophet, lies in its faith in the *akhirat* and a disaffection with the world. Its degeneration would emerge from its unlimited aspirations for worldly honour and privileges.

(*f*) The plight of man-in-the-world is also constructed through a complex imagery. A man is portrayed as being chased by a lion (death) who seeks refuge on a tree branch. But he is staggered to find that the branch bends over a pond where several crocodiles (graves) wait for prey, their mouth wide open. The branch as a life-line is being hollowed out by a wood pecker (ailments and anxieties which reduce life). The man hanging from the branch suddenly forgets his agony as he tastes a drop of honey that falls from a bee hive (worldly allurements) on the tree top.

Such abominable images of the world are certainly not an invitation to renunciation. It is merely to caution the believer that a constant vigil is required during one's engagement in the world to eke out a living.

Absolute trust in Allah's succour is what equips a *tablighi* to render the dark and deceptive alley-ways of the world safely negotiable. A total submission to Allah's will not only bestows huge reserves of strength but also other resources which hitherto lay unrecognized and unrealized, such as deep sleep or uninterrupted breathing. When a *tablighi* seeks Allah's proximity through a sincere observance of mandatory prescription (*faraiz*) and optional prayers and practices (*nawafil*), such a believer is chosen as his beloved. In the state of love, Allah becomes the ears of the believer, his eyes, hands and feet. And if he supplicates, he is blessed and if he seeks shelter he is duly protected. But Allah also puts one to a trial in order to ascertain if a blessing reinforces faith in the divine or promotes self-conceit.

One *tablighi's* father suffered from terminal cancer but this made him turn to the *faraiz* and *dua*, and he received from Allah an immense contentment of heart. Without this blessing, the family would have had to contend with two patients. Another respondent, a school teacher by profession, and the only breadwinner of the family, finds in a family hostile to his engagement with the *dawat*. In an otherwise spacious apartment, he is relegated to a small room. But he is not alone in the room. With *namaz*, *tilawat* (recitation of Koran), *zikr*, he relates to Allah, and in turn, to a world larger than the one in which he lives physically. Although the world places several odds before a *tablighi* when he sets out to labour for *din*, Allah intervenes with a *ghaibi madad* and the believer finds himself equipped with such mental and physical powers as enable him to conquer adversity.

There are innumerable experiences amongst *tablighi* to warrant how, if you walk towards Allah, he runs to receive you. One *tablighi* claims that a *jamaat* staying in a certain mosque in Bhopal found themselves untouched by the poisonous fumes of the gas leak from the Union Carbide factory in December 1984.

In their intervention in the world, the *tablighis* do not seek to struggle for control of the larger institutions and apparatuses. One worker, in a fertilizer industry (also a *tablighi*), commented how the trade union institution in its politics was un-Islamic, as it either aroused emotion or suppressed them. In the work of *dawat*, emotions are shaped and given a direction. Yet *tablighis* do not propose retreat from the grotesque world into a hermit existence. They engage in a moral struggle against the established order by living out a blueprint of an ideal life through proposed programmes of the *jamaat*. The basic concern is to demonstrate that the world can be 'saved' from the fire of hell, if it comes to be organized around the dictates of *din*.

The discursive presentation of their experience by respondents is primarily to familiarize listeners with *tablighi* ideology. It may also be a part of the recurrent exercise to build up an atmosphere for reinforcement of conviction. But, one is constantly reminded that the tongue is not as reliable as the body which practices faith.

Tablighi ideology thus deepens into the province of emotions, affectivity and body language. Tears are a more reliable sign of communion with divinity than an appropriately chosen expression. A *Dua* interspersed with intense emotional outbursts of the listeners is closer to the marrow of true worship than a forceful *bayan*. The oral narrative of the *tablighi* ideology is replete with the anecdotes and associations which convey importance of tears in communication with Allah. One *sahabi* is said to have been weeping while supplicating: the tears that rolled down his eyes carried a tint of blood. He was asked about the agony that struck him so deep, he replied that this was his repentance for not fulfilling his duty towards Allah. The blood in the tears ensured that tears were authentic.

The entire cosmological and organizational complex of *tabligh* may be viewed as a delimited terrain (the ensemble of valorized meanings and their concretizations) from whose vantage point the affective weakening becomes thinkable and definable. This performative, discursive and affective terrain is neither arbitrary nor fortuitous. The performative is entailed in the given *tablighi* schedule. The discursive is the experience of the Islamic tradition stored up in the fifteen-hundred-year-old narratives of the biographies of the prophets up to prophet Mohammad and his companions.

The Islamic tradition which the *tablighis* invoke is older than the customary cultural traditions of most Muslims. Most common tradition of the recent past of the Muslims in India is one which organizes the community to secure a lager slice of the share in material resources and power in society. In this logic, according to a *tablighi*, one is using *asbab* (instrumentalities) as both means and ends. One is really caught up in the vortex of *asbab*. In the commonplace tradition among Muslims, one's eyes are focused on this world but not on the world that one enters after death. The endorsement of the tradition of *tabligh* implies a rejection of the immediate past of the believer where the relation of the person with things is not mediated by any reference to Allah. The rejection is in favour of something rarefied and is experienced as a substantial overturning of recently-held values.

In a sense, the *tablighi* is attempting to wrest their version of Islamic tradition away from an uncritical conformism to the 'rule of fashion' in this world that is always waiting intently to overpower it. As religious practice wholly distinct from everyday life is hardly ever absorbed in it fully, it has a remarkable capacity to hold the world at a critical moral distance.

The transformation which *tabligh* brings about in the life of an individual is in fact a transformation of identity. The world becomes a floating signifier, the fixity of its signs and referents are subverted.

From the vantage point of a *tablighi*, the world of *asbab* is devoid of a permanent ground. All identities have a relational character. The *tablighi* identity while grounding itself in commands of Allah and the recognition of *akhirat* as the beginning of an eternal life, transform the identities forged for and through this world.

The *tablighis*, in making the Muslim identity, have shifted their attention from the naturalized social and cultural endowments attributed to the Muslim community. The focus shifts to the physical being of an individual *tablighi* as a major province of the world, as a site which establishes the living nexus of meanings. The focus on the body of the believer gives *tablighi jamaat* a different political orientation. The group ceases to be a competitor for the scarce values and endowments to which others aspire. Its quest for meaning centralizes collective attention on the objective forms which scarcely have a value outside the intersubjective fold of the group. Thus, *saat batein* becomes the synopsis of the relationship between the *tablighi* and Allah. It is the site where the components of Muslim identity are constituted. And, as a matter of principle, the *tablighis* desist from contesting over a matter which deflects their attention from the prescribed schedule of *tabligh*. The project which the *tablighis* have charted out is intended for all humanity, and a typical *tablighi* is forever catching up with unfinished tasks.

The *tablighi jamaat's* activities are constituted within a sphere of society that is intended to remain outside the fold of economy and state. It remains in the intimate shere of family and neighbourhood, and the sphere of associations (particularly the *jamaat* itself). The network of associations of *tablighi jamaat* are periodically reproduced through enduring forms of self-constitution and self-mobilization. It is institutionalized and generalized through rules and resources and a cosmology and moral injunctions of right and wrong. The focus of ideology, mobilization and communication remains the individual Muslim with his/her relation to Allah. The individual as receptor of ideas and affect is not a mere listener. He realizes in a short time that there is a network of association waiting to include the novice. The principle of admission of new members and their placement inside the organization offers space to graduate from one position to the other. Self-motivation (the felt need to participate in the programmes) is perhaps the only criterion to move from one status of responsibility to other.

Further research is required to analyse those contexts of *tablighi* life which limit and constrain identity. Also the *tablighi* identity is limited by the active presence of identity constructs upheld by other traditions of Islam. A *tablighi* is 'looked at' by those who share his social space but not his identity. This non-sharing expressing itself as indifference or serious disagreements and even opprobrium generates serious processes in the defence and propagation of meaning. Research seeking to explore *tablighi* identity should also unravel the complex mediations (sacred or secular) which have a bearing upon practice. Surely, ideological claims are seldom consummated in reality in conformity to the wishes of the proponents. A *tablighi* always exists in a state of constant tension with realities which enjoin a different theory and practice. There are other constructions of identity which compete for allegiance. Further research should adequately portray the polyphony in the ideological voices and contested character of the social and cultural space where the *tablighi* identity is formed.

Traditional Rites and Contested Meanings: Sectarian Strife in Colonial Lucknow

MUSHIRUL HASAN

The truth is that in those days the whole year was spent waiting for Muharram. . . . After the goat sacrifices of Baqr Id the preparations for Muharram began. Dadda, my father's mother, started to softly chant elegies about the martyrs. Mother set about sewing black clothes for all of us; and my sister took out the notebooks of laments . . . and began to practice them to new airs. In those days film music had not taken grip of *nauha* melodies. They were simple and at the same time deep, like the folk-music of villages and small towns, and when my sister, mother, or an aunt wore black clothes and stood up to recite,

Sleeping spoke out the dreaming Sakina,
The lord's breast's no more, so no more Sakina . . .

the wrists supporting the book of *nauhas* were immediately transformed. It seemed to the listeners as if the lament was issuing straight from the jail in Damascus where Imam Husain's sister Zainab was trying to comfort his beloved daughter Sakina in a subterranean dungeon. . . . I don't know about Lucknow—I don't even know about Ghazipur—but I certainly do know that among the Saiyid families of Gangauli, Muharram was nothing less than a spiritual celebration.

Rahi Masoom Reza, *The Feuding Families of Village Gangauli*,
translated by Gillian Wright, Delhi, 1994, pp. 9-10.

I

As darkness descended on Lucknow, once a prized city of Awadh, some people huddled together in a cafe or on the terraces with their eyes fixed on the distant horizon. After a long and anxious wait, the city comes alive: the moon is sighted in the middle of dark clouds hovering over the Gomti river. The deafening sound of crackers from Nakhaas and the loud and clear call for prayers from Shah Najaf mark the beginning of the holy month of Muharram. Lakhnavis would observe the next ten days with solemnity. They would, moreover, reaffirm their unflinching devotion to those Islamic principles for which Imam Husain, grandson of the Prophet of Islam, and his companions laid down their lives on the banks of the river Euphrates in AD 680. Once more, they would, in their imagination, rally round those gallant men and women at Karbala who kept the Islamic flag flying without capitulating before the evil and tyrannical forces. They would once again desire to share in their *karb* (pain) and *bala* (trial). The ritual recreation of Karbala creates an environment that, in Clifford Geertz's terms, can 'establish powerful, pervasive, and long-lasting moods and motivations in men by formulating conceptions of a general order of existence and clothing those conceptions with such an aura of factuality that the moods and motivations seem uniquely realistic'.

Come day one of Muharram and life in Lucknow comes to a standstill. Perfume and tobacco shops wear a deserted look. Trade is no longer brisk. Business has slackened. The busy and noisy bazaars of Aminabad and Nakhaas are subdued. The city is robbed of its buoyancy and festive look. Meer Hasan Ali, an English lady married to a Shia and living in Lucknow in the 1820s, contrasted the profound stillness of an extensively populated city with incessant bustle usual at all other times.[1]

The change is also manifested in other ways. Women, including the newly-wed, remove their jewellery, their bangles and flashy clothes; 'the hair is unloosed . . . and allowed to flow in disorder about the person; the coloured pyjamahs (loose trousers) and duppattas (long scarf) are removed, with every other articles of their usual costume, for a suit that, with them, constitutes mourning— some choose black, others grey, slate, or green'.[2] Comfort, luxury and convenience are set aside. The *pallung*, the *charpoy* (the two descriptions of beds) and the *musnad* are removed. Instead, women of all classes use a date mat or simply sleep on a matted floor.[3] Men are equally abstemious, sporting white *angarkhas* (a combination of the *jama*, a collarless shirt and *balabar*) or *achkans* (knee-length tunics) in dark shades. Poets, accustomed to regaling large audiences with *ghazals*, switch to writing *marsiyas* (elegies) and *soz* (dirges).

---

[1] Meer Hasan Ali, *Observations on the Mussalmans of India* (Delhi, 1982 rpt.), p. 30.

[2] Ibid., p. 46.

[3] Ibid., p. 43.

Their chief patrons, the rajas and nawabs, abandon their favourite pastimes to lead a pious and abstemious life. Their palaces, *havelis* and forts bear a sombre look during Muharram.

Courtesans and their retinue in Chowk put away their musical instruments, their *ghungrus, payals* and the *tabla*. Umrao Jan Ada's 'Khanum' commemorated Husain's martyrdom on a more elaborate scale than any other courtesan in Lucknow, decorating the place of mourning with banners, buntings, chandeliers and globes. She was herself an accomplished *soz-khwan* (reciter of dirges). The most celebrated professionals dared not perform in her presence.[4] Her account finds resonances in Attia Hosain's description of her visit down 'the forbidden street whose balconies during the first days of Muharram were empty of painted, bejewelled women when visitors climbed the narrow stairs only to hear religious songs of mourning'.[5] There was the glass *tazia*, the miniature domed tomb, shining, gleaming, reflecting the light of many crystal lamps.

The city's black clad men and women set aside their daily chores to sorrow for the martyred Imam and his loyal and courageous companions. They marched through the lanes and bylanes in fervent lamentation chanting 'Ya-Husain, Ya-Husain', rhythmically beating their chests, self-flagellating, carrying replicas (*tazia*) of Husain's tomb, his coffin (*tabooi*), his standards and insignia (*alam* and *panja*) and his horse (*dul-dul*). One of the most impressive religious spectacles, commented William Crooke, was the long procession of *tazias* and flags streaming along the streets with a vast crowd of mourners, who 'scream out their lamentations and beat their breasts till the blood flows or they sink fainting in an ecstasy of sorrow' [6] Notice, the following description:

The sun was high above the church steeple when we heard the distant chanting, 'Hasan! Husain! Hasan! Husain! Haider!' It came nearer and the measured sound of bare hands striking bare breasts, the monotonous beat of drums and cymbals made my heart beat with a strange excitement. Then the barefooted, bareheaded men came in view following the *tazias* carried shoulder-high. There were *tazias* of peacock's feathers, of glass, of sugar,

[4] Mirza Mohammad Hadi Ruswa, *Umrao Jan Ada*, translated by Khushwant Singh and M.A. Husain (Hyderabad, 1982), p. 48.

[5] Attia Hosain, *Sunlight on a Broken Column* (Delhi, 1992), p. 64.

[6] W. Crooke, *The North-Western Provinces of India: Their History, Ethnology, and Administration* (Delhi, 1975 rpt.), p. 263.

of bright-coloured paper, intricate, beautiful arched domed, some as high as telegraph poles, others from poor homes so small that they could be held on one man's head, all hurrying to join the main procession at the allotted time, for burial or, consecration.[7]

Such devotional activities in public were just a small part of Muharram ceremonies. The imambaras (literally, the house of Imam), many of which symbolized Lucknow's Shia past and present, served as central organizing spaces, physical statements uniting the populace of the city,[8] symbols of communitarian solidarity, and as platforms for articulating individual and collective experiences. Here the gatherings (*majlis*) were structured, adhering to a pattern laid down by the Shia nawabs of Awadh. Beginning with *soz-khwani* (recitation without the aid of musical instruments), a *majlis* would be followed by a sermon or *marsiya-khwani* (reading of elegy), a style of rendering inspired by the legendary Lucknow poet, Mir Anis (1802-75) and conclude with short dirges. 'As soon as the impressive and heart-rendering notes of dirges were chanted by Mir Ali Hasan and Mir Bandey Hasan', wrote the essayist-novelist Abdul Halim Sharar (1860-1926),

hundreds of men from élite families began to sing them, and then the women of noble Shia families also intoned them with their matchless voices. Matters have now reached the stage that during Muharram and on most days of mourning, heart-rending sounds of lamentation and the melodious chanting of dirges can be heard from every house in every lane in old Lucknow. In every alley one will hear beautiful voices and melodies which one will never forget.[9]

The sermon is an elegiac account of the episodes in the Karbala story, a moving narrative of the pain, anguish and agony of Husain and his companions. Year after year speakers detail the sequence of events, retaining the order in which individual members of Husain's family were killed. Thus the sixth of Muharram is connected

[7] Attia Hosain, op. cit., p. 72

[8] J.R.I. Cole, *Roots of North Indian Shi'ism in Iran and Iraq: Religion and State in Awadh 1772-1859* (Berkeley and Los Angeles, 1988), p. 98; and Sandria Frietag, *Collective Action and Community: Public Arenas and the Emergence of Communalism in North India* (Delhi, 1990), p. 237.

[9] A.H. Sharar, *Lucknow: The Last Phase of an Oriental Culture,* translated and edited by E.S. Harcourt and Fakhir Hussain (London, 1975), p. 149.

with Husain's young nephew, the seventh with his 18-year old son, the eighth with the brave and devoted brother Abbas, the ninth with the 6-month old son Ali Asghar, and the tenth with Imam Husain's own martyrdom. Qasim, Ali Akbar, Abbas, Ali Asghar and Husain himself exemplified the enormity of the tragedy; so that days linked with their martyrdom convey deep meanings, special attachments and associations. Their experiences, narrated by an *alim* or a *mujtahid,* move audiences (*azadars*) to mourn, wail and lament, beat their chests (*matam*) and share in the sufferings of the martyrs by self-deprivation and mortification. Attia Hosain captures the mood in Lucknow:

It was the ninth night of Muharram. On the horizon there was a glow as of a forgetful sun rising before moonset. The glow of a million lamps from the illuminated Imambaras where *tazias* and banners were laid to rest, lit the sky, and the city was alive, crowds forgetful in that bright beauty of the month of mourning. . . . When he (Asad) read of the agonies of thirst of the children of the Prophet, cut off from the river by their enemies, the women sobbed softy. Ustaniji began beating her breast, saying 'Hassan Husain' softly, with a slow rhythm. Ramzano stared at her strangely and joined in. The others still sobbed softly.[10]

Ten days of mourning ceremonies culminate on *Yaum-i Ashura* with the *Majlis-i-Sham-i Ghariban* at the famous Ghuframab Imambara, the final mournful tribute to the *Sayyid-ash-Shuhada* (Lord of the Martyrs). The final curtain is drawn on Chehlum, the fortieth day. Sharar described a procession of women carrying *tazias* at the Talkatora Karbala. All were bareheaded and their hair hung loose. In the centre a woman carried a candle. By its light a beautiful, delicately formed girl read from some sheets of paper. She chanted a dirge along with other women. Moved by the 'stillness, the moonlight, those bareheaded beauties and the soul-rending notes of their sad melody', he heard the following lament as the group passed through the gates of the shrine:

When the caravan of Medina, having lost all
Arrived in captivity in the vicinity of Sham
Foremost came the head of Husain, borne aloft on a spear
And in its wake, a band of women, with heads bared.[11]

[10] Attia Hosain, op. cit., p. 68.
[11] Sharar, op. cit., pp. 149-50.

II

Muharram, Husain and Karbala signified different things to different sections of Lucknow society. Some saw in the observances the potential for political mobilization. The Khilafat leadership and the votaries of Pakistan could therefore employ the paradigm of Karbala and harness the most evocative themes of Shi'ism to provide depth to their movements.[12] Husain's martyrdom also served, to the Shias of all times and in all places, as an everlasting exhortation to guard their separate identity and to brave their numerical inferiority in the face of firmly established and sometimes oppressive majorities. It made sense, according to Hamid Enayat, on two other levels: first, in terms of a soteriology not dissimilar to the one invoked in the case of Christ's crucifixion—just as Christ sacrificed himself on the altar of the cross to redeem humanity, so did Husain allow himself to be killed on the plains of Karbala to purify the Muslim community of sins; and second, as an active factor vindicating the Shia cause, contributing to its ultimate triumph. When one adds to all this the cathartic effect of weeping as a means of releasing pent-up grief over not only personal misfortune but also the agonies of a long-suffering minority, then the reasons for the popular appeal of Muharram ceremonies become apparent.[13]

Husain stirred the passions and sensitivities of several groups. On the night of ninth Muharram, groups of women, largely Hindus, moved about the villages wailing and reciting *dohas,* mostly improvised lyrics, on the epic tragedy. Urban and rural Hindus venerated Husain and incorporated his cult into their rituals.[14] They offered flowers and sweets at local Karbalas, participated in processions, decorated and kept *tazias,* and sought Husain's intercession to cure the diseased, avert calamities, procure children for the childless or improve the circumstances of the dead. The

---

[12] See Mushirul Hasan, *Nationalism and Communal Politics in India, 1885-1930* (Delhi, 1991), and *Legacy of a Divided Nation: India's Muslims since Independence* (London, 1997).

[13] Hamid Enayat, *Modern Islamic Politcal Thought* (London, 1982), p. 20; and V.J. Schubel, 'Karbala as Sacred Space among North American Shia', in Barbara Daly Metcalf (ed.), *Making Muslim Space in North America and Europe* (Berkeley and Los Angeles, 1996), pp. 186-204; Farnk Korom, 'Identity on the Move: A Trnidadian Shia Ritual in Transnational Perspective', unpublished paper presented at North Carolina State University, Raleigh, 22-5 May 1997.

[14] Cole, op. cit., pp. 116-17.

Imam's trial and tribulations inspired faith in a universal nemesis ensuring justice for oppressed souls. In popular belief and mythology he was the Ram of Ayodhya carrying his crusade into the wilderness; his brother Abbas personified Lakshman—devoted, energetic and brave; his sister Zainab and wife Umi-i Kulsoom—the surviving witnesses to the slaughter at Karbala—were cast in the image of Sita, caring, dutiful and spirited. Yazid, the Umayyad ruler and Husain's persecutor, was Ravan—greedy, corrupt, ambitious, cruel and ruthless.

W.H. Sleeman found Hindu princes in central and southern India, 'even of the brahmin caste', commemorating Muharram with 'illuminations and processions . . . brilliant and costly'. In Gwalior, a Hindu State, Muharram was observed with splendid pomp. So also in Baroda, where the ruler sent an exquisite prayer carpet of pearls to Mecca.[15] Travellers discovered Hindus clothed in green garments and assuming the guise of faqirs.[16] So did Jafar Sharif.[17] A Hindi newspaper reported in July 1895 that Muharram had passed off peacefully in Banaras. 'When it is Hindus who mostly celebrate [sic] this festival, what fear can there be?'[18] In Lucknow, 'thousands of Hindus chanted dohas along with the Shias and Sunnis'.[19] Shiva Prasad kept a tazia in a specially prepared shed. On the tenth of the month, the elaborate man-high tomb made of bright-coloured paper and tinsel was carried to its burial in procession. The Muslim servants recited dirges, while Shiva Prasad and his sons followed in barefooted, bareheaded respect.[20]

This was not all. Munshi Faizuddin's reminiscences, published in 1885, described Muharram rites in the court of the last two Mughal

---

[15] P.D. Reeves (ed.), *Sleeman in Oudh: An Abridgement of W.H. Sleeman's Journey Through the Kingdom of Oude in 1949-50* (Cambridge, 1971), pp. 158-9; Walter Roper Lawrence, *The India We Served* (London, 1928), pp. 292-3; Bampfylde Fuller, *Studies on Indian Life and Sentiment* (London, 1910), pp. 125-6; W.S. Blunt, *India Under Ripon: A Private Diary* (London, 1909), p. 72.

[16] Frietag, op. cit., p. 259.

[17] Jaffur Shureef, *Qanoon-e-Islam*, translated by G.A. Herklots (Madras, 1863), p. 123; see also Omar Khalidi, 'The Shias of the Deccan: An Introduction' in *Hamdard Islamicus*, vol. 15, no. 4, 1992.

[18] Nita Kumar, *The Artisans of Banaras: Popular Culture and Identity 1880-1986* (Princeton, 1988), p. 216.

[19] Sharar, op. cit., p. 149.

[20] Attia Hosain, *Phoenix Fled* (Delhi, 1993), p. 176.

emperors.[21] So does Syed Ahmad Dehlawi's (b. 1946) *Rusum-i Dehli* (Rituals and Traditions of Delhi), written some decades later.[22] The Sunni raja of Nanpara had Shia *ulama* read to him elegies for Husain.[23] In Allahabad, Sunnis took out 122 of the 220 *tazias*.[24] Rural Muslims, Crooke declared in 1897, joined the Muharram observance 'almost without distinction of sect'.[25] A Western scholar of Indian Islam was struck by the Shia influences on 'the length and breadth of the Sunni community'.[26] In a small north Indian princely state, a British civil servant found that every Muslim guild—the painters, the masons, the carpenters, the weavers—had their own *tazias* and their own troupes of actors and mourners who reproduced scenes of the struggle at Karbala.[27] Here and elsewhere, Shia-Sunni relations were not structured around sectarian lines. Some people nursed sectarian prejudices, but most consciously resisted attempts to create fissures in the broadly unified and consensual model of social and cultural living. Regardless of the polemics of the *ulama* and the itinerant preachers, bonds of friendship and understanding remained intact among Shias and Sunnis of all classes who shared a language and literature and a cultural heritage. That is probably why Sharar declared that no one in Lucknow ever noticed who was a Sunni and who a Shia.[28]

Lucknow was, both before and during the Nawabi rule, relatively free of religious insularity or sectarian bigotry. The Shia nawabs took their cue from their Sunni overlords in Delhi to create a broad-based polity and a cosmopolitan cultural and intellectual ethos. They adhered to the policy of *sulh-i kul* (peace with all), pioneered by the Mughal Emperor Akbar. Wajid Ali Shah is reported to have said that 'of my two eyes, one is a Shia and the other is a Sunni'. Sunni officials occupied important positions in the middle and lower echelons of government department. The highest officials in Wajid

---

[21] Munshi Faizuddin, *Bazm-i Akhir* (Delhi, 1986), pp. 63-6.

[22] Syed Ahmad Dehlawi, *Rusoom-i Delhi* (Delhi, 1986), pp. 178-80.

[23] Cole, op. cit., p. 105.

[24] C.A. Bayly, *The Local Roots of Indian Politics—Allahabad 1880-1920* (Oxford, 1975), p. 81; for Bilgram see Syed Athar Raza Bilgrami, 'Bilgram Ki Azadaari' in *Islam aur Asr-i Jadid*, Delhi, vol. 25, no. 2, April 1993. For a brilliant description see Rahi Masoom Reza, *The Feuding Families of Ganguli*, translated from Hindi by Gillian Wright (Delhi, 1994).

[25] Crooke, op. cit., p. 263.

[26] Murray T. Titus, *Indian Islam* (Oxford, 1930).

[27] Penderel Moon, *Strangers in India* (London, 1943), pp. 86-7.

[28] Sharar, op. cit., pp. 74-5.

Ali Shah's court, including the vazir and paymaster, were Sunnis. Sunni officers also managed the Sibtainabad Imambara and the *baitul buka* (house of lamentation).[29] Generally speaking, the Shi'ism of Awadh rulers provided both a liminal cultural glue and a set of structural lines of schism along which conflict could be routed.[30]

Shia-Sunni controversies did not plague most princely States. Several Shia families from Awadh, such as the Syeds of Bilgram, sought and secured lucrative positions in Hyderabad. Shia-Sunni marriages were commonly contracted in princely States like Rampur, as also in *taluqdari* families. Shias and Sunnis forged a common front in literary and political associations, acted in unison during the Urdu agitations against the April 1900 Nagri Resolution of the government in UP, and shared the Muslim League platform. They were one in agitating over the Kanpur mosque, the Aligarh Muslim University issue, and, much to everybody's surprise, on the Khilafat question. The raja of Mahmudabad (1879-1931), a devout Shia, kept these causes alive. He patronized the 'young party', funded their news-papers and their agitations. James Meston (1865-1943), Lieutenant-Governor of UP, reported that a 'clique of noisy and aggressive Muslims of the young party' made the raja's house their headquarters and lived and agitated at his expense'.[31]

Urdu prose and poetry, too, offers no clue to polarized Shia-Sunni sentiments. The writings of Syed Ahmad Khan (1817-98), Altaf Husain Hali (1837-1914), Shibli Nomani (1857-1914), Maulvi Zakaullah (1832-1910), Maulvi Nazir Ahmad (1836-1912) and Abdul Halim Sharar were free of sectarian claptrap. In 1889, Sharar wrote *Hasan aur Anjalina*; Shia-Sunni relations was its theme. The great Urdu poet Asadullah Khan Ghalib (1797-1869) wore no sectarian badge, no sectarian colour. He was 'a pure unitarian and true believer'. Suspected by some to be a Shia and by others as a *tafazili* (one who, though a Shia, acknowledges the pre-eminence of Ali), Ghalib revelled in the ambivalence. In fact, there was some confusion at his death as to whether his funeral rites should follow Shia or Sunni rituals.

---

[29] Ibid. This is not to suggest that the Awadh rulers did not express their solidarity with the Shias or that the Shias were not given preference in appointments. See Michael H. Fisher, *A Clash of Cultures: Awadh, The British and the Mughals* (Delhi, 1987), pp. 65-6.

[30] Frietag, op. cit., p. 250.

[31] Meston to Chelmsford 20 Aug. 1917, Meston Papers (1), IOLR.

Dakhni and modern Urdu poetry were both rich in *manqabat*, poems in praise of Ali, and in *marsiyas*, authored by both Shias and Sunnis. Husain is everybody's hero, the embodiment of Islamic virtues of piety, courage and commitment. He laid down his life but did not compromise with a bloody-minded tyrant, who presided over a degenerate political and social order. His exemplary courage inspired Mohamed Ali (1878-1931), the volatile Khilafat leader, who believed that while Yazid won on the bank of Euphrates but Husain 'reigned and still reigns over the hearts of a faith of God's human creation, while the soul of humankind in its entirety applauds the victory and final triumph of the victims of Karbala and shall continue to do so . . .'.[32]

> *Qatl-i Husain asl me marg-i Yazid hai*
> *Islam zinda hota hai har Karbala be baad.*

> Husain's assassination, in reality, symbolizes, the death of Yazid.
> Islam is revived in the wake of every Karbala.

Mohammad Iqbal (1876-1938) echoed similar sentiments: 'Strange and simple and colourful is the story of Kaaba; its end is Husain, its beginning Ismail.' Husain was a model of the perfect man who becomes a martyr in his strife for God's unity against the rulers of the world. Every age brings forth a new Yazid, but resistance to tyranny, as evident in Husain's legendary example, is incumbent upon every believer.[33] Employing the paradigms of Husain and Karbala, Iqbal sent forth the message:

> *Nikal kar khanqahon se ada kar rasm-i Shabbiri.*

> Emerge from the confines of the Khanqahs and,
>   re-enact the example set by Husain.

All of this underlined the importance of Husain, Muharram and Karbala as living and vibrant symbols of India's composite cultural interaction, the intermixing of religio-cultural strands and the fusion of religious beliefs and practices. Yet by the end of the nineteenth century, such representations of unity gradually gave way to symbols of discord. They served, in the hands of the politician-priest combine,

---

[32] Mohamed Ali to A.A. Bukhari, 19 Nov. 1916, in Mushirul Hasan (ed), *Mohamed Ali in Indian Politics: Select Writings 1906-1916*, vol. 1, (Delhi, 1985), p. 301.
[33] Quoted in A. Schimmel, *Gabriel's Wing: A Study into the Religion Ideas of Sir Muhammad Iqbal* (Leiden, 1963), p. 167.

to heighten sectarian consciousness, assert judicial and political rights and widen areas of competition and disharmony. Each side came to nurse profound grievances about the other based on mutually exclusive interpretations of history.

The first ominous sign surfaced around 1906, when some Sunni zealots constructed their own local Karbala at Phoolkatora on the north-eastern edge of Lucknow, opposite the existing one in Talkatora. The fires of sectarian unrest were then stoked by the public praise (*madhe sahaba*) of three Khalifas—Abu Bakr, Umar and Usman—whom the Shias regarded as 'usurpers' of Ali's claim to be the successor of the Prophet.

The Shias retaliated with a vilification (*tabarra*) campaign. Sunni preachers, on the other hand, declared Muharram observances as acts of *biddat* (heresy). They exhorted their followers to avoid them scrupulously.[34] Zafarul Mulk, secretary of the Lucknow Madhe Sahaba Committee, struck a sharp note by declaring *taziadaari* 'deleterious to the spiritual and temporal well-being of the Muslims'.[35] The nature of the Shia-Sunni engagement inevitably led to the appropriation of certain symbols and the rejection of others.

The writing on the wall was clear; Muharram was no longer a common symbol of veneration but an exclusively Shia concern in its format as well as in the composition of the participants.[36] By the 1930s, its popular appeal had considerably diminished, though less so in the rural hinterland.[37] A powerful symbol of unity was transformed into a potent vehicle for sectarian mobilization; in consequence, Shia-Sunni strife became much more common in certain north Indian towns than Hindu-Muslim riots. Shia-Sunni frictions were sparked off in Lucknow in the 1880s and 1890s and 1907-8. 'The feeling of tension between the Sunnis and Shias of

[34] Selection from Native Newspaper Reports UP (hereafter SNNR), for the week ending 19 Dec. 1936, and 20 March 1937.

[35] Zafarul Mulk, *Shia Sunni Dispute: Its Causes and Cure*, Servants of Islam Society Publication no. 3, n.d., p. 1.

[36] The process was not confined to Lucknow; for Bombay, see Jim Masselos, 'Change and Custom in the Format of the Bombay Muharram during the 19th and 20th Centuries', *South Asia* (Australia), Dec. 1982, p. 61; and for Banaras, see Nita Kumar, op. cit., p. 216.

[37] C. Khaliquzzaman, *Pathway to Pakistan* (Lahore, 1961), p. 149. Referring to the Bakhshu's *tazia* procession in Lucknow, Sharar commented: 'Nowdays, because of the quarrels between Shias and Sunnis, this procession lost its original form', Sharar, op. cit., p. 151.

Lucknow had reached its climax', reported the *Gauhar-i Shahwar* in April 1907.[38] Allahabad, Banaras and Jaunpur witnessed widespread violence. What began as small-scale skirmishes during the last quarter of the nineteenth century (many of which went unnoticed in official despatches because of their listing in the category of 'Native Societies and Religious and Social Matters' in the 'Selections from the Native Newspapers') escalated into bloody feuds involving scores of people and turning several areas, including Lucknow and its adjoining districts, into a cauldron of sectarian animus.

The lines of cleavage were sharply demarcated by the mushroom growth of sectarian organizations, such as the Anjuman-i Sadr-us Sudoor, floated by Maulana Syed Agha Husain in 1901, and the Anjuman-i Jafariya, established by the Syeds of Barha four years later. A Shia conference was set up in October-December 1907, some months after the Muslim League came into being. There was much talk of 'Shias of light' leading the way and mitigating the economic and educational backwardness of their community. Some were keen to take their grievances to the British government, including the viceroy.[39]

The depth of sectarian feelings surfaced at the first Shia Conference in 1907. Delegates delivered fiery and intemperate speeches against the Sunnis. The atmosphere was so vitiated that Gulàm-us Saqlain (1870-1915), Editor of *Asr-i Jadid*, left the meeting in disgust. The hardliners seized the initiative in renaming the organization as the Shia Political Conference, petitioned the government in December 1909 to enumerate the Shia population separately in the census, and insisted on their separate and distinct identity.[40] The conference, initially formed to foster cultural and educational goals, turned into a platform for articulating sectional political aims.

In the mid-1930s the Shia Political Conference, now firmly controlled by Syed Wazir Hasan (1874-1947), the architect of the Congress-League scheme of December 1916, rallied round the Congress and supported the Muslim Mass Contact Campaign, Jawaharlal Nehru's brainchild. At the same time, it continued to clamour for separate representation in the Legislative Councils, a

[38] April 1907, SNNR, UP, 1907.
[39] *Surma-i Rozgar*, 1 Feb. 1907.
[40] *Asr-i Jadid* (Meerut), Oct.-Dec. 1907.

demand spurred by the defeat of two Shia candidates in the 1937 elections. The *Sarfaraz*, a Shia weekly from Lucknow, attributed their defeat to 'venomous' Sunni propaganda and called for safeguarding Shia 'national and political rights'.[41] The Anjuman-i Tanzimul Muminin expressed lack of faith in the Muslim League, a body controlled by the 'Sunni Junta'. So did Syed Ali of the Shia Students' Conference. The Majlis-i Ulama, held at Lucknow on 5 July 1945, endorsed the memorandum sent by Hosseinbhoy A. Laljee to Wavell as well as the Congress High Command. The Shia Federation threatened to organize strikes, boycotts and demonstrations if its demands were not fulfilled.[42]

These were empty threats. Although sections in the Congress were sympathetic to Shia aspirations, they were not willing to raise the 'Shia case' in negotiating with the British and the League. Likewise, the government had no reason or compulsion to recognize the Shias as a major political force. 'We cannot give them special help' was how an official reacted. 'We cannot contemplate', commented a senior member in the Home Department, 'treating religious sub-division of Muslims as a new minority'. Inevitably, the future editors of the transfer of power documents ignored Shia petitions in their compilation. 'Not wanted: I don't think we need bother at all with those cables from the Shias.'[43]

III

Lucknow was the scene of violent Shia-Sunni riots in 1938-9. These were a sequel to a protest movement, launched in May 1935, against an official suggestion to forbid *madhe sahaba* on certain days.[44] The agitation gained intensity a year later. It turned violent in May-June 1937, when frenzied mobs in Lucknow and Ghazipur went on a rampage. Trouble in Ghazipur was instigated by some Sunnis from Jaunpur. Enraged mobs burnt and looted property and killed at will.

---

[41] *Sarfaraz*, 6, 7 and 13 May 1939.

[42] Syed Ali to Jawaharlal Nehru, 6 Dec. 1945, Jawaharlal Nehru Papers, vol. 4, New Delhi; Hosseinbhoy A. Laljee's Cablegram to Wavell, 6 April 1945, in *Shia Muslim's Case* (Bombay, n.d.), pp. 1-2, 6-96; L/P and J/8, 693; Transfer of Power Papers L/P and J, 10/64, IOLR.

[43] 18 Feb. and 16 Dec. 1946, 16 Dec. 1974, ibid., L/P7/J, 10, 64.

[44] Note by the Intelligence Department on the Shia-Sunni controversy in Lucknow, Home Poll. D., File No. 75/6, NAI.

The summer of discontent rumbled on. Sectarian strife, hitherto dormant, became a common occurrence in the daily lives of Lakhnavis.[45]

More trouble was fuelled during the next two years against a committee's ruling against *madhe sahaba* in Lucknow.[46] Husain Ahmad Madani (1879-1957), principal of the renowned seminary at Deoband, along with some other Jamiyat al-ulama leaders, advocated civil disobedience. Thousands courted arrest. Although a fervent advocate of secular nationalism and a principled critic of the 'two-nation theory', the Maulana stirred sectarian passions with remarkable tenacity and fervour. He spoke at a public meeting in Lucknow on 17 March 1938, sharing the platform with the firebrand Maulvi Abdul Shakoor, head of the Dar al-Muballighin, and Maulana Zafarul Mulk, chief exponent of *madhe sahaba* in Lucknow.[47] Elsewhere, the Ahrars and the Khaksars developed common cause with the Jamiyat al-ulama. The mercurial Khaksar leader, Allama Mashriqi, mobilized his followers from different places, although police vigilance made sure that not many sneaked into the city's municipal limits.[48] The Ahrars, fresh from their successful agitation against the maharaja of Kashmir, organized bands of volunteers (*jatha*) in Lucknow. They came from neighbouring Malihabad, Kanpur, Delhi, Meerut and from as far as Peshawar. By the end of March 1939, hundreds were arrested. 'Tension in the city', wrote Lucknow's deputy-commissioner, 'has increased and is now nearing breaking point'.[49]

On 30 March, the Congress ministry bowed to such pressures and

[45] Shia-Sunni riots broke out in May-June 1937. The provincial government believed that they were provoked by the Shias to indicate that any change introduced in their past practices would be resisted. See Harry Haig to Linlithgow, 7 June and 4 July 1937, 2-4 June 1938, 10 and 23 Oct. 1939, L/PJ/5/264-6.

[46] The government appointed the Piggot Committee in 1907 to regulate Muharram observances. This was followed by the Justice Allsop Committee recommendations of 15 June 1937. The high court judge endorsed the Piggot Committee's report on *madhe sahaba*, Government Gazette of the UP, Extraordinary, 28 March 1939, L/P and J/ File No. 265, pp. 139-50, IOLR.

[47] G.M. Harper to Jasbir Singh 18 March 1939, General Administration Department (GAD), File No. 65, Box 607, Lucknow, Harry Haig reported that Madani insisted that the Sunnis should be allowed to assert their right to recite *madhe sahaba*. To Linlithgow, 23 Oct. 1939, L/P/266.

[48] Haig to Linlithgow, 6 Sept. 1939, L/P and J/5/26.

[49] Jasbir Singh to Harper, 24 March 1939, op. cit.

allowed *madhe sahaba* on *Barawafat*, the Prophet's birthday. While the Sunni leaders promptly called off civil disobedience and organized a 30,000 strong *Barawafat* procession to register their victory, the Shia confidence in the Congress ministry was jolted. The *Sarfaraz* chided Pant and his ministerial colleagues for their capitulation.[50] An impression gained credence that the Congress had played a 'double game' by contravening established conventions in Lucknow, sowed the seeds of Shia-Sunni dissension and stoked the fires of sectarian unrest to weaken the Muslim League's claim to be the sole representative of the Muslim community. This was not an uncommon occurence. Christopher Bayly's study has shown how the Muslim leadership in Allahabad, poorly integrated into both the formal and informal system of power, had become an object of attention for political orators to exploit sectarian fissures.[51]

The Shias responded angrily to the ministerial decree of 30 March. A large crowd assembled a day after at the imposing Asafud-daula Imambara, indulged in *tabarra* and excitedly climbed the upper stories of the gateway. Some rushed towards the nearby Tila Mosque, though the police blocked their onward march. Pandemonium prevailed; others set fire to nearby shops. A free exchange of brickbats ensued, with people waving weapons they had acquired from the *shamianas* and palisades. The police opened fire, dispersed the mob and imposed curfew.[52] The scholar S. Khuda Bukhsh (b. 1842) was anguished to see a posse of police with glistening bayonets in Lucknow. 'Well might we heave a deep sigh at sight such as this? Has time turned its (Islamic) precepts of brotherly love and fraternal unity into sad, mocking derision? These were the mournful thoughts as my carriage glided down the road.' He was sorry that

. . . the fabric of Islam is torn by dissensions, fierce and bitter; and that nobody was trying to restore peace, concord and harmony among Muslim. What a noble sight it is to see the police officers interfere at Muharram between the followers of the Prophet to prevent a breach of peace.[53]

Harry Haig, Lieutenant-Governor of UP, felt that sanctioning *madhe sahaba* set up among Shias conditions of intense emotional

[50] *Sarfaraz*, 30 March 1939.
[51] Bayly, op. cit., p. 130.
[52] Harper to Chief Secretary, 16 March 1939, GAD, File No. 65, Box No. 607.
[53] *Essays: Indian and Islamic*, London, 1912, pp. 215 and 273-4.

hysteria and stiffened their resolve to indulge in *tabarra*.[54] As he had foreseen, Shias assembled each day at the Asafi Imambara, recited *tabarra* on the Husainabad Road, and then courted arrest chanting '*Ya Ali*', '*Ya Ali.*' Tension mounted each day. 'No one knows', wrote an exasperated official in March 1939, 'from hour to hour—let alone from day to day—what will happen next.'[55]

There were other outward signs of protest. The Shia *mujtahid*, Maulana Nasir Husain, threatened to court arrest. So did the wife of Wazir Hasan, member of an influential family, and their son Syed Ali Zaheer.[56] Trouble spread to other areas as well. Volunteers from Agra, Kanpur, Fyzabad, Barabanki and Rampur sneaked into Lucknow in early April to assist their beleaguered brethren. Plans were set afoot in Rae Bareli to congregate in Lucknow on *Barawafat* and participate in the planned *tabarra* agitation.[57] A batch of burqa-clad women from Rae Bareli turned up at Kazimain, a predominantly Shia locality, to court arrest, though the Shia *mujtahid* did not allow them to do so.[58] In August, Shias of Kanpur observed hartal against the police firing in Lucknow, wore badges on their arms and fluttered black flags on their houses. Riots also broke out in Banaras.[59] A report published in August 1941 suggested that the 'attempt to find a solution to the Shia-Sunni dispute in Lucknow appears to have been abandoned'.[60]

Jawaharlal Nehru, who spent some time in Lucknow trying to resolve the Shia-Sunni deadlock, felt that his colleagues had been tactless in dealing with the disputes. 'I fear there has been much bungling about this issue', he wrote to Maulana Abul Kalam Azad

---

[54] Haig to Linlithgow, 18 April 1939, Linlithgow Papers (microfilm), New Delhi.

[55] Jasbir Singh to Harper, 13 March 1939, op. cit.

[56] Wazir Hasan's wife was Chairman of the All-India Shia Women's Association.

[57] Harper to chief secretary, 16 March 1939, op. cit.

[58] Ibid.

[59] *Pioneer*, 24 Aug. 1939, Kanpur's superintendent of police reported a Shia-Sunni riot and the impending threat of the Ahrars to take out a *madhe sahaba* procession defying government orders, 10 June 1939, Diaries, Harold Charles Mitchell Papers, IOLR. For Banaras, see Charles Allen (ed.), *Plain Tales from the Raj* (London, 1981), pp. 246-7.

[60] L/P and J/5/272. See also fortnightly report, second half of March 1940, L/P n.d. J/5/270. In 1943, Sunnis in Lucknow tried to revive the *madhe sahaba* agitation and defy the ban on the *Barawafat* procession which fell about the middle of March. This led to the externment of some Sunni leaders from Lucknow. Fortnightly report, second half of Jan. 1943, L/PJ/5/272.

(1888-1958), who was not consulted before the ministry executed a volte-face. The matter was decided, he told the Maulana, 'without full consideration of the consequences'.[61] Rajendra Prasad, having been closely associated with some leading Shias of Bihar, such as Ali Imam, Husain Imam and Sultan Ahmad, was equally wary of the consequences. He observed:

I presume the Shias will continue civil disobedience and will be courting jail. . . . It must be very distressing to put nine thousand people in jail who are apparently not opposed to the government and many amongst whom are widely respected for one reason or the other. What troubles me even more is the propaganda which is gaining ground that the Congress stands to create division amongst Musalmans and what I apprehend is that after a time both will be more united against the Congress than they have ever been before.

Rajendra Prasad added that the Shias were ardent nationalists and the Shia Political Conference had consistently acted in unison with the Congress. For these reasons, the ministry should not have allowed anti-Congress sentiments 'to grow in any community and more so in a community sympathetically inclined'.[62]

IV

The Shias were few in number, not exceeding 4 per cent in any of the provinces in British India (Tables 1–2). They were most numerous in Lucknow and the satellite townships, where the imambaras and mosques stood as reminders of Shia domination under the nawabs. Elsewhere in UP, they were unevenly distributed in Jaunpur where the Sharqis once held sway, in Machhlishahar,[63] Bilgram, Sandila, Allahabad, Jalali in Aligarh district,[64] Jansath in Muzaffarnagar, Moradabad, Amroha, Sambhal, Budaun and

[61] Nehru to Azad, 17 April 1939, S. Gopal (ed.), *Selected Works of Jawaharlal Nehru*, vol. 9, pp. 334-5.

[62] To Nehru, 16 May 1939, Valmiki Choudhary (ed.), *Dr Rajendra Prasad: Correspondence and Select Documents*, vol. 3 (Delhi, 1984), p. 77.

[63] 'Many of the respectable Mussalmans of Jaunpur and the town Machhlishahar belong to this (Shia) denominaton.' *District Gazetteer* (*DG*), UP of Agra and Oudh, vol. 28, Allahabad, 1908, p. 85.

[64] For Syeds of Jalali, see Syed Mohammad Kamaluddin Husian Hamadani, *Siraj-i Manir* (Garhi, Aligarh, 1978).

TABLE 1: SHIA AND SUNNI POPULATION IN INDIA, 1921

Provinces and Princely States	Muslim Population	Shias	Sunnis
		(percentage)	
Assam	2,219,947	Nil	100
Baluchistan	773,477	1	96
Bengal	25,486,144	1	99
Bihar and Orissa	3,706,277	1	99
Bombay	4,660,828	3	88
CP and Berar	528,032	2	98
Madras	2,865,285	2	94
NWFP	2,084,123	4	95
Punjab and Delhi	12,955,141	2	97
Baroda	162,328	10	88
Kashmir	2,548,514	5	95
Rajputana and Ajmer	1,002,117	2	98

NOTE: Figures for Bombay, Baroda and Rajputana and Ajmer include Khojas, Bohras, and in some cases, even Memons.
SOURCE: *Census of India*, 1921, vol. 1, p. 120.

TABLE 2: DISTRIBUTION OF SHIA AND SUNNI POPULATION IN UP, 1882

Division	Percentage of Total Muslim Population	
	Shias	Sunnis
Agra	1.5	98.5
Allahabad	5.3	94.7
Banaras	2.0	98.0
Fyzabad	3.6	96.4
Jhansi	0.8	99.2
Lucknow	10.7	89.3
Meerut	2.3	97.7
Rae Bareli	1.8	98.2
Rohilkhand	1.6	98.4
Sitapur	1.7	98.3

Source: *Census of India*, NWFP and Oudh, 1882, vol. 1, p. 74.

Rampur.[65] The nawab of Rampur and the raja of Mahmudabad and his kinsmen in Bilehra and Bhatwamau were Shias. Successful professional men were few, although some like Hamid Ali Khan, a Lucknow lawyer, Syed Raza Ali (1882-1949), Syed Ghulam-us-Saqlaim, Syed Wazir Hasan and his son, Ali Zaheer, Syed Hyder Mehdi, Congressmen and Chairman of the Allahabad Improvement Trust, occupied prominent positions in public life. Some achieved fame as writers and poets in the early 1940s or thereafter, notably, Syed Ehtesham Husain of Lucknow; Khwaja Ahmad Abbas (1914-87), a descendant of Altaf Husain Hali; Syed Sajjad Zaheer, son of Wazir Hasan and co-founder of the Progressive Writers' Movement; Ali Sardar Jafri of Balrampur state, an Aligarh student expelled from the university in the mid-1930s for his radical activities; and the poet Kaifi Azmi, who spent years in Bombay in the company of socialists and communists.

Yet the success of such men does not reflect the condition of their Shia brethren, many of whom were backward and lagged far behind their Sunni counterparts. They were few in the professions and fewer still in trade and commerce. The substantial group of poverty-stricken *wasiqadars* clung to the crumbling remains of their ancestral environs. Most lived in ghettos or in the narrow lanes and alleys of the old city of Lucknow and Allahabad. In 1913, there were 1,661 *wasiqadars* in Lucknow, many of whom lived very much in the past. Some held durbars even until the early 1920s.[66] Their condition symbolized the decline of a class which owed its survival to nawabi patronage. Other Shia groups were not able to move up the ladder because they were poorly equipped to seize the opportunities in trade, business, professions and government service. Meston commented that the Shias were 'a community backward beyond all normal degrees of backwardness'.[67]

There can be no doubt that Shia-Sunni estrangement was related to the decline of the Shia aristocracy in the second half of the nineteenth century, the impoverishment of their less privileged brethren, and the relative prosperity of some Sunni groups which

---

[65] *DG*, Muzaffarnagar, vol. 3, pp. 114-15; *DG*, Sitapur, vol. 11, pp. 105-6.

[66] Sarojini Ganju, 'The Muslims of Lucknow, 1919-39' in K. Ballhatchet and J. Harrison (eds), *The City in South Asia: Pre-Modern and Modern* (London, 1980), p. 286.

[67] UP Govt. (Education Department), File No. 398, 1926, UPSA.

deepened Shia anxieties about their future.[68] They were estranged from a world dominated by the 'other'. The British contributed to this process insofar as they gave legal definition to the Shia-Sunni divide. The approval or ban of religious commemorations, arbitration of disputes and regulating religious procession routes transformed latent doctrinal differences into public, political and legal issues.[69] An even more powerful current that was at work towards the end of the nineteenth century appeared in the form of religio-revivalism, affecting the structure of both inter-as well as intra-community relations. Therefore, the Shia-Sunni schism in Lucknow, notwithstanding its local specificity, needs to be located in the context of such countrywide religio-revivalist trends and tendencies.

It is widely known that cow-protection societies, Hindi Pracharni Sabhas and the Arya Samaj movement were designed to hegemonize Hindu society with the aid of common cultural and religious and symbols. Similar currents, some in response to the intellectual and cultural hegemony of the West but most in reaction to Hindu revitalization campaigns, gripped Muslims as well. Towards the end of the nineteenth century, in particular, the notion of a sharply defined communitarian identity, distinct and separate from others, had acquired greater legitimacy among the north Indian *ashraf* Muslims. In the political and educational domain, Syed Ahmad Khan plotted his trajectory within a communitarian framework. The Aligarh College, the All-India Muhammadan Educational Conference, the Urdu Defence Associations and the Muslim League were concerned to create a Muslim identity in the public and private spaces.

Such concerns were exemplified in the activities of Aligarh's 'first generation'. They were matched by a concerted drive to create an ordered, unified and cohesive religious community within the Islamic paradigm. Such was the goal of the founders of the Dar al-ulum at Deoband and the Nadwat al-ulama in Lucknow. They asserted their role as interpreters and guardians with greater vigour and consistency and insisted, through sheafs of *fatawa* (religious decrees), on imposing a moral and religious code consistent with Koranic

[68] Imtiaz Ahmad, 'The Shia-Sunni Dispute in Lucknow', in Milton Israel and N.K. Wagle (eds.), *Islamic Society and Culture: Essays in Honour of Professor Aziz Ahmad* (Delhi, 1983); Ganju, 'The Muslims of Lucknow', op. cit., pp. 290, 292.

[69] Keith Hjortshoj, 'Shi'i Identity and the Significance of Muharram in Lucknow India' in Martin Kramer (ed.), *Sh'ism: Resistance and Revolution* (London, 1987), p. 291.

injunctions and free of accretions and interpolations. Not surprisingly, over 200 books listed in London's India Office Library catalogue, compiled by J.M. Blumhardt in 1900, dealt with ceremonial religious observances and includes compendia of religious duties, treatises on lawful and unlawful actions and collections of religious precepts. In a nutshell, the growth of the printing press, the proliferation of vernacular newspapers and the expanding educational networks served as powerful instruments for restructuring an ideal community that would conform to and reflect the Islamic ethos that prevailed during the days of the Prophet and his successors.

Initially confined to northern India, the Islamic resurgence spread to other areas rapidly. Religious revivalism, conducted under the aegis of the *faraizis*, had already swept the rural Muslims in the Bengal countryside. The dominant strain of the Islamization drive there and elsewhere was to reject composite and syncretic tendencies and create instead a pan-Islamic or a specifically pan-Indian Muslim identity. Rafiuddin Ahmed has shown how religious preachers prompted the masses to look beyond the borders of Bengal in quest of their supposed Islamic past and attach greater importance to their 'Muslim' as opposed to their local or regional identity. This new emphasis proved crucial to the subsequent emergence of a measure of social cohesion in a diversified and even culturally polarized community.[70]

In relation to the Hindu 'other', the meaning of being a Muslim was translated through late nineteenth-century religious and political idioms. Shias and Sunnis, on the other hand, discovered new symbols of identification in the form of separate graveyards (*qabristaan*), separate mosques, separate schools, separate religious and charitable endowments.[71] These institutions defined the boundaries within which Shias and Sunnis were required to stay apart. They were to live as separate entities in a world fashioned by the religio-political leadership. Attempts to disturb the status quo encountered strong resistance.

Sunni Islam was just as much 'corrupted' by the incorporation of Hindu beliefs and customs, as by the adoption of Shia practices. So

---

[70] Rafiuddin Ahmed, *The Bengali Muslims 1871-1906: A Quest for Identity* (Delhi, 1981), p. 184.

[71] As early as 1871, Shias and Sunnis, in separate formal representations, demanded 'distinct and separate burial grounds'. V.T. Oldenburg, *The Making of Colonial Lucknow 1856-1877* (Princeton, N.J., 1984).

a campaign was mounted at the turn of the nineteenth century to question shared cultural, religious and intellectual paradigms and revive those controversies that had been dormant for long. The *madhe sahaba* processions were, for example, organized with much greater fanfare in Fatehpur, where Maulana Syed Abid Husain first started the practice in 1901, and in Lucknow around 1908-9 with the backing of Maulana Syed Ainul Qazat, tutor of both the Firangi *alim* Maulana Abdul Bari (1878-1926) and Maulvi Abdul Shakoor, one of the chief architects of the Sunni agitation in Lucknow and the Dar ul-Mabbalighin.[72]

There was, in addition, a concerted move to discourage Shia-Sunni marriage, to portray Shias as promiscuous heretics and traitors to the country and to Islam. Frequently singled out as traitors were Mir Sadiq, Diwan of Tipu Sultan, Mir Alam, Diwan of Hyderabad, Mir Jafar, Diwan of Siraj-ud Daula, and the Bilgrami family.[73] 'Among the people classed as Muslim', observed Zafarul Mulk,

the Shias and the Ahmadis are the two sects which have basic differences with Muslims and are a constant source of internecine trouble and discord. . . . *It would be a real gain to the health of the body politic of Islam if these two sects were lopped off and treated as separate minorities.*[74] (emphasis added)

Muharram practices were the chief target of attack. The central theme, underlined years later by an *alim* of Nadwat al-ulama in Lucknow, was the impropriety of giving 'vent to one's feeling of sorrow through wailings and lamentation' and crying over a past event.[75] Around 1933-9, considerable polemical literature surfaced against *azadari*.[76] *Taziadari* was denounced as *bida* and *haram*.[77] In February 1939, the Tahaffuz-i Millat sought permission to take out small processions to dissuade Sunnis, by word of mouth, from *taziadari*.[78] Sharar, who bemoaned Shia-Sunni differences, observed how Maulvi Abdul Shakoor perfected the art of public debates (*munazirah*) with his Shia counterparts.[79]

[72] Zafarul Mulk, *Shia-Sunni Dispute*, op. cit., p. 11.
[73] Omar Khalidi, op. cit., pp. 39-40.
[74] Zafarul Mulk, op. cit.
[75] S. Abul Hasan Ali Nadwi, *The Mussalman* (Lucknow, 1974 edn.), p. 65.
[76] See, for example, Proscribed Publications (Urdu), 52, 93, 139, IOLR.
[77] SNNR, UP for the week ending, 19 Dec. 1936, and 20 March 1937.
[78] Jasbir Singh to Harper, 10 Feb. 1939, op. cit.
[79] Sharar, op. cit., p. 95.

The indictment of Muharram rites was by no means a new development; the severity with which it was done in Lucknow during the 1930s was somewhat unusual and had few historical precedents. It is true that orthodox Sunni treatises were critical of and averse to the Shias. In the sixteenth century, Shaikh Ahmad Sirhindi, chief exponent of the Naqshbandi *silsilah* in India, began his career by writing a pamphlet against the Shias. Shah Waliullah (1702-63), one of the foremost original thinkers in the history of Indian Islam, discussed the question of whether Shias were *kafirs*, apostates or just immoral. Shah Abdul Aziz (1746-1824) wrote a highly polemical book in 1889 to prevent 'Sunnis from straying away from their faith in polemics with the Shias'. Deoband's Dar al-ulum, inspired by the Waliullah and his disciples, was antithetical to Shia beliefs and practices. Syed Ahmad's invitation to Deoband's founders met with an emphatic refusal: they would not associate with a college that had room for Shias.[80] One of its foremost *ulama*, Husain Ahmad Madani, shared this antipathy towards the Shias, though he was at the same time a major proponent of secular nationalism. Yet the diktat of an *alim* here or a theologian there did not undermine those values and customs that people had shared for generations. There were other schools of thought in Sunni Islam which advocated reconciliation and rapprochement. In fact, many of the Shia *mujtahids*, including the renowned Maulvi Dildar Ali, were products of the Firangi Mahal in Lucknow, and there were forces within Sufi Islam that cemented unity and integration.

Sectarianism in the 1930s, however, was of a distinct nature. The debates then were no longer restricted to the Khilafat. Nor were the age-old controversies confined to the learned and holy men. The energy released during the decade, spurred by newly-started organizations wedded to separate Sunni and Shia world-views, substantially altered the structure of social relations. They imposed severe strains on the overall consensus, achieved through long-standing social cultural and economic networks. People were encouraged to transgress traditional codes of conduct and behaviour and organize themselves as a separate entity in opposition to the

---

[80] David Lelyveld, *Aligarh's First Generation: Muslim Solidarity in British India* (Princeton, N.J., 1978), p. 134; see also, S.A.A. Rizvi, *Shah Abd Al-Aziz: Puritanism, Sectarianism, Polemics and Jehad* (Canberra, 1982), p. 256. For Deoband, see B.D. Metcalf, *Islamic Revival in British India: Deoband, 1860-1900* (Princeton, N.J., 1982). See also, Sharar, op. cit., p. 95, for a brief history of public debates in Lucknow.

'other'. The emotional charge deepened the intensity and depth of sectarian conflicts, competition and rivalries.

The Shias were not far behind in fortifying their claims. They tried, first of all, to rejuvenate their educational institutions which had virtually collapsed in the absence of nawabi patronage. They regarded the MAO College at Aligarh as a 'Sunni' institution, though Syed Ahmad Khan had, in recognition of Shia-Sunni differences, made a provision for teaching Shia theology. They had no theological seminary of their own. And because entry to Deoband or Nadwa was restricted to Sunni students, those Shias who aspired to become religious leaders received education not in India but in Iran and Iraq. Thus Syed Abdul Qasim Rizvi (d. 1906) studied in Lucknow and Najaf in Iraq. Back in Lahore, he promoted Usuli Shi'ism in the second half of the nineteenth century, founded congregational prayer mosques in the city and in Peshawar further north, built edifices for commemorating Husain's martyrdom, and establishing an *imami* seminary in Lahore with the backing of Nawab Ali Raza Khan Qizilbash, a wealthy Shia landowner of Iranian origin.[81] Maulana Syed Ali Naqi (1903-88), a descendant of the learned Ghufranmaab family, also studied in Iraq. He returned to Lucknow in 1932 and founded the Imamia Mission and a weekly magazine *Payam-i Islam*. He wrote over 300 books. Many of his writings in the mid-1930s were in defence of *azadari*.[82]

The establishment of the Nadwat al-ulama led to the founding of a Shia school in Lucknow. The scheme for a Shia College, floated in March 1914, was the brainchild of Fateh Ali Khan Qizilbash (1862-1923), a landowner of Lahore with large estates in eastern UP, but was backed by Nawab Hamid Ali Khan of Rampur (1875-1930) and the UP government. The idea caught on fast. By mid-June 1916, Rs 3,17,410 was raised. Because contributions came mainly from UP, there were demands to locate the college in the same province. The Syeds of Jansath in Muzaffarnagar district preferred Meerut. So did Rampur's nawab, though his preference for a city so far removed from his own area of influence is incomprehensible. Some suggested

[81] See 'Introduction' in J.R.I. Cole and Nikkie R. Keddie (eds.) *Shiism and Social Protest* (New Haven, 1986), pp. 66-7; Cole, op. cit., pp. 288-9, and Frietag, op. cit., p. 263, for the contribution of Maqbul Ahmad to reformist tendencies among Shias.
[82] This information is based on Salamat Rizvi, *Syed al-ulama; Hayat aur Karnamen* (Lucknow, 1988).

Agra, so that students 'do not imbibe political ideas in tender age and may cause inconvenience and trouble to the government'. But most settled for Lucknow, where the college gates were opened in 1917.[83]

Shia societies mushroomed in every quarter of Lucknow, the hub of Shia intellectual and cultural life. Prominent amongst them were the Madrasatul-Waizeen, organized on the lines of the Shibli Academy at Azamgarh and funded by the raja of Mahmudabad; the Imamia Mission, set up by Maulana Ali Naqi; and the Tanzimul-Muminin, the Shia answer to the Tahafuzz-i Millat, which was patronized by affluent manufacturers of tobacco and perfumes like Mohammad Umar and Asghar Ali, Mohammad Ali. These bodies were backed by an aggressive Shia-owned press—the *Sarfaraz*, an organ of the Shia Political Conference, *Shia*, printed in Lahore, and *Asad, Nazzara* and the *Akhbari-i Imamia*, published fortnightly.[84]

With the country heading towards greater Hindu-Muslim friction, sectarian competition began to resemble inter-community conflicts. Not surprisingly, the process structuring sectarian conflict paralleled that of Hindu-Muslim friction in other urban centres of UP. This was, in part, because Sunnis and Shias of Lucknow could draw on the reservoir of experiences and models developed in the subcontinent during that period. That is, the nationwide impetus to define one's community provided material that could be used by both groups of Muslims.[85] In general, such tendencies were not countered by a parallel ideological crusade, though individuals like Maulana Abul Kalam Azad tried in vain to cement the divide, heal the wounds and keep the recalcitrant parties in check.[86]

The Congress in UP also tried to defuse the mounting sectarian tensions in Lucknow, though most settled for a 'divide and rule'

[83] 'Establishment of a Shia College at Lucknow', 25 Oct. 1917, UP Govt. (Education), File No. 398, 1926, UPSA; Fateh Ali Khan to Meston, 21 Oct. 1915, File No. 136/15, Meston Papers. The raja of Mahmudabad and Syed Wazir Hasan were the only two prominent Shias who were initially opposed to the Shia College. They believed it would weaken the Aligarh Muslim University movement and accentuate Shia-Sunni differences.

[84] For a summary of 'Shia Awakening', see Rizvi, *A Socio-Intellectual History*, Chapter 5.

[85] Frietag, op. cit., p. 249.

[86] Azad was deputed by the Congress High Command to resolve the impasse. His personal stature aided the process of reconciliation. The Shia *ulama*, in particular, agreed to suspend the *tabarra* agitation at his instance.

policy doling out concessions first to Shias and then to Sunnis. This strategy worked for a little while. Shia leaders, having rallied round the Congress in the past, expected to be rewarded for their loyalty. The bulk of Sunni leadership was, on the other hand, enthused by Pant's gesture on 30 March 1939 and stayed put in the Congress. But their support, having been tied to short-term communitarian interests, was rapidly eroded when the Muslim League raised new hopes and expectations in the early 1940s.

Both the context and the reference point of Shia and Sunni leaders were rapidly evacuated by the powerful drive for a separate 'Muslim nation'. The options were suddenly diminished. The forces of an overriding and hegemonic 'Muslim nationalism' subsumed sectarian allegiances. A British official had urged the Shias in 1946 'to sink their fortunes with the Sunnis and be treated as Muslims'.[87] So they did. Once the creation of Pakistan became imminent, both Shias and Sunnis buried hatchets, hitched their fortunes to the Muslim League bandwagon, and undertook their long trek towards the promised *dar al-Islam* (land of Islam). They emerged from the ruptures of history to find that strength lies in forging ahead, exploring new choices and options in the future homeland. They were tantalized by a new ideal exemplified by a new leader. The ideological conflicts were, however, carried over to the new nation, where the inconclusive debates resumed with the same intensity and fervour.

On 14 August 1947 Pakistan was born on the principle of Muslim solidarity. But its rationale is tested year after year as Shias and Sunnis continue to fight each other on the streets of Karachi and Lahore. A BBC report in mid-February 1995 showed live pictures of a Sunni leader in the North-West Frontier pouring venom against the Shias. A hysterical audience chanted anti-Shia slogans in a country created for Muslims in the name of Islam. A news agency reported widespread sectarian violence and the arrest of scores of people in Punjab, the chief battleground of warring Shia and Sunni activists.[88] A day later, gunmen burst into two Shia mosques in Karachi and killed eighteen men. Women wailed in agony and young men spoke angrily of revenge.[89] Such incidents serve as sharp reminders of the deep fissures that plague Islam in the subcontinent. They are, some might also say, an indictment of the 'two-nation' theory.

---

[87] 16 Dec. L/P and J/8/693, 1946.
[88] *The Times of India*, 25 Feb. 1995.
[89] Ibid.

Varying Identities of Nepalese Muslims

MARC GABORIEAU

In the first legal code promulgated in 1854 by Jang Bahadur Rana, the first of a line of hereditary Prime Ministers who governed from 1846 to 1951 (Whelpton 1991), Nepal is defined as 'the only remaining Hindu kingdom in the Kali Age'. The phrase 'Hindu kingdom', which appears for the first time in this text, has remained the official definition of Nepal down to this day; it has been retained in the last 'liberal' constitution promulgated in 1990.

If, in its essence, Nepal is fundamentally Hindu, one would expect to find in its institutions a reflection of traditional Hindu attitudes toward Muslims: one would be tempted to see Nepal as a kind of museum in which medieval identities would be preserved to this day. This paper intends to show that this is not the case. The identities of the Muslims, as those of the other religious minorities, have been continually changing according to context and epoch. We will try to sort out the factors which led to these variations. After presenting the Muslim minorities in Nepal, we will inventory the elements they have used to construct a variety of identities; we will be then in a position to explain when, how and why they choose (or are compelled) to emphasize one or the other of these identities.

HINDU NEPAL AND HER NON-HINDU MINORITIES

Nepal and Her Hindu Population

The present Kingdom of Nepal was built by the Gorkha Dynasty of king Prithiwi Narayan (1742-75) and his successors, who conquered Kathmandu Valley from the previous Newar kings and annexed about fifty hill principalities (Gaborieau 1995, pp. 54-66). This dynasty used Hinduism as an instrument to unite under a common ideology the various populations of the country. Prithiwi Narayan had already endeavoured to turn his newly-founded kingdom into a 'true country of the Hindus (*hindu-stān*)' (Stiller 1968, p. 44).

At that time, however, not all his subjects—perhaps not even the majority of them—were Hindus. Of course the ruling people, the Nepali-speaking high castes and their untouchable service castes (who had all of them been migrating from the central Himalaya for about a thousand years), were Hindu. But they had to contend with older settlers who were not all of the same religion. There were, of course, a majority of Hindus among the Newars of the Kathmandu Valley and among the Hindi-speaking dwellers of the Tarai along the Indian border. But in the rest of the population, in the hills as well as in the plains, there were people who were not *sanatani* Hindus. According to the criteria used by the new dynasty, these fell into two categories.

One category included people who could gradually be absorbed into the Hindu fold. Among them were a sizeable number of Newars who still practised a form of Indian Buddhism, and several tribes of the northern areas of the country who followed Tibetan Buddhism. In addition, other tribes who practised various forms of animistic religion also fell into this category. Buddhists and animists alike were legally 'Hindu'. And from the eighteenth century the Gorkha Dynasty encouraged them to become *sanatani* Hindus by adopting Vedic rituals and the rules of the caste system.

Non-Hindus: Muslims and Christians

The second category included two religions considered alien (*bi-deshi*) and legally classified as non-Hindu: Islam and Christianity.

Muslims had come first, preceding the Gorkha dynasty. The letters of Christian missionaries who entered Nepal at the beginning of the seventeenth century bear testimony that Muslims were already present in Kathmandu at that time; if we believe the chronicles, they arrived as early as the fifteenth century. Most of them lived in the districts of the plains, which had submitted to the Delhi Sultanate and later to the Mughal Empire. But tiny Muslim groups have also lived for centuries in the Hills: Kashmiri and Hindustani traders in Kathmandu valley, and the bangle-makers in the western Hills. The various Muslim minorities of Nepal which have survived to this day make up around 3 per cent of the total population of about 20 million people: there are approximately 600,000 Muslims in Nepal.

But this sketch would not be complete if we did not take into account the Christians, for their peculiar situation gives us a clue to the problems of the Muslims in modern Nepal. They too preceded the Gorkha dynasty since the missionaries were allowed to make converts from the time of their arrival in the early seventeenth century; but the number of local converts was always limited, less than a hundred in 1768! Numbers are not the issue, but rather the attitude of the Nepalese authorities to non-Hindu minorities.

The policy of the various regimes to religious minorities provides a chronological framework in which we can study the evolution of Muslim identities. We have clearly three periods:

(1) before the conquest of Kathmandu by the dynasty of Gorkha in 1768: preaching was allowed, Hindus were allowed to convert to Christianity and presumably also to Islam.
(2) from 1768 to 1990, both preaching and conversion were *de jure* and *de facto* banned; Christian converts were definitively, and Muslims temporarily, expelled.
(3) from 1990 when both preaching and conversion are again *de facto* allowed.

But before studying how Muslim identities varied over these periods, we must inventory the elements out of which they were constructed.

ELEMENTS OF MUSLIM IDENTITY IN NEPAL

It must be emphasized that not all the following elements of identity are chosen by the Muslims themselves. Some derogatory ones are imposed on them by the Hindu majority. We will start with them for fear that they would otherwise pass unnoticed. We will then review common descriptive elements agreed upon by Hindu and Muslims. We will finally list elements of self-praise chosen by Muslims.

Derogatory Epithets Conferred by the Hindus

The elements imposed from outside by the majority are founded on religious affiliation; emphasis is placed on the social and ethnic consequences of being Musalman, as Muslims are called in Nepal (Gaborieau 1972; Gaborieau 1977, part II).

Although the neutral concept of religion (*majab*, from Arabic *mazhab*) does exist in Nepali legal texts, Islam is not spoken about in a neutral way in those texts or in common parlance. In a polite conversation a Hindu may grant to a Muslim or a Christian that his religion is *dharma* in the same way as the Hindu religion is, but in the legal codes it is derogatorily called an opinion, *mat*, with often pejorative epithets such as 'foreign' (*bideshi*), or even 'irreligious' (*bidharmi*) (for instance code of 1935, vol. 5, pp. 15-16, § 29; code of 1963, p. 223, chap. 19, § 1).

All who adhere to these debased religions are considered impure and consequently socially inferior. This stereotype, which had already been noticed by Al-Beruni in the beginning of the eleventh century, has persisted to this day. According to the caste rules which were enforced by law in Nepal up to 1963, Hindu people belonging to clean castes were not allowed to accept water or have sexual relations with Muslims. The latter were placed in the last but one tier of the caste hierarchy, among the impure but not untouchable castes (at the same level as for instance butchers, oil-pressers or washermen) (Gaborieau 1972, pp. 94-104).

Finally, even if in reality most Muslims are originally Hindu converts, they are catergorized as foreign, often mythical, tribes and called *Mleccha*, barbarians, or *Yavana*, Greek, or *Turk*.

Descriptive Elements Shared by
Both Muslims and Hindus

Both Hindus and Muslim also use common terms to designate Muslims. As with other South Asian Muslims, Nepalese Muslims have both ascriptive identities transmitted hereditarily, and acquired socio-economic status which may vary.

All Nepalese Muslims ultimately came from India, but at different times, from different areas and from different social backgrounds. This variety of origin furnishes the most common labels. The small community of Kashmiris in Kathmandu is opposed to all the other Muslims who, coming from the north Indian plains, are known as Hindustani or Deshi (the two terms being synonymous in Nepali). When one needs to be more precise, reference is made to caste affiliation. It is well-known that the Kashmiris of Kathmandu claim descent from high caste converts. On the contrary, the Hindustanis of the same town are converts from lower castes: the 'Araqis, locally called Ranqi, who have their own bazaar with their mosque in the old Kathmandu town, are an offshoot of the Hindu caste of the Kalwar; alcohol-distillers (Blunt 1931, p. 206); Dhuniyas, cotton-carders; and Julahas, or weavers. Similarly, the bangle-makers of the hills are traditionally designated by their caste name in its original Hindi form, Churihara, or nowadays more commonly in its Nepali form, Churaute. The use of this caste name enables us to distinguish between actual dealers in bangles and a small minority of religious mendicants of the Madariyya sect who settled among them, the *Fakirs* (*faqir*), who make up another caste. In the Tarai, as in the Indian plain across the border, there exists a whole range of Muslim castes from *Ashraf* and converts of the high castes at the top, to untouchable tanners at the bottom (Blunt 1931, Chap. X; Gaige 1975, *passim*; Gaborieau 1982a, pp. 85-9). When one needs to designate precisely one or the other group at various levels of the hierarchy, caste names are used.

In other contexts, when such precision is not needed, various groups of Muslims are referred to by their socio-economic status, which may or may not correspond to their caste status. All Kathmandu Muslims, irrespective of their ethnic and caste affiliations, are considered traders, as are a sizeable number of the plains Muslims. Hill Muslims are more often seen as farmers, for dealing in bangles is in fact a secondary occupation for them. Most of the Terai Muslims, irrespective of caste, are agriculturists: few are rich zamindars, many are small farmers; and there is an increasing number of landless labourers. A small proportion of the low caste people still follow traditional handicrafts and services (see Gaige 1975; and Gaborieau 1977).

Elements Chosen by Muslims

First, emphasis is placed on religious affiliation, and Muslims will usually refer to themselves proudly as Musalman. This term designates originally, and in most cases today as well, all adherents of Islam, whatever their origin or ethnic or caste affiliation.

But one must be aware that traditionally in some contexts it may have had a more restricted sense, as Adrian Mayer emphasized long ago (Mayer 1960, pp. 34-5 n.1), viz., a Muslim of foreign origin, the so-called *Ashraf*. This excludes the local converts who are designated by their caste names. This restrictive sense is also found in Nepal both in the speech of high status Muslims and in legal documents (Gaborieau 1993b, p. 336).

And this leads us to the most common element of identity among high status Muslims: the vindication of a foreign origin. In Islamic law, anteriority of conversion means social superiority, and is taken into account to establish parity (*kafa'a* in matters of marriage (Blunt 1931, 191-5; Gaborieau 1993b, pp. 362-5). The Arabs, who were converted to Islam before all others, rank highest; and the other conquerors, the Turks and the Afghans who entered India as Muslims, are superior to the local converts. In this way in Nepal and India the so-called *Ashraf* are considered superior to all the other castes of Muslims; they are the Syeds and Shaikhs who claim an Arab origin, the Mughals (believed to be of Turkish stock), and finally the Pathans who are Afghan. While other caste names are grounded in Indian social structure, the *Ashraf* are designated by foreign terms indicative of a higher status in Muslim society.

There is, finally, at a lower status, another element of identity which is peculiar to some Muslims. It is a character acquired by renouncing the world and becoming hereditary members of a Sufi order, which is called *Faqirs*. Like the hereditary *sanyasis* and yogis, the *Faqirs* are religious mendicants associated with cults of saints. In the hills of Nepal, as in most villages of northern India, they usually belong to the heterodox Madari Sufi order (Gaborieau 1977, pp. 122-30). *Faqirs* belonging to a higher order, probably the Qadiriyya, were attested in Kathmandu Valley in the eighteenth century.

Let us turn to these *Faqirs* to start analysing the variations in Muslim identity over time.

THE HEROIC PERIOD: KINGS, MERCHANTS AND WONDER-MAKING *FAQIRS*

We now consider how various concepts are combined, in ways which vary according to time and context, to construct a variety of Muslim identities. We will proceed chronologically, following roughly the three periods we distinguished in the first part of this paper. The data we have for the first period, which preceded the unification of Nepal, concern the mountainous part of the country, Kathmandu and the Western Hills.

The Bangle-makers of the Western Hills

For the bangle-makers of Western Hills no contemporary evidence is extant (except for a very vague letter of an Italian missionary); but a series of official documents written at the end of the eighteenth and the beginning of the nineteenth century enable us to reconstruct a rather precise picture. These Muslims came as artisans and dealers in auspicious ornaments for women; they appear to have been close to the local kings who gave them religious rights and land to settle in. They provide ornaments for queens and for goddesses: to this day they bring twice a month a fixed amount of bangles to the main temple of Kali in Gorkha, the historical seat of the present dynasty (Gaborieau 1977, pp. 89-139).

The Kashmiris of Kathmandu

The rare original documents which have survived from the period preceding the unification of Nepal are all from the Kathmandu Valley. They emanate not from the Muslims themselves, but from outsiders: a Newar king and Christian missionaries. They concern only the Kashmiris. From oral traditions and the evidence left by the missionaries we know that Kashmiris came as traders and settled on the commercial road which linked Patna to Lhasa and Sining; a few Muslims were also recruited as military experts. Two official orders of 1737 and 1738 (texts in Gaborieau 1977, pp. 34-7 and facing p. 128) were issued by the last Newar King, Jaya Prakash Malla (1737-68), to a *Faqir* called Ghasi Shah, identified with Shah Ghiyasuddin whose tomb is still worshipped. They confirm the possession of a plot of land on the eastern side of Kathmandu town, where the *Faqir* had his hospice (*takya*) and from where he could exercise his authority on all the 'Sufis-Faqirs' of Kathmandu Kingdom: this place, where the mosque of the Kashmiris and their old cemetery stand, is still known as *takya*. Thus, before 1768, the Kashmiri community appears to have enjoyed religious rights and to have been close to the royal palace. Their religious leader, who acted as an intermediary between the king and the merchants, was a Sufi. In the oral traditions which complete these documents, emphasis is placed on the supernatural powers of this mystic who could compel the king to help the Muslims. To this day the Newars believe that Muslims have miraculous powers, notably, to stop cholera epidemics. Similar traditions of encounters of Sufis with the Dalai Lama are found among the Kashmiris of Lhasa (Gaborieau 1989 and 1995 b).

In brief, in the surviving evidence, Muslims in Nepal before 1768 appear as merchants dealing in rare and precious goods and led by Sufis with miraculous powers. In these quasi-mythical images nothing is said about their place in Hindu society.

FROM 1768 TO 1920: KEEPING A LOW PROFILE

From 1768 on enough evidence has survived to provide a comprehensive picture of the situation of the Muslims in the newly-unified Kingdom.

First let us emphasize the novelty of the order which banned Christian and Muslim proselytization for more than two centuries. It is probable that before this time Muslims were allowed to make converts in the same way as Christians were. King Prithwi Narayan was suspicious of the Christian missionaries whom he saw as the spearheads of a British conquest. After conquering Kathmandu Valley he immediately expelled the Christian missionaries and their Newar converts: preaching Christianity was banned and conversion was prohibited. These measures, which were specifically aimed at Christians, had repercussions on Muslims. Since the latter fall in the same legal category as Christians, they were also persecuted; they were even driven out of Kathmandu for a short period. They were allowed to return but the ban on proselytization stayed: as Francis Buchanan (later Lord Hamilton) testifies, Muslims were punished for making converts in 1802-3 (Hamilton 1819, pp. 37-8).

There are two other rulings concerning Christians and Muslims which were more likely in force before 1768, but which are attested only later: prohibition of cow-slaughter and enforcement of purity rules to prevent pure caste Hindus from being polluted by Muslims or Christians. Hamilton and later Hodgson (who was the first British resident in Kathmandu from 1820 to 1843) testified that these rules were enforced in the first half of the nineteenth century (Hamilton 1819, pp. 20-1; Hodgson 1834, *passim*). After 1854 these rules were written down in detail in the legal codes (see relevant rules of the code of 1854 as translated and analysed in Gaborieau 1972, pp. 94-105; and Gaborieau 1977, pp. 212-21).

It is in this context of rules imposed from above on the Muslims of Nepal that we now try to understand which elements they used to construct a viable identity. We will first define a common basic identity of Muslim groups. In the fifth section of the paper we will outline the more composite identities forged by particular groups to enhance their social or political status after 1920.

Basic Identity Model

Identity at that time rested on four main ingredients: religion, ethnic affiliation, caste affiliation and personal political representation.

Conservation of the religion was, of course, the primary ingredient; and the piety of the Muslims made it possible. But the importance the Nepalese authorities attached to the maintenance of the boundaries of the Hindu community also played its part. Muslims had always been free to practise their religion, to have Sufi hospices, mosques and religious schools which were sometimes built on land donated by the kings; they were able to create religious foundations for the maintenance of their religious institutions. But they had to keep to themselves: the law stipulated that they would not convert or pollute Hindus. Conversely, they were unable to cross over into the Hindu fold; being impure, they could not, even if they wanted, be admitted into any Hindu caste, even the lowest. In any case, they had no choice but to remain Muslim. In order not to offend the Hindu majority they had to keep a low profile and remain in their place.

The emphasis being not on religion, it fell on ethnic affiliation and caste. It is remarkable that all of the Muslims of Nepal kept their affiliation to Hindustani ethnicity. Of course, those living in the plains spoke Hindi dialects; but in Kathmandu, in a Newar environment, they speak a kind of Hindi (even the Kashmiris who came through Patna). Even in the Hills, where they lived for several centuries among Nepali-speaking people, they have retained a Hindi dialect (Gaborieau 1977, pp. 99-113). Wherever they go, Nepalese Muslims can be easily recognized as of north Indian stock.

To this ethnic identity they always added an element of status. It was not enough to pose as a Muslim of north Indian origin. One had to enhance one's own status by claiming a prestigious origin which would guarantee a respectable place in the caste hierarchy. The easiest and more specifically Muslim way was to claim to be of foreign origin and pass as Syed or Shaikh. But to be a convert of a high caste would suffice. An illustration is provided in Kathmandu itself: the opposition between the Kashmiris and the Hindustanis is founded less on ethnic origin than on caste. The former claim to descend from high caste converts. One of them, Khwaja Ghulam Muhammad (1857-1928), whom we will meet again later in this paper, wrote in his autobiography that, when he visited Kathmandu for the first time in 1872, 'he discovered through old documents that they [the Kashmiris who resided in Kathmandu] were rich and noble merchants: they belonged to the families of the Pal, Khajval, Khallu, Harif, Mattu and other princely families of yore'. This high status is always reaffirmed in opposition to the Hindustanis who come from lower castes and illustrated by an event in the beginning of this century. The Rana Prime Minister of Nepal, who was building a new palace, ordered that both Hindustanis and Kashmiris should stop burying their dead in separate cemeteries around their mosques on the eastern edge of Kathmandu town; in exchange he gave a big plot of land for a new common cemetery outside the town. The Kashmiris protested, saying that they would not be buried in the same cemetery as the low status Hindustanis; and the government had to build a wall to make two distinct cemeteries.

Caste identity is even affirmed at lower levels. For instance, in the hills the bangle-makers always insist on their identity as Churiharas or Churautes, a term which in Nepal means a landowning group, to assert their superiority over the landless Muslim Faqirs and Hindu untouchable artisans (Gaborieau 1993b, 335-44 and 380-6).

In this traditional model there was no way for Muslims to enter politics and find a way into the apparatus of government. Whenever there was a serious problem, self-appointed eminent personalities approached the government, acting as intermediaries. The names of two Kashmiris survive: Akhund Amiru'd-Din Wasiq and his above mentioned son-in-law, Khwaja Ghulam Muhammad (1857-1928), who has left an autobiography (see Gaborieau, 1973, pp. 7-12); he was a regular courtier of Prime Minister Chandra Shamsher (r. 1901-27). Two of their interventions in this century remain famous: they secured for Muslim children the right to enter government schools (from where they had been hitherto excluded because they were classified as impure) and they obtained a division of the new cemetery into separate sections for Kashmiris and Hindustanis.

To sum up, this basic identity model allied a low religious profile with a strong affirmation of ethnicity and caste. It was in consonance with the hierarchical model imposed by the Nepalese Government through its legal codes. Muslims were placed in a subordinate position and could have access to the political field only through the personal representation of a few notables who managed to win the ear of the Prime Minister. By keeping such a low profile and acquiescing to their subordinate position, Muslims gained one reward, security. They remained free to practise their own religion; they were physically secure and no anti-Muslim riot occurred in Nepal before 1947.

TWO ALTERNATIVE MODELS AFTER 1920

Yet this low profile was not maintained by all Muslims until the constitutional change of 1990. Conflicting identities were framed in opposite directions. An earlier one, from the 1920s onward, was an assertion of Islamic identity; the other, from the 1960s, was an affirmation of Nepalese identity.

Islamization as a Tool of Social Mobility

The basic model, as we have already seen, insisted on the social superiority of the higher castes. This was resented by the lower castes. It is well-known that in India, from the beginning of this century, lower Muslim castes, particularly the weavers, resented the domination of the higher castes and organized politically to voice their grievances. One way to claim equal status with the *Ashraf* was to outdo them in religious matters, to claim to be better Muslims than them. That is how the weavers gained the epithet of 'bigoted'.

A similar phenomenon occurred in Nepal. In Kathmandu the Hindustanis, who had been hitherto staunch believers in the intercession of saints, converted to 'Wahhabism' (in fact the Indian Ahl-i Hadith school). They could claim to be better Muslims than the Kashmiris who continued worshipping their saints. In the 1960s, they even tried to take control of the mosque of the Kashmiris, who resisted with the help of the Nepalese (Hindu) police. While the Kashmiris have traditionally exercized religious leadership in Kathmandu, the Hindustanis have now claimed it and declared their own mosque to be the Juma Masjid of Kathmandu.

I had the opportunity to study in detail a similar development among the bangle-makers of the hills. Up to the 1920s they had to accept their low caste status. With increasing pressure on the land many of them started migrating to find work in the towns of India and Burma; they got the opportunity to attend Koranic schools and fell under the influence of the Deobandi seminary. When they came back they built mosques and Koran schools in their villages. They proudly claimed to be Musulman on par with the *Ashraf.*

In both instances Islamization ensured social mobility that was impossible in the basic model.

Nepalization under the Panchayat System after 1960

Constitutional changes took place in the 1950s and the 1960s. After the collapse of the Rana regime in 1951, there was a short-lived period of 'democracy'. In 1960 king Mahendra (r. 1954-73) took over and established for thirty years the partyless autocratic Panchayat regime. The 1962 Constitution had special clauses prohibiting discrimination on religious grounds (Constitution of 1962, Part III, § 10). But these changes did not alter fundamentally the situation of Muslims. Nepal reamined a 'Hindu State' (Part I, § 3); every one was entitled to practise his/her own religion, but proselytization and conversion were banned (Part III, § 14). The legal code of 1963 abolished the caste rules and the Muslims could no longer be prosecuted for polluting Hindus. But the two main clauses against Christians and Muslims were maintained: the ban on cow-slaughter (Code of 1963, pp. 190-1); and the ban on proselytism and con-version (p. 223, § 1). The last mentioned paragraph makes it clear that this legislation is directed at Christians and Muslims.

Although their legal status did not really improve, Muslims now had the opportunities to enter the political process. Their representation in various bodies, from the village panchayats to the state panchayat remained minimal and far below their proportion to the total populations (for comprehensive statistics see Gurung 1992, pp. 19-21; Dastider 1995, pp. 88-90). But this should not be taken as a complete failure: it is a radical departure from the past; and now Muslims have an avenue to enter into the government machinery.

What is interesting to note is that this entry was not used to claim a separate Muslim identity. In accordance with the Panchayat ideology, which stressed a common Nepali national identity, and tried to erase all ethnic and religious cleavages, Muslims who collaborated with the Panchayat system by being elected to various bodies, or even by being appointed in the National Panchayat, chose to affirm a Nepalese identity, insisting on wearing the Nepali dress and speaking Nepali.

An Unstable Situation

At the end of the 1980s the situation was quite uncertain. The basic model no longer worked. Nepalese Muslims followed two contradictory trends. One was a process of Islamization which would logically widen the gap between Hindus and Muslims, in addition to fostering conflict among Muslims. The other was a process of Nepalization which would logically underplay Muslim identity. The two trends could coexist for some time. In 1975 I saw in a hill village in Central Nepal two people of the same lineage. One was the elected head of the village panchayat: dressed in the Nepali fashion, he addressed the village assembly where all male adults, Hindu and Muslim, sat; he urged Nepalization. Next Friday his cousin, in the main mosque of the village, led the afternoon prayer in Muslim dress wearing a turban, and preached Islamization. How long could both these trends coexist?

A HIGHER RELIGIOUS PROFILE AFTER 1990

Events proved that the Nepalization trend was fragile. It collapsed with the Panchayat system in the riots of the spring of 1990. King Birendra, who had ruled since 1973, had to give way and abandon the autocratic regime which had lasted for thirty years. A new Constitution was drafted and promulgated in the autumn of 1990. Political parties were again permitted; a regime of parliamentary monarchy was established; there are now two assemblies, an entirely elected Lower House, and part-elected and part-nominated Upper House. The Prime Minister, nominated by the king, must be chosen by the majority party of the Parliament (Ellington 1991; Dharamdasani 1992; Shaha 1993). During these events the traditional way of handling ethnic and religious problems was questioned. Did this result in substantial changes?

The Constitutional Debate and its Consequences

Radical questions were raised during the negotiations which took place during the summer of 1990 for the framing of the new constitution. For the first time demands were made to abolish the Hindu character of the kingdom, establish a secular state and grant real freedom in matter of religion; they emanated from a large array of Buddhist, Muslim and Christian associations; the demand received support from organizations representing Buddhist and animist tribal groups as well as from leftist and liberal politicians (Hutt 1991, p. 1029). The need for constitutional change was particularly acute for the Christians, several of whom were serving jail sentences for proselytizing and conversion. Significantly, for the first time Muslim associations joined in the demand.

A counterattack was launched by traditional Hindus and two of their organizations, the Sanatan Dharma Seva Samiti and the Vishwa Hindu Parishad (Nepal committee). The spectre of mass conversions to Christianity was raised. The demand for a secular state was finally turned down. The 1990 constitution, in matters of religion, retained the clauses of the 1962 one: Nepal remains a 'Hindu State'; prose-lytizing and conversion remain banned. If we keep to its letter, the 1990 Constitution was a non-event as far as the status of non-Hindu minorities is concerned.

But the practice of both the government and the concerned people considerably changed in the wake of the constitutional debate. In June 1990 an amnesty was promulgated for thirty Christians convicted of proselytism or conversion, and for 200 more under prosecution on the same grounds. And no prosecution has been launched since. There is now in Nepal complete religious freedom in fact, if not in law.

Rise of Ethnicity and of Religious Identities

This *de facto* liberalization has had far-reaching consequences. The old Hindu Nepali norm, which all had to accept, was shattered. All suppressed tendencies surfaced. What is striking is the explosion of ethnicity: all non-Nepali ethnic groups in the Hills and plains claim cultural and even political autonomy. Religious groups, which up to now had kept a low profile, became more and more conspicuous. This is true of the Buddhists who, as we have seen above, are legally within the pale of Hinduism: they have built, with Western, Thai and Japanese money, about twenty new huge monasteries in Kathmandu Valley.

Profiting by the new liberal attitude of the government, all Christian organizations, mainly Protestant, have become active: hidden converts now openly practice their religion, thousands of people are converting to various Protestant denominations in the villages, mainly among the Buddhist, animist or superficially Hinduized tribals; hundreds of churches are being built. By the end of 1993, the figure of Nepalese Christians was considered to be as high as 200 000, that is to say one per cent of the population.

Raising the Muslim Profile: Benefits and Dangers

These events induced a similar change among Muslims. A Muslim identity can now be openly affirmed. Mosques in Kathmandu Valley were up to that time inconspicuous: one had to know where they were to be able to find them. In Kathmandu the Hindustanis, who now style themselves Nepali, have recently built with Gulf money, on the eastern edge of the old town, a huge Juma Masjid, visible from afar: Islam has entered the landscape. Nearby, one can also see on the street an 'Islamic Library' and a bookshop, the Everest Book Store, owned by a Muslim, where Islamic books are on sale. For the first time, a book *Muslims in Nepal* was published in Kathmandu by a Bangladeshi woman (Siddika 1993): the book is a symbol of the affirmation of a Muslim identity. Two Nepalese Muslims had previously published short papers about their community (Ansari 1981; Ansari 1991).

Muslim associations in Nepal were few until recently: the only one which counted was the All Nepal Anjumani-i Islah, which was pro-government in the time of the Panchayat; and it was not very active. With the constitutional change, Muslim associations literally mushroomed and there are now not less than nine different associations for the socio-cultural needs of the Muslims. The most active of these are the Islamic Yuwa Sangh and the Iqra Model Academy, both located in Kathmandu, and the Ittihadul Muslimeen, situated in Nepalganj in the Western Tarai (Siddika 1993, pp. 235-9; Dastider 1995, pp. 92-3).

Muslims have also become more involved in the political process. A recent study has shown that they have become active in several political parties (Gurung 1992, Table 2) and that they were slightly better represented than in previous assemblies in the Parliament elected in 1981: 2.3 per cent as against 1.8 (Gurung 1992, pp. 20-1 and Table 3; Dastider 1995, pp. 89 and 109-11). But in spite of this progression, they have yet to reach—in politics as in the administration—a representation equal to their proportion in the total population, i.e. 3 per cent.

Raising thus their own profile as a distinct religious and political group may not be without danger for the Nepalese Muslims. The building of the new Juma Masjid in Kathmandu raised hostile comments even from liberal Hindus. Up to now communal riots have been few in Nepal and were quickly quelled. But the affirmation of a Muslim identity may be seen as a provocation. A few incidents are ominous. In October 1992, in the Western Tarai, Muslims objected to Hindus playing music in front of a mosque; this started a riot which extended to several districts; later the same year the Ayodhya affair created a tense situation in Kathmandu (see Dastidar, 1995). We have seen earlier that previously, by keeping a low profile, Muslims had their security guaranteed. Raising their profile may have the opposite effect: by openly affirming a distinct identity Christians and Muslim are coming into competition with Hindus and this may lead to conflict (Gaborieau 1994, p. 69).

REFERENCES

Ansari, Hamid, 'Muslims in Nepal', in *Journal, Institute of Muslim Minority Affairs*, vol. 3, no. 1, 1981, pp. 138-58.

Ansari, Tahir Ali, 'Muslim Minorities in Nepal', in *Journal, Institute of Muslim Minority Affairs*, vol. 9, no. 1, 1988, pp. 159-66.

Bista, Dor Bahadur, *People of Nepal*, Kathmandu, 1967.

Blunt, E.H.A., *The Caste System of Northern India, with Special Reference to the United Provinces of Agra and Oudh*, (London, 1931, rpt. 1969).

Code of 1935, *Muluki ain*, Kathmandu, Law Ministry, vol. 5, VS 2005 (=AD 1948).

Code of 1854, *Sri S. Surendra Vikram Saha deva-ka shaan kal-ma banrko muluki ain*, Kathmandu, Law Ministry, VS 2022 (=AD 1948).

Code of 1963, *Muluki ain*, Kathmandu, Law Ministry, VS 2020 (=AD 1963).

Constitution of 1962, *The Constitution of Nepal*, Kathmandu, Law Ministry, 1963.

Constitution of 1990, *Constitution of the Kindgom of Nepal 2047 (1990)*, Kathmandu, Law Ministry, 1992 (reproduced in *Himalayan Research Bulletin*, XI/1-3, 1991, p. 18f).

Dastider, Mollica, *Religious Minorities in Nepal: An Analysis of the State of the Buddhists and Muslims in the Himalayan Kingdom* (Delhi, 1995).

Dharamdasani, M.D. (ed.), *Democratic Nepal* (Varanasi, 1992).

Eellington, Ter, 'The Nepal Constitution of 1990: Preliminary Considerations', in *Himalayan Research Bulletin*, XI/1-3, 1991, pp. 1-17.

Gaborieau, Marc, 'Muslims in the Hindu Kingdom of Nepal', in *Contributions to Indian Sociology*, n.s., 1972, VI, pp. 84-105, rpt. in T.N. Madan (ed.),

Muslim Communities or South Asia, Culture, Society, and Power (Delhi, 1995, 2nd edn.), pp. 211-39.

————, *Recit d'un voyageur musulman au Tibet*, Nanterre, Societe d'ethnologie, 1973. [Account of a travel in Tibet in 1882: Urdu text, translation and commentary; extracted from the autobiography of Khwaja Ghulam Muhammad.]

————, *Minorites musulmanes dans ie royaume hindou du Nepal*, Nanterre, Societe d'ethnologie, 1977. [Muslim Minorities in Nepal: an ethno-history.]

————, 'Peasants, Urban Traders and Rural Artisans: Muslim Minorities in the Kingdom of Nepal', in *Journal, Institute of Muslim Minority Affairs*, vol. 3, no. 2, 1981, pp. 190-205.

————, 'Muslim Minorities in Nepal', in Raphael Israeli (ed.), *The Crescent in the East: Islam in Asia Major* (London, 1982), pp. 79-101.

————, 'Les rapports de classe dans l'ideologie officielle du Nepal', in Jacques Pouchepadass (ed.), *Caste et classe en Asie du Sud* (Paris, 1982), pp. 250-90. [Class relations acording to Panchayat ideology in Nepal.]

————, 'Pouvoirs et autorite des soufis dans l'Himalaya', in Veronique Boullier and Gerard Toffin (eds.), *Prêtrise, pouvoirs et autorite en Himalaya* (Paris: 1989), pp. 215-38. [Powers and authority of Sufi in the Himalaya.]

————, 'The Transmission of Islamic Reformist Teachings to Rural South Asia: the Lessons of a Case Study', in Hasan Elboudrari (ed.), *Modes de transmission de Ia culture religieuse en Islam* (Le Caire, 1993), pp. 119-57.

————, *Ni Brahmanes, ni Ancetres, Colporteuer musulmans du Nepal* (Nanterre, 1993). [On kinship and caste among Muslims in Nepal and northern India.]

————, 'Une afaire d'Etat au Nepal depuis deux siecles: le proselytisme chretien et musulmans', in *Archives de Sciences sociales des religions*, no. 87, 1994, pp. 57-72. [State attitude to Christian and Muslim proselytism in Nepal.]

————, *Nepal, Une Introduction a la connaissance du monde nepalais* (Pondicherry, 1995), 2nd edn. [An introduction to Nepalese studies.]

————, 'Power and Authority of Sufis among the Kashmiri Muslims in Tibet', *The Tibet Journal* (Dharamsala/Delhi), vol. xx, no. 3, Autumn 1995, pp. 21-30.

Gaige, Frederick H., *Regionalism and National Unity* (Delhi, 1995).

Gurung, Harka, 'Representing an Ethnic Mosaic', in *Himal*, May-June 1992, pp. 19-21.

Hamilton, Francis, *An Account of the Kingdom of Nepal* (reprinted with a preface by Marc Gaborieau, Delhi, 1971).

Hodgson, Brain H., 'Some Account of the System of Law and Police as

Recognized in the State of Nepal', in *Miscellaneous Essays relating to Indian Subjects* (London, 1880), pp. 211-49 [first publihed in *Journal of the Royal Asiatic Society*, London, 1834, I/2, pp. 258-79].

Hoffer, Andras, *The Caste Hierarchy and the State in Nepal: A study of the Muluki ain of 1854* (Innsbruck, 1979), p. 240.

Hutt, Michael, 'Drafting the Nepal Constitution', *Asian Survey*, 1991, vol. XXXI, no. 1, pp. 1020-39.

Joshi, B.L. and Leo E. Rose, *Democratic Innovation in Nepal: A Case Study of Political Acculturation* (Berkeley, 1966), p. 551.

Mayer, Adrain C., *Caste and Kinship in Central India: A Village and its Region* (London, 1960).

Shah, Saubhagya, 'The Gospel comes to the Hindu Kingdom', in *Himal* Sept.-Oct. 1993, pp. 35-40.

Shaha, Rishikesh, *Politics in Nepal 1980-1991: Referendum, Stalemate and Triumph of the People* (Delhi, 1993).

Siddika, Shamima, *Muslims in Nepal* (Kathmandu, 1993).

Stiller, Ludwig F., *Prithwinarayan Shah in the Light of Divya Upadesh* (Ranchi, 1968).

Whelpton, John, *Kings, Soldiers and Priests: Nepalese Politics and the Rise of Jang Bahadur Rana, 1830-1857* (Delhi, 1991).

The 'Bihari' Minorities in Bangladesh: Victims of Nationalisms

TAJ UL-ISLAM HASHMI

Successive governments of Bangladesh, along with the vast majority of Bangladeshis, have consistently denied the existence of any discrimination against the ethnic, religious or linguistic minority groups living in the country. The case of the 'Biharis' in Bangladesh is different from the other minority groups. In the first place the average Bangladeshi does not accept them as members of a minority of citizen status, let alone agree with the view that the 'Biharis' were (or are) ever discriminated against or victimized. Bangladeshi intellectuals, politicians, businessmen and others argue that

(*a*) the 'Biharis' in general collaborated with the Pakistani occupation army during the Liberation War in 1971 and were responsible for the killing of thousands of Bangladeshis

(*b*) they are nothing short of 'war-criminals', and

(*c*) are 'stranded Pakistanis', who should be sent back to Pakistan.

One is not likely to hear from them that just a handful of 'Biharis' actively collaborated with the Pakistanis in 1971 (as did many Bengali Muslims), and that is no justification for treating about a quarter million of them as pariahs, crowding them into unhygienic 'refugee camps' in Dhaka and elsewhere. Few Bangladeshi talk about thousands of innocent 'Bihari' men, women and children being killed during and after the war by Bengali 'freedom-fighters' and others, or about hundreds of thousands of them losing their properties in the wake of the independence of Bangladesh in 1971.

Many Bangladeshi Muslims would argue that (*a*) Bangladesh is a secular country although Islam was declared as the 'state religion' in 1988; (*b*) communal rioting and discrimination on the basis of race,

* Presented at the 20th Anniversary Conference of the Asian Studies Association of Australia (ASAA), Melbourne, 8-11 July 1996. I am thankful to Andrew Major, Mushirul Hasan, Javeed Alam, Ruchira Ganguly-Searse, Moazzem Hossain and Gyanesh Kudaisya for their comments and suggestions.

religion and language are matters of the past, prevalent only during the colonial and Pakistani periods; (c) Bengali Muslims are different from fellow-Bengalis or Muslims elsewhere in South Asia in that they are mild, gentle and non-communal by nature; (d) people in Bangladesh live in peace and harmony with their neighbours; and (e) that the creation of Bangladesh signalled the death-knell of 'communal' forces.

The imposition of a ban on Islam-oriented political parties by the government in 1972 may also be cited to highlight the secular nature of the polity. The subsequent lifting of the ban on parties like the Jamaat-i Islami and Muslim League by the military government of General Ziaur Rahman (1975-81), may also be cited by some as a step taken in the opposite direction. The adherents of such views impute communal behaviour and anti-Hindu incidents of loot and arson in Bangladesh in the early 1990s to the unhindered political activities of the Islam-oriented groups, implying, most apologetically, that only the Islamists are communal (anti-Hindu) but all other Bangladeshi Muslims are free from the virus.[1]

What is even more interesting is that although some Bangladeshi Muslim intellectuals would agree with the view that Bangladeshi Hindus (about 10 per cent of the total population) in general enjoy second-class status in almost every sphere of life, very few would accept that tribal groups in the Chittagong Hill Tracts have been living in a much more difficult situation than the Hindus. Only a handful of Bangladeshi Muslims would agree with various international human rights groups and individuals who have documented incidents of mass-murder, rape, looting and arson, committed by both Bangladeshi security forces and civilians against the Chakma and other ethnically non-Bengali minority groups in the Chittagong Hill Tracts since 1972. A recent book by a Bangladeshi intellectual and a former minister under the Ershad regime (overthrown in December 1990 by the people) is not only defensive about Bengalis but also portrays tribesmen as outlaws and killers. A minister of the Khalida Zia government has also been very critical of them, denying them any right of autonomy or separate identity.[2] It is equally interesting that those intellectuals, politicians and others who are

---

[1] See for details Shahriar Kabir, *Bangladeshe Samprodaikotar Chalchitra* (Bengali) (Dhaka, 1993); Mahmudur Rahman Manna, *Samprodaikota O Jamaat* (Bengali) (Dhaka, 1993); and Taslima Nasreen, *Lajja* (Bengali) (Dhaka, 1993), *passim*.

[2] Mizanur Rahman Shelley (ed.), *The Chittagong Hill Tracts of Bangladesh: The*

critical of Islamic groups like the Jamaat-i Islami and Muslim League are hardly critical of Sheikh Mujibur Rahman, 'the Father of the Nation' (who advised the tribes to become 'Bengalis') for denying the tribes rights to retain their culture, language and separate ethnic entity.

This paper aims at exploring the reasons why the 'Bihari', Urdu-speaking Muslim refugees from India, who migrated to East Pakistan in the wake of the Partition of 1947, were not assimilated into the mainstream and why and how Bengali Muslims persecuted and exploited them. This is an attempt to understand why and how nationalist movements, especially in the 'Third World', breed chauvinism, and to show how the bulk of the 'Bihari' refugees were misguided by their West Pakistani patrons and their local non-Bengali agents, alienating them from the bulk of the Bengali population in East Pakistan. Later, during and after the civil war of 1971, this alienation was far more pronounced. In short, the 'Biharis' have been the victims of two divergent streams of nationalism—the Pakistani from 1947 to 1971, and the Bengali/Bangladeshi from 1971 to the present.

The origin of the problem lies in the Partition of the Indian subcontinent in 1947. Prior to this Muslims had constituted a minority of four million out of nearly thirty million of the total population of Bihar. The large-scale exodus of Muslims from Bihar, Uttar Pradesh and West Bengal started in the wake of the massacre of thousands of them in Bihar and Calcutta in late 1946 and in 1947 and 1950 by Hindu and Sikh extremists. The Great Bihar Killings of October-November 1946, preceded by the Great Calcutta Killings of August 1946, alone led to the extermination of about thirty thousand Muslims. Consequently more than a million Bihari Muslims sought refuge in East Bengal after Partition. Another thirty thousand entered East Bengal from other parts of eastern India, especially eastern Uttar Pradesh and West Bengal. They were followed by more migrants from eastern India after the communal riots of 1950 and 1964. Since the majority of these Muslim refugees were Bihari Muslims from Bihar and Calcutta, all of them were collectively known as 'Biharis' in East Bengal or East Pakistan.[3]

Untold Story (Dhaka, 1992), pp. 168-77; Oli Ahmad's (Minister of Communications, Government of Bangladesh) interview with the BBC Television, 31 May 1995.

[3] Minority Rights Group, 'The Biharis in Bangladesh', Report no. 11, 4th edn. (London, 1982), p. 8.

By 1971 their numbers had swollen to more than 1.5 million and often they were subsumed under the broad category of 'non-Bengalis' which included various refugee groups from Uttar Pradesh, Punjab, Maharashtra, Gujarat and other parts of north-western India. There were a few West Pakistani businessmen, pedlars, money-lenders and security guards (mostly Pathans) throughout East Pakistan.

When the bulk of the 'Bihari' refugees arrived in East Pakistan there was no land for them. Not being peasant or agricultural workers, they settled in urban and semi-urban centres. Many were self-employed small traders and mechanics, while others were government officials and clerks, teachers and professionals and skilled workers on the railways and in the mills and factories. By the early 1960s most of them were provided with cheap housing in the refugee colonies of Dhaka (Mirpur and Muhammadpur), Chittagong, Syedpur, Rangpur and elsewhere in northern and western East Pakistan. The well-to-do section of the 'Biharis' lived in private residential areas in Dhaka, Chittagong, Khulna, Sylhet and other big towns.[4]

During the early days of the Pakistani government programme for refugee rehabilitation in East Pakistan, the local Bengali population did not resent the arrival of displaced 'Biharis'. They were welcomed as fellow-Pakistanis, who had suffered and sacrificed for the attainment of Pakistan. Up to the early 1950s the bulk of the East Pakistani Muslim middle and lower middle classes were in a state of euphoria, created by their birth of Pakistan.

By 1951, a large number of Hindu professionals, clerks and petty officials, landlords and businessmen had emigrated to India. The East Bengali Muslims grabbed the vacant positions and 'abandoned enemy properties' left behind in the urban and rural areas. They regarded the 'Bihari' refugees as comrades-in-arms. Sheikh Mujibur Rahman, who later created Bangladesh, is said to have brought many Bihari Muslims over to East Pakistan in the wake of the Partition of 1947 by touring around Bihar, urging them to migrate to East Bengal.[5]

The Pakistani Government for quite some time succeeded in portraying the 'Biharis' as the *muhajirin* of Pakistan. Although the

[4] See Map-Source, ibid.
[5] Maulana Bhashani (1880-1976), one of the political gurus of Sheikh Mujibur Rahman, is said to have told this to Basant Chatterjee. See Basant Chatterjee, *Inside Bangladesh Today: An Eyewitness Account* (New Delhi, 1973), p. 85

term literally means refugees, it has a much deeper religious connotation. Prophet Mohammad and his early followers from Mecca who emigrated to Medina were also known as the *muhajirin*, who received the support and protection of Medina's Muslims or *ansars*. Similarly, Pakistani ruling elites, a few of them represented in East Bengal as well, might have adopted the term *muhajirin* with a view to making East Bengali Muslims duty-bound to help and accept them as their own people. This scheme worked for some time and not simply because of government machinations. To understand why the average Bengali Muslim did not resent the presence of the 'Biharis', one must understand how desperate he was to overthrow Hindu hegemony represented by the *zamindar-mahajan-bhadralok* (landlord-moneylender–middle class), especially during the four decades up to 1947.[6]

However, the honeymoon was short-lived. M.A. Jinnah's speech in Dhaka in March 1948, stressing that 'Urdu and Urdu alone shall be the state language of Pakistan' caused widespread consternation. To the surprise and dismay of most East Bengali Muslims, who had unflinching faith in Pakistan, Jinnah also declared that anyone opposed to Urdu as the 'state language' was an enemy of Pakistan.[7]

What a handful of Bengali intellectuals and politicians realized not long after the creation of Pakistan—that East Bengal had virtually become a colony of the western wing—was soon realized by many due to the speech of Jinnah of March 1948 and a chain of events and political developments that highlighted the preponderance of 'non-Bengalis' in important sectors of administration. The Urdu-speaking East Bengali Prime Minister, Khawaja Nazimuddin, further enraged East Bengali intellectuals, students, politicians and others by unwittingly favouring Urdu as the 'state language' in January 1952.[8]

Thereafter the eastern and the western wings of Pakistan gradually drifted apart. The West Pakistani civil and military rulers, the bureaucracy (mostly manned by 'non-Bengalis') with its colonial

[6] Taj ul-Islam Hashmi, *Pakitsan as a Peasant Utopia: The Communalization of Class Politics in East Bengal, 1920-1947* (Boulder, 1992), *passim*.

[7] Badruddin Umar, *Purbo Banglar Bhasha Andolon O Tatkalin Rajiniti*, vol. 1 (Bengali) (Dhaka, 1970), pp. 104-22; Keith Callard, *Pakistan: Political Study* (London, 1957), p. 182.

[8] Kamruddin Ahmad, *The Social History of East Pakistan* (Dhaka, 1967), pp. 124-5.

structure and mentality, 'non-Bengali' business interests and other 'non-Bengalis' living in East and West Pakistan aided the process of disintegration. West Pakistanis behaved as if they, as members of a racially and intellectually superior race, had the divine mandate to rule East Pakistan. The upper echelons of the 'Biharis' in East Pakistan, as junior partners of West Pakistani business groups, believed that their existence and continued prosperity in East Pakistan depended on the goodwill of the Pakistani ruling and business elites. Consequently, they also joined the anti-East Pakistani and pro-West Pakistani stream, mobilizing the half-educated or illiterate, poorer working class sections of the 'Biharis' against their Bengali neighbours, thus forsaking the economic and political interests of their adopted home. On several occasions, 'Bihari' mill-workers at Narayanganj, Dhaka, Khulna and Chittagong took part in anti-Bengali communal riots whipped up by their Pakistani masters in the 1950s and 1960s.[9]

The Pakistani ruling and business elites successfully hegemonized the 'Bihari' mass consciousness by distributing a few favours—jobs in mills and factories, railways and postal departments and cheap housing in several 'refugee colonies' in Dhaka and elsewhere in the province, concentrating them in ghettos and isolating them from the Bengalis. Pakistani elites and their Urdu-speaking junior partners in East Pakistan exploited 'Bihari' loyalty to Pakistan,[10] regarded by many as their 'promised land'. They often regarded them as 'semi Hindus', pro-Indian and disloyal to Pakistan.[11]

Most 'Biharis' believed that as Urdu-speakers they were not only better Pakistanis than their Bengali neighbours but were also racially superior. They regarded themselves important partners of the Punjabi-Urdu-speaking oligarchy of Pakistan and accepted the West Pakistani ruling and business elites as their sole patrons, guides and protectors. They had neither any representative in the Provincial or Central Legislatures nor any leader to promote understanding between themselves and their perceived 'friends' and 'foes', West Pakistanis and Bengalis, respectively. Consequently they failed to understand that the Pakistani rulers were using them by alienating them from the indigenous population as European colonists had used

---

[9] Abul Mansur Ahmed, *Amar Dekha Rajinitir Panchash Bachhar* (Bengali) (Dhaka, 1970), p. 335; Kamruddin Ahmed, op. cit., pp. 174-7.

[10] Basant Chatterjee, op. cit., pp. 102-3.

[11] Kamruddin Ahmed, op. cit., p. 176.

Asian migrants against indigenous people in Africa.[12] Some scholars compare them with enterprising Jewish minorities, who 'succeeded through hard work induced by their feeling of insecurity'.[13] However, from their extra-territoriality and almost total indifference to the development and welfare of East Pakistan, it seems they had more similarities with Asian migrants in colonial Africa than with hardworking and intelligent Jews of Europe and America. Consequently, not long after the 'Biharis' had settled in different urban areas of East Bengal, their anti-Bengali attitude and sudden prosperity (both due to hard work and government patronage) soon turned them into the most undesirable elements or 'parasites of East Bengal' in the eyes of many Bengali intellectuals, traders, workers and professionals.

By the late 1960s when most East Pakistanis started demanding more autonomy for their province, some 'Biharis' openly sided with the quasi-military regime of President Ayub Khan. In contrast most 'Biharis' and Indian migrants in Karachi openly defied Ayub Khan, demanding more rights and opportunities for Karachi: unlike the 'Biharis' in East Pakistan, Indian refugees in Karachi had leaders from within their own community who did not want to compromise with the central government at the expense of the interests of their adopted home, Karachi.

In East Pakistan, the arrest of Sheikh Mujibur Rahman and other Bengali nationalist politicians in 1966 led to widespread violence and many Bengali students, intellectuals and politicians raised the cry for an independent state. By early 1969, due to the concerted efforts of all the leading opposition parties of both East and West Pakistan, President Ayub Khan relinquished power. The mass upsurge of 1969 also led to the release of many political prisoners, including the Awami League (People's League) leader, Sheikh Mujibur Rahman and his 'co-conspirators'. Soon, the militant, pro-independence 'leftist' sections of the pro-Awami League student and youth organization began to raise slogans demanding total independence for East Bengal. *Jai Bangla* (Victory to Bengal) was one such slogan.

Other slogans were far more provocative. By late 1970 and early 1971, the Dhaka University campus was reverberant with

---

[12] 'The Biharis in Bangladesh', p. 8.
[13] Ibid.

Ekta-duita maura dharo
Sakal-bikal nashta karo

Catch one or two *maura* ['non-Bengalis']
Every morning and evening and eat them up.

Graffiti proclaiming Bengalis as the 'most superior race in the world' (*Bangali bishwer srestho jati*) started appearing in the universities by early 1970.

II

By the time of the December 1970 parliamentary elections, anti-'non-Bengali' feeling was whipped up to such an extent throughout East Pakistan that attacks on 'non-Bengali' shops and properties by Bengali mobs were quite common in Dhaka and Chittagong. The day (1 March 1971) President Yahya Khan announced his decision to prorogue the impending parliamentary session, Bengali mobs in big cities, especially Dhaka and Chittagong, targeted 'non-Bengali' homes and establishments. These attacks continued unabated, especially in the peripheral districts, until Pakistani control was re-established between late March and late April 1971. Thousands of 'Bihari' men, women and children were killed. In many places, especially in the northern and south-western districts, thousands of 'Biharis' were burnt alive or simply hacked into pieces by Bengali marauders.[14]

After the liberation of Bangladesh on 16 December 1971, and in some cases after the liberation of certain districts even earlier, more 'Biharis' fell victim, to the terror let loose by genuine and pseudo-Bengali freedom-fighters. Many 'Bihari' and Bengali collaborators of the Pakistani armed forces during the Liberation War of 1971 were gunned down during December 1971 and early 1972. Unlike the Bengali collaborators the 'Biharis', whether they collaborated or not, faced the wrath of Bengali freedom fighters and supporters/workers of the Awami League twice—once before the Pakistani crackdown on 25 March 1971 and later when they were charged with colla-boration. However, most managed to survive either by handing over their entire properties—houses, shops, cars, cash and jewelleries—to the mobs, or through the direct intervention of the Indian army

[14] Lawrence Ziring, *Bangladesh from Mujib to Ershad: An Interpretive Study* (Dhaka, 1992), p. 65; Qutbuddin Aziz, *Blood and Tears* (Karachi, 1974), *passim*.

and Border Security Force in the wake of the Liberation.

According to a report of the London-based Minority Rights Group, over 300 'Biharis' were killed by 'extremist mobs' at Chittagong in early March 1971, and at Jessore, Khulna, Rangpur, Saidpur and Mymensingh. Some estimate that several thousand 'Biharis' were killed prior to the Pakistani army's ruthless intervention on 25 March 1971 and that further reprisals against them followed when Yahya Khan arrested Sheikh Mujib and outlawed the Awami League.[15] However the non-Bengali version of the story does not tell us how 'Bihari' marauders persecuted Bengalis under the protection of Pakistani authorities during April and December 1971.

The following account by Anthony Mascarenhas, author of *The Rape of Bangla Desh*, highlights the plight of the 'Biharis' as well:

Thousands of families of unfortunate Muslims, many of them refugees from Bihar, . . . were mercilessly wiped out. Women were raped or had their breasts torn out with specially fashioned knives. Children did not escape the horror: the lucky ones were killed with their parents; but many thousands of others must go through what life remains for them with eyes gauged out and limbs roughly amputated. More than 20,000 bodies of the non-Bengalis have been found in the main towns such as Chittagong, Khulna and Jessore. . The real toll, I was told everywhere in East Bengal, may have been as high as 100,000; for thousands of non-Bengalis have vanished without a trace.[16]

In another report sent from East Pakistan *The Sunday Times* of London, gave similar information about 'the brutal massacre of thousands of non-Bengalis—men, women and children' at the hands of Bengalis, holding that 'more than 20,000 bodies have been found . . . in Bengal's main towns but the final count could top 100,000'.[17]

In the light of scores of eyewitness accounts of the civil war in East Bengal in 1971 and the subsequent Liberation War (from 25 March to 16 December), it is no longer possible to argue that the assault on innocent civilians was a one-sided affair—Pakistanis and 'Biharis' victimizing Bengalis—and that the Bengalis retaliated only after the 'Biharis' had taken part in persecuting them in the wake of the Pakistani crackdown on 25 March.

[15] 'The Biharis in Bangladesh', pp. 8-9; Kazi Anwarul Huque, *Under Three Flags: Reminiscences of a Public Servant* (Dhaka, 1986), p. 569.

[16] *Sunday Times* (London), 13 June 1971.

[17] *Sunday Times*, 2 May 1971.

Malcom Browne of the *New York Times* reported from Chittagong in May 1971, that before the arrival of Pakistani troops 'when Chittagong was still governed by the secessionist Awami League and its allies, Bengali workers, apparently resentful of the relative prosperity of Bihari immigrants from India, are said to have killed the Biharis in large numbers'.[18] The same reporter in another report from Khulna in early May narrated how thousands of 'non-Bengalis' were butchered by Bengalis, tied to frames specially set up 'to hold prisoners for decapitation'.[19] *The Times* of London cites a British technician who said that 'hundreds of non-Bengali Muslims have died in the north-western town of Dinajpur alone'.[20] From a memorandum submitted to the British Parliamentary delegation in Dhaka by Diwan Wirasat Hussain, a 'non-Bengali' leader of the East Pakistan Refugee Association on 20 June 1971, it appears that out of more than 50,000 Muslim refugees of Dinajpur 'barely 150 survived the March-April 1971 [prior to the arrival of Pakistani troops] massacre of non-Bengalis'.[21] Other eyewitness accounts corroborate this.[22] Scores of other Western media reports substantiate the assertion that thousands of 'Biharis' were killed in different districts of East Bengal prior to the arrival of Pakistani troops.[23] It is difficult to agree with Mascarenhas that the military action of West Pakistan preceded and did not follow massacres of non-Bengalis.[24] Not only do the testimonies of hundreds of victims contradict his assertion, but a report of the Minority Rights Groups also affirms that thousands of Biharis were killed at Chittagong, Jessore, Khulna, Rangpur, Saidpur and Mymensingh in early March 1971, before the military action.[25]

Significantly enough, the fifteen volume *History of the Freedom Movement of Bangladesh* (in Bengali) and scores of other studies are either silent about the massacre of 'Bihari' civilians by members of the rebel Bengali troops and civilians or else defensive about

[18] *New York Times*, 10 May 1971.
[19] Ibid., 9 May 1971.
[20] *The Times*, 6 April 1971.
[21] Q. Aziz, op. cit., p. 121.
[22] Ibid, pp. 118-21.
[23] *New York Times*, 7 May 1971 (cited in Q. Aziz, op. cit., pp. 183-4); I am an 'eyewitness' to how 'Bihari' businessmen and their family members were gunned down and how about 700 'Biharis' were kept in jail and later killed by Bengalis at Sirajganj town in April 1971, prior to the arrival of the Pakistani army.
[24] Anthony Mascarenhas, *The Rape of Bangla Desh* (Delhi, 1971), p. 119.
[25] 'The Biharis in Bangladesh', p. 8.

Bengalis reacting to 'non-Bengali' being armed by the Pakistani army. Consider the following accounts of the Bengali-Bihari encounters during the liberation war of Bangladesh given by three Bangladeshi freedom-fighters.

Rafiqual Islam (retired Major, who actively took part in the Liberation War), in *A Tale of Millions* gives a sketchy account of what happened in Chittagong on 3 March 1971 between Bengali and 'non-Bengali':

In the early hours of the day, a procession was heading towards the city centre of Chittagong raising nationalistic slogans. When the procession reached the Wireless Colony—a non-Bengalee populated area of the city—some unknown persons opened fire with rifles and physically assaulted the demonstrators. The Bengalee hutments in the adjacent areas were set on fire and many people were burnt alive. News of this incident spread immediately and enraged the city people. *There was serious breach of law and order. EPR* [East Pakistan Rifles, para-military border security force] *was called out to assist the civil administration. It was around 9 o'clock in the morning when I reached the Wireless Colony. By that time, serious rioting was reported* [sic] *from other non-Bengalee areas of the city—Ispahani Colony Ambagan Colony, Kulshi Colony, and Sadar Nagar* [emphasis added].[26]

We also learn how Pakistani troops of the 20th Baluch Regiment were responsible for the deaths of several Bengali demonstrators. Of late, one Bengali journalist in a self-congratulatory style has praised his countrymen and the Government of Bangladesh for looking after thousands of 'stranded Pakistanis' living in refugee camps in Bangladesh.[27]

What is not revealed in such accounts is how thousands of 'non-Bengali's or 'Biharis' were killed in Chittagong alone between 3 March and 2 April 1971 from the beginning of the mass insurgency up to the reoccupation of the city by Pakistani troops. It is, however, difficult to ascertain the death toll in Chittagong. While the Government of Pakistan's White Paper on the East Pakistan Crisis (published in August 1971) estimated the 'non-Bengali' death toll to be 15,000, some eyewitness accounts mentioned the figure to be

---

[26] Rafiqul Islam, *A Tale of Millions: Bangladesh Liberation War-1971* (Dhaka, 1986), p. 37.

[27] Ibid., pp. 37-8; Obaid ul-Haq, 'Bastuharar Votadhikar, Nirbachan O Geneva Camp', *Janakantha* (Bengali Daily), 13 June 1995.

more than 50,000.[28] According to eyewitness reports, late in the night of 3 March, 'a violent mob, led by gun-totting Awami League storm troopers, invaded the non-Bengali settlements in the city and looted and burnt thousands of houses and hutments'. Wireless Colony and Ferozeshah Colony, along with other 'Bihari' settlements at Raufabad, Halishahar, Dotala, Kalurghat, Hamzabad and Pahartali in Chittagong city, were attacked by Bengali civilians and rebel soldiers. The same sources also reveal that while the East Bengal Regimental Centre in Chittagong (the headquarters of Bengali troops) was the operational headquarters of the 'rebels' (freedom-fighters), 'the principal human abattoir was housed in the main town office of the Awami League'. Another eyewitness account by a Western reporter corroborates the foregoing assertion:

The events of March and April until recently remained a mystery to the outside world. Today they speak for themselves. The headquarters of outlawed Awami League leader Sheikh Mujibur Rahman at Chittagong are still caked with blood, a grim memorial to a slaughter of Urdu-speaking Biharis by Bengalis.

In Thakurgaon, a town in northern East Pakistan which has a large non-Bengali population, the killing may have been even worse. There I saw hundreds of women crying in the streets—widows of some of the 7,000 Biharis reported to have been massacred.[29]

To turn to the other Bengali accounts of what happened in Chittagong and other towns in 1971, we may refer to Major General Safiullah's book on the Liberation War of Bangladesh. It is noteworthy that like Major Rafiqul Islam, Safiullah was also a sector commander (a Major in 1971) during the war (chief of the Bangladesh army up to August 1975). Safiullah's account is not very different from Rafiqual Islam's However, by portraying the 'Biharis' of Chittagong as allies of the Pakistani troops Rafiqul Islam has used the evasive expression of 'serious rioting' to misconstrue the facts, Safiullah's portrayal of the 'non-Bengalis' of Chittagong is of 'looters' and 'killers' of Bengali civilians.[30]

Barrister Moudud Ahmed (a freedom-fighter and a well-known politician), on the other hand, offers a relatively objective account

[28] Q. Aziz, op. cit., p. 48.

[29] Ibid., pp. 48-51; Werner Adam, 'Pakistan: See for Yourself Yahya', *Far Eastern Economic Review*, 19 June 1971, p. 5.

[30] Maj. Gen. K.M. Safiullah, *Bangladesh at War* (Dhaka, 1989), p. 40.

of the Bengali-'Bihari' problem during 1971. He argues that the Pakistani army quietly distributed arms in the 'non-Bengali' ghettos in Mirpur and Muhammadpur in Dhaka, Pahartali (Chittagong) and Syedpur (Rangpur). He narrates that, prior to the military crack-down on 25 March, 'some non-Bengalis killed some Bengalis' with impunity and the army shot the Bengalis down when they tried to retaliate. At the same time he points out that Mujib urged the Bengalis to continue their struggle in a 'peaceful and disciplined manner', and on the other, assured the 'non-Bengalis' living in East Bengal fair treatment as 'sons of the soil', he urged Bengalis to protect the life and properties of 'every citizen whether Bengali or non-Bengali, Hindu or Muslim'. Mujib is said to have sent some top Awami League Leaders to Chittagong in early March to maintain peace in the area.[31] What is missing in this account is that, long before the deadlock over the transfer of power to the majority party (Awami League) in early March 1971, different section of Bengali students, workers and others had already started a bitter anti-'non-Bengali' movement throughout East Pakistan.

According to Lawrence Ziring, Mujib's call to strike on 1 March 1971, 'was also taken as a call to arms and a bloody campaign of murder, arson and looting seized the province, especially the capital. . . . The East Pakistani Bihari community was the target . . . and many of their numbers were butchered in wild orgies that the authorities [Sheikh Mujib and his party] seemed unable or unwilling to prevent.'[32] Ziring also writes about the large-scale looting and burning down of 'non-Bengali' properties during 1 and 25 March, and the initial flight to India of tens of thousands. Many 'non-Bengalis' were also flown to West Pakistan in the wake of the military crackdown on 25 March.[33]

Another account by Mascarenhas (who had been sympathetic to the Bengalis) of the persecution of 'Biharis' in East Pakistan reveals how the masses and their leaders, including Bengali military officers, were prejudiced against the 'Biharis'. Major Ziaur Rahman (later Lieutenant General and President of Bangladesh until his assassination in 1981), a leader of the freedom-fighters, is said to have

[31] Moudud Ahmed, *Bangladesh: Constitutional Quest for Autonomy* (Dhaka, 1991), pp. 206-7.
[32] Lawrence Ziring, op. cit., p. 64.
[33] Ibid., p. 65.

remarked in 1971, 'Those who speak Urdu are also our enemies because they support the Pakistan army. We will crush them.'[34] In another episode we are told how Major Zia treated some 'Bihari' prisoners at Kalurghat in Chittagong on 28 March 1971, after his troops had brought them to him. He is said to have ordered them: 'Take the men out and shoot them'. Then, pointing to the women prisoners, he told his troops: 'You can do what you like with them'.[35]

III

The killings of 'Biharis', were not solely motivated by the patriotism or communal frenzy of Bengali nationalists. Petty bourgeois social envy and the lumpen proletariat's proclivity to violence and anarchy were directly involved in the killings. The participation of peasants in some peripheral towns seems akin to Russian peasant involvement in the pogroms in the late nineteenth century.

As stated, the persecution of 'Biharis' did not cease with the liberation of Bangladesh in December 1971. Although only a handful of 'Biharis' had joined the East Pakistan Civil Armed Forces (EPCAF) and other auxiliary forces (*Razakars* and *Al-Shams*) raised by the Pakistani authorities, hundreds of 'Bihari' men were captured by Bengali freedom-fighters and taken blind-fold to 'execution' by locally organized 'firing squads' on flimsy charges of collaboration with the Pakistanis and killing of Bengalis during the Liberation War. An international observer points out how 'Tiger' Kader Siddiqui, the leader of guerrilla group from Tangail district, killed several Biharis two days after the Liberation before a crowd in Dhaka Stadium, 'an act which was seen widely on television and in the world's press, but for which he has never been tried'.[36] Yet many Bangladeshis, since the Liberation, have been blaming 'Biharis' for the killing of several Bengali intellectuals in December 1971.[37] International observers have also pointed out that the 'nationalist local press' repeatedly fuelled the Bengalis' hatred of the 'Biharis', leading to the

[34] Anthony Mascarenhas, *Bangladesh: A Legacy of Blood* (London, 1986), pp. 118-19.
[35] Ibid., p. 122.
[36] 'The Biharis in Bangladesh', p. 9.
[37] Ibid., pp. 8, 21; Carol Rose, 'Living on Hope', Newsletter, Institute of Current World Affairs, 30 June 1992, p. 6.

mass looting and expropriation.[38] After visiting some refugee camps in Bangladesh, Basant Chatterjee observed in 1973:

Perhaps no other class of people in the world today is as ruined, economically and socially, as smitten and smashed up as the community of the former Indian refugees in Bangladesh who are known here by the general term "Bihari". . . . Today in Bangladesh, to be a Bihari is the worst crime. . . . Thousands have been discharged from service on the ground of "long absence without leave", But their salaries and funds have not yet been paid. . . . Many persons rejoined duty on the strength of "clearance chits" given by Awami League M.P.'s. But they did not return; even their bodies remained untraced.[39]

Chatterjee asserted that 'no Bangla leader, of the ruling party or the opposition' ever took the trouble to visit the camps where the 'Biharis' lived 'not even like vermin because vermin move . . . looking at them in their mat-cells, one can scarcely believe that these lumps of bone and skin can be living human beings. They all appear to be dead.' He rejected the Bangladeshi government assertion that 260,000 'Biharis' opted for Pakistani citizenship as fictitious.[40]

While thousands of 'Biharis' fell victim to the wrath of Bengali nationalists during early March to late April 1971, many were actually killed or ousted from their properties by Bengalis having connections with the ruling Awami League Party. With a view to acquiring 'Bihari' properties in big towns, especially in Dhaka and Chittagong, these properties were initially decorated with Awami League banners or sign boards portraying them as Awami League or pro-Awami League student, worker or youth organization offices. Many 'Biharis' were forced by Bengalis to sign documents indicating transfer of ownership of cars, houses and shops to their names.[41]

Order No. 1 of 3 January 1972 (issued before the release and arrival of Sheikh Mujibur Rahman to Bangladesh on 10 January) stipulate that the government could take over the control and management of those industrial and commercial concerns whose owners, directors and managers had left Bangladesh or 'were not available' to control and manage the concerns or 'could not be

[38] 'The Biharis in Bangladesh', p. 9.
[39] Basant Chatterjee, op. cit, pp. 102-13.
[40] Ibid., pp. 112, 115.
[41] 'The Biharis in Bangladesh', pp. 9, 14, 16; Hasan Zaheer, *The Separation of East Pakistan: The Rise and Realization of Bengali Muslim Nation* (Dhaka, 1994), p. 431; Siddiq Salik, *Witness to Surrender* (Karachi, 1978), p. 212.

allowed to run them in public interest'. It empowered the new administration 'to operate bank account of the owners, the directors and managers'.[42] Not long after this order came the Bangladesh Abandoned Property Order (also known as the President's Order No. 16) on 28 February 1972, which had a far-reaching effect. It empowered the government to dispose of 'abandoned' properties. The vagueness of the definition of 'abandoned property' was taken advantage of by the government-appointed 'administrators'. Consequently the property of many bonafide citizens of the country, living within Bangladesh, was expropriated. One prominent legal expert, Moudud Ahmed, defended the rights of some Bangladeshi citizens whose properties were brought under the broad category of 'abandoned'.[43] 'Almost every property of every non-local or Bhiari who migrated originally from India years ago and settled and had not opted for Pakistan was taken over as abandoned property or was under the threat of being taken over. The politicos took the advantage of the miserable state of these people.' Moudud Ahmed has pointed out how local leaders of the ruling party or 'officers enjoying their patronage' took full advantage of the government order. Ghazi Gholam Mostafa (a stalwart of the ruling Awami League Party and chief of the Bangladesh Red Cross, who was also notoriously known as the 'Blanket Thief') supervised, and expropriated 'non-Bengali' industrial, commercial and residential properties in Dhaka and its suburbs at Tejgaon and Tongi.[44]

Following the withdrawal of the Indian army in late January 1972, the Bangladesh Government sent soldiers to the 'Bihari' enclave at Mirpur in Dhaka who, in the name of recovering arms, killed and arrested many Biharis though the Bangladeshi press, with the sole exception of the left-wing Sunday paper, *Holiday,* remained silent.[45] The toll in Khulna alone reached 1,000 on 10 March 1972. Many more were killed by Bengali extremists after the Liberation, mainly with a view to grabbing their properties.[46] This fact was also not reported by the press.[47]

[42] Moudud Ahmed, *Bangladesh: Era of Sheikh Mujibur Rahman* (Dhaka, 1991), pp. 14-16.

[43] Ibid., pp. 16-19.

[44] Ibid., pp. 21-2 and 41, n. 20.

[45] 'The Biharis in Bangladesh', p. 9.

[46] Ibid., pp. 14 and 16.

[47] Talukder Maniruzzaman, *The Bangladesh Revolution and its Aftermath* (Dhaka, 1988), pp. 93-5.

A somewhat balanced assessment of what happened during and immediately after the Bangladesh Liberation War of 1971 was made by the late Hamidul Huq Chowdhury, a Bengali politician (Foreign Minister of Pakistan in 1956) and the founder of the daily *Pakistan Observer (Bangladesh Observer)*:

During the whole period, a large number of Bengali private citizens were killed. On the other side the Urdu speaking citizens in East Pakistan, who were considered to be Pakistanis, also suffered grievously. No real figure of the total loss of lives, has ever been collected by any authority. Some said it could exceed a hundred thousand. My guess was it might be something like 10 to 15 thousand.

Almost all the businesses and industries set up by the non-Bengalis were looted, damaged and forcibly occupied by rowdy elements. Many leading non-Bengali businessmen succeeded in leaving East Pakistan in early 1971 fearing the break-down of law and order and thereby saved their lives. Otherwise no mercy would have been shown to women and children of the Urdu-speaking citizens.

Large numbers of Bengalis suffered in the hands of non-Bengali elements in different parts of East Pakistan. I lost more than one relative in the hands of some Urdu-speaking rowdies, though they were not connected with politics.[48]

The plight of the 'Biharis' of Bangladesh and those who managed to sneak into Pakistan after 1971, has been succinctly narrated in an Urdu short story by Ibrahim Jalees. To him, these people 'from the moment they are born till their last day, [they] neither want to live nor wish to die—disgusted with life and afraid of death!'[49]

IV

The roots of the conflicts which divided peoples of the subcontinent in different phases —first, Hindus were separated from Muslims and then the line of separation was drawn between different ethnic and linguistic groups—are by-products of elite conflicts, and competition between unequal middle classes. Consequently, the concept of nationalism, as developed in the subcontinent during the last one hundred odd years, has been germinating conflict. In short, the

---

[48] Hamidul Huq Chowdhury, *Memoirs* (Dhaka, 1989), pp. 322-3.

[49] Ibrahim Jalees, 'A Grave Turned Inside-out' (translated by V. Adil and A. Bhalla), Alok Bhalla (ed.), *Stories About the Partition of India*, vol. II (New Delhi, 1994), p. 141.

Hindu-Muslim, Bengali-'Bihari' and Bengali-'Tribal' conflicts in Bangladesh are part of much larger conflicts and identity crises in the subcontinent. So far as East Bengal is concerned, the Partition of 1947 and the creation of Bangladesh in 1971 have neither benefited the minorities nor resolved the problematic issues of nationalism in Bangladesh. Hindu Bengalis and 'Bihari' Muslims, along with the 'tribals', have consequently suffered most due to the changes in the political geography of the region since 1947. The persecutions have been a byproduct of peasant xenophobia, petty bourgeois greed and intolerance, class conflict and racism/communalism nurtured and exploited by ultra nationalist Bengali leaders.

However, unlike the anti-Jewish pogroms in Russia, Ukraine and Poland in the late nineteenth and early twentieth centuries, the killings in Bangladesh were neither an inevitable, precipitous outcome of class conflict nor a by-product of any spontaneous 'primitive rebellion' of the peasantry. The 'Biharis' had hardly any conflicting class-interests with the peasants and the bulk of them did not represent the mythically prosperous 'non-Bengalis' in the region. Their segregation from the Bengalis in towns and small trading centres, retaining their own distinct identity, which parallels the prevalence of Jewish ghettos in Russia and Poland in the nineteenth century, alienated them from the indigenous people. By 1971 they further alienated themselves from the bulk of the Bengali population becuase they nursed the illusion of being part of the Punjabi civil and military ruling elites.

One needs to understand why 'these non-Bengalis, who had no other place on earth to live in except Bangladesh, put their sole reliance on the military masters of the West although in any system of government it was the Bengalis—and not the Punjabis—who were bound to enjoy the substance of power'.[51] As discussed earlier, the main reason for their lack of commitment to Bangladesh, especially during the Liberation War of 1971, was because they were not sure of securing equal citizenship rights in the event of the emergence of Bangladesh. Already stigmatized as vicious, conspiring agents of exploitation long before the civil war started in March 1971 by

---

[50] Mafizullah Kabir, *Experiences of an Exile at Home: Life in Occupied Bangladesh* (Dhaka, 1972), p. 55.

[51] Ibid.

different sections of the Bengali bourgeois and petty bourgeois classes, the 'Biharis' were victims of wild rumours about their participation in the mass-killing of Bengalis and as co-conspirators of the Pakistani military junta. Consequently under the leadership of those Bengalis who had an eye on 'Bihari' property, Bengali peasants, soldiers and other lumpen elements let loose a reign of terror.

Their acts of unbriddled terror have striking similarities with those committed by Russian, Ukrainian and Polish peasants who took part in the anti-Jewish pogroms under local leadership believing their victims to be potential enemy agents—'pro-Polish' or 'pro-German' from the Russian point of view and 'pro-Russian' from the Ukrainian and Polish points of view.[52]

In sum, with the annihilation, mass expropriation and disclaimer of almost all the 'Biharis' of Bangladesh as citizens, they are today not longer components of the minorities in the country. They are, in a way, victims of nationalism—Pakistani as well as Bengali/ Bangladeshi, and subjected to persecution and discrimination.

---

[52] See for details Michael Aronson, *Troubled Waters: The Origins of the 1881; and Anti-Jewish Pogroms in Russia* (Pittsburgh, 1991); and John D. Klier, *Imperial Russia's Jewish Question, 1855-1881* (Cambridge, 1995).

Muslim Identity in the Balkans in the post-Ottoman Period

NATHALIE CLAYER
ALEXANDRE POPOVIC

The Muslim communities living in the Balkans were formed during the long Ottoman rule extending from a hundred and fifty to five hundred years, depending on the region, from the late fourteenth to the early twentieth century. These communities were formed after Turkish (or Turkish speaking) immigrants from Anatolia settled in the Balkans, other non-Turkish speaking Muslims (e.g. Tatars, Tcherkesses, etc.) migrated, and the local population in regions like Bosnia-Herzegovina, Albania, Crete, Macedonia, Bulgaria and Greece became Islamized.

At the end of the Ottoman rule, which occurred at very different times in different regions (between 1699 and 1912), these communities—or at least what remained of them after the fairly large-scale migration—found themselves living with the surrounding Christian (and other) communities in the following nation-states: Romania, Bulgaria, Yugoslavia, Greece and Albania (in Hungary, the Muslim community has disappeared completely). Except for Albania, everywhere else they have become a religious and/or an ethnic minority. Immersed in essentially Orthodox Christian, and possibly also Catholic, surroundings (as in Northern Albania, Bosnia-Herzegovina), they have lost the privileged status they enjoyed during the Ottoman period.

Such religious, economic, social and political changes could only have serious repercussions on the position of these Muslim peoples in twentieth-century Balkan society. Forced to define themselves in relation to their 'motherland' Turkey and the Muslim world, to the new states and, finally, to the surrounding Christian communities with whom they do not share the same vision of the (particularly Ottoman) past, they had to resort to manoeuvre or compromise or make certain choices, according to the circumstances. It will therefore be easily understood that their feelings regarding their identity changed from region to region and from time to time. A case study follows of the two most important Muslim groups in the Balkans at present: those of Bosnia-Herzegovina and the Albanian Muslims—two groups of native peoples who were converted to Islam. We will later make a rapid survey of the situation of other Muslims in the Balkans before drawing our conclusions.

THE MUSLIMS OF BOSNIA-HERZEGOVINA

For the Muslim population of Bosnia-Herzegovina, 'Muslim identity' is a complex and changing concept which (for historical and political reasons we shall try to explain later) they have had to modify constantly in order to adapt to the current situation. This has obliged their 'theoreticians' to expunge some established historical facts or falsify the past in order to present a 'new version' of Muslim identity in a *ne varietur* continuity, proving 'conclusively' and 'scientifically' (once more) the soundness of that new version.[1] It will however be easily understood that this Muslim identity was not perceived in the same manner by the concerned persons during the Ottoman and post-Ottoman periods.

During the Ottoman period (1463-1878), the Muslims of Bosnia-Herzegovina (a little more than one-third of the total population) perceived their Muslim identity at two levels as was usual during this period. Within the Muslim world (the Ottoman *umma* or the universal *umma*) they were known by their regional name, as Bosnians, just like the other Balkan Muslims, the Arnavoutes (Albanians) and the Pomaks (Bulgarian Muslims).[2] But to distinguish themselves from the surrounding non-Muslim world (in the Balkans and elsewhere), they called themselves 'Musulmans', using a single term to convey their religion and their ethnic group, or even their nationality. Since the latter did not exist as yet (in some regions and

---

[1] For example the top-ranking leaders of Bosnia-Herzegovina's Muslim religious community (not only the successive *Reis ul-Ulema* but also other high-ranking dignitaries) have been depicted after every change of direction (which obviously calls for a purge *a posteriori*), either as traitors to the community in the pay of the previous regime, or at best as senile, useless and incapable persons.

[2] It needs to be emphasized that the Pomaks of Bulgaria, the former Yugoslavian Macedonia and Greece have a specific name which distinguishes them immediately from their non-Muslim compatriots, which is not the case with Albanian Muslims or those of Bosnia-Herzegovina.

periods) or because, in the case of Muslims of the Ottoman Empire, it did not have any meaning, for a long time the words 'Musulman' and 'Turk' were generally synonymous.

Obviously, it was only after the fall of the Ottoman Empire and the setting up of Balkan nation-states in the nineteenth and twentieth centuries that things changed permanently (and painfully) for the Balkan Muslims and generally for those in South-Eastern Europe, obliging the theoreticians of Bosnia-Herzegovina to revise the concept of Muslim identity continually. Thus there were several different versions corresponding to five successive historical periods.

The Austro-Hungarian Period (1878-1918)

Occupied by the Austro-Hungarian Empire in keeping with t[h]e decisions of the Berlin Congress of 1878, Bosnia-Herzegovina [an]d its Muslim population (like the other peoples of these two regi[on]s[3]) lived under a 'double monarchy' for forty years. As Muslim id[ent]ity (based on a religious criterion) no longer sufficed a section [o]f the Muslims very rapidly declared themselves (or identified emot[io]nally as) 'Serbian Muslims'; some others called themselves 'Cr[oat]ian Muslims' while the majority called themselves just 'Musli[ms].[4] Subsequently, they were all helped in their search for nationality [to] a large extent by a political decision conceived and implemente[d] by B. Kallay,[5] finance minister of the two-headed monarchy and also a well-known historian, as explained by Branislav Djurdjev who writes:

[3] According to the official census of 1879, the total population of Bosnia-Herzegovina was 1,58,440, of whom 496,761 (42.86 per cent) were Orthodox Christians (Serbs), 448,613 (38.72 per cent) were Muslims and 209,391 (18.07 per cent) were Catholics (who would gradually end up calling themselves Croats). According to the 1910 census, the total population was 1,898,544 of whom 825,918 (43.49 per cent) were Orthodox Christians, 612,137 (32.25 per cent) were Muslims and 434,061 (22.87 per cent) were Catholics.

[4] It is quite reasonable to imagine that the last group contained, in addition to native Slav Muslims, a handful of other Muslims: Turks, Albanians, Gypsies, etc.

[5] To explain the reasons for the Islamization of a large part of the population of Bosnia-Herzegovina, Kallay also propounded the 'Bogomile Theory' which claims that in this case it was an 'ideological' choice (exercised immediately after the Ottoman conquest in the fifteenth century) made by the Bogomiles of Bosnia (a 'dualist heresy' of Paulician origin) who were persecuted by the Serbian Orthodox Church and the Catholic Church, and for whom the arrival of the Ottomans provided (finally!) an

In order to maintain Bosnia and Herzegovina as two separate bodies within the dual monarchy, and to put an end to the spread of Serbian and Croatian nationalism, Kallay tried to create a 'Bosnian nation' and a 'Bosnian language'. But this policy did not succeed (at that time) in winning over a sufficient number of followers among the native population, because the Serbs and the Croats had already acquired a national awareness, and the majority of Muslims of 'undeclared nationality' considered Turkey as their motherland. Besides, a large number of Muslim families had always invoked the sovereign rights of the Ottoman Sultan over Bosnia and Herzegovina. There was only a small number of Muslim intellectuals and landowners who adopted the cause of Bosnian nationalism.[6]

We must also add that during this period (more precisely after 1906), the first Muslim political parties of Bosnia-Herzegovina were created under the leadership of the important local landowners. The latter began to act as a counterbalance to the Ulema and contributed in large measure to making more complex, for the Muslims of Bosnia-Herzegovina, the perception of their Muslim identity. It was all the more complex because from then on these party leaders naturally took part with gusto in the one-upmanship with the political parties of the other two religious groups of these two regions, allying themselves with them when the need arose, or with the Austro-Hungarian authorities, thus blending in an unprecedented manner the strictly religious with 'nationalist' and 'ethnic' loyalties.

The Kingdom of Yugoslavia (1918-41)

As the very name of the new state created on 1 December 1918 indicates ('Kingdom of Serbs, Croats and Slovenes' which later became the 'Kingdom of Yugoslavia'), the only chance it gave the Muslims of Bosnia-Herzegovina to identify themselves[7] was through a compulsory option: they could opt either for the Serbian nation

---

unexpected opportunity. Cf. B. Djurdjev, 'Bosna', *Encyclopédie de l'Islam*, s.v., t.I, p. 1304 (of the French edition) and T. Kraljacic, *Kalajev rezim u Bosni i Hercegovini (1882-1903)* (Sarajevo, 1987), pp. 80ff.

[6] B. Djurdjev, p. 1313. The details regarding this concept, its launching and the reasons it was abandoned a few years later, can be found in the information gleaned from the personal diary and notes of B. Kallay in T. Kraljacic, *Kalajev rezim*, pp. 186-201, 210ff and 272ff.

[7] During these twenty years, the Muslims represented 31 per cent, the Orthodox Christians 44 per cent and the Catholics 24 per cent of the total population of Bosnia-Herzegovina.

or the Croatian nation. The Muslims in these regions (and most of all the local intelligentsia) were courted by the Greater Serbia and Greater Croatia movements and books entitled *Famous Serbian Muslims* and *Famous Croatian Muslims* containing the biographies of these persons were published. In this changed situation, many Muslims in Bosnia-Herzegovina continued to call themselves Serbs of Muslim faith, while others called themselves Croats of Muslim faith. A third group desperately tried to bypass this absurd situation by calling themselves 'Yugoslav Muslims'.[8]

Two other phenomena concerning this period must also be mentioned. First, there was greater cohesion between the three different religious communities of Bosnia-Herzegovina than between the Muslims of Bosnia-Herzegovina and those of Eastern Yugoslavia (the Albanian, Turkish and Slav Muslims of Kosovo and Macedonia) as revealed by the Yugoslav Muslim press of the period. Also there was a total separation between the various Muslim political parties of these two groups. At the same time a new 'pan-Islamist' current emerged among the Muslims of Bosnia-Herzegovina (in addition to the two 'customary' currents seen in the entire Muslim world at the end of the nineteenth century, namely, the 'traditionalist' and 'reformist', already seen in Bosnia-Herzegovina during the Austro-Hungarian period) which crystallized in 1941 in an organization called 'Mladi Muslimani' (Young Muslims). Its members later (long after the organization was dismantled by the Communist government in 1946 and 1949) played a significant role in the 're-Islamization' (from about 1970 onwards) of a section of the Muslim population of Bosnia-Herzegovina and the Sandjak region of Novi Pazar, as also in the 'politicization of Islam' and the 'Islamization of politics' which followed.[9]

World War II (1941-45)

During these five years, several new phenomena deeply influenced Muslim identity in Bosnia-Herzegovina.

On the one hand, a major section took an active part in the affairs

[8] For more details regarding this period, cf. A. Popovic, *L'Islam balkanique. Les musulmans du sud-est européen dans la période post-ottomane* (Berlin-Wiesbaden, 1986), pp. 312-36.

[9] Cf. on this subject, X., Bougarel, 'Un courant panislamiste en Bosnie-Herzégovine', in Gilles Kepel (ed.), *Exils et royaumes. Les appartenances au monde arabo-musulman aujourd'hui* (Paris, 1944), pp. 275-99.

of the fascist state created by Hitler's Germany and in the mass killing (several hundred thousand) of Orthodox Serbs of the region. The 'Tchetniks', a group of Serbs belonging to the pro-royalist and anti-Communist underground, retaliated by destroying Muslim towns and villages. On the other hand, all the existing Muslim political parties disappeared and then formed within the community two diametrically opposite camps (leaving out the 'silent majority' and several minor groups):

(a) Those Muslims who had collaborated openly, either with the fascist Croatian government, or directly with the German authorities to the extent of enroling not only in various policing agencies and local militias but also (under the influence of Amin al-Huseini, Mufti of Jerusalem) in regular military units (including the 'SS', like the 'Handjar' division) to fight in Bosnia-Herzegovina and on the Soviet front; and

(b) Those who joined the 'partisan' armed forces to fight under the orders of the Communist Party against the occupation forces and local ideological enemies.

The following tactics were adopted at the time by the leaders of these two camps against the Muslims of Bosnia-Herzegovina. As far as the Oustachis (the Croatian fascists) were concerned, the Muslims of Croatia (and therefore also those of Bosnia-Herzegovina) had to be considered as Croats—they were even called in the then prevalent terminology 'the flower of the Croatian nation'. As regards the leaders of the Yugoslav Communist Party, it had to attain two major goals: first, it had to make sure (according to the prevailing Soviet model) that the local Muslims were considered not a religious group but an 'ethnic' group. This gave rise to the idea that the religious component should be relegated to the background or obscured right from the beginning; second, it had to reassure the local civilian Muslim population by refraining from offending their religious sentiments and by pretending to believe that, strictly speaking, it was more a matter of 'customs' than religious practices.

Finally, for reasons that are not easy to understand, the Muslim religious functionaries who took part in the armed anti-fascist struggle within the ranks of the 'partisans' were small in number, while it was not so in the case of those belonging to various pro-German and Oustachi civilian and military organizations. This explains why many Muslim religious functionaries and members of the Muslim religious intelligentsia of Bosnia-Herzegovina (most of whom were subsequently pardoned) spent some time (even a few years) in prison after 1945.

Communist Yugoslavia (1945-92)

Evidently, the manipulation of the 'Muslim identity' of the Muslims of Bosnia-Herzegovina reached its highest point under the Communist dictatorship, because it was possible to impose a 'scientific, general, compulsory and clear-cut' line of conduct on the entire population. There were many reasons for this.

The first was that the Tito government had to find an effective remedy to counter the formidable religious revival because, as in other Eastern countries, in Yugoslavia too religion was the only 'legal' means of asserting the strength and the aspirations of local nationalistic sentiments.[10] What did this religious revival correspond to in the case of the Muslims of Bosnia-Herzegovina? The principal factor was the strong religious sentiment of the Muslim population and the need for religion in urban and rural areas. Another factor, no less important, was the need to assert local nationalism which, for the Muslim inhabitants of Bosnia-Herzegovina, could refer only to Islam, a term which was coloured either with secularistic socialism or to a lesser extent with religiosity.

Two other factors, both equally important, must be underlined. There was a combination of complex circumstances, created by several long-standing problems like the multiplicity of religions and nationalities and aggravated by a precarious economic condition. The Tito government tried to exploit the situation by employing a national, ethnic and even religious solution to regulate the distribution of government jobs and to keep a close watch over the country's entire population. This was followed by a certain number of political options judged advantageous by the Tito government at a particular time in order to play a leading role in the bloc of 'non-aligned' countries dominated by Muslim states. This led to the official recognition in 1967 of the 'Muslim' nation of Bosnia-Herzegovina as distinct from the 'religious' Muslim community. At the same time, since the new situation was likely to create problems for the non-practising, secular and atheist local population (the Communists), it was 'scientifically' explained that in Bosnia-Herzegovina 'Muslim' did

[10] Cf. Patrick Michel (ed.), *Les Religions à l'Est* (Paris, 1992).

not mean belonging to a religiously defined community but 'a meaning totally different and far from the original'.[11]

It goes without saying that the 'Muslims' of Bosnia-Herzegovina (and all leaders of the Muslim religious community) seized the opportunity to make the most of the ambiguity of the new situation, constantly trying to confuse the two terms (just like the leaders of the Communist Party, but in the opposite direction!). Once the new situation became official (if not consecrated), there followed a spate of publications in which a multitude of writers (both believers and atheists), often starting from diametrically opposite premises invariably ended up by recognizing the indisputable existence of a Muslim nation of Bosnia-Herzegovina which excluded other Yugoslav Muslims (Albanians, Turks, Macedonians, Gypsies, etc.).[12]

Many other events have a bearing on the 'history of Muslims' of Bosnia-Herzegovina, among them the flowering of Islamic religious radicalism, which directly concerns the problem of the 'Muslim identity'. As a matter of fact, it seems perfectly clear from the analysis of Xavier Bougarel (1993 and 1994) that two distinct groups served as a vehicle for Islamic religious radicalism: the leaders of the Muslim community of Bosnia-Herzegovina of the Tito period and an infinitely more radical group formed by the true 'Apostles of Islam', whose core consists of a few survivors of the 'Young Muslims' of the past and the present president of Bosnia-Herzegovina and leader of the major Muslim political party (*Savez Democratske Akcije, S.D.A.* or 'Union for Democratic Action'), Mr. Alija Izetbegovic. This group which tries in the most explicit manner to re-Islamize the entire Muslim population of Bosnia-Herzegovina, openly spews out venom [see X. Bougarel's articles and two 'theoretical' works by Mr. A. Izetbegovic, *La déclaration islamique* (1970) and *L'Islam entre l'Est et l'Ouest* (1980)] not only against past leaders (all considered to be in the pay of the Tito government and earlier governments) and the non-religious, secular and atheist Muslim intellectuals of Bosnia-Herzegovina, but also (an argument we have frequently heard in some other Muslim countries) 'Western' secularism and democracy accused of all the present misfortunes of the Muslim world.

---

[11] Cf. Atif Purivatra, *Nacionalni i politicki razvitak Muslimana* (Sarajevo, 1969), p. 5.

[12] The most complete work of this type (and in our opinion the most serious and honest) is the one by Muhamed Hadzijahic, *Od tradicije do identiteta. Geneza nacionalnog pitanja bosanskih Muslimana* (Sarajevo, 1974), vol. 1, p. 264.

After April 1992

For a variety of reasons, the numerical proportions of the three religious groups in Bosnia-Herzegovina changed during the preceding period. When the civil war broke out in Bosnia-Herzegovina in April 1992, their population stood at: 44 per cent 'Muslim', 33 per cent Orthodox Christian (Serb) and 18 per cent Catholic (Croat). This new situation and the consequences of the war have once again radically modified the notion of Muslim identity among the Muslims and the 'Muslims' of Bosnia-Herzegovina, impelling religious and political leaders of these two groups to seek new options and mystifications. The explanation briefly is as follows.

The first free elections in Bosnia-Herzegovina after World War II led to the defeat of the Communist Party and the victory of the newly formed Muslim Political Party which brought together in a 'holy union' all the existing tendencies. Shortly afterwards and well before Alija Izetbegovic, the main accused in the famous Sarajevo trial of 1983 (then sentenced to fifteen years imprisonment) became the new president of Bosnia-Herzegovina, this Muslim political party split into several factions. The main factions could be described as 'religious', 'secular' and 'leftist'. The leftist branch was rapidly dissolved (but it probably continued underground), while the 'secular' branch after officially withdrawing from the political scene has reappeared in diverse and complex incarnations. So, the 'religious' branch of Alija Izetbegovic's 'Union for Democratic Action' (SDA) has been in power since then.

This new 'continuity with change' has given rise to a new version of 'Muslim identity' in Bosnia-Herzegovina. Having realized the disadvantages of the excessively long 'underhand collaboration' with the dying Tito regime in Yugoslavia and the 'Muslim Nation', the new Muslim leadership has decided to solemnly reject the so-called 'Muslim nationality' (naturally claiming that it was forced on them by the previous Communist rule!), and to henceforth make themselves known (for obvious political reasons) to western international institutions as 'Bosnians', returning thereby to the postulates formulated almost a century ago by the Austro-Hungarian authorities.[13] That is where matters stand at present.[14]

---

[13] It is instructive to read at this juncture, from this new point of view, the numerous official publications of Bosnia-Herzegovina's major Muslim theoreticians of the 'Muslim Nation' of the Tito period, e.g. Mustafa Imamovic's *Muslimani spram Bosnjyastva* 'The

II

What, then, can be said about the true feelings of Bosnia-Herzegovina's Muslims about their identity? Quite naturally, these feelings are complex and change according to individual personalities; each personality has multiple facets consisting of religious and/or secular sentiments which are intricately mixed with the feeling of belonging to a particular region, family, culture and ideology. This is, furthermore, complicated by the absence of a specific name that would designate this category of the population in a simple and precise manner.

THE ALBANIAN MUSLIMS

The case of the Albanian Muslims is different in many respects from that of their coreligionists in Bosnia-Herzegovina. Their version of Islam has different characteristics. Further, since the eighteenth and nineteenth centuries, they are more numerous than Albanian Catholics and Orthodox Christians[15] and, unlike the Croats and Serbs in Bosnia-Herzegovina, they have never had a neighbouring country which they could identify with (except for some Orthodox Christians who tend to lean towards Greece).[16] However, just as the Muslims

---

Muslims confronted by Bosnism' which appeared in the official cultural review of the time and set the tone and the 'final official line to be followed', *Knjizevna Revija*, Sarajevo, Aug.-Sept. 1990, pp. 8-9 and 13 where it is said 'Just as "Bosnism" (Bosnjastvo) is an outdated term to define the Muslims [of Bosnia-Herzegovina] at the national level, similarly for the majority of inhabitants of Bosnia-Herzegovina, their faith notwithstanding, this term is unacceptable as a common national name for the future!' Cf. an excellent analysis of this phenomenon by Darko Tanaskovic, *Hercegovina of Srednjeg Veka do novijeg vremena* (Belgrade, 1995), pp. 47-56, where further details and a more developed bibliography are available.

[14] Let us add that at long last a final variation of this new denomination seems to have made an appearance a short while ago, viz., the use of the term 'Bosnian Muslims'.

[15] The Islamization of Albanians was a slow and gradual process which picked up in the seventeenth century in Northern Albania and after the eighteenth century in Southern Albania. At the end of the Ottoman period, about 70 per cent of Albanians had been converted to Islam.

[16] Many Orthodox Albanian-speaking people took part in the struggle for the creation of a Greek state at the beginning of the nineteenth century, or were later attracted by Greece and/or by Hellenism due to their common religion. As regards the position of the Orthodox Christians and the Catholics in the newly created Albanian state, it is interesting to note that in 1920, after the upheaval caused by World

of Bosnia-Herzegovina share their language with the Serbs and Croats, the Albanian Muslims speak the same language as their Catholic and Orthodox compatriots. In addition to political factors which were generally underestimated, language was one of the main vehicles of unification which led to the creation of an Albanian state and nation.[17]

Very few studies have so far been devoted to this question of the Muslim identity of Albanian Muslims because there was an attempt to create the impression that it was a question of secondary importance. As a matter of fact, this question has often given rise to cliches derived from the slogans coined by nationalists in the late nineteenth and early twentieth centuries like 'an Albanian is an Albanian before being a Muslim or a Christian' or 'the Albanians' religion is Albanianism',[18] inciting the Albanian people to set aside existing religious divisions. While rejecting this paradigm we will consider how the Muslim identity of Albanian Muslims is reflected since the late nineteenth century. In order to do so, we will take into account the diversity of Albanian Islam and the disparity between different socio-political contexts. Divided earlier between two states[19]—Albania and Yugoslavia—and today between three states—Albania, the 'new' Yugoslavia—and the Republic of Macedonia—the Albanian Muslims have lived since the beginning of this century and continue to live in different political, economic and social environments in these two (and now three) countries.

If one goes back to the end of the Ottoman period when there was no border separating the Albanian Muslims from one another,

---

War I, the Orthodox and Catholic Churches declared themselves in favour of a non-centralized cantonal state. Bernhard Tönnes, *Sonderfall Albanien* (Munchen, 1980), p. 345; Michael Schmidt-Neke, *Entstehung und Ausbau der Königsdiktatur in Albanien (1912-1939)* (Munchen, 1987), p. 75.

[17] On the Albanian national awakening, see the excellent study by Stavro Skendi, *The Albanian National Awakening* (Princeton, 1967).

[18] The latter slogan was taken from a poem written by Pasha (or Pashko) Vasa Efendi, an Albanian Catholic who was a senior official in the Ottoman Government. Here are a few lines from the poem: 'Albanians! you are killing your brother/ You are divided into a hundred parties/ One says I am a Christian, another says I am a Muslim/ One: I am a Turk, the other: I am a Latin (Catholic)/ Some say: I am a Greek, Slavs say some others/. . ./Awake Albanians from your sleep/ Don't pay attention to churches and mosques/ The Albanians' religion is Albanianism.' S. Skendi, *The Albanian National Awakening*, pp. 169-70.

[19] Until the end of World War II, there were Albanian Muslims also in Greece (to

they were still far from being a homogenous group. The most important 'dividing line' was between the Sunnis and the Bektachis. The latter belonged to a *tarîkat*, a mystic Muslim brotherhood from Central Anatolia[20] who followed an extremely heterodox and syncretic doctrine. The Bektach brotherhood, already established at some places in the Albanian territory since the middle of the nineteenth century, gained many followers among the Albanians, especially in the southern half of the present Albania and also further north, particularly in the Kruja, Martanesh, Tetovo (in Macedonia) and Djakovica (in Kosovo) regions.[21] Other more or less visible 'dividing lines' were created by various peculiarities: ethnic peculiarities (between two Albanian ethnic sub-groups—the Gegs in the north, in Kosovo and in the major portion of Macedonia, and the Tosks in the south);[22] regional peculiarities (in the Dibra region, for example); and peculiarities related to clans (in the mountains in the north of the present Albania), without forgetting the social disparities (from the beys who were big landlords to the shepherds in the mountains and the officials in the Ottoman Government). Besides, since Islamization was an on-going process at the time, there were Muslim groups who had been Islamized quite recently, which gave rise to some crypto-Christian groups.[23] It is easy to imagine that in this context the sentiments of Albanian Muslims regarding their

---

the south of the border between Greece and Albania). They were known as Cams (Tchams) or Tsamides. There are only a handful of them today, the majority having taken refuge in Albania or having perished at the end of World War II. On this subject, see Pierre-Yves Péchoux and Michel Sivignon, 'L'éviction des Tchamides d'Epire occidentale en 1944', *L'ethnographie*, 85/2, 1989, pp. 113-19. It should be noted that there are still some Orthodox Albanian-speaking groups in the same region as in other parts of Greece.

[20] On Bektachism, see A. Popovic and G. Veinstein (eds.), *Bektachiya. Etudes sur l'ordre mystique des Bektachis et les groupes relevant de Hadji Bektach* (Istanbul, 1995).

[21] On Bektachism in Albania, see N. Clayer, *L'Albanie, pays des derviches* (Berlin-Wiesbaden, 1990); on its spread in Macedonia and Kosovo, see F.W. Hasluck, *Christianity and Islam under the Sultans* (Oxford, 1929), pp. 523-5; and also the contributions of Nimetullah Hafiz and Liliana Masulovic-Marsol, in *Bektachiyya*.

[22] The line dividing these two sub-groups is generally drawn along the river Shkumbi which passes through the town of Elbasan in Central Albania. The Gegs and the Tosks differ from each other on many counts: linguistic, historic, cultural, social and even religious. As a matter of fact, the majority of Gegs are Sunni Muslims and Catholics while the majority of Tosks are Orthodox and Bektachis.

[23] There were crypto-Christians mainly in Central Albania (in the Elbasan region),

identity were extremely varied. This diversity was reflected very precisely in the key period which witnessed the Albanian national awakening at the end of the nineteenth century and in the early twentieth century, i.e. in the years that preceded and followed the creation of an Albanian state in 1912-13.

Actually, among the Albanian Muslims, the members of the Bektachi brotherhood took a clear stand during the national awakening. They played an active role in its promotion by distributing books and periodicals in the Albanian language among their compatriots, by teaching them to read and write their mother tongue, by promoting the Roman script and by supporting from 1905 to 1906 the armed guerilla action (çeta).[24] At the same time, the spread of Bektachism among the Albanian population was unprecedented. It appears that this version of 'non-conformist' Islam evolved in response to a peculiar political and social situation where some groups among the Albanian population were not tolerated. This reveals the ability of Bektachism to 'refuse the established order' and revolt. In fact, there was a strong opposition in these regions to the central government after it brought to heel the prominent citizens of the area in 1830, and later tried to enforce the reforms of *tanzimat*. After 1878, 'Albanian Bektachism' distanced itself from 'Turkish Bektachism' because, owing to its syncretic nature, it rallied to its beliefs a constituent of the Albanian nationalist movement.

The attitude adopted some years later by a large number of Muslims (Sunnis) of central Albania denotes a totally different assertion of identity. They revolted in 1914-15 following the constitution of an independent Albanian Principality under the Christian Prince of Wied. The insurgents, probably incited by the Young Turks and other governments interested in destabilizing the newly-born political entity, declared that they wanted to join the Ottoman Empire or at least have an Ottoman Prince appointed under the suzerainty of the Sultan, according to the Shariah. As for the rest, the Bektachis were their main adversaries and they destroyed many of their institutions.

---

in the Lurja region (near Dibra) and in some parts of Kosovo and Macedonia where there were Albanians who had recently emigrated from the mountains of North Albania and who had been converted to Islam on their arrival in the plains or shortly afterwards.

[24] N. Clayer, 'Bektachisme et nationalisme albanais', in A. Popovic and G. Veinstein (eds.), *Bektachiyya. Etudes sur l'ordre mystique des Bektachis et les groupes relevant de Hadji Bektach* (Istanbul, 1995), p. 281.

The split between the Sunnis and the Bektachis was recognized de facto on the political plane when Albania was reorganized in the 1920 following World War I: a High Regency Council of four prominent citizens was formed consisting of a Sunni Muslim, an Orthodox Christian, a Catholic and a Bektachi Muslim.[25] Besides, as far as the administration and leadership of Albanian Muslims were concerned, there was also an unofficial separation between the Sunni and Bektachi communities. Further, even within the Sunni community, several currents emerged: the traditionalists (especially in the northern half of the country among the Gegs, particularly in Shkordra and in the Kavaje, Tirana and Elbasan regions) and the reformists (especially among the Tosks and the Dibrans). It is also necessary to underline the existence of an important Sufi current.[26] The reformists, who took over the community's reins, tried to make it accept the reforms launched by the Albanian government[27] who gave the country a secular constitution, abolished the Shariah and adopted a Civil Code in 1928, and stopped religious instruction in schools for some time. Nevertheless, it seems that in reality things had not changed much as compared to the Ottoman period and the great disparities persisted, not only between Sunnis and Bektachis, but also between Muslims of different regions in the country: some continued to react primarily, as Muslims, e.g. with hostility to King Zog's marriage to a Christian, others gave priority to their regional or clan identity, while still others (notably the Bektachis) insisted on their national identity.

The Communist period (1944-92), on the contrary, had severe repercussions on religious identities in Albania. After 1967 all forms of religion were banned and religious practices and worship and even names having a Christian or Muslim connotation were forbidden. In these circumstances, religious feelings weakened and they could not develop among the younger generation, except in

---

[25] The country's four main religious groups were not represented proportionately in the High Council because in a total population 830,000, there were approximately 55 per cent Sunni Muslims, 20 per cent Orthodox Christians, 15 per cent Bektachis and 10 per cent Catholics (the figures usually cited do not count the Sunni Muslims and Bektachis separately).

[26] Different brotherhoods were established in the country: first and foremost, the Halvetiyye in the South, the Centre and the North-East, but also the Kadiriyye, Rifaiyye, Sadiyye, Tidjaniyye, Djelvetiyye and Güsheniyye.

[27] It must be noted that the government was dominated by the beys or big landlords.

certain circles or families which managed to secretly keep alive some elements of their tradition. It would be wrong to believe that religious identities (both Christian and Muslim) were eradicated in Albania, the only country in the world to have an officially atheist government. The situation following the reopening of places of worship at the end of 1990 illustrates this fact.

It is certain that many Albanian Muslims—Sunni and Bektachi—have not started practising their religion (or their parents' religion) in the changed circumstances after the fall of the Communist regime. Many young people do not know what it means to believe in God. But they are all aware of their religious origins, including the Bektachis, which shows that this mystic brotherhood has become a full-fledged religious community in Albania. Yet awareness of belonging to a particular community should not be confused with feelings about religious identity. Some have already embraced Christianity in spite of their Muslim lineage, others are making an effort to understand Islam (Sunni or Bektachi) and practise it while yet others remain atheists or agnostics. Logically, it would appear that the Muslim identity would be stronger in the old strongholds of traditional Sunni Islam in northern and central Albania (Shkoder, Durres, Kavaje and Tirana). It is also more noticeable among those who were born before the establishment of Communist rule. It is also more visible in the rural areas than in cities (except of Shkoder, Durres and Kavaje). Muslim identity is also more pronounced in the families of former Ulemas and Sheikhs who hope to regain their position in society.

Faced with the desertion by a large part of the Muslim population and the propaganda of different Christian sects, the cadres of the Sunni and Bektachi Muslim communities have sought to combine national (ethnic) and religious identities by explaining that the degree of love for the country depends on devotion and faith. Sunni leaders have resorted to a theory which claims that Albanians embraced Islam to preserve their ethnic and national identity when threatened with assimilation by the Greeks and Slavs.[28] The president of the

---

[28] N. Clayer, 'Identité nationale et identité religieuse chez les musulmans albanais', in: Michel Bozdémir (ed.), Islam et laïcité. Approches globales et régionales (Paris, 1996), pp. 137-49. It is to be noted that these same Sunni leaders tend to deny at present that the Albanian Bektachis are entitled to a separate identity. They think that there is only one Muslim community to which all Albanian Muslims belong, without taking into account the important doctrinal differences of the Bektachis.

Association of Muslim Intellectuals said in reply to a journalist that the idea of establishing the association came from a group of Albanian intellectuals 'firmly convinced of the positive role of the Muslim religion throughout history in the formation of the collective and individual identity of the Albanian people'.[29]

In the political domain, the right-wing nationalist party (Party of the Democratic Right) and its leader Abdi Baleta (former Albanian ambassador at the United Nations during the Communist regime) did not hesitate to take up these questions. Abdi Baleta declared, 'Islamization occurred as a natural historical process; it had lasting historical, religious, ethnologic and even national consequences for the Albanians. Islam has become an internal characteristic in the psychological makeup of Albanian Muslims and the Albanian national identity.'[30]

At the state level, President Sali Berisha, who himself has descended from a Muslim family from north-eastern Albania, did not hesitate to make Albania a member of the Islamic Conference in 1992. Although he has been received by the Pope and close ties have been formed with Italy, Germany and the United States, his action has given Albania a Muslim identity to a certain extent. At least, that is how it is viewed by a section of public opinion in Albania which has severely criticised the decision. The religious revival has triggered off a debate in Albanian society and its main theme is the country's position between the East and the West. The 'Muslim' arguments are naturally not acceptable to Albanian Christians or atheists who are bent on turning to the West. From their point of view, Muslim identity is not conterminous with the Albanian identity.[31]

III

The situation of Albanian Muslims living at present in the 'new' Yugoslavia, i.e. in Kosovo and Montenegro and also in the Republic of Macedonia, is quite different in several respects from that of their

[29] *Dituria Islame*, vol. X, no. 72, Prishtinë, Sept. 1995, p. 2.

[30] *Drita Islame*, vol. VI, no. 2 (63), Tirana, February 1995, p. 4; *Dituria Islame*, vol. X, no.71, Prishtinë, August 1995, p. 39.

[31] N. Clayer, 'Islam, State and Society in Post-communist Albania', to be published in Suha Taji-Farouki and Hugh Poulton *Muslim Identity and the Balkan States* (Hurst: London).

coreligionists in Albania. Since the demarcation of borders has left them outside the Albanian state, they are an ethnic and political minority in a region dominated by Slavs, but part of a vast majority of Albanians who find themselves in this situation together with some Catholics and Bektachis and a handful of Orthodox Christians. Their ethnic and religious identities are therefore closely bound in these areas. The Albanians were Muslims, Islam was a part of their ethnic identity and the Muslims were first and foremost Albanians. It has been seen that their relations with the Slav Muslims of Bosnia-Herzegovina remained distant. Besides, following the return of a large number of Turks to Turkey, Albanian Muslims have become a predominant component of the Muslim communities of Kosovo and Macedonia. This is responsible for the continuation of a process which started in these regions during Ottoman rule: the Albanization of a section of local Muslims.

As in Albania, the setting up of a Communist regime in Yugoslavia affected the religious freedom of Albanian Muslims just like the other ethnic and religious groups. However, from the 1970s, the Communists became more flexible in this regard. Sufi networks became stronger as a result, especially in Kosovo, and a process of re-Islamization started. It does not seem that the Muslim identity of the Albanians of Kosovo was directly reflected in the troubles which broke out in this region in 1981.[32] The list of demands was of a nationalist, not religious, nature. Since then the situation has changed. Political upheavals have led to the suppression of the autonomous status of Kosovo province, the separation of Yugoslavia from the other predominantly Muslim region of Bosnia-Herzegovina, whose Ulema had until then dominated the highest organs of the Yugoslav Muslim community, and the establishment of the independent Republic of Macedonia. A new generation of religious leaders fresh from Islamic Universities in Arab countries occupied the top ranks of the restructured Muslim communities within new political organizations. On hearing the arguments of these Muslim leaders, it would appear that we are witnessing the same phenomenon as in Albania: a constant attempt to promote a Muslim identity among the Albanian population by making it correspond to the national identity by explaining that it is one of the key elements. This strategy, whose main aim is to re-Islamize the Albanian

[32] Cf. A. Popovic, *L'islam balkanique . . .* , p. 359.

population, has been more successful in these regions than in Albania. As a matter of fact, in Kosovo as in Macedonia, the political trial of strength between the Albanians (the majority of whom are Muslims) and the Orthodox Serbs and Macedonians makes this combination of nationalism and religion more effective than in Albania where Albanian Muslims are faced with other Christian and atheist Albanians.[33]

IV

As for the other Balkan Muslim groups (Turk, Pomak, Torbesh, Gypsy), each case presents certain peculiarities as compared with Muslims of Bosnia-Herzegovina and Macedonia. For the Turks, who have a motherland (Turkey), Muslim identity generally seems less important that their ethnic and Turkish national identity to which it is linked more closely when there is a high degree of religiosity. But for the Pomak and Torbesh, it is the Muslim identity which is preponderant most of the time as it distinguishes them from Christians, Bulgarians or Macedonians. In the case of Muslim Gypsies, the problem is still different.

Without entering into the details about these diverse groups, in the light of what has been said in the preceding pages it can be asserted that Muslim identity is for all of them a complex and changing concept. It depends on the groups themselves, but also on the political and social climate in which they live, and on the country and the period of time. In the first place, Muslim identity depends on religiosity or else on religious affiliation, or on belonging to a community of Muslim descendants who have become more of less secular. Even in the case of a very widespread religiosity, re-Islamization is always possible because religious Muslims always try to attract secular Muslims to the 'common abode'.

But Muslim identity is also a product of factors imposed on these communities, either by their own religious or political leaders, or by the state to which they belong, or by the surrounding population, or even by fundamentalist movements sweeping the Islamic world (pan-Islamism, radicalism, fundamentalism, or the pan-Turkish movement). Thus Muslim identity will be strengthened by the rise of nationalistic sentiments among local non-Muslim populations as

[33] Cf. N. Clayer, 'Identité nationale . . .'.

these sentiments generally have a religious facet (Christian or anti-Muslim) and a totally different vision of the past, especially of the Ottoman period.

Even if it is advisable to differentiate each of these ethnic groups in each Balkan state, certain general tendencies can be observed in the entire Balkan zone during the successive phases that followed the dismantling of the Ottoman Empire. In the years immediately after the disintegration, the Balkan Muslims (except the Albanian Bektachis) clung to the Muslim component of their identity. With the coming to power in the early 1920s of Mustafa Kemal Ataturk in a secular and reformist Turkey, a similar trend was at work among the Balkan Muslims. In the early 1940s, small pan-Islamist groups or those advocating an Islamic revival were born all over the area. But soon World War II broke out and the Communists came to power in all Balkan countries except Greece. Muslim identity was disguised in a non-religious garb. It became, even more than before, a communal, ethnic and even national identity in the case of Bosnia-Herzegovina, following the establishment of a 'Muslim nation'. However, for the last twenty years in Yugoslavia, and more recently elsewhere, the influence of Islamist movements from the rest of the Muslim world is evident and re-Islamization is taking place. This phenomenon is associated today with the flare-up of nationalist sentiments and Muslim leaders are trying on the one hand to re-Islamize their communities and, on the other, to respond to the nationalist sentiments of non-Muslims. The latter often invoke the danger of a 'green axis', which will bind together the various Muslim groups in the Balkans right from Turkey to Bosnia-Herzegovina and passing through Albania. This would amount to ignoring the peculiarities of each of these groups whose feelings about identity cannot be so easily reduced to a strictly religious one.

Bosnia in the Annals of Partition: From Divide and Rule to Divide and Quit

RADHA KUMAR

When the Yugoslav federation began to disintegrate in the late 1980s, most analysts were concerned that the ethnonational principle on which representatives were claiming independence might spark a partition war in Bosnia because, like Macedonia, it did not have a clear ethnic majority-minority division. It was instead defined as comprising three 'constituent nations', Muslims, Serbs and Croats.[1] Subsequent events were to prove these fears well-founded, but even then few envisaged how prolonged and bitter the conflict would be, or that in the end the partition for which the war was fought would remain undecided as peace was established. Fewer still thought that an international intervention, when it came, would end by itself espousing partition as the most satisfactory of a set of highly unsatisfactory solutions.

Describing the Partition of India in 1947, the historian and former civil servant Penderel Moon summarized the British role in pushing Partition through without establishing the boundaries of the new states or planning for the wars which might ensue as 'divide and quit'.[2] The phrase followed on an earlier description of the partition

---

*This paper is, in some ways, outside the scope of this volume. It is, however, included to serve as a background, especially for readers in the subcontinent, to the other contributions on Yugoslavia and its fragmentation. Moreover, as India and Pakistan celebrate fifty years of their independence, the theme of Radha Kumar's paper would surely interest those social scientists who are engaged in exploring the roots of India's Partition.—*Editor*

[1] The Muslims were recognized by Titoist Yugoslavia as a 'nation' in 1974. Communist Yugoslavia espoused a watered down version of the Leninist definition of nations/nationalities as well as the Soviet institutionalization of a nationality policy combining some degree of self-administration (in autonomous territories) with some degree of demographic engineering (the strategic placement of autonomous territories).

[2] Penderel Moon, *Divide and Quit* (London, 1961).

of Bengal in 1905 as 'divide and rule'.[3] Both phrases underline the role of the colonial power and point to the fact that decisions to divide are most commonly impelled by considerations which have little to do with the needs or desires of the people who are to be divided. This truism of the history of twentieth-century partitions has acquired a new twist in the Bosnian partition war which began with the avowed divide and rule intentions of the Presidents of Serbia and Croatia—Slobodan Milosevic and Franjo Tudjman—but ended with the international community's adoption of what was essentially a British colonial formula of divide and quit. This shift from regional divide and rule ambitions to international divide and quit policies, and the accompanying intensification of communalism[4] in Bosnian society and politics, are the subject of this paper.

I do not intend to imply that the partition of Bosnia is a *fait accompli*. It is not certain that Bosnia will in fact be partitioned; indeed, there are signs that the shift from divide and rule to divide and quit might in itself portend a move away from partition. The thwarting of Croatian and Serbian ambitions to divide and rule Bosnia, which grew to be one of the aims of the international community's involvement in the region, also challenges the core of divide and quit, because it asks who will then keep the division in place. In other words, the moot point is whether there can be divide and quit without divide and rule.

The war in Bosnia began with an episode of the kind which has commonly prefaced the outbreak of communal violence in India. On 1 March 1992, as a Serbian Orthodox wedding procession wound its way through the old Muslim section of Sarajevo known as Bascarsija, the wedding guests brandished Serb flags. This was interpreted by Muslims as an act of deliberate provocation at a time when the republic had just held a referendum on independence, and the majority of Bosnian Croats and Muslims had voted for independence while the majority of Bosnian Serbs had boycotted the referendum. Unidentified gunmen opened fire on the procession

---

[3] As Home Secretary Risley frankly confessed in 1904, 'divide and rule' was an important motive in the plan to partition. Sumit Sarkar, *Modern India* (Delhi, 1983), p. 107.

[4] As used in the Indian context, to mean conflict based on religious identity.

and the groom's father-in-law was killed and an Orthodox priest wounded. The Bosnian Serb leader Momcilo Krajisnik, then Speaker of the Bosnian Parliament, declared the shots were 'a great injustice aimed at the Serb people', and barricades went up overnight all over Sarajevo.[5] Barricades had gone up only a few days earlier, after the referendum, but had been dismantled by the police. This time joint patrols of the Bosnian police and the Jugoslav National Army (JNA) persuaded people to dismantle them.

Less than a month later, fighting began in a small town on the Bosnia-Croatia border called Bosanski Brod which had been previously used by the JNA to launch attacks on the Croatian border town of Slavonski Brod (which housed a JNA barracks). Known as the Krajina, the Bosnia-Croatia border divided a large swathe of Serb-populated territory that had been settled as the Austro-Hungarian barrier to the Ottoman Empire. In the early communal hagiology of the war, radical Serbs created an imploding symbol of the Krajina as both the defence of Christendom against the Orient, and the defence of Western democracy against the Nazis. How that symbol imploded is one of the strands of the partition process in Bosnia.

From the border, fighting then spread inward to Bijeljina and Zvornik, towns which formed crucial links between the majority Serb communes in the north-west (whose population was 63 per cent Serb, 15 per cent Muslim and 9.5 per cent Croat according to the 1981 census[6]) and the west bank of the river Drina, which continued down to eastern Bosnia. The effort to consolidate contiguous Serb territories was, therefore, a primary aim in what followed. On 1 April one of Serbia's most infamous paramilitary groups, Arkan's Tigers, led by a former sweetshop owner who was also said to have been a hitman employed by the Ministry of the Interior,[7] moved into Bijeljina. They had been in Eastern Slavonia the previous year, where they had pioneered 'ethnic cleansing', a term used to describe the pattern of mass murder and forced expulsion which grew to characterize the war in Bosnia. The strategy of Arkan's Tigers, which was adopted by other Serb paramilitaries, was to surround a village

[5] Laura Silber and Allan Little, *Yugoslavia: Death of a Nation* (London, 1996), p. 205.

[6] Its figures have to be treated warily, as it was carried out in volatile circumstances.

[7] Tom Gjelten, *Sarajevo Daily: A City and Its Newspaper Under Siege* (New York, 1995), pp. 88-9.

or small town,[8] enter it, block off the entrances and exits, go from house to house ordering people onto the main street, separate the men from the women and children, and allow the latter to leave the village after robbing them. The house would then be plundered and destroyed, generally by fire. Some of the men would be murdered, others put to forced labour or herded into makeshift prison camps. The paramilitaries would come equipped with a list of prominent local Muslim community leaders: they would get one of their prisoners to point them out and they would be the first to be killed.[9]

Though the war in Croatia had demonstrated JNA complicity with Serb paramilitaries, and Bosnia itself had suffered the destruction of a mosque in Trebinje during the shelling of Dubrovnik by JNA reservists from Montenegro in November 1991, President Izetbegovic appeared to believe that the JNA would behave differently in Bosnia, and asked them to defend Bijeljina against Arkan's Tigers.[10] At this stage, the chief threat appeared to be from Croatia; already by early February the Bosnian region of western Herzegovina was being mobilized along ethnic lines. The spillover of the war in the Croatian Krajina, initially through a series of small clashes between the Serb and Croat refugees and local militias, had rapidly caused a buildup of ethnic tensions, and barricades had gone up in the western Herzegovinian town of Mostar. The JNA moved into Bijeljina on 3 April, but the violence continued unabated, and the next day Ejup Ganic, the Defence Minister, and the Croat members of the coalition government pressured Izetbegovic into calling for a mobilization of the territorial defence. The SDS members of the Presidency, Nikola Koljevic and Biljana Plavsic, resigned in protest at the mobilization and a day later Serb paramilitaries laid siege to the Sarajevo Police Academy.

Although most accounts of the wars in former Yugoslavia take either the position that religious enmity is 'ancient' (and therefore unchanging) in the Balkans or that communalism was chiefly a

---

[8] According to David Owen, the Serbs discovered in their attacks on Vukovar that capturing larger towns or cities in modern warfare extracted a terrible price and so turned to 'the medieval siege, putting citizens under barrage and psychological pressure but not launching a frontal attack'. This was the tactic adopted with Sarajevo. David Owen, *Balkan Oddyssey* (New York, 1995), p. 84.

[9] Silber and Little, op. cit., pp. 244-7.

[10] Izetbegovic distinguished between the JNA proper and the reservists; the latter, he said, had caused havoc in the republic.

rhetorical device (and therefore did not seriously affect the course of the war), historical accounts of the Bosnian war indicate that communal categories gained in potency—especially via those two others, the Serbs and Croats—as Yugoslavia hurtled from economic to political disintegration.[11] The Serbian President Slobodan Milosevic, in fact, came to power on a wave of economic discontent in the 1980s, caused largely by the withdrawal of international aid, and both Slovene and Croatian nationalism were fuelled by the richer republics' resentment at subsidizing the poorer ones. The rise of the nationalists was also a crisis of the Communist Government, and its effect was to accelerate the fragmentation of most institutions of governance. Paramilitaries like Arkan's Tigers had already begun to undermine police and army functions by the late 1980s, first within Serbia and Croatia (in Kosova and Knin), and then across Bosnia.

Contemporary accounts indicate that the Bosnian Government was in disarray at the point when the war began. On the same day as paramilitaries laid siege to the Police Academy, a small demonstration appealing against ethnic conflict became a procession of thousands streaming across the Vrbanja bridge into the majority Serb-inhabited area of Grbavica to show that the city 'belonged to all the people'. As the crowd moved towards the Police Academy en route to Grbavica, Serb paramilitaries opened fire and a young woman was shot. The crowd turned back to the Parliament building, where a hastily formed National Salvation Committee began discussions on the demand for fresh elections. On 6 April, the day the European Community recognized Bosnia, discussions were still on about whether or not to hold fresh elections, when Serb snipers opened fire at the Parliament building.

The call for fresh elections was especially significant. The first free elections in Bosnia, on 9 November 1990, had brought in a coalition government formed by three ethnic and communally-based parties, the Muslim Party of Democratic Action (SDA), the Serb Democratic Party (SDS) and the Croatian Democratic Union (HDZ). They had between them won 202 of the 240 seats in the two houses of Parliament.[12] All three had been founded in the summer; the SDA in

---

[11] See, for example, Michael A Sells, *The Bridge Betrayed: Religion and Genocide in Bosnia* (Berkeley and Los Angeles, 1996); Roy Gutman, *Witness to Genocide* (New York, 1993).

[12] The SDA won 33.8 per cent of the seats, the SDS 29.6 per cent and the HDZ 18.3 per cent. Of the remaining 38 seats 18 were won by reform Communists and 13

May, as a 'political alliance of Yugoslav citizens belonging to Muslim cultural and historical traditions',[13] and the SDA and HDZ in July 1990. The latter two are Bosnian branches of parties formed in Croatia and underline the way in which diaspora nationalism can influence native ethno-national consolidation, especially when the diasporas are contiguous. The SDS was founded by Croatian Serbs in the Krajina region and the Bosnian Croat HDZ was a branch of the ruling party of nationalist Croats. SDA leader Izetbegovic was the guest of honour at the SDS founding congress, and at a memorial meeting for World War II victims, Izetbegovic and the radical Bosnian Serb leader Radovan Karadzic had pledged that 'blood must never flow down the Drina river again'.[14] The SDS branch was especially active in the eighteen Serb majority communes adjacent or close to the twelve Serb majority communes in the Croatian Krajina, and the founding of a Bosnian branch of the HDZ in western Herzegovina can be seen as at least partly a counter to the SDS. Though the three parties formed a joint front against the Communists, they were already divided over power-sharing: the SDS and the HDZ wanted ethno-national parity, while the SDA preferred the majoritarian democratic system of one man one vote.[15] The election law which was formulated took an intermediate position between the two: it accepted the ethnic principle but made it proportional. The elections to the bicameral Assembly were 'to reflect ethnically, within 15 per-centage points, the population as a whole'. The ethnic identity of the candidates was listed on ballot papers alongside their party affiliations.[16]

The 1990 election results have been widely seen as a vote for ethnic nationalism and as evidence that the Muslims, Croats and

---

by the Ante Markovic alliance. The ethno-communal breakdown of deputies elected in the 1990 Bosnian elections was: 39.5 per cent Muslim, 35.4 per cent Serb, 21.6 per cent Croat, 3.3 per cent Yugoslav. Lenard J Cohen, *Broken Bonds: Yugoslavia's Disintegration and Balkan Politics in Transtition* (Boulder, 1995), p. 146.

[13] Silber and Little, op. cit., pp. 206-7.

[14] David Owen, op. cit., p. 186.

[15] Silber and Little, op. cit., pp. 209-10. According to the Bosnian Constitution of 1974, however, Muslims, Serbs and Croats were constituent nations, and so ethnic representation was written into the elections.

[16] The Commission on Security and Cooperation in Europe (CSCE), *The Referendum on Independence in Bosnia-Herzegovina*, Report of the Helsinki Commission Delegation to Bosnia-Herzegovina, 12 March 1992, p. 6.

Serbs put communal or ethnic identities above secular or pluralist ones, but the results were more mixed than this. In parallel elections, Serbia and Croatia had voted overwhelmingly for the ethno-nationalist leaders Slobodan Milosevic of Serbia and Franjo Tudjman of Croatia. In Bosnia,[17] in contrast, even though the extremist Radovan Karadzic had been voted in chiefly by the Serbs, nationalist Croats had voted for the relatively moderate Stepan Kljuic and the Bosnian Muslims were divided between ethnic and secular identity. The north-western Bosnian Muslim leader Fikret Abdic, who had once headed the Yugoslav agro-industrial company Agrocomerc[18] and who was known as a pragmatic Yugoslavist, got more votes than anyone else (beating Izetbegovic by over 150,000 votes). This entitled Abdic to become President but he traded the presidency to get an ally, Alija Delimustafic, made Interior Minister, and Izetbegovic became President. According to Delimustafic, ethnic patronage now became common and the administration began to be 'Lebanized' with the police, in particular, being segmented along ethnic and communal lines.[19] Internal dissension snowballed into political disintegration. In February 1991 the SDA and the HDZ proposed that Parliament declare that republican laws would hold precedence over federal laws and in April the SDS riposted with a proposal to divide Bosnia into ethnoeconomic regions, with each 'nation' administering its economic and political interests, and declared a 'Serb Community of Krajina' in western Bosnia.[20] The proposal followed earlier meetings between Milosevic and Tudjman in January (which continued through March), at which they discussed dividing Bosnia between Serbia and Croatia. In its turn, the discussion was prompted partly by negotiations over the possible secession of Slovenia and Croatia and the search for a *quid pro quo* for the displacement of populations entailed in establishing ethnic majorities in the territories under each leader's political control, and was spurred by the conflicts between Serbs and Croats in Croatia's border regions which had

---

[17] In this sense, the Macedonian elections had the most pluralist result, with a predominantly social-democratic coalition coming to power, headed by Kiro Gligorov, whose first cabinet included members of all the minorities.

[18] And was later implicated in a scandal comprising oversubscription to the company.

[19] Cohen, op. cit., p. 161, fn. 16.

[20] Janusz Bugajski, *Ethnic Politics in Eastern Europe* (New York and London, 1995), pp. 34-5.

begun during the late eighties and were spiralling into war. War was precipitated soon after by the Slovene and Croat declarations of independence at the end of June. The Slovene war ended ten days after it had begun, principally because Slovenia was at one end of Yugoslavia and its population was ethnically homogeneous. In Croatia, by contrast, the war was intense not only because of the large Serb population but because they were concentrated in areas adjoining the multi-ethnic republic of Bosnia—with an even larger number of Serbs—and Serbia proper. In May 1991, when Croatia held a referendum on independence, the Croatian Serb SDS held a separate referendum and declared themselves an autonomous region of the Yugoslav federation. They had been arming themselves for some time, with the help of Serbian President Milosevic. Alarmed by the threat of war in Croatia, and what such a war might spell for Bosnia, Izetbegovic toured West Europe and the US to ask for the preventive deployment of UN peacekeepers, but was turned down.[21]

Within three weeks of the outbreak of war the Dutch, who were then holding the European Community (EC) presidency, suggested that the option of negotiated internal border changes be explored because the Serb political leadership and the JNA 'would not tolerate' an independent Croatia with an 11 per cent Serb population. The EC support for changing internal borders, they added, could be justified on the grounds that the provisions of the Helsinki Act included the right to self-determination of national minorities within republics. At the same time, it was clear that this was a daunting option.

In the first place it is impossible to draw Yugoslavia's internal borders in such a way that no national minorities would remain. Many minorities reside in relatively small pockets of even isolated villages. On the other hand it cannot be denied that, if the aim is to reduce the number of national minorities in every republic, better borders than the present ones could be devised.'[22]

The Dutch proposal was rejected by the other EC member states not only becuase of the problems which the Dutch had anticipated, but also because 'it was out of date to draw state borders along ethnic

[21] Warren Zimmerman, 'The Last Ambassador: A Memoir of the Collapse of Yugoslavia', *Foreign Affairs*, March-April 1995, p. 16.
[22] David Owen, op. cit., pp. 31-3.

lines'.[23] Two months earlier, in May 1991—in a last-ditch effort to stave off the Slovene and Croat declarations of independence—the EC had pledged its support to a unified Yugoslavia and offered it the carrot of a $4.5 billion aid package.[24] Nevertheless, the conflict developed along the lines sketched by the Dutch. Although Izetbegovic had manifested his commitment to rescuing Yugoslavia from disintegration by a series of confederalist proposals, it began to be rumoured that he was prepared to restructure Bosnia on ethnic lines. Less than ten days after he and the Macedonian President Gligorov had suggested a 'Community of Yugoslov Republics',[25] it was reported that at a mini-summit on 12 June 1991 he had discussed plans to either divide Bosnia into ethnic cantons or restructure it as a union of three constituent nations with Presidents Milosevic of Serbia and Tudjman of Croatia. President Tudjman later admitted he had suggested the latter plan but Izetbegovic had categorically rejected it.[26]

By autumn 1991, the Bosnian Serbs had begun declaring Serb 'autonomous regions', first in the western and south-eastern Serb-majority areas and then in a narrowing spiral of smaller and smaller pockets such as the Romanija mountainous regions east of Sarajevo. In September, the SDA accused the SDS of violating the governing coalition agreement. Matters came to a head in the 14-15 October parliamentary session, in which the successful secession of Slovenia and the secession war in Croatia led to a debate on the eventual

---

[23] David Owen, op. cit., p. 33.

[24] On 29-30 May, EC President Jacques Delor and Luxemberg Prime Minister Jacques Santer visited Belgrade and the former promised to request $ 4.5 billion for Yugoslavia in return for economic reforms aimed at turning it into a free market and political reforms aimed at maintaining its territorial unity. Susan L Woodward, op. cit., p. 160. The offer was too much, too late: the market reforms would have had to have built on the failed structural adjustments and depended on financial centralization while the political reforms were open to decentralization.

[25] On 3 June 1991, in a last ditch effort to save Yugoslavia, Izetbegovic and Gligorov proposed a 'community of Yugoslav Republics', with common market and common defense and foreign policy institutions, though each republic would also maintain its own armed forces and embassies. The proposal was first rejected and then conditionally approved by Milosevic, and was also approved by Croatian President Tudjman and Slovene President Kucan, though the approval of the latter was disingenuous as the Slovenes were already preparing to declare independence on 26 June. Given this, the proposal came too late.

[26] Cohen, op. cit., p. 217.

secession of Bosnia if Yugoslavia disintegrated; the SDA and HDZ deputies proposed a memorandum on the sovereignity and neutrality of Bosnia, the SDS deputies walked out, and the remaining deputies adopted the memorandum. The memorandum was again an attempt to find an intermediate position between being part of a Serb-dominated Yugoslavia and being torn apart by moving too quickly to independence, but the SDS was in no mind to appreciate the attempt. On 9-10 November, the SDS retaliated with a referendum in which only Bosnian Serbs could vote, and they voted to remain with Yugoslavia.[27]

HDZ support for the sovereignty and neutrality of Bosnia appears to have been so much lip service, for in the same month a 'Croatian community of Herceg-Bosna' was declared in the thirty Croat-majority communes of western Herzegovina and central Bosnia and a 'Croatian Community of the Bosnian Sava Valley' was declared in the eight Croat-majority communes of northern Bosnia. HDZ leaders explained that this was primarily a protective measure against SDS pressure for Bosnia to remain in Yugoslavia: these communes would only recognize a government committed to independence.[28] But in December the SDS leader Nikola Koljevic and the HDZ leader Franjo Boras began a series of talks about an ethno-territorial division of Bosnia. The aim of the talks, according to Boras, was to prevent a war by mutually agreeing to a division, and in late November the two visited President Tudjman to lobby his support for the idea. (As Tudjman and Milosevic had already agreed to try and partition Bosnia, presumably the purpose of the visit to Tudjman was to show that in fact the partition scheme was internally rather than externally initiated.) According to Stipe Mesic, 'The talk was about creating ethnically clean areas. In other words, the problem of Muslims had to be solved, since it was obvious that Boras and Koljevic had already agreed on the borders among themselves.'[29]

International mediation played point-counterpoint to this process. In September 1991, the EC formally accepted responsibility for mediating the conflict and set up a Peace Conference for former Yugoslavia. Its chairman Lord Carrington, had previously served

[27] Ibid., pp. 214-16.
[28] Janusz Bugajski, op. cit., p. 34.
[29] Silber and Little, op. cit., pp. 306-7.

during the partition of Palestine and had been part of a mission to South Africa during discussions of a possible partition of that country; he had subsequently steered Zimbabwe to independence and democracy in 1980. In the early months of the Peace Conference, Lord Carrington's efforts were to avert partition wars by combining decentralization with the protection of minority rights, but he soon moved to combine decentralization with ethnic power-sharing (building on the trend of the 1990 election), an approach previously adopted by the British in India in the years before Partition, and tried again in Cyprus in the constitution of independence, in both cases with dismal consequences. In the case of Bosnia the approach was further muddied by its tentative and staggered application first to the whole Yugoslav federation and then in isolation to the republic of Bosnia-Herzegovina. Indeed, the effort to combine ethnic politics with decentralization was made in Bosnia just as it began to be given up in Yugoslavia; while in May-June 1991 the EC and the US had affirmed their support for a unified, perhaps confederal, Yugoslavia, after the outbreak of war attention turned increasingly to the issue of recognition of its republics as independent states. Thus, EC negotiations for a Bosnian confederation of ethnic nations took place at the same time as the EC gave up negotiations for a Yugoslav confederation, and implied that the EC might do as little to stop the disintegration of Bosnia as it had done in the earlier years of Yugoslav disintegration. In November 1991 the EC asked a five-member judicial commission headed by Judge Robert Badinter of France to draw up the conditions which each republic would have to satisfy for recognition as an independent state, chiefly on human rights and minority rights protection. In the same month the EC, meeting in the Hague, secured an agreement to ceasefire in Croatia. The agreement was an impetus to the push for independence: both Austrian and German leaders, then the most open supporters of Slovenian and Croatian independence, argued that European recognition could prevent the further outbreak of war. In fact, the agreement did not bring about an immediate ceasefire in the Croatian Krajina; instead, conflict intensified as Serb and Croat leaders jockeyed to improve their bargaining power by territorial control.

While the Badinter commission was still at work, Germany announced at the EC Foreign Ministers' meeting on 16 December that it would unilaterally recognize Slovenia and Croatia on Christmas day.[30] In the nine-hour debate which followed Lord Carrington argued that

early recognition would torpedo the (peace) conference. . . . And that if they recognized Croatia and Slovenia then they would have to ask all the others whether they wanted their independence. And that if they asked the Bosnians whether they wanted their independence, they inevitably would have to say yes, and that this would mean a civil war (in Bosnia).[31]

The same points were made by Cyrus Vance, the UN negotiator, and President Izetbegovic had already cautioned against early recognition,[32] as had a series of Conference on Security and Cooperation (CSCE) meetings through 1991. The French and US Presidents, Francois Mitterand and George Bush, and the British Prime Minister, John Major, had already written to German Chancellor Helmut Kohl stressing the probability of war in Bosnia if Germany went ahead with recognition.[33] The EC debate was resolved only when Germany reminded Britain that it had acceded to Britain's demand that the social chapter of the Maastricht treaty be dropped.[34] In a compromise formula, the EC announced that applications for recognition would be decided on 15 January 1992, and meanwhile the Badinter Commission would assess applications for recognition. Germany then decided in any case to recognize Slovenia and Croatia on 18 December 1991.[35] On 2 January 1992, the November ceasefire agreement for the Croatian Krajina was expanded into a comprehensive truce by Cyrus Vance. By this time, thousands had died, some 700,000 people had become refugees, and Croatia had suffered enormous physical damage.

[30] It has been argued that as Germany's announcement came six months after the war began in Croatia, the Germans cannot be held responsible for (indirectly) worsening the conflict. However, the announcement was made while Croats and Serbs were discussing a ceasefire and the creation of UN Protected Areas in the Krajina, and while Lord Carrington was negotiating a series of domestic and bilateral agreements between the Croat and Serb leadership. Its impact was to weaken Carrington's bargaining position with the Croats and intensify Serb fears.

[31] Silber and Little, op. cit., pp. 199-200.

[32] Cohen, op. cit., p. 239.

[33] Interview with Czech Foreign Minister Jiri Dienstbier, then chair of the CSCE, 19 Oct. 1992.

[34] It is probable, too, that the French *quid pro quo* for acquiescence was a greater role in European security.

[35] European public opinion appears to have supported the German decision. A poll conducted in December 1991 showed that the percentage polled who were in

Meanwhile, the Bosnian Government prepared for independence. In December President Izetbegovic applied to the EC for recognition but in January he was told that the 'expression of the (people's) will' for an independent state was not 'fully founded'. Recognition might still be possible, the Badinter Commission advised, if Bosnia held a referendum under international supervision.[36] At the same time, though the Badinter Commission had said that Croatia did not meet the human rights standards for recognition, the EC decided to recognize Slovenia and Croatia. The decision was so controversial that it was openly criticized by the wider European organization of which EC states were members, on the grounds that it was

destabilizing to those it left behind. This was apparent in press coverage of Yugoslavia on the very day that Croatia and Slovenia were recognized—January 15, 1992—which indicated that "secret" talks were taking place between Serbia and Croatia, along with ethnic Serb leaders from Bosnia-Herzegovina, to divide Bosnia-Herzegovina between them as a way of resolving their own differences.[37]

The SDS was quick to strike: in the same month, while continuing to remain in the Bosnian Government, they declared a Serbian republic of Bosnia-Herzegovina, proclaiming it part of the Yugoslav federation. On 25 January the SDA and HDZ announced that the referendum on independence which was required by the EC for recognition would be held at the end of February and the SDS called for a Serb boycott; Serbs were warned that those who voted would be considered traitors, and in several Serb-majority areas local SDS officials prohibited the setting up of polling stations and refused to release voter lists to the Election Committee until Serb names had been excised. In the SDS-dominated town of Banja Luka, more radical than thou Serbs formed their own Assembly and proposed that the Bosnian Krajina join with the Croatian Krajina to form an autonomous territory of the Yugoslav federation.[38] On 21 February,

---

favour of preserving Yugoslavia's territorial integrity were 18 per cent in Germany, 20 per cent in France and 17 per cent in Britain. As against this, support for 'respecting democracy and self-determination (including possible independence)' was 63 per cent in Germany, and 73 per cent in France and Britain. Eurobarometer No. 36, Dec. 1991, p. 41.

[36] CSCE Report, op. cit., p. 10.

[37] Ibid., p. 11.

[38] Ibid., pp, 13-14, 20.

a week before the referendum, the EC sponsored Lisbon Conference hosted talks led by Lord Carrington and Ambassador Cutileiro on Bosnia-Herzegovina at which the major topic was the possible cantonization of the republic into three ethnoterritories. Cantonization had become something of a buzz word following the Milosevic-Tudjman talks of early 1991: in October, the moderate Croat nationalist Kljuic had repeated Tudjman's proposal for ethnic cantonization and in January 1992 the militant Serb nationalist Karadzic was talking about Bosnia as a 'Balkan Switzerland'.[39] The Serb, Muslim and Croat delegations to the Lisbon Conference came equipped with copies of the Swiss Constitution (as had Greek and Turkish Cypriots, Sinhalas and Sri Lankan Tamils, and Indians and Kashmiris before them). Why the Swiss Constitution became the model for ethnonationalists is not the question here, but one response to cantonization proposals is germane. When a Swiss constitutional model was proposed by Tamil federalists in Sri Lanka in 1956 during a constitutional conflict over whether the Sri Lankan state would be unitary or federalized along ethnic lines, it was an independent candidate from a region with a large Tamil population who pointed out that such a model could not work in the demographically dispersed conditions of Sri Lanka. 'Let the federals produce a map of Switzerland. Does it make as ridiculous a map as the one of Ceylon produced by them? Does not even common sense suggest to them that there should be geographical continuity among the cantons of the various states?'[40]

The map which was produced at the Lisbon discussions would have drawn a like howl from our 1956 interlocutor. None of the three ethnic groups had contiguous territories, but the Muslim cantons were the most scattered.[41] It seems Radovan Karadzic also proposed partitioning Sarajevo—by a 'green line' as had been deployed in the partition of Nicosia, the Cypriot capital—but this was not accepted.[42] President Izetbegovic agreed in Lisbon to the formation of ethnically-based territorial units in Bosnia—not yet partition but a step in its direction—but when details of the Lisbon agreement, including the

[39] Woodward, op. cit., p. 281.
[40] Cited by A. Jayaratne Wilson, *The Break Up of Sri Lanka: The Sinhalese-Tamil Conflict* (Honolulu, 1958), p. 85. This makes ironic reading in the context of the Bosnian war and the international peace plan.
[41] Lee Bryant, 'Bosnia-Herzegovina', *War Report*, Nov.-Dec. 1992, p. 12.
[42] Woodward, op. cit., p. 281, fn. 12.

map, began to be rumoured in Sarajevo there was such an immediate outcry that he withdrew from the agreement. While Izetbegovic announced his withdrawal in Sarajevo, Radovan Karadzic and Josip Manolic (a Tudjman aide representing the Bosnian Croats) held a secret meeting in Graz at which Karadzic told Manolic that any agreement would have to include Serb control of the northern corridor. Apparently, this was the first time that Bosnian Serb and Croat leaders had pored over the map together. There were extensive discussions on population transfers.

In the event, populations were transferred by force rather than agreement. In late March Arkan's Tigers began moving to create the eastern crescent of the ethnic territory later named Republika Srpska. When the EC recognized Bosnia on 6 April, following an over-whelming vote in favour of independence,[43] Arkan's offensive gained momentum. On 8 April Serb paramilitaries and JNA forces, massed outside Zvornik, began shelling the town from inside Serbia, and on 9 April Arkan issued an ultimatum to the majority Muslim population of Zvornik (60 per cent) to surrender. The next day Zvornik fell. Arkan's Tigers moved on to Srebrenica, where the town's Muslim leaders were urgently negotiating with local Serbs for an agreement which would protect the town, but the Tigers' arrival disrupted the negotiations. The Tigers encountered their first resistance in Srebrenica where a Muslim militia, led by a policeman named Naser Oric who had once been in Milosevic's bodyguard, succeeded in routing the Tigers at the the end of April.

At the same time as the Tigers moved towards Srebrenica, Serb forces began bombing Sarajevo. The bombs fell as Easter was being celebrated by the representatives of four faiths in a bid to resist the growing communalization of Bosnia: the Fransciscan monk Marko Orsolic, the Serbian Orthodox priest, Krstan Bjeljac, the Sarajevo Imam, Ibrahim Seta, and the Jewish community president, Ivan Ceresnjes.[44] While Sarajevo was being shelled, Momcilo Krajisnik slipped into the city to propose to Izetbegovic that the Serbs would

---

[43] The referendum turn out was roughly 63 per cent of eligible voters, as the majority of Serbs did not vote, but though Serb opposition to independence had been the reason for the EC's suggesting a referendum in the first place, the outbreak of war had convinced them that withholding recognition would be worse than granting it.

[44] Zoran Pajic, 'Where Do You Go From Here', paper presented at the Helsinki Citizen's Assembly Meeting on 'The State of Europe', London, 6-7 July 1995.

stop the war if he would agree to partition Sarajevo into twin cities. This push for a two-level partition, of the cities and the country, was to characterize the war for the next three and a half years. By the beginning of May Serb forces had begun establishing a northern corridor by consolidating their hold on Brcko and Doboj. 'Bureaus for Population Exchange' began to be set up all over northern Bosnia, which functioned for the most part as extortion dens. Muslims and Croats not only had to pay in hard currency to be allowed to leave, but had to sign over properties and assets. Refugees were packed into sealed trains at Doboj and sent to Zagreb. On 2 May Serb forces turned their attention to Sarajevo. Serb troops moved from the surrounding Vraca and Trebevic mountains into Grbavica, but this first attempt at forcibly partitioning Sarajevo was half-hearted as they lacked an infantry. Nevertheless, they got to the suburbs of Grbavica, Momjilo and Nedzarici and cut Dobrinja off from the rest of the city (the suburbs suffered a siege within a siege for the best part of the war). These areas now constituted the inner city front lines and bacame a *de facto* partition of the city, albeit only of areas at its periphery.

On 6 May a second secret meeting between Serbs and Croats took place at Graz airport, this time between Karadzic and the maverick Croat leader Mate Boban. A former clothing store manager, Mate Boban emerged through Tudjman's partonage as the *de facto* leader of the Croats, eclipsing the more moderate HDZ leaders Kljuic and Boras. Karadzic and Boban had detailed discussions on Croat and Serb territories in Bosnia. The SDS had initially planned that the south-western boundary of their greater Serbian state would lie along the Neretva river, partitioning Mostar and bringing east Mostar into Republika Srpska. But Karadzic agreed to Mate Boban's suggestion that instead the main street running through Mostar, 'Marshal Tito', should be the boundary of the Croatian territory of Herceg-Bosna, and also agreed that Herceg-Bosna would comprise the Croat-majority coastal areas, an adjoining Serb-majority area, Kupres (which was 51 per cent Serb) and the mixed Muslim-Croat central Bosnian areas.[45] The talks were deadlocked on the very issue which was to remain unresolved in the war, the northern corridor comprising the Posavina and Brcko regions which linked the Bosnian side of the Krajina with eastern Bosnia, but, in an agreement prefiguring the

[45] Silber and Little, op. cit., pp. 307-8.

eventual agreement after four years of war (the Dayton Peace Agreement of November 1995), Karadzic and Boban decided they would accept international arbitration for the region around Kupres and seven towns in the Posavina.

Soon after, the JNA withdrew from the east bank of Mostar and on 17 June Croatian forces, comprising units of the Croatian military which had originally entered Bosnia in pursuit of the Croatian-Serb war, the Croatian Defence Council (HVO), the progenitor and military arm of Herceg-Bosna, and the paramilitary arm of the radical nationalist Croatian Party of Rights (HOS),[46] drove the Serbs out of Mostar. How far they had to use force is debatable, given the Karadzic-Boban agreement. The HVO now began to consolidate its hold on territories, with cash and *materiel* from the main HDZ and from other supporters in Croatia. The first small steps towards integration with Croatia had already begun: the Croatian dinar had replaced the Yugoslav currency in some parts of Herzegovina by 1991, partly because the Bosnian state had no currency and partly bacause the choice of currency used marked ethnonational affiliation. On taking over Mostar Boban dismissed almost all the Muslims in public life and replaced them with HDZ members loyal to his hardline nationalism, mounted road blocks around the city, and curtailed Muslim movement both into and out of the city.

By autumn 1992 there were three armies in Bosnia: the RSA, the HVO (Croatian Defence Committee) and the ABH. On 25 October, a gangland fight over a gasoline consignment in Prozor sparked war between the Muslims and Croats. Local units of the HVO and the ABH sprang to the defence of their (ethnically-bound) mafiosi and there were gun battles in the streets. A resultant breakdown of communications between the HVO and the ABH led both to desert their positions at Jajce which was surrounded by Serb forces but not in any danger until 29 October when 40,000 panicked Muslims and Croats poured out and the RSA walked in. Two days earlier an SDS proposal to create a confederation of 'three territorially distinct states based on ethnic or confessional principles' had been rejected by the international mediators Cyrus Vance and David Owen on the grounds that

such a plan could achieve homogeneity and coherent boundaries only by a process of enforced population transfer—which has already been

---

[46] Cohen, op. cit., p. 276.

condemned by the International Conference, as well as by the (UN) General Assembly. . . . Furthermore, a confederation formed of three such states would be inherently unstable, for at least two would surely forge immediate and stronger connections with neighbouring States of the former Yugoslavia than they would with the other two units of Bosnia-Herzegovina.[47]

Thanks to the Karadzic-Boban agreement, by winter 1992 the RSA and HVO had no more territory to fight over and turned to attacking the ABH. As a joint RSA-HVO attack on the ABH intensified, the Bosnian Government itself began to become ethnically divided. Logically the 'war cabinet' began to be dominated by the SDA, and the more moderate Serbs and Croats in the government began to be marginalized in the process of political and military decision-making. Additional obstacles to international negotiations emerged. The SDA began to be openly criticized as a culprit: privately, UN forces responsible for humanitarian aid had long criticized the Bosnian Government for being neither grateful enough nor compromising enough, but now the mediators began to actually canvas opposition. According to David Owen, the international mediators had regarded President Izetbegovic as intransigent for some months. In December, meeting Fikret Abdic for the first time, Owen was struck by his criticism of Muslims who 'blocked' compromises with Serbs and Croats and urged him to join the Bosnian Presidency and pull his weight at their meetings.[48]

In early January 1993, when Cyrus Vance and David Owen presented a plan to create ten ethnically-based provinces or cantons[49] under a weak federal government, the plan benefitted nobody but the Croats, who stood to gain larger territories than they either controlled or could claim on the basis of ethnic weightage. The plan was intended to forestall partition by scattering the cantons so that three ethnoterritories could not be formed, but in a war situation its other key elements, the devolution of most civil powers including policing to cantons, and the acceptance of the ethnic principle—at military, territorial, administrative and political levels—gave the partition process a degree of immediacy. David Owen later remarked that he and Vance had been careful not to label any of the provinces Serb, Croat or Muslim; but when the military arrangements envisaged

[47] STC/2/2, Geneva: ICFY, 27 Oct. 1992, pp. 4-5.
[48] David Owen, op. cit., pp. 82-3.
[49] Three Serb majority, three Muslim majority, two Croat majority, one combined Muslim-Croat majority and a multi-ethnic province around Sarajevo.

by the plan were that RSA troops would withdraw to Banja Luka, Bijeljina and East Herzegovina and the HVO to the Posavina (and so each ethnonational party would have its own armed wing) the ethnic principle was clear. Moreover, by 14 January Owen was exploring the possibility of a territorial exchange between the HDZ and the SDS, by which the Bosnian Serbs would be able to link their western and eastern territories and the Croats would control Bosnian territory adjoining Croatia's eastern border.[50] Owen omits to mention that the 'swaps' he was so blithely attempting to arrange would entail the massive displacement of populations, and gave a fillip to the ongoing process of ethnic cleansing. Though the Bosnian Government, which had presented a proposal for thirteen multi-ethnic regions which would 'dilute Serb majority areas' in December,[51] protested that the plan was a prelude to ethnic partition (as the weakness of the federal govern-ment meant the provinces would be effectively self-governing), in March Izetbegovic accepted it, arguing in Sarajevo that he was doing so because he was confident the Serbs would reject it.

By March 1993, when the Bosnian Government reluctantly accepted the Vance-Owen plan, the SDS rejected any form of centralized government, arguing that all that was needed was a central coordinating body. As far as the Serbs were concerned, the Vance-Owen peace plan demanded large territorial concessions at a time when the only areas remaining as obstacles to Serb territorial ambitions were the eastern enclaves of Srebrenica, Zepa and Gorazde. Under the Vance-Owen plan all three were in the Muslim-majority Tuzla province, a jagged area curving aroung the Serb-majority Pale province, which was itself in three pieces dotting east Bosnia. A Serb acquiescence to the plan would mean effectively giving up Greater Serbia, and early 1993 appears to have seen a two-pronged Serb strategy to acquire eastern Bosnia through negotiation and force. At the same time as Srebrenica was being attacked, Bosnian Serbs were demanding a territorial exchange in the negotiations which would allow them to link Zvornik and Sekovici.[52]

Srebrenica had remained a thorn in the RSA side since April 1992, when the local Muslim militia had driven Arkan's Tigers out. In January 1993, Serb forces surrounded the town and blockaded aid

[50] David Owen, op. cit., pp. 90-9.
[51] Ibid., pp. 78-9.
[52] Ibid., pp. 133-43.

convoys, and Srebrenica began slowly to starve. In March 1993, in an attempt to draw international attention to the plight of Srebrenica, the Bosnian Government announced it would accept no more aid for Sarajevo while Srebrenica starved. On March 11 the new UN Protection Forces (UNPROFOR) chief, General Morillon, went to Srebrenica to negotiate the opening of aid routes. The first convoy to come in was besieged by women and children desperate to leave the town, and the UN High Commission for Refugees (UNHCR) found itself a reluctant assistant to ethnic cleansing.[53] In April the Serbs issued an ultimatum that if the Muslim militia did not surrender and the Muslims leave Srebrenica, they would attack the town. Though the UNHCR began to evacuate Srebrenica, on 12 April the Serbs shelled it. The town's militia were outgunned and on 14 April the local authorities smuggled a message to the UNPROFOR headquarters in Belgrade that the Bosnian defence was about to collapse, and requested the UN to broker a surrender. The request placed the UN in a quandary as Srebrenica was in a Muslim canton under the Vance-Owen plan and the UN feared that international pressure for military intervention to defend Bosnian Muslims would mount if it was seen to broker the surrender of an area which had been internationally allocated to the Bosnian Government. On 16 April, the UN Security Council declared Srebrenica a 'safe area' and the surrender was produced as an agreement to disarm as part of the process of rendering the enclave safe.[54]

Though the Vance-Owen plan did not initiate the Croat-Muslim war, there is little doubt that the Croats saw a sympathetic view of Croat territorial ambitions in it. By the end of April there was allout war between the HVO and the ABH. Meeting David Owen on 21 April, the Croatian Defence Minister Gojko Susak said that the Croats were beginning to prefer an alliance with Serbs to one with Muslims; on the same day, RSA commander Ratko Mladic told Owen that the Serbs would defend Croats in the Mostar region, the heartland of Herceg-Bosna.[55] Some of the nastiest fighting now took place in central Bosnia. In Kiseljak, Croat militiamen entered the only Muslim village in the area, Ahmici, slaughtered dozens of villagers

---

[53] This was not, however, the first time the UNHCR had found itself assisting in the forcible expulsion of population: in late September 1992, UNHCR vehicles had transported Muslims from Banja Luka and Prijedor. David Owen, op. cit., p. 55.

[54] Silber and Little, op. cit., pp. 266-75.

[55] David Owen, op. cit., pp. 137-9.

and set the village on fire, ostensibly as preventive action against a wave of Muslim refugees following the surrender of Srebrenica. In Travnik the HVO demanded the ABH disarm and disband on the grounds that Travnik fell in a Croat governed province under the Vance-Owen plan, and in Zenica, which was an ABH stronghold, talks between the Muslim mayor and the local HVO commander broke down when the HVO started shelling from the surrounding hills.

The Bosnian fight back began in central Bosnia with troops composed of refugees. The 3rd Corps of the ABH formed two new brigades, of men driven from north and east Bosnia, the 17th 'Krajiska' Brigade in Travnik and the 7th Muslim Brigade in Zenica. The Krajiska Brigade was led by Colonel Mehmet Alagic, a refugee from the Kozara mountains in north Bosnia, the 7th Muslim Brigade was aggressively Islamic, arguing that Bosnian adherence to the principles of multi-ethnic tolerance had led to the destruction of Muslims, and it was now time for Bosnian Muslims to defend themselves as Muslims rather then Bosnians. Within Zenica the 7th Brigade made periodic attempts to Islamicize daily life, smashing alcohol shops and destroying pigs.[56]

By the summer of 1993 the territory under government control was a smattering of isolated enclaves, none viable without the life support of international aid, and arguments for the establishment of safe areas began to become compelling. On 6 May the UN passed Resolution 824 (1993) extending the safe areas to Sarajevo, Tuzla, Zepa, Gorazde and Bihac, but on 13 May the French circulated a 'non-paper' to the United States, Britain and Russia in which they suggested that any ideas of reconquering territory around the enclaves or providing them with complete armed protection be given short shrift; instead the safe areas should function as 'sanctuaries'. With the example of Srebrenica before them, the United States voiced concern that the safe areas could become euphemisms for giant refugee camps; at the same time, the situation on the ground led them to conclude that the Vance-Owen plan was unfeasible, for as the Serbs extended their domination over eastern Bosnia it became more and more evident that only defeat could lead them to relinquish these territories. The United States now moved closer to support for the ethnic trifurcation of Bosnia, joining in an initiative involving

[56] Silber and Little, op. cit., pp. 297-9; David Owen, op. cit., p. 143.

Russia, France and Britain initially, and, when other members of the European Union protested at the 'Great Powers' reference, Spain. On 22 May the United States, Russia, Britain, France and Spain put forward a Joint Action Plan for a union of three republics, the sealing off of Bosnian borders, and the extension of the UN mandate to include the protection of the six safe areas (the UN subsequently extended UNPROFOR's mandate by Resolution 836 of 4 June and requested 7,600 additional troops). The Joint Action Plan was widely seen as a harbinger of the next stage of talks, towards a three-way partition. The seamy side of Owen's Balkan Odyssey was beginning to emerge.

Its first sign was that the international community now chose to preside over partition negotiations in which the territorial control exercised by rebel Serb and Croat leaders was acknowledged as giving them parity with Bosnia's official leaders (now almost all Muslim). In Washington, President Clinton announced that the US would accept partition as long as it was freely accepted by the parties themselves. In Geneva, Owen was told by US Ambassador Victor Jackovitch that Silajdic and Ganic could live with the new proposals, even the map (with some qualifications). On 22 June Owen suggested to the EU Foreign Affairs meeting that the Carrington-Cutileiro plan for a three part confederation and cantonization should be reconsidered and on 23 June Owen and Stoltenberg had a meeting with Presidents Bulatovic (of Montenegro), Tudjman and Milosevic at which nine constitutional principles for a Union were formulated. Owen then wrote to Izetbegovic about the meeting (why Izetbegovic was not present is not explained). Izetbegovic's response was that the public was not ready to face the fact 'that partition had taken place on the ground' and he would need to discuss the issue before he could agree to negotiate. Owen interpreted this response as a demand for more territory and on 9 July he and Stoltenberg persuaded Tudjman and Milosevic to 'try and get' 30 per cent of the country's territory for the Muslims. On 12 July Izetbegovic said he was ready to attend the talks. On 27 July Karadzic presented a map under which the Serb republic would have 54.3 per cent of Bosnian territory, the Muslim republic (to which the Bosnian Government was reduced by implication) would have 28.4 per cent and the Croat republic would have 17.3 per cent. On 28 July Boban countered with a map giving the Serb republic 52 per cent of Bosnian territory, the

Muslim republic 26.7 per cent and the Croats 21.3 per cent.[57] The 30 per cent which Owen believed was the US bottom line was finally made up by the Croats agreeing to 'give' the Muslim republic Stolac. On 30 July Owen and Stoltenberg announced that a map had been agreed on, but this announcement, like the previous announcement on the Vance-Owen Plan, proved to be premature. By 20 August the mediators had carved a rough agreement on the boundaries of the three republics, and it had also been agreed that Sarajevo would be placed under UN administration and Mostar under EU administration, but Brcko and the eastern enclaves remained sticking points. The Bosnian republic remained fragmented, with Bihac isolated in the north-west and the three eastern enclaves connected only by a road.[58] Nevertheless, the agreement was put to the vote: the Serb Assembly voted 55 to 14 in its favour, the Croat Assembly was near unanimous in its favour (with only one dissenting vote) and the Bosnian Parliament (which was the only legitimate body of the three) voted to continue negotiations on the plan. After nearly a month of hectic negotiations over some 2.3 per cent of Bosnian territory, a map giving 53 per cent of Bosnia to the Serb republic, 17 per cent to the Croat republic, and 30 per cent to the Muslim republic was agreed during talks on the HMS *Invincible* on 20 September 1993. Two days later Izetbegovic turned down the plan: he was concerned about the eastern territories.

The Bosnian Serbs and Croats, however, interpreted the new formula of a union of three republics as tantamount to recognition of a three-way partition and Boban and Karadzic confidently styled themselves the Presidents of Herceg-Bosna and Republika Srpska. At the same time, Fikret Abdic began negotiations with the Bosnian Serbs and Croats to establish his independent control over the north-western region of Bihac. This was perhaps the finest hour of Owen's Odyssey: some nine months of political finagling (he first met Abdic in December 1992) had at least yielded a concrete result. Abdic was expelled from the Bosnian presidency, and war broke out in Bihac

---

[57] From the beginning, negotiations over the maps bore an uneasy relation to the ethnic composition of Bosnia, in which Muslims comprised some 44 per cent of the population, Serbs 33 per cent and Croats 17 per cent. A majority of Muslims, however, were concentrated in the towns.

[58] UN S/26337 of 20 Aug. 1993.

between Muslims loyal to Abdic and Bosnian Government forces.[59] On 21-2 October, at the joint initiative of Presidents Tudjman and Milosevic, Abdic signed separate agreements with the HDZ leader Mate Boban and the SDS leader Radovan Karadzic, under which an 'Autonomous Province of Western Bosnia' was established by the self-styled Presidents of Herceg-Bosna, Republika Srpska and now the 'AP Western Bosnia'. The agreement with Mate Boban specified that the Croatian paramilitary HVO units in Bihac would 'remain incorporated' into the armed forces of Abdic's province, while the agreement with Radovan Karadzic called upon the Bosnian Government to recognize Bihac as an autonomous province of the Muslim republic proposed by the EU and set up a boundary commission to establish the borders between Bihac and Republika Srpska.[60]

Bosnia was now about to enter its third year of war. While communal cartographies were being negotiated the real process of establishing them on the ground through mass murder and forced expulsion was in full sway. Although Tudjman and Izetbegovic had signed an agreement for a ceasefire between the HVO and the ABH in September, the war between Croats and Muslims in central Bosnia—which had grown partly as a conse-quence of the cantonal maps drawn by the Vance-Owen plan—intensified in October. The fighting was now concentrated in areas where the issue of who would control the multiethnic cantons was still to be resolved. In the town of Vares, whose pre-war population had comprised equal numbers of Muslims and Croats and a Serb minority which had fled when the war first broke out, Croats and Muslims had worked hard to preserve communal peace, even through the summer of 1993 when the Croat-Muslim war was far advanced. But the town's resources were first strained by waves of Croat refugees from surrounding towns and villages, and then cracked under communal pressure as refugees accused the local Croat leadership of collaborating with the enemy. In October an armed HVO unit from

[59] Silber and Little, op. cit., pp. 304-6; Liljana Smajlovic, 'Buddies in a Clinch', in *Vreme*, 11 Oct. 1993, pp. 25-7. Smajlovic also interprets the falling out as a portent of the emergence of a Muslim state in Bosnia.

[60] Joint Statement issued by the President of the Croatian Republic of Herceg-Bosna, Mate Boban, and the President of the AP Western Bosnia, Fikret Abdic, Zagreb, 21 Oct. 1993, Declaration issued by President Dr Radovan Karadzic of the Republika Srpska and President Fikret Abdic of the Autonomous Province of Western Bosnia of the Republic of Bosnia, Belgrade, 22 Oct. 1993.

Kiseljak arrived in Vares and first jailed and then replaced the town's Croat mayor and police chief. The town's Muslims were rounded up, and their houses were raided and plundered. Within a few days almost all of them had left. Surrounded by ABH-controlled territory, the Croats could not defend Vares. On 3 November the HVO evacuated Vares' Croats and on 5 November the ABH 7th Brigade, itself formed of refugees, walked in. The town's Muslims returned and now a wave of Muslim refugees replaced the Croat refugees who had earlier flooded the town. The entire town of Crna Rijeka in northern Bosnia, which had been cleansed by Serbs, was resettled in Croat homes in Vares.[61] A new demographic engineering, using refugees, had begun.

On 7 November the foreign ministers of Germany and France, Klaus Kinkel and Alain Juppe, wrote to the President of the EU Foreign Affairs Council, Willy Claes, arguing that the Muslim-majority republic should comprise at least one-third of Bosnia's territory (that is, that the 30 per cent negotiated by Owen was too little). In December the EU persented an Action Plan with a new map which provided the proposed Muslim republic with expanded territory to link the eastern enclaves of Gorazde and Zepa, and a corresponding link for the Croat republic of territory between Jajce and Gornji Vakuf (which was to be supplied in exchange for territory between Zenica and Sarajevo). This would allow the Muslim republic 33.5 per cent of Bosnian territory and the Croat republic 17.5 per cent. Though the plan was following through on the proposal for a union of three republics, it also set the lines for a tripartite partition. Certainly the view that partition might now be internationally acceptable was one factor in the HDZ and SDS rejection of the plan's other proposal, that Sarajevo be reunited under a two-year UN administration and Mostar be reunited under a two-year EU administration (to which Serbs and Croats had agreed in earlier talks in August 1993)[62].

Meanwhile, the contours of an eventual settlement began to take shape. While supporting the EU plan for a union of three republics, the US was also seeking means of controlling or limiting the conflict bilaterally: beginning in August 1993, Charles Redman, the US special envoy to Bosnia, held a series of meetings aimed at brokering a

---

[61] Silber and Little, op. cit., pp. 300-1.

[62] An EU administration for Mostar was agreed following Croat opposition to a UN administration.

Muslim-Croat federation. The idea was first discussed by Redman, Silajdic (the then Bosnian Prime Minister), and Mate Granic, the Croatian Prime Minister. Silajdic and Granic both expressed an interest in the proposal and in September 1993 they came to a rough agreement on a federation, but the agreement had little chance of being mooted while the Croat-Muslim war worsened. US pressure on Croatia to stop supporting the Croat offensive in Bosnia had grown sharper as Tudjman resisted it and in the late fall Redman had begun to threaten sanctions. In December 1993 the US ambassador to Croatia, Peter Galbraith, was told that the hardline Croat leader 'Mate Boban would be taking, as it was put to me, a long vacation'. In Bosnia Haris Silajdic and Ivo Komsic of the Bosnian-Croat Peasant Party began working on a federation structure which incorporated several elements of the Vance-Owen Plan, including ethnic cantonization. The limits of agreement, however, were soon revealed: at a meeting in Germany, the following January, when discussing a Croat-Muslim Treaty of Cooperation (including the confederation option), when the Bosnian leaders asked the Croat leaders to agree to demilitarize central Bosnia, the answer was no. Ten days later, Tudjman and Milosevic agreed to formally recognize each other's new countries; significantly, Bosnian Serbs and Croats followed suit with an agreement to place liaison officers in Pale and Mostar, respectively proclaimed the capitals of Republika Srpska and Herceg-Bosna. Neither Bosnian Croats nor the Croatian Government were ready to give up the Tudjman-Milosevic partition plan. At the end of January, Bosnian Prime Minister Haris Silajdic complained to the UN that the Croatian army was engaged in the Bosnian Croat-Muslim conflict, and UNPROFOR estimated that there were anything between 3,000 to 5,000 regular Croatian army troops in Bosnia.[63] The UN gave Croatia a two-week deadline to pull its troops out of Bosnia and implied that failure to do so would be met with the imposition of sanctions against Croatia, but by 18 February no troop withdrawals had taken place. Sanctions were not imposed, partly to give US diplomacy a chance. While Komsic presented the federation proposal to a special Croat Assembly called in Bosnia, which was attended by Croats from all over former Yugoslavia (and some from abroad),

---

[63] Department of Public Information, UN, 'The United Nations and the Situation in Former Yugoslavia', Reference Paper Revision 4, p. 19.

Redman and Galbraith pressed Tudjman to support a Croat-Muslim federation with the option of confederation with Croatia.[64] At the end of February, four days of proximity talks in Washington yielded a 'Framework Agreement for the Muslim-Croat Federation' and a preliminary agreement on confederation with Croatia. A ceasefire took force across central Bosnia and UNPROFOR troops began to be moved to the Croat-Muslim frontlines.

In the same month, a series of events forced an agreement to lift the siege of Sarajevo. On 4 February, Serb snipers killed ten people in the government-controlled Sarajevo suburb Dobrinja. The next day a bomb in the crowded Sarajevo marketplace killed 49 and wounded 200, and NATO issued an ultimatum to the RSA to withdraw their heavy weapons to a 20 km distance from Sarajevo (an 'exclusion zone') within ten days. The ultimatum also called on the Bosnian Government to place any heavy weapons they had in the exclusion zone under UNPROFOR's control, and threatened air strikes against either party for failure to comply. Four days before the NATO ultimatum was due to expire, British Prime Minister John Major went to Russia to canvass Yeltsin's support against the ultimatum. Yeltsin appealed to the Bosnian Serbs to pull back their heavy weapons and guaranteed to place Russian troops in the areas from which they pulled back, and Russian officials met with Bosnian Serbs in Pale. Karadzic and Mladic agreed both to withdraw their heavy weapons and to allow a UN administration for Sarajevo, and 400 Russian troops were moved from eastern Slavonia to the hills surrounding Sarajevo (though UNPROFOR estimated that 4,600 troops would be required to truly secure freedom of movement for Sarajevans).[65] The UN line on negotiations had triumphed over the NATO initiative at peace enforcement, but only at the cost of indefinitely postponing peace in Bosnia. The positioning of UN peace-keepers along the Sarajevo confrontation lines ended by reinforcing the *de facto* partition of the city in Bosnian Serb favour. The Serbs viewed the Russian troops as temporary guardians of their heavy weapons rather than confis-

---

[64] David Owen, op. cit., pp. 319-23.

[65] UN S/1994/291 of 11 March 1994, 'Report of the Secretary-General Pursuant to Security Council Resolution 900 (1994)'. Resolution 900 (1994) dealt with lifting the siege of Sarajevo and appointing a 'senior civil official to draw up an assessment and plan of action for the restoration of essential public services in the various *opstine* of Sarajevo'.

cators.[66] In March, when a framework agreement for a Muslim-Croat federation was signed by the Bosnian Government and Croat representatives, the SDS interpreted the agreement as a sign that the international community was ready to accept a two-way partition of Bosnia and demanded recognition of Republika Srpska.[67]

Moving on this assumption, the Serbs started shelling Gorazde in early April. Despite a UN Security Council demand that the attacks cease and the threat of NATO air strikes on Serb positions, the attacks continued. Air strikes were ordered but they were so limited as to be counterproductive. Bombs were dropped on 10 and 11 April. The Serbs retaliated by seizing 150 UN personnel on Mount Igman and shelling Tuzla, and continued the assault on Gorazde. They then stormed the UN weapons' collection point at Sarajevo's Lukavica barracks and seized anti-aircraft guns. NATO issued an ultimatum that the RSA would face further air strikes unless there was an immediate ceasefire, troops were pulled back to a 3 km distance from the centre of Gorazde, and heavy weapons were withdrawn to a distance of 20 km from the town. Just before the ultimatum expired, the UN sent in an aid convoy, in a move widely seen as preempting air strikes against the Serbs. Though the RSA had only just begun to withdraw from Gorazde, no attacks were launched when the deadline came and went. Instead, the British and Ukrainian peacekeepers administered an agreement along the lines of the Srebrenica Agreement: the demilitarization of the enclave and the interposition of the UN troops between the RSA-ABH front line and the town. The agreement was achieved under Russian pressure. Following the US and Russian initiatives a Contact Group was set up to mediate the Bosnian conflict, which was composed of the Foreign Ministers of France, Germany, Russia, Britain, the EU Commissioner for Foreign Affairs and the two Chairmen of the ICFY Steering Committee.

On 10 May the Bosnian and Croat Governments and the leaders of Herceg-Bosna signed the Washington Accords for the establishment of a Bosniac-Croat Federation and both the Bosnian Government and international mediators held out the hope that pressure on Serbian President Milosevic would bring the Bosnian Serbs into a similar agreement. The Accords specified that the Bosniac-Croat

---

[66] Silber and Little, op. cit. pp. 313-18.
[67] David Owen, op. cit., pp. 269-70.

Federation was formed by two constituent nations, and allocated political, judicial and administrative functions by ethnicity. The Federation would be cantonized along the lines of the Vance-Owen Plan, under which cantons would have wide autonomy. The ABH and the HVO would be unified under a single command. Fighting between the Bosnian Government and Bosnian Serb forces continued, and another round of international negotiations yielded a one-month ceasefire agreement. Like countless other agreements, it was violated within days of being signed. By the end of June it was clear that any hopes that the Serbs would enter the Federation on the same terms as the Croats were dead: instead, the Federation constitution was beginning to be viewed primarily as an interim war-time arrangement to form a joint front against the Serbs until territorial divisions were agreed. The agreement also meant that Bosnians might now finally have a land route open by which to get arms (though the Croat practice of levying a fee on the goods rather limited the arms they were able to bring in). One of the first acts of the Federation was to launch an offensive against Fikret Abdic's forces in Bihac, in which the HVO units which had been pledged to him by Mate Boban in October 1993 now fought alongside the ABH against him. The offensive routed Abdic, but made thousands of his Muslim supporters refugees in the Serb-populated area of Croatia which was under UN protection.

At the same time, the ethnic principle which informed the constitution, from the naming of two 'constituent nations' of Bosniacs and Croats to the allocation of political and executive positions, had a series of immediate consequences. The relegation of Serbs to the category 'Others', while officially defended on the grounds that the SDS-led Bosnian Serbs were not ready to join the federation, implied that there was little space for the Serbs who had remained in Bosnian Government-controlled territory, and more and more of them began to leave. Politically, the ethnic allocation of seats in a constitution which was chiefly a war-time standoff between recently embattled parties increased rather than decreased the strength of ethnic nationalists. In the June assembly elections the SDA and HDZ pushed out most of the smaller and non-ethnic political parties; the moderate Croat leader, Ivo Komsic, who had been a key figure in the negotiations for a Federation, was more or less retired and an HDZ leader who had been prominent in Mostar during the Croat bombardment of the Muslim-populated east Mostar, became Vice-President.[68]

International negotiations now came closer to a two-way partition. The Contact Group presented a map dividing Bosnia between the Federation and a Bosnian Serb entity with 51 per cent of the territory (the sum of the 33.5 per cent and 17.5 per cent agreed under the Joint Action Plan negotiations, to go to the Bosnian and Croat Republics respectively) to go to the Federation and 49 per cent to a Serb Republic. The map preserved the eastern enclaves as Federation territory, and at the end of July the Federation, Croatia and rump Yugoslavia accepted it, but the Bosnian Serbs rejected it. Under last-minute pressure by Milosevic, Bosnian Serb leaders agreed that as a compromise Republika Srpska would treat the Contact Group plan as a starting point for negotiations, but the compromise was rejected by the Serb Assembly in Pale.

The winter of 1994 was dominated by two conflicting last-ditch efforts: the first, mediated by former US President Jimmy Carter, to wrest a ceasefire between the Federation and the RSA, and the second a joint initiative of Bosnian and Croatian Serbs, to join their territories by conquering Bihac before the UN mandate in Croatia expired in March. Tudjman had threatened that the mandate would not be extended, and the Croatian army was by now both trained and equipped to reconquer the Krajina without too much difficulty. Despite the ongoing war in Bihac and west central Bosnia, both the Federation and the Serbs agreed to a four-month ceasefire, but this had little more than symbolic meaning as most prior ceasefires had also been agreed for the winter months when the climate slowed much of the fighting. Carter had attempted to transform this cease-fire into a separation of forces agreement, but the Bosnian Government feared that the interposition of UNPROFOR on the front lines would impose a *de facto* partition of the sort which had occurred in Cyprus, and demanded the SDS accept the Contact Group map as a negotiating point, which they refused to do.[69] The Croatian Serbs and rebel Muslims were not bound by the ceasefire agreement and attacks on Bihac continued through the winter.

Meanwhile political conflict within the federation mounted. In

[68] Radha Kumar, 'Dying in Sarajevo', in *Index on Censorship*, 4/5 1994, pp. 186-7; 'Report of Two-Day Workshop on Human Rights, Minority Rights and Collective Rights', Sarajevo, 25-6 June 1994, *Helsinki Citizens Assembly*, 29 June 1994.

[69] *NYT*, 21 Dec. 1994, 24 Dec. 1994.

February, reports of the presence of Iranian and Afghan *mujahedeen* in Zenica started a debate within the Bosnian Government, in which the Presidency was split between those who protested that Bosnia's only hope was to preserve a secular and multi-ethnic army and those who said they 'had to tolerate the *mujahedeen* because of the money coming in from fundamentalist countries'. Though HDZ and SDA leaders had agreed to submit problems within the Federation to an international arbitrator, preferably appointed by the US, and a retired US general had been appointed to help unify HVO and ABH units into a single army, the Croat Defence Minister of the Federation, Jadranko Prlic, threatened that the Federation would fall apart if the *mujahedeen* were not expelled.[70]

By the spring of 1995 Bosnia was again sliding into a full-scale war. When the ceasefire expired the RSA began shelling Bihac again. In a sudden attack, the Croatian army attacked west Slavonia and captured it, sending thousand of Croatian Serbs fleeing to Bosnia. The attack had been planned some time ago but had been scheduled for the autumn so as to avoid a falling off in summer tourism; the RSA shelling of Bihac, however, forced the pace of the attack on west Slavonia because Croatia feared that if Bihac fell the Krajina Serbs would have a rail link through to Belgrade.[71]

The election of Jacques Chirac as Prime Minister of France signalled a shift in what had hitherto been a kind of minimal West European consensus on Bosnia. Chirac argued for a more robust approach to the UN mandate. After hundreds of UN peace-keepers were taken hostage by the RSA in May, France pushed for the creation of a 'Rapid Reaction Force' which would respond more aggressively to Bosnian Serb fiats. In late June, the US committed itself to providing $50 million towards the costs of the Rapid Reaction Force (it was estimated the Force would cost $700 million per year).[72] While the Rapid Reaction Force was being discussed, the RSA began to mass around Srebrenica. Though the build-up to the Serb assault on Srebrenica took a few weeks, the assault itself took only days and the consequent ethnic cleansing was brutally quick. On 6 July the RSA began shelling the enclave and the commander of the Dutch battalion stationed at Srebrenica asked for NATO planes to be put

[70] Ibid., 5 Feb. 1995, 18 Feb. 1995.
[71] Ibid., 13 Aug. 1995.
[72] *Associated Press*, 29 June 1995. Henceforth *AP*.

in readiness for air strikes, but his request was turned down by the overall UNPROFOR Commander, General Janvier. The RSA then moved against UN observation posts in Srebrenica and forced the Dutch to withdraw, and while refugees from surrounding villages flooded the town, the Serbs took some peace-keepers hostage. The UN again turned down requests for close air support from the Dutch batallion commander, and when a fourth request was made, General Janvier is reported to have said in a staff meeting, 'Gentlemen, don't you understand? I have to get rid of these enclaves.' When air strikes were finally ordered, the pilots were told only to fire at tanks or artillery seen firing. After hitting two tanks, the NATO aeroplanes withdrew. The Serb forces threatened to kill Dutch peace-keepers and the Dutch Government asked NATO to suspend air strikes. Srebrenica fell at 6 p.m.[73] On 12 July, 1500 Serb troops marched into the town, backed by tanks, and under the supervision of Ratko Mladic, the Commander of the RSA, the Bosnian men of military age were separated from the others, taken away and massacred. The UN Secretary-General, Boutros Boutros-Ghali, ruled out air strikes and the UN spokesman, Alexander Ivanko, announced that the most the UN had been able to negotiate was that a Dutch soldier be allowed to travel on each bus, to 'monitor human rights abuses'.

Britain, who had troops in neighbouring Gorazde, responded with warnings of withdrawal, while France pushed for troops reinforce-ment to recover Srebrenica. The UN Security Council demanded the return of Srebrenica but stopped short of supporting the French proposal.[74] In the US, pressure for lifting the arms embargo intensi-fied.[75] The next day, as refugees began to surge into Tuzla, reports of the carnage of male civilians in Srebrenica filtered through. Zepa was already being targeted as the 'next' safe haven on the Serb list of attack. UN military officials stated that the eastern enclaves were undefensible, they had been able to survive thus far only because of Serb acquiescence. In an illuminating aside, a British officer said that Gorazde was less likely to fall than Srebrenica or Zepa, because it 'was never demilitarized', as the other two had been when they

---

[73] Robert Block, 'Betrayal of Srebrenica', citing a leaked report of a Dutch Government investigation, *The Independent*, 30 Oct. 1995.

[74] *NYT,* 13 July 1995.

[75] See William Safire, 'The Time Has Come', in ibid., 13 July 1995; Anthony Lewis, 'Weakness as Policy', in ibid., 14 July 1995.

were declared safe areas, implying that the international community would not act to save Zepa.[76]

On 14 July, the Serbs encircled Zepa and began shelling the three UN observation posts there. The Ukrainians had already been told not to resist: the Serbs had 450 Dutch troops at their mercy in Srebrenica, together with some 62 Dutch hostages. In London, NATO allies met to discuss the French proposal, largely in relation to Sarajevo, Tuzla and—perhaps—Gorazde. Zepa had already been given up, though it had not yet fallen. When the Bosnian Serbs pushed past UN observation posts into the Zepa enclave they were met by some resistance from Bosnian troops who had seized the weapons of the Ukrainians. In Paris, European officials said there was 'little prospect' of military intervention to save Zepa. Zepa did not fall until ten days later.[77]

Meanwhile Krajina Serbs and Fikret Abdic's troops attacked the Bosnian Government's V Corps who were holding Bihac, a move which military analysts saw as attempting to consolidate Bosnian and Krajina Serb communications and supply lines before the Croatian attack on the Krajina began.[78] The Croatian Government warned the UN that if Bihac's status was threatened Croatia would intervene.[79] On 22 July President Franjo Tudjman and President Izetbegovic agreed in a meeting with US Ambassador Peter Galbraith that Croatia would militarily assist the Bosnian Government to retain Bihac,[80] and would seize towns and villages just across the border to ease pressure on the enclave.[81] The next day Croatian artillery began to move in range of Serb supply lines in the region. In London, European and US officials and diplomats admitted that the fact that the threat of retaliatory air strikes was limited to an attack on Gorazde alone might be construed by the Bosnian Serbs 'as a green light' to attack other areas with impunity.[82] RSA shelling and sniping had killed 140 people and wounded 722 in Sarajevo in the past three weeks. Then two French peace-keepers were killed in an attack on Sarajevo.

[76] Ibid., 14 July 1995.
[77] Ibid., 16 July 1995.
[78] Ibid., 20-1 July 1995.
[79] Letter from Croatian Foreign Minister, Mate Granic to UN Security Council, ibid., 21 July 1995.
[80] Ibid., 23 July 1994.
[81] Ibid., 13 Aug. 1995.
[82] Ibid., 24 July 1995.

Seeing that international frustration with the Serbs might have reached its zenith, Croatia began an attack on the Krajina border, severing supply routes between Knin and Bosnian Serb-controlled territory. In a last attempt to secure both Croatia's territorial integrity and Serb rights as a community in Croatia, the US and Russia proposed that the Krajina would be autonomous and would have its own flag, currency, parliament and police force, and its citizens would be entitled to dual nationality, but the Croatian Serb leaders turned down the proposal. On 4 August, Croatian forces bombarded villages along the entire 90-mile Krajina. Knin was hit by over 1,500 shells. Like the RSA, advancing Croatian army troops attacked UN observation posts and seized UN peace-keepers, on several occasions using them as human shields. In Washington, White House and Pentagon officials said they 'understood the motive' for the Croatian attack, which, President Clinton said, 'was animated by the Serb attack' on Bihac. The US had given the green light, officials specified, to an attack on Serb forces in and around Bihac, but a red signal to a broader Krajina offensive. In Belgrade, President Milosevic ignored the Croatian SDS leader Milan Martic's appeal for help.[83] The next day, the Croatian army took Knin, and the largest exodus since the war began took place, of Serbs from Croatia into Bosnia. In Bosnia, the government feared that the retreating Croat Serb forces would swell the RSA, but a more serious worry was that the Krajina refugees would settle the Serb-controlled territory, which had been progressively depopulated during the war by a flow of Bosnian Serb refugees to Serbia, and thus provide demographic grounds for an acceptance of partition. These fears were partly substantiated when US Secretary of State Anthony Lake and Under-Secretary Peter Tarnoff went to canvass British, French and German leaders on a US proposal to exchange Gorazde for land around Sarajevo, widen the Brcko corridor, and offer the Serbs the option of confederation with Serbia and the Bosnian Government a 'mini-Marshall Plan' to rebuild the remains of their country

Croat forces meanwhile advanced on Serb-held territories in the north-west around Banja Luka and in the south-west towards Trebinje, and the RSA found itself engaged on several fronts with the Croats and with the ABH in central Bosnia.[84] On 28 August, the

---

[83] Ibid., 1-5 Aug. 1995. The UN, Russia and Britain condemned the Croatian attack.
[84] *NYT*, 5-18 Aug. 1995.

Serbs shelled the Sarajevo market place, killing 37 and wounding 80. At 2 a.m. on the 30 August, NATO responded with massive air strikes on Serb military targets around Sarajevo, Srebrenica and Gorazde. After two days of air strikes, the SDS appointed President Milosevic to represent the Bosnina Serbs at peace talks. Air strikes were suspended pending a NATO ultimatum to the RSA to comply with the weapons exclusion zone around Sarajevo and halt all attacks on Tuzla, Bihac and Gorazde by 11 p.m. on 5 September, and when the deadline expired without RSA response, NATO embarked on a sweeping attack, targeting 50 military sites.The air strikes continued until 14 September when the RSA finally pulled its heavy weapons back. By now Bosnian Serb missile defence and communications systems had been destroyed.[85]

Bosnian Government and Croat forces now began a joint offensive in western Bosnia. Within a few days they had captured hundreds of square miles between Bihac and the rest of the federation. The foreign ministers of Bosnia, Croatia and the rump Yugoslavia then arrived at a broad agreement in New York on a constitutional framework for a Bosnian confederation, but—despite having accepted a *quid pro quo* in the shape of international acquiescence in his expulsion of close to 300,000 Serbs as a return for cementing the Federation—President Tudjman commented in Paris, 'the problem of how Muslims and Croats will live together remains open' and referred ominously to growing Islamic fundamentalist tendencies.

Despite a broad agreement having been reached there was still no ceasefire. Sarajevo, Gorazde and Brcko remained unresolved issues and the Bosnian Government wanted the option of force should the agreement fall through, as so many had done before. The tensions between the Croat and government forces were also heightened; while the ratio of federation and Serb-controlled territories now pretty well tallied with the 51:49 proposed by the Contact Group, Croat forces now controlled some 21.8 per cent of the 51 per cent and the Bosnian Government held 29 per cent. A small battle between ABH and Croat forces took place near Bosanski Petrovac but did not spread; the conflict continued to be chiefly between ABH and RSA forces, supported by Arkan's Tigers, who had reappeared in western Bosnia after Srebrenica.[86] Under intense international pressure, the fighting waned in October, and tentative agreements were reached on the reunification of Sarajevo, a road connection between Sarajevo and Gorazde, and that Brcko would be placed under international arbitration. In November 1995, the Dayton Peace Agreement was signed in Ohio. Bosnia would comprise two 'entities', the Bosniac-Croat Federation and the Republika Srpska, each with their own parliaments, armies, police forces and law courts. The stage appeared to be set for partition.

Appearances are frequently deceptive. While the main thrust of the Dayton Agreement was towards partition, it also included an option to exit from partition, in clauses relating to arms control, a common economic space and the rights of refugees to return to their original homes (i.e. the multi-ethnic towns or dispersed countryside which they had fled). As the international community moved towards consolidating a peace based on divide and quit, sending 60,000 troops to man the partition borders and dissolve some of the internal battle lines, they were faced with the inverted issue of divide and rule; it was not clear either that there were any political groups who could form stable enough governments to permit the troops to withdraw without renewed conflict, or that the regional leaders they relied on to contain the conflict, Milosevic and Tudjman of Serbia and Croatia, were in any position to do so. Close to a year after the Agreement was signed, the Bosnian peace continues to smoulder and neither entity can be said to have political leaders in a position to rule. Moreover, Milosevic and Tudjman are under increasing political pressure domestically. If anything the processes of internal political disintegration in former Yugoslavia (and the accompanying criminal militarization of society) which were crucial elements of the war's beginning are continuing.

Reading present signs is always dangerous, but the fact that NATO has set up an international paramilitary force for the arrest of war criminals, and formed an international civilian police force to assist in reestablishing law and order and the return of refugees, indicates that divide and quit may gradually cease to frame international policy towards Bosnia. Bosnia may yet be the turning point in partition theory.

[86] Ibid., 23-9 Sept. 1995.

Problems of Identity and the Use and Abuse of Religion in Transcaucasia and Yugoslavia

IVAN IVEKOVIC

There is no comprehensive and final answer to the question—what is identity? It seems that the concept was first used as 'psychological identity' by Erik Erikson, a post-Freudian,[1] who reunified under this label the 'self' psychoanalysts had fragmented into ego, super-ego, id, object relations and so forth. He argued that a person's identity grows in the course of the life-cycle, or it may degenerate, as in negative identity or identity diffusion. According to Erikson, identity is defined as a relationship between the self and others; it 'connotes both the persistent sameness within oneself (self-sameness) and the persistent sharing of some kind of essential character with others'.[2] Not entering this debate, I will only say that the term was immediately adopted by the behaviourists who incorporated it into anthropology, sociology, political science and related disciplines. From this inception, it became a preeminently socio-political category and it should be treated as such. Genetically, philosophically or/and culturally predetermined and static 'identities' belong to the realm of wishful thinking. The Marxists would say that whatever meaning is given to 'identity', it belongs to the 'social superstructure', which is a more or less deformed reflection of the material reality. Besides, we are all bearers of multiple and overlapping identities which make up our consciousness and usually they are not mutually exclusive, although we may arrange and rearrange them in different hierarchical orders. These hierarchies are related to the perception of our changing overlapping and often contradictory power, material and or status interests. Having this in mind we may speak of our gender, class, caste, national, ethnic, professional, political, cultural, linguistic or religious identities. As we are all 'social animals', each one of these identities is also related to a specific group or community, which

---

[1] See Paul Roazen, *Erik Erikson: The Power and Limits of Vision* (New York, 1976).
[2] Erik Erikson, 'The Problem of Identity', in Maurice Stein *et al.* (eds.), *Identity and Anxiety* (Glencoe, Ill., 1960), p. 6.

serves as positive or negative reference. It may be the family, clan, tribe, craft-guild, caste, territory, nation-state, religious congregation, political party, football club and so forth, with which we identify ourselves and to which we are more or less loyal, or which we reject. Sometimes these loyalties clash because the social and political environment has changed and this change affects our interests. Then we may speak of an identity problem or crisis.

Lowell Dittmer and Samuel Kim, describing 'China's quest for national identity', argued that 'identity is a series of descriptions that define a person in terms of networks or categories of membership and location in the stream of time and human history'.[3] But to define today what precisely is the Han 'national' identity is probably as difficult as to define what is 'Muslim' identity. Identity is certainly associated with ideology, but the problem is, whose ideology? It is a slippery zone in which only unperformed culturologists dare to venture asserting for example that whatever happened in Chinese history is the consequence of 'Confucianism' and whatever happened among the Muslims, now or before, is the result of a dogmatic, 'fundamentalist' interpretation of the Koran.[4] We may add Max Weber and his 'Protestant' work ethic, which allegedly blessed North-Western European societies with the 'spirit of Capitalism', rationality and later democracy, and using such a pseudo-logical procedure we will end up with the inevitable 'Clash of Civilizations'.[5] Such Euro-centrically biased conceptualizations of 'cultural diversities' found an automatic echo among Second and Third World intellectuals who perceive the 'West' with its 'perverted materialist values' as a direct threat to the 'cultural identity' of their own societies. Stereotype against stereotype and a mirror-like image of the 'Other' which is just the deformed reflection of the 'Self'.

Sidney Verba and Lucian Pye linked 'National Identity' directly to the nation-state. According to Verba, national identity is 'the set of individuals who fall within the decision-making scope of the state'.[6]

---

[3] Dittmer, Lowell and Samuel S. Kim (eds.), *China's Quest for National Identity* (Ithaca and London, 1993); 'The Search for a Theory of National Identity', p. 12.

[4] Lucian Pye's writings offer a typical example of such an approach. See his *Asian Power and Politics. The Cultural Dimensions of Authority* (Cambridge, Mass. and London, 1985). Although such culturologist bias is essentially ideological, this school of thought, as we will demonstrate, has produced a number of valuable concepts.

[5] Samuel Huttington, 'The Class of Civilizations', in *Foreign Affairs*, Summer 1993.

[6] Sidney Verba, 'Sequences and Development', in Leonard Binder (ed.), *Crises and Sequences of Political Development* (Princeton, N.J., 1971), pp. 283-316.

In their conceptualization, determining national identity becomes determining who is included and who is excluded by national boundaries, however the state chooses to draw them. These boundaries, either physical territorial or social, are arbitrarily determined by the 'sovereign state' carving out a precarious identity by force and guile in a competitive international environment. In the same arbitrary way 'sovereign states' determine the criteria for citizenship. Given the crucial importance of boundaries, an identity crisis occurs when those boundaries blur, or are challenged. As Pye puts it,

In the process of political development an identity crisis occurs when a community finds that what it had once unquestionably accepted as physical and psychological definitions of its collective self are no longer acceptable under new historic conditions. In order for the political system to achieve a new level of performance . . . it is necessary for the participants in the system to redefine who they are and how they are different from all other political and social systems.[7]

Pye identifies four 'fundamental forms' of national identity crisis, based on territory, class, ethnicity nationality, and historical cultural exclusiveness. However, 'national identity' as Verba and Pye put it, is not a mere addition of personal identities, it is not 'the largest and most inclusive megacollectivity', but is defined both by the dimensions/characteristics of the social group 'nation' and by the group's subordination to a 'sovereign authority' which appropriates the right to include/exclude. That means that the inclusion into the nation is not completely voluntary: it does not depend exclusively on the subjective feelings of the individual, or even of the sub-group to which he or she belongs, but more so on the criteria for inclusion exclusion fixed by the 'authority'. Amending Verba and Pye, I would add that this authority is not necessarily the 'nation-state' with its legal monopoly of coercion, but may also be a 'moral authority' such as the Church or the religious establishment. Indeed, before the emergence of modern state-entities, 'religious authorities' set rigid criteria of the inclusion (and exclusion) of individuals in a given community. The individual had practically no choice. That is the point when Weber's concept of legitimation of authority becomes

[7] Lucian Pye, 'Identity and Political Culture' in Binder (ed.), op. cit., pp. 110-11.

crucial. As Verba argued, 'identity directly affects the institutionalization of legitimacy, and legitimacy in turn affects penetration'.[8]

'National' and/or 'historical-cultural' identities are circumscribed
by their boundaries, which may more or less coincide with such
'objective criteria' as common ethnic or racial origin, common
language and/or religion, but in practice these boundaries change
not according to the subjective feelings and wishes of those who are
included/excluded, but according to the whims of external political
constraints, both internal and international. That means that 'national'
or 'religious' identities are not static, but evolving and sometimes
blurred categories whose boundaries, both physical and social, are
continuously constructed and reconstructed. There is nothing
'natural' or 'God-given' in these boundaries, because they were
always precarious and changeable human conventions imposed on
the individual and entire collectivities from outside themselves. A
short review of the maps of any atlas of world history would confirm
that there are few state boundaries which have not been changed
over the last hundred years. My father was born in Austro-Hungary,
myself in the kingdom of Yugoslavia, my two sons in the SFR of
Yugoslavia and I am actually a Croatian citizen living temporarily in
Egypt, but I cannot predict where my grandchildren will be born
and how they will identify themselves. Those are situations which
were/are forcefully imposed on my family from outside and there
was/is little we could do to influence the course of political events,
except that each one of us has had to adapt himself to new
circumstances redefining his own social identity. That means that our
personal identity crises were generated by events from outside
ourselves and outside the family or group to which we think we
belong, by political changes in our social environment. There was
no way that our subjective feelings of belonging could influence the
political set-up of 'the society at large'. As put succinctly by Leonard
Binder, the problem of identity results from 'the tension between the
culturally and psychologically determined sense of personal-group
identity and the political definition of the community. . . . The
modern identity crisis arises, in part, from the insistence that
subjective identity and objective political identification coincide.'[9] In

[8] Verba, ibid., p. 311.
[9] Binder, 'The Crises of Political Development', in Binder (ed.), *Crises and
Sequences of Political Development*, pp. 53-4.

other words, identity is essentially a socio-political and not a cultural phenomenon.

The state-entities mentioned earlier and that succeeded each other emerged from legitimation crises of previous state-formations, of their socio-economic orders and political systems, and their dominant state imposed ideologies. In Jurgen Habermas' systems approach, although he had in mind something else (the 'fundamental contradictions' of the capitalist social formation and its class conflicts), crises erupt when

individuals and groups repeatedly confront one another with claims and intentions that are, in the long run, incompatible. . . . As long as the incompatibility of claims and intentions is not recognized by the participants, the conflict remains latent. Such forcefully integrated action systems are of course, in need of an ideological justification to conceal the asymmetrical distribution of chances for the legitimate satisfaction of needs (that is, repression of needs). Communication between participants is then systematically distorted or blocked. Under conditions of forceful integration, the contradictions cannot be identified as contradictions between the declared intentions of hostile parties and be settled in strategic action. Instead, it assumes the ideological form of a contradiction between the intentions that subjects believe themselves to be carrying out and their, as we say, unconscious motives or fundamental interests. As soon as the incompatibility becomes conscious, conflict becomes manifest, and irreconcilable interests are recognized as antagonistic interests.[10]

Although Habermas spoke of class conflict, his description may be applied to 'ethnic', religious' or 'communal' conflicts as well, because they all belong to the category of 'ideological conflicts' that mask more fundamental contradictions of our class-divided societies.

Robert Cox has succinctly explained how new states, new historical structures and political realities come into existence, how and why they do emerge. A 'historical structure' or a historically evolved 'social formation' is a picture of a particular configuration of forces which has nothing to do with the naïve vision of an immutable and eternal state-entity, ethno-national and/or religious community. In his words,

[T]his configuration does not determine actions in any direct, mechanical way but imposes pressures and constraints. Individuals and groups may

---

[10] Jurgen Habermas, *Legitimation Crisis* (Boston, 1973), p. 27.

move with the pressures or resist and oppose them, but cannot ignore them. To the extent that they do successfully resist a prevailing historical structure they buttress their actions with an alternative, emerging configuration of forces, a rival structure.[11]

Or, I would add—an alternatively redefined state and/or community. Such alternative new communities and/or state-entities may emerge out of new perceptions of reality and of available resources, of the surrounding world, or of that aspect of the world that impresses itself upon individuals who found themselves in an environment that they suddenly perceive as inimical. The subjective perception of resource scarcity perhaps plays the decisive role. Cox continues,

This picture, shared among many people defines reality for them; and because they think of reality in the same way, their actions and words tend to reproduce this reality. These realities go by various names—the state, the family, the job market, and so forth. It does not matter whether we approve or disapprove of them. They constitute the world in which we live. They are the parameters of our existence. Knowing them to be there means knowing that other people will act as though they are there, even though none of these entities exists as a physical thing. There is no clean separation between objectivity ("out there") and subjectivity (in the mind). The ontology which defines the "real world", the world of non-physical realities that shape our existence, is sustained by inter-subjective meanings derived from long years of collective experience.

Or, to put it simply, both the former Soviet Union and Yugoslavia, as well as our new nation-states, were/are precarious human constructs, historical creations providing responses to certain conditions which are not immutable, although each one of them may be glorified as the ideal (or 'natural') type of state-entity and/or community, or for the matter of fact—denigrated as 'artificial constructs' or as 'prisons of people'. Having said that, it is important to underline together with Cox that such historical constructs generate new contradictions and points of conflict that bring about their further transformations, which may displace again the formerly dominant structures, retaining some of their features and transforming others.

The collapse of the Soviet and Yugoslav federations may be interpreted as a consequence of unresolved systemic problems these

[11] This and the next quotation: Robert W. Cox, 'Critical Political Economy', in Bjorn Hettne *et al.* (eds.), *International Political Economy: Understanding Global Disorder* (Halifax, 1995), pp. 35-7.

two state-enmities carried-on. The new states that took their place, imposed 'from above' a new formula of social integration based on forceful ethnic inclusion/exclusion. It remains to be seen how such a formula may work internally and in a growingly interdependent international environment. It also remains to be seen how much the ethnocentric formula of legitimation used by our new authorities will be successful. The previously described shift from one state-entity to another directly affected personal and collective identities. In the words of Habermas, a legitimacy crisis 'is directly an identity crisis'.[12] Similarly, Ernest Gellner asserted that nationalism 'is a theory of political legitimacy, which requires that ethnic boundaries should not cut across political ones'.[13] In a more cautious way, while admitting that problems of identity and legitimacy are related and that they overlap in many aspects, Lucian Pye pointed out that the satisfactory resolution of the identity crisis may not involve the settling of legitimacy crisis. Indeed, all over Eastern Europe and in the former Soviet space we have recently witnessed a massive and aggressive reaffirmation of separate ethnic identities, but this 'resurgence' has not resolved the legitimacy problem of our newly-established regimes which remains problematic in spite of repeated election and plebiscite exercises. Pye defined the legitimacy crisis 'as a break down in the constitutional structure and performance of government that arises out of differences over the proper nature of authority'.[14] He equated the parallel eruption of the crises of identity and legitimacy with the crises of a given political culture, a theme beyond the scope of this short sketch.

Interestingly enough, the more the new legitimation formula is challenged, the more it is aggressive and vociferous. Dankwart Rustow found it striking that 'the talk about the nation has been the loudest where the sense of nationality has remained the weakest-among the nineteenth century Germans and Italians and among the twentieth century Arabs, Asians, and Africans, rather than among English, Frenchmen or Japanese'.[15] He also remarked that '[P]roposal for the redefinition of national identity are most ardently formulated by marginal nationals, individuals who have been through a

---

[12] Ibid., Habermas, p. 46.

[13] Ernest Gellner, *Nations and Nationalism* (Ithaca and New York, 1984), p. 1.

[14] Pye, 'The Legitimacy Crisis', in Binder (ed.), op. cit., p. 136.

[15] Dankwart Rustow, *A World of Nations: Problems of Political Modernization* (Washington, D.C., 1967), p. 22.

Fremdheitserlebnis (the experience of being a stranger), who have reasons to question and then vigorously reassert their personal identification with a nation.'[16]

Concluding this sketch but not capitulating, I would certainly agree with Denis Goulet who wrote that '[M]odern men and women must come to recognize that they are the bearers of multiple, partial, overlapping identities and loyalty systems, no single one of which can claim their total allegiance.'[17]

II

In times of acute social crisis when the individual and whole social groups feel marginalized, insecure or threatened in their very existence, people tend to seek security and protection within positive reference groups with which they share common interests, historical memories and systems of values. Among these reference groups religious sects and communities play distinctive roles. The moving relationship which is established between the individual and the group is however ambiguous and there is no automatic reciprocity, because the sect or the religious community is invariably hier-archically organized and subjected to a spiritual/formal authority which has the power to include or to exclude. An individual, born in the community, may be ostracized if he does not conform with the expected code of conduct or simply because he is not of the liking of the priest, sheik or whoever has the moral/formal authority. But even the excluded one remains in a way linked to group, because the 'Others' often perceive him as belonging to that group. During political conflicts in Yugoslavia and Transcaucasia, as well as in Northern Ireland, or some places in India or Pakistan, individuals and whole families were killed just because they were born in the 'wrong' reference group.

The conventional assumption of modernization theories was that religious influence necessarily wanes with the growth of modernity. It was even suggested that modern nationalism replace traditional religious identity.[18] Today, witnessing the 'revival' of both religion

---

[16] Dankwart Rustow, ibid., p. 161.

[17] Denis Goulet, 'Development: Creator and Destroyer of Values', in *World Development*, 20, No. 3, 1992, p. 473.

[18] Bendedict Anderson analysed the transition from religious to national identity in *Imagined Communities* (London, 1990). Hans Kohn, the influential post-World

and nationalism, we know that the two identities are not mutually exclusive. They may in fact reinforce each other. It seems that the general crisis of the Communist model of modernization has generated a moral crisis in which individuals and entire social groups seek spiritual comfort in religions, both in traditional denominations and new sects and millenarian cults. In reshaping the shattered bonds of solidarity and in redefining their group identity, people use the 'raw material' available to them. They use also religious beliefs and memories as well as existing or newly-created religious institutions. Religion and ethnicity have an advantage that they seemingly re-establish the psychological link with the pre-Communist past (historicism again!), and they may, as is the case in the contemporary laboratories of the Balkans and Transcaucasia, become part of the same process of construction of new political identities.

Religion always played an important social and cultural role in our societies, even when Communist messianism suppressed its visible public manifestations.[19] Religion contributed substantially to the shaping and re-shaping of our cultures and political identities although religion was to a great extent secularized. Here is a short reminder.

THE LABORATORY OF TRANSCAUCASIA

In the Caucasus contact-zone religions traditionally delimited different cultural and political spaces. It is beyond our scope to discuss here the role of the All-Russian Orthodox Church, which was used by the czars to legitimize their absolutist rule and imperial conquests. From the seventeenth century onward the church increasingly fell under the bureaucratic domination of the Russian state and played a supporting role in the state's expansion into non-Russian land.[20] It amalgamated with the state and was used as a tool of political

---

War II expert on nationalism, emphasized that secularization is an integral part of the modernization process and claimed the national and religious identities are incompatible. See H. Kohn, *The Age of Nationalism: The First Era of Global History* (New York, 1962).

[19] For a general overview of the relationship between the party-state, religion and nationalism, see Pedro Ramet (ed.), *Religion and Nationalism in Soviet and East European Politics*, (Durham, NC, 1989 rev. ed.).

[20] Robert L. Nichols and Theofanis G. Stavrou (eds.), *Russian Orthodoxy under the Old Regime* (Minneapolis, 1978), pp. 128-37.

indoctrination: the Czars were attributed 'divine rights' to rule their subjects, and even 'to protect' all the Christians in the Ottoman Empire. In the conquest of the Caucasus, the 'protection' card was used to win the collaboration of local Christian Armenians and Georgians against the Muslim Persians and Ottomans. Once Soviet power was consolidated after the civil war, the atheist state pushed all the churches out of the public space and established a firm control over their hierarchies and institutions. However, the policy of the state towards religion changed over time. It was relatively tolerant during the N.E.P. period, only to become extremely brutal in the 1930s. It relaxed during the Second World War, when the Russian Orthodox Church was called to contribute to the war effort, but the process was reversed afterwards. After the hectic and inconclusive deStalinization under Khrushchev and its parallel anti-religious rhetoric, Brezhnev's 'mature socialism' used clerics of various religions for international propaganda campaigns. The churches themselves were assigned a strictly limited and controlled public role but ceased to be harassed. It is only with Gorbachev's *perestroika* and *glasnost* that they re-emerged from the shadow of the state. 'Today, as Russia sheds the Soviet legacy of state-enforced atheism and reaches back into its history for guidance, religion once again seems destined to play an important political role.'[21] This is valid for all Soviet successor states as well.

Split from the rest of Christianity over the Monophysite controversy since the fifth century, the Armenian Apostolic Church, also called Gregorian, turned inward and became the key source of the continuity of Armenian cultural identity. It is within its frame that a distinctive Armenian script was developed and the Church became the guardian of the language after the fourteenth century when the last independent Armenian principality fell to foreign invaders. Many Armenian Christians looked to the czars for protection, contributing to the integration of parts of their ancestral territories into the Russian Empire. Others, who became Ottoman subjects, preserved not only the religious autonomy of their Church within the *millet* system, but also the Armenian cultural identity. During the nineteenth century it emerged as a major instrument of Armenian national self-assertion in the Ottoman state. It was implicitly recognized by the Soviet authorities as a national cultural institution, and the 'Catholics of all

---

[21] K. Dawisha and B. Parrott, 'Russia and the New States of Eurasia', p. 93.

Armenians', the head of the Apostolic Church, was encouraged to maintain intensive relations with the Armenian diaspora abroad and to counter the influence of a rival Catholicos located in Lebanon. Since his appointment in 1955, Catholicos Vazgen I has travelled extensively. For many of his co-nationals he became the living symbol of national continuity and connection with the homeland. A rather unique relationship had been established between the Armenian Church and the Soviet state, which for its own reasons systematically courted the influential Armenian diaspora. But the Church's domain in the Armenian SSR itself had been considerably reduced.[22] Even so starting with the 1960s the Church was in the forefront of the movement to commemorate the victims of the Turkish genocide which has played a central part in the Armenian national mythology since the beginning of this century. During Gorbachev's *glasnost* policy the ecclesiastical hierarchy at home abstained from antagonizing Soviet authorities, but was instrumental in the mobilization of political and financial support of the diaspora for the emerging Armenian nationalist project, focused on the Nagorno Karabagh issue. Aided by gifts of the diaspora its activities tremendously expanded: churches were reopened and renovated, new ones built, new priests ordained, and parish groups proliferated. In practice, it became the church of the new secular state. The new Catholicos Karekin I is present at all state ceremonies and his priests enthusiastically bless whatever is offered to them, including 'volunteers' units that ethnically cleansed conquered Azeri territories. As it was reported, 'His Holiness Karekin I was present and blessed the first plenary session of the National Assembly' issued from the first-Soviet parliamentary elections of 5 July 1995.[23]

In contrast, the Georgian Orthodox Church, which lost its independence and was forcibly absorbed into the imperial Russian Church in 1811, carried on a living memory of oppression under Russian rule. Church Slavonic was even imposed as a liturgical language. The *millet* system on the other side preserved the religious autonomy of the Georgians who were Ottoman subjects. However,

---

[22] For an account of Soviet religious policies and the position of different churches in the Soviet system see Bohdan Bociurkiw, 'Nationalities and Soviet Religious Policies', in Lubomyr Hajda and Mark Beissinger (eds.), *The Nationalities Factor in Soviet Politics and Society* (Boulder and Oxford, 1990), pp. 148-74.

[23] Thomas Gorguissian report from Yerevan published in *Al Ahram Weekly*, 17-25 Aug. 1995.

many of them converted to Islam (Meshketian Turks, Adzhars) and ceased to be considered Georgians. Only after the 1917 Revolution did the remaining Georgian bishops declare the restoration of Georgian religious autonomy reconfirmed during the Second World War by the Soviets. It should be remembered that Stalin himself was previously a student of a Russian Orthodox seminary and that he was certainly aware of anti-Russian sentiments of his fellow-Georgians. In another concession to his compatriots, the Soviet dictator deported, in 1944, the Meskhetian Turks to Central Asia. However, without a numerous and prosperous diaspora, the Georgian Orthodox Church, unlike the Armenian, was more vulnerable to the pressures of the atheist regime. Leading Georgian dissident, Zvaid Gamsakhurdia,[24] who will become later President of the Republic, campaigned in 1977 against the corruption and the submissivness of the Georgian Church. Receiving support from the ranks of Georgian intelligentsia and even from certain party cadres, the Church began in the 1970s[25] to play a more visible role in the national revival process. Most of its hierarchy openly supported the ultra-nationalists Zviadist project, and once in power, Gamsakhurdia promoted the Christianization of the republic. He publicly denigrated Islam, provoking a counter-reaction of the Abkhazs, Adzhars, local Azeris and others. For him, the Georgian Church was the embodiment of Georgian nationhood. His most popular work, 'Georgia's Spiritual Mission', depicts Georgian Christianity as a militant ideology in defence of the nation, but at the same time as a source of Georgia's 'special spiritual purpose' to mediate between East and West.[26]

Soviet Azerbaijan and the Northern Caucasus were covered by two separated officially sponsored Islamic *muftiates* (spiritual directorates) whose main role was to control the religious life of the Muslim population of these two regions, traditionally associated with the Middle Eastern Muslim world. They have also been employed by the Kremlin propaganda abroad to support various Soviet foreign policy initiatives. The Baku *muftiate*, one of the four established in the USSR, was unique because it integrated both the Sunni and Shia

---

[24] For a biogaphy of Gamsakhurdia, see *Sakartvelos Respublika*, no. 89, 8 May 1991.

[25] Early protests againt the repression of the Georgian Orthodox Church are desribed in *RCL*, vol. 9, no. 1, Spring 1985, p. 78.

[26] Stephen F. Jones 'Georgia: A Failed Democratic Transition', in I. Bremmer and R. Taras (eds.), *Nations and Politics in the Soviet Successor States* (New York, 1993), pp. 304-5.

denominations which coexist in Azerbaijan without apparent tensions. Nevertheless, unofficial Islam, upheld by Sufi brotherhoods and disseminated by kinship networks, escaped the control of obedient establishment, which was accused of the betrayal of the basic tenets of the faith. It seems that the 1979 Islamic Revolution in Iran, with its Shia fundamentalism, had little repercussion among the Caucasus Sunni populations. The Shia segment of the Soviet Azeri population was on the other hand antagonized by the perse-cution of fellow-Azerbaijanis in Iran. It was even reported that the USSR opened its borders to receive Iranian Azeri refugees.[27] With Gorbachev's reforms the underground brotherhoods appeared publicly. The *Naqshebandi tariqa* in Chechnya associated itself with the separatist project of General Dudayev, and Iman Shamil, who fought the Russians in the last century, became the symbolic hero of the new resistance to Russian rule.

During the events of winter 1989-90 that saw the outpouring of nationalist and autonomist sentiments in Azerbaijan, Gorbachev blamed disturbances on 'Muslim fanatics'. He accused Iran of igniting the fires of fundamentalist fervour and warned it to stay out of the republic's affairs. These accusations were dismissed by the nationalists of the Popular Front, who were rather looking toward secular Turkey for a source of inspiration. Although citizens of Azerbaijan have recently shown a widespread interest in Islam, most foreign observers concluded that the level of secularization of the population is rather high and that only one tiny segment supports the notion of creating an Islamic state.[28]

THE YUGOSLAV LABORATORY

In the Yugoslav space also three religions played major social roles. They were and they are still associated with different ethno-national projects. The frontier-line between Eastern and Western Christianity roughly cut the space into two, with the massive presence of the Muslim element in Bosnia and Herzegovina and Sandzhak (Muslim

---

[27] *Sunday Times* (London), 11 Sept. 1983.

[28] Shireen Hunter cites an unpublished opininon survey conducted in Azerbaijan in 1990, according to which 77 per cent of the respondents wanted to learn about Islamic culture, but only 19 per cent favoured full integration into the Islamic world and 3.8 per cent endorsed the idea of an Islamic republic. See ibid., 'Nations and Politics in the Soviet Successor States', p. 238.

Slavs), in Kosovo (ethnic Albanians) and in Macedonia (ethnic Albanians, Pomaks and Turks).

The Serbian Orthodox Church preserved its religious autonomy under Ottoman rule and played a central role in the shaping of the Serbian ethno-national project in the last century. The pre-World War I Kingdom of Serbia promoted it into a *de facto* state religion, although the country, with its successive territorial acquisitions, incorporated a growing number of non-Serbs and Muslims. With the annexation of Macedonia after the Balkan wars, Macedonian Slavs came under its jurisdiction, and were labelled 'Southern Serbs'. The Montenegrin Orthodox Church lost its religious autonomy with the integration of the kingdom of Montenegro into the newly-created state of the Serbs, Croats, and Slovenians at the outcome of World War I. The situation did not change after the Communists took power in 1945 and recreated a Montenegrin state-entity within the Yugoslav federation. Accused of having 'invented' a Montenegrin nation, the Communist authorities did not attempt to re-establish the religious *status quo ante*, and probably for the same reason did not intervene in favour of the Macedonian Orthodox Church, which seceded from the Serbian Church and in 1967 proclaimed its autonomy with the active support of local Communist officials.[29] The autonomy of the Macedonian Orthodox Church, which elected its own Archbishop, was never recognized by the Serbian and other Orthodox Churches. It became a source of hidden tensions already within the SFR of Yugoslavia, but erupted publicly in the mass media war when the Serbian Orthodox Church was given an important role in Milosevics's political strategy. Even before the actual collapse of the Yugoslav federation, the Serbian Orthodox Church marked the political space of 'Greater Serbia' by carrying around the earthly remnants of 'Emperor' Lazar, the mythical figure who was killed at the Battle of Kosovo with the Turks back in 1389 when Serbian principalities lost

[29] After the abolition of the eight hundred-year-old achibishopric of Ohrid in 1767, the first demand for the revived independent Macedonian Church was made in 1891 by Metropolitan Teodor of Skopje, when the Macedonian eparchy of Veles was administratively part of the Bulgarain exarchate. The same demand was repeated in 1945 by a council of local clergy and laity in the partisan-held Skopje. The first step toward autonomy was taken in 1958 when the archibishopric of Ohrid was re-established. See Steven Pavlowitch, 'The Orthodox Church of Yugoslavia: The Problem of the Macedonian Church' in *Eastern Churches Review*, vol. I, no. 4, Winter 1967-8, pp. 380-1.

their independence. According to the popular tradition, the Serbs lost the battle because of the betrayal of Prince Vuk Brankovic, while Turkish Sultan Murad I was killed by Milos Obilic, who later became the symbol of resistance to Ottoman rule. The Kosovo myth was subsequently incorporated into the popular imagination, carried on by the Orthodox Church and remoulded in the last century to serve the cause of Serbian national awakening and territorial expansion. The myth was appropriated by the Karadjordjevic Dynasty, and was an integral part of the *Chetnik* ideology during the Second World War. It recently became the battle-cry of resuscitated Serbian nationalism. The Milosevic clique used the myth, the willing Orthodox hierarchy and the related religious iconography for ethnoreligious popular mobilization. At the mammoth rally organized at Kosovo Polje in the summer of 1989 which brought together perhaps as many as half a million of Milosevic's supporters, his portraits were interspersed with icons, religious banners and crosses. Milosevic openly threatened war as a warning not only to Kosovo Albanians, but also to all others who might dare to oppose his project. The Orthodox hierarchy and a number of priests took an active part in wars in Croatia and Bosnia whose declared aim was to 'gather all the Serbs in one state'. Priests blessed publicly known war criminals and the blowing up of mosques and Catholic churches, and found justifications for the genocide of Muslims. When Milosevic started to advocate 'peace' and when a fault-line appeared between him and Bosnian warlords, the Orthodox hierarchy switched sides and began to support Karadzic's war option.

The Catholic hierarchy in Croatia had unsettled problems with the Communist regime dating back to World War II and the ambiguous relationship of Zagreb's Archbishop Stepinec with the *Ustashi* puppet-state. Alojzije Stepinec was only following the then prevalent policy of the Vatican, but he was perceived by the victorious Tito partisans as an ideological enemy, which he certainly was. He was arrested, judged in a mock-trial and sentenced to prison, where he died. With the Cold War was raging in Europe, he was made Cardinal, and was promoted into a symbol of resistance to Communist rule. For Croatian nationalists he became a martyr. Although the diplomatic relations between the new Yugoslav state and the Vatican were later normalized, the relationship between the atheist state and the local Catholic Church remained tense. The Catholic hierarchy, both in Croatia and Slovenia, proved to be less compliant than the Orthodox or Islamic hierarchies. In 1978 Polish Cardianl Karol Wojtyla was elected Pope and initiated Vatican's new *Ostpolitik*, the main concern of which was to improve the condition of believers in Eastern Europe and the Soviet Union and to bolster the status of national Catholic churches. Propagating the new ecumenical spirit, the previously self-centred local hierarchies opened to the public and initiated a dialogue with various sections of society, a dialogue including Marxist intellectuals. Although the regime proved incapable of adapting itself to the new flexibility of the Catholic Church, it was forced to give concessions which included massive public religious ceremonies and a relatively free religious press. These public liturgies often associated Croatian national symbols and Catholicism, while the religious printed press voiced ethnic-religious grievances. When the Communist regime was finally on the verge of collapse and when the first free elections were scheduled in Slovenia and Croatia, the Church put all its moral weight and logistical support behind anti-Communist groups and parties. In both republics, the League of Communists, whose local leaderships were already taken over by reformers, was defeated. The electoral victory paved the way to the separation from Yugoslavia and to the political independence of the two republics. The Catholic Church played a prominent role both at home and on the international level and was associated with the independence project. The Vatican was among the first to give diplomatic recognition to the established regimes, which meant enhanced popular legitimacy. Priests who had until the day before been invisible suddenly invaded the public arena seemingly endorsing the exclusive nationalist discourse of ethnocrats. The ruling HDZ portrayed itself as the most faithful defender of Croatian Catholicism, which was *de facto* promoted into the sole state religion. It had devastating effects in ethnically mixed regions of Croatia, and even more so in neigbouring Bosnia and Herzegovina, where the electorate split along ethno-religious fault-lines. Probably the atrocities of the war in Bosnia finally prompted the Vatican to re-define its relationship with the 'holy Croatian cause'. The dilemma was self-evident: either the Vatican will accept that Catholicism may be used and abused by various enthnocrats and warlords for their selfish aims, and then accept its share of moral responsibility for the committed crimes, or the church should be separated from the state, any state, because Catholicism is supposed to be a transnational religion. The second option would help to avoid the repetition of past blunders, when the Vatican did not recognize the totalitarian character of Nazi-Fascist regimes, and would enable the Church to extend its pastoral mission to all people, irrespective of their nationality or even faith. John Paul II clearly repeated the message in summer 1994 when he visited Zagreb, but I am afraid that he was understood only by a part of the auditorium, bishops and priests included. His message of peace was definitely not heard by those priests who in Mostar bless usurped and stolen property, or who by their silence condone the systematic destruction of mosques and Orthodox Churches.

As for the Bosnian Muslims, or Bosniaks as most call themselves, it should be remembered that they were probably the most secularized ethno-national group in Bosnia and Herzegovina. The rather misguiding appellation of 'Muslim' is a cultural one, not religious. It was given a preference, because using the name of Bosniak would imply that Bosnia is only their national territory, and not the homeland of local Serbs and Croats as well. There are many possible explanations to the phenomena of the secularization of the Muslims, but I will cite only two: first, they are predominantly an urban population living traditionally in ethno-religiously mixed surrounding (the exception is Western Bosnia, where they represent a compact rural group) and because they are urban they have benefited the most from Communist modernization; second, they were for more than hundred years separated physically and culturally from the rest of the Muslim world. On the other hand, those among them who remained practising believers know well that the Koran categorically commands the protection of monotheistic communities. It is not by pure coincidence that most church-buildings belonging to Orthodox and Catholics which are located on Muslim-held territories are still there, while most mosques in Serb or Croat-held territories have been blown up. However, the war which has been imposed on the Muslims and whose main victims they are, gradually changes their attitudes.

In fact in Bosnia we are witnessing a process of de-secularization of the three ethno-national identities. The Muslims are not an exception. It should be noted however that Alija Izetbegovic, the President of the internationally recognized Republic of Bosnia and Herzegovina, started his political career as an Islamic thinker. His intellectual and political activities were penalized by Communist authorities. In 1949 he was sentenced to 5-year hard labour for his association with an illegal 'Young Muslims' Organization, and in 1983, together with twelve other Muslim intellectuals, to 14 years imprisonment. A lawyer by education, he published in 1984 *Islam between East and West*,[30] a work expressing ideas along the lines of neo-fundamentalist thinkers such as Mawdudi and Qutb. In short, in this book he advocates the establishment of an Islamic society, with its own laws, where Muslims are the majority and in which non-Muslims would be treated as a 'protected minority', not as full citizens. When pluralism was introduced in former Yugoslavia he was a founding member of the Party of Democratic Action (SDA), which adopted as moderate and secular public programme, and won the majority of Muslim votes. With war sufferings, people increasingly look for spiritual comfort in their religion, and so did the Bosniaks exposed to a real genocide. In Bosnia and Herzegovina all religions have been gradually, politicized in order to reinforce the legitimacy of mutually opposed ethno-national projects. The Muslims were perhaps the last to follow suite. A neo-fundamentalist group emerged within the SDA and gained political influence. Part of its influence is due to the quasi-monopoly it established on non-governmental sources of aid from Islamic countries.

Both in Transcaucasia and in the Balkans we have now the impression that religions, which were more or less effectively excluded from the formal organization of society under Communist rule, suddenly re-emerged from the partly forgotten past. Religions, churches, mosques, priests and *imams* have been reintroduced into public life and in different ways integrated into official power structures. They filled the vacuum created by the delegitimation of the Communist project and provided an integrating framework for post-Communist societies which have problems to define their new identities. As the religious institutions, in spite of secularization and atheization policies of the previous period, retained a margin of autonomy (some more and some less), they spontaneously started to speak for the emerging civil society the moment Communist regimes were unable to contain popular discontent. While opposition groups were still suppressed, and opposition parties did not yet emerge, religious institutions offered a platform where dissident ideas could be articulated with relative impunity. All over East Central Europe and in the former

---

[30] The first version was written in 1983. See Alija Izetbegovic, *Islam Between East and West* (Indianapolis, 1989).

Soviet Union long deserted churches, mosques and temples became places for public reunion. Although the religious hierarchies were careful to avoid a direct confrontation with the party-state, a number of clerics had no such inhibitions and played active and more or less visible roles in the process of emergence of new nation-states. In the Balkans, Transcaucasia and the Baltic, they associated themselves with new ethno-national projects to which they brought a feeling of historical continuity with the pre-Communist past. Religious symbols, banners and icons appeared in mass political rallies giving legitimacy to pro-independence movements and their leaders. Even former prominent Communists played the religious card. Orthodox and Catholic priests were called to bless newly elected parliaments, national flag, coats of arms and to preside over state-sponsored ceremonies. Less visible in the beginning, Muslim *imams* in Bosnia and Azerbaijan also joined the bandwagon. At least in this stage of our development religions have been extremely politicized and we are witnessing a process of religionization of politics, which is not only a phenomenon restricted to the two regions under investigation here.[31]

In an effort to reconquer the social space which was denied to them by previous atheist regimes, religious activists and church hierarchies engaged a battle for the de-secularization and clericalization of our societies. It is a kind of religious fundamentalism which really belongs to a rather distant past, which views religion, society and the state as one inseparable and immutable entity. Profoundly traditional and suspicious of any questioning or scientific inquiry, this type of theological approach emphasizes non-negotiable and eternal truths, giving, as Srdjan Vrcan wrote,

religious attributes and connotations to some key political ideas in everyday usage, even if of mundane origin, with the visible intention of increasing their non-negotiable attraction and intensifying their emotional charge as well as protecting them by explicit sacralization from possible political critique and immunizing them from public dissent.[32]

It proceeds with a 'a factual ontologization of the existing social, political and cultural differences or othernesses' into 'conflicts

---

[31] See, for example, R. Robertson, 'Globalization, Politics, and Religion', in J. Beckford and T. Luckmann (eds.), *The Changing Face of Religion* (London, 1989).

[32] Srdjan Vrcan 'The War in ex-Yugoslavia and Religion', in *Social Compass*, vol. 41, no. 3, Sept. 1994, p. 417.

between different and opposed human types, between irreconcilable types of culture, between antagonistic types of civilization',[33] between different religions. Echoing such an analysis, Gertrude Himmelfarb described the contemporary superimposition of religion and nationalism as 'the dark and bloody crossroad'. She remarked that in defiance to our expectations we are today

confronting a lethal combination of nationalism and religion—and not in one region but all over the globe. The 'national question', which not only Marxists but most enlightened intellectuals (again, conservatives as well as liberals) had consigned to the ashcan of history, is threatening to become the question of the present and the future. How else are we to understand what is happening in the Middle East (and not only the Arab-Israeli conflict but religious conflicts within the Arab world), or in the former Soviet empire, or what was once Greater India, or in Yugoslavia, or—let us not forget just because it is so tragically familiar—in Northern Ireland? These are the realities of our world, "the bloody crossroads" where nationalism and religion meet.[34]

However, our wars have nothing to do with traditional 'religious' wars, although the attitude described previously by Vrcan certainly contributed to the legitimization of political violence in our current conflicts. Religion have always been used and abused for political ends, including in the most advanced liberal democratic countries. They are apparently the most enduring method of legitimation of political power. Church hierarchies or clerics on pay-lists of different rulers more or less graciously supported their secular projects, or upheld their challengers and their equally mundane counter-projects. Even Communists attempted to impose their doctrine as a kind of civic religion and in many cases subdued the traditional churches. Our ethnocrats are not an exception, but the crucial question is who manipulates whom? Times have changed and the monotheistic religions are supposed to carry a universal message addressed to all people regardless of race, ethnicity, tribe, nation or gender. The message, at least theoretically, should be a message of peace, tolerance and mutual understanding. The extent to which it penetrates the parochial thinking of our separated denominations and churches is dubious. Even the Catholic Church, with its multinational leadership, brain trust and official ecumenical message, presents an ambiguous face in Croatia and Bosnia.

---

[33] Srdian Vrcan, ibid., p. 418.

[34] Getrude Himmelfarb, 'The Dark and Bloody Cossroads where Nationalism and Religion Meet', in *The National Interest*, Summer 1993, p. 56.

The Bosnian Tangle:
Is Bosnia-Herzegovina Multicultural?

RADA IVEKOVIĆ

We are reaching the end of a paradigm of perception and of explanation of the world, the end of an epistemological, i.e. Enlightenment, paradigm. I take it that this Enlightenment pattern of modernity lasted until the end of the twentieth century. We seem to have exhausted most attempts at the old historicizing and evolutionary scheme of the nineteenth century, and we find ourselves without references. We have come to doubt the idea of development through the increasing mastery of nature towards a level thought to be more 'advanced'. The pattern of the latter was usually given as Western and European. The economic development as well as the development of sciences came to break the (symbolic) primeval unity. This primeval unity was given, in olden times, as the Revelation. In modern times, the much-desired-but-lost unity was proposed as (the discovery) of the universal: unity to be re-conquered. The universal is being proposed as neutral regardless of its (particular) origin. But its origin lies in the ruling culture (Western, white, male, Northern).

Paradoxically, most cultures seem to strive to restore the supposedly lost 'original' unity through a *distanciation* which is felt as a constitutive injury. This distanciation (from the 'origin') is culture itself, and its different expressions are all aspects of culture, of science, of the ways of (acquiring) knowledge, etc. This distanciation takes the form of man stepping back from the world—in order to better encompass it. So the necessary step towards restoring the imaginary and symbolic lost unity of the world ends up with its opposite—a big divide. This partition (of the world), a necessary going towards the other through the mastering of the other, has shown to be suicidal *because* it is murderous. This is the situation of post-Yugoslavia, and of Bosnia-Herzegovina. All partitions have been made in the name of a better and 'more' original unity. They are being expressed through myths of historic re-foundation.

The tendency to this cleavage was expressed, in science, through an increasing divorce between 'natural' and 'human' or 'social' sciences. But writing, philosophy, culture in general express it. They are, paradoxically, as many attempts to mend and stitch together the wounded world. Language does the same. Time, distance acquired with time, is that which permits this cunning of the language, since language precedes us.

With the temporal gap (from the origin narrated in the Text)—appears abstraction. Abstraction is a precious intellectual tool, but it has its price. All cultural activities are this abstraction. In periods of crises, when the cleft between the real and the ideal becomes deeper, when the consensus-lie does not hold any more, the efforts to mend the cleavage double; they also often deepen the cleft itself. At other times, the Third World, rapidly caught up with, nowadays, by Eastern Europe, by the once Yugoslav countries and by the inner wounds of the 'First World', represented the fragmented 'remains' of a world thought wholesome. One part of this whole is nowadays anticipated *as* the world of Islam. So we produce the world of Islam *as* the Other (of) the West, in a new dichotomy which may be (re)constituted since the end of the Cold War. (But Islam is not the only possible figure of the other for the West, other options too could be imagined.)

As for Revelation, the dream of utopia of a world as the Whole, it is indeed a world in itself, or a parallel world of sorts. Nobody has direct access to it. There are mediators who legitimate it through the self-legitimation of their own privileges. They allow the foundation of law and order, justifying their own power. This self-foundation hides the void of foundation, of the origin; it hides the fact that no foundation is possible starting from the same, but only from the different, and from crossings. A foundation or an origin *in* or simply from the neighbourhood of the other (the other principle, the other sex, the other tribe) *threatens* the identity of the same when it is particularly under interrogation (in times of a crisis). Thus the origin from the other should be hidden. The ideal is to be *svayambhu*, as if any origin were possible without another. To show that is the task of Revelation, of the Farther's Law and, in the last consequence, of literature too: culture thrives on difference. Official or nationalistically (communally) politicized culture has the aim of hiding the origin *in and with* the other, and the task of homogenizing. Yet a culture of resistance does not have to do that. On the contrary.

Over the centuries, philosophy, as much as literature, has done both: it has both hidden the foundations by self-founding in an autistic origin and unmasked the non-existence of any foundations. It thus has proceeded to reveal the untenability of the thesis of autistic origin from oneself.

Culture, as much as life in the biological sense, needs the other and needs mixture. There is no life or culture where there is no mixture. In fact, where there is no exchange, no communication—there is war. It is even one of the definitions of war.

Homogenization is achieved through the identification of all individuals at the cost of their individuality, with a higher instance/office thought to be universal and neutral, for example the figure of the father of the nation, the Saviour, the Political Leader or God the Father (politics function here in much the same way as monotheistic religions do). It is also achieved through terrorizing the (Leader's) own people. This is how a nation is constituted, first of all as a community—not as a society—in its quest of a state. If there already is a state—as there has been one in the case of Bosnia-Herzegovina, though federal and not quite autonomous, *but* with all elements of a stately structure, then the reformulation of the nation(s) will *disrupt* the existing society framed by the current state, and impose communities in order to reshape the state to the measure of the (new) nations(s).

Bosnia-Herzegovina was, before this war, much more of a society than communities. In fact, what we call nationalism in the former Yugoslavia and in post-Yugoslav states is quite comparable to communalism in India or elsewhere. Particular nationalisms are *all* accompanied by some degree of religious or national fundamentalism. But although religion and/or nation may be the expression of the peak of the conflict, they do not explain it and they are not the *cause* of the Balkan conflict (the causes are multiple and partly extra-Balkanic too, we cannot go into that here). They are being used as its pretext and as the justification, on all sides, of further aggression. (When I say all sides, I mean that all parts in conflict share the responsibility, but not that they share the same guilt: aggression is aggression, whether you consider it a civil or 'ordinary' war, and the Bosnian cities of Sarajevo and Mostar know and can name their different aggressors.)

For a war to break out, especially a civil war, you need a narrative preparing it and sustaining it. Whose story is this master narrative in the making through blood and flesh? Whose is the political will endorsing it? And is the scribe of this story (the intellectual) the willing medium of someone else?

In the West, there appears a paradoxical figure with philosophy and with literature, and that is the author, a form of the subject (agent). The pleasure of the author (the intellectual) in analyzing the symbolic order (the asymmetry) we live in is paradoxical. This role is at the same time subversive, masochistic and one of enjoyment (pleasure); the enjoyment is that of one who is 'at the origin' because the intellectual (re)produces (besides simply reflecting) the symbolic order he criticizes. His is a situation of double-bind. He may be the author of *text* of the *narrative* which founds the creation of a nation, although the true subject-agent is symbolically a much more powerful figure than he is (unless they are one and the same person, which has also happened a lot). Without a narrative, without the creative power of a narrative, the nation would remain what it is: wishful thinking at best, a concept, in any case an idea relating only to the imaginary dimension. Whereas the narrative is the (re)foundation myth given through Revelation, the one ascertaining, promising the lost unity. In order to create a future (nationalisms are pseudo-historicizing narratives), the intellectuals working for the war lords have to rewrite or invent the past.

In nationalism, a pseudo-past is proposed instead of a programme for the future. This is why we are at the end of the Enlightenment: the Enlightenment gave utopia, a historicizing explanation of the world as progress towards a better and *new* future. In this sense, Yugoslavia (the previous state going by that name, called socialist) was an Enlightenment and historicizing project with an idea and an ideal, and with a universal and non-discriminative claim. (There is no doubt that there were many discriminations, among others the one against Albanians, or by general consensus, against women; but these discriminations were not being *theorized* as such, were treated as exceptions to the rule when at all noticed, and bore testimony to a split paradigm of knowledge. When I say that the project of a society for Yugoslavia as a state had a universal claim, I refer to its publicized intention, not to its results.) The new nationalisms have no universal claim whatever, and no true political, social, project: they are explicitly content with referring to restricted communities, ethnic groups or religions, not to society as an integrated whole where individuals from different communities mix. Instead of a project, the nationalists propose their own reduced vision of the past which invariably comes out in national epic form, about 'our' nation having been here *before* the others, *without* the others, and claiming the right to the whole territory (and usually also to women as territory). The non-universality is explicit in such claims as 'all Serbs in one state' (the Serbian nationalist slogan), or such as 'the Young Croatian democracy' (the Croatian nationalist slogan). The same is being imposed on Bosnia-Herzegovina by the international community by reducing it to a mainly Muslim and dependent Bantustan, which will end up as an enclave, curiously called 'entity' here! The Dayton compromise is surely the official, internationally willed, end of Bosnia-Herzegovina as a society, and its resolute transformation into juxtaposed communities which live with minimal exchange (and the exchange, nowadays, goes over racketeering and mafia). In fact, these communities do not really live together, but side-by-side, and a new word has been forged to this effect in the once common language of the area which now bears three names: the term is *suživot* (co-life) as opposed to simply *život* (life). The Dayton compromise is not the outcome of ethnic cleansing or of genocide: it is their definite enforcement.

The narrative, however, anticipates the threat of its own inconsistency, a menace that comes from the proliferation of multiplicity and from mixture at the very spot which should guarantee unity. The possible polysemics of any Revelation (for example of the Koran, where it is even explicitly given by the classical tradition), questions the Law and represents at the same time (symbolically) the transgression of the (paternal) interdiction of freedom and transformation. It represents the paternal pattern *and also* a blow to the phallic construction of the (male) lineage which, should it collapse, threatens to sweep *us all* down to the abyss, since the paternal law *is* the only 'universal' framework available. Therefore the danger of *writing* (narration) is immense, and the responsibility and risk of intellectuals (who mediate it) is enormous. They let themselves be hired by the politicians and warlords. They can also resist, and many do too. It is thus the function of the national fiction (narrative about the), the nation, to weld the community around a first differentiation which also means around a fundamental exclusion. The other nation will be excluded and made the enemy, regardless of the fact whether the nations in question have already acquired some historic reality or not. The one has become multiple—

paradoxically—through its will to cover the world with its unity: this has been, at least, the Western gesture, and European, although only historically Western and European (by which I mean to say that it was no fatality).

The same mechanism is actually the one used by post-Communist nationalisms (although nationalisms are *not* particularly post-Communist, but are certainly post-dichotomous, post-Cold-War, post-East/West-division), by communalisms and fundamentalisms. These trends only replace the once universal ideal by their own particular ideal, and it holds as good. They tear down a myth, and replace it with a new myth of independent origin. Croat nationalists will look for a pre-Muslim Iranian or Aryan origin as far as possible from the neighbouring Serbs speaking a slightly differently standardized form of the same language; the Serb nationalists will look for a hyperborean or 'Indochinese' (in the topographical sense) pre-Asiatic origin, or for a vetero-Slavic origin; Slovenes will insist on their Illyrian, non-Slavic origin. (The Serbian and Croatian languages, and of new the Bosnian one too, stand related to each other the way Hindi and Urdu are, with probably even less distance. Until recently, they all went under the common name of Serbocroatian.)

So Europe (the West) came to found itself by offering to be a model for the rest of the world. The tearing of the prevailing myth of origin, and the post-Communist change of paradigm is at the same time (symbolically) the tearing of some supreme authority. Narratives get supplanted, each accompanying a historic subject (agent) on to the stage, through the assertion and exclusive claim of a territory. Exile is given *immediately* and not as a consequence of any territorial definition.

In an anthropological and universalizing (as much as historicizing) projection, man is now founded in himself, i.e. in his Western and masculine image. At the same time, the recognition of the *particular* origin (Western, European) of this universal is refused. This universal has the advantage, before the lost totality, of bringing desire and enjoyment, and in any case the pleasure of transgression and treason.

In cultures adhering to their (new) myths of origin, the transgression of the text's injunction may be fatal (be it religious Revelation, secular Law, the Nationalist pseudo-historic written and non-written *moral* narrative, etc.). People die for it or because of it. Wars and ethnic cleansing show the truly narrative and creative force of those myths of the renewal of the origin. But the 'praxis' of ethnic and ideological cleansing is much more functional in stopping the narration that threatens the founding fiction of the origin (which is but the fiction of a foundation) in the same (the One), as far as possible within the narrative itself.

Writing then becomes unnecessary, or it becomes just a bad copy of the physical violence, because the Writer/Master/War Lord sends every reference back to the revelation, understandable in itself, of his own particular truth as being the only truth, that by which he self-proclaims and self-legitimizes himself, and that by which he announces his State (a State for His people only) and thus his own Law. This manner of stitching the unity of the world in the bleeding social fabric is the most efficient of all. The aim of an 'as if' turn (a *narrative force*) in time is then attained, the past itself is changed, a new beginning is made-up right within the past which becomes a pattern for the new desired commencement. Nothing in common, nothing contaminated by the proximity of the others will be tolerated, changes of names and calendar are undertaken and (the new) history starts again at zero. The difference between good and evil is lost for quite some time, until new values (in general, thought to be opposite to the previous ones) are given within some new dichotomy hiding a hierarchy.

In these conditions, we need no culture any more. War is much more efficient than any narrative, it *is the best narrative*.

The described situation is ours. This is the relationship of Serbia and Croatia (even though in asymmetry) to each other, as well as the relationship of both to Bosnia-Herzegovina. In these conditions, there can be no question of any interest whatever for philosophy. Writing, inasmuch as it maintains differences, has always had the function of guaranteeing peace and unity. When the war becomes an institution, when it is expected of the war to solve the problems, when the war replaces thought itself, as is the case here, then language loses sense (in spite of—if not because of—the attempts at its purification), philosophy loses its *raison d'etre*, and literature has nothing more to say. The philosopher becomes then the theoretician of ethnic and other cleansing, the 'Ethnic Cleaner' himself. Culture is successfully replaced by an order of brigands, by a policed discipline, by military law.

It is starting from this limit of thinking that we nowadays observe the frightening abyss of a possible end (or an impossibility) of philosophy. Some philosophers have opted for the war lords, and have become the exponents of the nationalistic aggressors' ideas. If it is too late for these philosophers, there may still not be too late for thinking.

The Bosnian society was an integrated one, which means that the communities were completely interrelated, interactive, mutually inherent, and could *not* be identified as separate. The individual, as a Bosnian (and, for many previous decades, as a Yugoslav), came before his or her community, and many individuals could not be described in terms of community. The communities were defined by admission and integration and not by the exclusion of others. People intermarried, even though it was not seen as 'inter'-marrying, they didn't live in separate ghettos, towns or areas (these are the result of the recent ethnic cleansing), they were to a very large extent all secular, and big portions of the population did not fit into any of the communities ethnically or religiously defined. They did not have separate cultures, but shared *one* Bosnian culture which had historically integrated elements of different origin. They were no communities in the sense of rigid castes, or in the way ethnic communities coexist in the United States of America. In Bosnia-Herzegovian, in general, an individual came before an ethnic or religious community, and was a Bosnian before he was member of a particular community. To a lesser degree, this was true of all Yugoslavia. I am not going into the reasons of the collapse of Yugoslavia, which are many and complex,[1] but one of the many compostie and complementary reasons may be the not sufficient social integration of Yugoslavia, the lack of a numerically relevant all-Yugoslav middle-class, and possibly the social over-integration, on the other side, of Bosnia-Herzegovina, which had to be destroyed in order for disintegration to proceed. The several ethnic, religious or national groups making Bosnia-Heregovina (mainly Muslims, now called Bosniaks as opposed to Bosnians; Croats, Serbs, Gypsies, Jews and also others) never exhaustively defined the identity of a Bosnian citizen who was generally first a Bosnian and then only anything else, if at all. The 'Bosnian' type is at this level the 'concrete universal' respecting particularities, much as the 'Yugoslav' type was for the

---

[1] On such topics I have written in many articles, and in particular in three of my books: *Briefe von Frauen über Krieg und Nationalismus*, with Biljana Jovanović, Marusa Krese, Radmila Lazić, Suhrkamp (Frankfurt a/M, 1993); *La Croatie depuis d'effondrement de la Yougoslavie*, ed. by R. Ivekovic (Paris, 1994); *La balkanizzazione della regione* (Rome, 1995).

former Yugoslavia (although the terms of Yugoslav, Yugoslavia, have now become compromised through nationalist misusage and cannot be utilized any more). The 'Yugoslavs' in the non-nationalistic meaning of the word have symbolically dis-appeared, because of the semantic turn and change. When you have no more name to claim, you don't exist symbolically and are not present in the public space (you are not a subject-agent). During this war and after the collapse of Yugoslavia, Bosnians have been fighting to resist some such and even bloodier disappearance (while keeping their own characteristics), both physical and symbolical, in the same way in which the vanished Yugoslavs (in the first, non-nationalist, meaning of the word) have.

If the process goes to its end, one day there will be nobody there any more to call themselves Bosnians (Western press and governments have been using indiscriminately 'Muslim' for 'Bosnians' all through the war). Consequently, Bosnians will disappear from representation, from the media, from public space, from public opinion, as they have already disappeared from the news supplanted by more recent genocides. If they disappear, there will remain only people called Serbs, Muslims (Bosniaks), or Croats. This is a good example of 'history' going backwards at the hands of men. Bosnia may indeed one day become multicultural or multiethnic. Yet in spite of the many influences, in that patch of concentrated history, both from the East and from the West, and also from the West's East and from the East's West, one could say that no one there comes from different and separate cultural origins. That culture has always been composite.

Afterword

AZIZ AL-AZMEH

The papers in this volume concern the notion of identity as it impinges on several issues of current importance. This reflects the use (and in my understanding the overuse and indeed abuse) of this notion in recent academic writings and political pronouncements. Identity is an issue that must be squarely faced and soberly addressed.

The analytical value of the notion of identity is of some dispute. Its profligate and uncritical use is very recent, the conditions for which are primarly political the world over. There is a tendency to substitute 'identity' for 'social group' or 'community' today, which I discuss below. Such substitution assumes a somewhat infra-historical substance as the subject matter of society and history, endowed with miraculous powers of resistance, a substance whose definition in present discourse veers towards a subjectivism and a view which regards cultural elements and ostensibly primary social bonds as paramount in historical development, and which regards social transformation as over-determined by decisions and shifts in perspective somewhat entirely endogenous. Such an identity merely 'expresses itself' as one contributor to this collection states. Ethnic groups and religious communities are portrayed as somehow pre-existing. There is also in this drift of thought and imagination the tendency to presume that Muslims have a specific proclivity for self-definition in terms of religion. Indeed, more than one paper displays different shades of this tendency.

But there are other means of dealing with the concept of identity, means which take as their primary points of departure the primacy of social, ideological, social, and more broadly historical considerations for the construal of identity, its constituent elements and its shifting references. Correlatively, questions are posed as to the reason why identity is invoked as an analytical tool rather than other, in my view more adequate concepts. A number of contributions to this collection make the implicit and explicit parameters of this critical view and historical use of the notion of identity abundantly clear.

Popovic and Clayer display for example a keen eye for the career of political identities and the politics of naming, but alas confine this to Bosnian Muslims to the exclusion of Serbs and Croats. The contributions of Joya Chatterji and Mohammad Ishaq Khan are, to my mind, good cases in point. Hamza Alavi speaks of identitiy in the political context from which it is inseparable, and by means of identifiable social carriers.

Given that I have stated a number of opinions concerning the notion of identity. I feel they must be explicitly defended. I, wish to do so not only because I regard this as an adequate context in which to treat the histories and societies of Muslims, but also because I believe the uncritical use of this notion is ultimately, in a sort of objective Machiavellism of unintended complicity, grist to the mill of communalist politics in India and elsewhere. Rather than provide a theoretical critique of 'identity' and correlated concept such as 'authenticity', and of the analytical models it normally entails in its uncritical use, it would perhaps be best to contribute an overview on Muslim reactions to colonialism, most particularly in the Arab world, not only for the comparative perspective that this would invite, but also because the ensuing historical and geographical stretch will enable the reader to form an opinion on the analytical salience of the notion of identity in a concrete and specific situation.

I

Two matters need to be stressed so that the parameters informing my considerations will be clear and unambiguous. The first concerns the geographical scope of this paper. I do not believe that it is possible to talk in general terms about a 'Muslim World', or to assume commonalities between the situations in Sinkiang, the Comoro Islands, Arabia, or the Ottoman Empire and successor states. For one thing, such an assumption would imply that these are territories whose societies, polities, and cultures are overdetermined by religion, assumptions and presumptions I consider to be unfounded: the imperatives that determined the forms and means of religious and cultural reaction to colonialism are specific to the territories in question. It must be added that even as colonialism is not only a tangible and nameable beast, but a vast historical process of capitalist globalization in a specifically political form, political specificity implying forms of direct political rule is not the sum total of colonialism. It is a system of relations not entirely encapsulated in specific colonial regimes.

Back to Islam: it is undeniable that forms of intellectual and activist Muslim internationalism did exist. Yet these changed profoundly over time and space, and were not self subsistent impulses arising out of the natural proclivities of Muslims overall, but rather the outcome of determinate conjunctural configurations. Pan Islamism in the latter part of the nineteenth century was an Ottoman diplomatic instrument with some Indian resonance, energized here and there by the enigmatic Jamaluddin 'Afghani'. Indian Khilafatist sentiments after the First World War and before were encouraged by Britain; pan-Islamism under Saudi direction in the 1960s constituted the cultural arm of the Truman Doctrine, which over a number of years spawned a variety of networks and infrastructures which fed alike the protests against Salman Rushdie, the war in Afghanistan and today's radical, mass pathological fringe of Algeria, United States and elsewhere. And though Mahdism in the Sudan can arguably be construed as anti-colonial, in its specific conditions it was the response of an élite socio-economic configuration sustained by the East African slave trade against British control over territories where this trade was carried out, and organized its contestation through a network of mystical fraternities. The Lybian Sanusiyya was similarly constituted in a situation of dispute over the control of territorial networks. Wahhabis in Arabia was made possible by imperatives of territorial unification connected with diversions of trade routes involving maritime Arabia, without any sense of opposition to European control but indeed rather in terms of an accommodation with new circumstances whose distant origins and conditions were unclear to the Wahhabis.

Moreover, the religious response to European presence, with its vocabularies, means of mobilization, and institutional setting, does not in itself adequately describe the cultural response to colonialism. As will be shown, such a response is more pertinently identified with statist projects for cultural, social, and intellectual transformation in response to colonialism, correlative with political and other means of response.

I limit this discussion to the reformist Ottoman state in the second half of the nineteenth century and its successor states in the Arab world. But I will also venture farther afield and, episodically, highlight parallels and contrasts, always bearing in mind that the religious and cultural responses to colonialism were uneven. In other words, I will not speak of the religious and cultural reaction of Islam to colonialism, but of the reaction of varieties of practicing or sociological Muslims (those who are born Muslims) in different times and places, and in contexts that were not solely religious. I should also stress that the frame of reference was the nation state, with Christians participating as much as Muslims in processes of transformation.

The second preliminary point is that I will not be construing my analytical account in terms of the currently fashionable pseudo sociological brooding on the Self and the Other, or in terms of contrastive identities or dualities such as the inauthentic and authentic, endogenous and exogenous, the local and the imported, indigenism and Westernization. I find Identity and its correlative terms to be performative categories to be read symptomatically in their various times and fields of action, and not to be taken for analytical categories.

In view of this, the model of action and reaction, as though there were a conflict between two separate and essentially intransitive units, does not seem to me to be helpful for describing the religious and cultural transformations of various Muslim populations in the age of colonialism. Far more useful is the model of combined but uneven development on the world scale.

II

The nineteenth century was critical for the process I propose to relate, and much of the twentieth century was a period that witnessed the consolidation or else the relative destitution and atrophy of some of the most important cultural and religious developments of the previous century. It was a time when the Ottoman state, endogenously but according to models of statebuilding that were becoming universal, sought to reform itself in order the better to survive and to resist the encroachments into its territories in the Balkans and within its populations in the Levant. The model according to which these transformations were being instituted were not those imported from elsewhere. They were in the process of development globally; and indeed, in certain instances, certain cultural transformations that took place under state direction within the Ottoman Empire were far in advance of those in Europe. One case in point is non-sectarian education; another is the removal of legal disability related to religious denomination. Both were in advance of British developments, for instance. The abolition of slavery in the Ottoman Empire preceded that in the United States. The notion of Ottoman decline is a rhetorical convention which deduces from the technological, military, and economic empowerment of Europe the unjustified corollary that the weaker Ottoman state was declining internally.

The nineteenth century was the time during which the Bonapartist model of the state expanded worldwide into Italy, France, Poland, and partly Russia by direct Napoleonic influence; into Latin America by Napoleonic example in the form of Simon Bolivar; and into Ottoman lands by means of the institutional models of this state. Of these, the most crucial for my purposes is that this state was one which was highly interventionist in the domains of law, education, and culture more generally conceived. This interventionism derived from the need to produce a new body of functionaries on whom depended the expansion of the state's field of competence and the correlative emergence of a public sphere. It may be recalled that the emergence of sociology as a discipline taking society as its topic was also correlative with this recent visibility of a public sphere.

In Ottoman domains, the attempt to reform the state (under the title of *Tanzimat*) by instituting French republicanist arrangements which took the political form of Bonapartism, resulted in what I should like to call, without wishing to be ironical or paradoxical, a Sultanic Republicanism, the one term referring to the manner by which power is exercized, the other to the institutional form of state, especially its attempts at monopolizing legal and cultural hegemony. This was a state which had within it important emerging elements of a republicanist character, presided over by a Sultan who, much like the king of Morocco today, had a certain extra-judical character (whose ambiguity constituted a field of contest between the Sultan and the senior bureaucracy) and the power of veto. The constitutional experiment of the 1870s which granted the Sultan extra-judical status in the constitution itself in return for his agreement to be bound by the Constitution and by law, was thwarted by Abdulhamid II in 1879. This resulted in a major mutation within the body of the senior ranks of the administrative and political service, and in the marginalization of the more liberal and ideologically progressive elements, who had sustained positivist ideas of society and polity in the organizational context of Freemasonry. But the social ideas and administrative means of republicanism lived on in the daily workings of the state apparatus and the cultural and educational systems it spawned, and these matters, crucial for my argument, need to be explicitly highlighted.

What the Hamidian regime after 1879 meant for the emergent socio-cultural complex that the reformist Ottoman state was building was the continuation of modernist institutional and cultural transformation, but also the official downgrading of modernist political ideas, especially of constitutionalism, in a manner that approximated in its thrust rather similar transformations that were simultaneously taking place in Germany and Russia. That the Sultan was increasingly leaning towards legitimizing his authority by appeal to the notion of the Khilafat need not necessarily imply the institution of that system, but is more saliently to be interpreted as the arrogation of religious primacy to the Sultan at the expense of the religious and priestly institution personified by Seyhul-Islam, who was, from 1839, made a member of the Cabinet.

The two matters that needed to be highlighted are the reforms of the legal system and the institution and dissemination of a novel cognitive regime premised on new state educational institutions, the resultant of which was the formation of a new intelligentsia much like the German *Bildungsburgertum*, which displaced, against various forms of resistance, the cultural, legal, and educational hegemony of the priestly class and led to the emergence of the notion of nationality and ultimately nationalism. Later, in the twentieth century, this resulted in nationalism combined with socialism as the main instrument with which colonial and crypto-colonial relations and conditions were countered.

Although the Ottoman Empire was not a colony, much of its energies in its latest phases, before the era of political colonialism that followed the First World War, were directed at resisting or accommodating the pressures of the European powers, military and financial, the latter in the form of the Ottoman Debt administration set up in 1882. This was a time when parts of the erstwhile empire, Egypt, Algeria and Tunisia, had fallen under various forms of direct European domination. While Tunisian developments under French rule accelerated some pre-existing trends, and made Tunisian history in its wider processes run more or less parallel to that of the Levant, the situation in Algeria was very specific and aggravated, and tended to stem the glimmerings of Ottoman reform; this relegated the vast majority of Algerians to an enforced backwardness whose consequences are evident today. As for Egypt, developments can be registered which ran parallel to those in the Empire, the crucial difference being that the Egyptian educational system, as a result of the state fiscal crisis of the 1870s, was far more crucially dominated by the religious institution of Al-Azhar.

The reforms of the legal system comprised two strands. The first was directed at the substantive content of law, which was altered by codification and the increasing infusion of non-traditional, positive elements, most particularly from French, Belgian, and Swiss models. Starting with the codification of Muslim Hanafite laws of commercial transaction (the *mecelle* of 1839-76), this was to be a continuous process which ultimately led to the abolition of the *Sharia* in Kemalist Turkey and the institution within the Arab world, with minor exceptions, of codes of civil law quite independently of the *Sharia* and without engaging in the ideological battle attendant upon its formal abolition. These codes treated whatever institutes of the *Sharia* that were retained under the heading of custom and local practice, particularly in the field of agrarian legislation.

The *Sharia* is not a code of law but a body of precepts, canonical sources, and precedents with considerable latitude and internal heterogeneity. It is ultimately a form of judges law, where the legal process and the activity of the judge are crucial. The conversion of some of its elements into a law code is in fact therefore the first stage in its abolition as *Sharia*, for it is thereby transformed into a modern—albeit not modernist—legal system. The majority of its substantive components are rejected by a process of pruning and exclusion, and its internal structure and modes of procedure and legislation are ejected. The codification, in the famous Ottoman *mecelle*, of commercial law, and the later codifications of the Ottoman law of personal status and its Arab decendants, proceeded alongside piecemeal legislation in other domains, ultimately coordinated by Turkish republicanist legislation and Arab civil laws, and with very radical reforms in penal law and laws of evidence. Of the consequences of these reforms most germane for my purposes here are the abolition of the *jizya* paid by non-Muslims, the abolition of the legal disability in terms of testimony by non-Muslims and women, the abolition of the sultan's penal prerogatives on the principle that penalties for specific crimes, torts, and misdemeanours are to be exclusively limited by the provisions of the law, the abolition of the law of talion, and the exclusive title to Ottoman nationality for the inhabitants of the Empire, whatever their religion, to the exclusion of non-Ottoman Muslims.

Correlatively, and this is the second strand of Ottoman legal reform, the legal process was henceforth to be the prerogative of secular courts, although some of these were staffed by erstwhile members of the priesthood, who had been subjected to a conversion process by means of modern legal education and who consecrated this transformation by switching from priestly dress to state bureaucratic uniform. But these elements tended to become progressively replaced by civil employees who had been prepared for their task by secular law schools. Even the law of personal status, alone of all sectors of law to be almost wholly derived from the *Sharia*, was administered, once codified, by secular courts.

These developments occurred together with the reform of the educational system, which entailed state takeover, first with the establishment of specialist higher institutes of law and medicine (after the modernization of the military and its correlative schools of engineering), later by the establishment of preparatory schools—and later, of elementary schools—in the capital and the main provincial centres, which instituted a curriculum based on the study of modern disciplines like natural sciences, mathematics, languages, history, geography, geology, law and administration. In all these, as in the legal system, a transformation in the hegemonic cognitive regime was translated from knowledge based on canonical texts and other superstitions to positivist conceptions of knowledge, which privileged science and the modern organization of society, in which religion was to play a role, but not a cognitive, institutional, political, or organizational role.

Such was the ethos of the *Bildungsburgertum* that resulted from this process, and which prompted Ottoman army officers, lawyers, state administrators, teachers, and literati to read Condorcet, Rousseau and Voltaire in preference to al-Bukhārī and al-Ghazālī. It was precisely in this milieu that were nurtured ideas of Ottoman nationality, irrespective of religious affiliation and connected with the project of the secularizing—albeit not secular—Ottoman state towards greater control of society, bypassing the mediating elements of communalist organization. This secularizing proto-nationalist project encompassed, in an implicit and sometimes explicit procedure of positivist social engineering, the whole range of social, economic, and cultural life, from the creation of large landed property by the compulsory registration of land, to the formation of a state élite charged with the normal functions such a group would occupy in republicanist regimes, namely the function of ideological and legal hegemony. And it is in terms of this hegemonic project that the state multiplied, and indeed often monopolized, hegemonic functions, aimed at endowing it with the requisite ideological, political, and administrative coherence that were hoped to enable the Ottoman state to adapt to its times and survive. I prefer to speak of ideology rather than culture for I take cultural expression to be one subsumed under ideology, and would not concur with the Geertzian thesis of ideology as a cultural system.

There were of course resistances to this secularizing process. For one thing, in the natural course of events, these processes were uniform neither in their geographical nor in their social extent or reach. Muslim priestly resistance and the resistance of tribal and other provincial elements, were dealt with by a good degree of finality in the course of the nineteenth century and in the Young Turk *coup d'état* of 1909, respectively. What I wish to stress here is that these processes resulted, by 1909, in the genesis of a relatively cohesive group of Young Ottomans with nationalist and positivist ideas. The group included Turks, Arabs and other nationalities. There were indeed calls for local Arab autonomy, but this was virtually never conceived, except by individuals with close connections with foreign consuls, apart from the ambit of Ottoman nationality. And these positions, along with their modernist ideological under-pinnings, were held by persons connected intimately or more proximately with the Young Turks who were Muslims and Christians.

On the Hamidian camp were ranged persons of tribal origin recruited by the Sultan, in addition to subaltern officers who spearheaded the attempted counter-coup of 1909, and certain conservative Muslim elements, particularly among the lower ranks of the priesthood, all of which groups had in common the lack of exposure to the emergent state educational system and the network of relations it produced in the army, bureaucracy and intelligentsia. In the same, politically sultanic, institutionally unrepublicanist and socially communalist historical direction, ran the opposition of the European Consuls and the resistance of those parts of the Christian population under clerical control, especially that of the Western churches. These opposed the legal uniformization of the citizenry and the state educational system, and the setting up of non-denominational schools; they attempted to enclose the Christian populations, especially the Armenians, Greeks, Iraqi Assyrians, and Arab Maronites, within a communalist and secrtarian regime which, for the commercial classes, had the advantage of a certain European protected extra-territoriality. The Armenian and Roman churches vehemently opposed the abolition of the traditional Muslim law of apostasy. But this cannot be said for other Syrian Christians, who advocated and indeed actively participated in secular education and in the elaboration of the idea of Ottoman nationality based on civic as distinct from sectarian participation.

III

The First World War had a number of consequences salient for our topic. Chief among those was the break up of the Ottoman Empire and the onset of direct political colonization. The Turks under Mustafa Kemal Ataturk managed to save Turkey and indeed to constitute it as a national state, after a series of protracted military campaigns against Britain, France, Italy, and Greece, singly and in combination. The Khilafat was abolished while the Khalifa was fugitive aboard a British gunboat in the Sea of Marmara. This was followed by a highly accelerated realization of the processes in gestation that have been described, with the official abolition of the *Sharia* and the nationalist secularization of life generally and, not least, the formation of a Turkish bourgeoisie not only cultural but social and economic. Not the least important and significant of these instances of intensive secular nationalist acculturation was the banning of the veiling of women and their active induction into economic and public life.

Matters developed otherwise in the Arab provinces. Very important elements of the Arab-Ottoman cultural, bureaucratic and military élite turned against the Young Turk regime from about 1912, a trend that was accelerated during the First World War, with a growing authoritarianism and exclusive Turkism that conditions of war made all the more intense. A number of these Arabs were hanged in Beirut and Damascus in 1915; they had, almost to the man, been associated with varying degrees of involvement with the Young

Turks. It is noteworthy that the primary theoretician of Arab nationalism in the twentieth century, who had such an important role in reforming the educational systems of Iraq, and later of other Arab countries, Sāṭi al-Ḥuṣrī, had been closely associated in Salonika with Ziya Gökalp, a Kurd who became the prime exponent of Turkish nationalism.

Thus the drift from Ottoman to Arab nationalism was ideologically imperceptible and almost automatic, as the nationalisms expounded were both premised on a positivist understanding of history that regarded the nation state as the highest form of social development. Some of these persons joined in the later stages of the Hijazi rebellion of 1916 (habitually misconstrued as the Great Arab Revolt) which had been a pan-Islamic Khilafat movement fleetingly supported by Great Britain. When the Sharif of Mecca, al-Husayn bin'Ali, declared himself Khalifa, this assumption was ratified by an assembly consisting of a medley of Afghans, Indians, Javans, and others, and included only one Arab, Mohammad Rashīd Riḍā, the spiritual and ideological founder of the tendency that was later to become the Society of Muslim Brothers.

One result of this rebellion was the division of eastern Mediterranean Arab lands between France and Britain, the latter allocating Palestine for colonization by the Zionist movement. The resistance to these developments took the primary form of constituting nationalist movements whose cultural outlook was largely modernist and in continuity with late Ottoman developments, although there were marginal uses of religious motifs in nationalist discourse, and even more marginal religious movements that conceived their primary task as less the direct opposition of colonialism than the reversal of the socio cultural advancements of the previous century, under the title of socio religious moralization, of moral re-armament by means of religion, which included the veiling of women, the re-institution of the by now forgotten *Sharia*, and the rest of the familiar repertoire, not to forget episodic agitation in the name of the Khilafat, particularly the fiasco on behalf of King Fuad I of Egypt in the 1920s. Much of the religio-culturalist nationalism in the Arab world, marginal until two decades ago, had married a religious xenophobia and intolerance with political collaborationism under the pretence of being religious and moral rather than political. The famous Algerian Society of the *Ulama* under Ibn Bādīs is a case in point, as is overall the history of the Muslim Brothers. The explicit aversion to politics itself reflects socio-political marginality in the overall public sphere.

Pan Arab and local nationalism (Egyptianist, pan-Syrian) perpetuated the trends already in place, and accelerated them with their advent to power after independence in Syria, Iraq, and elsewhere. But this is not to say that the movement of history was in abeyance during the mandatory period, which saw significant modernist cultural movements allied to nationalism in countries mandated (Syria, for instance), nominally, independent (Egypt, for example) or colonized (Tunisia and, to a lesser extend, Algeria). The same period also saw further extension of modernist cultural institutions, under private impetus in Egypt and upon French initiative in Syria (and under the impact of Ḥuṣrī in Iraq), and further modifications to the legal systems.

The nationalist movements came to power in the period following the Second World War (with the exception of the annexation of much of Palestine to the Jewish colonies by military action, terrorism, the expulsion of Arabs, and the confiscation of land). Regardless of political or ideological complexion—liberal and patrimonialist in Syria until the Nasserist and later the Baathist era, liberal in Egypt until Nasser, socialist and nationalist in the Nasser-Baath period, with important admixtures of other political orientations, particularly Communist in Iraq, Sudan and, Syria, and, not the least significantly, Kemalist in Tunisia—the general thrust of state-building resulted in further institution and dissemination of the secularizing culture of statist modernism, under conditions of extreme adversity and considerable external pressure, and of profound internal transformation.

The combination of socialism and nationalism as political ideologies, and the scientistic conception of education and of culture as the path to development and true decolonization, are the main cultural planks in the Arab response to colonialist conditions and relations in the period following the Second World War. Indeed, this was the period that witnessed the almost profligate flowering of Arab modernist culture in all its fields as a hegemonic instance, with the efflorescence of Marxism and existentialism as the left and right extremities of nationalism, and of modernist poetry, highly potent in the Arab world, which domesticated religious symbolism, blended it with the pagan mythology of the renewal and regeneration of Adonis and Baal, and put forward an almost redemptive expression of national liberation and regeneration. This was also the period which saw the beginnings of the criticism of religious representations, ideologically and historically but most particularly in terms of the connection between religion and social backwardness, a combination which was regarded as a fundamental cause for continuing Arab disempowerment against formerly colonial and neoimperial hegemonic campaigns, locally symbolized by Arab incapacity against the particularly acute and aggressive form of colonialist implantation in the form of the Zionist state in Palestine.

None of this is surprising for the post-War period was one of much optimism. It was a period which, in an international capitalist system mindful of the disastrous consequences of its pre-war workings, instituted a system of Keynesian prophylaxis, including by extension the welfare state (or the New Deal), in the face of the alternative that emerged from the revolution in Russia and the emergence of the Socialist bloc. The Third World correlative of this was projects of development allied to modernist culture; the one being thought to be the necessary complement of the other, and it is well to remember this today, rather than succumb to the current anachronistic shibboleths which seek to portray the modernist nationalist regimes in the Arab World, India, and elsewhere as a mirage. We should especially resist such statements from individuals who owe the education, culture, and careers which enable them to speak about these matters in this way to the very cultural and educational institutions they describe as having been illusory.

The crucial development leading to the present situation I have just described with its fraudulent vocabularies and historical implausibly (and which describes itself, entirely without irony, as post-colonial) has explanations of the order of history, history that is not only local but unevenly global. None of the matters addressed so far are open in any meaningful way to the vocabularies of identity. Culture was regarded, all along the very long nineteenth century (which has terminated in 1989) as correlated with progress and advancement, although romantic political and ideological currents construed it as a selfsubsistent national medium impervious to history meaningfully conceived. These romantic currents, most highly developed in a theoretical sense in Germany, but effective in many varieties of nationalism and populism world-wide, and highly salient to Zionism, were generally associated with the Right, and were indeed the ideological bedrock of the chauvinism and jingoism with which socialist movements were countered in Germany and elsewhere, culminating in National Socialism.

These romantic visions of history and community are back in vogue today under the signatures both of racism and chauvinism on the one hand, and of the post-modern delight in the pre-modernity of others, distributed as deregulated cultural goods in the present era of globalization. The thrust of these ideological—not cultural— goods in the South is the economic, social, and cultural dis- empowerment of the state in the name of the local. It must be noted that these cultural goods are now distributed with massive intensity by non-governmental organizations, both as theoretical wares (post- colonial discourse), and programmes for social organization that seek to deprive the state of the republicanist prerogative of providing its citizens with social and cultural advancement. This culturally hegemonistic project of the state has always been the mainspring of attempts to countervail the pressures of colonial and quasi colonial relations, as we have seen. Projects of state disempowerment are inserted within the regime of cross-conditionalities imposed by the World Bank and the IMF. That they are identified with calls for local democracy and 'civil society' is a matter less to be taken at face value for the agreeable aural effect, than appropriately scrutinized in the light of the structural and political conditions in the present phase of globalization.

The incidence of romantic ideas of community and of history in the Arab world, before and after the Second World War, is undeniable but marginal. Most saliently, these conceptions were deployed in the context of Islamist political movements from the 1950s, tapping the resources of social conservatism and xenophobic cultural nationalism, projecting phantasmatic ideas about 'identity', against the national Arab state, which had taken a decidedly modernist direction. In the period before the crisis of Nasserism and Baathism following the war of 1967, they constituted the cultural plank of the Truman Doctrine, locally translated as the Baghdad Pact followed by CENTO. Over several decades now, they have circulated in the context of Islamist movements, supported by cultural, educational, and administrative infrastructures accruing from petro-Islamic largesse.

Subsequently, they came to take on the aspect of an ideological sublimation and condensation of structural marginality and estrangement within Arab countries whose causes are identified with the state which had seen, particularly after 1989, development projects atrophy and its republicanist functions diminish. These same politico cultural romantic conceptions also came to function as ideological condensations of a situation of national disempowerment, particularly well illustrated in the Arab-Israeli dispute. The heady mixture of eschatological and other phantasmatic solutions to local problems which the Arab world shares with other countries of the South, most particularly to problems of structural marginalization with no end in sight of the structural blockages to the social mobility of the subaltern and lumpen-intelligentsia, and of the seemingly incomplete process of nation-building, provide fertile grounds for that Islamism which presents itself as a hypernationalist programme of liberation, not only from neo-colonial relations, but also from a state which is post-colonial.

There seems in the currently fashionable anti-state, putatively democratist rhetoric, an argument from imperfection: having decided that post-colonial states (but perhaps not societies) are neither cherubic nor ever consummate, and hence imperfect, they are *ipso facto* unjustified in their prerogatives and functions and their history is one of an unauthentic misadventure. I find it astonishing that this argument from imperfection is bandied about by those who ought to know very much better. The leap from the state within the bounds of history and its structures, and from society as historical process, to society unburdened of modern history and restored to a prelapsarian originality, is marked in India and in some Western social science by the transition between Subalternism Mark I, to the post-modernist Subalternism Mark II, from history to the mystique of representation, from Bengali peasants to the voices of designer Angst, matters so perceptively studied by Aijaz Ahmad.

It goes without saying that this attempted reversal of the modernist cultural trend in Arab societies and polities is not in any con-sequential sense a process for countering neo-colonial relations, but for their reconfirmation and legitimation, on the assumption that Arab societies are incapable, by the very nature of their putatively Muslim identity, of developing. This Islamist doctrine of congenital incapacities premised on unhistorical notions of identity is structurally sustained by the disintegrative thrust of contemporary conditions of globalization, not only respecting the world, which is described in terms made universally familiar by Samuel Huntington and which is clearly to be construed as a policy for confirming the exclusive control of the United States and its allied for hegemonic relations premised upon the impermeability of North and South, and the confirmation of the latter in its relative but fated backwardness. For this unhistorical notion of identity is also premised on the disintegration of the South into so many impermeable and incommensurable phantasmatic identities, each with its culturally appropriate political system (Islamic in Afghanistan, for instance), but everywhere on the assumption that state republicanism should be minimized, economies transnationalized, and societies and cultures in involution sustained by post-colonial social theory.

It is only under the conditions of today that we may meaningfully speak of cultural and religious resistance. But it is resistance to the very instruments that have enabled the Arab world, no matter how partially, to resist colonial relations.

Glossary

Ahl-i Hadith:	Muslims who prefer the authority of Prophetic tradition (*hadith*) over that of a ruling by one of the schools of Islamic jurisprudence.
Ahl al-dhimma (*zimmi*):	the people with whom a compact was made, who paid the poll-tax called *jizya*.
Ahmadiya:	messianic movement founded by Mirza Ghulam Ahmad (d. 1908), in Qadian, a village in Punjab.
Ahrar:	'the free'; political party founded in Punjab in the late 1920s.
alam:	flag of Imam Husain, the grandson of the Prophet, carried in procession during Muharram.
alim :	see *ulama*.
Amir-i Jamia:	Chancellor of Delhi's Jamia Millia Islamia, founded in 1920.
angrez:	the British; hence *Angrezi sarkar*, the British Government.
anjuman:	an association, usually of Muslims, i.e. Anjuman-i Khuddam-i Kaaba.
Anjuman-i Islam:	*lit.* 'Association of Islam'.
Anjuman-i Jafariya:	Shia organization named after the fourth Shia Imam, Jafar-i Sadiq.
Anjuman-i Tamir-i Millat:	*lit.* 'Association for the Regeneration of Muslims'.
ashraf:	term (as opposed to *ajlaf*, the 'low-born') to describe those Muslims descended from immigrants in India; the Syeds (descendants of the Prophet) and Shaikhs (descendants of his Companions).

azadaars:	mourners of Imam Husain's martyrdom on the 10th day of Muharram, A.H. 61 (A.D. 680).
Bakr Id:	*lit.* 'the feast of sacrifice', Muslim festival.
bala:	*lit.* 'calamity'.
barawafat:	twelfth day of the month Rabiul-Awaal, observed in commemoration of Mohammad's death.
Barelwis:	followers of Maulana Ahmad Riza Khan (1856-1921), resident of Bareilly in Uttar Pradesh.
basti:	locality.
Bayt al-Islam:	*lit.* 'House of Islam'.
bhakt:	devotee.
biddat:	*lit.* 'innovation'; innovation in religious ritual or belief.
bigha:	just over half an acre.
biradari:	community.
burqa:	veil observed by Muslim women.
charpoy :	cot; a bed.
dar al-harb :	'the abode of war'; territory not under Islam Law.
dar al-Islam:	'the abode of Islam'.
Dar al-ulum:	'abode of knowledge; also the theological seminary at Deoband in Uttar Pradesh.
dargah:	Muslim shrine or tomb of a holy person.
dharmik sabha:	religious organization.
dharm yudh:	*lit.* 'religious war'.
din (*deen*):	religion, i.e. Islam.
dohas:	songs written mostly by Hindi poets.
durbar :	public audience; *durbari*—one who joins the court.
Fatimid Khilafat:	(909-1171), the only Shia Khilafat with its seat in Cairo.
fatwa:	written opinion on a point of Islamic law (plural: *fatawa*).
fiqh:	the science of Islamic jurisprudence, that is of the religious law.

firangi:	a European; also Firangi Mahal, a theological seminary in Lucknow.
Gaurakshini Sabha:	organization for the protection of the cow.
Gharib-Nawaz:	patron of the poor, i.e. Khwaja Muin-uddin Chishti, the Sufi saint in Ajmer.
ghair-mazhabi:	irreligious.
ghazal:	poetic form in Urdu.
Haj:	pilgrimage to Mecca and Medina; an incumbent religious duty.
Haram:	the sacred precincts of Mecca and Medina; the apartment of women in a Muslim household.
haraam:	*lit.* 'prohibited'; That which is unlawful.
hartal:	strike, work stoppage.
haveli:	mansion.
Hijaz (Hejaz):	name given to that tract of land which the Muslims consider the holy land. Within its limits are the sacred cities of Mecca and Medina, and most of its places are connected with the history of Mohammad.
hidaya:	*lit.* 'guidance'; title of the well-known book on Sunni law.
hijrat:	act of migration; *muhajir* (pl. *muhajirin*), migrant.
Hukumat-i Ilahi:	Kingdom of God.
Id:.	Muslim festival at the end of the month of fasting; Id-al Fitr as opposed to Id-al Zuha or Bakr Id, 'the feast of sacrifice'.
iddat:	term of probation for a woman in consequence of a dissolution of marriage, either by divorce or the death of her husband.
ijtehad:	*lit.* 'exerting oneself; technical term in Islamic law, first for the use of individual reasoning in general, and later, in a restricted meaning, for the use of the method of reasoning by analogy (*qiyas*).

ijtima:	religious congregations; especially organized by Tablighi Jamaat.
Imam:	title indicating leadership, governance or rule; 'the one exercising general leadership in both religious and political affairs.' Shias refer specially to the twelve Imams, starting with Ali, cousin and son-in-law of the Prophet.
Imambara:	*lit.* 'House of the Imam'; place where *tazias* (lath and paper models of the tombs Imam Husain and his family) are kept and also carried in procession.
jagirdar:	an assignee of the right to collect the state revenues from a specified area, in Mughal times in lieu of a salary from the royal treasury.
jamaat:	assembly; organization.
Jamaat-i Islami:	a religio-political body founded by Ali Ala Maududi.
Jamiyat al-ulama-i Hind:	the political wing of the Deobandi *ulama* founded in 1919 during the Khilafat movement in India.
Jazirat al-Arab:	'the island of Arabia; the area bounded by the Mediterranean, the Red Sea, the Indian Ocean, the Persian Gulf and the rivers Tigris and Euphrates.
jehad (jihad):	religious war undertaken by the Muslims against the unbelievers.
jizya:	the poll-tax levied in *dar al-Islam*.
qabaristan:	Muslim graveyard.
kafir :	a non-Muslim; one who practices *kufr*, infidelity.
kalima:	Muslim attestation of faith in the Unity of God and the finality of Mohammad's Prophethood.
karavan:	caravan.
karb :	pain
Karbala:	about twenty-five miles north-west of Kufa; the site in Iraq where Imam Husain was assassinated.

karkhandar:	artisan.
khadi (*khaddar*):	hand-spun cloth.
Khair-i Umma:	welfare of the Islamic community.
Khalifa (Khalifah: Caliph):	'to leave behind'; a successor; a vice-regent or deputy.
Khilafat (Caliphate):	the office of Khalifa. The last great Khilafat of Islam was non-Arab, that of the Ottoman Turks in Constantinople (1517-1924). *See* Umayyad.
Khilafat-i Rashida:	*see Khulafa-i Rashidun.*
khilat:	a dress of honour presented by a king/nawab as a mark of distinction.
Khudai Khidmatgars:	*lit.* 'Servant of God', movement of Khan Abdul Ghaffar Khan.
Khuddam-i Kaaba:	*lit.* 'Servants of Kaaba'; Anjuman-i Khuddam-i Kaaba founded in 1913.
khula:	an agreement for the purpose of dissolving marriage.
Khulafa:	plural of Khalifa, 'successor' of the Prophet Mohammad,
Khulafa-i Rashidun:	'the well-directed Khalifas'; the four pious *Khulafa*—Abu Bakr, Umar, Usman and Ali.
la-dini:	irreligious.
lashkar:	army.
marsiya:	elegiac poem describing the tragedy of Karbala.
muhajir:	refugee (singular: *muhajirin*).
mujahid:	holy warrior; freedom fighter (plural: *mujahidin*).
Nadwat al-ulama:	'an assembly of meeting place of Muslim scholars'; name of the famous seminary founded in Lucknow by Shibli Nomani.
namaz:	the prescribed prayer in Islam.
Naqshbandi:	a sufi order.
Nawabi:	style of the Nawab.
noha (*nauha*):	'lamentations for the dead'; a short lament; written and sung to the sufferings of Husain and his companions.
pagri:	head-gear.

panchayat:	village council.
pandal:	a covered stage.
pir :	a Sufi master on the mystical path; also known as *murshid*.
puja:	Hindu religious worship.
purdah:	Muslim women are required by religion and custom to be secluded from the male adults. See *burqa*.
Qaid-e-Azam: (Quaid-e-Azam)	great leader, title attached to M.A. Jinnah, founder of Pakistan.
qanun-i falah:	law for the welfare of the community.
qasbah:	town.
Qurayash (Quraish):	the Arabic tribe from which Mohammad was descended.
salaar :	head; leader; commander.
sabha:	an assembly, usually of Hindus.
sajjada-nashin:	successor to the leader of a *pir* and custodian of a sufi shrine.
satyagraha:	'truth force'; 'soul force'; Gandhi's passive resistance movement.
Shab-i barat:	Muslim festival to pray for the dead.
Shair-i Mashriq:	'Poet of the East', the poet Mohammad Iqbal.
shaheed:	martyr.
Shariat (*Sharia*):	the Islamic Law, including both the teachings of the Koran (Quran) and of the traditional sayings of Prophet Mohammad.
sharif:	*lit.* respectable; also used for the upper castes among Muslims.
Sunni:	'one who follows the trodden path'; applied to the largest 'sect' in Islam.
tabligh:	the Muslim conversion movement, e.g. Tablighi Jamaat.
Tablighi Jamaat:	Muslim organization established in the 1920s to spread the word of Allah.
talaq:	divorce.
taluqdar :	in Awadh, *zamindars* with proprietary rights.

tanzim:	Muslim consolidation movement.
taqlid:	*lit.* 'winding round' in the sense of blind acceptance of the *Shariat.*
tariqa:	a way, the term for the Sufi path, or school of guidance along that path.
tashadud:	oppression.
tauhid (*Tawhid*):	a fundamental doctrine of Islam; belief in the Unity of God.
Tahaffuz-i Millat:	*lit.* 'defense of the community'.
thana:	police station; police headquarters.
ulama:	plural of *alim*, *lit.* 'man of knowledge'.
umma:	term occurs sixty-four times in the Koran and is used to express the essential unity of Muslims in diverse cultural settings.
Umayyad:	the first dynasty in the history of Islam. Their Khilafat (661-750), with its capital at Damascus, was followed by the Abbasids (750-1258) at Baghdad. Another Umayyad Khilafat at Cardova in Spain lasted from 929 to 1031.
Wahhabi movement:	puritanical movement founded on the teachings of Mohammad Ibn Abd al-Wahab (1703-1791).
waqf (plural *auqaf*):	*lit.* 'confinement' or 'prohibition'; Muslim charitable endowments.
zamindar:	landholder.
zamindari:	land held by the *zamindar.*

List of Contributors

AZIL AL-AZMEH was formerly a Fellow of the Institute of Advanced Study, Berlin. He is the author of several books in English and Arabic, including *Ibn Khaldun, Islams and Modernities* and *Muslim Kingship: Power and the Sacred in Muslim, Christian and Pagan Polities*.

HAMZA ALAVI is co-editor of *Rural Development in Bangladesh and Pakistan* (1976); *Introduction to Sociology of the 'Developing' Societies* (1982); *Capitalism and Colonial Production* (1983); *State and Ideology in the Middle-East and Pakistan* (1988); *South Asia—Sociology of Developing Societies* (1989).

JOYA CHATTERJI, senior Research Fellow at the Hinduja Cambridge Project, is the author of *Bengal Divided: Hindu Communalism and Partition, 1932-1947* (1994).

IAN COPLAND, Associate Professor of History at Monash University, Australia, is the author of *The British Raj and The Indian Princes: Paramountcy in Western India 1857-1930* (1982); *The Princes of India in the End-Game of Empire, 1917-1947* (1997).

MARC GABORIEAU, head of the Centre of Indian and South Asian Studies in Paris and Professor at the School of Higher Studies in Social Sciences, has written many books in French, including *Account of a Muslim Traveller in Tibet* (1973); *Muslim Minorities in the Hindu Kingdom of Nepal* (1977); and *No Brahmans, No Ancestors: Muslim Pillars in Nepal* (1993).

NATHALIE CLAYER is senior researcher at the CNRS Paris, she has written a number of scholarly articles and books in French.

PAPIYA GHOSH is Associate Professor in the Department of History, University of Patna.

MUSHIRUL HASAN, Professor of History at Delhi's Jamia Millia Islamia, is the author of *Nationalism and Communal Politics in India, 1885-1930* (1991); *A Nationalist Conscience: M.A. Ansari, the Congress and the Raj* (1987); *Legacy of a Divided Nation: India's Muslims since Independence* (1997). He has edited *India Partitioned: The Other Face of Freedom* in 2 volumes (1997 rev. and enlarged edn.).

TAJ UL-ISLAM HASHMI, senior Lecturer in the History Department, National University of Singapore, Singapore, is the author of *Colonial Bengal* (1985) in Bengali; *Pakistan as a Peasant Utopia: The Communalization of Class Politics in East Bengal, 1920-1947* (1994).

IVAN IVEKOVIC, Professor of Comparative Politics at the American University in Cairo, Egypt, has authored several books in Croation language, including *Africa in the Struggle for its Second Independence* (1990), *Africa in Transformation* (1984), *The Palestinian Resistance Movement* (1980). His forthcoming book in English is entitled *Social Change, Politics and Ethnic Conflict in Yugoslavia and Transcaucasia*.

RADA IVEKOVIĆ, Associate Professor of Philosophy, Philosophy Department, University of Paris-8, St. Denis, has authored and translated several books, including *Early Buddhist Thought* (1977); co-authored *Indian and Iranian Ethics* (1980); *An Outline of Indian Philosophy*.

NIRAJA GOPAL JAYAL, Associate Professor at the Centre for Political Studies, Jawaharlal Nehru University, has edited *Sidney and Beatrice Webb: Indian Diary* (1987), and co-authored *Drought, Policy and Politics in India* (1991).

MOHAMMAD ISHAQ KHAN, Professor of History, Kashmir University, Srinagar, is the author of *History of Srinagar, 1846-1947: A Study in Socio-cultural Change* (1978); *Perspectives on Kashmir: Historical Dimensions* (1983); *Kashmir's Transition to Islam: The Role of Muslim Rishis* (1994); *Experiencing Islam* (1997).

RADHA KUMAR is a Warren Weaver Fellow at the RockeFeller Foundation in New York. She has written *The History of Doing: An*

Illustrated Account of Movements for Women's Rights and Feminism in India, 1800-1990 (1993); *Divide and Fall? Bosnia in the Annals of Partition* (1997).

SHAIL MAYARAM, Fellow at the Institute of Development Studies, Jaipur, is the author of *Resisting Regimes: Myth, Memory and the Shaping of a Muslim Identity* (1997); *Counterperspectives on State Formation in India: From a Marginalized World between Hinduism and Islam,* (forthcoming); and has co-authored with Ashis Nandy, Shikha Trivedi, Achyut Yagnik, *Creating a Nationality: The Ramjanambhumi Movement and the Fear of Self* (1995).

GAIL MINAULT teaches History at the University of Texas, Austin. She is the author of *The Khilafat Movement: Religious Symbolism and Political Mobilization in India* (1982). She has also edited several important books and translated Urdu texts.

A.G. NOORANI, a lawyer, is the author of *The Kashmir Question, Badruddin Tyabji; Dr Zakir Husain; The Trial of Bhagat Singh* (edited).

ALEXANDRE POPOVIC is a senior researcher at the CNRS, Paris. He has written a number of scholarly articles and books in French.

MOHAMMAD TALIB is Associate Professor in the Department of Sociology, Jamia Millia Islamia.

DIETRICH REETZ is a scholar at the Centre for Modern Oriental Studies, Berlin. His recent English-language publications include a research monograph on the *Hijrat—The Flight of the Faithful. A British File on the Exodus of Muslim Peasants from North India to Afghanistan in 1920*. His current research project is on the 'Political project of Islamic movements in colonial India 1900-1947'.

Index